Gods, ghosts, and black dogs

The fascinating folklore and mythology of dogs

Stanley Coren

Hubble & Hattie

The Hubble & Hattie imprint was launched in 2009 and is named in memory of two very special Westie sisters owned by Veloce's proprietors. Since the first book, many more have been added to the list, all with the same underlying objective: to be of real benefit to the species they cover, at the same time promoting compassion, understanding and respect between all animals (including human ones!) All Hubble & Hattie publications offer ethical, high quality content and presentation, plus great value for money.

More books from Hubble & Hattie –

Among the Wolves: Memoirs of a wolf handler (Shelbourne)

Animal Grief: How animals mourn (Alderton)

Babies, kids and dogs – creating a safe and harmonious relationship (Fallon & Davenport)

Because this is our home ... the story of a cat's progress (Bowes)

Camper vans, ex-pats & Spanish Hounds: from road trip to rescue – the strays of Spain (Coates & Morris)

Cat Speak: recognising & understanding behaviour (Rauth-Widmann)

Charlie – The dog who came in from the wild (Tenzin-Dolma)

Clever dog! Life lessons from the world's most successful animal (O'Meara)

Complete Dog Massage Manual, The – Gentle Dog Care (Robertson)

Dieting with my dog: one busy life, two full figures ... and unconditional love (Frezon)

Dinner with Rover: delicious, nutritious meals for you and your dog to share (Paton-Ayre)

Dog Cookies: healthy, allergen-free treat recipes for your dog (Schöps)

Dog-friendly Gardening: creating a safe haven for you and your dog (Bush)

Dog Games – stimulating play to entertain your dog and you (Blenski)

Dog Relax – relaxed dogs, relaxed owners (Pilguj)

Dog Speak: recognising & understanding behaviour (Blenski)

Dogs on Wheels: travelling with your canine companion (Mort)

Emergency First Aid for dogs: at home and away Revised Edition (Bucksch)

Exercising your puppy: a gentle & natural approach – Gentle Dog Care (Robertson & Pope)

Fun and Games for Cats (Seidl)

Gods, ghosts, and black dogs – the fascinating folklore and mythology of dogs (Coren)

Helping minds meet – skills for a better life with your dog (Zulch & Mills)

Home alone and happy – essential life skills for preventing separation anxiety in dogs and puppies (Mallatratt)

Know Your Dog – The guide to a beautiful relationship (Birmelin)

Life skills for puppies – laying the foundation of a loving, lasting relationship (Zuch & Mills)

Living with an Older Dog – Gentle Dog Care (Alderton & Hall)

Miaow! Cats really are nicer than people! (Moore)

My cat has arthritis – but lives life to the full! (Carrick)

My dog has arthritis – but lives life to the full! (Carrick)

My dog has cruciate ligament injury – but lives life to the full! (Haüsler & Friedrich)

My dog has epilepsy – but lives life to the full! (Carrick)

My dog has hip dysplasia – but lives life to the full! (Haüsler & Friedrich)

My dog is blind – but lives life to the full! (Horsky)

My dog is deaf – but lives life to the full! (Willms)

My Dog, my Friend: heart-warming tales of canine companionship from celebrities and other extraordinary people (Gordon)

No walks? No worries! Maintaining wellbeing in dogs on restricted exercise (Ryan & Zulch)

Partners – Everyday working dogs being heroes every day (Walton)

Smellorama – nose games for dogs (Theby)

Swim to recovery: canine hydrotherapy healing – Gentle Dog Care (Wong)

A tale of two horses – a passion for free will teaching (Gregory)

Tara – the terrier who sailed around the world (Forrester)

The Truth about Wolves and Dogs: dispelling the myths of dog training (Shelbourne)

Waggy Tails & Wheelchairs (Epp)

Walking the dog: motorway walks for drivers & dogs revised edition (Rees)

When man meets dog – what a difference a dog makes (Blazina)

Winston ... the dog who changed my life (Klute)

The quite very actual adventures of Worzel Wooface (Pickles)

You and Your Border Terrier – The Essential Guide (Alderton)

You and Your Cockapoo – The Essential Guide (Alderton)

Your dog and you – understanding the canine psyche (Garratt)

Back cover photo courtesy University of British Columbia

 For post publication news, updates and amendments relating to this book please visit www.hubbleandhattie.com/extras/ HH4860

www.hubbleandhattie.com

First published March 2016 by Veloce Publishing Limited, Veloce House, Parkway Farm Business Park, Middle Farm Way, Poundbury, Dorchester, Dorset, DT1 3AR, England. Fax 01305 250479/email info@hubbleandhattie.com/web www.hubbleandhattie.com
ISBN: 978-1-845848-60-6 UPC: 6-36847-04860-0 © Stanley Coren & Veloce Publishing Ltd 2016. All rights reserved. With the exception of quoting brief passages for the purpose of review, no part of this publication may be recorded, reproduced or transmitted by any means, including photocopying, without the written permission of Veloce Publishing Ltd. Throughout this book logos, model names and designations, etc, have been used for the purposes of identification, illustration and decoration. Such names are the property of the trademark holder as this is not an official publication.
Readers with ideas for books about animals, or animal-related topics, are invited to write to the editorial director of Veloce Publishing at the above address. British Library Cataloguing in Publication Data – A catalogue record for this book is available from the British Library.
Typesetting, design and page make-up all by Veloce Publishing Ltd on Apple Mac. Printed in India by Replika Press.

Contents

An introduction to this book of dog tales ...

It was just a gathering of casual friends who work together, sitting on a miscellaneous collection of chairs, eating sandwiches and drinking coffee from thermos bottles, or soda pop from cans. The conversation was gentle, and mostly meaningless: designed to pass the time rather than to educate or illuminate. Someone in the group mentioned that he had read an article in the newspaper reporting a new entry in the *Guinness Book of World Records*. It described what was supposed to be the world's largest dog — a Great Dane named Gibson — who, at around 42 inches at the shoulder, was nearly 7 feet tall when standing on his hind legs.

One of my friends chuckled and said, "Now, that's not all that tall. My grandfather used to tell me the story of a dog who was so tall he had to climb a ladder in order to scratch his own ear!"

A ripple of laughter at this was followed by: "It's been a long time since I heard tell of it, but, on the flip side, there's a story about a really tiny dog who probably made it into the *Guinness* book. I believe the details were that this dog was *so* small, it took two men and a boy just to see him!"

As often happens in such situations, the telling of a tall tale or two simply opens the floodgates, and sooner or later everybody has to chime in with their favourite story, even if it is abbreviated into a short comment rather than a full-blown narrative. Before we finally drained the last of the coffee, tossed away the empty pop cans, and made ready to go back to work, many more familiar and unfamiliar tales had been told, and included stories about a large collection of dogs who should have been listed among world record holders for their species ... if only they really existed.

There was the story of the fastest dog in the world, for example, who was so quick that he reached home a second-and-a-half before his bark did. Another was the one about the dog who was so fat that NASA orbited a satellite around him; his littermate was a dog who was so skinny that he could run through a rain shower and never get wet. Then there was the dog who wagged his tail so fast the weather department had to put out a tornado advisory warning every time he was happy. And the best herding dog ever was a Border Collie (of course), who was so smart that the farmer who owned him trained him to herd bees. That dog could direct a swarm of bees from one meadow to another two miles away without losing a single bee.

Our human-canine bond

It is at times like these that my feeling is reinforced that the universe is not composed of atoms, the way that scientists would have us believe, but, rather, that it is composed of stories, which have to do with the things that concern us the most. They are stories of love, power, greed, children, and, of course, dogs. Over the years I have collected many of these stories about dogs – a large number of which have to do, in some way or another, with the emotional bond between people and their dogs. My collection includes tales of all genres: folk, fairy, and tall. There are complex myths and simple anecdotes, and some that may be, or at least try to masquerade as, true history.

When I was in university I was majoring in the science of psychology. However, because of my love of stories, I made time to take an elective course in folklore. The course did not have a focus on dogs, but on some of the classical Greek and Norse myths, plus a few African tales, and a smattering of stories from the Americas. However, it was during this course that my professor explained that each story could be reduced to a motif, which is a core idea, stripped of all of its embellishments.

One of the books that we were asked to consult was Stith Thompson's *Motif-Index of Folk Literature*, which attempted to organize all of these motifs into sensible groups, and to assign each of them a code consisting of a letter and a set of numbers. Although it was not part of our assignments, I remember poring through this index and finding 537 motifs featuring dogs in the collected folk tales of the world. But as I scanned the pages of this compendium I wondered whether it was possible to ever build a complete index of all of the ideas that make up folk tales, simply because these stories are always changing, evolving, and often expanding.

I suspect my feeling was based on a much earlier encounter that I had with Brother Solomon,

a Baptist preacher I had met while on leave from the army, and traveling through South Carolina. Brother Solomon loved to collect and tell folk tales which could be traced back to the Africans who were brought to America as slaves. After I heard him tell one particular story, another listener in the group protested that Solomon had changed the story, and it wasn't the same as when she had heard it from him on a previous occasion. Solomon simply smiled and said, "Of course I changed it. I always change the stories when I tell them, otherwise you would have no reason to listen to me telling them a second time. But you can change the story back when you tell it to someone else if you like."

I suppose that that is the joy of telling folk tales: namely, that every storyteller can put part of his or her own character into the story, and throw in a pinch of flavour from the place he comes from, and the time in history in which he or she lives to create something new and entertaining. The stories are not fixed in stone, and there really is no right or wrong way to tell them. The only requirement is that they must be interesting, and engage the listeners' attention.

Tall tales

Consider, for example, the 'tall tale,' which, for centuries, has formed the core of American folklore and literature. The essence of a tall tale is that it starts out as if the storyteller is relating an actual event – part of their own personal history – or a reminiscence about what happened, either to the narrator or an acquaintance.

To work successfully, a tall tale has to start with a familiar and believable setting or circumstance. Next, it must include some commonplace details and situations which, almost imperceptibly, evolve into the outrageous. This means that every telling of the tale must be different because the time, place and life history of the storyteller and his listeners are always changing. The author Mark Twain loved these tall tales, and many of the things he wrote were presented in much the way that tall tales would have been told while sitting around a fire after dinner. He observed

Gods, ghosts, and black dogs

that, for such a tale to work, you have to tell the story as if you believe every word, and can't understand why the audience is laughing.

An example of such a tall tale came to me the other day, whilse I was standing in line at a coffee shop. The man behind recognized me from a recent television appearance, and greeted me pleasantly. He noticed that I was wearing a pin in the shape of a Greyhound on the lapel of my sports jacket. He pointed at it and commented, "I once owned a Greyhound. Fast as blazes, he was. He was so fast that he could outrun his own shadow. But my problem with him was that he was so skinny that he kept escaping from the yard. He would find the narrowest little space between the slats in the fence, and he would be gone. I kept making the fencing tighter and tighter, but he would still find spaces where he could wriggle his way through.

"Then, one day, I was listening to the radio, and they had this dog expert on (someone just like you), and the radio show was taking telephone questions from listeners. So I figured I would phone in and see whether this clever professor guy who studied dogs could solve the problem of my skinny Greyhound escaping all the time. Sure enough, my phone call got through, and that dog expert told me, 'That's no problem at all. You don't even need any special training for your dog. All you've got to do to keep him from escaping through the cracks in your fence is to tie a few really big knots in his tail.' It was good advice, and it worked like a charm!" We both laughed, and I added another tall tale to my collection.

Perhaps because I was training to be a psychologist, what I had hoped to get when I took that folklore course so many years ago included, not just a record of the folk tales themselves, but a chance to study the people who made up these stories. My particular interest in the stories involving dogs might have been linked to my own research interests, which has to do with the psychological nature of the bond between people and dogs. Certainly, many such tales emphasize the way we think about dogs when the narrator describes events associated with the love and loyalty shared between humans and their cherished companion animals. However, it is also the case that,

throughout my life, I have really collected stories and folklore just because I like to hear them, and retell them when I get a chance. My methods do not involve a deliberate search for the lore of the dog, but most of the stories I have collected have come to me in casual ways as I have interacted with the various individuals with whom I crossed paths, and who were willing to talk to me: modern-day versions of bards and minstrels, maybe, but also typically down-to-earth people who are willing to take the time to tell me their favorite stories, or their most amusing tall tales. Sometimes, they tell me some fable that has been handed down through the years in their family as a special anecdote, or a story that has been passed on with the claim that it is a true piece of history.

Obviously, all of the dog stories that I cherish had creators, although, in the main, their names have not been included in the sagas I have heard. This is because the authors of these tales consider themselves to be ordinary people, not creative geniuses, and neither authors of books, articles, or blogs who demand a royalty, or at least a byline.

The storytellers

So, just who were these storytellers and yarn spinners? Well, some of them were bookless people who couldn't read and write, but still shaped fables which came to life in shanties, around hot stoves in cold winters, surrounded by the damp smell of mittens and wet dogs drying; the aroma of tobacco smoke and coffee, and the sound of laughter mocking the cold weather outside. You knew that one of these tellers of tales was about to begin creating when they moved their chair closer to the fire or the stove, reaching down to give a little pat to an old hound resting at their feet, before clearing their throat, and leaning back in their chair in a manner probably familiar to everyone present. It was then that the storyteller, beginning a story with an idea or an observation, would spin a web of fantasy for the others in the room.

In truth, it was the case that, often, the narrator himself didn't really know which direction the plot would take, or how the saga would end until it was told and the words had finally stopped flowing.

Some of the people who shaped these tales were educated, and, often, they created their particular brand of stories for those occasions when with companions and wine-filled crystal glasses, time was moving slowly. Such an individual might reach out and touch his well-groomed companion dog, before proceeding to spin out a story about some fantastic canine, in order to bridge a gap in the conversation. If this storyteller had not told their little anecdote at that moment, doubtless someone else in the group might have tried to use the lull in the discussion to talk about politics or finance, the state of the world or how human morality is going to pieces – the kind of topics that stir the emotions and the intellect, rather than encouraging comfortable social interaction.

Stories about dogs are safe, and don't impinge on anybody's political ideology, religious beliefs, or economic motives. Such stories simply pass the time, and allow people to interact; maybe laugh a bit, or give a surprised, "Where did *that* come from?" Meanwhile, the dogs in the room scrounge around, under the tables, beneath the chairs, hoping (the way that all dogs have always hoped), that maybe something edible might have fallen on the floor, while, above them, the fables about real and imagined and invented canines grow fatter with each telling, and rich in the embellishment of each successive storyteller. These stories are not intellectual constructions, or deep analyses of situations, but part of the social fabric of that moment: an expression of the good feelings of people chatting about nothing at all, and occasionally telling tales of fantasy, wonder, amazement and entertainment. As such, the stories do not have to be part of a grand mythology, and can be a short, simple parable that becomes part of a conversation or social interaction, and disappears from consciousness, even before the wine in the glass has been drained.

My collection

So, at this late stage in my life I have decided to crack open my own personal collection of folk tales, anecdotes, and stories about dogs. Some are short, some are long, some draw upon old and ancient myths, some claim that they have some foundation in history, and some are just simple fables that are passed around by family members and friends. But all of my stories have to do with dogs., and whether the stories involve kings, knights, elves, ogres, talking animals, fairies, witches, demons, gods or just plain folk, they all tend to shed some light on the way we think about dogs and relate to them.

In many instances I try and relate the circumstances in which I first heard the tale, and perhaps say something about who told it to me, because all of that detail is part of the magic of the story. I can't always provide that information, since, at my age, my memory is broken in a few places. Names of the tellers of the tales often become lost, and sometimes, when several stories are told, one after another, around a mug of hot buttered rum, it is difficult to sort out who told which story the next morning. I try to tell each story the way that I remember it, of course, with a few of my own embellishments here and there, since telling a story without adding something is no fun at all. I don't think that the original storytellers would mind that, though, as all of us have the feeling that each story we tell is something that came *to* us, rather than something that was created *by* us, and we are merely borrowing these stories for a while, decorating them, and then passing them on.

I give you these stories that I have preserved simply because they amuse and fascinate me, and I think that you might enjoy them as well. They are not meant to be part of your education, even though some contain valuable insights into the way that we think about dogs. Hopefully, a few of these stories might turn out to be ones that you will remember, and you might find yourself inclined to take the opportunity to slip one of them into a conversation somewhere, or turn another into a bedtime tale to catch the imagination of a child. If any of these folk tales do not work to your satisfaction, feel free to change them to make them better, and then hand on the improved version to someone else as part of your contribution to the fabric of the universe of stories ...

Why dogs chase cats

I was at the University of Pennsylvania's Museum of Archaeology and Anthropology, standing in what served as the 'artifact laboratory' of a friend of mine. Since its founding in 1887, the museum has collected more than a million objects, many of which have come from field excavations and expeditions, while others have been obtained by collectors who scour the world for interesting historical and culturally significant items. My friend is an archaeologist, and he and his students have unearthed and collected many of the objects now stored in the museum. Once these ancient items are gathered, they're brought back to Philadelphia, where the hard work of analyzing and reconstructing what has been collected on the expeditions begins. This phase of the work often involves collaboration with paleontologists, historians, biologists, and other specialists.

Although the analysis of archaeological artifacts can often require some very complex scientific equipment, much of the important work involves just the use of the researcher's trained eyes and some fairly simple measuring devices, which means that an artifact lab might not always look very laboratory-like. This particular room looked more like a warehouse than a laboratory, with rows of metal shelving containing white cardboard boxes. Most of the boxes were the size in which manila file folders and bank documents are commonly stored in, although other shelves contained brown cardboard boxes that looked like oversized versions of the boxes that pizzas are delivered in. All were neatly labelled with white, orange or pink tags.

In the middle of the room stood a long table, on which were magnifying glasses, rulers, calipers and measuring tapes, as well as an array of photographic equipment. Next to it was another long table, and it was the one that I was leaning against while my friend took one of those 'pizza boxes' from a shelf, checked its label, and then placed it down in front of me. Opening the box he extracted a large clay brick which he carefully placed on the table, and began explaining its significance to me.

"I thought that as a psychologist who studies dogs, this artifact would make you smile. It really is a record of behaviour, and it shows how constant and predictable certain behaviours can be."

He went on to explain, "Now, if you ask people to tell you about the most typical, or characteristic behaviours that dogs are known for, I think that high on the list would be the observation that dogs chase cats. In fact (if you forgive me for my undue emphasis), it seems to me that if there is any one thing which is an absolute and universal truth in the world, pertaining to behaviour, at least, it is that dogs do chase cats.

"Lying in front of you is evidence of that psychological and behavioural truth, and the neat thing is that it comes from 3000 years BC. One of our University of Pennsylvania teams collected it around 60 years ago in India, in the province of Sindh from one of the ancient Harappa cities. If you study this carefully you can see that this brick is a record of a cat being chased by a dog. It seems clear that the two animals raced across it when the clay was soft and unbaked, and if you look here you can see the deep impressions of the front edge of their foot pads, as well as their degree of spread, which indicates that the animals were running very fast. And over here you can see that the dog's footprint slightly overlaps the cat's, which shows that he was running behind."

I let my fingers gently rove over the surface of the brick, feeling the indentations that made up the footprints, while picturing in my mind the image of a cat fleeing from a dog in that ancient land, 5000 years ago. It gave me a sort of spooky feeling as the nerves in my fingertips seemed to make contact with living things that were so long gone, but which had been acting in the same way that their great, great, great grandchildren were acting today. It also gave me a feeling of continuity and predictability in their behaviour.

I smiled, then playfully said to my friend, "This is wonderful. Now if you could also explain the reason why it is true that dogs chase cats, then that would be a real contribution to behavioiral psychology."

He laughed and wandered over to a counter that contained an electric coffee maker. As he poured coffee into two white mugs bearing the university's crest, he replied, "I can't give you the explanation with certainty, but my grandfather could."

He returned to the table and handed me one of the mugs of coffee. Since no cream or sugar was evident, I simply sipped the bitter hot black liquid, giving a shrug and wave of my hand to encourage him to continue.

"Well, Dedushka (that is what we kids called my grandfather) was from Russia, and was a reservoir of what I like to call 'why?' stories. No matter what question any of us kids asked him — why is the sky blue or why the sea is salty, he had a story to explain it. When I was around eight or nine years of age, my grandparents had some kind of mixed breed terrier called Filat, and they also had an orange tabby cat called Lyov. That dog was always chasing that cat, and I remember asking Dedushka to tell me why that was the case. He assured me that this chasing behaviour was not unique to Filat and Lyov, but that all dogs chase all cats. He then told me one of his 'why?' stories to explain this. As best as I can remember, the story went something like this.

"Way back in the beginning, a short time after people were created, God created dogs. This was so long ago that there was only one kind of dog, and they all looked the same: smaller than wolves; their short hair a light brown colour. They all had foxy faces, sort of pricked-up ears (bent over a little at the top), and long tails that were not bushy.

"God knew that people were smart, but he also knew that they weren't wise in the ways of the world yet. So when he created dogs, he whispered in their ears, telling him: 'I am giving you a task, and if you succeed at it, you and all the generations of dogs who follow you will be rewarded. I'm putting you on earth as a companion to and protector of the people I have created. As animals I know that you are wise in the ways of the world, and alert to what is going on around you. Use your wisdom and what you gather from observing the world to help educate my fragile humans, and make their lives more successful and more comfortable.'

"These animals, the Mother and Father of All Dogs, accepted their task willingly, and carried it out diligently. Firstly, they looked around to see what conditions the people were living in in order to decide what, as dogs, they might do to improve the lives of their human charges, who were really not in good shape, and barely surviving. These first people were cold and miserable, because they had not even learned how to make fire for themselves, so, when night came, they would huddle together and share their body heat, hiding in the darkness of their caves, hoping not to be noticed by the wild beasts who roamed nearby. The dogs knew about fire because they had seen it a few times after lightning bolts had struck trees, and thought to themselves that this fire thing might be useful for their human charges, if it could be tamed and understood. The dogs watched carefully whenever there was a storm, hoping that they might have the chance to capture some fire.

"One day, there was a brief storm with thunder and lightning, and the ever-watchful dogs saw a lightning bolt hit a tree not far from the cave that the people were hiding in, and immediately ran to it to see if the lightning had caused some fire. The dogs were in luck, and, with the help of his mate, the Father of All Dogs managed to break off a burning branch with his mouth, which he carefully balanced as they started back toward the cave. It soon became clear, however, that the branch would be completely burned up before they reached the people, so the Father of All Dogs laid down the flaming branch for a moment to try and think what to do.

"As luck would have it, he happened to lay the branch next to another branch that had blown from a tree, and the fire touched this new branch and set it alight. Cleverly, the Father of All Dogs realised he had discovered the secret of how to keep fire alive.

"Using his newly-acquired knowledge, the dog carried the branch a little farther. Meanwhile, the Mother of All Dogs ran through the forest and found another dry branch. Then, as the branch the Father Dog was carrying began to burn low, he set it next to the piece of dry wood that his mate had found to ignite this. The dogs repeated this process until they returned to where the cold people were huddled together, trying to keep warm in the darkness of their cave. The dogs brought them this wondrous hot thing, which also shed light, and the people were amazed. The Mother of All Dogs placed another dry branch nearby, and touched the flame to it to show the

people how one flame could be used to start another fire, keeping the flames alive forever.

"Fire was the key to human progress, and, soon, it was not only used to provide heat and light, and cook their food, but also to extract metal from the ground and forge it into tools and weapons. These new tools meant that houses could be built, and also that plows, hoes and rakes could be fashioned to allow humans to grow their own food rather than rely on hunting alone.

"God saw how the dogs had improved the lives of people by teaching them about fire, and he was pleased. He did not forget the promise that he had made to the dogs, and whispered into the ears of the people 'Look at this animal. These are the dogs that I have created and fashioned to help make your lives so much better. Remember what this Father of All Dogs and Mother of All Dogs look like because you owe them, and all of their children who may be born in future generations, a great debt. When you see an animal who looks like this, remember that it was such an animal who helped bring you fire, and who has earned the right to live in your homes and sleep in front of the fire. You must also grant dogs the right to eat any food that falls on the floor, and any leftover food that might be scraped from the cooking pots or the dinner bowls before you clean them. Remember what these special animals look like and treat them well.'

"The people heard what God was saying, so they looked at the dogs and forged a memory of what such an animal looked like. As instructed, they remembered to show the dogs respect, and give them access to food (the leftovers and food that the people did not need) when they saw a dog. The dogs were pleased and happy and comfortable. The dogs were also glad that they were allowed the sleep by the fire that they had brought to mankind.

"With the new metal tools that the fire allowed them to create, the people soon began to clear the land, and plant crops, growing grains like wheat, corn, oats and barley. Such grain was special because it could be dried, and stored, and would provide food during the barren months of the winter when no fresh vegetables were available, no nuts or berries to be gathered, and the wild animals sheltered in caves or under the snow, and were difficult to hunt. It was then that the grains could be crushed and milled and made into bread or hot mush porridge to keep the people alive and well-fed.

"But the world was filled with many animals, each with their own needs, and it is true to say that many of them did not care about the welfare of people. It was not long after humans began to store grain that rats and mice discovered the places where all of this food was stockpiled for the village – a great bonanza to these creatures – who snuck into the storerooms and tore into the sacks that contained the grain. They ate much of it, scattered much of it in the dirt on the floor, and fouled and spoiled much more grain than they actually ate. As a result much of the precious food that the people had planted, harvested and stored became unfit for human consumption. Because of the loss of so much of their accumulated provisions, the people began to worry about having enough food to make it through the year.

"It was then that the cat entered the picture. Up until then the Mother and Father of All Cats had wandered the forest, catching mice, rats, rabbits, squirrels, birds, lizards, and whatever else they could hunt in order to feed themselves. This was hard work, which could often be very uncomfortable, especially when the weather was cold, when rain was falling, or when there was snow on the ground.

"But cats are clever and observant, and could see what was happening in the villages, quickly realising that mice and rats gathered in great numbers in the places where people stored their grain and other food. It would be an easy matter for cats to get all of the food they needed by hunting the rodents who gathered around the humans' storerooms. What is more, the cats would not have to stalk or track the rodents, but could simply wait until their prey appeared, and even better was the fact that, since they would be inside a house, barn or storage building, hunting could be carried out in relatively warm and dry conditions. The felines concluded that this might be a really good deal, and so presented themselves to the humans, who accepted their presence, allowing them to live inside, and share

their warm dwelling. The cats would hunt the rodent pests to earn their living, killing and eating the mice and rats, the meat from which would sustain them. The humans liked this idea since it would reduce the population of pests in their villages, in turn preserving the precious grain that they needed to survive.

"All went well for a while. The dogs did not mind when the cat's joined them in laying on the rug in front of the fire; the cats grew fat from eating the rodents, and the amount of grain that was spoiled was greatly reduced.

"But cats are basically lazy beasts, and would rather not have to work for their food if at all possible. Cats are also jealous and envious creatures who do not often live in peace with others: always evaluating their own situation in relation to that of others, and unhappy when another appears to be faring better than they.

"The cats regarded the dogs with envy, and one day the Father of All Cats asked the Mother of all Cats: 'Why should we have to work all night hunting rats and mice to feed ourselves, while the dogs are treated like royalty and allowed to eat the scraps of food that fall on the floor? Why should the humans act like the dogs' servants by taking the scrapings from the cooking pots and their own dinner plates, putting them in a bowl, and placing this in front of the dogs as if they were honoured guests?' and the Mother of All Cats replied: 'Think about this, if there were no dogs in the humans' house, or if there were fewer dogs, at least, that would mean that there would be more food, on the floor or scraped from the pots, and certainly the humans would give it to us, their hard-working cats.'

"The Father of All Cats thought about his mate's words, and his envy of the dogs grew, and he became more and more bitter. As it happened, the first Mother of All Dogs was pregnant, and due to give birth to her litter of pups in a few weeks. The cat knew that this meant there would soon be even more dogs around: more dogs to crowd around the fire; more dogs to gather scraps of food from the floor, and more dogs to eat the scrapings from the pots and plates, making it even less likely that the cats would get food without having to hunt. The Father of All Cat's intense

Gods, ghosts, and black dogs

envy drove him to hatch a plan — a violent course of action that would prevent those puppies from ever coming into the world.

"That night, while the people lay in their beds, and the two dogs slept by the fire, instead of hunting rats and mice the Father of All Cats climbed up on the mantelpiece of the fireplace. Then, without warning, he hurled himself down from that height, paws straight, claws out, aiming straight for the belly of the pregnant dog. He hit her full force, and then jumped up and down as many times as he could and as hard as he could. The Father of All Cats might have damaged the Mother of All Dogs permanently if her mate had not awakened and chased the cat away, across the room and out through an open window.

"The cats hid behind the sacks of grain in the storeroom, where the Father of All Cats laughed and told his mate 'There will be no puppies this time, and if I can do that every time the dog becomes pregnant there will not be enough dogs in the world to compete for the food that the people would otherwise waste. This plan will surely work, and we will not have to hunt all night while the dogs sleep.'

"When morning came the cats were pleased to hear the Mother of All Dogs wailing in pain. The cat's attack had started her labour much earlier than it should have, and the puppies were being delivered. It might be said that the cat's plan failed, as, in fact, there were puppies. But, oh what puppies! The cat's vicious attack had done something to change the puppies in the womb, and now, instead of them all looking the same, each appeared different. One was tiny — no larger than a teacup — while another looked large enough to eat all of his siblings. Some had pricked ears, some floppy; some had long hair, some short; some had spots or patches of colour; some had flat faces, some had sharp faces; some had bushy tails, some had tiny little stumps. They were all dogs, but they no longer looked like the first dogs at all.

"When the humans came to see the puppies they did not recognize them as dogs, as they certainly did not look like the image of dogs that God had asked them to remember and honour with the warmth of their fire and the excess food in their home. They did not trust these strange beings, and certainly would not give them all of the benefits that they gave the first dogs. If it had not been for the fact that the Father of All Dogs and the Mother of All Dogs stood between the confused and unhappy people and their newborn pups, the puppies might've been killed, and certainly would have been driven out of the humans' home.

"Although the cats' plan had not worked in the way they had hoped, the damage was done, and it was to be many years before humans accepted that these differently shaped and sized creatures really were dogs, and many more years still before they truly believed that, although each dog looked different, they were still the descendants of the original helpmates who had brought them the gift of fire: the very animals that God had instructed them to honour. Over those long years, some dogs did come to be accepted, and were allowed to sleep by the fire, while others were forced to live outside because they did not resemble the first dogs.

"And this bias is still evident in people today. Some accept and love dogs with a particular appearance, but reject those who look different. This may have to do with the way in which the human memory tries to recall the image of the first dogs, and reconcile this with the many different shapes and sizes of dogs that exist today.

"But one thing that remains the same is the memory which dogs have of that night when the Father of All Cats attacked the Mother of All Dogs. Because of this no dog now fully trusts cats. In fact, whenever a dog sees a cat and remembers what was done to their ancestor, he or she will give chase, just as the Father of All Dogs did all those years ago. Dogs will chase cats to drive them away from the fire. Dogs will chase cats to drive them away from unearned food which might come from the hand of humans. Dogs will also chase cats to protect their unborn puppies.

"it's not clear whether or not dogs fully understand that the reason they are compelled to chase cats stems from this incident so long ago. Maybe a trace of memory of what that first cat did, and what he looked like has passed down through the generations of canines, and now become part of the dog's DNA. Cats look much more similar to one another than do dogs, so the memory of what a cat looks like is certainly clear in a dog's mind. It is therefore likely that the dog simply reacts to the sight of a cat, and the feeling that this is something that should be chased."

My friend laughed and said, "And that's the way that Dedushka, my grandfather, explained why dogs chase cats. Of course, he would have told it with a glass of vodka in his hand, which I am sure would make it more convincing."

I laughed and assured him, "It works pretty well with just a cup coffee." Placing my own coffee mug on the table, I ran my hand over that ancient brick once again. As my fingers traced the indentations of the paws of those long-gone animals, I imagined the Father of All Cats being chased by the Father of All Dogs. Here was 5000 year old proof of my friend's claim that one of the great universal truths is that dogs chase cats.

Visit Hubble and Hattie on the web: www.hubbleandhattie.com
www.hubbleandhattie.blogspot.co.uk
• Details of all books • Special offers • Newsletter • New book news

Dogs, rice and sex

It was around two o'clock in the afternoon, and I was sitting in a modest, family-run Thai restaurant with a friend. Because it was a small operation with few employees other than the family, the restaurant opened for lunch between the hours of 11am and 1:30pm, and then closed for the afternoon; reopening at 5:30pm for dinner service. I had been coming to this restaurant for a number of years, and particularly liked to use it when I wanted a relaxed lunch and quiet place to talk to someone. The family knew me, and liked me because I had helped solve a house soiling problem they had with their dog. They never rushed me out in the afternoon if I stayed beyond the usual lunch hours, and also made sure that I had hot tea, and otherwise treated me as if I was visiting family.

Lawan, the restaurant owner's wife, came by and deposited a new pot of tea on the table, returning a few moments later carrying a bowl that contained mostly rice with a few vegetables. Sitting down at the table next to ours, she was followed by a small, white-and-black fluffy dog, which I guessed was most probably a Shih Tzu, although quite a bit larger

than the average size for that breed. I knew, from my previous experiences with the dog, that his name was Phueng, which was the Thai word for 'bee.' This label suited the dog well since Phueng tended to buzz around much like his namesake. I bent over to give him a pat, and he happily licked my fingers.

Lawan scooped a little rice from the bowl in front of her with a flat spoon, and offered it to Phueng. Looking up, she smiled, saying, "It is a tribute that one should offer to a dog if one is around when we eat rice."

Sensing that there was a story behind this, I tried to encourage her a little, asking, "So tell me the story behind this tribute."

Lawan hesitated for a moment, waving her hand in front of her, "Oh, it is just a kind of tradition that comes from a sort of folk tale. The story tells how it came to be that dogs are fed and can live in our houses, but don't have to do any work to earn their living."

I chuckled, "Then you must tell me so that I can also learn the secret of how to be fed and housed, and not have to do any work to earn my living!"

At this she laughed also, then paused to give the dog a few more grains of rice before responding. "There are really two parts to this story, one of which I've already told my children, but the other is . . . Well, I will wait until they are older before I tell them that part.

"Before they came here my grandparents were part of the Lisu people. They are hill people; part of a group of tribes who live in northern Thailand. Because of where they are located they hear many different stories: some are Hindu; some are Buddhist, and some are just handed down word of mouth through the generations. They all get mixed up, and although the names of the gods and demons stay the same, they often become stories which belong only to the Lisu people and nobody else.

"Like the Hindus, the Lisu believe that the world has been created and destroyed many times. Only it seems that in this current creation we have been much more clever, and have managed to survive much longer than any of the other worlds that were made before this one. It is the god Brahma who creates the worlds, but once they are made 'The Grandfather' doesn't pay very much attention to them. If the people in the world become old and weak, or if they fail to do good deeds, the god Shiva comes along and destroys the world. That wakes up Brahma again, and he goes about the task of re-creating the universe.

"One of the reasons that people became weak in earlier creations of the world was because they did not have enough food. Human beings had to survive on what they could scrounge, like berries, grasses, bark, and roots. They were not very good hunters (and animals were much smarter in that earlier time), so they very seldom had any meat.

"Fortunately, the great god Vishnu liked the people in our particular creation, and felt he would like this world to continue for a long time. He knew that people must stay healthy, otherwise they would attract the attention of Shiva, the destroyer of worlds. Vishnu also knew that to stay healthy the people must have proper food. So the god came to earth dressed in white and riding a great bird, and told the people that, behind the great mountains, was the land of the Daityas, who were great and dangerous giants, led by the brothers Hiranyaksha and Kumbhakarna. What was important for the people to know was that the Daityas were growing rice. The god Vishnu assured the people that if they could obtain some rice seeds and plant them, they could grow enough food to be healthy and to live long lives.

"Getting the rice was not going to be easy, however. The problem was that the land of the Daityas was completely surrounded by mountains which were much too high and too dangerous for humans to climb. The only other way into and out of the land of the giants was through the back of a certain cave: if you looked hard enough you could find the entrance to a narrow tunnel, which was much too small for any human to go through. But Vishnu had an idea.

"Brahma had given the people dogs of many sizes to help them with tasks. Some were guard dogs; some were noisy little dogs that were supposed to sound the alarm if strangers came near the village. Some dogs had to wear packs and saddlebags to carry tools and other possessions; some were trained to find roots and berries to help feed the people, and others had jobs to do with hunting rats and vermin, and so on. The dogs worked hard, but lived mostly on scraps left over by the people, or bits of food that they might forage for themselves. In addition, they were forced to stay outside in the cold and wet, since it was considered improper to have a dog inside the home. Vishnu suggested that it might be possible for one of the smaller dogs to make it through the tunnel, and get some rice seeds for the people.

"So, this tribe of the people that Vishnu favoured chose a small, fluffy, black-and-white dog named Dao, which means 'star,' to help them in their quest, as Dao seemed to be a very bright and clever dog. They led him to the mouth of the cave which Vishnu had pointed out, and asked Dao to go through and bring them back some rice seeds.

The dog eventually made his way through the tunnel and reached the land of the giants. Once there, Dao carefully and cautiously explored the land around him, and managed to find his way to the place where the Daityas dried their rice, next to a great open shelter where the giants kept all kinds of foodstuff,

Gods, ghosts, and black dogs

including salt, meat, honey, and even bread.

"The dog considered the situation, and realized that, even if he was able to safely make his way down to where the rice was drying, he had no way of carrying the rice seeds back to the people. He had no sack; no basket, and even if he had had a container for the rice, he was too small to carry such things. It was then that the Dao had a sudden inspiration.

"The giant, Hiranyaksha, was supposed to stand guard that day, but the sun was hot and he had lain down and was dozing, which made it easy for the dog to make his way to the entrance of the shelter where the food was kept. Dao stood next to the pile of food, and began to bark loudly. Hiranyaksha woke up with a start, grabbed his club, and lumbered off to attack the intruder. But the dog was small and fast, and he easily avoided the giant's weapon, while trying to manoeuvre him into a certain position at the same time.

Once Dao felt that the giant was in the right spot, he barked loudly and stood in place until the giant again swung his club. At the last moment the dog dodged away, and the club smashed several jugs that contained honey. While Hiranyaksha stared in dismay at the mess, Dao quickly rolled in the sticky honey. As the giant let out a roar of anger and raised his club again, the dog managed to dart between the giant's legs, and run to where the rice was drying. He rolled in the pile of rice, and many hundreds of seeds stuck to his honey-covered fur. After a mad dash to the tunnel entrance, Dao worked his way back to where the people were waiting.

"The people carefully cleaned the rice seeds out of the dog's coat, and planted them the way that Vishnu had told them to, so that it would grow quickly and provide food for everyone. The people remembered Vishnu had said they should honour kindness done to them by bestowing kindness in turn, and so, as they washed the honey out of the dog's hair, they promised Dao that for bringing them the rice, he and all other dogs would be fed by humans forever. And it is in memory of that promise — and as a tribute to the race of dogs for what one of their number did long ago to ensure that people have food

to eat — that we offer dogs a few grains of cooked rice at each meal."

Lawan smiled, and said, "And this is the story that I have told my children."

"And the part of the story that your children are not yet old enough to hear — what about that?" I asked.

Lawan's face reddened a little with a blush, "Ah, yes. That story . . . well, it again begins with the god Vishnu, who looked at the world, and was pleased that the people were now growing rice and had enough food to keep them healthy, since this meant that Shiva would not soon come to destroy the world. But when he looked more closely, he noticed that the people of the world were growing old, and even though they had plenty of rice to eat, they soon grew frail and weak simply because of their age — a weakness that would soon attract the attention of Shiva the destroyer.

"When Brahma created the world, he realised that the animals had short lives, so if their species was to survive, they must have some way to regenerate, or at least have offspring. He divided the animals into sexes — male and female — and gave them sex organs that allowed them to quickly couple, and then get on with other business while their progeny grew inside of the female. For some reason, Brahma did not consider this aspect when it came to humans, so there was no such thing as different sexes. Vishnu knew that this was a problem, and that people, like animals, would have to reproduce. People would have to have children who could replenish their species, and keep their race populated and strong, allowing the world to continue, and escaping the attention of Shiva the destroyer.

"So Vishnu gathered all of the people (there were not so many then) and split each one, so that one half of each person's body became male, with the other half female, which, of course, meant that humans could now have sex, the result of which would be children.

"It is important to realise that humans of this time were not the same as the people of today; some details of their anatomy were rather different, for example. The story tells us that people did not really want to be split into male and female parts, and when men and women engaged in sexual intercourse, it felt so natural to be reunited into a single whole entity again that they did not want to separate from each other. The anatomy of their sex organs was such that their desire to be one unified being again actually caused them to become locked together, and they would have trouble separating from one another for a long period of time — until all of their passion had drained away.

"As you might expect, this led to all sorts of problems: for example, if someone came to the house to ask for coals for the fire, or if they needed assistance, or if an alarm was sounded because of a problem in the village, a couple could not get up from their sleeping platform to help, but could only lie there, locked together, until their passion had completely drained. And because of the nature of human desire, men and women would often end up locked together for long periods, at the most inconvenient times, interfering with their work in the fields, including the harvesting of rice, and even caring for their children. All in all, their lives had become very complicated because of this inconvenient aspect of the design of human bodies, which resulted from when they had unwillingly been separated into men and women.

"So the people petitioned the gods to ask for help. However, Brahma was unconcerned, since he was convinced that the way he had created the world was perfect, and needed no change. Shiva was not bothered by the situation either, because if the people did not create enough children, or did not care for them adequately, the world would grow weak, and he would simply destroy it so that it could be created again.

"However, Vishnu *did* care, since he liked this creation of the world and its inhabitants, and had already invested a lot of work in trying to make sure that the population remained healthy, and that the human race would continue. So, once again, Vishnu appeared in front of the people, this time in the form of a giant blue-skinned person with four arms.

"The god Vishnu then said to the people, 'I cannot create, or uncreate, or re-create you or parts of your world. Only Brahma has the ability to do that. I can, however, move things around, exchange them, or rearrange bits and pieces of them, but only if all of the individuals involved agree. So I have a proposal for you that might solve your problem. If you, and the race of dogs, agree, I will exchange your genitals so that humans will have those that belong to dogs and dogs will have those genitals that now belong to people.'

"Vishnu continued, 'This will be good for the humans because this change in anatomy would mean they will be free to have sex and then go about their business. But if dogs agree to this plan, then all humans must promise that they will not give dogs work to do except for those tasks that the dogs themselves consent to. With no chores or designated work, it should not be so great an inconvenience for males and females of the canine species to be stuck together for long periods of time after they have sexual intercourse. But remember that, if everyone is willing to accept this proposal, it means that if a dog feels that eating, sleeping, and playing with your children are the only tasks that he is willing to do, then you must accept this.'

"Both the people and the dogs consented to this arrangement, and so it has been since that time."

Lawan smiled broadly, and added, "I will not tell that part of the story to my children until they are old enough that I do not have to explain to them what sexual intercourse is — even if they are already asking me why they have so many chores to do while our dog just lies on the carpet and relaxes."

We all laughed at this. Phueng gave a little bark and twirled a little, as if to acknowledge that he and his species had come out of this cosmic bargain the clear winners!

How the dog made
man fit to live

One of the things that emerges over and over in the folklore of dogs is the importance of the bond that they share with people, which many stories seem to suggest existed from the time that dogs and people were created.

A professor from the University of New Mexico at Albuquerque told me one such story, which he claimed to have heard from a member of the Tinde Indians tribe, best known outside of the tribe as the Jicarilla Apaches. As far as can be determined by oral account, the Jicarilla migrated from Canada in the 1400s, and settled on land bounded by four sacred rivers in northern New Mexico and southern Colorado. These sacred rivers are what we now call the Rio Grande, Pecos River, Arkansas River, and the Canadian River. Inside that area are the sacred mountain peaks and ranges which serve as landmarks in many of the Indians' stories.

According to the Jicarilla Apaches, Black Hactcin was the creator of the world. He created the sky, the Earth, the rivers and lakes, and all of the animals in the world. As each species of beast was created, Black Hactcin asked it where it chose to live

and what it chose to do. The birds chose to fly and live in the sky, while the fish chose to swim in the water, and other animals chose to be hunters, or to live a more quiet life grazing, and eating the food that the plants of the forests and plains provided.

One of the animals that Black Hactcin created was the dog. When the dog was asked what he was going to do in the world, he replied, "I am comfortable here with you, Grandfather, and I would really like just to be your companion. Is that possible?"

Black Hactcin smiled, because he liked the dog, but said, "That cannot be, since I have much to do, and will soon be journeying into the night sky. I believe that it would be good for me to make stars to decorate the sky, and serve as a map to guide all living things in their travels. Making stars is hard work, and will take me a long time, and you, as a mortal being, would not be able to find a place to stand in the sky with me while I shape the stars."

This made the dog unhappy, since he was a sociable beast who liked company, and often felt depressed when there was no one around for him to be with. After a little thought the dog asked, "Oh,

Grandfather, then can you make me a companion? I know that no companion will ever be as great and good as you, but can you make me a companion who is fit to be in the world with me, and could remain behind to take care of the world when you go into the night sky?"

"I don't know if I can create a proper companion for you," replied Black Hactcin, "I have given great thought to all of the animals, and I created each with qualities that make them special. It may be difficult to create another which is special enough and different enough to add to the set of animals that are already here ... but I will try. Firstly, I will lie down and you must draw a circle around me with your paw."

So the dog carefully scratched a circle in the earth, making sure that it went all the way around the great Creator. Black Hactcin stood up and looked at it: he said, "That should do." Carefully stepping out of the circle that the dog had drawn, he walked around it three times before saying to the dog, "Go a little way from here and don't look back, while I do my work here."

The dog went off a little way, as instructed. He was a dog, however, and curious and impatient, so in a few minutes he looked back. From where he stood he could see something, and exclaimed in surprise, "Oh, Grandfather, someone is now lying in the place where you were lying."

"Don't look. Walk further off," replied Black Hactcin.

The dog obeyed and went a little further away, but he was still a dog, and again he could not help himself looking back. When he did he blurted out, "Now someone is sitting there."

Black Hactcin laughed at the dog's eagerness, but repeated, "Don't look! Walk further off."

The dog walked some distance away again, and paced, and turned in circles, until at last the creator called him. "Now you can come back and look," he said.

The dog raced back so quickly that he collided with Black Hactcin. The god laughed and gave him a gentle pat on his head, while the dog peeked around the god's legs to see what was in the circle.

"Oh, Grandfather, he moves," cried the dog.

Together, they stood by the newly-created man and looked him over.

"He's wonderful!" replied the dog.

Black Hactcin walked behind the man and lifted him to his feet.

"Now run," Black Hactcin said, and took hold of the man and showed him how to run. And so the man ran.

"Now talk," said Black Hactcin, but the man said nothing. Four times his creator told the man to talk, to speak, to make a sound, to say something to prove that he could talk, but still the man said nothing. The god cast his eyes down and took a deep breath. Sadly, Black Hactcin said to the dog, "He is not right. He is not fit to live as your companion. He must be undone."

"Wait, please, Grandfather; let me try," said the dog.

The dog walked in front of the man-thing, looked up at his face and barked, "ruff!" The man stepped back in surprise, and said "Huh?"

The dog then barked twice, "ruff! ruff!" and the man said in a puzzled voice, "Huh? What?"

"Is this talking?" asked the man.

"Yes, you are learning. This is a good start," replied Black Hactcin, and the dog barked in agreement.

"Now shout," said Black Hactcin, and he gave a big yell to show the man how to do it, while the dog barked and howled to make a great sound as well. The man looked at the two of them, and listened and understood. Soon, he also began to shout.

"Well, what else? There is something missing ..." said Black Hactcin, "something which he yet needs to be fit to live."

Black Hactcin thought for a minute, then turned to the man. "Laugh!" he commanded. The man did not understand, so Black Hactcin repeated "Laugh! Laugh! Laugh! Laugh!" and each time he did so his voice became louder, and by the fourth repetition he was becoming frustrated and his voice was loud and angry. The man, who did not understand, was becoming afraid of the anger in the creator's voice.

Annoyed and discouraged Black Hactcin said, "He is not ready. He is not fit. He must be unmade."

Gods, ghosts, and black dogs

"Wait, please, Grandfather," said the dog again, and stepped between the man and the angry god. When the dog did this, the man was less afraid, and relaxed enough to smile just a bit.

Then the dog turned back to the man, and jumped up on him and licked his face and his hands. He then backed up and ran off a little way, running back to jump up on the man again and lick him, his tail wagging. He kept on jumping up on the man, and dancing around in front of him, the way that dogs do today when they are full of love and delight. And as he did so, the man's smile grew wider and he began to laugh.

The dog ran off and grabbed a stick, returning with it and dropping it at the man's feet. The man picked it up, and the dog backed away with a happy bark. The man understood what he wanted, and tossed the stick in the direction of the dog. The dog chased after the stick and brought it back, and when he did the man took it and tossed it again, and, as he did, he began to laugh more. He knelt down in front of the dog, took his head in his hands, ran his hands through the fur around the dog's face, and tousled his ears, and all the while he was laughing. He laughed and he laughed, and Black Hactcin began to laugh as well at the sight.

"Now the man is fit to live," said the creator of all things. Turning to the dog he said, "Finally, you have a worthy companion, my dog," and looking at the man he said, "Go and make a home together with the dog. I am going into the sky now, but I will look down on you, and I expect to see you walking together with the dog, and to hear from you the sound of the talking and laughter that he taught you."

The man took his dog as the god instructed, and man and dog have been together ever since.

Sir Bedivere and the dragon

Of all of the folk tales that originate from England, many of the most familiar — and certainly some of the most complex and exciting — have to do with the legend of King Arthur and the Knights of the Round Table. The story of King Arthur has been told and retold by a great many people, and has been rewritten as literature many times, and by many different authors. With so many stories of Arthur and his Knights in existence it's hard to tell which are parts of the original legend and which are newer literary elaborations. Then again, don't all folk tales arise and grow as a series of elaborations by those who tell and retell the story?

Let me tell you one such story of King Arthur's time which tells of the courage of men and dogs. I no longer remember when or where I first encountered this story, but it is a particular favourite of mine — probably because all of the characters and settings are so familiar.

This story begins on a morning when Sir Bedivere was called to King Arthur's chambers. Sir Bedivere had been a trusty supporter of King Arthur from the beginning of his reign, and one of the first knights to join the fellowship of the Round Table. Sir Bedivere helped Arthur fight against the Giant of Mont Saint-Michel, and he would be present at Arthur's last battle — the fateful Battle of Camlan against the forces of the King's illegitimate son, Mordred. Sir Bedivere and Arthur alone survived that fight, and it was Bedivere who was given the task of returning Arthur's sword, Excalibur, to the Lady of the Lake while the great King's life-force slowly ebbed because of the wounds he had received. But that sad ending was still many years away, and these were happier times when the fellowship of the Knights of Camelot was still strong.

"Bedivere," began the King, "I have a problem, and will need your services, and perhaps even your strong arm and your sword, to resolve it. I have been receiving reports from one of our towns located next to the River Tweed on the border of Lothian. It is a region under the care of Sir Hywel, who was a strong knight in his time but who was wounded in battle, and is now rather frail. If I had received only one such report, I would have considered it a bit of madness or fantasy, but there have now been several

Gods, ghosts, and black dogs

similar dispatches from the region, and each new version contains a deeper note of fear and panic.

"The reports have to do with a dragon." Arthur raised a hand to silence the protest he saw forming on Bedivere's lips.

"No, I do not really believe in the existence of dragons. Even though my family name is Pendragon, which means 'head dragon' or 'chief dragon.' It is not a name that my father, Uther, earned by fighting dragons, but rather it comes from the fact that his father was born when a great comet was in the sky, and that comet was in the shape of a dragon. Still, there are respectable people in many places around the world who claim to have seen dragons. Lancelot says that when he was in France, he encountered two villages that had been burned to the ground, and the surviving residents claimed that this devastation resulted from the anger of a fire-breathing dragon.

"The reports that I have been getting say that this dragon has taken up residence in a cave near the River Tweed, and has been demanding to be fed, or otherwise he will ravage the countryside with fire. So every week the people bring him an ox, or a horse, or two sheep. Some children and older people have also begun disappearing, and Sir Hywel fears that the dragon may be taking these as well.

"I'm told that two of Sir Hywel's knights and a squad of soldiers were sent to kill the dragon, but were never heard from again, and reports are that the dragon still lives, and is still demanding tribute. I am going to send you to confirm that such a beast really exists, and, if so, then I give you the task of ridding the countryside of the dragon. I would give you a comrade-in-arms, but none of the other knights can be spared at this time, so, instead, I will give you my favourite dog, Cavall, who is a proven hunter and fighter."

Arthur looked across the room to where a large gray dog was resting on a mat in front of the fireplace. Upon hearing his name, Cavall stood up and walked over to stand by the King. Bedivere looked at the familiar form of Cavall, who often trotted beside Arthur when he travelled the countryside. Cavall was a huge dog. His shoulder reached almost to the King's waist, and his gray and grizzled head seemed as high as the middle of Arthur's chest. Courage and intelligence seemed to shine from his eyes.

Arthur gently stroked the dog's neck, and said "It was Cavall who helped me hunt the great boar, Twrch Trwyth. We had the beast trapped; however, it turned on our hunting party and injured many of my companions. I was fighting it when the beast unhorsed me. I dropped my lance and fell on my side, and could not free my sword. I could see that the boar was charging me. It was then that Cavall leapt forward and grabbed the boar's throat. It screamed in pain and veered away, giving me time to recover and draw Excalibur. Thus, it was because of Cavall's courage that Twrch Trwyth died that day and not me.

"I fear that if there really *is* a dragon it will be a more significant foe than the great boar, so I have ordered some armour to be prepared for Cavall. He will go with you, and will obey your commands. It is difficult to know exactly how intelligent he is, but he often appears to understand human speech well enough to carry out complex plans on the basis of what he has heard. Cavall will also protect you, since I have reminded him that you are a beloved comrade of mine that I wish to keep safe."

As Bedivere walked from the room, Cavall followed him, glancing back at his King only once. The knight and the dog went immediately to the armoury, which a man by the name of Leonard had run for many years: his staff of blacksmiths and craftsmen did wondrous work.

Leonard held up the armour which had been specially made for the dog, Cavall. "I have made his armour out of leather, which we have boiled so that it is almost as hard as steel, but is much lighter and will not restrict the dog's movements in any way. We have also added metal studs and a steel collar to provide extra strength and protection."

Leonard showed Bedivere how to fasten the armour onto the dog, and Cavall stood patiently while they fussed with the buckles and straps. Then, together, Arthur's dog and Bedivere went off to collect the knight's own armour and his powerful horse, Ifor, to begin the journey north in search of the dragon.

Four days into their trip north, Bedivere and Cavall came across a tall man standing in the middle of the road. He was dressed in gray robes and wore a soft, gray, pointed hat that folded to obscure much of his face, although it was still possible to see white hair and a long, white beard emerging from under the hat. In his left hand the man carried a long staff, which seemed to have runes carved into it, and a tip made of silver.

Bedivere's horse seemed uneasy at the sight of the man, and Bedivere himself was also a little suspicious of this encounter, since he had heard of cases where bandits had ambushed people on this road, after first enticing them to stop and talk with someone who seemed to be merely another traveller. As a precaution, the knight reached down his hand and made sure that his sword, Cadwgan, was loose in its scabbard.

Cavall seemed unfazed by the appearance of the man, and walked up to him to nose his hand. The man looked down at the dog, and said, "So, the Prince of Dogs is now the companion-in-arms for Sir Bedivere."

He reached out and rubbed the dog"s head, "How goes it, Cavall, in your new and elegant armour?"

As Cavall wagged his tail in response, Bedivere breathed a sigh of relief, since he now recognized the voice. "What brings the wizard Merlin so far north of Camelot?" he asked.

"I come with information important to your quest. Things do not go well by the River Tweed. The dragon is angry because Sir Hywel sent knights and troops to try and slay him. He now claims that he will no longer accept livestock as his food, but is demanding that his tribute be paid by feeding him members of the human population, beginning with the youths. The people are in great fear of this beast, and it appears that their terror is driving them to agree to his terms."

"Can dragons actually speak?" Bedivere asked.

"The ancient ones can speak in your mind, so that you know what they are saying, even if there is no sound. This particular dragon claims that his name is Aeddan. According to lore passed on about dragons, that is certainly the name of one of the old ones. This

seems to be confirmed by the fact that he can make his meaning clear to anyone.

"You must understand that dragons live so long because they are very difficult to kill. The scales of a dragon are very tough; even more resistant to weapons than the strongest armour. There are only a few places where the dragon's skin is exposed, and where a blade or spear might penetrate. One such place is at the base of the dragon's neck where the scales descend down the head to meet the scales rising up from the shoulder. This allows a small crease of skin to be exposed – his most serious weak spot – and where a well-placed blow from a sword or axe could mortally wound the beast.

"Unfortunately, the dragon is very large, and this target is above his front shoulder, making it very difficult to reach. There is also a small space at the top of each of his legs (think of these as the equivalent of your armpits), and these places contain soft skin which can be pierced by a weapon. Wounds in these locations will certainly hurt the dragon, although sword cuts there will not kill him, unless much blood is lost.

"Now listen carefully. People believe that dragons breathe fire. Dragon's want people to believe this, and this particular dragon's name – Aeddan – even translates to 'fire.' In fact, dragons do not breathe fire, but rather the dragon spits out a stream of venom, which – a few seconds after being exposed to the air – bursts into flame. The secret weakness of dragons is that they are actually vulnerable to fire, but no one thinks to use it against them since it is believed to be their weapon, and it is hard to imagine that a creature would be vulnerable to his own weapon. Since the venom is hurled a distance away from the dragon, the fire that it causes does not harm him, and so his susceptibility to damage from the flames remains a secret. If you can bring enough fire to the dragon, you may stand a chance of killing him.

"Bedivere, you are a great knight and you are clever, but you are hunting a very dangerous beast. Cavall is a better hunter than you, and he has killed many a legendary monster, even though some of those, like the great boar, were aided by magic. So when you enter combat with Aeddan you must look to Cavall and follow his lead. He is not only brave, he is also wise. That is all that I can offer to you, except to wish you Godspeed."

With that Merlin reached down, gave Cavall another pat on his head, and then walked swiftly past the mounted knight, heading south toward Camelot.

Two days later Sir Bedivere and Cavall stood before the door of the modest-sized castle owned by the Lord of this region, Sir Hywel. The guards stepped aside to reveal a distraught older man who was leaning on a cane. He was dressed in simple clothing except for an ornately embroidered tabard.

"You come alone?" Hywel seemed on the verge of tears. "You come alone, and you come too late. I asked King Arthur for help and he sends me one knight? Doesn't he know that two of my best and bravest knights and a company of soldiers who went out to face the dragon are already dead?" Hywel leaned heavily on his cane, and seemed to be struggling to regain his composure. Finally, he said in a voice full of despair, "And now my daughter, Arwen, shall be dead also."

"What do you mean?" asked Bedivere.

"We have just agreed to the dragon's terms, which are that every week, on Sunday morning, we will bring him a human to serve as a sacrifice, and upon which he can feed, in return for which he will not destroy with fire the villages and towns along the river. Because we displeased him by sending out knights and soldiers, he now mocks the misery of our failure. He has forced us to surround the space in front of his cave with bright banners and bunting, as though our arrival with one of our own people destined to die by his foul jaws is part of a festival or county fair. To add further to our shame, when we bring the person to be sacrificed they must be accompanied by the elders of the city, who must then bear witness to the slaughter, and swear that we will never again attack the dragon.

"I refused to be the one who would decide who must die, so we agreed to set up a lottery, in which all of the names of all of the young people in this town would be entered, and from which one name would be drawn each week. My own children insisted that to prove to the townships that we were

being fair, they must also bear the risk, as do the rest of the people. So, the names of my son and two daughters were included in the lottery. Now we have had the first drawing of the lottery. Fate can be cruel, even when you are trying to do the right thing, and by some stroke of evil luck the very first name drawn to be sacrificed was that of my youngest daughter, Arwen.

"The Council of Elders has taken my daughter, and they are already walking along the way to the dragon's cave."

"So they walk to the dragon, while I am mounted upon Ifor, who can run like the wind!" exclaimed Bedivere. "That means that there may still be time to save her. Show me where they are going."

Hywel pointed to a road that ran past the castle. "It is down this road. Follow it until you see the river, and you will see a side trail to the right, between a pair of old, crooked oak trees. Travel that path just a short way and you should see the banners at the mouth of the dragon's cave. But I fear that you're already too late."

Bedivere did not stop to give a polite farewell, but snatched a spear from one of the guards and spurred his horse forward. He was racing down the road as fast as Ifor could carry him, but, as fast as he was, the dog, Cavall, was even faster. They veered to the right when they reached the pair of oak trees, and ahead could see the slowly moving party, led by the lovely, dark-haired maiden Arwen. The group was just some hundred yards away from the ring of banners in front of an open cave.

Bedivere called the party to a halt. "I will precede you, and you will follow slowly. I want you to stay back a safe distance while I deal with the dragon."

"Sir Knight," it was Arwen speaking, "already two of your kind have perished fighting this beast, and the monster has promised that it will do great harm to the population of our towns if we try to harm it again. It is best that you leave me to my fate. In the end it will be for the good of all."

Cavall walked to where the young maiden stood. She was small, and the great dog was very tall, so he only needed to lift his head a little to lick the tears from her cheeks. He then turned to Bedivere and barked twice, before dashing into the circle of banners. Bedivere looked at Arwen and said, "I believe that my comrade-in-arms has said that we are here to defend you, and this we will do."

Moments later, arriving at the mouth of the cave, Sir Bedivere was astonished to see what Cavall was doing. The dog had systematically torn all of the banners from their staffs, and was arranging them in a line before the cave's opening. He then looked toward the cave and began to bark. Bedivere remembered what Merlin had told him, and vowed to himself that he would indeed follow Cavall's lead in the imminent battle. Raising his spear the knight shouted, "Aeddan, I know your name and I am here to deal with you and your threats. You are old, and, some say, wise, but you are unwanted here, and by order of King Arthur you must leave this land. If you do not leave this land you will be punished, and will be lost to the world forever."

A great red head — around which shimmering scales formed a ring and a crest — appeared at the mouth of the cave. As the dragon advanced, huge claws on his feet and folded wings on his back became visible. His long, thick, scaly tail culminated in a vicious-looking spike. For all the world he looked exactly like the red dragon on King Arthur's banner.

A voice formed in Bedivere's head, although his ears heard nothing more than the rumbling growl of the great beast. "King Arthur has the audacity to wear my image on his crest, so it is only fair that he should pay tribute to me by feeding me the most select and tender of his subjects. Understand, Sir Knight, that many of your kind have gone before you. Understand further that no feat of arms, or protection of armour, has ever prevailed against me. Prepare to meet thy doom, and let the population of the countryside know that it shall feel my displeasure after I have disposed of your dead body."

As the dragon lumbered forward, Cavall barked loudly, and the beast swung his head in the direction of the sound. The dog darted to the right, and as Aeddan moved to follow him, the dog darted back to his left, dashed under the great head, and between the front legs of the beast. The great, gray dog then leapt and managed to bite the soft spot

under the dragon's left front leg. It was hard to know whether Cavall had done much damage based upon the appearance of blood, since the red blood from a wound would have been lost against the red of the dragon's scales. However, the howl of pain that resulted from the big dog's attack left no doubt that the attack had been successful.

Bedivere said to himself, "As Merlin instructed, I follow the lead of the one he calls the Prince of Dogs." As the dragon swung his head to the left to follow Cavall, it gave Bedivere the opportunity to dodge under the beast's legs as the dog had done, and drive his spear into the soft spot behind the right leg. The spear went in and, as Bedivere pulled it free, blood spattered all over the knight. He crouched low on his horse, then drove his spurs into Ifor's flanks to urge him away before the dragon fell.

Now, with both front legs injured, the dragon sank to his knees, so that his eyes and his mouth were at the same level as the dog and the knight. Now, Cavall did something that amazed Bedivere by grabbing one of the cloth banners he had earler ripped from the staffs, and dashing straight at the dragon. Surely the dragon would now spit venom, and the dog would die in the gout of flame?

The dragon seemed as surprised as the knight, giving Cavall time to get close enough to the beast's mouth to snag the banner on one of his front teeth. A moment later, Cavall had run full circle to snatch up yet another of the colourful pieces of cloth, again dashing almost into the dragon's open jaws and snagging the flag on yet another tooth.

None of this made any sense to Bevidere, but, remembering the advice of the King's wizard, he reasoned that if Cavall wanted to stuff the mouth of the dragon with banners, then so be it. Urging his heroic horse, Ifor, forward, Belvedire bent low to hook a banner on the end of his spear , then charged straight toward the dragon. As soon as was close enough, the knight hurled the spear at the beast's mouth, where it firmly lodged. By the time Bedivere had retreated a safe distance from the dragon, Cavall had already jammed yet another banner into Aeddan's mouth.

Suddenly, the dragon's voice filled Bedivere's

mind once again: "You stupid fools. You think that you can harm me by throwing pieces of coloured cloth at me? You will burn for this!" With that, the dragon spat a stream of venom, but the three banners hanging from his teeth – and the one in his mouth – meant that, instead of a jet of fluid, the venom spattered upward, filling the beast's mouth and soaking the colourful flags. It was now that Cavall's plan became clear to Bedivere, and seconds later the venom burst into flames, filling the dragon's mouth.

As Merlin had said, the dragon was vulnerable to the flames, as evidenced by the screams of pain resounding in their ears. The enormous beast was swinging his head back and forth, trying to free himself of the burning pieces of cloth, though with little success.

The dragon turned and made a dash to the nearby river with the idea that the water would quench the flames. Bedivere and Cavall pursued him, and when the dragon lowered his head into the water, Cavall leapt upon his back and began running toward his head. At once, Bedivere understood and followed suit, clambering up towards the dragon's shoulders, drawing the great sword Cadwgan, and plunging it into the tender, unguarded space between neck and shoulders that was exposed as the dragon lowered his head to gulp the water.

The dragon started to raise his head, and Bedivere began to slip backwards, but Cavall leaned against him, pushing his paws against the folded wings of the beast, and bracing Bedivere to keep him from falling. This gave the knight the chance he needed, and he hoisted Cadwgan to plunge it into the exposed area yet again. As quickly as he could Bedivere managed to stab the dragon a third time before Aeddan lurched violently enough to throw off both man and dog.

Unfortunately, Bedivere's sword had not come free when he had fallen, and now the dragon was swinging his head toward the two of them, great jaws agape. Bedivere felt a huge weight hit his chest as Cavall knocked him out of the way of the long, sharp, snapping teeth just inches away. The dog stumbled as he landed and tried to regain his feet, but was not quick enough. The dragon swung his huge

head in Cavall's direction, sending him flying him far away and into a tree. Turning his attention once again to the knight, Aeddan took a step in his direction, but the loss of blood from his wounds was too great and he collapsed in a heap. Bedivere painfully climbed back up onto the dragon to his sword, still visible in the dragon's neck. Summoning his strength he wielded Cadwgan until, at last, the head of the dragon fell free from his body.

Bedivere looked around for Cavall. Not seeing him he climbed down from the dragon, and walked toward where the brave dog had been thrown. Cavall was lying next to the tree that he had hit with such force, blood around his mouth.

Bedivere bent down to gently touch the dog's head and Cavall opened his eyes. Slowly and painfully, the great, grizzled grey dog stood. His superb hardened leather armour was torn and bent in places, and showed many dark scorch marks, but it had worked well enough to keep him alive.

Two months later, Bedivere returned to Camelot, and with him as his wife was the Lady Arwen. He had been so taken by her kindness and bravery when she knew she was to be sacrificed to the dragon that he fell in love with her. Beside them walked the tall, gray dog Cavall, no longer in his leather battle armour, but a fine suit of ceremonial armour trimmed in gold, given to him by Lord Hywel in grateful thanks for his part in saving his daughter, Arwen.

Later that day, when all of the official greetings had been completed and Cavall's ceremonial armour had been removed, Bedivere came to King Arthur's chambers to return his dog. Over a glass of hot mulled wine, the knight was able to tell the King the full story of the part Cavall had played in slaying the dragon. After the tale was told, he paused for a moment, then said to the King, "On our way there we met the magician Merlin, who gave us valuable advice. He told me to trust the judgement of your dog, Cavall, which I did, and it saved my life. It also allowed our victory. In jest, Merlin called Cavall 'Prince of Dogs,' which, if there were such a title, surely Cavall deserves."

King Arthur laughed heartily, and replied,

"Then let there be such a title, and let Cavall be the first Prince of Dogs."

On seeing his master laugh, Cavall approached with tail wagging, and leapt up to lick his master's face. At that moment, he was just a dog, reunited with the man he loved, and although he might have been intelligent enough to know and understand the honour bestowed upon him, the truth is that dogs really care very little for titles ...

Visit Hubble and Hattie on the web: www.hubbleandhattie.com
www.hubbleandhattie.blogspot.co.uk
• Details of all books • Special offers • Newsletter • New book news

Odysseus and Argus

I was recently attending a university-sponsored event, and found myself chatting with some of the other professors in attendance. As often happens when there are no momentous or significant issues to be dealt with, the conversation drifted aimlessly from topic to topic, and it was then that one of my academic colleagues turned to me and asked if I believed that dogs really had feelings of love for humans, or were they just hanging around us and acting friendly because we are their meal ticket, and give them food and shelter. I have been asked variations of this question many times, and on this occasion I answered by mentioning to the group that I had just come across a wonderful quotation by Roger Caras, an author who also served as president of the ASPCA (American Society for the Prevention of Cruelty to Animals). It went "We give them the love we can spare, the time we can spare. In return dogs have given us their absolute all. It is without doubt the best deal man has ever made." I mentioned the quote because I thought that it nicely summarized my own feelings about dogs, and the reciprocal bond that we have with them.

A professor from the English Department, who was standing with the group, gave a little snort of disdain, and proceeded to tell me, "I am amazed at how a scientist like you has been sucked into this sentimentality for dogs. This idea that dogs feel any loyalty and love for humans is a modern invention. In fact, the idea that people form sentimental attachments for dogs is probably the result of very recent cultural trends. I would bet that the keeping of dogs solely for companionship is something which only became acceptable in modern times, probably as the result of people moving into cities with their high population density. Despite the number of people crowded into such areas, many individuals often feel emotionally isolated in cities. Family members often live far away, and with the pressure of work filling up many hours each day, there are limited opportunities for emotional and social interactions with others. As compensation, a lot of people will focus some of the feelings that otherwise would have been directed to family and friends on their pets. Look back at the literature from two or three centuries ago and you won't find any mention of the loving loyalty of dogs;

nor will you find mention of any ancient warrior prince shedding a single tear for one of his dogs."

Now, this is a common argument, which, in its various forms, suggests that the people of today have all gone soft. Part of the evidence offered for this is the fact that we form deep emotional attachments with our pet dogs, and also anthropomorphize them to suggest that they also have a deep emotional attachment for us. Certainly, the argument goes, the tough, independent people of years gone by had no such feelings for or about their dogs; it must be that soft-headed, romantic writers of modern popular literature have spread these sentimental ideas concerning dogs.

However, such arguments are false. Dogs have been in our emotional lives for virtually all of recorded history. Western literature is generally marked as having begun with two epic poems by Homer. The first is *The Iliad*, which describes the Trojan War, and the second is *The Odyssey*, which tells the story of the Greek hero Odysseus (or Ulysses, as he was known in Roman myth), and his long journey home following the fall of Troy. The poems were probably composed near the end of the eighth century BC, somewhere in Ionia, which was then a Greek-speaking coastal region in what is now Turkey.

In Homer's epic work, after the end of the Trojan War, Odysseus took ten years to return to his home in Ithaca, and along the way he encountered many strange beasts and magic-wielders, and ultimately became an item of dispute among the gods on Mount Olympus. After being away for so long, those who had remained in Ithaca assumed that Odysseus had died, and his wife, Penelope, and son, Telemachus, were forced to deal with an unpleasant group of suitors who had taken over his house while competing for Penelope's hand in marriage (and, of course, possession of her estate and remaining wealth). Penelope was trying to delay naming someone to take her husband's place, but her suitors were becoming impatient, and were putting great pressure on her.

Upon his return to Ithaca, Odysseus learned about what was happening, and decided to secretly re-enter his house, disguised as a beggar,

with the idea of ultimately springing a surprise attack on Penelope's suitors to drive them off or kill them. To complete his disguise, Odysseus arrived at the mansion in the company of the swine herder, Eumaeus, who did not realise that he was accompanying a returning hero.

It is at this point in the story that my colleague's theory that there was never any feeling of attachment to dogs, nor any belief that dogs shared a similar affection for humans in antiquity fails. In this ancient story, we are told that as he approached his home after his long absence, Odysseus encountered his dog, Argos lying neglected on a pile of dung: old, weary, and decrepit. Argos was the only one who recognized Odysseus and, despite his age and infirmity, the dog tried to greet him. A modern text version of this portion of the story goes –

As Odysseus and Eumaeus were talking, a dog who had been lying asleep raised his head and pricked up his ears: this was Argos, whom Odysseus had bred before setting out for Troy. As a young dog, Argos had been his master's constant companion, and would go out with Odysseus and some of the other men when they went hunting wild goats, or deer, or hares. But when he was barely more than a year of age, Odysseus left for Troy. Now that his master was gone, Argus was lying neglected on the heaps of mule and cow dung that lay in front of the stable doors till the men should come and draw it away to fertilize the fields, and he was full of fleas. As soon as he saw Odysseus standing there, Argus dropped his ears, wagged his tail in joyful recognition, and tried to rise, but was too feeble, and could not get close to his master. When Odysseus saw his dog on the other side of the yard, he wiped a tear from his eyes, careful to make sure that Eumaeus did not see it, and said, "Eumaeus, what a noble hound that is over yonder on the manure heap: his build is splendid; is he as fine a fellow as he looks, or is he only one of those dogs that come begging about a table, and are kept merely for show?"

"This hound," answered Eumaeus, "belonged to him who has died in a far country. If he were what he was when Odysseus left for Troy, he would soon show you what he could do. There was not a wild beast in the forest that could get away from him when he

Gods, ghosts, and black dogs

was once on its tracks. But now he has fallen on evil times, for his master is dead and gone, and the women take no care of him."

So saying, they entered the mansion, and made straight for the ill-behaving pretenders in the hall. Behind them, Argos lay back down and finally allowed himself to pass into the darkness of death, now that he had seen his master once more after more than ten years.

I turned to my colleague and asked, "Then what about the literary description of the relationship between Odysseus and Argos? *The Odyssey* was composed some twenty eight centuries ago. As I recall, there is only one time in that entire epic where the bold and brave warrior, Odysseus, sheds a tear, and that is when he sees his old loyal, faithful dog Argos, struggling to approach him after his many years away."

I will give my colleague credit for having the humour and humility to laughingly respond, "Well, perhaps some modern inventions, like the human-dog bond, and the idea of reciprocal feelings of love and loyalty between people and dogs, simply arrived a little bit in advance of the rest of our modern age."

The dog of Montargis

The emotional bond between dogs and people works both ways — we love our dogs and they form attachments to us which are equally strong, if not stronger. This is the basis of many of the myths and stories about dogs that work their way through history and folklore, and are so common that it is difficult to dismiss all of them as simply homespun fantasies. Indeed, sometimes, tales that are taken to be folklore and which, like folklore, have been passed down through the ages by word of mouth, turn out to be something more, with a degree of historical support. Such is the case with this story — The dog of Montargis, which, like most of the scholars who study such things, I took to be simply another myth about the human-canine bond.

I began to reassess my feelings about this story when I recently came across a document describing an incident in France that occurred around the year 1380, during the reign of Charles V. The story that it told sounded — both in general and in many specifics — very much like *The dog of Montargis* story that I was familiar with, which concerned a greyhound named Dragon, who belonged to Aubrey

De Montdidier, a nobleman, and the nephew of the Count of Montargis. Dragon accompanied his master whereever he went, and slept in his bedroom on a braided rug.

One day, Aubrey was supposed to meet with a friend, Sieur De Narsac. The two had been friends for a long time, and Sieur had also become quite friendly with Dragon, who would often accompany his master on visits to his home. De Narsac was also well known at court since he was a knight and captain of the king's men-at-arms. Aubrey had planned meet with his comrade to watch a local sporting contest that afternoon, but did not show up at the agreed time. Although De Narsac searched and made inquiries about him for the next three days, no one seemed to know Aubrey's whereabouts.

Early on the morning of the fourth day, De Narsac was awakened by the sound of scratching at his door, and, on opening it, found Dragon standing unsteadily on the threshold. He looked weak and starving — he had clearly lost weight since the captain had last seen him. The poor dog was in great distress, whining and looking up piteously into De Narsac's face. When food and water were brought to him, Dragon gulped it down gratefully: it was obvious he had had nothing to eat for several days.

As soon as the dog finished eating he seemed to regain much of his strength. He nuzzled De Narsac's hand, and began running back and forth between the knight and the door, looking toward the outside and barking at the end of each run. It seemed clear to De Narsac that the dog wanted the young captain to follow him. The dog's movements were so unusual that De Narsac wondered if the behaviour might have some connection to the disappearance of his master. Perhaps he was trying to bring help to Aubrey who might be injured?

De Narsac decided to follow the big dog, and Dragon led him down the stairs, into the streets, over the bridge, and out of the Porte St Martin. It was clear that Dragon intended him to follow, since, every few yards, the dog would turn back to check that De Narsac was behind him. Together they went on until they entered the Forest of Bondy, which was considered a dangerous place, especially at night, since it was infested with bandits and brigands.

Dragon led De Narsac through several narrow forest paths until they arrived beneath a large spreading oak tree, where he lay down at full length and refused to move. De Narsac had a feeling of foreboding about this, and decided to return to the city for help. He tried to induce the Greyhound to follow him, but Dragon protested with a combination of growls and whimpers. Returning as fast as he could to Paris, De Narsac gathered help, and when the party arrived, they began to dig up the ground where the dog had been stretched out. There they found the body of Aubrey De Montdidier. The corpse showed evidence of a violent death. When they took the body to Paris for final burial, the faithful Greyhound followed.

After this incident Dragon attached himself to De Narsac, and they lived as close friends for some weeks. Then, one fine day, as they walked out together along the Rue St Martin, De Narsac was startled when Dragon began to growl fiercely. The dog broke from his side and attacked a young man named Macaire, who was wearing the uniform of the King's

bodyguard, and who had been walking quietly along the opposite side of the street. Two people nearby used their walking sticks to beat off the dog, and he was led away by his new master. A few days later Dragon again encountered Chevalier Macaire, and once more tried to attack him.

With the second attack, people began to talk. Talk of these strange attacks by the dog of an officer of the King's men-at-arms, directed at one of the King's own guardsman, soon reached the ear of the monarch himself, along with whispers of a long-standing quarrel between Aubrey De Montdidier and Macaire. King Charles decided to determine the substance of the matter, and had the young Sieur De Narsac and his Greyhound brought before him at the Hôtel St Pol. The young man entered and bowed low before the King, but the dog broke from his side and charged through the crowd of courtiers near the throne to once again single out Macaire. He was beaten off, but his action led Charles to conclude that there must be a good reason for Dragon's hatred of Macaire. Although the guardsman protested that he didn't know why the dog was attacking him, the King suspected that this was not true, and decided to put the issue to the time-honored test of trial by combat, the traditional way of letting God decide who the guilty party was.

That very afternoon a strange confrontation took place with the King and his courtiers all acting as witnesses. Chevalier Macaire was armed with a stick, and the dog was given an empty barrel as a refuge to retreat from his opponent's attacks. The big dog seemed to understand the importance of this extraordinary fight, and the moment he was released he darted at his enemy, growling and snapping. Macaire seemed to lose his nerve. His swings of the stick went wild and hit only air, and in what seemed like little time, the dog found an opening, and managed to pull down the man, tearing at him viciously with his teeth. In abject terror, Macaire pleaded to the King for mercy, shouting out a confession that he had murdered De Montdidier. The King allowed that God had indeed judged the matter and no further trial was needed. Macaire was executed that same night.

The story of this powerful bond between a dog and his owner has become known in the retelling as *Aubrey's Dog*. It was also memorialized in a scene depicting the combat, carved upon the stone mantelpiece of a fireplace in the old castle of Montargis. This bas relief illustration was supposedly carved shortly after the actual incident occurred, and many believe that it was meant to be a record of an actual event, rather than an illustration inspired by a folk tale.

Visit Hubble and Hattie on the web: www.hubbleandhattie.com
www.hubbleandhattie.blogspot.co.uk
• Details of all books • Special offers • Newsletter • New book news

The fox and the dog head

It was a hot, muggy, July day in the low mountain area of South Carolina. As I drove down the highway, I noticed a little place with a sign that read 'Bar and Grill,' so I steered my car into the small parking lot with the idea of stopping for something cold to drink.

The inside of the place was dark, with the windows covered, and, even without air conditioning, it was a lot cooler inside than it was out. There were maybe half-a-dozen tables scattered around the room, and a small bar, perhaps 12 or 15 feet long, with four tall barstools leaning against it. The only other person in the room was a thin, gray-haired man behind the bar. I could see some beer taps in front of him, and the idea of a cold draft beer seemed very appealing at that moment.

I went up to the bar, hopped onto a stool, and ordered a mug. It was then that I noticed, beside a set of mirrored shelves that contained a variety of liquor bottles, a mounted fox head on the wall. What was unusual about it was that in the mouth of the fox was a leather dog collar. I smiled and said, "I don't remember seeing something like that before. There must be a story that goes with it."

The bartender scraped foam from the mug of beer he had just drawn and set it down. "There is indeed," he replied.

"My grandfather gave me that. He said it came with a story, and if I wanted to keep it I had to promise to tell that story to anybody who asked about it — whether or not I believed it. It really is a Br'er Rabbit kind of story, with talking animals and a moral, and the moral of this story is that even a dead dog can still hunt.

"According to my grandpa, he got that fox head from one of the sons, or maybe it was a grandson, of Roger Lee. Now, Roger Lee was a rich, important plantation owner before the Civil War, who not only owned a big plantation, but also hundreds of acres of forest land nearby. It was good forest land because it was chock-full of deer. Although Mr Lee was known to harvest a few deer to put some venison on the table, the entire wooded area was posted with 'No Hunting' signs, and it was widely circulated that Mr Lee could get rather testy if he caught somebody poaching on his land. "So, let me give you the Uncle Remus version of the story the way it was told to me.

The fox and the dog head

"It seems that Br'er Fox and Br'er Coyote would sometimes walk by Mr Lee's forest and see all of those deer just wandering around. Now, both their mouths would just water at the thought of some fresh venison, but neither of them was strong enough to kill a deer by themselves, and even if they could somehow muster the strength, neither had the know-how necessary to stalk and catch a deer.

"It was on one of those walks past the woods that Br'er Fox said to Br'er Coyote, 'You know, dogs have been bred to hunt deer, and a good strong dog naturally knows how to hunt down any one of those deer and kill it easy. Just give a listen for a minute because I have a plan that can keep our bellies full of venison. I have been thinking that there is this man who lives not far away from here who collects special mushrooms – those spotty brown ones – to sell in the city. The city folks really like that kind of thing, and pay a lot of money for them. He also sells really good hunting dogs, and I'll bet that if we found a whole bunch of those special brown mushrooms we could trade them and get ourselves a hunting dog each. If we had a hunting dog we could catch ourselves enough deer so that we could be fat the whole year long.'

"Br'er Coyote agreed, and started the plan rolling by getting two baskets: one for him and one for Br'er Fox. Next, the two of them set off to collect those mushrooms. Now, the reason that those mushrooms are so expensive is because they are hard to find, and once you do find them you have to scrabble around in the cracks under logs where they grow in order to gather them. Br'er Coyote worked hard for three whole days in order to fill his basket, but Br'er Fox was lazy, and not at all happy about the amount of work involved in gathering mushrooms, so he gave up after only a few hours on the first day. Br'er Fox could see what a pitifully small collection of mushrooms he had in his basket but he wasn't worried. He had a new plan.

"You see, after Br'er Fox hatched his scheme to use dogs to hunt for deer, he began to think about the situation. The fact of the matter is that foxes and dogs don't get along very well, and one of the sports that the rich plantation owners used to enjoy was getting up on horseback, and following a pack of hounds sent out to hunt for foxes. Br'er Fox began to get a bit anxious about having a dog around, and thought to himself, 'What if that hunting dog that I get wants to hunt foxes more than he wants to hunt deer? That might not be a good thing.' That wily fox was a clever scoundrel, and he worked out a scheme which would allow him to take advantage of Br'er Coyote's hunting dog without any risk to himself.

"Br'er Coyote didn't suspect anything, and the next day he and Br'er Fox took their mushrooms to the man who lived at the edge of the woods. Br'er Coyote had enough mushrooms to trade for a really fine hunting dog, but Br'er Fox had only enough mushrooms to trade for the head of a dead dog.

"Br'er Coyote laughed at Br'er Fox and his dog head. 'You can't catch nothin' with a dead dog's head,' he said.

"Wily Br'er Fox replied, 'You are wrong, Br'er Coyote. The dog head has teeth, and that's what you need to kill yourself a deer. And I'll wager that my dog head is going to kill more deer than your whole dog.' Giving a little huff of satisfaction, he grabbed his dog head and marched on down the road in the direction of Mr Lee's private woods.

"The two would-be poachers quietly slipped past the 'No Hunting' signs, and, within a minute or two, saw a deer in the bush. Br'er Coyote sent his dog in pursuit, and Br'er Fox ran after it, carrying the dog's head by the collar it was still wearing. Br'er Coyote's dog reached the deer first, cornered it, and killed it. Br'er Fox arrived a minute or two later. (Foxes are faster than coyotes, especially in dense woods where the fox can duck under bushes that the coyote has to run around.)

"Now the tricky fox put his plan into action. First, he chased Br'er Coyote's dog away from the fallen deer. Next, he opened the jaws of his dog head, and clamped the teeth onto where the deer had been bitten by the dog. When Br'er Coyote arrived, Br'er Fox cried, 'It is my dog head that killed it, so I should get to keep as much of the meat as I want, and you'll get whatever is left "Br'er Coyote did not utter one word of protest, even though he noticed that his dog had some blood on his mouth, and he had some

Gods, ghosts, and black dogs

suspicions that Br'er Fox was trying to cheat him out of this venison. Instead, he said, 'You go get some rope so that we can drag this deer out of the woods before Mr Lee catches wind of the fact that we have killed one of his animals. I'm told that he owns a big shotgun, and can be quite nasty when he catches poachers.'

"Br'er Coyote moved a short distance from where the deer's carcass was lying. He had thought up his own plan to deal with the situation, and waited until he heard Br'er Fox returning with the rope. He slapped a branch against a tree several times, and each time it made a loud slapping noise Br'er Coyote gave a loud howl of pain, and shouted 'No, Mr Lee, please stop whipping me. It was not my dog that killed your deer. It was Br'er Fox's dog head that killed him. You just go behind those bushes there and you'll see the deer with Br'er Fox's dog head still biting him.' Then he slapped the branch again and howled once more, crying 'Please stop hurting me! Just check behind the bush, Mr Lee!'

"Br'er Fox heard all this and feared for his life and safety. He shouted out, 'Don't listen to him, Mr Lee. Everybody knows a dog head can't kill nothin'. It was Coyote's live dog who killed the deer.'

"It was then that the sly fox hatched himself another plan. It seemed to him that Mr Lee must be a little distance away, behind some bushes, beating the coyote, so there was still a chance he could hide the evidence, and let Br'er Coyote and his dog take the blame. Br'er Fox called out, 'Wha's more, Mr Lee, if you check the deer you won't find any dog head just the bite marks from a dog.'

"And as he finished telling that lie, that devious fox made a dash for the body of the deer to grab the dog head, pry it out of the deer, and, holding it by the collar, attempt to toss it high up into a nearby tree where it could be hidden in the branches unseen, especially by Mr Lee who, the fox thought, would be coming into sight any minute now with his whip in his hand. Although Br'er Fox was a crafty animal, he

was not very strong, and nor very accurate when it came to throwing things. Also, he was not very lucky this day. He was in the process of swinging the dog head as hard as he could in order to throw it high enough to become tangled in the tree branches when, at the last moment, that old head came free of its collar. The head flew high into the air cracking against a tree branch and then coming straight down with its jaws still open and its teeth still sharp. The open mouth of the dog head landed on the neck of Br'er Fox, and he was killed instantly.

"When Br'er Coyote arrived, he was mighty surprised to see his partner-in-crime laying there. He checked to be certain that Br'er Fox was no longer alive, and then he took the rope that the fox had been bringing and tied up the deer. Br'er Coyote and his dog then dragged the deer out of the woods, and the two of them feasted on venison for the next couple of weeks. Mr Lee found the body of Br'er Fox the next day. The fox still had the collar from the dog head in his mouth, and the jaws of the dog head were still locked on to the fox's neck.

"Mr Lee had been hunting foxes for most of his life using a pack of dogs, and knew that dogs and foxes are natural enemies. He understood that any dog worth his salt would do everything he could to kill a fox, but still had to admit that this was the first time he had ever seen or heard tell of a dog coming back after he was dead to hunt a fox. He told his son to gather up the body and to mount the fox's head with the dog's collar still in his mouth as a reminder of that event. And, according to my grandpa, what you see here is all that is left of Br'er Fox after his crafty plans to cheat Br'er Coyote fell apart."

The bartender refilled my mug of beer, then cast a glance at the fox's head. "I can't say I believe that story with talking animals and all that. But the evidence is hanging on the wall, and I promised grandpa I would pass it on the way I heard it from him. I have been told that after a couple of drinks it comes to feel a bit more believable."

The bear and Davy Crockett's dog

All of you have probably heard about Davy Crockett, the great bear hunter from Tennessee, who went on to serve in Congress, and who later died with the other heroes of the Alamo. In fact, there are so many stories about him, there had to be at least two Davy Crocketts: one of them the real genuine article, and the other the Davy Crockett that legends and folklore created.

The legends about Davy had already begun during his lifetime, and when he showed up at the Alamo to offer his services, William B Travis, the commander of the forces, is reported to have said, "Based on the reports that that I have heard about you, the real Davy Crockett has to be at least nine feet tall and have four arms!" To which Davy is said to have replied, "Those reports are true. I just lost a little weight and stature on the long trip here to Texas. I also left two of my arms back in Tennessee to keep a lovely lady company until I return!"

A lot of the legends about Davy Crockett have to do with his ability as a bear hunter, and the wonderful hunting dogs he had with him. I first heard this story about Davy Crockett's bear hunting from

someone who claims that he originally got it from a retired congressman from Tennessee. However, I heard a different version of the same story from a man who now lives in Nashville, but who traces his roots back to his Chickasaw Indian grandfather. When I later thought about the two versions, it seemed to me that each was telling only half of the story, so let me take the liberty of trying to fuse together the two halves to make a single story about a remarkably clever dog ...

Davy Crocket always hunted bears with a pack of eight hunting dogs. These were very special dogs, and one in particular was not only incredibly smart, but was supposed to have a certain magic in him.

The story goes that when Davy Crockett was young, he decided that he wanted to learn how to hunt bears. Bear skins sold for a lot of money at the trading posts, as did bear meat, and a family could stay alive and healthy during the hardest winter if they had a couple of bear carcasses in their smokehouse. The problem was the Tennessee black bears were really big, tough, and mean. You had to get close to them to make your rifle shot count, and the

Gods, ghosts, and black dogs

problem was that, by the time you were close enough to shoot, the bear had surely already seen you, and most likely was charging with your blood on his mind; a lot of hunters had been killed or badly hurt trying to hunt the big Tennessee bears.

Now, Davy Crockett had seen a lot of bearskins being worn by the local Indians, and reasoned that they must know the secret of the best way to hunt bears. With that in mind, Davy started asking around and discovered that, of the four great Indian tribes in Tennessee at that time (the Chickasaw, Shawnee, Cherokee, and Yuchi), it was the Chickasaw who had the reputation for being the best hunters. Furthermore, since the Indians did not have the really fine rifles that the Tennessee frontiersmen did, it was suspected that their success in hunting bears had to do with some kind of secret strategy, or maybe even some kind of native magic.

It was early one spring, just after the winter snow had melted, that Davy Crockett set off for Western Tennessee. Once there he managed to arrange a powwow with the Chickasaw Chief and his Medicine Man. When they sat down to talk and were passing around the pipe, the Chief began providing the information that Davy Crockett was looking for.

"The secret to hunting bears is not just the skill of the hunter but having a pack of special dogs. First of all the dogs can help you find the bear, no matter where he's hiding. Then, when the dogs find the bear and begin barking, they will keep the animal in place, and provide a signal for you: when you hear the noise the dogs are making you will know where to go. Now if a man comes up on a bear, that bear will surely see him and know that he is a threat, and his instinct will be to rush at the man as fast as he can and try to kill him. But if the bear is surrounded by dogs – tough dogs, and enough dogs – then that big black beast will worry more about those hounds than about the hunter, which means that the hunter can get close enough to get a really good shot at killing the bear, even if that hunter is using a bow and arrow, or a rifle that is not so good. In fact, if the dogs are working well, you can usually get off several shots, to make sure that the bear is dead, or is at least weak enough so that you can kill it with your knife.

"Many times, if you are hunting with dogs and get really lucky, the hounds will chase the bear up a tree. If the dogs are barking and growling at the bottom of the tree, the bear won't come down, and you can get really close and keep shooting until the bear falls from the tree. When that happens you know that he is likely to be dead.

"It is important that you have enough dogs. Two or three will usually not do very well since the bear can fight them off. Even if you have four, the odds are not all that good, since all the bear has to do is to hurt one, and he is left with a manageable number. I believe it is best to use at least six dogs. Many of our great hunters believe that, just in case you find yourself facing a really big bear, having a pack of eight dogs might be even better. We can find you such dogs, and even train them for you."

It was then that the old Medicine Man spoke up. "The number of dogs, and the kind they are, is important, but what may be even more important is the leader of your hunting dog pack. This must be a special dog if you are going to become a great bear hunter. The dog must have some magic in him, because he has to be able to understand everything you are saying to know what you want him to do. He must also be able to talk to the other dogs, and even the animals you are hunting. You will not be able to hear what the dog is saying, but the animals will hear, and the dog will understand what those animals are saying to him. Such a hound will be very clever, and will keep your other dogs – and most importantly you – safe.

"This leader dog must first be found (since they are not all that common), and then the magic must be put into him. After that, the dog must be trained. Only after you have a leader dog should you put together the rest of your pack of bear hunting dogs. With a good leader and a good pack of hounds, you can become a great hunter. But such dogs, and the leader, are very expensive. We will give you a leader dog, and seven other bear hunting dogs, but in payment you must hunt for us, the Chickasaw, for two winters. Each of those winters you must provide us with eight bears (one for each dog). We want this since it will guarantee that this village has enough food to make it through the hardest months of the winter."

Davy Crockett agreed to the terms. The Medicine Man then said, "There are two new litters of puppies in this village: let us see if one of them has a pup that can be a leader dog."

The three men got up and walked across the village to a yellow dog with a litter of seven puppies. The Medicine Man looked at each puppy in turn, and shook his head, moving on to a nearby shelter which housed a black dog with a litter of nine puppies. The Medicine Man stooped and picked up one of the puppies. It was black, like his mother, except for his chest, which was white, and there were two yellow spots, one above each of his eyes.

The Medicine Man smiled, "This is what we need: a four-eyed dog."

He pointed to the yellow spot above each eye, and said, "It is these other two eyes that will allow this dog to see into the minds of people and animals, and to understand the meaning of their words. Tomorrow night we will have a sweet grass ceremony, during which we will put the spark of magic into this dog. You cannot be here for that ceremony, since this magic is a secret that only the Chickasaw can know. So you must go now, but come back at the end of summer, and we will give you this dog and seven others. By then, they should be old enough and strong enough to hunt with you this winter, and help you fulfill your contract with us. Before you leave, you must give this dog a name, for I will need it for tomorrow's magic ceremony."

Davy Crockett considered for a moment, then said, "Since he is to be the leader of my pack of dogs, I will call him 'Leader,' if that is okay with you?"

Both the chief and the Medicine Man nodded, and without more ado, Davy Crockett shouldered his long rifle and set off for his home.

Late that summer Davy Crockett returned to the Chickasaw village. The Chief and the Medicine Man greeted him, and next to them stood a tall, young dog, black, with a white chest and a yellow spot over each eye. The Medicine Man spoke first, saying, "This is your dog, Leader. He has been given a spark of magic to make him wise and a great hunter.

Before you agree to take him, you should probably test him to see if he is what we promised."

Davy asked, "Since I don't speak Chickasaw, how will he understand what I'm saying?"

The Medicine Man answered, "His spark of magic lets him understand all languages, human and animal. Take him for a day or two, and see how cleverly he hunts. Do not hunt bear now, since his pack has not yet been gathered, but find a clever animal to hunt, and see if the dog's wisdom can help you catch it."

Davy Crockett introduced himself to Leader, who wagged his tail as if he understood that the frontiersman was to be his new master, and the two of them set off down the road.

They had not gone far when they came to a small settlement containing a few homes, a general store, and a tavern of the kind that was called a 'shantee' in those days.

Davy stopped in the shantee, and asked the bartender if there was anything worth hunting in the area. The bartender looked at him, and then down at the dog, and said, 'If that's a coonhound you could try and rid us of a nasty raccoon that's been hanging around here. He gets into the garbage and scatters it around, and if there is no garbage left out, he tears holes in the roofs or sides of buildings to get at food stored inside. He's ripped the shingles off the roof of my place here more than once and got into my food supply. The problem is that he is a very wily raccoon, and when he sees people he doesn't let them come close enough to take a shot at him. He keeps a careful watch, and always manages to run away and hide before he's in any danger. If you get rid of that pest I would certainly be in your debt."

So Davy Crockett turned to Leader and said, "Let's go hunt ourselves a coon." The dog seemed to understand, since he gave a decisive wag of his tail and started for the door.

Davy followed the dog around to the back of the shantee, which was where the garbage was dumped. Surveying the situation he decided to test his hound's intelligence and hunting ability, so, leaning against the building, he told Leader to find the raccoon; suggesting to the dog, "See if you can figure out some way to get him out of hiding and into some place where I can spot him long enough to get him in my sights." He then cradled his famous Tennessee long rifle, Betsy, in his arms, and waited to see what the dog would do.

Leader began to sniff around. His sensitive nose told him that the raccoon had actually been right where he and Davy were standing, not more than a minute or two before. Judging by what he had heard the bartender say, the dog reasoned that the raccoon knew that people were out to get him, and right now he was hiding from any hunters. But Leader was wiser than the raccoon was wily.

The dog made a big circle around the pile of rubble and garbage, and quietly moved through some trees. Eventually, he managed to circle around and come up behind his quarry, who was concealed between some old logs. Then, with the spark of magic that allowed him speak to all animals, he asked the raccoon in language that no human could hear or understand, "Why are you hiding?"

The raccoon was surprised to see the dog, but, showing no fear of the hound he answered, "There is a man standing there with a gun. I believe he wants to shoot me."

"Well, you certainly have that wrong," replied Leader. "That man there is Davy Crockett, the finest bear hunter in the world. He has come to this part of Tennessee to challenge the best of the Chickasaw hunters to see which of them can kill the most bears in a single day. He doesn't care about raccoons. It would be an insult for him to kill a raccoon, since the only things that he feels are worth hunting are bears – the bigger the better. He is so arrogant about that he even pretends not to see or notice little creatures, like squirrels or rabbits or raccoons. So you're wasting your time and effort by hiding from him. Davy Crockett doesn't care a lick about you."

The raccoon looked at Davy Crockett, who seemed to be staring off into the distance, not noticing anything. The crafty old animal thought to himself, "They have just put out the garbage from dinner, and it looked as if there were some meaty bones there. If I don't grab them quickly then the crows will get them and fly off. Since I am not a bear,

and the dog says that this man ignores anything which is not a bear, I should be safe going down there."

And, with that, the raccoon hopped up on the log and started to move toward the pile of garbage. When Davy saw him he immediately swung his rifle around and shot the raccoon. The grateful bartender was so pleased that he skinned the raccoon and used the hide to make a proper coonskin cap, which Davy Crockett proudly wore from that day on.

Davy Crockett was very pleased that Leader had figured out what he wanted, and the way he had cleverly lured the raccoon out into the open, so he happily returned to the Chickasaw village and gathered up the remaining seven dogs promised to him. He assured the Chief that he would return at the end of September when the bears were fat and slow, and hunt enough of them to ensure that the village would have meat all winter long. He also promised he would do the same for the next year.

Well, as you all know, Davy Crockett went on to become the best bear hunter that the state of Tennessee had ever seen. The bears would all hide when Davy was in their vicinity, though this didn't help them much because when Davy went hunting with Leader showing the way, the dogs found most of the bears, anyway. Once they found a bear, the hounds would keep it pinned down or up in a tree until Davy arrived with his rifle, Betsy, to finish the job.

The Tennessee bears were most upset at the success of Davy Crockett's bear hunts, and agreed that they had to do something about their problem. They planned that, during the summer, when Davy Crockett usually did not hunt for bears, they would take it upon themselves to hunt down Davy himself. The bears understood that it was not just Davy who was their problem, but also the dogs, and especially their captain, Leader. Although the bears usually tried to avoid Davy Crockett, they decided to keep an eye on his home and surrounding area all that summer, and even though it was unlikely that they would catch Davy (unless he got really careless), the bears were hoping that they might find one of the dogs out wandering alone, and take their revenge on the animal.

The bear and Davy Crockett's dog

Most of Davy Crockett's dogs spent the hot summer days lounging on the porch, or under a tree in the yard, trying to keep cool, but this was not the case with Leader, who was wise and very smart. He became bored easily, which made him restless. So, while the rest of his pack was trying to sleep and keep cool, Leader would carefully explore the forests that surrounded the cabin: often leaving the cabin early in the morning, and ranging far and wide; returning only when the sun was beginning to dip below the horizon.

It was on such a day when Leader was exploring that he found a cave. He poked his head into it, and sniffed around a little, but all he could see was a big mud puddle from recent rain. Then he heard a growl ... and turned to see the biggest black bear he'd ever come across. The bear looked angry, and was blocking the entrance to the cave.

"Hello, Davy Crockett's dog," the bear said. "You and your kind have hunted bears, and killed and eaten many of my brothers. Now, it is time for you to be *my* lunch."

Leader thought very quickly, and then said, "I'm sorry, bear, but I can't be your lunch. You see, the Governor of Tennessee and two congressmen are coming to visit Davy Crockett. They want him to run for Congress, and if they think highly enough of him when they meet him, he might just get elected. That is good news for you and the other bears since it would mean that Davy Crockett would be away in Washington, and not around here to hunt you. In order to get those politicians to like him, Davy Crockett has made a very special pudding and left it on the floor of this cave to set. It has a very special taste, which Davy feels will impress the Governor and the congressmen. I don't know what it tastes like, since Davy Crockett does not want anyone to taste it before it is served tomorrow night."

"Well," said the bear, "I would like to taste it."

"No," replied the dog, "the Governor and the congressmen would be very angry."

"Just one little taste, dog. The Governor and the congressmen will never know, and neither will Davy Crockett."

"Alright, then, bear, but first let me run away from here so that no one will blame me for disturbing the pudding before it was set."

"Okay, then, you can go. I will catch you later." And the bear stepped away, giving the dog a chance to dash past him and out of the cave.

"Imagine, the Governor's pudding," the bear said, as he marched over to the puddle and took a big gulp. Immediately, he spat it out in anger, shouting, "That's mud! I'll get you for this, dog!"

The bear raced out of the cave, moving as quickly as he could, and soon caught up with Leader, who had been moving much more slowly than usual since the hound couldn't help laughing, and rolling on the ground, thinking about how he had outsmarted the bear.

"You tricked me once, dog, but now you *will* be my lunch," roared the bear.

The dog looked about and thought quickly. He spied a wasps' nest in the tree.

"I did not trick you." cried Leader. "The pudding always tastes awful until it is set, and you simply ate it too soon. Besides, I can't be your lunch because Davy Crockett has asked me to guard his drum that is hanging in this tree."

"His drum?" asked the bear.

"Davy Crockett has made it especially so that he may beat it when the Governor and the congressmen arrive. He says that he will give a drum roll to honour their arrival."

"I would like to hit this drum to see what it sounds like," said the bear.

"Oh no, bear! The Governor and the congressmen would be very angry to find that the drum had been played before it was used to welcome them."

"Just one little hit, dog. No one will ever know."

"Well, alright, but first let me run far away so that no one will blame me for making such a sound."

"Go, then," said the bear with a wave of his paw; adding, "Imagine, the Governor's drum," as he reached up to pound on the wasps nest.

At once, hundreds of wasps swarmed out of the nest, and began stinging the bear. He ran away quickly, but the wasps followed, until he finally came

Gods, ghosts, and black dogs

to a pond and jumped in, remaining underwater as long as he could, until the wasps had left.

The dog watched this and thought it was very funny. He watched as the bear went underwater yet again, and because he was laughing so hard he did not see the bear sneak out of the far end of the pond and circle around him. He stopped laughing, however, when he heard the bear growl.

"You tricked me twice, dog, but *now* you will be my lunch."

"I did not trick you," said the dog, "it is just that you beat the drum with your paw, instead of using the special drumsticks that Davy Crockett has in his home. If you do not use the correct drumsticks, the notes come out sour and they sting."

"No matter," growled the bear, "this time I have you."

The dog quickly looked around for a solution to his latest problem, and spied a giant copperhead snake resting on a rock. "I cannot be your lunch," he told the bear, "since I have been asked to guard the elegant belt that Davy Crockett has made for the Governor to wear, and it is very special since it is made to look exactly like snakeskin."

"Well, the Governor does not need it, and I want it. I will wear this belt that Davy Crockett made when I kill and eat you. Then I will wear it so that I can show all of my fellow bears that I was cleverer than both Davy Crockett and his dog. I will wear my new belt so that I will look as elegant as if I were a high official in the tribe of humans."

The bear moved directly to the rock and snatched up the snake, giving Leader a chance to dart away. The snake, who had been sunning himself, awakened with a hiss, as the bear began wrapping his 'belt' around him, and began biting the bear again and again. The bear howled and growled, and finally managed to shake off the snake, though the copperhead's venom was already beginning to take effect, and he was becoming groggy.

Meanwhile, Leader ran to the top of the small hill overlooking Davy Crockett's cabin, and began to bark. Davy could not believe that he was hearing *that* particular bark, the one Leader always used in the fall when they went to hunt bears, which told Davy that the hounds had cornered or treed a bear. Grabbing his rifle, he called the other dogs, and ran to the top of the hill where Leader was standing.

When Davy looked down the slope, he saw the great black bear lying on the ground. The snake's venom had already rendered the gigantic animal unconscious, making it a very easy matter for Davy to dispatch him.

Davy Crockett turned to his dog, and said, "You are even cleverer than I imagined. You must be the smartest dog in all of Tennessee; maybe all of the world. I do not know how you managed to knock out a bear all by yourself. I am amazed that the bear was already senseless and half dead when I reached him. You must be the wittiest and most intelligent dog *ever*."

Because Leader was so wise, and had that spark of magic which the Chickasaw Medicine Man had put into him, the dog understood every word that Davy Crockett said. He wagged his tail and thought to himself, "You are correct in what you say. But you will never really understand just how *truly* clever I am!"

The Hounds of the Bayous

I was sitting at the Café Du Monde in the French quarter of New Orleans with a few friends and colleagues. We were attending a psychological conference in that fascinating city, but this was a slow day, and the talks that required our attendance were not until the afternoon. So we had gathered this morning to drink coffee laced with chicory, and eat beignets. For those of you who have not had the experience of eating beignets, you should know that these are relatively shapeless blobs of yeast dough, which are deep-fried, sprinkled with powdered sugar, and served hot. They are a cardiologist's nightmare, but a wonderful accompaniment to the dark, slightly bitter coffee served with them.

However, just like most other things that are full of fat and carbohydrates, beignets seem to be addictive, and I had eaten more than I probably should have. One of my friends, a professor at Tulane University, ordered another plate of these warm pastries, and when it arrived he grabbed one for himself, then pushed the plate toward me. Smiling, he said, "You don't get down here to the 'Big Easy' very often, so enjoy these while you can."

I waved my hand and passed the plate to the friend sitting at my left. "I do love these things," I admitted, "but I'm reminded of a greedy dog, who was even fatter than I am bound to get if I keep eating more. This dog was known around the neighbourhood for bullying or threatening any other dog that came near his bowl, or any place where food was available. On this particular day it happened that a bakery truck, delivering cakes to a restaurant, went around a corner too fast, and lost a good bit of its load. All that cake was lying in the middle of the street, and that greedy dog made a beeline for it. He started to eat, and eat, and eat, and then he ate some more.

"A couple of young puppies arrived while the dog was gorging himself on all that sweet stuff. The pups had been forced to live on the street, and were hungry a good deal of the time, so they looked on in envy while all this wonderful food was being consumed. It was one hefty dog that was doing the eating, though, and they certainly weren't going to rush up and try to grab some of his prize. Finally, however, when their hunger began to get the better of their fear of the big dog, they carefully approached

43

Gods, ghosts, and black dogs

to try and get a few crumbs of the cake and cookies lying on the ground.

"The large dog saw them, and gave a low growl (he was just as greedy as he was fat). The puppies held their peace and waited a while longer, then the braver of the two approached the big dog, and asked, 'Got enough, now, Sir?' 'No,' came the grumbled reply, 'but I've got down to where it don't taste so good anymore.'

"And that is where I am now, my friends."

My colleague from Tulane University (which is located inside the city limits of New Orleans), laughed, and said, "You obviously aren't a Louisiana hound. Our dogs here can be hard workers, but whether or not they are working, they are always on the alert for, or trying to scrounge, any morsel of food, and once they spot something they can eat, they jump at it. It doesn't matter whether they're hungry, or fat, or have a full belly. When they find some food they don't stop eating until they've nearly licked the ceramic glaze off their bowl."

"I don't know if that fits my observations," I protested. "A few years back, my friend, Peter, and I took a trip with our wives through the bayous. We saw a lot of hounds, but, for the most part, they were just lying on the front porch, or down at the foot of the stairs in the sunshine, dozing the day away. They didn't seem like they were in a frenzy to get food, or were spending much time or energy working for something to eat. In fact, as I remember from that trip, I don't remember most of those country hounds doing anything other than relaxing. They didn't move even when people came up and found them blocking the way. They just laid there, soaking up the sun and acting as if was not required that they do anything for anyone. I was quite surprised to notice that the folks who owned them didn't seem to mind having dogs lying around: they just politely stepped over those lazy hounds if they happened to be in their way. I don't think that those dogs even raised an eyelid; they just acted as though it was their God-given right to sleep out there in the sunshine, and they intended to exercise that right as long as they could."

My colleague laughed, and said, "Well, it is not their God-given right to lay on the porch in the sunshine and not be bothered, but it *is* a right that was given to them by the State of Louisiana. In the interests of furthering your education, let me explain to you how this all came about.

"It all began one summer quite awhile back, down in the bayous where things suddenly got really strange. I think the astronomers concluded that it was something to do with the solar cycle, maybe sunspots, or an increase of cosmic rays, all of which began to interact with global warming, or whatever. The result was that that year was particularly hot and damp, and also probably because of the cosmic conditions, the mosquitoes in the wetlands started growing, with reports that some mosquitoes were growing more than an inch every minute until they reached full size – which was really big.

"Now, mosquitoes need lots of protein to survive, and what these giant insects couldn't get from blood-sucking they began to get from meat-eating. Next thing anybody knew, these big, monster mosquitoes began to kill our farmers' chickens and pigs at an alarming rate. As you might expect, folks around here began to get very worried.

"Well, everyone knew we needed help, so we decided to call for assistance from a really smart professor that we'd heard of (from Tulane University, of course), who knew everything there was to know about insects. The folks living out in the countryside and the bayous put together a delegation, which visited the university and asked the professor, 'How do we take care of the problem that we're having with these giant mosquitoes? They are killing off all our livestock, and we're afraid that when these behemoths get finished with the pigs, they'll probably go after the cows, and then maybe the horses, and then maybe even people!'

"This erudite professor was not fazed in the least, and told the folks not to worry; explaining that he knew about a special strain of enormous bees which lived in Australia, and might be the solution to their problem. These giant bees didn't collect pollen like bees usually do, but rather, ate other insects. So the professor figured that if they brought in a truckload of these bees, they would wipe out the giant mosquitoes.

"Unfortunately, however, it turned out that this entomologist didn't know everything about the way that such a strange and unique insect species worked, and, because of that, his plan didn't quite go the way he had expected.

Instead of killing off the mosquitoes, the giant bees and the giant mosquitoes interbred, and the result was a nightmare. These hybrids were also gigantic, and had inherited the big front stinger from their mosquito parent, and the big rear stinger from their bee parent. With fearsome stingers on both ends, they became even more efficient hunters, and the number of livestock that were lost to insects began to skyrocket.

"As you might imagine, the folks who lived in the bayous were now really starting to panic, so the Governor of the State of Louisiana offered a reward for anyone who could resolve the problem of these bee-mosquitoes.

"Well, this very old, very wise bluetick hound heard about this. At that time, the hounds who lived in Louisiana were not really all that well respected, and had to work hard for a living, hunting, guarding, and running around all the time trying to spot any trouble that might require their master's attention. Any time a dog took the opportunity for a little snooze in the sun, maybe on the porch or on the stairs, he never really got to enjoy his rest, because, when folks saw them lying there, they would kick them out of the way, and send them off to find some work to do. It was a hard life. However, this bluetick hound thought that the insect invasion just might provide an opportunity for all of the dogs in the State of Louisiana to benefit ...

"This sagacious old hound went to the university (Tulane, naturally) to find a professor who could translate animal language. He convinced the professor to go with him to the capital building in Baton Rouge. The dog and academic marched right up to the Governor's office, where the latter informed the governor that they were there for a little chat about the insect problem in the bayous. The upshot of this conversation was that the Governor agreed that if the hound and his other canine colleagues could get rid of the giant bee-mosquitoes, all dogs in the State of Louisiana would be rewarded with the right to sleep, undisturbed, on their owner's porch in the sunshine, and not to be yelled at or kicked out of the way, with such rights to be granted in perpetuity. They shook hands (or paws) to seal the bargain.

"So, this clever old hound went back home to the bayous and set to howling until he had gathered all of the dogs in the region. Firstly, he told them about the bargain he had struck with the Governor, then outlined his plan. Groups of dogs were sent out to scour the countryside, and within a day were able to discover where the bee-mosquitoes were nesting.

"The next morning, just as the sun was rising high in the sky, and only a short time after the giant bee-mosquitoes had left their hive to go out on their daily hunt for food, the dogs gathered their courage and sneaked inside the massive insect hive. (You need to understand that these were country hounds living out there in the bayous, who, up to now, had not received a lot of care and grooming from their owners. One consequence of this (as might be expected) was that the dogs were infested with fleas.) Once inside the hive, the pack of hounds began to follow the plan that the wise old dog had outlined for them, and rubbed their hair against the walls of the giant insects' home, dislodging hundreds of thousands of fleas in the process. Next, as quick as a flash, and before any fleas could jump back onto the dogs, they dashed out, leaving the hive full of fleas.

"Of course, those fleas needed some place to live, and also needed the blood of something in order to survive, so when the bee-mosquitoes returned home, the fleas jumped on the enormous mutant insects and began to bite.

"You know what happens when dogs (or people) have fleas biting them? Well, exactly the same happened to those mammoth insects: their skin began to itch, more and more. And just like dogs or people with an itch, they started to scratch the irritations. If the itch was around their rear they would work their head around to try and scratch it with their big front stinger, and if it was near their head, they would try and scratch it with their big rear stinger. The problem was that, because these bee-mosquitoes had been born to sting other creatures to death and eat them, they weren't very good at scratching themselves with their own stingers, and usually drew blood in the process, accidentally injecting some of their own venom into themselves, with the result that they began to die, poisoned by their own weapons, and, ultimately, the entire hive was wiped out.

"The hounds got a big laugh out of all of this. Not only did they manage to wipe out the insect threat to the bayous, they also rid themselves of most of their fleas in the process. In fact, even without grooming from their owners, they would not be bothered by fleas for years to come since the fleas

now had this big pile of dead bee-mosquito carcasses on which to feast.

"And that, my friend," concluded my learned colleague, "is also the reason why, when you travel through Louisiana, you'll see so many hounds resting, undisturbed, on the sunlit end of the porch. The Governor kept his promise, and all of the hounds in the bayous have benefited from that promised reward ever since. It is their *state*-given right that they are exercising."

We all laughed, and I took another sip of my coffee, absentmindedly reaching for another beignet ...

Black Shuck

Early in 2001 I received a note from a woman named Florence Brown, who was contacting me about an incident involving a dog, in the hope that I could provide her with some explanation about a puzzling aspect of that encounter.

She and her husband, a retired Anglican priest, were taking a holiday in the north of Suffolk, in England, not far from the little town of Bungay, and staying at the Chequers Inn. They decided to take a long walk one day, and, it being wintertime, it was dark by the time they made their way along Ditchingham Dam, heading back to the inn.

According to Mrs Brown, "Suddenly, a huge black dog stepped out into the middle of the road directly in our path. Perhaps it was just the darkness, but the dog appeared larger than any I ever remember seeing. What was most striking about him, however, were his eyes, which were huge and glowed red, like burning coals. It was not as if the moonlight was reflecting in his eyes, more as if the light was coming from *inside* him, and resembling glowing red embers in a fireplace, only brighter. Even in the dim light provided by the moon, we could see incredibly large,

sharp teeth in his open mouth. It was very frightening.

"My husband froze in place, then made the sign of the cross. He told me to get behind him and not look into the dog's eyes. 'It's the devil dog, Black Shuck,' he said, and began loudly reciting a prayer. The dog simply stood there, making a cackling sound, like an old woman laughing. A few moments later, my husband clutched his chest and sank to his knees, gasping for breath. I ran around in front to help him up, but when I turned to look back at the dog, he was gone. I tried to catch a glimpse of him but couldn't see him either in front of me or off to either side of the road. Luckily, a few minutes later, an automobile came down the road, and the driver took us back to the inn. A doctor later told us that my husband had had some kind of heart attack, though, fortunately, with no major damage. However, the doctor warned us that my husband's heart may have been weakened by this event, and he might, therefore, be more susceptible to coronary problems in the future.

"My husband is a devout and religious man, but not a superstitious one. He spent some time living in Fakenham in Norfolk, however, where there are stories about ghostly beasts wandering the countryside at night, and he truly believes that we met some kind of demon or devil dog: perhaps the one he'd heard tell of called 'Black Shuck,' or 'Old Shuck.' I have tried to reassure him that it was just a large, black dog, and even if there were such a thing as Black Shuck, it would certainly not attack a priest. He refuses to be comforted by this, however, convinced that the proof lies in the animal's red, glowing eyes, and the fact that he was struck down after just looking into them.

"I am writing to you," continued Mrs Brown, "since you are a dog expert, and can, perhaps, explain the conditions under which a dog's eyes would appear to glow such a bright red in the darkness. I am seeking this information so that I may prove to my husband that this was some sort of natural phenomena rather than a kind of phantom or devil dog, since that thought is weighing heavily on his mind."

Throughout England, but particularly in Cornwall and East Anglia, there are many reports of ghosts and demons which take the shape of a large, black dog: phantom hounds who appear in a dramatic flash and then often disappear into a mist or a cloud. Their appearance portends bad things, and often death, and it is believed that it is the eyes of these devil dogs which cause the most harm. To stare once into the eyes of such a phantom, it is said, will make a man weak; to stare twice will make him ill, and to stare a third time will cause him to die. In general, these dogs are believed to be the devil's minions, or perhaps even Satan himself transformed into the shape of a dog.

However, in the counties of Norfolk and Suffolk, the folk there believe they actually know who this black demon dog is: the spirit of one extremely violent and wicked person who acted much like a demon when he was alive. This is one of those cases where the lore and the history are so intertwined that it is difficult to know where the truth stops and the folklore begins.

According to local tradition, Black Shuck, the devil dog who haunts Norfolk and Suffolk, is connected to a man named Hugh Bigod, who spent much of his life in Bungay Castle, not far from where

Mrs Brown and her husband had their frightening encounter. Hugh Bigod was the first Earl of Norfolk, and lived during the twelfth century. He was a treacherous man, with an appetite for power and control, and had a reputation for rarely keeping a promise. He was also quick to use violence for political or monetary gain.

It was after the death of King Henry I in 1135, that Hugh became a significant figure on the political scene. There were two contenders for Henry's vacant throne: his daughter, Matilda, and his nephew, Stephen. When the issue of ascension could not be resolved politically, the two sides went to war, and Hugh used this conflict as an opportunity for personal gain. At the outset he offered his support to Stephen, and in exchange was given the Earldom of Norfolk. Hugh and Stephen fought as allies in the battle of Lincoln, but when it appeared that they were losing the battle, Hugh deserted Stephen, and left him to fight on alone. As a result Stephen was captured and imprisoned.

Although Matilda's forces had won the battle, she could not claim the throne, because, up until that time, the monarch of England had always been a man, and nobles were hesitant to accept Matilda as the first woman ruler. Amidst all of the political wrangling, law and order broke down, and gangs of bandits roamed the land with little fear of capture or punishment. Hugh saw this as an opportunity to increase his wealth and holdings, and joined forces with another rebel, Geoffrey de Mandeville. Working together, these two spread terror throughout East Anglia, using force to extort money from the people in the region. In several instances, when Hugh's demands for funds were not met, he set fire to the villages in order to make sure that others in the area would be frightened into giving him what he wanted. Hugh also set about capturing and torturing people to pressure their families into paying large ransoms for their release.

Hugh Bigod was so violent and uncompromising that superstitions began to grow up about him during his lifetime: whispered rumours that he consorted with dark forces, and stories that he had a pact with the devil. Some even claimed that in the places where Hugh Bigod's shadow fell, the grass withered and died, and he became so dreaded that simply the mention of his name would cause people to make the sign of the cross to ward off evil.

Eventually, Stephen managed to regain the throne, but, as the countryside was in ruins, it was more important for him to try and restore peace, rather than seek retribution for past injuries and betrayals. Because of this Stephen made his peace with Hugh.

When Stephen died, Hugh sprang to the support of Henry of Anjou, who then became King Henry II, in repayment for which Hugh was allowed to keep his title of Earl, and the King turned a blind eye to the banditry and extortion that Hugh was engaged in. Hugh then built the castle at Bungay, which was virtually surrounded by the River Waveney, from where he continued to exploit the local population, relentlessly employing force to expand his territory until, ultimately, he had possession of the strongholds of Framlingham and Walton, as well as Bungay.

Although Hugh Bigod professed to be a religious person, he really had little respect for the church. Thus, when Pentney Priory refused to give him all of the tribute that he demanded, he simply seized the property, for which act the Pope excommunicated him in 1166. However, Hugh recognized that the Vatican was also subject to political pressure, and from his position of power he used bribery and threats against local churches and monasteries to force the Pope to give him absolution in this matter. Three years later, Thomas Becket again excommunicated him, citing the fact that Hugh was a corrupt, unholy, and unacceptable person. Against Becket's strong objections, political pressure was once more brought to bear and Bigod was again absolved.

Hugh eventually came to believe that his holdings and wealth were being threatened by Henry's growing insistence on a rule of law, and the King's desire to end ongoing violence against local citizens. Once again Hugh Bigod decided that his needs would best be served by betrayal and force, and, thus, in 1174 when King Henry II returned to England from a visit abroad, he found Bigod plotting sedition with the aid of his own sons. Ultimately, after the royal military was summoned, the rebellion ended with a temporary truce between Bigod and the King.

At this point the people of Norwich sensed that the throne was moving toward enforcement of justice and lawfulness, and that Henry was committed to taking steps against Hugh's banditry. They drew courage from this, and refused to give in to Bigod's continuing extortion: he would not tolerate such resistance, and, as had been the case in the past, his response was swift and brutal. He formed another army, which sacked and burned the city of Norwich, and massacred many inhabitants. King Henry could not stand for any more of this, so gathered a massive army and prepared to proceed against Bungay and Framlingham simultaneously. When Bigod saw how the the odds were against him he surrendered: forced to pay homage to the King, and then compelled to take the oath of a Knight Templar, and undertake a pilgrimage as part of the crusade to Palestine.

Bigod recognized that the forces against him this time were simply too great. Anyone else who had committed the serious crimes he had, which included murder, kidnapping, extortion, and treason, would have certainly been put to death, but, even in defeat, Hugh Bigod had enough power to avoid execution. Recognizing the need to at least appear repentant, despite his contempt for the church, Bigod adopted the uniform of a Templar, and went to the Holy Land. Unfortunately, his behaviour there continued in the same brutal mode, and he repeatedly demonstrated the same disdain for human life that had characterized his conduct during all of his years in England. Other members of his Templar order felt that his actions and methods dishonored their vows and beliefs, and it is believed by many that they arranged to have him assassinated. As a last insult, his body was sent back to England, and interred at Norwich, the site of his last domestic act of violence.

Bigod was buried on land owned by the Templars, which was considered holy, but when Roger de Pont L'Évêque, the Archbishop of York, heard of this, he felt that such a corrupt person on holy soil might cause it to lose its sanctity. He therefore travelled to Bigod's grave to say prayers and sprinkle holy water on it, and the story is told that, as the holy water poured

Gods, ghosts, and black dogs

out of the vessel, it immediately turned to steam, and never actually touched the soil. The Archbishop was clearly frightened by this, and declared the place profaned, polluted, and unhallowed; further asserting that Hugh Bigod must be considered a curse upon the earth, and not truly part of the church, regardless of the fact that he had been twice absolved by the Pope, and had been a member of the Order of Knights Templar.

It was not long after these events that the great black dog began to appear, and certain features of his description are common to all sightings. Most impressive are the large, burning red eyes, the enormous teeth, and fur so dark and shimmering you could see your reflection in it. The black dog first appeared in various places in Bungay Castle itself, and then began to appear in the lanes and byways nearby. Those people who encountered it often became sick, and many died.

In 1577, some of the local people went to the church and asked for help to rid themselves of this phantom. The priests did not know where to start an exorcism, since the appearance of the dog that the people were calling Old Shuck was unpredictable. Their best bet was at Bungay Castle where it seemed to have started. A priest was posted at the castle, and roamed the rooms at night looking for the phantom dog. He eventually encountered the monstrous beast standing in a corridor. The priest raised his crucifix and prepared to chant the exorcism rite. The dog made a sound — a combination of laughter and choking, it seemed — and then reared on his hind legs as though about to lunge at the clergyman. It was then that the astonished priest saw a faint red cross, starting low on the dog's chest and curving down under his belly, and he could not understand why this holy symbol of Christianity was emblazoned on what he believed to be a demon, nor why the mark of the cross did not destroy this devil, or at least prevent it from continuing its evil practices. However, the priest did not have time to study the mark on the dog, since, a moment later, the beast melted from his vision.

The priest was anxious and confused about what he had seen, and reported back to his superiors. A conclave was held to interpret these events, and one of the group remembered the story of Hugh Bigod, the vicious and corrupt man who had died as a Templar. A red cross on a field of white was the symbol of the order which the Knights Templar wore on the tabards that covered their armour. Perhaps this demon was the embodiment of the evil spirit of Hugh Bigod, who wore the Templar's red cross in life and might be branded with it in death. If this was some kind of demon or ghostly evil, the holy men reasoned that the spirit could be destroyed by carrying out an exorcism, and consecrating the place where Bigod was interred.

One of the older and more scholarly priests worried about this course of action, however. He had two concerns: the first being that the exact spot where Hugh was buried was in dispute, since he had been put in the ground nearly 400 years earlier, and, by order of the church, no marker was placed on the grave. And even if they could identify the right place, there was some concern about whether the usual procedures associated with exorcising demons would work, and whether the usual religious apparatus would protect those who carrying out the ceremony. The scholar was concerned because he felt that they were dealing with the spirit of a man who had been excommunicated twice and absolved twice by the Pope himself. Furthermore, he had gone on to take the vows of a Knight Templar (even though it was under duress), and may well have been killed by members of that group who, although they were warriors, were also considered to be holy men and priests. Perhaps because of this confused religious history, could Black Shuck have protection from Christian prayers and holy items? The old priest's concerns were ignored, however, and the rest the group set about to gather the material for the exorcism, and locate the likely place where Hugh was buried.

On a warm August Sunday in 1577, three priests gathered at what they believed to be the grave of Hugh Bigod, carrying holy water, burning incense, and crucifixes. They began to recite the words needed to exorcise a ghost or demon, and had uttered no more than a few sentences when the air was filled with a cackling sound, much like that the priest had heard in Bungay Castle. Then a voice whispered in their heads, "Your church has no sway over me," followed by a clap of thunder so loud that it drove the priests to the ground and rendered them insensible. Observers said that moments later the sky turned unexpectedly dark and a violent thunderstorm occurred.

Many people believe it was then that Hugh Bigod, whose spirit inhabitated Black Shuck, decided to wreak his revenge on the church that had insulted him, abandoned him, and ultimately may have been responsible for hi death. The storm grew in intensity, and soon thundered over St Mary's Church in nearby Bungay. Observers report darkness, rain, hail and thunder, and great strikes of lightning, which many feared might set a whole village ablaze. Such a quickly rising storm was terrifying, and many local people gathered inside the church, kneeling in fear and praying for mercy. It was then that Black Shuck appeared before them, wrapped in fire, with sparks of lightning flying from his sides. With incredible speed the demon dog raged through the church, attacking the congregation with his cruel teeth and claws. An old verse records –

All down the church in midst of fire, the hellish monster flew
And, passing onward to the quire, he many people slew.

Two people who were praying were touched by the black hound and killed instantly, while a third was "shrivelled up like a drawn purse." Others, he killed by breaking their necks with his teeth. Then he disappeared with the same speed with which he had arrived, apparenty dissolving from sight in an instant. At the time of the attack the Rector was on the church roof, cleaning out the gutter, and thus escaped the attention of the dog. Minutes later he rejoined his terrified congregation, which he tried to calm by leading them in prayer.

Very soon after these events the devil dog reappeared. The same storm that arose over St Mary's Church in Bungay swept over Blythburgh Church, some seven miles away, and it was in Blythburgh that the black beast next came to exact his vengeance. The church doors he threw open with a great scratching action, and, still wrapped in flames, the great beast ran down the aisle, slaying two men and a boy, and burning the hand of another person. At the foot of the altar the flaming black dog leapt high in the air; there was a flash – as if from a lightning strike – and the steeple of the church collapsed, the demon dog disappearing at the same time.

Later on, after the bodies had been removed and the injured person sent for care, the evidence of the attack could be seen burned into the door of Blythburgh Church in the form of scratch marks left by the devil dog's claws. No one dared try to remove these marks, and so there they remain to this day.

Many people believe that the attacks on the congregations at Bungay and Blythburgh were retribution by the spirit of Hugh Bigod for the attempt to exorcise him, and feel that these retaliatory attacks against the two churches were designed to demonstrate that this demon was immune to holy intervention. No further attempts have ever been made by the church to lay this phantom to rest or to again try to consecrate the place where Hugh Bigod is buried. Furthermore, it is now believed that Black Shuck specifically seeks out members of the clergy, such as Florence Brown's husband, and also pious people who truly believe in the Holy Scriptures, and those who believe that their innocence and goodness may bring them God's protection.

In answer to Florence Brown's message, I did not spell out the whole story that I have told you here, since I did not believe that this would be the best way to comfort her husband. Instead, I simply told her that I knew of no natural explanation for why the eyes of a dog should glow bright burning red on a dark night, but that, apparently, other people had reported such occurrences. Also, out of respect for the state of anxiety being experienced by her husband, I did not ask her if she saw a faintly glowing red cross on the dog's chest, which might identify it as the embodiment of the angry soul of a violent Knight Templar who roams the countryside in the form of a monstrous black dog. I would have certainly have liked to know the answer to that question, however ...

The black dog and the
Tollesbury midwife

I was sitting in a pleasant pub called the Jolly Sailor, in Maldon in the county of Essex, near the eastern coast in England. Across the table from me was a man in his early sixties who was puffing on an old briar pipe while we chatted over a couple of pints of bitter. The man was a breeder of Cavalier King Charles Spaniels, and I was considering getting a dog of that type. Given that it was a matter concerning dogs that had brought us together, it is not surprising that our idle conversation that afternoon was revolving around canine matters.

I did know of the tradition of ghost dogs and demon dogs that supposedly wandered the countryside in that vicinity, and asked if he, or someone that he knew, had ever encountered one? He nodded his head and smiled, took a puff of his pipe, and told me a story.

"You know people around here have a real fear of black dogs, at least certain black dogs that you meet at night. A big black dog with glowing eyes is supposed to be the devil, or to work for Satan, or something like that. Y'know that seeing such a dog in the darkness is supposed to predict that something terrible is about to happen to you or someone you know. I don't agree. I do believe that there may be some kind of spirit dog out there, but I think that the only bad things that the dog does are to those folks who deserve it. I think that our particular local spectral black dog has his own agenda, and is careful about who he chooses to hurt. Other folks might not agree, but I think that our black dog may even choose to help some people if they come up to his standards. Let me tell you why I believe that."

He paused a moment to relight his pipe with a wooden match from a little box that he pulled from his pocket. Then he continued, "Back in the 1960s, I was living in Tollesbury, which is just a few miles up the road from here. My Mum was a midwife; actually, one of only a few in the area. Because of her work, we had a telephone that hung from the wall in the kitchen, which would ring at all hours of the day or night to announce that someone was going into labour. Then, Mum would have to get out her bicycle and pedal over to someone's home to help whoever it was about ready to give birth to a child. My Dad didn't like it when Mum had to go out in the dark, but she was a tough old Essex lady, and nothing much scared her. Mum was born near the town and grew up knowing most of the roads and the lanes, and she could even tell you stories about most of the people who lived along them.

"In the beginning Dad used to offer to go out with her when the call came at night, but, according to Mum, he just got underfoot. Besides, he had his own job that he had to go to in the morning, which meant he often had to leave wherever they were before she was done. In the end, Dad gave up trying, and Mum would just hop on that old bike of hers and pedal off by herself, leaving Dad at home with me and my two sisters. Eventually, she would return, whenever the job was done, and the baby was born. Regardless of whether it was dark or light outside when the call came, she just rode out, and when the job was finished she rode home.

"Now, when I say that Mum was a brave woman I have to admit that there was one place nearby that did cause the hair on the back of her neck to stand up a bit, at least at night. Now and then she had to go to a little place called Tolleshunt D'Arcy, not far from Tollesbury, which sometimes meant that she had to use a road called Jordan's Green. There's a lane off that road that leads up to Gorwell Hall, which used to spook her. The way she told the story was that, when she was a child, there was a time when the whole region around here was in a state of panic. It seems that young children who were out playing, or just wandering around by themselves, were going missing. They would just leave their homes and not return. This panicked the other families in the neighbourhood who had young kids, and after the third or fourth child had disappeared, most of the other kids in the area were being kept inside, or only allowed out when there were adults with them.

"Anyway, one late night a local parish priest was cycling home in the dark from a visit with a family, when he heard the barking and growling of a dog near a little house just by the turn-off from Jordan Green. The priest stopped to see what was causing the commotion, and noticed a huge black dog digging and scrabbling in the ground. He leaned his bicycle against the fence, and walked over to see

what the dog was doing. As he did so, the dog looked up at him and, for a moment, it seemed as if he had large, glowing red eyes, although when the man later thought about it he felt that it was probably just the light of the full moon glinting off the dog's big eyes. In any event, the dog ran away at the clergyman's approach, and seemed to melt into the bushes to be lost from sight.

"When the man bent over the place where the dog had been digging, he was horrified to see what looked like a young child's hand, and immediately got back on his bike and raced to town to contact the police.

"When the police – led by the priest – returned to the spot in the morning, they found that the dog had been in the process of uncovering the body of a young girl: a child who had disappeared less than a week before. In nearby shallow graves they also found the bodies of the other three missing children.

"They arrested the man who lived in the house, and he readily admitted to the killings. He was not remorseful, and even argued that the murders were spiritually justified. It seems that his first wife died in the process of giving birth to their first child, and the child itself died a few hours later. He remarried, and when his second wife was giving birth to her first child, there were also complications, and both she and the infant died. Because of this, the man came to believe that children were tainted and cursed, and it was his duty to remove as many of them as possible from the world. However, before the man could be tried for his crimes, he managed to escape from the little local jail, and was later found to have committed suicide back in his home. He was buried nearby – some say in the same place where he had hidden the bodies of his young victims."

My storyteller laughed quietly, drew heavily on his pipe, and added in a conspiratorial tone, "There is a local legend which says that a group of neighbours and townsfolk later dug up his body, drove a wooden stake through his heart, and reburied him. They really thought that the man was evil incarnate, and when you become scared of something it does bring out the old ways and the old beliefs."

Gods, ghosts, and black dogs

His pipe apparently having gone out again (a continual problem for him, it seemed), he paused a moment to draw out another wooden match and relight the battered old briar. Taking a puff and exhaling some sweet-smelling smoke, he continued, "My mother knew this story. She was not a superstitious woman, but the thought of this wicked man and the children he killed made her feel very uncomfortable. Because of that, she would cycle as quickly as she could past the place where she'd been told he was buried.

"Then something happened that really frightened her. I remember clearly that it was late at night on the first day of May. She had gotten a call early in the day, and had spent many hours helping a woman whose labour was prolonged. Although she did eventually facilitate the delivery a healthy child, she was unhappy that the process taken so long. Her patient's prolonged labour and slow delivery meant that she missed the playful and colourful Mayday festivities held each year at the little school that my sisters and I attended. The full moon was high in the sky when she finally got on her bicycle and started home.

"She was pedalling home in the dark, and, as she neared the turn-off that usually made her anxious, Mum glanced up the hill and saw what appeared to be a man in black, with a faint orange shimmer (perhaps from the moonlight) around him. The man was walking in a direction, and at a speed, which looked as though his path would intersect with hers as she rounded the curve in the road. For some reason, the sight of this man, and the idea that he was about to catch up with her, made her anxious. Just then she saw a huge dark shape in the middle of the road. It was so large that she thought at first that it was probably a calf who had escaped from a nearby field, but when the shape turned to look at her, she saw that, in fact, it was a great black dog, with glowing red eyes. Those eyes were huge, and whatever light that was causing them to appear red also seemed to give them a yellowish flicker, like a dying flame. She hit her brakes so hard that she nearly lost her balance, then stood there, frozen in place, as the big dog approached her.

"The dog was so large that his head was actually higher than the handlebars of her bicycle. As Mum stood there, shaking, the dog sniffed her. She was about to call for help from the man, who, she presumed, was the owner of the dog, when the dog turned so that his body was between her and the approaching figure. The great beast looked up the hill and growled in a threatening manner, and then looked back at my mother. She wanted to get away from the dog since he was really frightening her, but also, for some reason, Mum felt even more uneasy about the man who was still moving toward her.

"She was off her bicycle and now positioned it between her and the big black dog. She wanted to get away from both him and the approaching man, and, with that in mind, began to slowly walk her bicycle along the road. As she did, the great dog kept pace with her, always glancing up toward the man, and staying between her and the man. When she had gone a short distance, mum looked back to see if the man was still following, and saw that he had stopped and turned so that his body was now silhouetted against the moonlit sky. She wasn't sure, but it looked as though he had something sticking out of his chest.

"My mother doesn't remember touching or saying anything to the dog, and except for that initial growl in the direction of the man coming down the slope, the dog never made another sound. In fact, she doesn't even remember hearing the sound of his footfalls against the road. She finally worked up the courage to get back on her bike, and now began pedalling down the road as fast as she could. The big black dog trotted along, keeping pace with her, and as the lights of Tollesbury began to come into view, he slowed a little so that her bicycle pulled ahead. Then, when she glanced back see how far back he was, he was simply no longer there. Mum was quite shaken by the event, although couldn't really explain why the whole episode made her feel anxious and uncomfortable.

"Mum was a churchgoing woman, and, as luck would have it, late the next afternoon the local vicar and his wife stopped by our home. Over a cup of tea my mother told him the story of what had happened the night before. The vicar's wife

The black dog and the Tollesbury midwife

seemed very interested, and a little concerned, and, after my Mum finished telling her story, she offered an explanation. 'There are some people who would probably say that the black dog was some kind of ghost or spirit, and it may have just saved you from the devil. You know that yesterday was the first of May, which witches call Walpurgis Night, or the Great Sabbot, when, they claim, supernatural beings — including evil things and dead things — grow restless because the wall between this world and the other world is very thin on this day. I'll bet if you asked one of those witches, she would tell you that the man on the hill coming toward you was the spectre of that child-killer from some years ago. Travelling down that road you still carried the scent of the newborn child you had been holding, and that may have been enough on that particular night to call back such an angry spirit. Perhaps his ghost was stirred to continue his earlier plans, and exact some form of vengeance against all children. Perhaps such a phantom was simply taking advantage of the opportunity that your presence provided, maybe to extend his distorted plan of vengeance to include someone associated with bringing the children he hated into the world. If you remember, it was a great black dog that brought to light that man's crimes by finding and exposing the bodies of his victims, and perhaps that black dog was itself an apparition bent on bringing justice. However, if the first black dog was a real flesh-and-blood animal, then it could be that the dog which you met yesterday, the one who seemed to want to protect you from the approaching man or spectre, might have been the spirit or ghost of that original helpful dog.'

"The vicar looked a little bit uncomfortable with his wife talking about such things as witches, spirits, and ghosts, so he intervened and added, 'That is, of course, if you believe in that sort of thing.'

"Well, my mother certainly did believe in 'that sort of thing' and, because she often told her family this story, I grew up believing in it, too."

The White Demon

I was walking down a busy street one warm summer day when I heard my name being called. Looking over I saw Katsuro, an acquaintance of mine that I knew from the university, sitting with an older man at an outside table in front of a coffee shop, so I wandered over and sat down. Katsuro introduced the man with him as Tadashi, his father, who had recently arrived from Japan. Tadashi was a retired university professor who had come to Vancouver to spend time with his son, after his wife (Katsuro's mother) had died. Tadashi was considering his son's offer to live with him permanently, since he had no other family members.

Katsuro had not actually called me over specifically to introduce his father, but rather wanted to speak to me about dogs. Apparently, his daughter was thinking about getting a dog, and since they had never had dogs as pets before, he wanted some advice about which breed might be best for her. One of the breeds they were considering was the Labrador Retriever, and, as chance would have it, just at that moment a young woman walked by with a black Labrador Retriever, and I observed, "It's interesting that Labrador Retrievers continue to be one of the most popular breeds of dog in the world, despite the fact that the majority of Labs are black in colour. You must understand that coat colour is not that important as an indicator of a dog's overall behaviour, but many people seem to shy away from black dogs. Animal shelters report that black dogs are harder to get adopted: it seems that, in the minds of many people, black dogs apparently appear to look more threatening: a bias which has been confirmed by some research that was done in my laboratory. It is also likely that some people still associate black dogs with the devil, or demons of some sort — the demon dogs who supposedly wander the English countryside are always said to be black."

Tadashi seemed interested in my observations, and joined the conversation in perfectly accented English. "That is not the case in Japan. In my country, especially outside of the big cities, it is big, white dogs who people are afraid of. The ghost dogs, the evil dogs, the devil dogs, are all large, white dogs; usually with long hair. They are very special and bring bad luck to anyone who comes near them, and they bring even greater misfortune to those who try to interfere with them."

He paused for a moment, and looked off into the distance as if observing a scene there, then continued, "You will not believe me, I think, but I once had the poor fortune to meet a white demon dog.

"I had just finished my first year of university, and needed employment to earn some money before the next semester started. My uncle knew of a job which he thought I might be able to get. He lived in a fishing village which had recently suffered a spate of thefts during the night. There was only one policeman in the region, and he was badly overworked. He was supposed to take care of not only that particular village, but also another, nearby village, and much of the area surrounding these two communities. The residents wanted some additional help for him, and decided that they would hire someone to fill in for their overworked constable, at least by patrolling at night. They thought it possible that this additional guard could catch, or at least identify, whoever might be carrying out the thefts, and if even this wasn't possible, it seemed likely that having someone keeping watch at night might just serve as a deterrent.

"I was not really supposed to be a policeman – more a watchman – and my job was to walk around the dock area and nearby streets, from one edge of the small village to the other. They gave me a white helmet and a white shirt, and armed me with a big, wooden baton, a flashlight, and a whistle on a string that I was to wear around my neck. If I saw anything untoward I was supposed to blow the whistle to raise the alarm, and wave the big baton as if I was about to attack – they never taught me how to actually use it as a weapon. So, basically, I walked back and forth along the edge of the village from sundown to sunset every night, which seemed to have the desired effect as the number of nighttime thefts dropped to almost none.

"However, some bad things did still happen in the village, even though they did not seem to involve thieves.

"It all began one night when I was at the edge of the village. Looking down the road, a short distance away from me I could see a big, white

dog, so tall that his head actually seemed higher than my waist. I was struck by the way that his fur seemed to glow – it was like looking at snow in the moonlight, only there was no moon in the sky that night. The dog stared at me. He had a big, square jaw, which was open just enough for me to see his long, sharp teeth, and I thought that if he decided to bite someone he could do a lot of damage. But what disturbed me more were his eyes: large and black, they reflected back no light, although there appeared to be some kind of bluish shimmer around the outside of each. To me, those big, black eyes looked like they were just empty holes in his head, surrounded by a flickering ring. Seeing the dog made me feel very uncomfortable: I suppose I was actually feeling a little afraid because I remembered stories I had heard when I was a child about white ghost dogs.

"I stared at the dog, but was then distracted for a moment by sudden squealing from a nearby pig pen. When I turned back to look at the dog again he was gone.

"I chided myself for being silly. I was a university student studying science, and knew there were no such things as ghost dogs or demon dogs. Subsequently, I didn't mention the incident to anyone: it didn't seem important, and I didn't want to sound like a fool.

"Late the very next night, as I approached the place once more, I saw the big, white dog again, and this time he walked down the road and over to the pig pen. The pigs were whining and squealing, and milling around, and, although I knew very little about farm animals, it was clear to me that they were in a panic. The dog disappeared around the edge of the pen. I was afraid that he was going to attack the animals so I ran forward and shouted, but when I reached the pen the dog was gone. Although the pigs were still agitated, I believed that my shout had scared away the dog.

"That morning I was finishing my rounds and getting ready to go to sleep when I heard some commotion and loud voices near where I had seen the dog. I went over and found a villager and his family at the pig pen. I asked what the problem was, and was told that all three of the pigs were dead. I told him,

Gods, ghosts, and black dogs

'Look carefully. Are there any bite marks? Do they look as though they have been attacked?' When he looked puzzled at my remarks, I told him about the white dog I had seen, and which I thought I had chased away. He inspected the animals, and told me that there were no wounds; no sign of blood or bites. However, my story of the white dog seemed to disturb him.

"Word spread very quickly through the village about the mysterious deaths of the pigs, and the presence of a large, white dog. By the time I was ready for my patrol that night, several people had already warned me that I should be on the lookout for the white dog, and if I saw him I should sound the alarm; this time using my whistle, which would carry better than my voice.

"Nothing happened until late that night. The thin sliver of moon had already disappeared below the horizon, and it was quite dark when I again caught a glimpse of the white dog, this time on the other side of the village, away from any place where farm animals were kept. He was standing on a little street which was lined with a number of small houses spaced a little apart. As I watched, the dog turned from the street and walked up onto the porch of one house, acting as if he didn't know – or care – that I was there. "Grabbing my whistle I began to blow, running so fast to the house that the whistle dropped out of my mouth and I had to put it back in to blow again. By the time I got to the porch, the family was awake, and so were the neighbours. I rushed in and cried 'I saw a white dog come in here. Look carefully.'

"It was a small house, so it was easy to search through it. There was no dog, but the back door was open a little, and everyone thought that the sound of my whistle must've frightened the dog enough to make him run out the back way. The people asked me to describe the dog, and when I told them how big and white he was, and how dark and strange his eyes were, they appeared very concerned and anxious, warning me to be especially careful, and keep a special lookout for the animal.

"Later, as the sun was just coming up and I was getting ready to end my rounds, I heard a woman scream. I ran toward the sound, which turned out to be coming from the same house where I had earlier seen the dog. I rushed to the door and arrived at the same time as a small group of residents of nearby houses. The woman of the house was standing there sobbing as she looked down on the tiny body of her infant girl. The child was dead but there was not a mark on her.

"This mysterious death of a child following so soon after the strange death of the pigs was worrisome enough, and the fact that both events occurred after the sighting of a white dog seemed like no simple coincidence to the villagers. The people were clearly becoming frightened, and I overheard several of them talking about demon dogs. By late morning the residents had called in a local priest to look at the child. The priest blessed and purified the body, and agreed with the villagers that the white dog might possibly be a devil, though tried to calm them by saying he would see if something could be done to keep it away, and prevent it from doing harm. The priest warned that if it was an evil spirit of some sort, rather than a real flesh-and-blood dog, it probably could not be killed, and trying to destroy it could bring great misfortune to everyone around.

"It seemed that, as night drew closer, most of the population was lighting lamps outside their doors, and anxiously scanning the streets for the white dog. I admit I was very nervous as I patrolled, especially when I moved far from the centre of the village toward the darker outside boundaries. However, I did not see the dog.

"It was well past midnight when my patrol brought me back again to the docks where the fishing boats were moored. I thought I saw the white dog standing on one edge of the dock. I wasn't sure at first because there were two oil lanterns burning near the entrance to the pier, and at first I thought it might just be the reflection of those lights on the water. However, as I drew closer, it became clear that it *was* the same large dog I had seen before. I observed him as he walked out on the dock, climbed a ramp and walked onto one of the fishing boats. I ran forward, again blowing my whistle as loudly as I could, thinking to myself that now there was no way that the dog could escape: he would be trapped on the little boat and we would catch him, and, once, captured that growing fear that something supernatural and evil was attacking the village would certainly end.

"I stood at the foot of the ramp blowing my whistle, my baton in my hand ready to defend myself should the dog reappear. In a short time, people from the nearby houses came to see what was happening, and this included the owners of the boat. We went aboard and searched the boat, but there was no dog to be found.

"I felt like an idiot. Maybe it had been just a reflection of the oil lights after all, and perhaps this was just a false alarm caused by my own nervousness. But those who had come down to the wharf thought that perhaps the dog really had been there, and had jumped off the boat when I sounded the alarm. With the lapping of the water against the dock it would have been hard for me to hear the sound of a dog swimming away.

"I did not sleep well that day, and just past sundown when I began my patrol again, I found a knot of people standing by the dock looking out to sea, and muttering anxiously among themselves. When I asked what was happening, they told me that a boat, *Hoshi*, had left in the morning to go fishing, just as it usually did at this time of year. It always returned just about the time that the sun was touching the horizon at the end of the day, and was now overdue, and none of the returning boats could remember seeing it that afternoon in the usual fishing grounds. Although this would normally cause some concern, this evening, the village people were much more worried than usual since the *Hoshi* was the boat that had been visited by the white dog the previous night. The vigil continued all night, and well into the next day, but the boat did not return, and the crew was never heard from again.

"By now, the people in the village were becoming convinced that they were being haunted or hunted by a demon in the shape of a white dog. The priest was again called out, and he agreed that there was a strong case suggesting the presence of some kind of devil. He assured the people that he had taken their concerns to the temple, and in just a day or two his brethren would bring the villagers some form of protection. But the people were frightened, impatient,

and angry. They would not let this beast plague their village for another night, and agreed to gather together when darkness came to hunt the white dog.

"The priest was very apprehensive. 'You cannot kill such a demon. Your weapons will not work. It will only cause him to retaliate. You can only ward off the coming of such devils. Perhaps scare them away, or use some form of protection. If you attack him he will bring fire and pain and suffering to all of you.'

"The villagers ignored the holy man's advice, and the village leaders said that they must take action to protect themselves now. Of course, these were not soldiers, and they had no real weapons such as rifles or guns. Nonetheless, the people gathered pitchforks, axes, sharpened hoes, sharp sticks, clubs, sickles, kitchen knives, and anything else which they felt could be used as a makeshift weapon.

"At nightfall they gathered and formed a long line along one edge of the village. The men were spaced only a few yards apart, and included in the line of men were some carrying oil lamps and flashlights to help light the way in the darkness. The idea was that with this line of men they could flush out the white dog and kill him. They had me walk up and down the line since I had a whistle and could make a loud noise if the dog was sighted. At the sound of my whistle they all were to rally around to help in the fight. The idea was to sweep through the village from one end to the other, in much the same way that people in India move a line of men through the jungle to drive out and capture a tiger that might be preying on one of their villages.

"We were well past halfway through the village, on a little street where tiny houses huddled close together, when someone saw the big, white dog. I blew my whistle and a lot of villagers went to surround the animal. The townsfolk yelled in anger, but not a single sound, not a growl, not a bark, came from the white dog. One man with a pitchfork rushed in to stab the beast. He clearly hit his target, but no sound came from the white dog; instead, the animal spun around, grabbing the man in his jaws and tossing him across the street. The pitchfork was still lodged in the side of the white dog, but

Gods, ghosts, and black dogs

the animal spun around in a circle twice and that sharp tool worked loose and fell to the ground. I was astonished to see that there was no blood on the pitchfork, and none on the side of the white dog to indicate where it had entered. Another man came forward carrying an oil lamp in one hand and a club in the other. As he raised his club to hit the animal, the dog darted forward and grabbed the oil lamp by its handle, spinning in a circle twice before releasing it: like a discus thrower might spin to throw his disk. The lighted lamp hit the roof of a nearby house, which burst into flame. In seconds the sparks had leapt across to the house next to it, and it soon was also ablaze. The villagers recognized that they were now facing a greater peril than even the dog, namely, the likelihood that much of the village, with all of its structures made of wood, would be set on fire. They forgot about the hunt and immediately began working to keep the fire from spreading to the rest of the village.

"In all the commotion I never saw what happened to the dog. It simply was not there when I looked for it again. Four homes were completely destroyed by the flames, and two others badly damaged. The man who had stabbed the dog with the pitchfork was found dead with no marks on him; the man who had had the lamp snatched from his hand discovered that his arm no longer worked, and it remained paralyzed for the rest of his life.

"In the middle of the next morning several priests arrived from the temple with a bundle of Omamori: little silk bags which each contain a special prayer written on a slip of paper. The little bags are meant to be worn on a cord like a necklace, and were designed to protect the people of the town. The priests also brought with them slices from silver coins. Each coin had been cut into eight pieces so that each piece looked like a tiny dagger or a sword. A small strand of silk was attached through a hole drilled in the wide end of these miniature 'blades,' and they were then tacked onto doorways of houses and barns, and entrances to animal pens. The priests assured the people that this would help to ward off the demon, and keep it from entering the places protected by the silver blades.

"The white dog was not seen again that summer. I left there when the university term was about to start, and have never gone back to that village."

Tadashi paused, then stared down at his coffee cup as if embarrassed to continue. However, he then spoke again, quietly. "I am a university professor – a man of science – and I do not believe that there is any evidence to support the existence of devils or demons. But I saw with my own eyes a white dog, whose eyes looked like empty black holes, and who was stabbed in such a way that he should have died, though he did not bleed or make a single sound. I saw a big, white dog who came and went at will, and seemed to bring evil and misfortune to everything that he touched. I do not believe in devils, but I will not touch, or even go near, any large, white dog, because such an animal frightens me to this day ..."

Campfire tales

It was the third week in August, and the corn crop was coming in. John, the father of one of our grandchildren, Centainne, had asked if he could use our little farm in Chilliwack, British Columbia, for a party. The idea was to celebrate the end of the summer, and a number of his friends and our family were to be invited for a camping-style overnight stay. The guests were supposed to bring tents or campers, or just sleeping bags, and we would hold a big barbecue, and boil up a bushel or two of corn on the cob. John also thought it might be fun to put together a campfire before bedtime.

Guests began to arrive a little before noon on Saturday morning. Some came as couples, and some came as families with kids. All told, we ended up with around two dozen adults, and perhaps nine or ten kids (five of whom were our grandchildren). People began to set up behind the house, and by four o'clock or so, most of them had dragged folding lawn chairs up to the patio area where the food and drink were located. John and our middle son, Geoff, had appointed themselves masters of the barbecue, and were contemplating matters having to do with

what would be grilled first, and how. Our oldest son, Kevin, and my wife's brother-in-law, Cameron, had taken on the task of filling up a large metal cauldron with water, in which to cook the corn, and started to heat the contents. People were happily taking bets on how long it would take for the big pot of water to reach the boil, given that it was being heated by one small propane cooker. Meanwhile, other guests were arranging bowls with salads, and baskets with buns and potato chips. Several coolers packed with ice had also appeared, and folk were already rummaging through them for bottles, and cans of beer or soda pop.

Most of the kids had made their way into the fenced area which I use as a training field for my dogs, and could be heard laughing and screaming in delight as they ran around the field, tossing objects to one another, and driving my two dogs absolutely crazy as they tried to intercept all of those things whizzing through the air.

By the time the sun drew close to the horizon, and the light began to dim, we had all consumed massive amounts of grilled meat and corn

Gods, ghosts, and black dogs

on the cob, and the adults had washed it all down with copious amounts of beer. The party had swelled somewhat, as several of our neighbours had come by to join in the festivities. There was a pleasant drone of conversation, punctuated by laughter, as people got to know one another, or renew acquaintances, or simply interact with friends and family.

Before the light had faded completely, a small party broke off to go further back into the field to where they had dug a shallow fire pit, and lined the outer rim with stones and bricks. They piled up a large amount of wood, and, as the last light faded from the sky, returned to announce that everyone should grab their chairs, the sacks of marshmallows, and the sticks to roast them with (and, of course, the coolers that contained what seemed to me to be an undiminished treasure trove of beer and pop).

By the time everyone had reassembled in the back field, there was a roaring campfire, which had been kindled under the supervision of my wife, Joan, who seems to be attracted to open fires in the same way that moths are attracted to burning candles. People soon settled in around the fire, and the kids were being instructed on how to roast marshmallows, which they were doing with great glee, even if demonstrating little skill at the task. Every now and then one of them would jump up and offer a family member a burning mass of charcoal on the end of the stick, which, apparently, had started out as a marshmallow, but somehow had caught fire when it was held too close to the flames.

Most of the adults were comfortably settled in, and the majority of them were engaged in the happy pursuit of consuming one or two bottles of beer beyond their usual limit. Thus, there was a mellowness in the air, and not a high enough energy level for anybody to propose anything strenuous or exciting.

I believe it was our granddaughter, Cora, who announced she thought that people were supposed to tell scary stories when they sat around a campfire.

"What kind of scary stories?" I asked, and then, using my fingers to make something that looked like devil's horns on my forehead, gave my best imitation of an evil villain's laugh.

"Well, any kind of scary stories. Since we are out here on your farm, and you are the dog guy, maybe they should be scary stories about dogs."

Someone from the other side of the fire chimed in, "I don't think I've ever heard any really scary stories about dogs."

I was sitting next to a big hulk of a man named Miles, a longtime friend of John's, he had done a good deal of carousing with before he had married our daughter. Miles had a great sense of humour, and, more importantly for this particular evening, a deep, booming voice that was perfect for telling spooky campfire tales.

"Well, I can tell you one," he said, leaning forward with his elbows on his knees. "It was told to me by someone who actually thought that it might be true. Furthermore, it was supposed to have happened in Aldergrove, which is one of the places we passed on our way here.

"Anyway, it starts with a guy named Bud, who was an automobile mechanic, and ran an emergency tow truck service. Bud married a tiny little blonde woman named Sally. Now, Sally was a pretty thing, but she looked kind of fragile, weighing in at only around 90 pounds. Bud worried about her some, since the house they had bought was not far from the edge of town. His concern was that there wasn't much in the way of streetlights, so it got pretty dark at night, and the houses were quite widespread. The real reason for his concern was that Bud was always on call, and sometimes car crashes or breakdowns would occur in the middle of the night. When he got the call for one of those, it meant that he would have to leave Sally by herself while he went out to tow a car that was in trouble. Bud was afraid that the isolated location of the house might make it a tempting target for thieves, and that if somebody tried to break in when he was gone, Sally would not be able to defend herself.

"Bud came up with a solution, however. He got Sally a Doberman Pinscher dog, fully trained for guard dog work. The dog's name was Sting. Let me tell you, Sting and Sally clicked like Romeo and Juliet. Nobody could get near Sally without her permission if Sting was around, and Sting had no hesitation about using his teeth to make sure that Sally was safe. If Bud and Sally were out of the house, Sting would patrol from room to room, and Bud knew that the place was as secure as if he had hired a Special Forces commando with a military rifle to protect his home. But when he wasn't needed for protection, Sting just loved Sally, and would snuggle up next to her like one of those little lap dogs, and wag that little stump of a tail. You can be sure that Sally loved him back just as much.

"Well, one night, Bud and Sally were invited out to a barbecue, just like this one. They had a really good meal, and, if the truth be told, Bud drank just a little bit too much beer for it to be safe for him to drive home (just like some of you folks here, I'm sure). So when it came time for them to leave, Sally put Bud in the passenger side of the front seat, and she drove them home.

"Well, they got to their front door, and Sally helped Bud inside. They only went a step or two through the door when Sally saw Sting. The big dog was standing there, gasping for breath, clearly in distress. He seemed to be choking on something, and in trying to dislodge it from his throat. Sting's breathing efforts were clearly harsh and damaging because blood was visible, dripping out of the side of his mouth.

"Sally immediately bent down and tried to pry open his mouth. She couldn't see anything, but Sting was coughing and gagging, and she started to panic. She raced to the telephone and called Dr Ford, a local veterinarian who had been a friend of the family for a long time. When she gave him a description of Sting's symptoms, he told her to bring the dog to his office right away.

"Bud was still a bit dopey from all the beer he had drunk, so Sally walked him over to a chair and had him sit down. 'I have to take Sting to the vet,' she told him, 'you stay here and I'll be back quick as I can.'

"Sally rushed Sting into the car. He was still gagging and coughing and spitting up blood when they got to the vet just a few minutes later. The veterinarian took one look at the Doberman and announced that the dog had to immediately go into surgery.

"So Sally went home, and there was Bud still sitting on the chair. She tried to get him to stand up and walk upstairs to their bedroom, but Bud was still way too groggy for this. As Sally was simply too small to be able to drag Bud upstairs by herself, she decided that maybe she should try to get some coffee into him so that he might sober up enough to make it up to the bedroom without too much assistance. Sally left him, still slumped in the chair, and went into the kitchen and began to brew a pot of coffee. When it was done, she helped Bud drink two cups of it, and it began to look as though he was finally going to be able to move on his own without her help. It was just as she finally got him to stand up, and had walked him to the foot of the staircase, that the phone rang.

"Sally was tempted to let the phone ring, because she didn't want to miss her chance at getting Bud upstairs to the bedroom now that he was on his feet. However, she thought to herself that no one would be calling this late at night unless it was important, and then she thought that it might just be the veterinarian calling about Sting, so she picked up the phone.

"She had barely said 'Hello' when she heard the vet's voice, shouting as if in a panic, 'Thank God I got you in time! Leave the house! Now! No time to explain, just get out of there!'

"The veterinarian had been a friend of the family for a long time, and Sally trusted him. She didn't understand what was going on, but if he knew something that meant she should get out of the house then she wasn't going to question this. She carefully turned Bud toward the front door and virtually pushed him outside onto the front steps, just in time to see two police cars pull up in front of their home. The next thing she knew the police officers were pushing their way past her and into the house with their guns drawn.

A few minutes later Dr Ford arrived in the van that he used as an animal ambulance. He jumped out and rushed up to Sally, breathlessly asking 'Have they got him? Please tell me, have they got him?'

"Just then, the police who had been in the house stepped back out through the front door, accompanying a big, burly man dressed in a T-shirt

Gods, ghosts, and black dogs

and combat camouflage pants. The man was holding his handcuffed hands clutched in front of his chest. The hands looked like they were leaking blood which was now seeping onto his shirt. One of the policeman called out, 'Hey, Sarge, we found him upstairs. He was in the bedroom. He closed the door, I think maybe to keep the dog out, and was hiding in the closet. He had this,' and the policeman held up a 10 inch long combat knife, the kind used by Special Forces assassins.

"Sally was completely confused. She grabbed the veterinarian's arm and demanded 'Who is that, and how did you know that he was in our house? For the love of God, please tell me what is going on.'

"Dr Ford took a deep breath which seemed to be an expression of relief more than anything else, then straightened up to compose himself. 'Well, I found out what Sting was choking on. It was a human finger, and it was very fresh'"

There was a moment of silence when Miles stopped speaking, finally broken by Cora's younger brother, Matty, who announced "That's yucky!"

"I can tell you a scarier dog story than that," a mellifluous male voice announced from across the fire, which I recognized as coming from another of John's friends, though I could not remember his name. "You see, there was this girl called Katie, who lived in a town called Hope (about an hour or so from here). One night, her parents had to go to a meeting at their church, and Katie stayed at home. She didn't worry about being alone because she had a dog. The dog's name was King, and he was a really big Collie dog — something like Lassie, only bigger.

"Anyway, Katie settled in to watch some television with King lying on the sofa next to her, and everything was fine until the 10 o'clock local news came on. Its main story was about the gruesome murder of a couple who lived in Hope. Katie knew them since they lived just a short distance from her home. The news report ended by saying that people should be careful; stay inside, and lock their doors and windows.

"All of this spooked Katie. King seemed to recognize that she was uncomfortable, and reached over and licked her neck reassuringly. Together, the

girl and the dog went through the house, closing and latching windows, and locking doors. Katie thought that she had just about finished when she remembered to check the basement. She went down there and found one of the basement windows open, which seemed a little strange to her since she didn't remember any family members spending any time recently in the basement. Nonetheless, she closed and latched the basement window and went back upstairs.

"Katie felt too tense to go to bed just then, so she and King sat on the sofa and watched some late night TV. King snuggled up next to her and occasionally licked her hand. The dog's warm, soft tongue against her skin was reassuring: his touch reminded her that she was not alone, and made Katie feel safe. Around midnight, Katie was finally getting really tired, so turned off the television and changed into her pyjamas. Getting into bed, King nestled beside her in the blankets, the way he always did for the first half hour or so when she got ready to go to sleep, although on hot nights, like this one, King would often hop off the bed and lie on the floor, but always within Katie's reach: she could simply drop her hand over the side of the bed and touch his fur for reassurance.

"Katie fell asleep right away, but awakened a little later for some reason. She wondered whether it was her parents coming home which woke her — glancing at the clock she saw that it was nearly 1am — but her folks had warned that they might be late home that night. Listening more carefully, Katie heard a faint noise coming from the bathroom: kind of a 'drip, drip, drip . . .' and thought that maybe that was what had woken her. She'd probably not turned off the sink tap properly, and it was leaking a few drops of water, and perhaps the disturbing news about the nearby murders had made her so nervous that her sleep could be disturbed by such a small sound. The idea that a murderer might be in her neighborhood made her nervous, and she looked for King, who already jumped off the bed. She lowered her hand over the bed to reach for him, and felt him comfort her with a few warm licks of her fingers.

"Katie considered getting up to close the

taps more tightly, but felt too comfortable in bed and dropped off to sleep again. She could not have been asleep for more than half-an-hour when she woke again to the 'drip, drip, drip. . .' sound coming from the bathroom. Feeling a flash of nervousness, Katie reached down and again felt the comforting lick of the dog's tongue on her hand. Once again, she drifted off to sleep, but this time only for a few minutes. Again, there was only 'drip, drip, drip . . .' to be heard.

"At this point Katie felt she had had enough. If she was going to have trouble sleeping because of the dripping noise the obvious thing to do was get up and close the tap, so she got out of bed and walked into the bathroom. There, hanging from the shower curtain rod, was her Collie dog, his throat cut and most of his skin peeled off. The dripping noise that she had heard had been drops of King's blood falling and forming a puddle of the floor.

"As Katie turned, she caught sight of the medicine chest mirror, on which was a chilling message written in her dog's blood "Humans can lick, too." And behind the message she saw in the mirror the reflection of a man with a knife in his hand ..."

There was a moment of absolute silence at the end of the tale, finally broken by Cora shrieking

"That's awful!" I could see that she was covering her eyes, which seemed like a strange response to hearing something frightening!

Just to join in to the spirit of the proceedings I offered, "I suppose I should add to the merriment by telling the story of the dog whose barking woke the Devil."

At that moment I felt a pair of hands on my shoulders, and looked up to see my wife, Joan. "That's enough of all this nonsense. I won't have the children having nightmares over frightening stories like these. If you want to tell a story, how about the one which tells how the Pekingese learned to bark?"

"But,'" I protested, "that's a funny story, not a scary campfire story."

"If you tell another story that frightens the children, you'll see just how scary I can be," Joan said, wagging a finger at me.

I gave a theatrical sigh, and began my story. "Back in the days when China was ruled by a mighty Khan, and all of the dogs in China bowed down to the Pekingese, no dogs knew how to bark. The only sound that dogs could make was a kind of chirp – like a bird who ..."

And God had a dog

It was August, and I had arrived at Santa Rosa, California, late on a Sunday morning, to teach a week-long course at the Bergin University of Canine Studies. The course I was teaching was about dog behaviour and how dogs think, and was a graduate course for students who were there to earn a Master's degree.

Bergin University is an interesting institution, which had begun life as the Assistance Dog Institute, but then later became an accredited university, and is one of the few places in North America where students can get a Bachelor's degree or a Master's degree in the area of canine studies. Many of the students are studying to be service dog trainers, and some graduates go on to start schools for service dogs: the kind who can help disabled people live independently. These dogs can open doors, pull a zipper, turn a light on or off, and so on. The graduate programme leading to the Master's degree not only provides practical skills, but advanced academic and research information for those students who want to become specialists in the area of canine behaviour.

This particular year I was staying on the campus in student housing, in a separate little room set aside for visiting faculty. I picked up my key and dropped off my suitcases. Nothing had been scheduled for me that day until the evening, when I was supposed to have dinner with the university's president and founder, Bonnie Bergin, and her husband, Jim, so I decided to take advantage of the sunshine and my rented car by taking a little ride north toward Mendocino County, with the idea of trying to find an interesting place to have lunch. I had a recommendation from a friend, and, after about 30 minutes' driving, I came across the place. It was a big, wooden building with a large, shaded outdoor porch area, on which there stood several wooden tables.

I walked up the two or three steps, and a waiter waved his hand nonchalantly at me. "Sit anywhere you like." Only a few people sat at the tables, and I noticed one man wearing a western-style hat, with a light, colourful, beaded vest decorated in the native Indian style over a light-coloured cotton shirt. At his feet rested a large, shorthaired, hound-type dog. The dog caught my attention because of his red colour — as red is any Irish Setter I had ever seen.

And God had a dog

"I walked over to the man, and bent down to give the dog a pat. The man looked up from his menu, and I said to him, "That's a handsome dog. It is probably the deepest red colour that I've ever seen on a hound."

"Red dog for a red man," he laughed. "Don't recognize you. You from around here?"

"No," I replied. "I'm here in California just to teach a course at Bergin University, where the Assistance Dog Institute is. Somebody told me that this might be a good place to get lunch and a pitcher of beer, and since I don't have to start teaching until tomorrow morning, I decided to give it a try."

"You know about dogs, huh? Well, I'm just getting ready to order, and if you'd like some company why don't you sit down here with me?" responded the man.

I pulled out a chair and sat down, and moments later the waiter dropped off a menu for me. I quickly selected something from it, along with a pitcher of a local draft beer, and waited for my companion to finish giving his order.

"My name is Kuzih," he told me. "That's an Athapascan name which means 'great talker.' I was given it because my father had a dream right before I was born, and in that dream he saw me growing up to be some kind of medicine man: what you university types would call a shaman. It appears the dream was a bit prophetic, because when I'm not on the job (I work for the California Department of Agriculture), that appears to be one of my functions in the band."

"Band?" I queried.

"That's a tribe, or native nation, not a rock band," he laughed. "I'm a member of the Cahto people. We are located mostly north of here but south of Eureka — around Cahto Valley and Long Valley, between the headwaters of the two main branches of the Eel River. If you know where Laytonville is, we are close by there. Like other California tribes, our ancestors were hunters and gatherers. Besides gathering nuts, seeds, berries, roots, and tubers, we hunted for deer, rabbits, birds, and fish to provide additional food for our people. The dog was our only domesticated animal. Nowadays, we are a pretty modern people, and keep up with contemporary standards, but we are trying not to lose the traditions. So, mid-summer and sometime in the winter we hold a kind of camp-out, to which we take the kids and try to teach them the traditions and folklore of our tribe. That is when I get to be a teacher, shaman, and the great talker my father dreamt I would be. I just try to pass on what I know about our tribal history and culture to the next generation."

The waiter came by and placed a pitcher of pale beer on the table, along with two glasses, which he filled for us before wandering off. I looked down at the deep red dog and asked, "So, is this dog a breed created specifically by your tribe?"

"Nobody created dogs, they just always were." he replied.

"Well, most cultures have some sort of folklore about how dogs were created; isn't that the case for the Cahto people?"

"We do have stories about the creation of the world, and we do have stories about dogs, but we have no stories about how dogs were created. Dogs were just always there. In fact, according to our folklore, dogs were present when the world was created, and played a bit of a part in shaping the end result.

"You see, according to our tradition, we Cahto people have two great gods, Chenesh, who is the first creator of the universe, and also the God of thunder and lightning, and Nagaicho, a wanderer who shaped the Earth, and brought living things into it. Chenesh was the more powerful of the two, but also lazy.

"One day, Nagaicho said to Chenesh, 'My dog and I are getting bored, and we would like some place to wander through and explore. Can you make such a place?' Notice that the dog is just there; nobody has created it. I guess the idea was that wherever living things were — especially people, and even gods — there were dogs. Since dogs are always around, they are already here, and gods don't have to spend time creating something which already exists.

"Anyway, according to the way we tell the story, Chenesh yawned and said: 'If you must have such a thing, here it is,' and he brought forth a great ball which was the world. It was round because

Gods, ghosts, and black dogs

Chenesh was too lazy to separate the sky from the oceans and the land, and Nagaicho had first to erect four great pillars at the corners of the world to separate the sky from the earth.

"When Nagaicho first looked at the world, all he could see was ocean and sky. The ocean was beautiful, and waves danced along its surface, so he created all of the creatures of the sea to swim in it and be happy. The dog looked down at this and began to bark. At first, Nagaicho was confused by this, but then understood and said, 'Oh my dog, there is only water and you need a place to stand, so let me create dry land.'

"Once the land was made, Nagaicho and the dog stepped upon it. Nagaicho took a handful of the dirt, and from it shaped the first man. The dog was pleased to see that here was someone who could work and play with him, though he also needed someone who would care for his kind and feed him, so from a whale in the ocean the god shaped the first woman. Nagaicho turned to the dog, and said, 'Because she is from a whale she will be soft, but as she grows old she will become fat. I have put into her a special feeling so that she will look at puppies as though they are her children, and she will want to tend and care for all puppies and dogs until they are old enough to work and hunt with the man.'The dog wagged his tail, and was very pleased.

"The sun was hot, and the dog was panting, and Nagaicho saw that he needed something to drink. So the god dragged his feet deep into the Earth and created rivers; then poked his fingers into the Earth and created flowing springs with cold, fresh water.

"'Drink,' Nagaicho said to the dog, 'for I have made this water sweet, not salty like the water of the ocean.' So the dog drank from the sweet water until his thirst was gone, and then Nagaicho himself lay down and drank.

"'Soon, the elk and the deer will come to drink at the rivers and springs,' said Nagaicho to the dog, 'This will good. They will all drink the water — even bears and people.'The dog sat down and gave a little bark, leaning his head to one side in the way that everyone knows means he is interested in what is going on, but doesn't quite understand the meaning.

"Nagaicho looked at the dog and tried to figure out what was puzzling him, then nodded as he understood. 'Oh, it is the deer and bear that you don't recognize. I haven't made them yet. Thank you for reminding me. Just wait a bit because first I want to finish working on the water.' So the god piled rocks around the edge of the water to make lakes and ponds, and put salamanders and turtles and little eels in the creeks.

"Afterwards, Nagaicho walked around the world, creating the creatures. He put all kinds of bear and deer in the mountains and forests, and made panthers and jack rabbits, and all manner of living things after he had created the places where they should live. As he made each creature he gave it a name, and told the dog what that name was so that he would remember and understand.

"After a while the god said, 'Walk behind me, my dog, and let us look at all that is made.'

"The trees were tall; the streams were full of fish. The little valleys had grown wide and full of flowering brush. Acorns and chestnuts hung on the trees; berries crowded the bushes. There were many birds and snakes. The grass had grown. Grasshoppers were leaping about. There was clover and flowers. The dog was happy and chased the rabbits and the deer, and when he had a chance the dog would bark loudly at the bears and wolves (although usually only from a safe distance). Nagaicho smiled to see this. Neither the god nor the dog felt bored any longer.

"'We made it good, my dog,' said Nagaicho. And so they started back, walking to the north, the god and his dog, who had always been with him."

The big, red dog lying at Kuzih's feet looked up momentarily when he stopped speaking. He gave a loud thump of his tail on the wood floor as if agreeing with the truth of the story, then dozed off while the two humans at the table continued to talk about gods, and dogs, and traditions, and drink cold beer on a warm summer's day.

The foredoomed
Prince

Egypt might seem like a good place to look for myths and legends about dogs, since the ancient Egyptians were one of the few cultures to actually worship dogs as gods. The dog god of Egypt is Anubis, who is associated with resurrection. His job is to guide the dead to the place where they will be judged. Anubis has the head of a dog, although some say that it's really the head of a jackal. However, that is wrong, since another god, Upuaut, truly has the head of a jackal, while the face of Anubis is really much like the prick-eared, long-faced Greyhounds depicted on the walls of tombs and pyramids. Still, the truth of the matter is that the Egyptians did not have animal gods, but believed that the spirit of each god resided in particular animals, and for each god there was an animal that was sacred to him. To attract the attention and favour of a particular god, the Egyptians offered sacrifices of that god's animal.

It is not because of Anubis, however, that Egypt is full of tales about dogs, but rather because in Egypt it was universally accepted that people could have an emotional bond with their dog. In recognition of that, by law, the killing of an owned dog (that is one with a collar) could be severely punished – sometimes by death. If the pet dog in a household died, the grief expressed was as if a person had died. The dog's master shaved off his eyebrows and the hair on his head and body. (If a cat died, a man was required only to shave off one eyebrow.) Virtually every large ancient city had a cemetery where the mummified remains of much-loved dogs could be placed along with inscriptions containing words such as 'beloved,''companion,''blessed,''faithful,' and 'we will be united in paradise.'

Although dogs were used as guards, weapons of war, hunters and shepherds, some were simply companions, and often treated as if they were family members, the affection that people had for their pet openly displayed. For example, many pharaohs were buried with effigies of their dogs: Rameses II was buried with the names and statues of four of his dogs, and Tutankhamen with images of two of his dogs. For those who could afford it, perhaps the greatest expression of caring was to have their dog's body mummified and interred with them, the canine mummy often placed on a reed mat at the foot of the bed or near the feet of his master's sarcophagus.

Cheops, the pharaoh who built the Great Pyramid at Giza, had a dog named Abarkaru, who is described as the pharaoh's companion and protector, and whose mummified remains were placed in the same chamber where his beloved king lies. There are even a few instances where the mummy of the dog was actually placed in the sarcophagus of his master. In one woman's burial, the container which held her dog was laid by her feet, and carried the inscription: 'a hound of the bed who his mistress loved.' In another, the mummy of a man rests next to his dog with the words: 'An unfailing friend. His name was Abu.'

From the period of the pharaohs come many stories and myths about the love, devotion, and heroism of dogs, and one of the most popular of these demonstrates the value that was placed on the friendship of a dog in those ancient times. The story has to do with the royal family. Apparently, the Pharaoh's sister had been thought to be barren, but, unexpectedly late in life, she had a son. She believed that her child was a favour granted by the gods so she named him Baraka, meaning 'gift' or 'blessing.'

As was typical in the royal family, the priests were called in to bless the child and to foretell his future. The soothsayer among them prophesized that "The death of this child will be determined by the actions of a crocodile, or of a serpent, or of a scorpion, or of a dog."

Pharaoh's sister became quite frightened by these predictions, especially the idea that so many types of creature might bring her son to an early death, and, in order to protect her child, she asked the Pharaoh to provide her son with a large house near the edge of the royal quarter of the city. The boy would be raised in isolation, and never allowed to wander in the desert, near the river, or in the streets where he might encounter any of those creatures who might bring about his death.

One day, some time later, Baraka stood on the roof terrace of his home, and looked at the nearby street where a cart was rolling by. In the cart were a young boy and girl, and they were playing with a litter of puppies. Baraka could hear their laughter, and asked one of the household servants, "What are these things? Could I have one of those things which might make me laugh like those children do?"

The Pharaoh, who loved Baraka dearly, learned of his nephew's request and consulted the priests. They told him that allowing the child to be near any of the four creatures that had been named might place him in immediate danger. On the other hand, they told him "Fate cannot be cheated. If the child is doomed, then the god Set will claim him, no matter what you try to do."

The Pharaoh was a doting uncle, and he interpreted the analyses of the priests as meaning that a dog would not place his nephew in any greater danger than his fate already decreed. So the King chose a puppy sired by his favourite dog, which was to be a gift for Baraka. However, since he still worried about his nephew's wellbeing, he first had the dog blessed in the temple of the god Horus, who defends people from evil. Then he named the dog Uzat, after the eye of the god Horus, in the hope that this might attach the favour and protection of the deity to both the dog and the child. The King then sent the dog to be a pet for Baraka, "lest his heart be sad."

In that lonely and isolated house it is not surprising that Uzat became Baraka's most intimate companion and best friend. Still, Baraka longed to see more of the world, and, one day, as boys might be expected to try and do, he managed to sneak out of the house. That morning, Baraka and his dog explored the nearby bank of the Nile River, poking around the bushes and reeds, and splashing in the water. As the sun rose toward noon, the boy sat in the shade and fell asleep.

He was suddenly awakened by Uzat's barking, and, when he stood up, he saw a crocodile had reached the shore of the river, and was charging toward him. The dog's barking not only alerted Baraka, but also distracted the crocodile long enough to give the boy a chance to run to safety, followed moments later by Uzat: his vigilant guard had also escaped the hungry crocodile. That night, Uzat was rewarded with a bowl of fine meat in thanks for his heroic actions.

Time passed, and when Baraka came of age, as was the custom for members of the royal family, the prince's marriage was arranged by the Pharaoh. When he first met Shepsit, his bride-to-be, they spoke of many things, including the fate that had been predicted for him.

When she heard the prophesy that had been made when Baraka was born, Shepsit was fearful for his safety, and said, "Then you must kill that dog to keep yourself safe."

Baraka was horrified by the suggestion, and answered, "I will not kill my dog. I raised him from when he was small. He is my friend and he saved my life from the crocodile."

Shepsit was insistent, however, and would not drop the matter, "I do not want a husband who so carelessly flirts with death," she replied.

Baraka sat silently for a few moments, then finally asked in a quiet voice, "Would you rather have a husband who cares nothing for his friends, and would turn on those that he loves?"

Shepsit listened to his words, and felt both ashamed at the demands that she had been making, and proud of the loyalty and love that her future husband was displaying. She took his hand in hers and said, "Then when we marry it appears that we will have a dog in our family."

As the years passed, Uzat grew old and died. The well-loved dog was succeeded by one of his own puppies, who was also blessed in the temple of Horus, and who, like his father, was also named Uzat. When Baraka went off to serve in the army, as a member of the royal house he was allowed to take his dog with him, even when the army went out on campaign. One morning, Baraka awakened and reached for his boots. Suddenly, Uzat began to growl. The young man wondered if this was the sign of the long-feared attack that would kill him. He reached for the boot again, and the dog charged across the room, grabbed the boot by its tip, and shook it from side to side. Out of the boot fell two scorpions who might well have killed Baraka had he stepped into the boot.

Still more time passed, and this second Uzat died; replaced, as before, by yet another blessed dog named Uzat, This dog had been sired by Baraka's previous canine companion, and was, therefore, the grandson of the first Uzat.

Shepsit never forgot the prophesy of the priests, and still occasionally found herself looking at the current version of Uzat, and worrying about whether this dog might someday be the instrument of her husband's doom. Every now and then she would bring up the matter with Baraka, reminding him of his fate as predicted by the priests. However, the prince still insisted on having his dog with him, reminding her that twice, already, a dog had saved his life, rather than bringing harm to him.

It was long after one of these conversations between Shepsit and Baraka that a servant brought in a basket of figs which had been harvested nearby, placing the basket in front of her master and mistress. Baraka thought that the figs looked quite ripe and good, and was reaching for one when Uzat leapt forward and knocked him down. Shepsit screamed and grabbed a knife to protect her husband from the death that she long feared the dog intended for him. However, the dog quickly turned away from Baraka, and, as he spun around, the basket of figs was knocked over. One servant ran over to help their master, while another went to retrieve the figs, giving a cry of fear when a deadly asp wriggled out of the basket. It was a serpent that could well have killed Baraka. Once again, his life had been saved by his dog. Shepsit dropped the knife and bent down next to Uzat, hugging his neck and whispering a quiet 'Thank you' to the dog. She would never again doubt his loyalty and fidelity.

More years passed, and still another Uzat sat by Baraka's side. The prince was now growing old and iill, and, at his wife's insistence, they called in the healer and a priest. With Shepsit sitting by his side, Baraka turned to the priest and asked, "My fate was to have my death determined by the actions of a crocodile, serpent, scorpion, or a dog. I am now old, and if the healer is correct, I will die of causes associated with advanced age. Does this mean that the original prediction of my death was wrong?"

The priest smiled, and said quietly, "No, your fate was as it should be. Because you accepted the friendship of a dog, and were true and loyal to him, you were saved from an early death by a crocodile, a serpent, and a scorpion. Thus, it is the actions of a

Gods, ghosts, and black dogs

dog that have, in fact, determined the nature of your death. The dog's actions will be what cause you to die of old age rather than some other cause. Through the friendship that you have shared with a dog, you have been blessed by Anubis, and by the god Horus who your dog was named after. That blessing and the protection of dogs who returned your love has given you a long life, and most likely you will be rewarded for that loyalty to your dogs in the afterlife."

The war steeds
of the fairies

Abbotsford, British Columbia, is a town located about one hour east of the city of Vancouver. I really can't tell you much about the people, commerce, or culture of the city of Abbotsford, since, for me, the main thing that draws my attention to this location is the fact that every year, in October, it hosts one of the largest dog shows in all of Canada.

I make it my business to always attend this dog show, even if my dogs are not competing in either the conformation or the obedience rings. One of the reasons I go to this show is obviously to see the handsome and well-trained dogs who attend, and another is in order to visit with the many 'doggy folk' who are there, some of whom have travelled a long way to enter their dogs in this prestigious show. However, there is one more reason for attending that is also important to me.

A dog show of this size attracts many merchants and vendors, who set up in stalls that encircle the competition rings, and fill the central area of the building. The products they are selling are dog-related, and many are specialty items that cannot easily be found anyplace else. You can not only find a sweater for your dog, elegant leashes and collars, beautiful beds, carrying kennels, and doggy toys, but also other, more obscure, items, such as beautiful jewellery in the shape of your favourite breed, various types of specialised training equipment, antique and contemporary art prints of dogs, and even high-tech gadgets such as a GPS built into a dog's collar so that you can always locate him, should he go missing anyplace other than on the moon.

It's always fun to browse through the various stalls to see what new items are available that I might want to purchase for the canines in my house, and so it was that I found myself standing in front of a large set of racks containing collars of all descriptions, including some Martingale-style embroidered offerings that were so elegant they could easily have graced the necks of King Henry VIII's Greyhounds. Beside me was a middle-aged woman — a brunette with streaks of gray running through her short hair — and in whose hand was a leash, on the other end of which was a handsome Welsh Corgi, with those great bat ears that make their faces so appealing. The young, blonde clerk was showing the woman a new

Gods, ghosts, and black dogs

line of dog collars which came in a great variety of patterns, although most important, according to the saleswoman, was the relatively new technology that distinguished these items.

"You see what they've done is to use a modified version of those quick-access plastic snaps that are used on hiking equipment, like backpacks, and even on parachutes. They're made out of this really strong plastic, and all you have to do is insert a tab into the slot and it snaps into place. There's no fumbling with buckles, or trying to get a chain collar over the dog's head. It just snaps in, holds tight, and when you want to release it you simply squeeze the two tabs on each side to get an instantaneous release. Since all of the parts of the mechanism are made out of plastic, they won't rust or corrode." As she spoke, the saleswoman enthusiastically clicked the tab of the collar she was holding in and out several times to demonstrate.

The woman with the Corgi looked at the collar, and asked, in a faint British accent, "So, there is no metal at all on this collar?"

"Exactly, not a single bit of metal," confirmed the clerk.

"Well, that won't do. You see, my dog is a Corgi, and there simply must be some iron or steel in her collar."

This rather strange comment caught my interest, and I dawdled a bit while the clerk rooted around her collection of canine neckwear until she found several handsome collars, with metal buckles, and stylish metal studs in the shape of stars, hearts, and even one with little metal dog bones affixed around it. The woman with the Corgi picked up a collar decorated with shiny metal stars, and asked "What kind of metal are these?"

"All of these collar decorations are stainless steel. They are fixed on to the collar really well, and shouldn't rust or give you any other problems."

The woman smiled, picked out a purple collar embellished with silvery metal stars, and paid for it with a credit card.

When she finished her purchase I wandered over to her, and gave her dog a friendly pat.

"She is a pretty little dog," I said. "I couldn't

help overhearing your comments to the clerk about needing a dog collar with some iron or steel on it for your Corgi. Could I ask you why that is the case?"

The woman laughed. As it happened, she had recognized me from some recent television appearances, and was willing to chat about her dog and her special needs. Her name was Rosalind, and she had had Corgis all her life. I offered to buy her a cup of coffee, and, as we wandered toward the little snack bar in the centre of the exhibition area, she told me her story.

"I grew up in England," she began, 'in a town called Wetherby, which is just a little to the southwest of York. When I was a little girl, I convinced my father to let me get a dog. I suppose it was because the young Queen Elizabeth had Corgis that I originally became aware of the breed, but it's also true to say that I really liked the way they looked, and they were the right size to fit into the tiny little house that we had in the city. So my dad went out and got me a Corgi.

"I fell in love with him the moment I saw him, and named him 'Toto' after the dog in my favorite film *The Wizard of Oz*. I know that he didn't look at all like Toto, and he certainly wasn't a Cairn Terrier like the Toto that Judy Garland sang to in the film, but I was eight years old, and the logic circuits in my brain really weren't mature yet.

"My father didn't believe in dogs wearing collars all the time – he said that they rubbed away the fur around a dog's neck, and left an ugly, worn streak of short hair – so he went out and got a fancy leash which had a cloth loop at the end that formed part of the leash itself, and acted very much like a slip collar that I could use when walking Toto. The rest of the time, my dog wandered around the house without any collar at all.

"One afternoon, when Toto was about nine or ten months old, I returned from walking him to find that my grandmother, who lived in the Welsh city of Cardiff, was visiting. Toto got very excited at seeing someone else in the parlour, and was spinning around and barking. He was tangling the leash as I was trying to slip the loop end of it over his head, and in all the confusion he got annoyed, and bit me on my thumb. It was a good deep bite, and I let out a yelp (I remember that some of the blood got on my white blouse).

"My grandmother got up and grabbed the leash, pulling it up hard enough so that Toto's front legs were off the ground, which stopped his snapping at me. A moment later, when he had calmed down, she slipped the loop off over his head. I was sucking my thumb by then, and the bleeding had stopped. My grandmother looked at my injured finger and announced 'You will be okay.'

"She then held up my father's fancy leash at arm's length, and looked at it with disgust. 'This is not a proper leash for a Corgi. Where is the iron or the steel that will hold his temper in check? Without it he will make you bleed a lot more.'

"To say that I was confused by her comments is an understatement, so I pleaded with her to explain to me what she was talking about because the idea of my dog biting me a lot in the future certainly didn't appeal to me.

"'Don't you know what Corgis are and where they came from?' she asked. 'Well, let me tell you. It all started in Wales, in Freni-fawr in the Preseli Hills of Pembrokeshire. Two children – actually brothers – were out playing around sundown. Just as the sun was about to disappear below the horizon, they saw some sparkling lights at the edge of the woods: most likely will-o-the-wisps that tend to hover around places where the fairies gather. The boys quietly crept closer to see what was going on, and found that they had happened upon a gathering of the Tywyth Teg, which is the largest tribe of fairies in Wales. These are not the gossamer-winged nymphs that most people think of as fairies today, but small, perfectly-formed beings who look very much like people, except for the fact that their adult height is only 18 inches. They looked very striking with their pointed ears, and sharp facial features.'

"'The men were all dressed in green, with leather vests or jackets. Most carried bows and quivers of arrows, and some carried what looked like silver swords. The women were also dressed in green, and several had a red sash that went around their waist and over their shoulder. They all carried small, lethal-looking daggers that appeared to be made of some sort of black glass. All of the fairies were standing in a ring around two pallets, which were covered with white cloth. One of them began to sing, and soon all of the group were slowly dancing around the white-covered objects.'

"'The boys were confused, and one was about to stand up to get a better look when he heard a faint voice instruct 'Stay quiet. Stay still. If they see or hear you they will kill you.'

"'The boys turned to see a small individual with pointed ears who, like the others in the group they were watching, stood about a foot-and-a-half tall. He was dressed all in red, with a red hat that covered his red hair and matched his red beard. 'My name is Far Darrig, and I mean you no harm. What you are looking at is a funeral procession for two of the Tywyth Teg warriors who have fallen in battle against the Gwyllion. The Gwyllion are an ugly and evil race that lives in the hills. They are an abomination to the rest of the faerie folk, and there never will be peace between the Tywyth Teg and the Gwyllion. Those evil hags have come down from the high places and have been raiding this area. They have also been taking human babies and replacing them with changelings. They intend to rear those babies to become soldier-slaves to fight their battles against the rest of the faerie folk. There was a bloody encounter just this morning, and although the Tywyth Teg won this battle, they lost two of their heroes. So now, before the sun rises again, the rest of their group must dance away their bodies. So stay quiet and watch.'

"'The dance went on for a few minutes, and the pallets began to fade, rising silently into the air and drifitng toward a nearby oak tree. The group followed the pallets which simply disappeared into the tree, and moments later the entire band of fairies also seemed to pass into the tree, as if it were not solid, but just some kind of curtain. All that was left behind were two dogs tethered to a nearby sapling, who seemed to be wearing saddles and bridles. One of the boys asked Far Darrig 'Why have they left their dogs behind?'

"'The red man answered 'Those are not dogs as you know them, but the war steeds of the fairies who died here. They are trained warriors in their own right. When they are excited, it is their job to bite anything that is in front of them. But they are more than warriors: they are great helpers for the faerie folk. The Tywyth Teg are not farmers, so when they need milk and meat for their great feasts, they come to the world of humans to steal a cow or two. This is where these dogs truly show their talent. The faerie rider only needs to point in the direction that he wants a cow to run, and then point at which cow he has chosen. His war dog runs directly toward the cow, and snaps at her feet to get her to move. The cow may kick but, because the dog is so short, the hoof will safely pass over his head. By cleverly nipping at one side of the animal or the other, this dog can drive a cow to any place that his owner desires.'

"'The boys looked at each other in wonder. Then the older one of the two said, 'My brother and I often have to drive some of the cows which our family owns from one field to another, and sometimes even down to the town when we are taking them to market. It is hard work because if there are more than two cows, one or another is apt to wander off in the wrong direction, and we are always chasing them and bringing them back to where we want them to go. Sometimes they kick us when they get angry, and it really hurts. If we had such talented dogs to help us drive our cattle, it would be a great blessing to us.'

"'The red man looked at the two children, and stroked his red beard for a moment. Then, finally, he spoke, 'Well, the funeral party won't be back for at least an hour, and you could take those two dogs with you. But you must understand that they won't go willingly. They are independent. They are fighters. Still, there is a way to control them. You must hang around their necks something which is made of iron or steel, metals which are poison to the faerie folk, which is why all of the Tywyth Teg weapons are made of silver, flint, or glass. The iron or steel will keep the faerie spells from reaching these dogs, and this will help to keep them from biting you. The metal will also cause those dogs to listen to you and obey when you tell them what to do. But, most importantly, having something made of iron or steel will keep the curse of the Cu Sith from ever falling upon you.'

"'What is the curse of the Cu Sith?' one of the boys asked.

"'Far Darrig answered, 'It is the final and most frightening weapon of these warrior animals. When their blood is hot and they begin to bark, they become very dangerous. And if they should ever bark three times, so quickly together that a man cannot hear a space between the barks, then whatever the dog is looking at will suffer grievous harm. Only iron or steel worn around their necks (so that the metal is near to their mouths) can prevent this.'

"'The boys nodded in understanding, then searched themselves to find some iron or steel. Ultimately, they decided to use their belts, each of which had a large, iron buckle. They could slip the belt through the buckle so that it formed a sort of collar at one end (where the iron could be close to the animal's neck), and the free end could act like a leash. They went to where the dogs were standing, causing the animals to look uncomfortable and snarl, but the moment that the belts were around their necks, and the iron was close to their skin, they calmed down.

"'If these dogs can drive our cattle the way that they did for the faerie warriors who were stealing cows, they will be of great help in our life,' one of the boys said. He then turned to the red man and asked, 'But when we are asked what these animals are, what shall we say?'

"'Well,' replied the red man 'You can just call them Corgis, since cor is the old name for the little people and gi is the faerie name for dog. Just remember to bind their spirits by keeping some iron or steel around their necks, and they will serve you well, and will even come to love you. But leave them without that special metal nearby and they will return to being uncontrollable and dangerous war beasts.'

"'So,' said my grandmother, 'it is your own fault that you were bitten. Corgis must have iron or steel around their necks in order to be safe from faerie spells, which may turn them against the humans who are near them.'"

Rosalind laughed and added, "Because I love them, and think that they are so handsome, I would much rather wrap my dogs' necks in collars studded with silver or gold, but if iron or steel keeps the nasty spells of the faerie folk under control, then I am willing to make sure that that is what they wear. I will say that ever since that day when my grandmother told me this story my dogs' collars have always had at least an iron or steel buckle. It is also true that I have never been bitten by a Corgi who was wearing such a collar. I don't know if that proves anything, but why take chances when dealing with special animals whose ancestors may have belonged to magical beings?"

Laelaps and Zeus

One of the greatest reservoirs of folklore and mythology has to be the stories of the Greek gods, whose home was supposedly on Mount Olympus. There are many variations of these tales, and while some are well known, others are not often told anymore.

One of the stories that has always fascinated me has to do with Zeus, the King of the Gods, and his relationship to a dog. This was a magical dog, and one who captured the affection of Zeus in a way that few things did. According to the epic mythology of the Greeks, this dog probably had more owners and masters than any dog in all of mythology, and according to the legend, he is still around today — and you can see him if you know where to look. This dog was born to the noble task of protecting a child, and he eventually became a pawn in a complex web of infidelity, deception, and revenge.

If we flash back to the beginning we find the original gods, Uranus or 'Father Sky,' and his wife, the first mother, Gaia or 'Mother Earth.' From their coupling, Gaia gave birth to the many gods, titans, and giants of mythology.

Uranus was not much of a father, since he considered all of his offspring as potential threats to his throne. Because of his paranoia, most of his children were exiled or imprisoned in the deepest places in the earth. Given the way they were treated, it's not surprising that, in those hidden places, the sons and daughters of Uranus began to plot against their father. The youngest son of Gaia and Uranus was the wily and ambitious Cronus, who would ultimately be the one to exact revenge on Uranus. With no remorse whatsoever, Cronus castrated his father, and took his place as ruler of the gods. What essence of Uranus remained was scattered across the sky that he had created.

Once he had assumed the throne, Cronus took his sister, Rhea, to be his wife, and sired several children with her. However, Cronus was not destined to have a peaceful reign. He learned that Uranus and Gaia had prophesied that once Uranus was gone, his replacement was destined to be overthrown by his own child, in much the way that Cronus had destroyed his father. Cronus was as clever as he was brutal, and, based upon the experience of Uranus, he recognised that exiling his own children, even into the most remote places in the bowels of the earth, would not protect him. He therefore decided to imprison his children within his own body, and so it was that Cronus began devouring his own children, who already included the familiar gods Hera, Hades, and Poseidon, and also Hestia (goddess of the household), and Demeter (goddess of the harvest).

Rhea was horrified at the fate of her children. Worse, was that, at the time Cronus was committing these atrocities, she was pregnant with Zeus. Since her baby's moment of birth was nearing, Rhea sought out her mother, Gaia, to help her devise a plan to save her child. Gaia agreed to help, in part because she remembered her own pain when her husband had taken her children from her.

Following Gaia's advice, Rhea fled to Crete to give birth to Zeus. Not surprisingly, Cronus soon discovered he had fathered another son, and, with an angry roar, appeared in front of his wife, demanding the child. Instead of giving him the baby, Rhea initiated the plan that Gaia had devised, handing Cronus a rock wrapped in swaddling clothes. As Gaia had predicted, Cronus was so angry at what he viewed as his wife's attempt to hide the child from him that he did not even check that she had given him an infant. Cronus made Rhea watch as he swallowed the bundle in front of her in an attempt to prove that he was still King of the Gods, and would always be her master. Cronus then returned to his abode in the sky.

Rhea hid Zeus in a cave on Mount Ida in Crete. Gaia feared that hiding Zeus would not be enough to keep this grandchild of hers alive, so she spent much time and effort trying to decide what kind of guardian should protect the child, Zeus. This guardian had to be loyal and brave, but not so large and spectacular as to draw the attention of Cronus. Finally, she decided that the most obvious, and least attention-grabbing, protector would be a dog, and she set about fashioning one as part of her plan.

Once the dog had been created, Rhea introduced him to her child, assigning the dog the task of guarding young Zeus. The infant god reached out to touch the dog, and smiled. The goddesses named this dog simply 'Golden Hound,' because his fur was the colour of burnished gold.

Golden Hound was a truly special dog, not because of his colour, but because of his abilities. The Golden Hound was capable of pursuing his quarry through any place in this world and all of the planes of existence, and catch any that he chased. Golden Hound also had infinite strength, and with that came the ability to kill and tear apart anything that he caught, regardless of his target's strength, or the thickness of his hide or armour.

Golden Hound was settled at the door of the cave that housed the child, and instructed to obey only Zeus or those who the god might instruct him to obey. With his strength and magical ability, this dog could deter even Cronus, and Gaia reasoned that, should another god or any other being dare to threaten baby Zeus, Golden Hound had the power to pursue and catch him, even if he fled to Mount Olympus, or tried to escape to the heavens.

As young Zeus began to grow, he became more and more fond of his guardian dog. One thing that bothered the young god was the fact that the dog's name was not a name at all, but a description. This dog was his friend and protector, and needed a proper name, so Zeus decided to give his well-liked companion the name Laelaps, which means 'the storm wind,' as a token of both his dog's strength and swiftness.

In time, Zeus grew strong enough to confront Cronus, and, after a long conflict, defeated him. In the end, Cronus was forced to drink an elixir which caused him to spew up his children, who, because they were gods, had survived all this time in the belly of their father. Cronus was then thrown into the pit at Tartarus, where he was fated to remain imprisoned for eternity with the other titans and giants. With Cronus out of the way, Zeus took over the position of King of the Gods.

Zeus was a god who had a great deal of passion — well, let's be honest about this: it was not so much passion as lust. He had had many affairs with goddesses, and other supernatural beings such as nymphs, and these had resulted in many children who became gods, or beings with great magical powers

Gods, ghosts, and black dogs

or strength. After six protracted affairs resulting in numerous offspring, Zeus turned his attention to his beautiful sister, Hera. He was attracted to both her beauty and her power, so began courting her (in secret, since his mother, Rhea, was already showing she was unhappy about his promiscuity). Hera, who no doubt knew that Zeus had already had many other lovers, spurned his romantic overtures.

Faced with Hera's rejection, Zeus decided that he needed another approach; one which he would come to use in many of his future sexual encounters. His new tactic involved guise and disguise. One day, Zeus appeared in front of Hera in the guise of a bedraggled, rain-soaked cuckoo. Hera saw the poor bird and felt pity for it. As a gesture of kindness, she took the bird into the shelter of her bosom to warm and dry him. Once nestled so intimately there, Zeus' passion could not be restrained, and he immediately returned to his true form. As he had done to many females before, he ravished Hera, and it is said that, by so doing, Zeus shamed Hera into marrying him, which she never forgave him for, although they ultimately had four children together: Ares (the god of war), Hebe (the goddess of youth), Eileithyia (the goddess of childbirth), and Hephaestus (the god of fire, craftsmen, and metallurgy).

Zeus was not a faithful husband, and had many more adulterous affairs, not just with goddesses, but also with mortals. He'd developed a fondness for human beings, and not only felt protectively toward them, but was often captivated and aroused by the beauty of mortal females. This led to many sexual entanglements with human women, resulting in many children – some of which became great heroes and demigods.

One of Zeus' liaisons was with a particularly beautiful and intelligent Phoenician woman named Europa. Zeus became enamored of Europa, and although it was often his habit to simply ravish women who aroused his lust, this one appeared to be special, as Zeus wanted more from Europa than he would get from a single forced mating. The god devised a plan which involved seducing her (here comes another case of guise and disguise), with the idea of getting her to voluntarily lay with him.

The plan began with Zeus transforming himself into a tame white bull, and acting as if he were just another animal in her father's herd. On this paticular day, Europa and her female attendants were gathering flowers, when she saw what appeared to be a particularly beautiful bull. She approached the animal, and caressed his flanks, talking gently all the while. In a humble and inviting way, the bull lay down, and Europa eventually climbed onto his back. Zeus seized the opportunity and quickly dashed to the sea, swimming with the young maiden clinging to his back with her arms around his neck. Zeus swam all the way to his own birthplace, the island of Crete, where he revealed his true identity once they were on shore.

In order to win Europa's favour the god ordained her as the first Queen of Crete, and showered her with many gifts, among which was a necklace made by the god Hephaestus, and a brass man named Talus also fashioned by that god. Talus was a robot soldier who would serve as a protector of the queen's realm.

It is now that we begin to see the way in which Zeus' dog, Laelaps, would be passed around – always as a token of love or esteem – but nonetheless viewed as a symbol or special piece of property. As events unfolded, it ultimately became clear that Zeus was the only one who truly loved the dog as a companion, though, nonetheless, it is here that Laelaps begins his journey through many households, going from the hands of one owner to another. You see, Europa was still not fully convinced of Zeus' affection for her, so the great god raised the ante. Because Europa loved to hunt, Zeus gave her a javelin that never missed, and, to demonstrate how fond he was of her, he also gave Europa his most beloved dog, Laelaps.

The seduction of Europa worked, and she ultimately fell in love with Zeus. He came to her many times, and she eventually gave birth to three of his children, one of whom was Minos, who succeeded his mother to become King of Crete. As a gesture of her love for her son, Minos (the first of her children to be fathered by the god), Europa gifted him both the magical dog, Laelaps, and the magical javelin.

When Zeus' wife, Hera, learned of his affair with Europa, she became angry and vindictive. Hera spent a lot of her time seeking vengeance on Zeus' lovers and his illegitimate offspring, and in this case she decided that, as retribution, she would end the royal line that began with Europa. Thus, she cursed Minos so that his sperm turned to spiders and he could not procreate, causing great horror and distress in the royal household.

King Minos had a general named Cephalus, whose wife, Procris, was a favourite of the hunter goddess, Artemis, with whom Procris would sometimes hunt. Artemis liked Procris a great deal, since she was an exceptional archer, and a pleasant companion. As a gesture of friendship, Artemis taught Procris the art of healing, and, thus, it came to be that, when Cephalus told his wife about the King's strange affliction, Procris offered to try and heal him. She created a series of elixirs which eventually purged Minos of all of the spiders within his body, restoring him to fertility and potency.

As you might expect, King Minos was extremely grateful for Procris' help, and wanted to bestow upon her some kind of gift which was truly special. The truth of the matter was that Minos had no real love for Laelaps, and had never once expressed any affection for the dog, regarding Laelaps as just a token, symbolizing that Minos' lineage traced back to the god Zeus through his mother. So Minos felt little pain in passing Laelaps on to Procris. Minos knew that Procris loved to hunt, and was a favourite of the goddess Artemis, so the gifts that he had received from his mother (the javelin that would not miss, and the dog, Laelaps, who had the power to catch anything that he pursued) would be appropriate and welcome rewards for the woman who had healed him. When Zeus learned that his dog was once again being handed on to someone else, he was not pleased, but Minos was his son, and he chose not to interfere.

For Laelaps, this period in his life was good, as Procris would frequently go out hunting, which gave him the chance to exercise, and also demonstrate his magical abilities. Procris loved hunting even more now that she had Laelaps, but her sporting activities did cause some problems. Many of her hunting expeditions with Artemis took Procris away from the royal palace; often for periods of several days. Procris' husband, Cephalus, was a good-looking man, and many women in the royal compound wanted to have a relationship with the handsome general. They were jealous of Procris, and so started rumours that she had been unfaithful to Cephalus, and was using these hunting trips to disguise the fact that she was really visiting her lover. Unfortunately, Cephalus came to believe these lies which claimed that his wife was an adulteress, and he angrily confronted her with charges of infidelity. Without knowing who her accusers were, there was little that Procris could do to defend herself, and she was hurt and ashamed by her husband's accusations. A proud woman who would not stand quietly and take the blame for sins that she had not committed, Procris gathered her magical weapon and her dog, Laelaps, and fled to the forest to be with her goddess, Artemis.

After a while, Cephalus began to pine for Procris, and soon began to doubt the stories of her infidelity. When word eventually reached Procris that her husband wanted her back, she took leave of the goddess and returned to the general. Cephalus no longer fully believed that his wife had been unfaithful, but there had been so much talk, and he still worried about the strength of her commitment to him, especially since Procris was so willing to leave him to go hunting. In order show how much she cared for him, Procris gave Cephalus her two most valued possessions: the magical javelin and the dog, Laelaps.

Meanwhile, Zeus' wife, Hera, was still raging around Olympus, angry about her husband's past and continuing unfaithfulness. She felt she would not be happy until she could find some way to publicly shame Zeus. She knew that the King of the Gods had a particular fondness for the dog, Laelaps, who had been his guardian as a child, and, even though the dog was now in the care of someone else, Zeus would sometimes come down to earth just to visit Laelaps, and watch the elegance with which he pursued and captured game. It was obvious that Zeus took great pride in the fact that nothing could escape his dog once the chase had begun. At banquets and parties

Gods, ghosts, and black dogs

that the gods held on Mount Olympus, Zeus would regale the other gods, telling them how proud he was of his magical dog, and the fact that there was no other animal like him, and no animal better than Laelaps when it came to the hunt. This clearly made the dog yet another target for Hera's rage.

Hera eventually hatched a plan to spite Zeus, and to shame him., and part of the plan involved demonstrating that his beloved dog was not so perfect. Hera went to her grandmother, Gaia, to enlist her aid. She knew that Gaia was not happy with her grandson, and that his numerous adulterous affairs bothered her. Furthermore, Hera was able to convince Gaia that Zeus was turning away from his relationships with the other gods and demigods, in favour of trying to improve the welfare of human beings, and that this was an inappropriate way for the King of the Gods to act.

"Grandmother," she said, "the only way that Zeus can be punished for his indiscretions is for him to be publicly humiliated. He cares more for the humans than for his own kind. They love him because they view him as a great protector. The only thing that he cares for more than the mortals is his dog, Laelaps. He has great pride in the skill of that dog – the dog you created for him. Although he has allowed the dog to live among the mortals, Zeus watches over him carefully. Did you know that when a man named Pandareus stole Laelaps with the idea of using the dog as a bribe to gain a position of power, Zeus turned him to stone, and then personally returned the dog to his human lover, Europa? Such a drastic action for a dog? For a human?

"Grandmother, I have a plan, but only you can help me. It is a plan which will let us chastise and punish my husband for his insults to all of us, and especially to me. Imagine an animal that only wants to hurt human beings, whose appetite can only be sated by eating the flesh of mortals. If such an animal were released on the earth, Zeus would be bound by his promises to humankind to protect it; compelled to bring the beast under control. If it is an agile animal, too quick to be taken down by an arrow, or even a thunderbolt, then what would Zeus do? Obviously, he would call for the assistance of his dog, Laelaps,

since you have given that dog a magical ability so that anything he pursues cannot escape him. But what if this new beast that you might create cannot be caught? Imagine the frustration that Zeus would feel: his pride would be hurt because he no longer owned the most perfect hunter in the world. Because of this he would doubtless feel shame, remembering that he had promised the humans he would protect them, and now clearly cannot. Perhaps if Zeus knows that his power is limited, if he learns that we will no longer tolerate his immoral and disrespectful behaviour, he might come to his senses ..."

Hera's words were convincing, and Gaia did not think through all of the ramifications of having an animal which would be so dangerous to all of humankind, and which could not be controlled or captured. In the end, Gaia was merely a grandmother who felt that her grandson had risen to such a position of power among the gods that he had become too proud. She felt that Zeus had become arrogant, and believed that he was entitled to behave in any way he chose, regardless of its morality. She felt that this grandchild of hers needed to be taught a lesson in humility, and perhaps the plan that Hera suggested could accomplish this. So Gaia created the Teumessian Fox, a giant, ravenous animal which Mother Earth endowed with the ability to avoid ever being captured or caught. In Hera's mind, such an animal would diminish the value of her husband's magic dog, and she hoped to use it to also diminish the respect that humans had for the King of the Gods.

Hera had not been completely honest and forthcoming with the old god, Gaia, however, and had intentions to not only shame Zeus, but also continue her vendetta against his various illegitimate offspring. Once she had control of the Teumessian Fox she launched her plan of attack, intending to use the beast as a pawn in a situation involving another one of the sons that Zeus had sired with a human woman, and the one that she singled out was Dionysus.

Dionysus was god of the grape harvest, winemaking and wine. He was also god of ritual madness and ecstasy; capable of great joy and abandon, but also easily stirred to anger and harsh retribution when he felt he had been slighted. At this time Dionysus was very angry with the city state of Thebes, which was ruled by Dionysus' cousin, Pentheus. Dionysus wanted to exact revenge on Pentheus, and all of the women of Thebes, particularly his aunts Agave, Ino, and Autonoe, because the people did not believe the claims of his mother, Semele, that she had been impregnated by Zeus. The people of Thebes mocked Semele for what they considered to be her false assertion of having lain with a god. Furthermore, their rejection of Semele's claim that she had given birth to Zeus' child served as justification for denying Dionysus' divinity, and their refusal to worship him as the god of wine.

Hera considered this situation to be an excellent opportunity to annoy her husband, so gave Dionysus the Teumessian Fox, telling him to let it loose upon the people of Thebes. Her reasoning was that, even if Dionysus succeeded in having his claim to divinity upheld, all of the people would eventually learn that the damage done by the fox had been initiated by a child of Zeus, so would tarnish Zeus' reputation, and greatly diminish the affection in which he was held. As a result, this would make her spouse less desirable as an object of worship. Since, ultimately, the power of any god depends upon the number of worshippers he has, this would eventually weaken Zeus, providing Hera with some sense of retribution.

Once Hera gave him the beast, Dionysus released the magical fox in the heart of Thebes, and the creature began to prowl the city at dawn and dusk, killing and eating young men and women in the street. This slaughter went on for many months, with young victims being lost almost every day. Pentheus called upon his General, Amphitryon, to rid the city of the fox. Amphitryon organized several great hunts, involving over a hundred dogs accompanied by hunters with bows and spears. However, the ability of the Teumessian Fox was such that none of the dogs even came close to capturing him. Despite their best efforts, the hunters never drew close enough to use their weapons on the beast, and the daily round of murders by Hera's fox continued.

Amphitryon had heard about Cephalus and his magical dog, Laelaps. Surely, this golden hound

was the answer to Thebes' problem? Amphitryon called upon Cephalus, and proposed what seemed like a brilliant plan. Laelaps, the dog who was destined to always catch his prey, would be set loose in the city, and, with his abilities, would certainly be capable of hunting down and tearing apart the great fox that was causing so much devastation.

It was thus that the remaining players fell into Hera's trap, and the stage was set for a dilemma of epic proportions, with an uncatchable fox being chased by an inescapable dog. Once the chase was on, the two animals tore through the city streets, leaping walls and toppling over anyone or anything in their path. They ran around the outskirts of the city at such speed that they tore up the ground, and left trenches in their wake.

Zeus had heard the people of Thebes' cries about the savagery of the fox, and had thought about the possibility of using Laelaps to hunt this giant beast. Now, he looked down and saw this amazing chase, amazed that anything was able to elude his dog, Laelaps. He called upon his grandmother, Gaia, to ask how anything could escape once Laelaps pursued it? It was then that the great goddess told him of Hera's visit, and the animal she had created for her. Zeus asked his grandmother to unmake the Teumessian Fox. Although saddened at the chaos she had unleashed, she had to refuse Zeus' request, however, reminding him of the role she had played in the war between the titans, cyclops, giants, and gods that had followed Zeus' ascension to the throne. To protect the gods, Gaia's powers had be called upon, and many supernatural beings, including some that she herself had given birth to, were unmade and dispersed into nothingness. This hurt Gaia's moral sense, and she had taken a vow to only create, and never to uncreate.

Now aware of the abilities that Hera's fox possessed, Zeus fully recognized the nature of the problem: the ultimate paradox. Once Laelaps had been set to the hunt, he was destined to pursue until he caught his prey, but this time he was hunting an animal which was preordained never to be caught. Zeus did not have the power to undo the magic that Gaia had put into these two creatures, and the only

Gods, ghosts, and black dogs

possibility that remained involved removing both animals from the face of the earth where they were presently doing such damage. Although he did not care about the fate of the fox, the idea of losing or harming Laelaps caused Zeus much sadness, but, with much regret, Zeus did the only thing he could to keep the countryside from being destroyed by this great chase between two magical beasts.

Reaching upward, he grabbed part of the essence of the sky, which was really part of what remained of his father, Uranus. He then shaped that essence into a ramp, and placed it right in the path of the fox. The two animals streaked up the ramp and a moment later found themselves in the sky, whereupon Zeus knocked away the ramp, so that neither animal could return to the earth. Finally, he turned the Teumessian Fox, and his own golden hound, Laelaps, into stars.

Gaia watched what Zeus did, and, looking at her grandson, was surprised to see him wiping a tear from his eye. In all of her memory Gaia could not ever recall Zeus crying. Zeus turned to his grandmother, and softly said, "I loved that dog. He was the only thing that gave me love and made me feel secure as I was growing up in that cave in Crete. I loved to watch him run. When I saw him running, or chasing something, I felt as if I was looking at a true expression of the harmony of the universe. He was beautiful; he made me believe that things could be perfect in this world. But now I know I will never see him run again, and it makes me feel hollow and empty."

Gaia walked over to Zeus and put her arms around him. "I will not allow such sorrow and darkness to enter your soul. Removing these animals that I have created from the world is almost like unmaking them, which is something that I have sworn not to do. So let me help you. Let me make it so that you can still see your dog, Laelaps, in full pursuit and still feel some love in your heart." With that, Gaia walked to what remained of the ramp Zeus had formed from the material he had torn from the sky. Gaia knew that these fragments of the heavenly firmament still contained the essence of Uranus and

his sky magic. She took all of the pieces of heavenly material and wove them into a net, which she cast net into the sky to capture the stars that Laelaps and the Teumessian Fox had been turned into. She then carefully returned each star to the heavens, but this time shaped the constellations and placed them in the sky according to a careful design. Once she finished it became clear what she had done. Now, each night, as the stars became visible and moved across the sky, Gaia's new constellations would become visible. First, would be the fox, soon after followed by the great hound, Laelaps. Thus, the pair would race across the firmament of the sky in an endless and eternal chase. Gaia turned to her grandson, and said, "You can watch your dog in his elegant chase forever, and perhaps the sight of him will bring you comfort."

Like Zeus, we can still see this endless chase, as the uncatchable fox and the inescapable dog run across the sky, and this is the way to find them. When the winter sky is clear, look until you see the three stars that comprise the belt of the constellation Orion. Follow the angle of Orion's belt downward (opposite to the side that holds his shield), and the next, very bright, star that you will come to is Sirius. Not only is Sirius the brightest star in the visible sky, it is also the primary star of the constellation Canis Major (the Big Dog), and serves as the nose of the dog, Laelaps.

Up and to the left of Sirius is Procyon, the primary star of the constellation Canis Minor (the Little Dog) which, in ancient times, was known as the fox, because it really is the Teumessian Fox. Procyon is the seventh brightest star in the sky, and forms a triangle of stars with Sirius in Canis Major and Betelgeuse in Orion, which is the eighth brightest star in the sky (and is easily recognized because of its distinctly reddish tint). Procyon, which marks the location of the fox, literally means 'before the dog,' since this star rises just before Sirius which marks the location of Laelaps, Zeus' magic dog. Thus, the King of Gods can draw comfort from seeing his beloved dog running in never-ending pursuit of Hera's magic fox, and we, too, can also see them in their endless pursuit.

Dogs and the Angel of Death

When my children were young I would sometimes spin a tall tale for them, only to be met at the end of it by my daughter, Rebecca's incredulous, "Daddy, you really don't think that that is true, do you?" My usual reply to her would be, "Remember that telling a thing isn't the same as believing a thing."

The fact that people tell folktales or recount myths to one another doesn't generally mean that anyone supposes that the story being told has any basis in truth. Although many of the stories involve elements of ancient religious beliefs, I doubt that any modern teller of tales actually accepts the existence of the gods Zeus or Odin, even though a story that they are retelling might concern the exploits and activities of those mythological beings.

When a religion dies, the stories which made up its bible or gospels can survive if they do a good job of illustrating a moral principle, or are simply interesting. Oral histories and cultural traditions, pictures carved into stone tablets or on the walls of tombs, fading ink marks on mouldering pages made of papyrus or parchment, which may have had sacred and holy significance in the past, are often preserved by becoming folktales, fairytales, and myths passed down the ages.

A lot of the stories and folklore about dogs started out as part of the fabric of various religions, and, certainly, nobody today believes that just because a folktale has it that our pet dogs have a connection to gods or ghosts or demons or saints, that we should accept this as the truth. At least, nobody believes this until the moment that our normally quiet and mannerly dog sits on our doorstep one night and produces a long and mournful howl. As we listen to that haunting sound, we might feel a momentary twinge of anxiety, and our minds may involuntarily bring up the thought of a loved one who is ill, or a family member who is late returning home, and has not called to explain the delay. In such circumstances we could well experience a chill of trepidation: a shiver running down our spine because *now* we remember the folktale which claimed that a dog's howl may predict that someone nearby is about to die.

Maybe you once heard tell of the Egyptian god, Anubis, who guided souls through the

85

Gods, ghosts, and black dogs

underworld with the aid of a legion of dogs, who howled as the soul broke free from the body of a dying person? Perhaps it was a less formal piece of mythology: maybe a favourite family anecdote about the death of your grandfather, which included the story of how his faithful companion dog suddenly began howling just half-an-hour before the old man died? And *then* you remember your mother observing that she was surprised by the dog's behaviour, since, "That dog never howled before. Could it be that he knew that the old man he loved was about to die?"

Perchance it is not the sound of a dog howling, but one barking in the dead of the night that elicits a twinge of fear in you. Not the frantic, excited barking that suggests something unusual is happening, or that someone has approached the house, but rather a more measured barking – slow and steady with pauses between each bark – which makes the hair on the back of your neck stand up ... Why is that?

Perhaps you vaguely remember once being told that Hecate, goddess of the dark, who brings death to those who have lived less than pure lives, is always accompanied by dogs. She sends those animals out into the world, and, when a dog finds an appropriate target, he stays close by to that person, marking his location with a series of widely spaced barks, to serve as a beacon to guide the goddess to her next victim. Perhaps hearing barking like this causes you to ponder on just how righteous your own life has been, thus far. Then again, you might remember an Irish friend telling you that dogs howl because they hear the noise of the hounds who lead the riders of the wild hunt as they race through the sky to collect the souls of the dying, or that those ancient mythical heroes, Achilles and Hector, who each in their own time knew that the fight they were about to begin would be their last because they heard a dog barking in that special way during the night.

When I hear a dog howl in the night I sometimes remember the ancient Norse legend, that explains the link between howling dogs and death. It speaks of the goddess Freya, the bearer of love, fertility and magic, but also the goddess of death, who rode the crest of storms on her chariot pulled by giant cats. Because cats are the natural enemies of dogs, it is said that dogs would begin to howl when they sensed the approach of Freya and her mystical felines, who may well be coming to claim the soul of someone nearby ...

In many religions dogs are considered to be psychopomps: a spirit or being that comes to you when you die and has the job of escorting you – or your soul, at least – to the next world. He is a guide and a protector who will show you the way, and guide you on your last journey, but, in order to serve as your guide, this canine psychopomp must be present when your soul leaves your body, so must arrive sometime before the time of actual death. Taking this requirement to the next logical step means that the psychopomp's presence is a sure sign that you are about to pass from this world.

Since dogs may be spirit guides for the dead, depending upon which religion or culture is involved, the appearance of a completely black dog, or a black dog with light spots over his eyes, or a red dog, or a spotted dog, or a totally white dog, or perhaps a dog with no tail, is to be feared, for, when such a dog appears at the door or near the home of a person who is lying ill inside, this could be a sign of the individual's impending death. You might remember your Aunt Sylvia or your Uncle Alex telling you that such a dog at such a time and place is 'bad luck,' and the half-remembered fragments of memories and folk stories such as these may account for why you might be feeling a little nervous right now, with a sick child in the house, and a large black dog standing under the street lamp in front of your home ...

You might not actually properly remember, or be able to recount such a story that links dogs to death and dying, but many do exist, and are practically unavoidable in the average lifetime. The snippets and fragments of this lore, this mythology, these emotional and spiritually-bound legends and parables have certainly reached your ears at some time in your life, possibly resulting in the association that dogs and death have more in common than simply starting with the same letter. Stories that we hear when we are young, or when we are relaxed and listening simply for the sake of doing so, often sneak past the logic filters in our brain and hide in the emotional centres of our mind, and is why, at night, when a dog barks or howls, we might feel a momentary foreboding or frisson of fear.

When I was training with the US. army at Fort Knox in Kentucky, I would take whatever free weekend time I had to wander through the countryside, and talk to people about their dogs, some of the motivation for which was that I was missing my own dog, but also that it was good to be away from the formality of life on an army base. Fortunately, rural Kentucky is filled with lots of people who like and own dogs, and who are willing to just sit and talk about them to pass the time.

One Saturday afternoon I found myself in the southeast corner of the state, talking to an old woman whom I knew only as Aunt Lila. Her son bred hounds — beautiful Redbone hounds, and we were sipping some lemonade that she had made while waiting for her son to return from the field with several of his dogs. The minister from the Methodist church that Aunt Lila belonged to came up the steps of her porch, and sat down with us, accepting a glass of lemonade. He had dropped by to check up on Aunt Lila, whose age had made her frail, and because of a few specific health problems, which gave the people she knew some concerns. Since her son spent part of each week trucking produce to the city, the minister decided to pay a visit, just to make sure that his parishioner was well, and to reassure himself she was being cared for.

"Now, don't you worry about me dying," Lila told the reverend when he asked about her health. "You and me will know when the time is coming because the dogs will tell you."

"Just how will the dogs tell you?" I asked.

"It ain't complicated," she replied, "If a dog gives two howls close together it means that Mr Death is coming for a man; three howls means a woman is about to die. You know which man or woman is about to pass away because dogs look in their direction. My daddy said it was good luck to have a dog howl with his back to you. So far, I can tell you, there ain't no dog that looked me in the face and howled."

I looked from the old woman, whose education had ended just short of finishing grade school, to her pastor, with his university training, and asked "Do you believe that?"

The minister smiled and said, "The bible certainly doesn't say yes or no about that. But I feel comfortable with it. Don't you get chills when you hear a dog howl? It may well be the fact that God has chosen the voice of the dog to send a message that something bad is about to happen, such as a person dying."

The idea that dogs can predict death was not new to me, and I believe I can still remember the first time I heard a snatch of lore connecting dogs to death. It was early one evening when I was about six or seven years of age. My dog, Skippy, a pleasant, playful, and generally unflappable Beagle, suddenly began to whimper, and make low, fearful, growling noises, looking with great apprehension at one end of the room where nothing seemed out of place.

I was at home with only my maternal grandparents, and my grandmother, Lena, looked up from her knitting and watched Skippy for a few moments. She had been born in Lithuania, and grew up in a time and culture when there seemed to be a story, or a myth, to explain virtually every event that occurred in the natural world. Although she was religious, I would not consider her superstitious, yet a lot of stories about supernatural and magical beings and events were tucked away in the hidden folds of her aged brain. One of them must have surfaced at that moment, because she turned to me and said, "He sees the Angel of Death. The angel's name is Azrael. When Azrael comes or goes, dogs can see him. They say that dogs have spirit sight, and can see devils and angels and ghosts. You can see them, too, at least sometimes, if you look at the exact place where the dog is looking. In order to see clearly, you have to look right over the top of the dog's head, and through the space between his ears."

My grandfather, Jacob, who had been listening, lit one of the cigars that were his passion in life, and took up the story from there. I never knew if my grandfather had the slightest belief in any of the stories that he told, or whether he just delighted in telling them. He loved telling stories

Gods, ghosts, and black dogs

to his grandchildren, if they would sit and listen to them. Mostly they were fables designed to explain the inexplicable, or perhaps provide comfort when things were going badly, or give the illusion that one could predict the unpredictable.

Taking a large puff on his cigar and exhaling it, as the blue/white smoke curled around his head, Jacob began to flesh out the story that my grandmother had hinted at.

"Yes, dogs can see the Angel of Death, the moment he comes close. If he is a brave dog — and if he really loves a person — he will give a special, growly bark, or make a whining sound, and look in the direction where Azrael is standing. If the dog is not in the same room, or is too far away from the person he loves, he will give a warning howl. It is a particular howl which starts with his head low, and rises louder and louder as the dog raises his head to point to the sky. When a dog barks that bark, or howls that howl, it calls the prophet Elijah, who will sometimes step in to save a good person from the Angel of Death. Sometimes, the barking or the howling wakes the ghosts of family members who have died, and they come to fight Azrael, to try and protect their loved ones. Other times, the noise convinces the Dark Angel that he'll have a strong fight on his hands, and he simply goes away. He is not gone forever, since when the dog is not around he may try to sneak back, so that he can get the job done without any trouble.

"No matter what, though, you should never stop a dog from barking or howling, since he may be trying to save the life of someone in the family; maybe even yours. When you hear your dog make those sounds, check that a door or a window is open a crack so that the prophet Elijah and the good ghosts can get in, and so that if Azreal wants to make a quick run out of the house, he can do so."

My grandfather took another long puff of his cigar, and studied the glowing ember at the end as if there were writing in it. Then, adjusting himself a little, he went on.

"They say that the reason dogs have such a short life is that sometimes Azreal won't give up, and decides to take the soul anyway. When that happens, good and brave dogs will try to stop the Angel of

Death from touching someone they love: appearing to be growling and snarling and barking at nothing, when what they are really doing is putting themselves between their loved one and the angel. If Azreal keeps coming, some dogs will actually try to jump up and bite him, while others will just block the way. Unfortunately, one touch from Azreal kills them, either fast or slow.

"You know, it's really a very heroic thing that dogs do for the people they love, and, what's more, it usually works. You see, the Angel of Death can only carry one life with him at a time. So when his hands are filled with the dog's soul, he has to run back and drop it off. Of course, this means that he is going home without his real victim. Anyway — and here is the good part — because old Azreal has taken a life (remember that's his real job in the first place), he gets to cross a name off his list. I don't know whether that angel likes dogs to begin with, or maybe just appreciates how courageous they are, but it seems that he often just crosses off the name of the person that the dog loved, and, at least for the time being, Azreal acts as though that name wasn't there in the first place. This means that unless God draws up a new list soon, Azreal won't be coming back for that person for quite a while, so even though it sometimes goes bad for the dog, it means that the person who the dog loved and tried to protect is usually saved."

I remember a great surge of panic as I dived across the room to grab my dog, shouting in my tiny voice, "No! Skippy, don't touch him! It's okay — we'll just run away!" while my grandparents looked on with somewhat bemused expressions.

I don't know if I can admit to believing in an Angel of Death named Azreal: a sinister, supernatural being that can be seen by dogs, but goes unnoticed by humans until he has claimed a life. My scientific education makes that sort of belief difficult. But I still experience a emotional response when I hear a slow, deliberate series of barks, or a dog howling in the night, to which logic is never an antidote. However, although I am somewhat ashamed to admit it, when I see my dog turn to look at an empty part of the room, and he gives a growl bark or a fearful whimper, I do get up to make sure that a window is cracked open. I don't know if I do that to make sure that the prophet Elijah and the good ghosts can get in, or so that a menacing angel named Azreal can leave the house.

Maybe it's just that it makes me feel a little more comfortable to do so ...

Visit Hubble and Hattie on the web: www.hubbleandhattie.com
www.hubbleandhattie.blogspot.co.uk
• Details of all books • Special offers • Newsletter • New book news

The Dog Father

I was attending a reception at the Museum of Anthropology at the University of British Columbia, which had recently undergone extensive renovation in order to allow more pieces in its huge collection to be displayed. Many of these newly-revealed items were art objects and ceremonial objects from the various northern and coastal native Indian tribes in Canada. Because of this, the guests at the reception included a number of dignitaries and representatives of the aboriginal tribes, as well as the usual collection of university faculty members, politicians, benefactors, and media representatives.

As I wandered around the showcases, my interest was caught by some of the Indian masks that were used in different ceremonies, dances, and plays. The ones I was looking at were from the Dene group of tribes, and my curiosity was stirred by one mask in particular, which was shaped like the head of a dog, but opened out to reveal a human face inside. The man standing beside me was clearly a native Indian. He had a weathered face, long, gray hair pulled back into a ponytail, and was wearing a colourful woven jacket with long fringes, and an intricate series of patterns which were composed of hundreds of shiny buttons.

"That's an interesting mask," I said, "I wish that the museum would give information about the stories behind something like that, instead of just telling us where and when it was collected."

The man turned to me, and I could see lines curving upward from the outside edges of his shiny, dark eyes. They were the kind of lines that might have been etched in the process of expressing many smiles, or much laughter, over a period of many years.

"That's a transformation mask," he said. "The dancer comes in with a mask closed so that all you see is the head of the dog. Later on, the mask opens up to reveal that the dog has changed into a human being. That particular mask is from the Tlicho or Dogrib tribe, which is part of the Dene Nation, and it is used to tell the story of how our tribe not only came to be, but came to be great hunters."

"Can you tell it to me?" I asked.

The man smiled, and, in the process, seemed to confirm my feeling that the lines around his eyes were evidence of many, many years of smiling.

"This story should be danced as well as spoken. It should be told after a meal, with lots of people, including the children, gathered around and relaxed at night. But I suppose I could give you an afternoon version of the story.

"It starts out in the long past time, after Raven had found the first men and put them together with the first women. These first people were human, but they were not like us. They were very ignorant, and had very few skills. They did not know how to hunt, so they could not get meat for themselves. They had to live on berries and nuts, maybe some eggs that they could steal from the birds, and sometimes clams, and other things they could gather along the shore. Sometimes they were lucky, when the animals – like the wolves, who hunt for a living – had killed something and occasionally left some scraps of meat behind, or sometimes those hunting animals could be chased away from their kill. That was about the only way that those first people could get meat. This meant that times were hard, and food was scarce – so scarce that the tribes would often wage war on one another just for a few baskets of food.

"This is really where the story begins. There had just been a great war between two hungry tribes, each trying to steal the small amount of food that the other had gathered. The fight was desperate and brutal, and, at the end of the battle, only one person, a young woman, remained alive. She must have had a name, but we know her only as Saymo, which means 'mother' in the Dene language. She was all alone, with no one to protect her, and no one to help her gather food.

"At that time the greatest hunters in all the world were the wolves, or, to be more specific, the members of the Wolf Tribe. You see, the Wolf Tribe was made up of all of those animals who look like wolves in one way or another, and included not just brown and gray and white wolves, but foxes and coyotes, and even some creatures who had wolf-like faces, but were beginning to look and act more like dogs. A time would come when the members of the Wolf Tribe would have a great falling out, and the clan would break apart, with each of the wolf-like animals going their own way, starting a family and tribe, and building their own history, but that time was still a long way off.

"The Wolf Tribe watched the battles between the tribes of men. After all, if the men killed each other, the wolves could feast on their remains without any danger to themselves. They also kept an eye on any humans who seemed weak and unprotected, since they might eventually become food as well.

"We don't know how or why, but it was one of these wolfie animals who saw the young woman, Saymo, and felt sympathy for her. After watching her from a distance for a long time, that sympathy began to shape into affection, and perhaps even into love. Some of our ancestors believe that it was these feelings which changed that wolf-like animal inside, and began to make him human, and also altered his outward appearance to become less wolf-life and more like a dog. So it came to be that the wolfie animal – who was now almost a dog – came out of the forest, and decided to be with the woman.

"At first, Saymo was afraid of the black wolfie beast who came into her camp, but he did not threaten her, and so she relaxed a little. Then, when he disappeared into the forest to return carrying a rabbit, which he laid at her feet so that she could cook and eat it, Saymo began to understand that he would not hurt her, and, in fact, wanted to help her. She decided then that she would try to make friends with this wolfie animal. Such a big, wild animal with teeth must have scared her, but Saymo nonetheless reached out to touch him. The wolfie animal did not pull away from her, but instead came close and lay down by her feet.

"Saymo looked at him, and said, 'I do not know your name. And since you are not speaking to me I will give you a name. I will call you Klee.'

"Klee was a word sound that had not been used before in the world, and the woman chose it simply because she liked the way that it came out of her mouth, and the way that it reached her ears. It did not have any meaning until Saymo made the sound, and, for her, it was just a new word to describe the wolfie animal who had come to live with their. For the people of the Dene nation, the word has become part of our language, and has come to mean 'dog.'

Gods, ghosts, and black dogs

"The black wolfie animal stayed with the woman. She soon saw that he was a great hunter, and brought her back much meat. He was also a great protector who chased away the cougar who tried to hurt her in the night. Because he was an animal first, he knew much about the plants and other things in the forest, and Saymo began to learn from him, about the plants, and barks, and grasses, even which would go together to make great medicine. She felt safe around Klee, and every night he would lie down beside her when she slept.

"Then Saymo began to have dreams, in which a handsome young man came to her as she lay in her bed. In her dreams the man held her and loved her. The dreams felt very real to her, but she knew they were not because she was the only human left in the world, and there were no men around anymore. One morning, after such a dream, she looked at the dusty ground around her bed, and noticed that, mixed in with the footprints of the wolfie animal Klee, were what seemed to be the footprints of a human man. This made her wonder, and started her thinking about what might be happening, and whether, in fact, her dreams *were* just dreams. Certainly, Klee would not allow a stranger to come to her in the night, because he cared so much about her protection, yet there were the footprints of a man mixed in with the footprints of the wolfie beast.

"Saymo decided that she would try to find out what was going on. Perhaps she would stay up late at night while pretending to sleep to see if something strange and wondrous was happening. Unfortunately, she was not to have the chance.

"Later that same day, just as the sun was beginning to fade from the sky, the Father of all Bears caught the scent of the woman. This great, ancient bear tracked the scent, and, seeing Saymo in the distance, noted that she had no claws; no sharp teeth, and no weapons, so he thought that this helpless animal might be something he could hunt and eat: easy meat to take back to his mate and their children. So the Father of all Bears made his way silently to the edge of Saymo's camp, and then bounded forward to kill her when her back was turned.

"At that moment Klee gave a warning bark and leapt up to bite the great bear on his face. The Father of all Bears swung his mighty paw and his sharp claws stabbed into Klee's side. The wolfie beast gave a yelp because he was badly hurt, but turned back, and, ignoring his wounds, he jumped again, this time biting the bear on his nose. This caused so much pain to the great bear that he shrieked, and swung his head to free himself from Klee. The wolfie beast held on as best he could, but eventually his hold on the bear broke. Klee flew through the air and hit a tree, hurting himself greatly, yet still he did not cease his attack. He rushed forward yet again, and the bear – realising that this was not going to be an easy hunt after all, and all the while hurting from the bites to his face and nose – turned tail and ran. The great bear swore to himself that he would never again be so bold as to try to enter a camp where a wolfie beast might be waiting, regardless of how vulnerable his human companion might seem.

"That night, Klee died of his wounds, and Saymo wept for the companion she had loved so much, and who had loved her so dearly that he gave his life protecting her.

"A short time later Saymo found, to her amazement, that she was pregnant. She did not know how this was possible, though had her suspicions, which all had to do with her dreams about the young man who would come to her, and the morning when she had seen human footprints mixed in with those of Klee.

"It was not many weeks later that she gave birth: not to a child, but a litter of eight puppies, which was so very strange. Saymo knew that if she had still been living in a village with other people, they would have been horrified and frightened at this, and probably would've driven her out, thinking that she was a witch, or some kind of demon. Saymo suspected that the puppies she gave birth to were actually fathered by Klee who, she was beginning to realise, had the ability to transform himself into a human. Out of love for her faithful and loyal wolfie beast, she decided to keep and nurture the puppies.

"But so many puppies! Saymo knew she would have to scavenge many hours each day to feed them, and, in order to keep them safe when she was out searching for food, she made a large bag from skin for them to hide in when she was away from the camp. Later that day she was returning with a basket filled with food, and, as she came near to the camp, thought she could hear the sounds of children laughing. She rushed noisily through the bushes to get home, only to find nothing but the bag with the puppies inside. She searched the area for children hiding nearby, but did not find any.

"The next day, again, she took her basket and went into the forest, with the thought that she might find some acorns in a grove of trees she spotted earlier, and she could grind them into flour to make flat bread for herself and the puppies. Once again, as she returned to camp, she heard the sound of children, and, as before, hurried home, only to find nothing but the puppies in the bag. This time when she looked around, she noticed that, in the ashes of the fire, were a mixture of footprints – those of puppies, and those of children. Now, she remembered her suspicions about her wolfie animal, Klee, who may have had the ability to turn himself into a human, in which form he had likely served as her husband, and made her pregnant. Perhaps the puppies had that ability as well? Perhaps there might be some way to get her children to retain their human form permanently ...?

"First, though, she had to catch the puppies in their human form. She suspected that one or more of the children were keeping watch for her return, so that they could return to the safety of the bag and their puppy forms before she saw them. So Saymo decided to trick them. She took a long stick and bound a crosspiece on it. The next morning when she went out to scavenge for food, she climbed a low, distant hill, and drove the long stick into the ground at its peak. Next, she hung her jacket over the crosspiece, so that, from the camp, it might look as if she was standing there, looking for something. Then, very stealthily, she stole back into camp.

"What she saw there was eight handsome children – four boys and four girls – and lying on the ground next to the open skin sack were the pelts of eight puppies. It was clear that the children had climbed out of the sack and taken off their fur skins to become human children. Saymo rushed forward

to grab them, and managed to get two of the boys and two of the girls, while the others escaped into the sack. Saymo pulled the sack closed, and tossed the four remaining puppy skins into the fire to keep the children from changing, but something fundamental happened as she did that, as, not only were the children she had caught fixed in human form, but the four puppies inside the sack were no longer able to change. Saymo now had four human children, and four puppy children.

"The four children now in human form were different from the humans who had lived before them. They had many of their father's wolf-like abilities, and were great hunters who could find game, no matter where it was hiding. They could make weapons to strike down large animals, which meant that they could bring home meat, and they were great, brave fighters, who would not run from cougars or bears, or even an angry moose, but would stand and defend themselves. They were great medicine men, who could find the most valuable plants, barks, and magical grasses which could be used for healing and for powerful magic. Together, these four had many, many children and those children became the first true people of the Dene tribe: it is to them that we owe our ability to hunt and fight, and find special things and magic things hidden in the forests.

"And what of the puppies who had returned to the sack? They were still wolfie animals, of course: still wonderful hunters, who could sniff out hiding prey, and could hear another animal trying to run away, even if half a mile away. They were swift and strong, and could run down a wounded animal, despite the fact that the chase involved running many miles. But they also had many of their mother's human qualities and feelings, and would stand by their chosen humans, being loyal and protective toward them, even if that meant risking their own lives. The greatest joy for these animals was being part of a family: staying by the fire, or sleeping at the foot of the bed where their beloved human rested. These were no longer wolfie beasts; these were the first true dogs, the *real* 'klee.'

"So, this mask represents Klee, the dog

Gods, ghosts, and black dogs

husband; the dog father: the spirit that could transform from dog to human and human to dog, and who is the father of both modern humans and modern dogs. And that is why the human face hides deep inside the wolfie head, showing not only his ability to change shape, but the fact that both the spirit of the man and the spirit of the dog are together in one being."

"That is a wonderful story," I said.

His face crinkled, deepening those smile lines even more, and he replied "It's an even better dance!"

Why we eat and drink

I was visiting Atlanta, Georgia, to give a public lecture and an all-day workshop about dogs and dog behaviour, when a friend – a professor at the University of Georgia at Athens – called to invite me to visit him. He promised me that if I agreed, he would arrange a little dinner party, which would include a few psychologists I knew, as well as some people who are active in dog-related activities. Since Athens is only a little more than an hour's drive northeast of Atlanta I accepted his invitation.

Shortly after I arrived at his house, we were joined by a dozen or so people, most of whom were associated with the university in one way or another, and their spouses. Many of them arrived with one or two bowls or casserole dishes, since this was intended to be a bit of a 'potluck dinner.' After I was introduced to all of the guests, we were directed to a table which contained a number of bottles of wine, and someone poured me a glass of a local red from a winery that I had never heard of. The wine was very nice, and I wandered over to a table which held a number of snacks, including a bowl of some interesting meat and vegetable fritters made with deep fried corn batter.

I was nibbling on a fritter when I was approached by one of the couples. The woman, who was a handsome, middle-aged black female, said, "That's a traditional Gullah dish. I learned how to make those from my grandmother."

"I must confess my ignorance," I said, "but what is Gullah?"

She laughed and said, "That's not a surprising question from someone who lives in the north. Actually, your question should be 'Who are the Gullah?' We are African-Americans, who mostly live in the low country and the sea islands off of South Carolina and Georgia. Back in the 1600s, English settlers, especially those owning land on the sea islands, got it into their heads that, in addition to cotton, a really good profitable crop might be rice. So they went into West Africa to capture themselves some black slaves who knew how to grow and harvest rice.

" Some people say that the name 'Gullah' is just a shortened form of Angola, and, for a while, about one third of the slaves sold in the Charleston market came from that country. The rice plantations

Gods, ghosts, and black dogs

were very successful, and Carolina Golden Rice brought a good price.

"After the Civil War ended the slaves were freed, but, since most plantation owners were not able to produce crops without slave labour, some of the land was sold to former slaves and plantation workers, one of whom was my great grandfather. His place was on St Helena Island, south of Beaufort. Most of the Gullah who stayed on the islands made a living by farming and fishing. We actually had very little contact with the mainland, because, at that time, the only way to get off the island was by boat. It really wasn't until the 1950s that they began to build bridges to connect some of the South Carolina and Georgia Sea Islands to the mainland, and it became easier to interact with the rest of the world. But that long period of isolation turns out to have probably been a good thing, as it meant that we Gullah got to preserve a lot of our traditions; even some bits and pieces of our original language, and some old recipes, like for those corn fritters.

"That isolation also allowed us to keep alive a number of our traditional stories. You know, according to one of our stories, you would not be eating those fritters right now – or, more precisely, wouldn't be eating anything else – if it wasn't for dogs."

"Now that sounds interesting," I replied, as I grabbed another fritter and motioned us toward some empty chairs,

"You must tell me that story."

The tale she told me that evening began with the fifth day of creation, and went something like this. God had already made the sky and the heavens by the fifth day, and had then made the earth and the waters. He had also made fish, birds, and even the nasty little flying bugs that are such a bother. Next, the Lord decided that he wanted to make some more interesting things to live on the earth.

God said to himself, "I'll start simple, then work my way up to creating some complicated beasts."

The first thing he created was a little mouse, and then he started on the next thing. However, the mouse was curious, so stuck around to see what the Lord would make next. The Lord made a snake,

and then both the mouse and the snake stayed and watched while God made a rat, then a rabbit, and next a pig, and then a deer . . . God was really on a roll with each new creature being a little more complicated than the last. Every one of the new animals had some special skills and a unique new shape, and each was made complete, with the spark of life wrapped up inside of them so that they would never need to eat or drink.

Meanwhile, all of the newly-created animals crowded about, waiting to see what God would produce next. It was getting to be late in the afternoon when God stopped to ponder a bit ... and then decided to make a dog. He told the watching animals: "I'm going to make me a right smart creature. He is gonna know how to help me keep all of you in your place."

When the dog was made, he was given knowledge about how to herd, how to guard, and how to watch and be alert: skills that were his from the first breath that he took. So, when God told him to move the animals away from the creating place because he wanted to rest a bit and grab a bite to eat, the dog knew what to do. God was so pleased with how the dog helped him, and how enthusiastically he worked, that, once the other animals were cleared away, God whistled for the dog to come along with him when he went home after work that night. He even let the dog lay by the fireplace, and then allowed him to watch God prepare his food, cook it, and begin to eat. The dog's eyes watched God eating, following every morsel and every spoonful as it went from plate to mouth; then he watched the spoon go back to the plate to fill up again, and deliver more food to the Lord's mouth.

Finally, God had had enough to eat, and he pushed his chair away from the table, and gave his stomach a contented pat.

God had noticed the dog watching him, and asked him "Do you want me to make you a mouth so that you too can enjoy eating?"

The dog nodded his head and wagged his tail "Yes!"

God said to him, "Now, you should understand that if I make you a mouth, the spark of life that I stitched up inside of you is going to come out, which means that you'll have to eat and drink every day."

The dog thought about it for a moment, and then remembered how pleased God seemed to be when he was eating and drinking. He thought to himself that doing that eating and drinking thing every day seemed like an interesting idea, so he wagged his tail and nodded his head again, and even stood up and danced around in a little circle to make sure that God understood that he wanted to have a mouth. His actions amused God, who was coming to feel a real deep affection for the dog.

So God cut him a nice, big mouth, filled with white teeth and a long, red tongue. The dog was delighted with his new self, and when God tossed him a bit of leftover corn fritter as a treat, the dog chewed and swallowed it, and felt happier than he ever had before. He danced around, bowing, and trying to express his joy to God. In the middle of his dance, he found that he could bark, and howl, and yip, and growl, and make all kinds of sounds, which made the dog even happier.

In the morning, God decided to spend a little time planting in his garden before he got back to the business of finishing creation. The dog came along, running and frolicking and barking for joy at the sight of the Lord. The dog was extremely happy now that he had a mouth which let him make sounds as well as allow him to eat. God smiled at the dog's antics, and reached into his pocket where he had stored a couple of corn biscuits left over from breakfast. He broke off a bit of biscuit, and tossed it to the dog as a treat, and the dog happily gobbled it up. The Lord thought how nice it was to have such a loving and appreciative animal around.

At that very moment, all of the other creatures arrived. They had heard the barking, and had come to see what the noise was, and where it came from. The sounds were coming from the dog's mouth, of course, and all of the other animals thought that this was a wonderful thing. It was not just the fact that he could eat with it and drink and bark with it, but he could do other things with it, too, such as pick up things, and carry them from place to place. If he

got a thorn stuck between his toes, he could pull it out with his teeth; he could even pick up a stick or a ball and play with it.

So the animals crowded around God and his dog, filled with amazement and envy, every single one of them clamouring and pleading for a mouth, too.

God was a bit annoyed by all this activity. Making mouths for all of the animals would take the better part of the morning, and this was the day that he was planning on putting together his most complicated creation, something which he planned to call 'people.'

The dog was a kindly animal, who felt sorry for his fellow beasts, so he looked into God's eyes and begged, "Please give them mouths also, My Lord."

God was uneasy about this, however, since giving mouths to the other beasts would mean them losing their spark of life also. He knew that some of the beasts would then eat the plants and flowers that he had created, while others would hunt and kill for food. Still, he understood that every living being should be given the right to choose his own place in the world, and, besides, the request came from his dog, who God knew felt he was doing a good deed by asking for this. In addition, this was the same dog who was so friendly and loving that he made God smile, which gave them a special place in the Lord's heart. God agreed to the request because it would make all of the animals happy, but really he agreed mostly because it would make the dog — whom he had grown to love — happy.

So God spent the morning creating mouths for all of the animals: some big, some small, some with flat teeth for munching leaves, some with pointy teeth for biting other animals. Then the Lord looked at how far the sun had travelled since morning, and knew that nearly half a day had already passed, and he had still not yet started work on creating people. Turning to the dog he said, "Clear all of these animals away from here, so that I can have some peace and quiet and go on about my creating."

So the dog used his new mouth to make loud barks, and rumbling growls, and to snap his teeth at the animals who were too slow to move.

Gods, ghosts, and black dogs

What the dog was doing with his mouth appeared fearsome and threatening to the other animals, so they scattered, leaving the place empty and quiet so that God could go about his work undisturbed.

When God saw what the dog had done he tossed him another piece of biscuit and smiled. As he returned to the complicated business of creating people, the dog asked, "These new creatures that you are making — these 'human beings' — could you give them mouths, too? They might like to eat and enjoy food also. And perhaps, maybe, you could give them hands so that they can make cornbread and fritters to eat, like you do? If cornbread is something they can make, and is easy for them to make, isn't it possible that they might like to share a bit of it with a friendly, hard-working animal like me?"

God laughed and said, "Sure. Because I love you as much as I do I will give these human beings mouths and hands, and even the recipe for corn fritters and cornbread!"

The happy dog lay down nearby to watch his Creator go about his business. He also kept a lookout for any curious beasts that might return, and need chasing away again with the sounds and snaps that he could make with his mouth. At the same time he wondered whether God might have yet another piece of corn biscuit in his pocket which he might be willing to place in the new mouth of his faithful and loving dog. The dog did not worry at all about the fact that he, and the human beings that God was now making to be his companion, would now have to eat and drink every day — in fact, he thought that it was a very nice idea, indeed!

Why the Pug has a flat, black face and a curled tail

I was standing by the side of a dog show ring, where the judge was awarding the best-of-breed ribbon to a Pug, and the various other colourful ribbons to the three runners-up. It was then that I heard a voice say, "They are a handsome group of bandits, aren't they?"

I looked in the direction from where the voice came, and saw a smiling, middle-aged, Chinese woman standing beside me. She was wearing a dark blue suit jacket over a red sweater and dark blue slacks. On her jacket was a silver pin in the shape of a Pug.

"Bandits?" I asked.

"Can't you see the black masks that they wear, like all outlaws and bandits?"

"I'll bet there is a story behind that. If you are willing to let me buy you a cup of coffee, I'd like to hear it." I replied.

"Oh, it's just an old folk tale," she protested.

"That's even better," I said, and the two of us drifted over to a section of the arena where one could purchase a cup of coffee to drink at a nearby table.

It turned out that the woman's name was Jaiying, but, although her parents were traditional Chinese, she was born in Canada, and preferred to be called Jane. She had owned Pugs all her life, and liked to come to the dog shows to see the various examples of her breed.

"I am second generation Canadian," she told me. "My grandfather and two of his brothers came to the city of Victoria in British Columbia, which then had a large Chinese population. They opened a restaurant, and a tailor's shop, and even though they were pleased to be Canadian citizens, they still tried to make sure that their children understood Chinese culture. That really helped my father, who now teaches Chinese and Asian studies at a college. He loves to tell stories, and I remember when I got my first Pug puppy – that is, the first dog who belonged to me and not the other members of my family – he began to tell me lots of stories about Pugs. But one story was my special favourite: the one about how Pugs came to look the way they do. I had him tell me that one many times.

"It was at the time when the world was still rather new, and the Jade Emperor, the one that we call the Heavenly Grandfather, still walked the earth, and could appear in a temple to speak to you if you prayed to him and had a good cause. Two brothers, one named Bo and the other Chonglin, came to the temple and called upon the Jade Emperor. They were wet and cold and exhausted from running a long way. They said that they had seen something frightening, and they thought that the God might need to intervene. The way they described it, they were walking across a field looking for shelter from a cold winter rain, when, suddenly, the earth at the base of a nearby mountain split open, and a fiery red light of blinding intensity appeared. At first, they thought that, perhaps, this was something like a volcano that was starting to erupt, but then, much to their horror, what they saw emerging from the great opening in the earth were monstrously large living beings, with sharp, rending claws, and great square mouths full of teeth. The beasts growled and howled, and began to move toward a nearby village.

"The men were terrified, and felt that they must bring this information to the attention of the gods. So they ignored the cold, wet fury of the storm, and travelled all night to reach the temple. It was clear to them that they had seen demons invading the world.

"The Jade Emperor suspected that these men were correct in their assumption, and that what they had probably seen were Mara: a particularly dangerous kind of demon. which can take many forms. The warriors among them have the large mouths with many fangs, and sharp claws, and are called Mogwa. They can do great harm to people, and even just the sight of them can drive men mad, or even stop their hearts from beating. The fact that these brothers had made such a long, hard trip to reach the temple quickly, rather than running and hiding to save themselves, proved they had courage and nobility, so the Jade Emperor told the men to stay in the safety of the temple, and he would go into battle with these Mogwa.

"The men did as they were told, and the priests gave them warm, dry clothes and found a place for them to stay in the temple. Less than a week later the Jade Emperor returned. He was tired, but had cleared the countryside of the demons. However,

he was saddened to find that all had not gone well with Bo and Chonglin in his absence. Because they had looked directly at the demon light coming from the pit where the Mara were emerging, their eyes had been damaged, and in the few days that the Heavenly Grandfather had been away, the men had gone completely blind. There was nothing that the god could do to reverse damage caused in this way, which made him very sad because the men had been alert and brave, and had sounded the alarm which saved many lives.

"So the Jade Emperor decided that he would provide for Bo and Chonglin. He built for them a small but comfortable house next to a river, and explained to them, 'Once each week someone from the village will bring you food. It will be meat, fish, and vegetables. Store it away so that no animals can get to it since you will only have one delivery each week. You will have to work a little harder for your water. I have provided a bucket attached to a rope, and all that you have to do is to throw the bucket out in the direction of the sound that the river makes. It will fill with water and you can drag it into your house.'

"The Jade Emperor then had an afterthought, and said to the men, 'I will also provide you with a companion: a dog who will serve as a guard and a guide. He will sound a warning if someone comes close to your house, and alert you if some person or some animal is trying to steal your food. He will also guide you if you need to go someplace. All that you need to do is attach a string to his collar, and to tell him where you want to go and he will lead you there.'

"He then gave the men a dog that looked like many of the other dogs that you could find in China at that time. The dog was small enough so that it would not take up too much room in the little house that the brothers now lived in. It was tan-coloured, with a sharp, foxy face, and it had a long, strong, whip-shaped tail. This kind of dog was known as 'Lo-chiang-sze,' and was smart, friendly, and understood his job. Although he did not look like it, this is the dog that would become the Pug, so let me call him the Pug dog from now on, just to make the story easier to tell.

"All went well for the men and their Pug dog

Why the Pug has a flat, black face and a curled tail

for several weeks. Bo and Chonglin lived a very quiet life, and because of their blindness mostly stayed in their home, and did not want the dog to lead them around the countryside. That meant their days were mostly uneventful, which, for an intelligent and playful dog like the Pug, was very boring, so the Pug dog decided he might engage in a bit of mischief to amuse himself.

"Every morning the blind brothers would throw their bucket into the river, and drag it back by the attached rope so that they would have water for the day. Since the bucket was quite heavy when it was filled with water, they took turns with that tiring chore each day. To ease his boredom the Pug dog decided to play a prank.

One morning, he slipped outside of the house and waited. It was Chonglin's turn to get the water, and the blind man threw the bucket toward the sound of the river, waiting a few moments for it to fill. The Pug dog quickly knocked the bucket onto its side to empty the water, and pushed very hard against its bottom so that it filled with sand. The sand was nearly as heavy as the water, which meant that it required considerable effort to drag the bucket across the ground, and into the house. When Chonglin found there was no water in the bucket, he emptied out the sand, put the bucket back in its usual place next to the door, and called out to his brother.

"In a worried voice he said, 'Bo, I'm afraid that the river has run dry. Today, I threw out the bucket and got back only sand.'

"'Let me try,' said Bo, as he hurled the bucket toward the river. Dragging the heavy bucket back into the house, he found that it was now filled with water. This made Bo quite angry, and he shouted at his brother, 'You are so lazy. I know that you do not like the hard work of dragging the water bucket into the house. So now you resort to tricking me into doing your morning's work.'

"Chonglin protested that it was no trick, but Bo was not convinced, and the two men argued all morning long over the water bucket incident. The Pug dog found this most amusing, and particularly liked the fact that when the men argued they became quite inventive as they tried to find new ways to insult each

other, which gave the dog an idea. If he could sow a little dissension among the brothers every now and then, it would provide an entertaining show for him, in much the way that watching a couple bicker on a TV sitcom breaks the boredom of a housewife stuck at home. So the Pug dog began to make plans.

"A day or two later, when it was Bo's turn to cook, the blind man carefully laid on the table two fish that he had grilled: one for his brother; the other for himself. He then went to get a pot of tea, and called Chonglin to dinner. The crafty Pug dog raced over to the table and grabbed not only one of the fish, but also the plate that it was on, quickly gobbling down the fish and licking clean the plate; placing it on the edge of the sink where the brothers washed their dishes. Chonglin, meanwhile, made his way to the table, only to find that, not only was there no food for him, but not even a plate had been set for him. When he protested to his brother that there was no food, an argument ensued, with Bo insisting that his brother was just being greedy, and had obviously quickly swallowed his food so that he could make a claim on the food on Bo's plate. As the brothers argued, the Pug dog rolled around on the floor, laughing at the scene.

"Every few days the Pug dog would try another variation of this prank. When it was Chonglin's time to cook, the animal stole some meat which was being set out for Bo, and a few days later he stole some pastries, and so on. The dog found his mischief-making all very amusing. Not only did he get to see the brothers argue and fume for hours, but got extra food in addition, and food that was much tastier than what he was normally given for his own meals.

"Because of the Pug's practical jokes, the tension between the brothers increased to such a point that they finally decided that when the food delivery arrived each week they would divide it in half, and each brother would hide his portion of the provisions to prevent the other from stealing it. Furthermore, they decided that each brother would cook his own meals separately. Bo chose to hide his portion of the food in the narrow space behind a clothing chest which stood close to the wall, and Chonglin decided to hide his portion of the week's rations in the narrow space behind another chest where the brothers kept their sleeping blankets. To prevent each other from knowing where the food was hidden, each brother would wait until the other had stepped outside the house, instructing the Pug dog to stand outside the door and watch to make sure that his brother did not come near the house until he had hidden his food. Because he was outside guarding the closed door, this meant that the Pug dog also did not know where the food was hidden, of course.

"Later that day when the brothers had both stepped out of the house, the Pug began to look around to see if he could find the provisions. Being a dog, he had a fine, long nose, which was very sensitive to smells, so it took only a short time for him to sniff out the hiding places. However, the brothers had hidden the provisions in narrow spaces, which were too small for the dog to get his short paw into. The Pug dog had an idea, though. Very carefully, he worked his long, strong tail into the space behind the chest, and – just as he had hoped – this allowed him to hook some of the hidden food and pull it out.

"Eventually, each of the brothers discovered that some of their food was missing, and, as might be expected, they blamed each other for committing the theft. As the dog had hoped, this started another argument, much to the amusement of the Pug. Each time the dog's thievery was discovered, the brothers would move their hiding place, almost always putting the food in narrow areas which were difficult to reach into, and difficult to find. None of this worked, since the Pug's sensitive nose would always discover the latest hiding place, and his strong, flexible tail would always be able to pry out enough food to cause an argument. As the arguments escalated, this provided endless entertainment for the dog.

"Eventually, the man who delivered the food each week to the blind brothers brought word back to the Jade Emperor that there was a problem, and a lot of conflict in the brothers' home. Bo and Chonglin were very special to the Jade Emperor because they had sacrificed their vision in order to bring a warning about the arrival of the demons. So the Heavenly Grandfather sent a small bird to watch the house and see what was happening. It did not take long for the bird to discover the mischief that the

dog was involved in, and to convey that information to the Jade Emperor. Once he understood who the culprit was the great celestial being made a trip to the brothers' home.

"When the Jade Emperor arrived he called Bo and Chonglin, and also the Pug dog, before him. He then explained to the brothers, 'This trouble between you two is not justified. Both of you are good men and have not slighted or stolen from your brother. This is all the fault of Lo-chiang-sze, your dog.'

"For the purposes of this audience with the Heavenly Grandfather, the dog was given the ability to speak, and protested,' But, Your Eminence, I meant no real harm. It is just so boring, because I have nothing to do. Bo and Chonglin don't go any place so I am not needed as a guide, and I am not involved in their daily chores, so there is nothing for me to do or to watch. I was just trying to stir up some emotion in this house so that I would not be so bored.'

"The Jade Emperor did not accept this excuse. 'I must prevent you from continuing to steal from your masters, and punish you for your thievery. So that all may know that you are a thief and a bandit, I will give you a black mask, just like those worn by the bandits and outlaws who roam the highways. Because you used your long, sensitive nose to find the food that you wanted to steal I am going to take that away from you, and leave you with just a short, flat nose that is good for breathing, but is of not much value for sniffing and finding things, and certainly can't be pushed into narrow spaces to discover if anything is there. Because you used your long, strong tail like a hook to drag things out of their hiding places so that you could take them, I am going to roll up your tail into a tight little coil, which cannot be used to lift or grab anything.

"'But I am not without compassion, and I understand your boredom. Since you find strong, human emotions to be amusing, I am going to grant you something which people will someday call 'empathy,' and this will allow you to interpret the slightest changes in human emotions, making you want to respond to particular emotions in a helpful way. It will compel you to want to watch your human masters very carefully, which is a job that will fill your

Why the Pug has a flat, black face and a curled tail

days, and keep you from getting bored. Because the changes in emotions in people are often very subtle, I will give you great round eyes so that you can see better, and study people more carefully.

"Then the Jade Emperor smiled and turned to the Pug dog once more, saying, 'By your black mask the world will know that, once in your life you were a bandit, but by your actions they will learn that you are now a dog who cares more about people and their feelings than any other dog in the world today.'

"The Pug dog bowed his head, then looked with his new large round eyes to see how his masters were reacting to it all. His new ability to empathise told him that they were feeling much happier, and were no longer angry with each other, and these positive emotions coming from the brothers made him feel better as well. The Pug dog then thought to

himself, 'Perhaps watching the feelings of my human masters will keep me from being bored. But still, even though I no longer have the nose or tail to steal or cause mischief, I do still feel like a bandit in my heart.'"

Jane deilvered the last part of her story, which represented the Pug dog's inner thoughts, in a high, squeaky voice, such as one might expect a small dog to have, and both of us laughed out loud. She then added, "Since, according to the story, Pugs still believe themselves to be bandits, and wear the bandit's mask that the Jade Emperor gave them, I feel that it is only fair that I think of them as bandits, and call them by that name."

"Reformed bandits, perhaps?" I asked.

"Perhaps reformed, or perhaps not," Jane answered with a little laugh.

How the Dalmatian got his spots

Although I am sure that many scholars may disagree, it appears to me that folklore, mythology, tall tales, and even casual anecdotes, are all cut from the same cloth: part of an oral tradition which involves passing time in an entertaining way by telling and listening to stories. Sometimes there are people who specialize in telling these tales, such as bards, minstrels, wise elders, shamans, teachers, and, of course, bartenders. While I have heard and collected many stories from settings where alcohol was flowing, and the air was filled with tobacco smoke, others have come to me while sitting with friends over dinner, and still others have been overheard when people are just trying to entertain children. Like many folk tales that get passed around in a specific culture, most are not written down, and there is no guarantee that the next retelling will contain the same elements. Part of the joy in both telling and listening to tales is the fact that the person spinning the story gets to elaborate and change bits and pieces to catch the attention of his particular audience, while the listeners – even if they know the general sense of the story – can appreciate its novel aspects.

Now, the reason that I began this chapter with such a rather formal opening is really only to justify the fact that I want to tell you a dog-related story that might be considered by some to be just an interesting, casual or amusing anecdote. This particular story might not meet some formal academic definition of what really constitutes a folk tale, although, for me, if 'ordinary folks' are telling the tale – even if they are inventing it on the spot – it qualifies as a folk tale. Having now doubtless incited the ire of any scholars who might be reading this book, let me tell you the story.

It was a hot Sunday in July; the kind of lazy day when you know that your kids were going to go crazy if you didn't find something to entertain them. Rebecca was eight years old at the time, and Benn six, and, by mid-morning, both were beginning to get twitchy, looking for something to do, or some trouble to get into to relieve their feelings of boredom. Fortunately, our neighbourhood fire station was having an open house that day, so I took the kids on a walk down to the firehouse. The big doors were wide open, and there was a large, welcoming banner above them. In addition, the door posts and the firetrucks were decorated with colourful balloons.

A big table was set up just inside the garage area, and on it was a large, insulated container that dispensed cold, grape-flavoured punch. Next to that was a big box containing cookies, and at the far end of the table was another box containing plastic badges in the shape of a fireman's helmet, each inscribed with the letters 'VFD' (Vancouver Fire Department). Although I could see several adults chatting with firemen, the majority of the visitors seemed to be primary school-aged children, clearly brought here by parents with the idea of filling a few hours of a slow-moving, hot Sunday afternoon, much as I was doing.

While the cookies, badges, and cold drinks were an immediate attraction for my kids, they quickly became more interested in the fact that this fire station had a mascot: namely a Dalmatian dog. The handsome spotted dog sat quietly next to a fireman, who, despite the heat, was wearing his fire helmet and yellow slicker simply because he knew that this was the way children expected to see a fireman dressed. However, the man and the dog were seated on the running board of a firetruck inside the rear of the station, which was a little cooler.

A small crowd of about a dozen children had gathered around the fireman and his dog. The fireman introduced the dog, saying, "This is Blaze. He is a Dalmatian. I know that you kids have seen TV cartoons and books which showed Dalmatians on firetrucks. That is because Dalmatians have been the mascots for fire companies for a long time."

One of the kids asked the inevitable follow-up question "Why is it that, out of all the different kinds of dogs there are, fireman always have Dalmatians with them?"

The firemen smiled and gave the dog a little pat. He had clearly heard that question before, and had a well-rehearsed answer ready.

"Well," he said in a leisurely voice, "it's really a tradition – kind of keeping a piece of history going. You see, way back in the early days, when fire companies were first started, the fire engines were large wagons, which were pulled through the streets by some really big horses. Dalmatians used to

be called carriage – or coach – dogs, because they were specially bred to be fond of horses, and to run alongside a horsedrawn carriage: usually right under the front axle, not far behind the horses' hooves. Dalmatians are fast dogs, who can easily keep up with horses, but they also had a job.

"While they were running, the dogs would bark, and their barking, along with the fire bell, of course, alerted people to the fact that there was a fast-moving wagon coming down the street, giving enough warning for them to get safely out of the way. But the Dalmatians were also a kind of guard dog, which means that when the fire wagons stopped and the firemen got off to go help put out the fire, the dogs would protect the firetruck. It was important to keep people from stealing stuff, or just messing around with the equipment, which they shouldn't be touching.

"Even though we no longer have engines that are pulled by horses, having that Dalmatian dog around became a tradition, and there are lots of fire stations that still keep a Dalmatian as their mascot. Nowadays, the dog rides in the firetruck, instead of running alongside it, but he still does feel that he is a guard dog, and barks if people he doesn't know get too close to the truck."

I felt myself smiling. His account was fairly accurate, and the kids were clearly interested. The next question from a child had a completely different flavour, however. "Well, that might be why you keep Dalmatian dogs in the fire station, but can you tell us why Dalmatians have those black spots all over them?"

My expectation was that the fireman would give a fairly bland and dismissive answer, something like "A dog has to have some colour; some are black, some are yellow, and Dalmatians just happened to have black spots," but, instead, he broke into a large smile, and leaned back a bit in the way I have seen so many storytellers do just before they launch into a favourite tale.

"I can only answer that question by telling you what I was told. You see, I am a fourth generation fireman. That means that my father was a fireman, and his father was a fireman, and his father's father

Gods, ghosts, and black dogs

was a fireman. Now, the story that I'm telling you is one that my dad told me, and he claimed that it came all the way down the line from my great grandfather, and my great grandfather claimed to have heard it from someone else older still.

"According to the way the story is told, the first Dalmatians were all white — not a spot of coloir on them. From the beginning they were doing the kind of work that I told you about before: running with the horses, guarding the fire company's stuff, and all of that. Although the work was important, there was nothing heroic about it, and the dogs were not considered to be real fireman, or real members of the fire company. Everyone regarded the dogs the same way that they did the horses who pulled the wagon: they were sort-of workers and helpers. but more like equipment and less like real companions.

"It's hard to know what the dogs thought their role was, but probably, in the way of all dogs, they liked the people that they worked with, and, of course, they liked children. Anyways, back then in that long ago, there was once this huge fire in an apartment building downtown, so big that one fire company just couldn't handle it all by itself. This meant that the fire crew which arrived first had to call for help,and it ended up that there were three fire companies all trying to pump water on that big, flaming building. Of course, each of the fire companies arrived with their fire wagons and their entire crew, which, in this case, included each company's white Dalmatian.

"You have to understand that the first job of a fireman is really not to put out the fire, but rather to make sure that all of the people in the building get out safe, and that was what the firemen really cared about this day. So everyone was running around trying to make sure that all the people who were in the apartments had gotten out of the building in time, and were no longer in danger. The fire companies thought that they had done a good job of clearing everybody, when a lady ran up to the captain of one of the fire companies. She was worried and crying, and it was hard to understand what she was saying. When the captain finally calmed her enough that he could figure out what she was trying to say, it became clear that there was a real problem. What the firemen hadn't known was that, down in the basement of the apartment building, where they thought there was just the furnace, the hot water heater, and that sort of stuff, there was actually one more apartment in the back corner. The woman was trying to tell the firemen that she had left her two children in that apartment when she had walked down the street to buy some milk for them. She had searched the crowd of people who had been rescued, and her children were not there. She was in a real panic.

"As soon as the fire captain understood the problem, he looked up to see whether he could get some of his crew to help rescue the children, and it was at that moment that he saw that all three of the white Dalmatian dogs had run over to one corner of the building, and were barking frantically, as if trying to call for help. The captain sent three firemen in the direction of the dogs, and when they got close the men could hear the faint sound of children calling for help. Unfortunately, there didn't seem to be much of a way into the building from where they were, so two of the firemen went around the side of the building to look for another way in. The remaining fireman stared in the direction that the dogs were looking, and although there was no clear passage, it seemed to him that maybe there was just enough space among the debris for him to wriggle his way through the wreckage where chunks of the building had collapsed, and find a way to the children. He lay down on his belly and began to crawl into the building.

"Unfortunately, the opening was just too small, and not only was it the case that he couldn't make his way very far, but he suddenly found he was stuck, and could go neither forward nor back, because debris was still falling from the fire above. An even bigger problem, however, was that nobody in the fire company had seen him crawl in there, and probably assumed that he was walking around the building trying to find a way in.

"Well, that last statement is not strictly true, as the three fire dogs, the white Dalmatians, had seen him go in, and they set up a such a commotion, barking fit to beat the band. One of them even ran back to the fire captain, grabbed him by his trouser leg, and began pulling to where the other two dogs were barking. The captain got the message that something was wrong, and called some men, who ran to the place where the dogs were barking and whimpering. When the men looked into the narrow passage, they could see the boots of their comrade, so one of them took a rope, got down on his belly, and looped the rope around the feet of the stuck fireman. By pulling on the rope, they managed to drag him to safety.

"Everybody recognized that the fireman had had a lucky escape, but there was no time to celebrate. Standing there, all of the members of the fire crew could still hear the children who were trapped in the apartment, crying and yelling for help. If the firemen didn't do something quickly, the flames would work their way down to where the children were, and burn them up, or the blaze burning on the top floors would make the building so weak that the whole thing would collapse on top of them. The only way in seemed to be that narrow, tunnel-like space that the first fireman had gotten trapped in. But considering the problems that the first attempt at rescue had run into, it didn't look as though that narrow space would work as an entrance for getting inside. Things looked very bad, and everyone was beginning to worry.

"When it comes to trying to save people, firemen don't give up, however: if they couldn't find a way in, then they were just going to have to *make* a way in to get those kids. The firemen grabbed axes, crowbars, and shovels, and desperately began clearing a way to the children, pulling away ash-covered pieces of wood, moving as quickly as they could. Covered with soot and charcoal and ash, they weren't making very much progress, however.

"I suppose we will never know what those three white Dalmatians were thinking, but it appears to me that they were just as worried about the children as everyone else, and, before anyone could stop them, the dogs had dashed into the narrow passage – all three of them. The firemen were even more anxious and upset at this because it seemed that not only the children, but also their dogs, were going to be killed.

"It couldn't have been more than a few minutes after the dogs disappeared into the basement that the firemen heard a loud barking, just off to the side of where they had been digging, so quickly changed direction. In a matter of moments they had cleared away the debris enough to see one of the dogs, wriggling his way out as best he could. One of the firemen grabbed hold of the dog and pulled, and it was at that moment that they all saw the hand of a little girl, hanging on to the dog's collar. Dragging both the dog and the girl to safety, they set to to widen the passageway so that another dog, and maybe even another child, might make their way out.

"The firemen were rewarded for their efforts when, a minute or two later, they saw the second dog pulling at a little boy, trying to get him to move down the narrow space. Behind the child they could make out the third dog, who seemed to be nudging and pushing the boy along. The firemen worked frantically to widen the tunnel, and in seconds were able to grab hold of the leading dog, and the young child. As soon as the boy was out, the third white Dalmatian scampered out behind him.

"The captain realised that the fire was not really under control, and the building was in bad shape, so yelled for everybody to get away from the side of the apartment building. The two kids were snatched up by the fire crew and carried to safety, with the dogs happily bouncing and barking around them. In seconds, everyone was out of harm's way, and the building collapsed almost immediately.

"Now, you've got to understand what had happened there. Those three white Dalmatian dogs (which, before this day, were thought of only as workers, not heroes, and not real members of the fire company), had just saved three lives. They'd not only guided the two children to safety, but also, by alerting the other firemen to the predicament that the first fireman had gotten into, had actually saved one of the members of the fire company as well.

"Everybody involved in the rescue gathered around the dogs to pat them, and, because they had been working in the soot and ash, each time a fireman's fingers touched the white coat of a dog, his fingertips left black spots. By the time the fire crew

Gods, ghosts, and black dogs

had stopped celebrating, the Dalmatians were no longer pure white, but, instead, had lots of black spots on their white coats.

"Here is where things get magical. You might think that when the dogs returned to their own firehouses and were given a bath, all of those black spots would've come off. But they didn't; it was as though God, or an angel, or a miracle, had decided to make those marks permanent. Those spots, which came from the soot, ash, and charcoal left by that burning fire, were like Medals of Honour, and it seems that someone who had the necessary magic meant for them to stay there to remind the firemen that their Dalmatian was much more than just a mascot. From that day on, a Dalmatian was no longer just a worker, nor a one-time hero, but a true fireman, with the courage to do the hard and dangerous work involved in saving lives.

"It wouldn't surprise me to discover that many of you don't believe this story is accurate and factual, and you should know that I found it hard to believe the first time it was told to me. Still, there is some proof which, at least for me, demonstrates the magic. The main piece of evidence is that the miracle which happened on that long-ago day repeats itself during the life of every single Dalmatian. All Dalmatians are born completely white, just like the old Dalmatians used to be, and just like the old time Dalmatians, it is only as they grow that they are awarded their permanent soot spots, which show that they were born to be firemen, and to help firemen. We know that those are magical miracle spots of soot and ash, because, just as in the case of the first three spotty Dalmatians, once the Dalmatian pup finally gets his black spots, they don't wash off and they don't rub off. Those spots stay right where they were put when those firemen patted those white Dalmatians with their sooty hands to congratulate them on being heroes and real fire dogs."

I didn't know whether I was hearing a real piece of folklore, or just a tall tale spun on the spot (excuse the pun), but it really didn't matter since the kids were entranced by the story. Afterwards, all of the children gathered around Blaze, the company's Dalmatian. Every one of them, it seemed, wanted a chance to pat the dog to confirm that those magical soot spots really would not rub off under their hands.

Why the Basenji doesn't bark

I was giving a series of talks in Toronto at the All About Pets Show, which is held annually on Easter Weekend. As often happens at such events, people stop me as I am walking around the hall to ask me questions, solicit advice, or offer their opinion about various aspects of dog behaviour, or events occurring in the news that may have an impact on dogs and dog owners. I usually enjoy these interactions, and try to be as helpful and open-minded as I can; to be honest, I am always looking out for interesting stories and observations about dogs and our human interactions with them.

This time I had arrived early at the stage where I was supposed to be speaking in order to plug in my computer, and check out the sound system and projectors. When I had finished this task, I turned and noticed that, although it was still nearly half-an-hour until my talk, a few people were already sitting in the front rows of chairs that circled the stage. One pair in particular caught my eye — an elderly woman sitting next to a middle-aged woman — but hat attracted my attention, however, was the handsome, sand-and-white-coloured Basenji resting next to their feet.

I have always liked the look of Basenjis, with their pricked ears and sharp, foxy faces. The Basenji is a medium-sized dog that originates from Central Africa; one of the more ancient breeds (there are records of Basenjis having been presented as gifts to the Pharaohs of Egypt). These dogs are still used by African natives to assist in hunting, where the dog's job is to chase birds and small game into nets that the hunters have set up in advance. However, one of the most remarkable features of Basenji behaviour is that these clever and resilient dogs do not bark.

With some free time before I had to speak, I wandered over to sit down on one of the plastic folding chairs near this group, and reached down to pet the dog. It turned out that the older woman was named Josette, and the younger woman was her daughter, Caroline. I learned that the dog's name was Ilo, which is from the African Bantu language meaning 'light,' chosen because of the dog's very light colouration. One usually does not find dogs in Canada with Bantu names, so I commented, "That's interesting. An African dog with an African name. Do you have some experience with Africa?"

Gods, ghosts, and black dogs

It was Josette who answered, speaking with a French accent, her voice conveying some of the raspy resonance that comes with age, though still with a playful, merry sound to it. "My father was a member of the Free French Forces in Africa during World War II. He was very much inspired by Charles de Gaulle. You might remember that De Gaulle was a French government minister who rejected the armistice with Germany that had been signed by Maréchal Philippe Pétain. De Gaulle's life was then threatened, and he escaped to Britain. He then somehow got the BBC to let him make a broadcast, the Appel du 18 juin [this translates to the 'Appeal of 18 June']. He had such a grand way of speaking, and he told the French people that they must resist what he thought was part of a master plan by the Nazi regime in Germany to try to take over the entire world. My father was one of those who was already in the army, and his entire military unit joined the resistance. Only a short time later they ended up in what was then called French Equatorial Africa, where, under De Gaulle's command, they fought in Chad (on the southern border of Libya) in what came to be known as the Battle of Gabon, or maybe you remember it as the Battle of Libreville. It was a glorious victory, and the battle resulted in Free French forces taking Libreville, Gabon, and all of French Equatorial Africa

"My father remained in Africa for the rest of the war, and after Germany finally surrendered, he found that there was no real reason for him to return to France. Our village in France had been completely destroyed by the actions of armies on both sides, and nothing worthwhile remained, so he sent for my mother and my sister and me. I don't know how he got the money to start a business, but he managed to go into partnership with two other men in a timber harvesting company. It made a lot of money, at least for that time and place. We lived in a big house with lots of African servants from the Nyanga tribe to do all of the work. There were many native dogs around in the villages, and a lot of these were Basenjis. I fell in love with the breed, so my father got me my first Basenji, a black-and-white puppy. I named her Habika – Bantu for 'sweetheart' – which is what she was."

I smiled, and asked in a teasing manner, "So,

it wasn't just the fact that you were looking for a dog who doesn't bark?"

Josette laughed, and replied, "It's not as if they are completely silent. In fact, Ilo makes this loud noise sometimes which sounds like one of those American cowboys yodelling. One of the men my father had hired to work around the house was Ashon (which means 'seventh born son'). I once was talking to him about the fact that Basenjis don't bark, and he told me that, while it might sound like a good thing to have a dog who doesn't bark, in some circumstance it can actually be a problem. When you are out in the field hunting with dogs, for example, it's important to know where your dog is at any moment in time. Obviously, with the majority of dog breeds, the sound of barking is the most usual way to locate a dog, so the absence of barking in the Basenji meant that sometimes the dogs would disappear in the high grass, and it could be very hard to locate them, and see what they were chasing. Some members of the Nyanga people solved this problem by hanging gourds with pebbles in them on the collars of their dogs, serving the same purpose as bells in that they make a noise when the dog moves, allowing the hunters to locate the animals. This helped, though was not a perfect solution.

"As a little girl I always wondered why, of all of the dogs in the world, the Basenji does not bark. One day, my sister and I were sitting with Habika, watching Ashon repairing a door that wasn't closing properly. Ashon liked to tell us about his people, and he also liked to tell stories, so I asked him if he knew why the Basenji doesn't bark. He said that the Nyanga people did have an answer to that question. The way I remember it, the story goes something like this ...

"In the distant past there were many gods, and there was some dispute about which would become the High God, or King. One day, long ago, there was a great storm in the heavens, and a piece of the sun broke off. It fell to the ground and started a fire, which was found by the god Nyamurairi, who recognized how important, useful, and powerful fire could be. Fire could provide a wonderful source of heat and light, but could also be a weapon that could destroy villages, forests, and even living things.

Yes, fire was a great power that could cause pain and provoke fear in animals, people, and even in gods. Nyamurairi now had possession of that fire which came from the sun, which obviously meant that he now had possession of immense power. So Nyamurairi declared himself the High God, and none disputed him.

"Nyamurairi built a big home with a fire pit inside, in which there were always flaming embers. The High God understood it was important that he should be the only one to possess fire, since anyone else who did so could also claim dominion over the world, or at least a big part of it. The fire had to be guarded and kept away from anyone else, so the god chose one of the most clever of animals, the dog, Rúkuba, (who was also the first Basenji) to guard the fire.

Rúkuba did not want to be a sentry, however, and would rather have roamed the forests, or run over the plains, or perhaps hunted and explored. He really wanted to live a life of comfort and freedom instead of being forced to eternally guard the fire in the god's home. The god Nyamurairi's will was strong, however, and he would not be denied. Rúkuba did try to run away to avoid being forced into being a sentinel for the fire, but you can't really hide from a god and, after a long, hard chase, Nyamurairi captured the dog, and used a strong rope to bind him to the door post of his home.

"Nyamurairi stood before Rúkuba and threatened him, 'If you will not serve as my sentry willingly, then you will guard my fire as a slave. If anything happens to the fire, or if anyone steals any of the fire, you will be severely punished.'

"Nyamurairi then went about his work, and mostly ignored the dog, feeding him but showing him no friendliness or warmth. The god was still angry at the effort he had been forced to make to capture the runaway dog, and often expressed this by kicking the dog if he got in the way. Almost every day he reminded Rúkuba that the dog's safety — and even his life — depended on no one ever getting any of the fire.

"This went on for many years, until a certain man named Nkhángo went into the forest looking for honey. He wandered through the cold, damp morning, and came upon the dwelling of Nyamurairi. The old god was out some place else doing the work that gods do, and Rúkuba was tied to the door post, looking very sad and forlorn.

"Nkhángo walked up to Rúkuba, and said 'You are such a beautiful animal, why do you look so sad?' and he stroked him gently.

"The way the man patted him, scratched his ears, and gently stroked him, made Rúkuba feel good (remember that Nyamurairi never showed him any affection or fondness), and he said to Nkhángo, 'I am sad because I have been tied to the door of this house to guard the fire.'

"Nkhángo asked, 'What is fire?'

"Rúkuba moved aside and said, 'Step inside and you will see.'

"Nkhángo entered the house and was amazed. The fire made him warm, and took away the morning chill. Even better, the fire lit the inside of the house, making it bright and cheerful. Nkhángo could also imagine how fire could dispel the darkness of night, making life safer, since it would then be difficult for evil things to sneak up on people unnoticed. 'Oh, what a wondrous thing this is. In my village there is no such thing as fire. My friend, please help me and steal a little fire for me. If you do and then come with me, I will take care of you forever.'

"Rúkuba said, 'Friendship is a good thing, and I'm tired of being a slave. Free me, and I will get some of the fire for you, and then we may sit and warm ourselves in front of it after you have brought the fire into your home.'

"Nkhángo untied Rúkuba, and the dog ran to the fire pit and grabbed a long, large stick with flame at one end, and the two of them ran back through the forest with it to Nkhángo's village. Once they reached his home, Nkhángo brought the fire to the headman, Iterere. The headman watched the fire burn, and felt it spread welcome warmth through his old body.

"Rúkuba then spoke. 'If you want to keep this fire you must share it with everybody. If only one person or just a few people have fire, then the god Nyamurairi can come and strike them down and steal back the fire. But if everyone has fire, the god will see that it can no longer be his alone, and it can no

Gods, ghosts, and black dogs

longer be taken back and again become his exclusive property.

"Iterere recognized that what Rúkuba was saying was truly wise, 'This fire is a good thing,' he said, 'and as you suggest, we must share it with everyone. Quickly, before the god comes to take the fire back, I want every house in the village to dig a fire pit and put fuel in it. We will light each one as soon as they are ready. The people will now have fire to warm and light their homes. Also, we must send runners with lit torches to all of the other villages, and have their chiefs distribute the fire among their people. Then, if all men have fire, the old god can never again try to hoard it for himself.'

"By the time that Nyamurairi returned home, all men had fire. Nyamurairi assumed that some human had managed to steal a bit of it, and either Rúkuba had gone off to chase him, or the dog had used the opportunity to run away. In any event it would do him no good to go after either the fire or the dog. The possession of fire was now too widespread for it to be possible to reclaim it. In truth, the dog only had value to the god as a guard for his fire, and now that a guard was not needed, the animal no longer mattered to him. Furthermore, Nyamurairi had important work to do now: set about laying plans to ensure that he could still remain as High God, which would be a difficult task once the other gods learned that he was no longer the only one who had fire.

"Nkhángo respected his bargain with the dog, and provided him with food, shelter, pleasant company, and, of course, a place to lie and sleep in front of the warm fire. In turn, Rúkuba was more than just a friend. For example, he now guarded the home of Nkhángo as a loyal companion, not a slave.

"One day Nkhángo said to his friend that he was going into the forest to seek honey, and Rúkuba went along with him. Suddenly, they heard a clamour in the bush, and then they saw wild boar. One man with his spear is not a good match against a wild boar, and Nkhángo would have tried to escape. However, Rúkuba went after the big animal, and seized it from behind, and while the great beast was distracted, Nkhángo was able to get close enough to kill it.

"'You are nearly a man! Your skill and

cleverness allowed me to finish this hunt as easily as if I had been with another human who also had a spear to help me kill the boar,' said Nkhángo.

"'It is you who are a man,' said Rúkuba, 'a man whom I have chosen to help, as a friend.' Nkhángo then cut off a fresh strip of meat and gave it to the dog as a reward, and this is the way in which the dog became a hunting companion of men.

"It seemed as if Rúkuba displayed new skills and abilities each day, and Nkhángo continuously regaled the headman with stories about what his dog could do. Soon, Nkhángo's exuberance about his companion's cleverness led Iterere to decide that the villagers could trust the dog's intelligence enough to use Rúkuba as a messenger. However, the dog did not want to be a messenger. He lay by the fire and thought to himself, 'I have a right to lie by this fire, because I brought it to men. For this and for my hunting skills, men owe me their friendship. I do not wish to be a slave again, to act only at the whim of some master. Now it appears that men will always be sending me here and there, taking messages and going on errands.' He thought to himself, 'All of this is happening because I can speak. If I couldn't speak, I could not be a messenger. So I know the solution to my problem, I will never speak again,' and from that day to this, the dog of the Nyanga people, the Basenji, has been barkless."

I laughed and said, "That is a pleasant little myth. But, you know, Ashron may have been more correct than you think — not about the gods, perhaps, but about the fact that it was the Basenji's own decision which resulted in him not barking. I was reading some recent research reporting the results of investigations in which scientists have been trying to determine why the Basenji does not bark. The researchers have conducted some detailed studies, which have included a number of autopsies and some careful microscopic examination of the sound-producing mechanisms in the Basenji. Their experiments also involved scans of the neurological connections from the dog's brain to his vocal cords. These scientists have found that the Basenji seems to possess a normal canine larynx, and there is apparently nothing neurologically different in the connections to the Basenji voice box that might make it different from any other breed of dog. When the scientists published their results, their conclusion was that it seemed the Basenji is, in fact, capable of barking, but apparently chooses not to do so.

"It does cause one to wonder a bit. The story says that the first Basenji, Rúkuba, chose not to bark so that he would not be forced to perform errands that would take him away from his warm, comfortable spot in front of the fire. Perhaps following the lead of their clever ancestor, the Basenjis of today have also simply taken a vow of silence."

Ilo, who had been lying comfortably at Josette's feet, looked up at me with his dark eyes, but did not offer any comment; nor did he say anything to suggest that he disagreed with my conclusion.

Visit Hubble and Hattie on the web: www.hubbleandhattie.com
www.hubbleandhattie.blogspot.co.uk
• Details of all books • Special offers • Newsletter • New book news

113

The fastest dog
in the world

I was travelling by car from Philadelphia to San Francisco, and had stopped in Chicago to drop off a package that my mother was sending to a cousin we hadn't seen in a while. My cousin, Fred, was an editor and author who worked for a trade magazine, although I no longer remember which industry was involved. He invited me to spend the weekend with his family at a little cottage they owned in Wisconsin, which he said overlooked a lake. The countryside was beautiful at that time of year, he told me, and, since I was not bound to any particular schedule, I agreed to stay.

After we had arrived, and settled in, Fred placed a bottle of beer in my hand, and asked me to follow him outside to take a look around. He particularly wanted me to look at some of the trees in the surrounding woods. "You've got to see the size of these things," he said, "they are just amazing."

I am not very knowledgeable about trees, and I only remember that these were some kind of evergreen, maybe a cedar or a fir, but I do recall that some of them were huge. Fred pointed to one of them, and said, "Four of us (me, my wife, and the two kids) tried to circle that tree while touching each other's hands, and there was still a gap. It is just one big, fat tree."

He took a swallow from his bottle of beer, looked up at the tree, and began musing out loud. "If you live in a place long enough you can't help but pick up bits of the lore of the region. I look at that huge tree and it starts me thinking that it was big trees like that which just about forced the loggers up around the Great Lakes to come up with some kind of folk hero. I think that, as a psychologist, you should appreciate that they might have an emotional need to imagine a logger like themselves, who was so gigantic that he could actually handle trees as large as this all by himself. So, to satisfy that need, they created Paul Bunyan."

Fred walked over to a nearby fallen log and sat down. He tilted his head back and took a deep breath, and the tone of his voice and the cadence of his speech changed. I have observed this happen hundreds of times, when people are about to launch into the telling of a story. Which he did.

"The people needed a big folk hero to handle

big timber, and Paul Bunyan was certainly large. Paul was so big that, when he was born, it took five giant storks, working overtime, to deliver him to his parents. When he was still a infant, they had to use a lumber wagon drawn by a team of oxen as a baby carriage for him. But then he grew up become really immense. For example, Paul was so big that they had to use wagon wheels for the buttons on his shirt. They say that, one time, after a hard day's work, Paul was feeling tired, and as he walked home he left his giant axe drag behind on the ground. You can still see the mark that the axe left — most folks call that the Grand Canyon. Another time, Paul started a campfire, which began to get a little out a hand since he had made it larger than he really needed. Paul didn't want that fire to damage anything, so he decided to pile some rocks on top of it to put it out. You can still see that pile of rocks — most folk call that Mount Hood.

"Those storytelling loggers gave Paul Bunyan some big, impressive companions as well, the most famous of which was Babe the Blue Ox. Some say that Babe grew so fast it seemed that every time Paul looked at her she was a little bigger, and this finally got to be a problem, since Paul was running into difficulty finding watering holes large enough for Babe to drink from. So he set to work to scoop out some big watering holes for his pet, and you can still see those watering holes — most people call them the Great Lakes. They also tell stories about how the 10,000 Lakes of Minnesota were formed from the footprints of Paul and Babe as they wandered around blindly during a big blizzard one winter.

"There are some people who feel that Paul Bunyan was just a literary invention by a north Michigan journalist named James MacGillivray, and was later popularised in some ad campaign for a logging company. But MacGillivray insisted he was simply retelling snippets of folk tales that circulated among lumberjacks here in the north central region of America, and up into eastern Canada. My wife's grandfather was a trucker who worked for one of the logging companies in 1910 — or maybe it was 1915 — anyway, sometime around then, so he spent a lot of nights with the loggers. As he remembers it, Paul Bunyan was at the centre of an awful lot of

the tales told in the camps back then. Paul Bunyan's exploits seemed to be told in every cedar camp, every fir camp, and every white pine logging camp in northern Minnesota, and each camp had its own set of stories. You have to understand that those old-time lumberjacks were rovers who tended to travel from camp to camp, always looking for those which had work available. So, as these guys went from one place to another, it made sense that they carried their stories with them. My wife's grandfather used to paint an image of big men, swapping yarns in the long, winter evenings, their socks hanging over the edge of a hot sheet iron stove to dry."

I looked at the big tree, feeling the need to contribute something to the conversation, so I said, "You know, I never thought about the fact that living around big trees would probably make you want to have big men as your folk heroes. However, it makes a lot of sense. I guess that the best folk heroes are those which are not blessed by magical abilities, but rather have the qualities that all of us common people have, only to a greater degree. So obviously loggers will tend to fashion tales of giant, powerful loggers. Now, because of my somewhat distorted mind, this sets me to wondering what type of folk tales dogs might create if they had the language ability to spin out stories.

"I think that, if they could tell tales, dogs would not be so concerned with size, or strength, so I don't think that there would be a giant canine folk hero. In my head, when I try to picture dogs sitting around the campfire, I imagine that they would be concerned about a dog hero who had a great nose that could sniff out anything, and I bet that very good ears would be something that doggy storytellers would also prize.

"To my mind, the canine equivalent of Paul Bunyan would be a very special dog that I once heard about named Sensilis. Now, Sensilis was big, nowhere near as big as Paul Bunyan or Babe the Blue Ox, but bigger than most dogs, a great white dog, with large, pricked ears, and a wide, black nose. It was not the size of his ears and nose which was important, however, but their sensitivity. Sensilis used to live in the far north, where all of the white dogs come from, although he had to move to the south, because his ears were so sensitive that the falling flakes of snow sounded like such a clatter to him that he couldn't sleep at night. So he moved to the south — the far south — to one of those dry states where the rain doesn't fall very often, and it never snows.

"Because the skies were clear, Sensilis could sit outside at night and look up at the sky. He liked to listen to the sounds that the stars made, some of which he thought were very musical, and he would sometimes sing along with them in a melodious series of howls, which made such a fine tune that the desert snakes would wish for legs so that they could dance to it. Sensilis' nose was so sensitive that, even if he was indoors; even if all of the shutters were closed and the curtains drawn, he could tell whether it was day or night simply because the sun and the moon smelled different to him.

"Sensilis ultimately got to use that nose in a unique way when he was hired by Allan Pinkerton, the first great private detective in North America. Pinkerton discovered that Sensilis could sniff trouble coming a day before it arrived, and could smell the difference between honest and dishonest thoughts, so he hired Sensilis, and that great white dog became the first police dog in the world."

My cousin laughed and said, "Well, I don't know what kind of folk tales dogs would tell, but I do know that, sometimes, when people are telling stories about Paul Bunyan, they do mention that he had a dog. As I heard it told, this was a big, black-and-white dog who started out with the name 'Sport,' but who eventually came to be known as 'Sport the Reversible Dog.' Of course, it shouldn't be a surprise to find that Paul Bunyan's dog was large — actually, Sport was very, very big — and Paul Bunyan liked to explain that the reason for Sport's large size was because the dog was part wolf and part elephant hound. And it was not just his genetic heritage that made him large, but also the fact that he was raised on bear milk.

"Sport's life started out as normal as could be expected for a dog of his size, but a certain event changed his life forever. When he was quite young, Sport was playing around in the horse stable. It was night, and when Paul entered the stable he saw some

movement in the back of the barn. Now, Paul Bunyan was strong and clever, but he tended to be on the impulsive side, and often acted without thinking, especially when he had had a drink or two, as he had that evening. Seeing a flicker of movement in the back of the barn, Paul thought that it might be a rat. Paul really did not like rodents, so he threw an axe at him. The axe cut Sport in half, right at his waist. When Paul saw what he had done he quickly stuck the two halves of Sport together, making sure that they stayed in place by using tree climbing spikes, and then bandaged him up. But that same darkness (and maybe the same alcohol) that had caused Paul to mistake his own dog for a rat, caused him to make a major mistake. In his hurry to save his dog's life he didn't stop to light a lantern, and so missed the fact that he had twisted the two halves of his dog, which meant that Sport's hind legs now pointed straight up instead of down. When the morning came, Paul saw his error, but it was too late to correct it since Sport not only grew fast, but healed fast also. Despite the strange orientation that his legs now had, with Paul's careful nursing, Sport had soon completely recovered.

"But what about Sport's mismatched legs? Well, Paul Bunyan's dog was not only big and strong, but also clever and persistent, and it occurred to Sport that having legs pointing both up and down gave him an advantage. Sport soon learned that he could run on one pair of legs for a while, and then flop over, and, without any loss of speed, run on the other pair! Because he could alternate his legs at any time, Sport never got tired, and anything that he ran after he eventually caught. In a long distance race he could run down anything.

"Then, one day, Sport disappeared from Paul Bunyan's logging camp. Apparently, Paul and the other loggers were sitting around one morning having breakfast, and someone asked him just how fast Sport could run. Paul Bunyan insisted that Sport could run almost as fast as the wind. Although Paul was trying to complement his dog, in Sport's mind, to say that he could run *almost* as fast as the wind was an underestimation of his true speed, since *he* believed he could run faster than the wind. To prove this, the dog set off to race the winter wind which was coming from the north. Sport disappeared over the horizon, and Paul never saw him again.

"There are reports that Sport just kept running, and since that wind didn't stop, neither did Sport. There are those who claim that Sport has circled the world thousands of times in his endless race with the wind. According to some, on a windy day you can sometimes catch a little glint, a flash of black and white whizzing past on currents of air, which they say is Sport, racing past, on one set of legs or another, trying to get ahead of the wind."

As if to punctuate the story, a gust of wind came up at just that moment, setting small leaves and twigs chasing each other across the ground. My cousin motioned for us to start heading back toward the house. As we came inside, I looked back at the big tree and asked, "Does that tree have a name?"

"Do you mean a name for the kind of tree that it is?" he replied.

"No, I mean a personal name, like Maximilian, or Cedric, or Arthur. Something as big and majestic as that tree should really have a name – a big-sounding name."

Fred pondered for a moment, "I had never thought of that. Paul, perhaps ...?"

The dog philosophers

It was a hot afternoon in Hutto, Texas, a small town located about a half-hour or so away from the capital of Texas, Austin, and I was there for a conference sponsored by the International Association of Canine Professionals. As is typical of such meetings, the day was filled with a number of talks about the science and practice of training dogs. I had given a presentation on the intelligence of dogs which had caused a bit of a stir and lots of conversation, and a number of conference participants (most of whom were dog trainers) had come over to me afterwards to talk about the topic, and give me some of their own observations.

When we got back to the motel late in the afternoon we were all tired, but still brimming over with information from the conference. It was way too early to consider going to dinner, and one of the people in the small group that I returned with suggested we get together at one of the tables out near the pool. She offered to provide some wine if the rest of us could find some glasses and snacks (and maybe some additional wine) to accompany it. A quarter of an hour later, the five of us reassembled at an outside table, which now held three bottles of wine, a bunch of heavy hotel bathroom glasses, and a variety of cellophane bags containing pretzels, nuts, and a few other salty treats.

Since I was carrying a pocket knife with a corkscrew attachment I had the task of opening the wine, after which someone else filled the glasses. We were just five people who worked with dogs gathering together socially. One of them, a dog trainer from Chicago, turned to me, sipped his wine, and said, "I liked what you said about dogs, and the idea that they are actually smarter than we tend to give them credit for. Obviously, dogs show their intelligence in a lot of different ways, such as when they become service dogs, assistance dogs, search and rescue dogs, performing dogs, and all that. But, tell me: if dogs are really so intelligent why don't we have philosopher dogs?"

Someone laughed, and said, "I don't know about dog philosophers, but I had an uncle who swore he had a dog who worried about certain questions that might be of a philosophical nature. The dog was a Basset Hound, and she loved to watch and listen to his daughter when she practiced on the violin. Sometimes, the dog would even disrupt the practice session by trying to sing along. At the end of each practice, when the girl put away her instrument, that old hound would sit there staring and sniffing at the violin case. My uncle swore that she was pondering the great philosophical question of 'Where does the music go when the fiddle is put in the box?'"

Another one of the group splashed some more wine into his glass and mused, "Dogs are not great philosophers, although when I was growing up there were some old storytellers who used to assure us that some dogs were born to be philosophers, and spent all of their lives thinking deep thoughts about their world, and pondering about what goes on in the human world.

"Let me tell you about an old man I met who lived in Richmond, Virginia, who had a fondness for hounds. He was a friend of my father's, who worked in the field of construction — building things all his life. When he was younger he helped build skyscrapers and bridges, and later on, when he was no longer agile enough to 'work the high steel,' or haul concrete, he changed his profession. He still worked with his hands, but now he spent his time making fancy cabinets for rich people's homes.

"Still, he had no regrets. He had earned an honest wage, and managed to save enough money to buy a tiny little house to retire to. It had a patio at the back, with space for reclining lawn chairs for him and his wife, and lots of space for his big, old Black and Tan Coonhound to sleep away the sunny afternoons while the man worked on odd jobs around the house. With his skill as a craftsman, he renovated the house, built new wooden fences and gates, hung a hammock in the back yard, built a brick barbecue, and fabricated a slew of other things to make their lives comfortable.

"One afternoon I visited him. I was sitting out on the patio with the old man when his eldest son dropped by to visit him. We were drinking beer from stubby-necked brown bottles, and talking about life, dogs, and philosophy of a sort. The old man motioned toward the dog lying at his feet, and said, 'Now, his daddy was a philosopher, and a great observer of human beings. You see, I worked all of my life using these hands of mine to hold tools and to shape things, and that dog would watch me doing whatever it was that I was working at. I could feel him analyzing my behaviour. Every time I picked up a tool I could feel that dog's eyes on me, and could almost hear the words in his mind, 'What cunning hands. How well they work the wood. Look at how they cut the leather or shape and twist and weave fibres to make ropes, and even my leash and collar. Ah, but those hands don't just work with soft things — those hands can work metal. Those hands grind iron, weld bronze and steel, smooth and shape concrete and reinforce it with metal rods to make bridges, buildings, dams, and breakwaters. Those hands can also be used to make bigger hands, mechanical hands, like giant claws and heavy hammers which work like hands, and also all kinds of diggers, haulers, derricks, and pile drivers. After all, what are the clamps of the big steam shovel if not just a man's hands made bigger and stronger?' Yes, it appeared to me that that dog's deep brown eyes were always wide with wonder, and he seemed to love to watch me working.

"'Then, one afternoon, after a whole lot of years of watching me, my old hound lay down to take a nap and just didn't wake up. It saddened me to think that his doggie philosopher's mind had closed down, maybe without ever finding any real answers to the questions he had pondered through his life. It was heartbreaking for me. However, that night, I had a dream which made me believe that maybe my dog's philosophizing had reached a final conclusion. In my dream, my old dog entered heaven, and was ushered to the foot of the throne of God Almighty. God spoke to him, and asked, "Tell me, since you are a philosopher dog, what gift should I have given to you, and all other dogs, to make your lives more perfect and productive?" And my dog, my old dog, stood proudly, the way that he always did in life, and said, "My beloved God, it really would've helped if you had given me thumbs."'"

There were some gentle chuckles, and then one of the group turned to me and said, "So, no doubt with your expertise about canine intelligence, you will have some kind of story about a philosophical dog?"

It was not the day or time to rummage

Gods, ghosts, and black dogs

through scientific facts to find a reasonable body of data that might answer the question, so, instead, I responded in the spirit of the conversation flowing around me. "Well, I really believe that all dogs are philosophers in one way or another – the sort of down-home, folksy kind of philosophers that we all love. Now, if someone will refill my glass of wine, and if the rest of you will allow me a little leeway, I will tell you about one such canine philosopher. I suppose that I heard this story in bits and pieces, and later it came together in my mind like a mental jigsaw puzzle – not in a dream, but a hypnagogic state [that state of reverie which is like a dream, and happens right before you fall asleep]."

There was a faint clink and a glugging noise as someone poured red wine into my glass. I picked it up, took a sip, and said, "Let me tell you this story the way that I see and hear it in my mind before I drift off to sleep on some nights.

"The philosopher in question was just a hound, sort of brown or tan, a common, doggy, forgettable colour. She had long, floppy hound ears, and a big, wide hound nose, and when called upon she worked diligently to find rabbits, and occasionally a deer. She was a responsible dog, and she gave a full measure of effort to accomplish whatever task she was given, so it was not surprising that she also worked really hard at being a good mother. Because of her efforts, her first litter of puppies had gone to their new homes well-educated: knowing how to bark, when to bark, when not to bark, when to wag a tail, where to sniff for rabbits, how to chase balls, and how to read the vast number of signals that human beings send out to their dogs. But the new litter of puppies that she was now caring for contained one pup whose mind was different. The puppy had a white tip on the end of his tail, and a white, star-shaped blaze on his forehead, and he asked strange questions, questions that forced his dam to ponder; questions that made her think very hard indeed.

"She was a clever dog, and the answers that she knew best had to do with the way that dogs and people behave. Those are, after all, the questions that dogs must answer for themselves in order to get along in the world – a world that consists of not just

other dogs but also people. Yet this puppy with the white tip at the end of his tail, and the star-shaped blaze was different. His questions were not about what people and dogs do, but rather how people and dogs are put together, and what they are made of. Unfortunately, the answer to questions about what things are composed of, or how they come to be, requires information that comes from what humans call 'science,' and dogs really don't 'do' science.

"But the puppy was very insistent, and again this morning he repeated the question that had been bothering him: 'What are people made of?' Now, what kind of question is that for a dog to ask? His mother wandered out of the house and stood in the yard.

"She lived on a small farm, just a mile or two from the edge of town. It was spring, the sun was shining, and new shoots of grass were poking their way out of the ground. 'What are people made of?' Her head was starting to hurt as she tried to deal with the question, so she absentmindedly nibbled on the tip of a piece of grass, and gazed at the field of oats beside the house.

"It was then that she had a flash of inspiration. Maybe people were made of grass? And, actually, when you thought about it, all flesh was grass, because it was out of the grasslands that people took their meat and milk, and all of the other things they needed to survive. Whenever there was a rich banquet, if you looked hard enough, you could see that it originated from grass. After all, there were so many grass families: wheat and oats and rye to make the bread, and the porridge that her human family seemed to sustain itself on. There was hay and alfalfa for the cattle, and that was turned into milk and cheese and meat. There was corn, which not only made flour and fine griddle cakes, but also fed the chickens, who then produced the eggs, and eventually became another kind of meat that humans loved so much. And there was the clover which attracted bees who made the honey ...

"Her reverie about what humans were really made of was disturbed when another dog came down the road, and paused by the open gate: a newcomer she had not seen before. He greeted her with a civil wag of his tail, looked toward the distant town, then back at her and asked, 'What kind of people live around here?'

"Now, this was the kind of question that she was happy to deal with. It had to do with the way that humans and dogs acted, and how to predict what would happen if a dog did this or that in front of a human or another dog. So she stood up, gave a courteous, acknowledging wag of her tail and a shake of her head, which caused her long ears to give a little flap, and asked, 'Well, stranger, what kind of humans were there in the country you come from?'

"'You might describe them mostly as a mean, selfish, hard group of folks, who would kick a dog out of the way, and not give a leftover scrap of bread to a hungry hound, even if they weren't going to ever eat it themselves.'

"'To tell the truth, I guess, stranger, that that's about the kind of people you'll find around here.'

"The stranger gave a sigh and moved on. She watched as the dog slowly walked toward the town. He had just about blended into the dusty background when another newcomer arrived at her gate. He sat down after giving a well-mannered greeting, and asked, 'What kind of people live around here?'

"'Well, stranger, what kind of people were there in the country you come from?'

"'I would describe them as mostly decent, hard-working, friendly and caring folks. If a dog needed something, there was always someone who would put out a bowl of water and toss him a crust of bread.'

"'Well, I guess, stranger, that that's just about the kind of people you'll find around here,' she replied.

"The newcomer stood up, gave a friendly salute with his tail, and moved off down the road in the direction of town. She watched him go, and thought to herself, 'Now, those kind of questions, about how people act around dogs, I can answer. But a question like, "What are people made of?" is much harder. Still, I do think I have come up with the answer. Humans are made of grass. Whenever people break bread together, or eat it alone, it is grass that is giving them life. I think that this is an answer which will work for my puppy. Of course, like all proper philosophical answers, it does raise some new

questions of its own. Like, if I am correct, why don't people begin each meal with a prayer that goes, 'Give us this day our daily grass?'"

With that, I lifted my glass of wine as if offering a toast at the beginning of a meal, and the person next to me tapped my glass with hers. I was taking another sip of my wine, when, from across the table, another one of my associates entered the conversation, saying, "Well, historically, there is a real candidate who we might count as a dog philosopher, even if some of the people who knew him would have insisted he was human. He was one of Plato's contemporaries, and named Diogenes. I think that most folks remember him as the philosopher who wandered the world with a lamp, claiming he was looking for an honest man. While Diogenes had some doubts about humans, he thought that dogs were extremely moral and intelligent, and even adopted the nickname 'Cyon,' which means 'dog,' for himself. The people who came to spread his philosophy called themselves "Cynics" although, as we all know, that label no longer carries much of a vestige of dogginess, the way we use it today. I've been told that, when Diogenes died, the people of Athens raised a great marble pillar in his memory, on top of twhich was the image of a dog. Beneath the dog was a long inscription that began with the following snippet of conversation, which, as I remember, went something like this –

'Say, Dog, I pray, what do you guard in that tomb?

'A dog
'His name?
'Diogenes'

"Now, I would not be so crass as to doubt the word of Diogenes. After all, his own intelligence and wit were so impressive that Alexander the Great, after meeting Diogenes in Corinth, went away saying, 'If I were not Alexander, I should wish to be Diogenes.' So, if he insisted that he was a dog, who are we to contradict him? And if we allow his statement to stand, then isn't this proof that there was at least one dog philosopher?"

The afternoon was warm, with the sun

Gods, ghosts, and black dogs

dropping slowly toward the horizon. Certainly, the sun was going down at a much slower rate than was the wine in the bottles on the table. For all our attempts at exploring the possibility that dogs could be sage thinkers, capable of deep intellectual analysis, we had not reached any definitive conclusions about the reality of dog philosophers, or the philosophy of dogs. Still, we were not bothered by this outcome since both the wine and the company were good, and we all understood that no philosophical discussion ever seems to end in a universally accepted conclusion.

Visit Hubble and Hattie on the web: www.hubbleandhattie.com
www.hubbleandhattie.blogspot.co.uk
• Details of all books • Special offers • Newsletter • New book news

The Devil and the seeing-eye dog

Religious writings and traditions are a rich source of folklore and mythology of all sorts; the great collections of myths we have gathered from places like ancient Egypt, Rome, Greece, and Scandinavia, were once part of religious doctrine, which means that there was a time when people actually believed that the Norse Thunder God, Thor, really did take his mighty hammer, Mjollnir, and go off to Jotunheim to fight the frost giants. I am sure that for most Christians, the idea of the Buddha riding a celestial lion through the skies sounds like a myth or a fairytale, while for Buddhists, the idea of Moses raising his staff and parting the Red Sea must seem like an equally incredible piece of folklore. Yet, each religion's collection of tales forms part of its dogma, used to justify current actions, teach moral lessons, explain events, or place restrictions on or serve as guidelines for daily behaviour. What this means, of course, is that these particular stories can have an influence that goes well beyond the simple entertainment value of a typical, non-religious tall tale or a bit of folklore. Every now and then the influence of these tales can be seen when their effects pop up in the news.

My attention was caught by an article in the *Reading Evening Mail* which described how George Herridge, a 71-year-old, blind Englishman and cancer sufferer, was forced to get off a bus. The incident was triggered by what was described by other commuters present as the 'hysterical reaction to his seeing-eye dog' by some Muslim passengers. Certainly in early Islamic tradition, as well as in early Judaism and Christianity, dogs were generally considered to be unclean. The stigma that dogs carried originated from the scavenging pariah dogs who roamed the cities and its outskirts, surviving on garbage discarded by the residents. Packs of these dogs were a major problem in many Islamic centres, as they carried rabies and various other diseases, and often could be quite vicious and aggressive towards humans.

However, at the same time it was recognized that the scavenging of these pariahs provided an important function. Thus, Xavier Marmier wrote in the mid-nineteenth century that "... disagreeable as these animals may be, in the State of Constantinople they are practically a necessary evil. Rectifying the lack of foresight of the city police, they cleanse the streets

Gods, ghosts, and black dogs

of a great quantity of matter which otherwise would putrefy and fill the air with pestilential germs."

The newspaper story that I read was concerned with an incident that occurred in modern England, where there are no pariah dogs, of course, and the dog in question was a calm Labrador Retriever under complete control, working as a service dog to assist a blind man.

Probably because I am a psychologist and a researcher, my curiosity about this event would not let me simply dismiss it from my mind. There had to be some reason – or at least some sort of religious doctrine – that accounted for the intensity of the emotional response of these Muslims toward the dog, and I wondered whether there was some kind of story, if not in the Koran itself, perhaps in some of the other traditional religious writings used by believers of Islam. Thus it was that this story from the English press was still on my mind when I attended a university function a short time later. Across the room I noticed a professor I had spoken with a number of times, who was an expert in Islamic matters. I wandered over to him, and, after we greeted one another, I described the newspaper report, and asked him about the relationship between dogs and Islam.

He sighed and glanced upward, then explained, "Muslim beliefs about dogs are sometimes confusing and contradictory. The majority of both Sunni and Shi'a Muslim religious scholars consider dogs to be ritually unclean, but these beliefs are not unanimous. There is a lot of disagreement about religious matters among the various Islamic sects, in much the same way that you would find disagreements between Catholics and Protestants in Christianity over many matters of belief, even though both groups claim to be Christians and claim to have the same basic underlying religion. The religious jurists from the Sunni Maliki School disagree with the idea that dogs are unclean, and those of the Sunni Hanafi School are ambiguous, allowing trade and care of dogs without religious consequences. However, all of these opinions are based, not on the Koran itself, but on the Hadith, which are not basic holy writings but, rather, a traditional compendium of commentaries, analyses, and interpretations of

the Koran. It is these Hadith which suggest that to be touched by a dog is to be defiled, and requires an act of purification. For instance, according to the Hadith, a bowl from which a dog has eaten or drunk must be washed seven times, and scrubbed in earth before it is again fit for human use.

"If we look directly at the Koran itself, it turns out that dogs are mentioned five times, and are never described as unclean there. In fact, the longest group of passages involving a dog is quite positive, and relates to the story of the Seven Sleepers. As the chronicle goes, during the short reign of the Roman emperor Decius in around AD 250, non-believers were systematically persecuted in an effort to strengthen the state-supported religion. In the city of Ephesus (now in western Turkey), seven faithful young men fled to a cave on Mount Coelius to avoid being tortured or killed because of their beliefs. The pet dog of one followed them in their flight. Once in the cave, some of the men feared that the dog – Kitmir by name – might bark and reveal their hiding place, so in their state of fear they tried to drive away the dog. At this point, God granted the dog the gift of speech, and he said, 'I love those who are dear unto God. Go to sleep, therefore, and I will guard you.' After the men then settled down to sleep, leaning on the back wall of the cave, the dog stretched out with his forelegs facing the entrance and began his watch.

"When Decius learned that religious refugees were hiding in some of the local caves, he ordered that all those cave entrances be sealed with stone. Kitmir maintained his silent vigil, standing watch and making sure that no one disturbed the sleepers. You know the story of Rip van Winkle who, according to the American folk tale slept for 20 years, well, that was the equivalent of an afternoon nap compared to what happened to the men in that mountain cave. These seven young men were clearly entranced, and they slept through all of the commotion involved with the sealing of the cave. Time passed and the men were forgotten. Still the men slept, while the dutiful dog, Kitmir, stood guard until a total of 309 years had gone by. When the sleepers were finally awakened by workers excavating a section of the mountain, the dog finally stirred, and allowed his charges to return to the world. He could do this because the world which these devout men would go out into now was finally safe for their faith. According to Moslem tradition, the faithful dog, Kitmir, was admitted to paradise upon his death.

"Certainly, an unclean animal would not be admitted to paradise," the professor commented. "There is another passage, however, that is often misinterpreted when the religious jurists who wrote the Hadith note that Mohamed once gave an order to 'Kill all dogs.'

"This command of the prophet resulted from an historical incident, where the Governor of Medina was concerned about the number of stray dogs overrunning the city. They had become a major health issue because the number of cases of rabies (which, at that time, was an incurable and always fatal disease) was rising so quickly, and the disease was clearly caused by the pariah dogs foraging through the garbage. At first, Mohammed took the uncompromising position that all the dogs in the realms under his control should be exterminated, and thus issued his command to exterminate all canines. After reflecting upon his decision, the next day, however, he mitigated his decree. He did this for two major reasons. The first was religious – namely that dogs constituted a race of Allah's creatures, and He who created the race should be the only one to dictate that it should be removed from the earth. The second was more pragmatic. The Prophet observed that some categories of dogs, particularly guard dogs, hunting dogs, and shepherd dogs, were useful to humans, and had hence earned their right to exist."

The Islamic professor smiled, took a sip of tea from his cup, and added, "Some scholars suggest that some personal aspects may have influenced Mohamed's reconsideration of his order to kill all dogs. A number of legends and stories say that the Prophet himself actually owned one or more Salukis, who he used for hunting. It is said that he truly loved hunting, and had great respect and affection for these dogs, which seems to be supported by the fact that one passage in the Koran quite specifically says that any prey caught by dogs during a hunt can be eaten. No purification, other than the mention of Allah's name,

is required of it. In any event, it is clear that Mohamed cancelled his early ruling, and rescinded the death sentence against the canine race.

"Further evidence which goes against the idea that all dogs are unclean comes from another passage in the Koran, which tells a story about a prostitute who noticed a dog near a well. The dog was suffering from thirst, and was clearly near to death. The prostitute was moved by pity for the poor animal, and, taking off her shoe, dipped it into the well to allow the dog to drink water from it. Because of this act of kindness, Mohamed absolved her of all of her sins, and allowed her to enter paradise. I find it hard to imagine that if he really felt that all dogs were evil and were to be killed, he would bless that woman for saving a life that he had condemned.

"I personally believe that the reason the Hadiths condemn dogs originates from another historical source. If you look at the way that the history of religious movements works, it is often the case that the gods of the old religion are converted into the devils of any new religion. Similarly, those things prized by an old religion are often held up as objects of hysterical hatred by the new. This explains Christianity's relationship to goats. In ancient times, goats were revered, and their image found its way into virtually every Pagan religion's list of sacred animals. In addition, the most frequent symbol of male dominance was horns, usually those of a goat, but sometimes also those of a bull or ram. The newly-developing Christian religion thus became fixated upon any image with horns; horns became a symbol of paganism, which is why the Christian devil and most demons are shown with horns.

"In the case of Islam, one of the major religions standing in the way of its spread was Zoroastrianism, which was quite successful, and had many adherents in the Middle East. Dogs were prized by Zoroastrians, and treated with great affection and reverence. To my mind, the current Muslim attitude toward dogs fits into this category. It is simply the case that the sacred symbols of the old religion are treated as profane or unclean by the new one. Since the Zoroastrians loved dogs, to show one's devotion to Islam, one must despise dogs."

Gods, ghosts, and black dogs

He suddenly stopped in his narrative, as if he had had a thought. "Tell me more about that seeing-eye dog on the bus; specifically what colour it was."

"It was a black Labrador Retriever," I replied.

"That may explain part of it," he said. "While Mohamed rescinded the sentence of death for dogs who worked and had a useful function, he allowed it to stand for one class of dogs — namely, stray black dogs. The reason for this is that he believed the Devil often masquerades as a black dog. Perhaps that Muslim family's concern was not because of their belief of the unclean nature of dogs in general, but because of their fear that they were in close proximity to the Devil —in the guise of that particular black dog."

Why the dog has a black nose

It was a day on which I was doing some historical research using material from the reference section in the central branch of the Vancouver Public Library. I had been at my task for several hours, and, although I was finding much of the information I needed, I was getting a bit stiff, and felt the need for a cup of coffee and a chance to stretch my legs and move around a bit. There was a coffee shop that I am fond of about a block away from the library, and I thought that a short walk and some caffeine would be refreshing, allowing me to continue with my work. I was not in any particular hurry, so decided to leave the library via the lower level, where all the meeting rooms are. It's also an area where the library uses the walls to exhibit various types of art, and, as these presentations change several times each year, I wanted to see if there was a new display.

While I was looking at some of the brightly-coloured prints in the current art collection, and moving toward the exit, I heard my name called. As I turned to the source of the sound I saw someone I recognized from the campus of the University of British Columbia. He was wearing a white shirt but,

more noticeably, he also wore a beaded necklace with a round medallion made of porcupine quills, and tiny red-and-black beads. The medallion was distinctively fringed in white fur. I rummaged through my mind to try and recall his name, and retrieve some information about which programme or department he worked with, but all I could remember was that he was a native Indian, and a member of the Heiltsuk tribe which lives in and around the island village of Bella Bella in British Columbia.

He was standing in front of an open door. Behind him, in the meeting room, I could see a number of children, aged, perhaps, 8 to 12 years old. They were sitting around in a circle of chairs that seemed to be centred on a woman, who looked like she was of First Nations extraction; perhaps in her fifties or sixties. Her shoulders were draped in a bright red woollen cape decorated with sparkly bits: shells, beads, and bright buttons. When she turned, I could see that these shiny baubles traced out the traditional shape of the mythical Thunderbird.

The man greeted me, and reminded me that he had attended a talk I'd given. "I don't know if

Gods, ghosts, and black dogs

you remember, but, after your lecture, I came up and asked for some advice about a behaviour problem I was having with my Malamute Husky dog — separation anxiety, I thought. Anyway, I just wanted to thank you, because the advice you gave me worked like a charm, and the problem is completely gone."

I smiled, and said something about being glad my advice had been useful, and then I glanced into the room behind him and asked about what was happening there.

"It's a culture camp," he explained. "It's designed to teach the language and culture of First Nation bands to the kids, or anyone else who wants a little education about our heritage. Most typically, culture camps run a few days, maybe a week in length, and very often involve actually camping out. However, we've found that that kind of arrangement doesn't work very well for city kids, so, every now and then, we hold a sort of day camp for native kids who live in the city here, where they get to spend six or seven hours learning about their parents' traditions. The kids are just back from lunch, and we like to start the afternoon with a bit of storytelling. Actually, I think I heard the storyteller say that she was going to start off with a tale about dogs. Maybe you'd like to stay and listen?"

It doesn't take much persuading to get me to sit down and listen to folk tales, myths, or virtually any story about dogs, so I wandered into the room, quietly taking a seat at the rear so that I would not disturb the proceedings. The woman was just getting ready to start, and, like many storytellers, she began with a question.

"Did you ever wonder why dogs have black noses?" Several young voices called out "Yes!" in unison.

"Would you believe it if I told you that the reason that dogs have black noses might be related to the fact that dogs are always hungry and looking for food?" This time the voices answered with the majority shouting "No!"

"Would you like to know why dogs have black noses, at least according to the old storytellers of our tribe?" Again a number of young voices cried, "Yes!"

The woman adjusted her cape with a short sweeping motion that momentarily reminded me of a big bird settling comfortably on a branch and folding her wings. Then, in a husky voice, she began.

"When Father Sky and Mother Earth created the world, next, they created all of the animals, and, of course, people. Of all the living things, they felt the most love for human beings, to whom they had given many qualities which made them special. Humans had the ability to think, and the desire to love and learn. They also had hands that could shape works of art and clever tools. In addition, humans had been given the knowledge that the gods existed, and that Father Sky and Mother Earth should be honoured with prayer and the burning of medicine spices and sweet grass, and with singing and dancing, and the sound of drums.

"Yet, Father Sky and Mother Earth knew that humans were far from perfect. The laws of the universe are very clear, and cannot be broken, even by the gods. Every living thing can be given only so many gifts when they are created, so some animals are given great strength, swiftness, sharp claws, great teeth; others are given the ability to fly, or to swim and breathe under water; others receive the ability to hear faint sounds or see things from very far away, and so on. However, most of the gifts that human beings were given had to do with intelligence, feelings, with abilities to make things and to shape the world, to compose music, and to tell stories. With humans getting all of those gifts to make them smart and special, there really was no room left to give them the power and strength of animals such as bears, or the swiftness of the fox, or any of that sort of thing. So the great gods decided to give people a protector and a helpmate to make up for some of these missing talents, and chose to do so by creating the dog.

"As Mother Earth shaped the dog, she spoke the words of making, and thus gave the dog his special abilities, his form, and his tasks in life. 'You will be the companion of humans. I give you teeth to protect them and to help in the hunt. I give you swiftness beyond that of humans, so that you may run down the fastest of animals and catch them with those great teeth. I give you the ability to hear the faintest of sounds, and a loud voice so that you may bark warnings to the people you protect. I also give you a fine, pink nose so that you may smell the faintest of scents and follow them to find game and to explore the world. Because you will be poking your pink nose in many places, I will make the skin on it rough and tough like cured leather. This will protect it from harm, but will make it difficult to clean, so I give you a long tongue to help clean it.'

"Then Father Sky added his words of making to give the dog a purpose. 'You will use your sharp teeth, your fine ears and your loud bark to protect people and warn them of danger. To help humans hunt you will use your very keen, pink nose to find game, or anything else that might serve as meat or other food. To make sure that you always search for food which might help keep your human companions from starving, I give to you a strong appetite and desire to search for food and meat for both you and your human companions. Your desire for food will be second only to your desire to love, help and protect people.'

"It may well be the case that Father Sky did not think carefully enough about how his words might make the dog behave. It is true that, as the gods desired, dogs did happily choose to be the companion and protector of people, and to help them on the hunt. But the dog's perceptive pink nose, which could smell the faintest of scents, combined with his desire to find food, would occupy the dog for many hours of every day when he was not protecting people, or actually out hunting. This often helped people in the tribe — for example, when the dogs found where rabbits or birds were hiding — information which allowed hunters to catch these animals to provide meat to feed the tribe. As they wandered around the woods, the dogs would sometimes find bushes with berries, or trees where there was fruit that had fallen to the ground. The happy barking of the dogs who had found something to eat would attract the people, who could also then eat and stay healthy.

"Human beings began to prosper, and their desire to learn new things gave them more and more knowledge. In time, they learned how to make fire to keep themselves warm, and not long after this they discovered how to cook the food and meat they had brought back from successful hunting expeditions with their dogs. Soon, in front of every home there was a cooking fire, with pots of vegetables, and spits on which joints of meat were roasted and turned. As the meat cooked, the fat and juice would drip into the ashes of the fire below, and, long after the fire had been put out, and the fire pit had cooled, the ashes still smelled of the meat that had roasted above them. Although people might not have been able to smell it, this scent was very evident to the dog's sensitive pink nose, however, and that was the problem.

"Father Sky's words when he was making dogs had placed upon them the duty to seek and explore any scent that might signal the presence of something that could be food. For that reason, a dog could not simply walk through the village and pass by the cooking fires, since each of the fire pits in front of homes carried the smells of the meat that had been cooked there.

"When the dog first encountered the cool ashes of the previous night's cooking fire, his perceptive nose caught the scent of the meat juices. His nose told him that there could be food in those ashes, so he sniffed harder. Then he thought, 'Perhaps the meat is *under* the ashes,' so he poked his pink nose deeper into the dark ash, and continued to do this until he had convinced himself that nothing edible remained there.

"When the dog finally stopped exploring the vestiges of the previous night's cooking fire, his pink nose was covered with fine, black soot, so he used his long tongue to try and remove it, but the leathery surface of his nose was rough, and a simple lick could not get it really clean.

"The dog then moved on to another cooking fire, and again caught the scent of the previous night's roasted meat. Once more, he poked his nose through the ashes, and gathered more soot on its tip. The same thing happened each time the dog passed by a fire pit. You see, although the gods had given dog a very keen nose and the obligation to use it to search for food, they had not given the animals the intelligence that people have, so even though the dog had poked his nose through the ashes from many other cooking

Gods, ghosts, and black dogs

fires, and not found anything to eat in the remains, he did not learn that this was a fruitless search. Because of the task that Father Sky gave him, each time the dog found the faintest scent of food in an old cooking fire, it had to be explored – but there were so many fire pits to sniff ...

"As the dog wandered around the village, sniffing at the cooking places, despite his attempts to lick his nose clean, it became darker and darker, and soon that light pink nose had turned black: black enough that he could not clean it, no matter how much he licked with his long tongue. It was so black that, soon, even his puppies would come to be born with dark black, leathery noses.

"So, the next time you look at your dog's black nose, remember it is black because Father Sky gave dogs the purpose and the task of sniffing for food; not just for himself, but for you, as well. Perhaps you can reward your dog for carrying out his duties by giving him a treat now and then when he sniffs at you."

I chuckled to myself, waved goodbye to my acquaintance, and began to move toward the door. I had a lot of work yet to do, and still wanted that cup of coffee. I also knew that if she began another story I might just get caught up in it and want to stay longer. As I approached the door I heard her ask the children, "Do you know why it snows in the winter?"

I stopped. This was no good. If I left now I knew I would stay up all night wondering about how some Northwestern Indians explain the existence of snow. I slowly turned back toward my chair as her husky voice continued, "It has to do with the Raven. We all know that the Raven is a very clever bird, but sometimes he is too smart for his own good, and he gets into trouble . . ."

The language of dogs

It was a warm spring day, and I had been walking across the university campus when the arthritis in my hip began to act up. I hurt, and I felt creaky and old, so I found a bench to sit down on until the aching subsided. As I sat there watching the flow of students, it suddenly occurred to me that I really couldn't be all that old since I still appreciated how pretty the young college girls looked, and how warm and pleasant the sunshine was.

I was jolted out of my reverie when I heard somebody ask, "Mind if I sit down beside you?"

The question came from a colleague of mine, a Professor of Linguistics. We had been on several university committees together, and I had once attended a public lecture that he gave in which he proved to be a wonderful speaker, as well as a fine scholar. As he sat down beside me he continued speaking, "I just finished reading your book *How to Speak Dog*."

The moment he said that, I thought I could anticipate how the conversation would go. I had written *How to Speak Dog* in order to demonstrate how recent scientific findings now allow us to understand a lot of what our pet dogs are trying to communicate. The book presented lots of information – not just on the sounds that dogs make, but also on their body language, and other means of communication. It has been very well received and is widely read, although its publication elicited a huge number of questions from readers. Many people now looked more carefully at the signals their dogs were giving, and because of this, many wanted to know whether a particular sound, bark, whimper, or a particular way of holding a tail or cocking an ear they observed in their own dog had really been intended as meaningful communication. Some of their questions about and observations of dog behaviour,were extremely interesting, and several had even prompted me to do further research – occasionally resulting in new information that provided me with a deeper understanding of the canine mind. Because of this, I always made time to listen to questions about dog communication and behaviour., although, in this case, something else was on my colleague's mind.

"I really enjoyed the book," he said, "and learned a lot from it. I suppose there were also

Gods, ghosts, and black dogs

some places where I might've disagreed with you, especially the way you use the concept of grammar when you're talking about dogs' language. However, the real reason that I wanted to speak to you is to tell you that all of the time you spent going through the scientific research literature in order to try to interpret what dogs are saying was really unnecessary. You could have gotten all of the answers about the nature of canine communication by simply asking my Uncle Harold."

I was immediately curious about where this was going, and asked, "Is your Uncle Harold a behavioural researcher, veterinarian, or dog trainer, or something like that?"

"No, Uncle Harold is just our family's resident storyteller. He picks up stories along the way, much the same as a fuzzy sweater picks up dog hairs. When he's had a little bit to drink, we have to shoo the kids out of the room because the stories sometimes get a bit raunchy, although they are usually funny. Most the time it seems as if, no matter what happens in the world, Uncle Harold has an interesting story that relates to it, which brings me to the case in point here. I was reading your book, and Uncle Harold noticed the title was *How to Speak Dog*. He laughed and asked me 'Are you trying to expand your knowledge of languages beyond those spoken by humans? It would be a good thing for a scholar, particularly a linguist like yourself, to do that. It would be especially useful to learn the language of dogs since we are around them all of the time. I know that scientists keep working to try to figure out canine language and communication, but I can tell you that all of that effort is much like trying to reinvent the wheel. You see, a great scholar already managed to translate what dogs are trying to say a long time ago, and I don't think that there's anything new for researchers to learn.'

"Now, judging by your expression, I sense some skepticism on your part about the validity of what my Uncle was saying." He gave a little chuckle which alerted me to the fact that nothing serious was about to be discussed, and continued. "I won't force you to track down my Uncle Harold to find the truth about the language of dogs; instead, for your scholarly edification – and so that you can include the real facts

about canine language in the next edition of your book – I will tell you the story the way that Uncle Harold told it to me.

"It seems that there was once a brilliant wizard, who – like most wizards –had an insatiable thirst for knowledge. Other members of the Wizard Guild called him the Language Wizard because the focus of his research had fallen on the study of languages. He spent all of his time exploring what words mean, how they are spoken, how grammar lets you string together sentences, and so on. The reason that he was obsessed with language was that this wizard believed that most of the things in the Bible were true. When he had first read the Gospel of John, where it says, 'In the beginning was the Word, and the Word was with God, and the Word was God,' this was a revelation for him. He thought to himself, 'Could language be the secret of the universe? Could language be the source of all things?'

"But, of course, he was a scholar, and, knowing that the Gospels were written later than the Old Testament and could contain some reinterpretations of the original text, he went back to the source. Sure enough, right there in the book of Genesis are examples where God simply utters the words to name a thing, and his words make it real. For example, I am sure you remember how we are told that it was when God said, 'Let there be light' that light came into being. The wizard felt that he had now discovered the secret of the basis of all magic: the source of magical power was in words and language. He thought to himself that this would explain how the Bible could give us examples of where *saying* a thing might cause it to come to be.

"Now, of course, if you or I are standing in the darkness, and say, 'Let there be light,' the room doesn't light up. In the wizard's mind, though, this didn't mean that the Bible was wrong, or that the magic could only be made to happen when God was doing the talking. No, the wizard had come to believe that creating things by uttering word sounds wouldn't come to pass unless those words were spoken in the right language, and said using the correct pronunciation. He reasoned that if he could find the right language, or some collection of languages from which he could select the appropriate words, then, just like God, all he need do was speak the words and magical things would happen at his command.

"With those thoughts in mind, the Language Wizard set out to learn every language, idiom, lingo, tongue or slang ever spoken on the Earth. It is hard to know how many languages he learned, but it had to be hundreds — after all, wizards have very long lives, and lots of time to study. However, like all wizards, he was a scholarly intellectual, so it was important to him that his research should be recorded to allow later generations to benefit from his work. Therefore, for each language that the Language Wizard studied, he also created a dictionary and grammar book, and these were stored in his library. Since he also collected other dictionaries and grammar books written by many different scholars who were also interested in language, his library was huge, and he had had to expand it several times to hold all of the books describing all of the languages he studied.

"As it happens, the Language Wizard lived in a tall tower on a remote island. He didn't need a cook or a housekeeper since the old-style wizardly magic he had already learned was sufficient to take care of his needs. He could simply conjure up a meal when he was hungry, or use an appropriate spell to clean up his tower, wash his clothes, or make his bed. He didn't have an apprentice because it took too much time and effort to teach one (it took even more time to correct the errors that apprentices always made when they were starting out in the wizarding business), and he didn't want to waste any of the time that could be spent studying languages. However, the Language Wizard did have a dog, and the dog kept him from being lonely.

The Language Wizard had a Border Collie because it was the breed recommended by the Animal Wizard (whose obsession was obviously the study of animals). The Animal Wizard had assured him that the Border Collie was the smartest of all of dogs, and suggested that a wizard as clever as the Language Wizard ought to have a particularly intelligent dog as his companion. The Language Wizard was convinced by this argument and agreed to accept the Border Collie the Animal Wizard offered as a gift.

"However, the Language Wizard was not adept around animals, and did not train his dog very much, or try to hone his dog's intellect to realise all of his potential. Essentially, the wizard wanted only that his dog be around to keep him company, and to socially interact with him when he wanted someone to talk with. Thus, when the wizard woke up in the morning he would greet the dog with an elaborate 'Good morning!' accompanied by some comment about the weather that he could see outside his window. The dog would listen, look at him intently, and respond, 'Woof.' When the wizard asked the dog, 'Are you hungry?' the dog would answer, 'Woof-woof.' Now and then, when the Language Wizard wanted to stretch his legs and take a walk, he would ask his dog if he would like to accompany him, and the dog would say, 'Woof.' As conversations go, these were not very detailed or complex, but they were adequate for the wizard, and kept him from feeling lonely.

"Well, the wizard worked for many years, adding to his list of languages, and testing each to see if the words in that particular tongue were magic, with the power to bring things into reality simply by saying let there be this or that, where 'this or that' was something the wizard wanted. Unfortunately, he wasn't achieving anything that might be termed a success.

"One day, he sat down after a long bout of learning a language, which was only spoken on a tiny island in the Pacific, and nowhere else. It was an interesting language, and, as usual, he had written a dictionary and a grammar book to describe it. Unfortunately, although the words and sentences in this language sounded nice, they — like the others he had studied before — held no magic.

The Language Wizard turned to his dog, gave a big sigh, and said to his pet, 'I have worked at this for so many years — trying to find the magic in language. But after all my efforts I don't know if I am getting any closer to achieving my goal. Tell me, do you think that I should continue in my research?' His dog looked at him and said, 'Woof.' It was at that moment that the wizard had an epiphany. He looked at his dog, and he asked, 'What did you say?' His dog looked back and said, 'Woof-woof.'

Gods, ghosts, and black dogs

"The wizard jumped up and shouted, 'That's it! I have concentrated only on languages spoken by humans. There is no reason why the language that God used, or the language that has the magic to make things come into existence, should be a human language. It could be an animal language. It could be the language of dogs, and that would make sense because God designed dogs to be around humans, and to be our helpers and companions.'

"So now the Language Wizard knew what he had to do: he had to learn the language of dogs. Even though he had spent many years studying language, he knew that this was not going to be easy, however, as there simply were no dictionaries of canine language (although maybe if he had waited a few hundred years he could've used the one in your book as a starting point). There were no written attempts at researching the language of dogs, and without a starting point it would be very difficult. He sat patting his dog, and asked, 'So, where do I start?' His dog looked into his eyes, and replied, 'Woof.'

"The wizard gazed at his dog, shook his head and said, 'As a Border Collie you are supposed to be smart, yet all you have to say is, "Woof?"' The thought occurred to him: 'I know you are a clever dog because the Animal Wizard has said so. Perhaps the Animal Wizard would have some information about the language of dogs.'

"Since this was long before the Internet had been invented, there was obviously no way to send an email to his wizardly colleague, but the next best thing was the CBCN (Crystal Ball Communications Net), which every wizard had a subscription to. So the wizard polished up his crystal ball and dialled up the Animal Wizard.

"Once the connection was made, he asked his friend and colleague how he might go about learning the language of dogs. The Animal Wizard could not give him a dictionary of canine language, and instead told him, 'On those rare instances when I actually want to talk to an animal, I give that animal the ability to speak like a human. I can then question the animal and get answers that I understand. I suppose if I wanted to learn about the language of an animal, then I would first cast a spell on a

wise member of that species, and ask him specific questions about the language he speaks. I think this would work in your case, especially since the dog you have is a very clever breed, and he clearly speaks the language of dogs.' On hearing the conversation the Language Wizard's own dog confirmed his agreement with a 'Woof.'

"The Language Wizard became very excited by this news, but the Animal Wizard added a caution, 'It's not easy to get an animal to speak a human language. One must first gather many ingredients from around the world to put together the appropriate potion. Furthermore, there are some things about this elixir business that I don't understand, but I'll tell you the part that I do: when the elixir is made, you can only give it to a specific kind of animal once, since it has no effect after the first administration. Each wizard gets to talk to one member of each species only once. Another problem is that the effect does not last very long – maybe half-an-hour at most – which means that the amount of information you can get is fairly limited. So, to make this worthwhile, you should prepare your questions well in advance to ensure you don't forget to ask about the most important points.'

"The Language Wizard was not fazed by this. He assured the Animal Wizard, 'A half-hour should do it. All I need is a starting place. I know enough about so many other languages I am convinced that if I have a place to start, and examples to listen to, I can re-create almost all of the rest of any specific tongue.' For the next hour or so the Language Wizard wrote down the list of ingredients he would need for the elixir as dictated to him by his friend. He also wrote down the details of how the ingredients were to be mixed and processed, and also carefully noted the incantation that had to be given when the potion was administered to the dog.

"There were lots of items to gather. Some were fairly simple to find, like dogwood flowers, a dogfish, cloth with a hound's-tooth pattern, horehound candy, or oil used to fry hushpuppies. Other items were more esoteric, such as drops of sweat from a dog-tired, dogmatic priest, a hair from the beard of a hellhound, a drop of saliva from a singing dog found only in New Guinea, or captured light from the dog star, Sirius, during the dog days of summer stored in a magic crystal. It took the Language Wizard more than a year to gather all of the ingredients he needed, and then an additional three days were required to actually prepare the magic elixir. The wizard then called his dog into his laboratory, and uttered the words of the incantation necessary to activate the potion. Finally, he put five drops of the precious fluid into the dog's mouth.

The Language Wizard flipped an hourglass designed to mark off half-an-hour, and looked expectantly at the dog. When he was greeted by nothing but silence, he finally asked, 'Can you speak?'

The dog seemed to clear his throat, and then said, 'I could always speak, only now I can speak your language as well as my own.'

"'I have some questions to ask you about the language of dogs, although I am unsure whether you can give me a full answer. After all, you have lived your entire life, from puppyhood, here with me in this tower. You may not have acquired the knowledge necessary to tell me about the language of dogs.'

The Border Collie gave a little thump of his tail and answered, 'Dogs do not write, so there are no journals or diaries to tell what an individual dog has learned. Dogs do not have libraries or electronic databanks to conserve and display any erudition or culture they have acquired as a species. Instead, what dogs know is encoded in their genes. Each and every dog has the knowledge he or she needs to be a dog, and this includes our universal canine language. This means that every dog can speak to any other dog and be understood.'

"'Well, then,' said the wizard, expectantly, 'let's start with something simple. When you say "Woof," which seems to be your favourite word, what does it mean exactly?'

"'Woof means "Woof." There are dialects and slang terms in dog language as there are in human language. Thus, you refer to someone who you are close to as a friend, while someone in Chicago might refer to them as their buddy, or someone in Texas might call them their partner, or someone in Australia might refer to them as their mate. They all mean the same thing, namely "friend." The same goes for dogs.

Instead of "woof" some dogs might say "arf," while others might say "ruff." These are just alternative ways of saying "woof," which is the correct usage as you might expect from a more cultured animal such as a Border Collie.'

"'Yes, I understand that,' said the wizard, 'but you haven't really given me the answer to what you mean when you say "woof."'

"'Woof means whatever I choose it to. It also means whatever the listener chooses to have it mean.'

"'But what if what you choose it to mean is not the same as what the listener chooses it to mean?'

"'Then the dog who says "woof," and the individual who hears "woof" don't really communicate very well, and that is how mistakes are made, especially when human beings are listening to us say "woof." But dogs are patient, and we know that if "woof" is misinterpreted, we can always repeat it, and if that doesn't work there is always "woof-woof," or, in extreme circumstances, "woof-woof-woof," or even "woof-woof-woof-woof," but that would imply that the listener is not attending very well, or the listener may be a little bit on the dull side of intelligence, or perhaps a little deaf.'

"'But,' protested the Language Wizard, 'that would mean that "woof" can mean anything, everything, or nothing in particular. You can't really call something a language if its words do not have precise meanings, and stringing them together in sentences, like "woof-woof" does not change the message as proper grammar or syntax should do.'

"'What is it about "woof" that you don't understand?' askd the dog. 'For a wizard you are acting exceedingly dense. When you ask me if I would like something to eat and I say "woof," you clearly understand me. If you ask me if I want to go out for a walk and I say "woof," you know what I mean. And if you ask me do I understand why you are feeling happy, grumpy, or sad on any given day, and I tell you "woof," you interpret my meaning quite well. Dogs are not lawyers who need special and precise language so that nobody can misunderstand what they are saying, lest somebody drag them into court on a technicality. Dogs are not scientists who must have words with precise nuances to make sure that the data

Gods, ghosts, and black dogs

is understood with precision. Dogs were designed to be the companions of human beings or of other dogs. Human beings, like other dogs, were designed to be intelligent enough to understand what is meant when a dog says "woof."'

"The Language Wizard was beginning to get a little frustrated. He listened to what the dog was telling him, and on one level he sort of understood what his dog meant, because he had always understood what he meant when he said 'woof' in their everyday interactions. He glanced at the hourglass and saw that the sand was running out. All of that effort in making the elixir and casting the spell for this? it seemed to him that he was not going to come away with a true dictionary of dog language, because how could it be a true dictionary with only one word in it? And even if there *was* only one word in the language, how could it be explained to the reader that the sole entry, 'Woof,' did not have a clear definition, but rather an infinity of definitions . . .

"In desperation, the wizard decided to try and salvage something from his efforts. Leaning over, he gave his dog a pat on the head. 'Perhaps it is the case that the matter of canine language is beyond me, or at least will take more thinking for me to understand. However, let me ask you one other question, which some might feel is more general

in nature. If I understand what you have told me, all of the knowledge, philosophy, and history of all the members of the canine race is encoded in your genes, which means that, within you, there must be a great realm of truths and insights that are of value not only to your own species, but also to others. If you search that library of information that dogs have within themselves, is there one thing you could call a universal truth that might help guide others in their lives?'

"The Border Collie looked into the eyes of the Language Wizard, gave an emphatic wag of his tail, and said, 'The core of canine philosophy as it is known to all dogs is, "Don't expect too much."'

"The Language Wizard sighed, then asked, 'And that is the great fundamental truth?'

"'Woof,' said the dog, and the wizard turned to see that the sand in the hourglass had run out, and the spell was ended."

I laughed and said, "Thank you very much for this vital information. It certainly helps clarify my understanding of what dogs are saying. I can assure you that if I use these scientific insights about canine language in a future book I will be certain to credit your Uncle Howard."

The Professor of Linguistics smiled, and said, "Woof!"

The old dog's new tricks

The elderly couple were sitting on the bench at the edge of the dog park, watching their black Cocker Spaniel play with a few of his friends. The dog's name was Lancaster, after some place in Pennsylvania where they had lived many years ago. I don't know how old they were, but there were lots of hints that they had many years behind them.

The man's name was Dan and the woman's name was Martha. They once told me that they had been childhood sweethearts, who had gotten married when he was just 19, and a newly-enlisted soldier getting ready to ship off to Europe to serve in the war against Hitler. He was in a muddy, cold, foxhole when he got the letter from home saying that his first son had been born. When the fighting ended and Dan made it back to his family, he took advantage of the veteran's benefits and went to college. A short time later they had two more children — both boys. They led a simple life and had a marriage that worked. Their sons, their grandchildren, and even their great grandchildren were close, and visited often. There were moments of pain, as in all lives. Martha once confided in me that, when they learned that their oldest boy had died at the age of 69, Dan had hugged her, and, with tears in his eyes, said "I told you long ago we'd never raise that boy." Martha remembers trying to console him with the words, "We tried, and we still have two more chances to make it work with the other boys."

The pair greeted me when I sat down beside them. All three of us were holding cardboard takeout coffee cups, and just watching the dogs play — merely casual friends who met now and then at the dog park when the weather was not too bad.

Martha turned to me and said in a playful tone, "I was thinking that since you are an expert on training dogs, maybe you could help me with a problem I have. It's not with Lanky out there, but my old dog here — Dan. The problem is that when we are at home, Dan carries around his mug of hot coffee, and always ends up putting it down on the nice wood end tables next to the sofa. The mug then leaves a white ring in the wood finish which won't come out. Recently, our youngest son, Tom [who was a retired carpenter], refinished the tables for us, so I wanted to know if there was some training trick which you use

Gods, ghosts, and black dogs

on dogs that I could modify to get Dan to remember to slip a coaster under his mug so that he won't mess up the new finish on the tables? Well, that was the plan, but the more I thought about it, the more I came to believe that your training advice probably wouldn't help because, as they say 'You can't teach an old dog new tricks.'"

Dan turned in our direction and smiled. "This business about old dogs and new tricks is really just a myth that young folks like to believe about those of us who are more senior than they are. Old dogs can learn new tricks if they are motivated to do so, and if they have some friends and loved ones to help them along the way. Why. old dogs can even think up some *new* tricks, which is better than just learning them from someone else.

"I remember hearing about one smart old dog when we were living back in Pennsylvania. The story was told to me by an old friend who used to be in the army with me. Nick grew up in the woods of West Virginia. The way I remember the story is that there was this old dog named Zeke. Of course, a dog with the name Zeke has got to be old, since nobody in their right mind would name a puppy Zeke. He was owned by a hardscrabble farmer, and was supposed to be a watchdog and a guard dog. The farmer and his wife had three children: two boys who were just toddlers, and the littlest (the girl) still a babe-in-arms.

"Zeke had done his job well, but he was getting old, and moved a lot slower. His teeth weren't as sharp as they used to be, and his bite wasn't as strong. On the other hand, his eyes and ears still worked well enough to stand watch over the house, and he could still sound the alarm with powerfully loud barking. However, the farmer had come to believe that Zeke couldn't do the guarding work anymore, and that it would probably be best to get rid of him, and maybe get a younger dog.

Zeke heard him talking to his wife about this, and telling her that he was thinking that he might just put the dog down in the next week or so, after he'd checked around to see if he could find a replacement. When Zeke understood what was happening, he got very depressed, and wandered out into the yard to lay down next to a big, old sycamore tree.

"Well, a couple of sparrows saw the dog just lying there, moping, and fluttered down next to him to see what was wrong. The sparrows who lived in that tree considered the dog to be their friend, since whenever Zeke saw one of the local cats stalking the birds, he would chase it away. After the dog told them what he had overhead the farmer saying to his wife, one of the birds suggested, 'Maybe we can help you. It certainly is not in your best interest to just hang around here and wait until the farmer picks up his rifle and shoots you, for no reason other than the fact that you've grown old. The village is not far away, and we can show you how to get food from the scraps that the humans leave there. Our friends, the crows, taught us how to do that. We've been there often and have seen a lot of stray dogs in the town who live reasonably well.'

"So, with the birds leading the way, Zeke headed off to the village. Just as they reached the little community they had to cross a low bridge over a clear stream. Zeke was a little tired, and he paused to look into the water where he could see the reflection of the nearby trees and the sky, and even his own face with all of the gray hair that had come to cover his muzzle as he had grown older. It was at that moment that a scrappy little terrier from the village came up to him, and wanted to know whether he was just passing through or whether he had any business in town. When Zeke and the sparrows told him that his plans were to live off of scraps from the humans in the village, the terrier shook his head sadly, and said, 'That would have been a good plan a while ago, but I don't know whether it will work now. Let me take you to some of my friends, and they can explain the situation to you.'

"A short while later, Zeke and the sparrows were sitting in a quiet alleyway. The terrier had gathered two of his friends, a Poodle and a Collie, both of whom were street dogs, like him. It was the terrier who began the conversation, 'We were living pretty well here until a wealthy banker from the big city retired, and bought a fancy house right at the edge of town. Because he is wealthy and has lots of expensive things, he got himself a really big, mean guard dog to protect his home. It would have been fine if that dog stayed near the door of his own house to watch it, but instead he wanders the streets during the day. He is a really greedy animal, and he likes to steal food from the street dogs.'

"The other dogs nodded in agreement as the terrier continued, 'Just the other day I visited the butcher. The butcher likes me because he knows that I kill any rats I see hanging around the shop. In appreciation of my work, he usually saves some of the fat he carves off the bigger pieces meat for me. He leaves it in a bowl by the back door in the late afternoon so that I can come by and eat it.'

"'Just about a week ago that big, mean banker's dog came up just as I was about to nibble on the chunk of fat that the butcher had left for me, and told me to give it to him or he would attack me. He then told me that he had learned my schedule, and would be coming around every afternoon, when I would be expected to stand aside and let him eat what the butcher had given me in appreciation of my work. Without that regular supply of food, I am having a hard time making do, and have been wandering around the streets getting hungrier and weaker every day.'

"It was the Poodle who spoke next. Although she lived on the street ,she was still a handsome animal, who tried to keep herself as clean and well-groomed as she could. 'I manage to get along because people think that I'm pretty. Lots of humans will tear off a tiny piece of their sandwich, and give it to me as a treat. That is nearly enough food to keep me alive, although the most important source of food for me comes from the baker, who I usually visit a few hours after lunch, around the time he has just finished baking the last batch of cookies for the day. He puts the cookies on trays so they can be brought out to the front counter to be sold, and, when he sees me, the baker takes a little whisk broom and brushes all of the cookie crumbs and broken pieces from the counter into a little bowl and puts it near the back door for me. It is such a wonderful treat, and it provides just enough extra food to keep me from feeling hungry. But that nasty banker's dog learned about my routine, and a while ago he began showing up and demanding my bowl of cookie crumbs. When I

refused and told him that it was my treat, he bit me.'

"The Poodle held up a front paw, which still showed signs of redness from the injury. 'Since then, he comes every day and snatches away my food and threatens me.'

"Finally, the Collie spoke, 'I only live part of the day on the street, and the rest of the time I work with the cheese maker. In the morning, I go out into the pasture behind his shop and round up his six cows so that he can milk them. Then, in the afternoon, I come back and gather the cows again for him. Each day, after he has finished the milking, the cheese maker leaves out a bowl of milk, and usually the rind he has cut from a cheese. The banker's dog has discovered this, and every day now he comes and steals my milk and cheese. When I try to resist, he bullies me, and threatens me by saying that he will hurt me, and chase the cows so that they will be too frightened to give milk if I do not let him have my food. All of the dogs here in the village are now living in fear of this greedy dog, and those of us who depend on the extra bits of food that the humans leave for us are now beginning to go hungry because of him.'

"Well, Zeke thought to himself that this was a bad situation. Even though he was larger than the Collie, because Zeke was old and his teeth were worn, he really couldn't fight off a big, mean guard dog. As he considered the situation in the town he knew that, under the present circumstances, if he came there to live, he would likely go hungry, just like the other street dogs. Nonetheless, although he was an old dog, he was smart, and could think up new tricks if he had to. So he told the sparrows and the three dogs that he had a plan to teach the banker's dog a lesson. If the scheme worked, it could make the town safer for the other animals, and a more inviting place for him to come to as well. But for his strategy to be successful, they would all have to work together. The birds and the dogs immediately agreed that it was worth trying something, rather than continuing to suffer because of the banker's greedy, intimidating dog.

"To put Zeke's plan into effect the sparrows first had to sneak into the butcher shop. When the butcher wasn't looking they took a nice cut of meat from the shelf, and placed it on the sill of an open window at the rear of the building. Then, at the usual time that the butcher left the fat trimmings for the terrier, and while the banker's dog was coming down the alley to grab it away, the Poodle joined the terrier, pretending that she did not know that the big, insatiable dog was approaching. She told the terrier in a conspiratorial tone 'You know, I see that the butcher has left a nice cut of meat on his windowsill today. You could just snatch it from there, and it would be a much tastier and a larger meal than your usual piece of fat, and there would even be enough of it for you to share with me.'

"The greedy banker's dog heard this, and stealthily crept up so as not to be noticed by the other dogs. He grabbed the joint of meat, and was about to make off with it, when, just then, the Collie came up to the other two dogs and said 'I also saw that piece of meat that the butcher left, but when I was crossing the bridge I ran into another dog — a stranger that I did not know — and he was carrying an even bigger piece of meat! I told him that he should be careful because the banker's dog might steal it from him, but he said that he was just going to hang out near the bridge and eat it all himself. I think he believes that he can finish it before the banker's dog knows that he has it.'

"On hearing this, the banker's dog became even greedier, and thought to himself 'This will be a wonderful day. Not only will I have this fine piece of meat that I have stolen from the butcher, but, in addition, I will steal and eat the meat that this strange dog is trying to keep from me.'

"The banker's dog dashed to the bridge at the edge of town, still carrying the piece of meat from the butcher shop, and looked around to see where the other dog might be hiding with his meaty treasure. As he peered over the edge of the bridge, he saw a dog with a big piece of meat in his mouth. The banker's dog's greediness had made him stupid, and he did not realise that he was looking at his own reflection. He gave a loud bark and growl, and leapt at the dog reflected in the stream, with predictable results, dropping the piece of meat he was carrying. Of course, there was no other piece of meat to be had, but the banker's dog's greed drove him on, and, in his addled

state, he still believed that there were two pieces of meat which now had been lost in the stream. Driven by his gluttony, he swore to himself that he would not stop looking for those pieces of meat until he had both of them, but a short distance downstream from the bridge the watercourse became a swift current, and, as the dog frantically searched for his missing treasures, he was carried further along. Before he recognized the danger, he was swept over a waterfall to disappear from sight. What happened to him is not clear, but it must've been drastic and hurtful because the banker's dog never returned to the village.

"The village dogs were very grateful to Zeke for planning the whole operation, and wanted to show their appreciation. That afternoon they sat and discussed the old dog's problem. The Poodle, who was not just a pretty, curly thing, but a very clever girl, observed, 'Zeke, you are a housedog who grew up with a family. You might be able to survive on the streets with our help, but I doubt that you would be happy here. So the best thing that we could do for you is to help resolve the problem that you have with your human family. Your people simply do not understand how intelligent and brave you are, and it should be our job to help them understand how valuable you really are.'

"The dogs and the birds sat and pondered for a couple of hours, and then it was Zeke who once again came up with a plan. As he explained it to the others, the Collie would become the captain of this operation, since he would have an important role to play, and knew where a critical piece of equipment was located. First, Zeke sent the sparrows to steal another slice of meat from the butcher shop. His instructions were that it had to be a large piece of meat, and freshly cut. Once the birds had their prize, Zeke gave it to the terrier with strict instructions that he must carry it to a place that the old dog had picked out, which was not far from the farmhouse where he lived. The terrier was supposed to wrap the piece of meat in leaves to keep it fresh and moist, and not to eat it under any circumstances!

"Next, the Collie arranged to get the most important gear for this caper, and went behind the cheese maker's house, where the little barn was that the cows slept in at night when the weather was cold. Last winter had been a hard one, and the wolves in the forest had had a lot of trouble finding enough to eat. Because of that, one large wolf became hungry enough that he thought that it worth the risk to come down to the village with the idea of killing a cow for food. When the Collie caught sight of the wolf, he had set up a great commotion, and the cheese maker came out with his rifle, and shot the big, gray beast. The cheese maker then had the wolf skinned, and tanned the hide, leaving the head on so that it was clear that this was the skin of a wolf. He then tacked it on the side of the barn as a warning to any other wolves who might want to try and take one of his cattle. The Collie needed this wolf skin, now, and, although it was difficult, he managed to pull the hide off the wall and carry it to the designated meeting place with the Poodle's help, where the terrier had already arrived with the still-wrapped slice of meat.

"The final preparations involved the sparrows. They punched neat little holes around the edges of the wolf hide, much like little buttonholes, and knotted bits of string they had stolen from various trash cans around the village through the holes to make laces. They fitted the wolf skin over the Collie, and tied it on with the string. They all agreed that the get-up was a convincing disguise, and made the Collie look much like a wolf — from a distance, at least.

"Next, Zeke hid in the bushes outside the farmhouse and waited until the farmer, his wife, and their older children were out in the yard while the baby napped inside. At Zeke's signal, the Collie sneaked into the bedroom where the infant girl was lying in her crib. He carefully cinched the blanket around her, and lifted her in his mouth. Then, as the Collie dashed out of the house, Zeke broke from the cover of the bushes and let loose a barrage of frantic barking directed at the Collie. The family looked up and saw what appeared to be a wolf carrying their infant daughter, but the farmer was too far away to react. Zeke made sure that the man could see him before he raced through the underbrush and chased after the imposter wolf. The farmer finally gathered his wits, and dashed into the house to grab his rifle, blundering through the woods a few moments later in the direction that the Collie and Zeke had run.

"Zeke caught up with his friend, and they both ran to where the Poodle and the terrier were waiting. The Collie carefully laid down the baby, and then he, Zeke and the Poodle began ferociously growling and barking and crashing around in the underbrush to make it sound as though a terrible fight was occurring. Meanwhile, the terrier had unwrapped the large piece of fresh meat he had stolen from the butcher shop., and slapped the meat against the white blanket that the baby was wrapped in, then slapped it against Zeke, especially around his face and his flank. With each slap a splash of blood from the fresh cut of beef stained the baby's blanket, and the fur of the old dog.

"A few moments later they could hear the farmer approaching. So the wolf-skin-covered Collie, the Poodle and the terrier quickly took off in the direction of the village, while Zeke — carrying the baby in the bloodstained blanket — made a good show of staggering in the direction of the farmer. When the farmer saw his daughter being carried by the blood-splattered old dog, he dropped his gun and snatched up the child. He was on his knees, sobbing with relief, hugging the little girl and petting Zeke with his free hand when his wife arrived. All he could manage to say was 'Zeke came back. He fought off the wolf and saved our daughter. He will have food and shelter and warmth and love from us for the rest of his life, even if he grows so old that all of the teeth fall out, and he can no longer bite anything.'

"And so it was that Zeke lived out a long and happy life. Although the family bought a new dog that was better at guarding and biting, Zeke was still allowed to rest by the fire, and play with the children, and he was fed and loved by his human family, and remembered fondly by his canine friends in the village.

"There is a moral to this story, my dear," Dan said to his wife with a broad grin. He reached over to put his arm around Martha, and continued, "We old dogs can learn new tricks if there is something in it for us. So if I learn this new coffee mug trick that you want to teach me, what is in it for me?"

Martha snuggled up against his chest.

Gods, ghosts, and black dogs

Smiling demurely, in a stage whisper she said, "I'm sure we can think of something."

I looked at the couple who had been married for more than 70 years ago, and thought to myself that the tricks they had learned and practiced regularly, like love, laughter, companionship, and storytelling, were probably enough, even if these 'old dogs' never learned another new trick in their lives!

Visit Hubble and Hattie on the web: www.hubbleandhattie.com
www.hubbleandhattie.blogspot.co.uk
• Details of all books • Special offers • Newsletter • New book news

The wet-nosed badge of courage

It has always seemed to me that some stories and folk tales were designed specifically for children. For adults, storytelling seems to reappear during lulls in conversation, periods of relaxation when nothing much else is going on, or at times when alcohol has lulled people into a more receptive mode that allows listening. In this era of electronics, where there is access to television, the internet, and video recordings in many formats, I fear that the practice of sitting and telling stories to children may well disappear. Even so, there are situations, still, when children will sit quietly and listen to and enjoy someone telling a story.

It was a late September day, and we were out at our little farm, which is located about an hour-and-a-half outside of Vancouver, Canada. Three of our grandchildren were visiting, and my wife, her son and daughter-in-law, and the eldest of the three kids had gone into town to purchase something, leaving me with the two young boys. They had stayed behind because they had noticed a video of Disney's *Lady and the Tramp* on one of my shelves, and they wanted to watch it. I remained behind to take care of them, and to begin preparations for dinner. Our kitchen is at one

end of a large room, while the other end serves as a family room, which meant that I could not only keep an eye on the activities of my grandsons, but also see and hear the television as well.

It was past 5 o'clock, and it was getting pretty dark outside when a storm with high winds and rain suddenly blew up. Inside the house things were still bright and warm, and the video had just got to the point where the nasty Siamese cats were singing their arrogant song (in Peggy Lee's voice, of course) when the power went out. This was not a particularly unusual event, since the power often goes out during high winds and inclement conditions in our little valley; however, the boys lived in the big city, where power cuts were rare, so, for them, this was a bit of an adventure, although also an annoyance since it interrupted their movie watching.

I dug out few candles and lit them, while Matty, the older of the two, curiously asked, "What are we supposed to do now? We can't just sit here in the dark."

"No problem," I said, "First, we have to light a fire in the fireplace, which will keep us warm and give us a little extra light." and I motioned for them to follow me into the garage, where we gathered up some firewood that was stored there to keep it dry, and then returned to the family room. In a few minutes we had a big, friendly blaze going. Next, I pushed the sofa up close to the front of the fireplace so that we could sit there and soak up the heat from the flames.

Obviously, I couldn't continue my preparations for dinner, and, besides, I was afraid that the kids would get bored just sitting there with nothing going on. I thought about offering to tell them a story, but somehow it seemed to me that the kids were too sophisticated to want to just sit there and listen to their grandfather prattling on about some made up world with heroes and princesses, and so forth.

It was then that one of my dogs came to the rescue. At that time I had two dogs, a Nova Scotia Duck Tolling Retriever, named Dancer, and a Beagle named Darby. Dancer jumped up on the sofa and nuzzled at the ear of my younger grandson, Santi, who giggled and pulled his head away, asking, "Why is Dancer's nose so cold and wet?"

This question seemed to provide the perfect opportunity to sneak in a story to occupy the time until the power came back on, so I said, "That's to remind you how brave dogs are, and to tell you that they will always care for you, and will protect you as well as they can."

I moved over to the refrigerator, and brought out two little containers of fruit juice, handing one to each boy, then splashed some bourbon into a glass for myself. The boys were looking at me expectantly, as if they knew that what I had just said was one of those things that requires a story to explain what it really means. Finally, Matty said, "I never heard about that before." So I settled down at one end of the sofa, and began to tell the story the way that generations of grandfathers have probably told it to their grandchildren.

"It all started back in the time of the Bible. People had gotten to be pretty wicked then, and God decided that he was going to wash all of the evil folks off the world in a great flood. He wanted to keep

some of the good people around to start over, and, of course, the animals had done no harm, so God wanted to keep a bunch of them to fill the forests, jungles and fields after the water had finally gone away.

"Now, in those days there was one special family, who God thought deserved to be saved from the flood that he was going to send. Noah and his family were good and righteous people, and they were really upset and scared when God told Noah that a great flood was coming. But God wasn't just warning Noah to give him a chance to run away, instead, he gave Noah instructions about how to build an ark." Santi, the younger of the two boys, fidgeted a bit so I explained, "An ark is really just a great big boxy kind of boat with no sails on it. Anyway, Noah was supposed to put his family on the ark to keep them safe from the water. But that wasn't all that God wanted from Noah. In addition, he was given the task of gathering up every kind of animal he could find and bringing them by twos or fours or sixes onto the ark. The people from Noah's family (which included his sons and their wives and their children) would become the parents of all of the whole next generation of human beings in the world, and the animals would become the parents of all of the other animals in the world, since only those on the ark were going to survive the coming flood.

"While Noah and his older sons worked on building the ark, his younger sons and their wives began to gather up the animals. The very first animals brought to Noah was a pair of dogs. Noah looked at them and said, 'Now, you are smart and reliable and intelligent animals. You see I need some help in watching over things, so I want you to make sure that none of my neighbours steals any of the precious wood or any of our other supplies that we need for building this ark, and getting it ready to sail on the floodwaters. I also need you to warn me if something goes wrong with the other animals, or if anything else goes wrong around here: you see, we will be really busy building this giant ark, and won't be able to keep a close watch on other things. Will you do that for me?'

"Of course (as you probably already know)

dogs had been created to love people, and it is in their nature to try to do anything that humans want when they are asked. So, as you would expect, the dogs agreed to take on the job, and began to patrol the area and keep watch.

"It wasn't long before the other animals began to arrive, and those who could help with building and preparing the ark did their best. Elephants and horses carried wood and other supplies to where the big boat was being built; giraffes used their long necks to lift things up to Noah and his sons when the men were working high on their ladders; cows gave Noah milk and chickens gave him eggs, while monkeys climbed high into the trees to gather fruits and nuts to serve as food supplies to feed everybody once the rain began to fall, and the ark was afloat. All this went on while the dogs served as watchmen, warning Noah whenever there was any sort of problem, and protecting Noah's possessions from his thieving, evil neighbours.

"Well, it wasn't too long after the ark was built, checked out, and found to be seaworthy, that the rain began to fall, so then Noah loaded everybody onto the ark. He depended quite a bit on the dogs during this time: you see, many of those other animals were not very bright, and kept forgetting why they had been gathered together at that time and place. For example, the sheep, cattle — and even the ducks and geese — would wander off into nearby fields just at the time that Noah's family was trying to get them all on board. With the rain now falling in earnest, it was the dogs' job to find the strays, herd them back to the ark, and then get them to walk up the ramp and into their pens. There was a lot of bleating and mooing and clucking in protest, but the dogs were good at their job, and everyone was onboard before the water rose high enough to be dangerous.

"Once that big, heavy ark was floating on the flood water, the dogs still had work to do, patrolling and watching for trouble as the boat drifted aimlessly on the water that now covered the earth. After forty days and forty nights of solid, heavy rain, the downpour ceased. A few days later, it seemed to Noah that maybe the level of water was dropping a little. He sent out a dove to see if she could find dry land. Since the ark was not a pleasure boat, but was built to protect its passengers from hard, driving rain, there was not much of a deck to stand on, and Noah sent the dogs out through a hatch he had built into the roof to watch for the dove's return — like a kind of doggy radar. Of course, the dogs were the first to see the white bird returning with an olive branch in her beak, which meant that the water *was* falling and the trees were now above the flood tide. The sound of joyful barking let everyone know that their long journey was coming to an end, and they would soon be able to walk on dry land again.

"But that happily-ever-after ending might never have happened if it hadn't been for the dogs demonstrating what kind of heroes they were a few weeks earlier. You see, the dogs were always on the lookout for trouble, since that was the job Noah gave them. Anyway, one night, when the dogs were patrolling the ark, they heard a big commotion. The sheep were bleating away at the top of their lungs, the cows were mooing, the horses were neighing, and everybody sounded really frightened. Since these animals were kept on the very lowest deck of the ark, the dogs raced down to see what was going on.

"When the dogs reached the bottom level, they saw that the floor area was filling with water. The dogs searched to find where the problem was, and quickly discovered, there in the hull of the ark, a neat, round hole, about the size of a coin. It was probably where a knot in the wood had been, which the water pressure had pushed out, leaving a hole that allowed the water to rush in.

"Of course, dogs are resourceful creatures, and looked around for something to stop the water coming in. There wasn't much about except for some hay that the big animals had been eating. The dogs took some into their mouths, and chewed it into a wad, with which they tried to plug the hole, pushing as hard as they could with their paws. The bad news was that, when you are way down below the waterline, like that bottom deck was, the water pressure gets kind of strong, and in this case it was strong enough to push out the emergency stopper that the dogs had made, and within minutes the water was flowing back into the ark.

Gods, ghosts, and black dogs

"The dogs figured that they couldn't handle this problem themselves, and needed humans with tools and wood patches to save the day. So the husband-dog motioned to his wife to tell her to go get help. She dashed for the stairs as fast as she could — and you know how fast dogs can go when they are running. The dog who stayed behind was smart enough to realise, however, that it would still most likely be a while before help arrived, since Noah and his sons and their families all lived on the top deck. The flow of water had to be stopped before too much flooded in, as water in the lower deck could drown the animals that the dog was supposed to protect. Since these animals were the last of their kind, if they drowned, their species would disappear from the earth, just as the dinosaurs had done many years earlier. The dog knew that he had to do something to at least slow the water's flow, and give everybody time to make the repair, so he braced himself against the side of the sheep pen to keep from being pushed back by the force of the water, took a deep breath, and shoved his nose into the hole!

"There is no way to tell you how strong the water pressure was but I can guess that it pushed really hard, trying to push the dog's nose out of the way. Not only that, but the water was really cold — so cold that the dog's nose began to tingle the way that your toes do if you get some snow in your boots. He was a brave dog and a strong one, but some of the water worked its way into his nostrils and dribbled down into his mouth. With his nose in the hole, and water filling up his mouth, it was really hard to breathe, but still that brave dog fought to hold his place. With his hind legs pushing at the slats of the sheep pen, and his nose plugging the knot hole, he managed to slow the stream of water to a trickle.

"No one knows how long it took the other dog to convince Noah and his sons that there was a problem, and to get them to follow her down to the bottom deck, but we can be sure it would've taken many, many long minutes for the people to work their way through the length and depth of that big old ark to reach the leak, and by the time they got there the dog with his nose in the hole was in great pain,

and barely conscious. Noah moved the dog away as carefully as possible (the dog was so weak that he nearly fell over when he was set down), then Noah and his sons hammered a great plug into the side of the ark to stop the water flow, and carefully sealed the side of the ark with pitch to make sure that there would be no new leaks.

"Afterwards, even with everyone working together and bailing out the water, it was several days before the lower deck was completely dry again. Seeing all of the water in there made it obvious just how dangerous that leak was ... why, if the dogs hadn't acted as fast as they did, and if that brave dog had not managed to stop up the flow of water as much as he did, it might well have been that, by the time help arrived, there would have been so much water that the ark might have foundered and sunk.

"When God looked down and saw the way in which the dogs had saved his project to clean up the Earth and start all over again, he smiled, and decided, there and then, that no one should ever be allowed to forget how loyal, faithful, loving, and clever dogs are. He awarded all dogs a special badge of courage in the form of a cold, wet nose, so that everyone would remember that cold water had nearly wiped out everything alive on the planet. If it hadn't been for the courage and intelligence of the dogs on the ark, there would be nothing living on this whole planet except for plants and fishes. So now you understand why, ever since that time, all good and brave dogs have cold, wet noses."

Santi giggled, and I could see that he was pushing Dancer away from his face again, while protesting, "Your brave, wet nose tickles my ear!"

Almost as if it had been scheduled, at that exact moment the power came back on, the television flickered back to life, and we could hear Peggy Lee singing, "We are Siamese if you please," while the evil cats destroyed furniture and tore up curtains in the house where the lovely Spaniel, Lady, lived. The boys turned their eyes toward the TV screen, and I accepted the fact that my moment of being a storytelling grandfather had passed ... and there was dinner still to be prepared.

The smartest animal

When they are relaxing, scientists can be just as frivolous and silly as any other group of people. I was attending a meeting of the Animal Behavior Society which, as is the case for such scientific gatherings, included the presentation of many papers and talks about recent research data on some of the more technical aspects of animal behaviour.

The conference organisers had arranged some entertainment, and this year it included an informal evening barbeque. When I arrived at the event I found a buffet with salads and the like, and a large barbeque grill with the usual collection of ribs, burgers, and hot dogs. The event organisers had also included a bar that served local wine, which could be purchased in large glasses or by the bottle to take to the tables where we were eating.

I was sitting at a table with several researchers, who had been sipping quite a lot of that wine to wash down the copious amount of grilled meat we were eating from paper plates. Several empty wine bottles stood on the table already, and one of the group arrived with two new, open bottles wine, then splashed some of their contents into our clear, plastic glasses. All that wine may explain why we were a lot more relaxed than usual! The conversation was pleasant and not very scientific, and I no longer remember who posed the question: which was the smartest of all the animals (leaving humans and aquatic creatures out of the mix). It was the kind of setting where scientific data was not expected in answer to such a query, but rather, anecdotes and opinions from the various members of the group.

One of the group poked my arm, and said "We all know that you would make the case for dogs being the cleverest beasts, so you don't get to offer your opinion."

I made a harrumphing sound, and agreed I would listen quietly, at least until my wine glass was empty. Someone laughed and grabbed a half-full bottle of red wine from the centre of the table, and placed it in front of me, with the comment that it should guarantee my silence, at least until the rest of the group had settled on an answer. So I refilled my glass and sat in polite silence.

The first person to suggest an answer proposed that the smartest animals would probably be found among the hunting cats. He argued, "I don't mean tigers and lions. They are so big, strong, and fast that they don't need a lot of intelligence; they just chase and pull down whatever they want to hunt. I'm thinking more of panthers and leopards, who are smaller and really have to out-think their prey. They have to understand the behaviour of whatever animal they are hunting, and figure out how to ambush or surprise their quarry before it runs away, or adopts a defensive stance that might make the whole enterprise more dangerous."

Across the table, another researcher suggested that the best candidate would be the monkey. "I won't propose any of the great apes, because I know that you will all complain they only differ from human beings by less than one half percent of their DNA, which means that to claim that apes are really smart is sort of cheating. But monkeys are certainly heading in the right direction along the evolutionary road, and everybody knows how clever they are." She paused, pushed a lock of her sandy-coloured hair out of her eyes, and continued, "After all, we've all heard of those folk tales in which monkeys are the clever tricksters, who outsmart all of the other animals to steal their food or other treasures. People who live in the bush with monkeys wouldn't have made them the heroes of such stories if they hadn't spent eons observing their behaviours, and judging them to be exceedingly clever."

One of the older scientists, who was sitting just at my right side, then joined the conversation. "Well, if we're going to use folk wisdom as the data to decide which animal is the smartest, then I have a contribution; one which I am sure will make Stan, our dog man here, happy." As if to punctuate his statement, he reached for the bottle of wine in front me, poured some into his glass, and then carefully returned it to me.

He continued, "Some years back, I was doing some research in Tanzania, not far from Ujiji and Lake Tanganyika, a very historically important region of Africa. Ujiji is the place where the explorers Richard Burton and John Speke first reached the shore of Lake Tanganyika in 1858, and is also the site of the famous meeting in October 1871 between Henry Stanley and Dr David Livingstone, when the former was supposed to have uttered the immortal words 'Dr Livingstone, I presume?'

"In the course of my studies, I met a lot of the local tribespeople living in the countryside and the bush. One was an old man named Erevu: I forget whether he was a chief, or a shaman, or just a local guy who liked to tell stories. He seemed to have an endless collection of stories about the history and goings on around the region, and was willing to trade his information and anecdotes for a bit of chocolate and a glass of gin. Every now and then he would wander into our camp accompanied by one or two of his dogs, who looked kind of like Basenjis only their coats were mostly tan and their tail wasn't curled like the Basenji tail. Erevu would settle down with us, and if we offered him something to drink, he would answer our questions, or just tell us some stories. I must admit that I spent some very pleasant late afternoons, while my associates and I sat around listening to Erevu talk. I scribbled down the gist of many of his tales, with the idea of doing something with them, but just haven't gotten around to it yet.

"One day, I asked him why he always travelled with dogs. 'Because dogs are the most intelligent animal in the world,' he said. 'Everybody knows that.'

"I told Erevu that perhaps all of *his* people might know that dogs are the smartest animals, but assured him that *my* people often think that cats or monkeys or whales are more intelligent. Erevu paused for a moment, then replied, 'I don't know about whales, since my people have never seen one, but I can tell you about dogs. Before I do that, though, you must first understand that all of the animals can talk to each other, and understand what other animals mean. It is not language as we know it, with words like ours, but it does have meaning which they understand. So, in this story, I will say what the animals would be saying in our words, as if we could translate animal talk.

"'This is a story of the dog, Mbwa.' (I should tell you that mbwa is the Swahili word for dog, and also seems to be the name of the dog heroes in a lot of the Tanzanian tales.) 'Mbwa was getting old, and his teeth were not as sharp and as strong as they used to be, and he was now not able to run as fast as he used to. But this old dog was still as clever as any dog. He knew all of the places where the birds hide, and could lead the hunters and the other dogs there so that they could catch the birds in nets. He could recognize all of the people who came to the village, and knew who were friends and who were not, and who was to be trusted and who must be watched. He could also recognize all of the animals by their scent, and warn our hunters away from chasing things that might be too dangerous.

"'One day, the dog, Mbwa, was sniffing around the outskirts of the village. He was out there for a while, just looking around to find likely places where birds and other animals might like to hide, and it was then that he noticed that the leopard, Chui, appeared to be stalking him, looking for something to eat. The dog was too old and slow to successfully run from the big cat, and not strong enough any longer to defend himself against him, so if he was to escape he would have to use his intelligence. Quickly looking around, he noticed some bones lying nearby, so settled down to chew on one of the bones with his back to the leopard. Chui was getting really close and crouching to spring when Mbwa announced very loudly in the language of animals "Wow, that was one delicious leopard! I wonder if there are any more around here?

"'When the leopard heard the dog say this, Chui stopped his attack in mid-strike, feeling a twinge of fear, and carefully slinkingaway into the bush, all the while thinking, "I must be more careful. That was a very close call. That old dog nearly had me!

"'Well, it turns out that, during this encounter, the monkey, Tumbili, had been carefully watching what was happening from a nearby tree. Monkeys are often very clever, of course, or at least think that they are, and they are always looking for things that they can turn to their advantage. This monkey had been in this part of the forest before, and knew that the bones the dog was chewing on were not those of a leopard, which meant that he also knew that the leopard had been tricked, and thus had lost his opportunity to capture an easy meal. The

monkey reasoned to himself that he could put this knowledge to good use.

"'You see, monkeys are afraid of leopards, since those big cats are very stealthy hunters, and can sneak up on monkeys, and even climb high enough into the trees to catch a monkey if he does not have enough of a head start. Tumbili the monkey thought that perhaps he could trade his information about the dog's trick for a period of protection from the leopard, and so, with that in mind, raced off after the leopard. You should know that monkeys are very noisy, and are always talking to themselves, which is why old Mbwa noticed the monkey dashing away in the direction the leopard had taken. Being as smart as he was, the dog guessed that something must be up. At the same time the dog also recognized that the village was too far away for his old body to get him to before a young leopard in hot pursuit could catch him, so Mbwa sat down and began to try and think of a solution to his dangerous problem.

"'It only took a minute or so for the monkey to catch up with the leopard, and tell his story to Chui. In exchange for the information about how the dog had tricked the leopard, the cat and the monkey negotiated a sort of truce. According to their agreement, the leopard promised not to hunt the monkey again until the end of the summer.

"'The leopard was not only hungry but also furious at being played for a fool, so he said, "Here, monkey, hop on my back, and see what happens when someone tries to deceive a mighty leopard.

"'However, by this time, the old dog, Mbwa, was ready. He had been watching for the return of the big cat, and when he saw the leopard coming with the monkey riding on his shoulders, he simply sat down with his back to the advancing, would-be attackers, and pretended not to have seen them. Just as the monkey and leopard got close enough to hear, the old dog exclaimed in animal language, "Where's that damn monkey? I sent him off half-an-hour ago to bring me another leopard!" The leopard stopped so suddenly that the monkey fell off his back. The leopard shouted at him "Traitor!" and chased Tumbili back up into the high branches of the tree. With all of the commotion of that chase going on behind him,

Gods, ghosts, and black dogs

the dog had plenty of time to safely return to his village.'"

The group laughed, and I pushed the wine bottle over to the storyteller, saying, "I don't need it any longer. I believe the case for the superior intelligence of dogs in comparison to cats and monkeys has been made by my esteemed colleague."

Visit Hubble and Hattie on the web: www.hubbleandhattie.com
www.hubbleandhattie.blogspot.co.uk
• Details of all books • Special offers • Newsletter • New book news

Why dogs sniff each other's rear ends

It was a late summer's day in Newfoundland, and I was sitting on a lawn chair talking with an elder of the Mi'kmaq Indians, who was also a member of the Benoit family. We had been talking about the fact that native people in North America used dogs that were only some 19 or 20 inches high at the shoulder to hunt big animals like moose or bears.

After a while, he poured each of us a large glass of screech: a rum whose origin can be traced back to the triangle trade in colonial times, when the same barrels were used to carry molasses and rum, and were only occasionally cleaned between loads. As a result, a deposit of strongly-sweet sediment built up at the bottom of the barrels, and the dockworkers would often liquefy the sediment with boiling water, and ferment it to produce a mind-numbing form of moonshine which contains about 40 per cent alcohol. This drink is now made commercially, in the same way that other rum is distilled, although I suspected that the drink I had in my hand had been made in something like the original way, since it had been poured from a clear glass gallon jug, with no label on it.

Newfoundlanders like to tell a story about how this rum got its name. Apparently, it had been just a homemade alcoholic drink until American servicemen came to the island during World War II, when, as the story goes, the commanding officer of the original detachment was offered a glass of it by an older fisherman, who downed his own drink in a single gulp. Being new to the island – and wanting to be as polite as possible – the soldier was trying to follow local customs as he observed them, so he also swallowed down his own tot just as quickly. Obviously unprepared for the strength of the drink, he let out a loud, painful bellow as it burned its way down his throat. His sergeant, who was standing outside, quickly opened the door, and asked, "What the hell was that ungodly screech?" The Newfoundlander who had served the drink answered, "Da screech? 'tis the rum, me son." So, in the retelling of this tale, the rum became known as 'screech,' and has remained so since then.

As we relaxed in the waning afternoon light (sipping – not gulping – our screech), we watched two dogs playing tug-of-war with a stick.

Gods, ghosts, and black dogs

Two other dogs appeared from around the side of the house and trotted up to them, and the two we had been watching dropped their stick, and all four dogs engaged in a round of sniffing each other's bottoms as part of the usual greeting ritual so common among canines.

My host turned to me with a smile, and said, "I know that you scientists can explain why dogs sniff each other's bottoms, but whatever reasons you come up with can't be as interesting as the way that my people describe it."

He leaned back and flicked his fingernail against the side of his glass to make a ringing sound, almost like a bell announcing that a story was about to begin.

"It was way back at the beginning, and Naguset, the creator, had done a whole lot of creating. He had made the earth and the sky, the sun and the moon, the oceans and the rivers, the mountains and the trees, and all that kind of stuff. He also created everything that was alive, starting with the plants, and then the insects, and finally he got to the hard part, which was making animals, birds, and fish. He was getting pretty tired after all this creating, and wanted to conserve some strength, because he had been pondering about making men and women. The idea which he had in his mind was pretty complicated, because he was thinking that he wanted these men and women creatures to have the ability to talk, think, sing, and dance, and that was going to take a lot of energy and effort on his part.

"Naguset was a really fair-minded god, not some kind of dictator or king who tried to tell everybody and everything what they had to do. And besides, he was too tired after all of that creating to make all of those millions of important decisions — where every animal was going to live, what they were going to eat, and so on — that still remained. So he leaned against a big rock (one he had created just for this occasion), and put his voice into the wind so that he could talk to all of the animals, and tell them that he was resting up so that he could create humans. After he explained what humans were going to be, and what they would be able to do, and how complicated they were going to be, he told the other animals that they had a bunch of decisions they needed to make.

"'I want all of you to decide where you want to live in this world; what you are going to eat; whether you're going to live on the land, or in the water, or fly through the sky. But I also want you to decide whether you want to get along with humans after I make them, or whether you want to go your own way, or even fight them.

"'Now, in order to make decisions like that you need to have a really big, long talk among yourselves. Don't worry: I know that I haven't given you the ability to speak and use language, because, to do that properly, so that each animal has his own language, would be a lot of work, and besides, I am saving this ability as a special gift for humans. But I *can* give you the know-how to speak to each other using wind talk, at least for a short while. Wind talk is where you think something, and the thought is sent to whoever you are trying to talk to, and they get that thought in *their* mind, just as I am talking to you now.

"'Now, listen carefully. I have built some big lodges made of magic bark and branches, and hides and stuff, and there is one lodge for each kind of animal. Each of these lodges is a sacred place; when you are inside, you will have the skills you need to wind talk the way that I do, so that you can speak to each other, work out all of the arguments, and reach a decision. Each animal will have a voice, and will have a say in the final resolution. I don't want there to be any chiefs, or big and important individuals taking over and choosing for you, because what you decide in that lodge is forever. Remember, every one of your kind will have to live by what you settle on.

"'It is important for you to know that I have put just enough magic in each of these lodges to hold them together for one day. You can go into them at sunrise, and you can talk and understand each other while you are inside. But the magic will wear off when the sun appears over the horizon the next morning, so you had better be outside the lodges then because the sun's rays will burn them into nothingness. Okay, now all of you go into your special lodge and decide on your future. I am going to take a little nap, and in the morning, when the lodges are gone and you have all agreed upon what you are going to do, I will sit myself down and make myself something that will be called 'human beings.'"

"With a giant gust of wind, Naguset lifted all of the animals and dropped each one in front of a lodge. The birds went into their lodge, and they decided that they would live in the sky and fly all of their lives. The fish decided that they wanted to live in the sea, and that this would be their last day on land. Bears decided they wanted to have nothing to do with these new humans, and would fight them if they came too close. Deer decided they wanted to run fast, and spend most of their time just eating and relaxing. Raccoons decided they wanted to play, and rabbits decided that they wanted to have lots of babies, and all that kind of thing. Every species worked out its destiny that night.

"However, when it came to dogs, things were a little different. The first thing dogs had to do was make sure that every dog in the lodge was equal. There was to be no fancy dress – no chiefs, no important individuals – because everyone was to have the same say in how they would live forever.

"For dogs, one thing served as a badge to differentiate between an animal who was high muckety-muck, important and powerful, and a plain working class dog, and this was the dog's tail, all of which were very different. Some were big and long, while others were short and stumpy. Some tails didn't have much hair, and looked like the tail of a rat, while others were flowing, with long, important 'feathers.' Each kind of tail had a meaning for dogs, and what that tail looked like told other dogs how important its owner was, and lets everyone know which family or tribe of dogs he came from.

"To ensure sure that everyone had an equal voice, each dog had to take off his tail and hang it near the door of the lodge when he went inside. The dogs asked Naguset for a place to store their tails for the duration of their powwow, but he was tired, and wanted to get on with his nap, so all he did was to take a long stick and drive it into the ground next to the door to the lodge, to serve as one of those standing coat racks that some folks have just inside their homes. The only difference was that it had

strings on it from which the dogs could hang their tails.

"It didn't take the dogs very long to make up their minds about what they wanted to do with their lives. The humans that Naguset said he was about to make sounded like pretty smart individuals, who would probably be great hunters, and clever enough to be able to make their own lodges, and warm them with fire. Since dogs are essentially easy-going creatures, and a bit on the lazy side, they decided to make no decision other than to opt to be with people, letting them help care of their kind, and make all of the hard choices.

"All of that took less than an hour to decide, and once that part of the powwow was finished, the dogs settled down to enjoy the food and drink that Naguset had left for them. It turned into a great celebration, with dogs using their temporary gift of magic wind talk to tell stories (and fibs) about themselves and their families, including all of their great accomplishments (some of which might even have actually happened), and so on. After a while, they got to singing and dancing, and, what with all the food and frivolity, the dogs simply forgot about the time as they partied through the night. No one noticed that the sun was beginning to nudge up over the horizon; at least, that is, until the first rays of sun hit the magic lodge, each ray setting the lodge alight, as Naguset had foretold.

"It didn't take long for the lodge to fill with smoke, causing the dogs to panic, and rush to get outside before the enchanted lodge was totally consumed by flames. With all of the dogs crowding the entrance at once, there wasn't time to sort through the tails hanging on the stick, so each dog just grabbed the nearest tail and rushed out.

"The dogs were standing outside, watching the last of the sacred lodge burn, when Naguset woke up, and felt that it was time to send the animals to start living their lives the way they had decided upon. Now, each of the dogs had grabbed a tail, but none of them had managed to grab their own in the confusion. Before they had the chance to sort things out, however, Naguset produced another great gust of wind, which sent every dog back to his natural home.

Gods, ghosts, and black dogs

"And there you have it. Every dog has a tail, but it isn't his own original family tail, which means that, whenever a dog meets another dog, he has to check around the back end to see if *this* dog has the tail that really belongs to him: the tail that his long-time-ago ancestor left behind when he was running out of the burning magical lodge.

"Dogs aren't all that happy about the fact that their proper tails went missing, but they are happy that they decided to live with people, and let humans take care of them and make all the important decisions. I am sure that even more puzzling to dogs than where their own tail has gone is why humans have no tails at all. But how that came to be is another story."

Visit Hubble and Hattie on the web: www.hubbleandhattie.com
www.hubbleandhattie.blogspot.co.uk
• Details of all books • Special offers • Newsletter • New book news

Why the Chow Chow has a black tongue, and a fuzzy, curly tail

Summer was winding down, and I was sitting at a table outside of a coffee shop just relaxing. I had one more chore to do before I could go home, and I was hoping that the caffeine in the coffee would give me the energy to complete it. Meanwhile, I was just watching the world go by.

A shadow fell across my table, and I looked up to see Luli, a secretary at the university. Luli came from a traditional Chinese family, although one of a second generation of children born in Canada. She was pretty, slightly built, and her eyes sparkled when she smiled, which she did a lot. A year or two earlier she had gotten an American Eskimo dog, named Snowy, who had some separation anxiety issues, and I had helped her deal successfully deal with her dog's problems. Afterwards, whenever I saw her, she always had a new picture of Snowy on her smart phone, and would usually show it to me, with a bit of a story about what was going on in her dog's life. Today was no exception, and Luli popped open her phone to show me a picture of her little white dog in a pointed, red-and-gold party hat.

Luli got herself a cappuccino and returned to sit down next to me. As we sat sipping our coffee and casually chatting, a woman walked by with a light tan Chow Chow by her side: a handsome dog, well groomed, and very fuzzy-looking. I smiled at the dog, then leaned over to Luli and said, "Sometimes, Chow Chows make me laugh. When they are coiffed like that they look to me much like one of those extreme, 1960s Afro haircuts, only these are hairdos that have four feet and a curled tail. Those blue-black tongues they have certainly don't make them look less surreal to me."

Luli looked at the Chow and smiled, "I never quite thought of it that way, but the original name of the dog breed probably says that other people have also thought about how fuzzy these dogs look. In Chinese we call them 'Songshi Quan,' which means 'puffy lion dog.' I always marvell at how their curled tails seem to get lost in all that fuzzy fur." She laughed, and added in a conspiratorial tone, as though she was telling me a cultural secret, "Do you know that the name Chow Chow is one of those funny mistranslations that pop up now and then? When the dogs were first imported into Germany, they arrived in

Gods, ghosts, and black dogs

crates marked 'Chow Chow.' The Germans, who were always careful about keeping records, took that label as indicating the kind of dog in the crate, so assumed that the breed of must be Chow Chow. What they didn't understand was that 'Chow Chow' was simply pidgin Chinese for miscellaneous merchandise."

She looked down at the picture of Snowy still showing on her cell phone screen, "My parents wanted me to get a traditional Chinese breed of dog instead of Snowy, and encouraged me to get a Chow Chow or a Pekingese. They liked to tell stories about how these breeds of dog were favourites in the royal palaces in China. Actually, one of their stories explains the fuzzy look, the curled tail, and the black tongue in the Chow."

I glanced at my watch, and thought to myself that my remaining chore could wait. I said, "Of course, you are going to tell me the story?"

Luli smiled. "I forgot you collect dog stories, don't you?"

I nodded, and she took another sip of her coffee, then began to tell the story in what seems to be the traditional manner that people always tell folk tales. "It was in the time of the first true Khan, when the great monks and sorcerers still had magic and could talk to animals. There were two kinds of dogs in the great palace, Pekingese and Chow Chow. The Pekingese were companion dogs, who sat on the laps of the royal family and kept them company. They were smaller than they are now, and, in the winter, could be tucked into the large, open sleeves of the traditional robes that high-born nobility wore. This was useful since, in there, they could serve as tiny little heaters to warm the aristocrat's arms. The Pekingese also played in small groups on the floor, sometimes with the children, much to the amusement of the nobility.

"The Chows of that time looked very different to those of today. Their long hair lay quite flat against their bodies, and they had a mostly straight tail — much like that on a Labrador Retriever now, but with longer hair. When the Khan came by, the Chows would stand respectfully at attention, with their tails pointing almost straight up, like the Chinese military flags. The Chow Chow's job was much more serious than that of the Pekingese: they were supposed to be guard dogs, protecting the palace, the temples, and other places of importance. For this reason, the King of the Chows, a dog named Chao (which means 'Great One') had been given the rank of Commander of the King's Guard.

"There existed a longstanding rivalry between the Pekingese and the Chows. You see, every year the Khan would have a formal portrait of himself painted, and would have his dogs with him in that painting. One dog would be placed next to the right hand of the Khan, in the position of honour, while the other would be placed to his left. The Khan would always decide which dog had pleased him the most that year, either by being the most handsome, the most useful, or the most clever. The dogs coveted that position of honour, and kept a running score of which breed had won that accolade the greatest number of times.

"It came to pass that, at this particular point in history, the King of Siam chose to give a gift to the great Khan: a beautiful pair of Siamese cats. In Siam, these cats were more often used as guard animals than as companions, and placed next to valuable objects in the Temple, sometimes on a short leash. Their task was to ensure that no one touched the objects or tried to steal them.

"The Khan received the gift of the two cats graciously, but did not know what he was going to do with them. Although beautiful, they were not friendly, companion animals he could leave with the children. He did not need them as guard animals, since that work was already being done by the Chow Chows. While he was musing about this problem, Chao came into the crown chamber. The dog saluted the Khan with an upright tail, and reported what had happened in the past hours. The monk who stood beside the Khan translated what the Chow said, 'Sire, we found an armed group of thieves trying to get into the royal treasury. I, and members of my dog guard, chased them out of the palace enclosure and through the woods until we finally captured them and recovered what they had stolen.' The dog then saluted again by holding his tail straight up.

"The Khan was happy with this report, and thanked the dog. He then noticed that the dog's fur was tangled. and that grass seeds and burrs were caught it, obviously from pursuing the thieves through the forest and the fields. He said to the dog, 'We must get you groomed properly, my Commander of the Guard, so that you will look clean and appropriately handsome if you are to sit at my right hand when I get my portrait painted early tomorrow.'

"It was then that the Khan had an idea about the cats.. He had been watching them groom themselves, their fine, sharp claws gently running through their fur to work out tangles, and remove anything caught in their coat. Perhaps he could assign the cats the task of grooming the dog? This would give them a job, make them useful, and not impinge on the duties of the Chow Chows, or any of the other animals in the palace. So the great Khan had the cats brought before him, to tell them of his plan to make them the personal groomers of his loyal dog.

"The cats regarded this suggestion as a great insult; the monk translating their indignant response: 'In Siam, we are members of the royal household, not servants. It would be an insult to the King of Siam, who gave us to you, if you should turn us into mere servants of a dog.'

"But the great Khan was a clever man, and he patiently explained to the cats that the Chow Chow, Chao, was not just any dog, but the official Commander of the King's Guard, often referred to as the 'Khan's Lion Dog.' He had the power to command all of the Chow Chows enlisted in the Khan's service, and, in his high office, Chao not only served as a representative of all Chow Chows, but was also a role model for them. As such, the dog was entitled to one or two aide-de-camps, who, the Khan explained to the cats, must also be an Officer of the Guard. In their role as aide-de-camp, the cats would serve as personal assistants to their Commander of the Guard. The Khan offered to grant both cats commissions in the Royal Guard, with the rank of lieutenant.

"The cats, somewhat mollified, agreed to this proposal, but only if their commissions in the guard granting their rank as officers was put in writing. This was needed, they explained, in case a member of the Siamese aristocracy should happen to see them performing their duties, and assume that they had

fallen from grace, and were now merely servants – or worse – slaves, carrying out menial tasks. The felines further decreed that their commissions must be written on very thin paper so that it could be folded to fit into a tiny, silk pouch that they would wear around their necks, and which could then be read by anyone who doubted their current status. The Khan agreed, and a royal scribe was called for to write out the cats' commission as lieutenants in black ink on thin paper, and the great Khan himself signed these documents in royal blue ink as befitted his rank. The documents were then placed in their little red, silk pouches and attached to the cats' collars.

"The dog, Chao, was next introduced to his new lieutenants, and the three animals returned to Chao's quarters in the barracks. The first task that Chao set for the cats was to clean his fur, to make sure there were no tangles, and nothing was stuck in it, such as seeds and burrs, because the Khan had said that he must look neat for his portrait in the morning. The dog then laid down to take a nap while the cats did their work.

"The cats knew little about military protocol, and were afraid that if they worked too hard at cleaning the dog's fur by raking their claws through it, they might wake their commander from his nap, which they feared would make him angry. So they worked very slowly, and very carefully, and by the time the dog awakened an hour-and-a-half later, they had only cleaned the fur around his face and ears. The dog was quite annoyed at the lack of progress the cats had made in grooming his fur, and told them 'In the morning, the Khan will have his portrait painted, and I am to sit by his right side in the place of honour, but only if I am well-groomed enough to look respectable when seated beside such a great and noble person. If you cannot discharge the duties which have been assigned to you, then I will have your rank stripped from you, and you will no longer be Officers of the Guard, and, indeed, will have to spend the rest of your life as servants, catching mice in the kitchen.'

"The cats protested they had done everything in the dog's best interests. 'We did not want to awaken you, or tug too hard at your fur since it might cause you discomfort, noble Chao.'

Gods, ghosts, and black dogs

"The dog said, 'I will arrange it so that you do not waken me or disturb me. However, the two of you will have to work through the night to comb out my fur, and if I find one grass seed or one tangle, then, as your commander, I will bring you up for charges of insubordination and failure to obey a command, and you will be punished under the code of military discipline. I have earned the honour to sit by the Khan's right side, and I will not have it lost by appearing unkempt in front of him.'

"So, that night, when the Chow Chow returned to his quarters, he ate his dinner and took a triple ration of brandy so that he could sleep through any tugging or pulling of his fur that might happen while the cats groomed him. Chao then lay down on his bed and fell into a deep sleep.

"The cats immediately went to work on him. They raked their fine, sharp claws through his fur, cutting through tangles, and pulling out debris that had lodged in the fur during the chase after the thieves earlier that day. As they worked on cleaning his fur, they noticed that the hair became soft and frizzy, much like what happens when a woman teases her hair because she wants it to look fuller. This pleased the cats because they liked the way that it felt when it was soft and fluffy.

"The job of cleaning up and combing out the Chow Chow's fur was done in a couple of hours. However, Chao's new lieutenants were cats, and cats must act as cats do. For example, cats like to scratch at things, and run their claws through soft, furry surfaces, which is why people buy scratching posts for them. So, all through the night, the cats continued to scratch and comb the fur of their commander, simply because they liked the way it felt. One of the cats worked away on Chao's body, and the dog's fur puffed out more and more, and his body began to look softer and rounder, much like a plush toy. The other cat was fascinated by the dog's tail, and combed and stroked it all through the night. Not only did the fur on the tail become long and soft and frizzy with all of that stroking and combing, but, much like a piece of leather that has been stroked on one side for a long time, it also began to curl, and almost into a full circle, looking more like a fuzzy wheel attached to the dog's

back than a traditional dog tail. After many hours of teasing and working Chao's fur, the cats lay down in the corner, content with a night full of scratching, expecting to be complemented in the morning for their work.

"When the dawn broke, Chao awakened, a bit groggy from the brandy he had drunk the night before. He checked the time, and saw that he was supposed to be in the Khan's chambers in just a short while to prepare to pose for the annual portrait. The Chow Chow glanced in the mirror and looked at his face, noticing that the hair was puffed out a bit, but clearly clean and untangled. He didn't have time to look at himself any further, but raced to the palace quickly in order to arrive at the royal chambers on time.

"When he presented himself before the throne, he was most surprised at the reception he got. At first, the Khan simply laughed, and asked 'What has happened to you? You no longer look like a guard dog. You certainly do not look ferocious enough to bear the title of Lion Dog. You look more like a kind of teddy bear to be fondled and nuzzled by children than the Commander of the Guard. If anything, you are now a Songshi Quan, a "Puffy Lion Dog." You no longer look military, and you do not even salute your Khan by holding your tail upright as a member of the guard should. I do not want you in my portrait looking like that. Not only will you not sit at my right hand, but I do not want you to be seen at all in the painting. I will sit this year with just the Pekinese.'

"The Chow Chow did not understand. He thought that he had held his tail in a respectful upright position as he always did. He could not understand that the cat had worked on his tail so long that it had now become permanently curled, and could never again be held straight up. Also, since he had not really looked at anything other than his face before leaving his quarters, he did not know how puffy his coat had become. Now, as he left the Khan's palace, he glanced in a mirror near the door, and saw what had been done to him over the night. He was angry at the cats for doing this, and ashamed at having lost his position at the right hand of the Khan.

"He rushed back to his quarters to confront

Why the Chow Chow has a black tongue, and a fuzzy, curly tail

the cats. 'What have you done to me? I am now disgraced and no longer look like a soldier with this fluffy coat you have given me. I also do not understand what you have done to my tail, since I it seems that I can no longer straighten it to salute Khan.

"The dog gave an angry growl and continued, 'You are no longer members of the Royal Guard, and I revoke your commissions.' He snatched at the two silk bags which contained the documents appointing the cats as officers, splitting open the little pouches, and pulling out the documents, which he chewed up, spitting out what was left at the feet of the frightened cats. However, the black and blue ink on the thin paper had dissolved in the Chow's mouth and stained his tongue a blackish blue. Seeing this, with a great snarl the disgraced commander chased the cats out of his headquarters, and swore to himself that, for the rest of his life, whenever he saw a cat, regardless of how royal or aristocratic it was, he would chase it and try to bite it.

"But this happened during the era of magic. In the sky that night and all through the events of the morning you could clearly see the moon, and it was coloured red. This was not just any red moon, however, but the eighth red moon of the year. In that magic time, things that happened under the eighth red moon became permanent and forever. Since Chao was the commander and the role model for all Chow Chows, what happened to him under that particular moon happened to all Chow Chows, and would be fixed that way always. And that is why all Chows have puffy fur, a permanently curled tail, and that unusual blue-black tongue. It is also one reason why Chow Chows never pass up a chance to chase a cat."

I looked at Luli and said, "I don't know if I can completely believe your story. You know, I once had a cat who liked to groom my hair, and look what happened to me." With that, I took off my hat and ran my hand over my bald head.

Luli laughed and said, "That's because the era of magic has passed."

The heroic dog
on the Titanic

Every now and then my study of the lore and mythology of dogs leads me to a surprise, which sometimes involves a particular observation of some aspect of canine behaviour that I had not known of or thought about before. Sometimes, the surprise has to do with an alternative way of looking at the relationship and emotional bond that we have with dogs, and sometimes it's that a story which is widely believed to be purely folklore turns out to have, at its core, a nugget of truth. Let me tell you about one such story, and also describe for you my investigation of the so-called 'myth' of the heroic dog on the *Titanic*.

For me, the tale begins in the year 2012, which marked the 100th anniversary of the sinking of the *RMS Titanic*. The great ship went down around midnight on April 14, 1912, and was lost to the cold North Atlantic Ocean. The *Titanic* was considered to be the most luxurious ship ever built, and it was also thought to be unsinkable. There are many stories about the ship, its passengers and crew, but I remember being caught by a story concerning an heroic dog who was on the ill-fated ship, and was credited with helping to save some of the passengers

on that night. Since, that year, it was exactly 100 years from the time of the sinking of the *Titanic*, I decided I would like to write an article about that particular dog, and his story, as a way of commemorating the event. I had been assured by several people who knew a bit about the history of the tragedy, that no dog was present on the voyage, or at least none who played any role in assisting the survivors. They told me that any story about canine heroism during the sinking had to be apocryphal; created after the event. Actually, hearing that the story of the dog on the *Titanic* was really a folk tale did not discourage me, since I thought that it might still be interesting to pursue it in order to learn when and why this particular story might have come about. My thought was that, in the end, such knowledge might shed some light on the bond and emotional feeling that people have for dogs in general, if not on an actual historical incident.

So I began my investigation by looking at the *Titanic's* highly experienced first officer, William McMaster Murdoch, a native of Scotland. All of the re-tellings of the story of an heroic dog on the great ship seem to begin with the observation that Murdoch took a canine companion with him to the *Titanic*: a large, black Newfoundland dog, named Rigel, who had also been with Murdoch when he was serving on the *Titanic's* sister ship, the *RMS Olympic*. If I could confirm that Murdoch did not have such a dog, or that the dog was not present on the *Titanic*, I reasoned, then at least the fact that the story was a modern piece of folklore would be proven.

My initial surprise was to discover that first officer Murdoch actually *did* have a large, black dog: there are two photographs of him on the *Olympic*, with the dog beside him, and statements from crew members suggesting that this dog was a common sight on the ship. However, that does not place the dog on the *Titanic*, but, although there are no photographs of Rigel on the *Titanic*, there are fragmentary reports which would suggest that Murdoch was seen on the ship with a black dog several times. Two of these reports come from passengers, and one from a crewman, who added that, on the fateful night when the great ship went down, the first officer's dog, Rigel, was safely housed in the *Titanic's* modern kennel facilities. Murdoch had placed him there because needed to focus on one of the major goals of this voyage – to reach New York in record time.

This piece of information poses a conundrum, since some of the individuals who have studied the *Titanic's* sinking say that no such dog existed. I therefore decided to look a little further, and it turns out that Rigel was not the only dog onboard: there were twelve others. In the kennels next to Rigel were two Airedales owned by John Jacob Astor, a Chow Chow owned by Harry Anderson, and a champion French Bulldog with the impressive name of 'Gamin de Pycombe,' owned by Robert Daniels. William Dulles brought a Fox Terrier, William Carter's family had two King Charles Spaniels, and Ann Isham had the largest dog, a Great Dane. Several other dogs stayed in the staterooms with their owners, and these included a Pekingese named Sun Yat Sen, owned by Henry Harper and his wife, Myra, and two Pomeranians belonging to Elizabeth Rothschild and Margaret Hays. The last of the canines onboard was a small dog of unknown breed named Frou Frou, who

belonged to newlyweds Helen and Dickonson Bishop, and who stayed in their room.

Each day, a crewmember would take the dogs for a stroll around the promenade deck, and these canine parades became quite an event, with guests scheduling their visits on deck to coincide with the walks. Everyone seemed to be enjoying the dogs so much that an informal dog show was scheduled by the first class passengers to be held on Monday, April 15th (unfortunately, that show would never take place).

In the fog and darkness on the night of April 14th, *Titanic* collided with an iceberg, tearing open five hull compartments. This was too much for the 'unsinkable' ship, and she began to go down. In the years which followed, the human tragedy and bravery of that night was well documented, and we know quite a bit about the fate of the 1522 people who were lost that night, and even more about the 714 people who survived. I was not surprised to find that accounts of what happened to the dogs are less clear. Some of the reports are confused or incomplete, but the following information appears in a variety of reputable accounts of that ill-fated night.

Although many people died because of the inadequate number of lifeboats onboard, it turns out that some of the first boats in the water had empty seats. Thus, Henry and Myra Harper boarded their boat carrying their Pekingese, and Elizabeth Rothschild and Margaret Hays each boarded different boats carrying their small Pomeranians. Because there was plenty of room on these lifeboats and the animals were small, the dogs' presence was not challenged. The Bishops' little dog was with them in their cabin; however, when it became clear that, by now, there were not enough lifeboats for all the passengers, Helen Bishop felt obliged to leave her much-loved pet behind. Later, she would tearfully tell how, as she left the cabin for the last time, Frou Frou grabbed the hem of her dress, trying to keep her from going.

In the case of Ann Isham, however, her dog was a Great Dane, and clearly too large for the lifeboats. Ann refused to leave her dog behind, insisting she would do whatever was needed to save him. Sadly, after the sinking, her body was observed

Gods, ghosts, and black dogs

in the water with her arms frozen around her beloved dog.

But what of Rigel, and the other dogs in the kennels? Murdoch had no opportunity to leave his post to rescue his dog: after the collision, he took charge of starboard evacuation. Crew members report seeing Murdoch hard at work, trying to free Collapsible Lifeboat A from the rope tackles used to lower it, when a huge wave washed him overboard, and he was not seen again.

In the midst of the chaos, an unknown passenger went to the kennels and released all of the dogs in an attempt to spare them the horror of drowning in locked cages. Sadly, most of the dogs simply disappeared in the cold water, but, according to the story, Rigel's fate was different to that of his kennelmates. Most of the passengers (and dogs) who ended up in the freezing water died from exposure, and it is for that reason that some have questioned whether a dog such as Rigel could have survived a long swim in the icy ocean. However, the Newfoundland dog was bred to function in the harsh conditions of the North Atlantic, and has webbed feet, a rudder-like tail, and a water-resistant coat: all of which make the dog a natural swimmer, whose body uses the same mechanisms as polar bears to combat hypothermia. This ability allows these dogs to help retrieve fishing nets off the shores of their original island home near mainland Canada, for example, and is actually 400 miles north of where the Titanic sank. There are also many stories of Newfoundlands rescuing people from the sea, while having to endure icy conditions for long periods of time to do so.

According to most accounts, Rigel swam around, at first apparently desperately looking for his master, but, after a while, choosing to simply stay close to Lifeboat 4. The dog was too large to take on board, even if there had been space to do so, but the people, in their exposed lifeboat, apparently suffered more from the effects of the wet and cold than did Rigel in the freezing water.

More than two hours after the Titanic went down, the passenger ship Carpathia finally arrived, and began to pick up the surviving passengers. It was still dark and a low mist hung on the water, so

Carpathia's crew was calling out to the survivors, waiting for them to respond in order to locate them. Unfortunately, Lifeboat 4 had become separated from the other lifeboats by some distance. Finally, the Carpathia began to pull away from the area, unknowingly on a course directly bearing down on the unseen little lifeboat. Its passengers were simply too weak to shout loudly enough to avoid being run down by the ship, yet, somehow, Rigel was still strong enough to bark. Carpathia's Captain, Arthur Henry Rostron, heard the dog, and ordered the ship to stop. Swimming in front of the lifeboat, Rigel marked the location of the survivors, and all were hauled up the starboard gangway, including the big dog.

But what happened to Rigel after he was picked up by the Carpathia? This is where things become a little confusing. There is a photograph of the Titanic's survivors on the deck of the Carpathia, in the background of which can be seen a crewman standing next to a large, black dog — presumably, Rigel — which reinforces the likelihood that he made his way to shore, along with the rescued passengers. The story of a dog alerting rescuers to a lifeboat lost in the mist would have received a lot of coverage, you might think, although it is possible that such a story might have been overshadowed by tales of heroism and loss among the wealthy and well-known passengers involved in the sinking. It's certainly the case that the day after the Carpathia reached New York with the survivors, the New York Herald carried a story about Rigel's significant role in the rescue of Titanic's passengers, but news reports about Rigel — except for an occasional passing reference — do not exist after that. Thus, the trail of what happened to him goes cold.

It seems to me that, if such a dog existed, and played any part in the rescue of passengers, lost and helpless on that cold, misty sea, there should be some account of what happened to him after. Certainly, in our modern era of intense media coverage, there would have been numerous pictures and stories about this canine who was present — and may have helped out — during one of the most significant tragedies of the time. However, Rigel seems to simply disappear ...

I tried to follow up various clues that might lead me to Rigel, the most promising of which seemed to be that the *New York Herald* reporter had noted that, since the dog's owner was dead, one of *Carpathia's* crew (supposedly someone named Brigg) had adopted him. I thought this might be a starting place, but it turned out that the report was in error, since 'Brigg' was the name of a passenger on the lifeboat that Rigel supposedly helped save, rather than a crewman on the *Carpathia*.

I recall I was pretty much at the point where I was about to conclude that the story of a dog named Rigel surviving the sinking of the *Titanic* was unproven, and likely to be just another modern myth, when one more scrap of evidence appeared in a most happenstance way. If I had not decided to undertake this research in the year 2012, when the 100th anniversary of this marine tragedy had stirred media interest in *Titanic*, I suppose I might not have had a chance to stumble across one last clue, or perhaps would not have been alert to it when it popped up in front of me.

In 1962, the BBC radio network decided to commemorate the 50th anniversary of the sinking of the *Titanic*, and, over the course of that year, conducted a number of interviews with a few survivors of the disaster, or relatives and descendants of passengers and crew. Most of the interviews were human interest pieces, endeavouring to provide more information and details of what went on that fateful night, and in the aftermath of the sinking. In 2012, a number of these interviews were dug up by various media outlets looking for information that might give a novel slant to the story. and some were re-broadcast on the radio in feature documentaries, and some on television. I seem to remember that I was listening to a radio feature about the *Titanic*, although only casually monitoring what was being said, when my attention was suddenly caught by the words of a woman, who I believe was the granddaughter of

John Brown. At the time of the rescue of the *Titanic's* passengers, Brown was serving as the *Carpathia's* Master at Arms. The comments which grabbed my attention had to do with her grandfather's description of the rescue of Lifeboat 4 – the lifeboat that was supposedly saved because of Rigel's loud barking. I thought to myself, "Perhaps there might be some mention of the dog," and I leaned in closer to catch what she was saying.

According to the woman, John Brown mentioned that they had almost not found that lifeboat. In his account, he says that as they were unloading its passengers, one of them refused to go below deck, and would not move away from the rail until she had assured herself that the big, black dog who had hovered near the lifeboat had also been hauled aboard. Could this be Rigel?

The woman's re-telling of her grandfather's account was winding down, and I feared that the canine content would end there. However her few closing comments included mention of the dog. She claimed that Brown, at the age of 62, was the second oldest crewman on the *Carpathia*. He had been active during all of *Carpathia's* attempts to rescue the *Titanic's* passengers, and was apparently touched by some of their stories of heroism and loss. According to her, it might well have been Brown's experiences that night which convinced him it was time to finally end his career at sea, and when he left the *Carpathia*, he took with him "the great, black dog who was rescued from the *Titanic*," and retired to his rural home in Scotland. I do not recall her ever mentioning the name of the dog, although she emphasized his size and his coloir – he was big, and he was black.

I thought to myself "If this account is correct, then it's likely that Rigel was not a myth, and, presumably, this canine hero of the *Titanic* tragedy saw out his natural life without ever having to face icy water again."

The morality of dogs

I found myself sitting in the 'green room' of a television station in New York City, waiting to be called in front of the camera for the taping of a magazine-type television show, where various guests appear on stage for a performance or an interview. For those of you who do not know, a 'green room' is the media term used to describe the space in a theatre, studio or similar venue that functions as a lounge or waiting room for performers or guests not yet required on stage, or in front of the cameras. I have only seen one which was actually green (the ABC television studios in New York), and that was a while back. Most green rooms provide a table, from which you can get yourself a cup of coffee or tea, and sometimes some cookies or other pastry, as was the case with this one

I have always liked the informal atmosphere of most green rooms, since this often gives me a chance to meet the other guests, and also provides an opportunity to chat with people who you might otherwise never have the chance to speak to. Depending upon the length of the show, and the efficiency of the crew (especially if it involves taping rather than a live broadcast), the wait time for guests

can be fairly long, which means that I can sometimes actually have a meaningful conversation with an interesting person before one of us is called out to sit in front of the cameras and microphones.

This particular morning I found myself sitting next to Job Michael Evans. I don't know whether you recognize this name, but you might recognize the religious sect he used to belong to – the Monks of New Skete – a small group of Byzantine-Rite Franciscan monks seeking to live a monastic life within the Eastern Christian traditions. The order resides in a rural section of upstate New York on the eastern edge of the low but beautiful Taconic Mountains. With the help of local residents, the Monks of New Skete learned farming, livestock keeping, and cheese making, and use these skills to feed themselves and support their religious and community activities.

However, the order is best known for one specific aspect of their activities; namely, the breeding and training of German Shepherd dogs. Each monk keeps one dog with him in his living quarters, and is responsible for training and socialising the animal, who is later sold to help support the order. In addition, the monks conduct dog training classes, and try to help people who have dogs with behavioural problems.

The Monks of New Skete became popular with the public because of a book, *How to Be Your Dog's Best Friend*, mostly written by Job Michael Evans, although authorship is attributed collectively to The Monks of New Skete on the spine. The first edition of this book contains some autobiographical accounts of Evans' personal interactions with the dogs, which are interesting, since he had not trained dogs before. However, most of the book focused on a solid, down-to-earth, set of training procedures focusing on a combination of rewards and discipline. Later editions of the book did not contain most of Evans' personal accounts of his experiences with the order, and updated the training methods somewhat, becoming more reward-based in method.

Once he had left the monastic life, Job Michael Evans came to New York City, and, trading on the popularity of the New Skete book, became a dog trainer to the rich and famous. He also went on to write a number of new books on dog training, and the solving of problem behaviours in dogs. He was appearing on this particular programme in association with the publication of one of those books.

As we sat in the green room waiting for our camera calls, one of the associate producers suddenly rushed in to say that there would be about a half hour's delay before we got started with taping the show. I don't remember what the problem was, but I took the opportunity to wander over to the table and refill my cup of coffee, and grab one of the chocolate chip cookies on a plate nearby. Evans seemed to have the same idea, and we ended up sitting down on the sofa next to each other.

Just to pass the time I started a conversation with "People are always asking me about the intelligence of dogs because of the work I have done in that area. I suppose, with your monastic background, that people are always asking you about the moral life of dogs?"

He smiled, and ran one hand through his dark, curly hair; then said, "Our order does have the belief that animals, and particularly dogs, have a certain innocent morality. Of course, when we were training our own dogs, or those of other people, we spent a lot of time dealing with the behaviour problems that certain dogs had, some of which – such as biting, stealing food or lack of house cleanliness – might be considered by some to be evidence that dogs do not have much in the way of a sense of morality. I used to think about these issues quite a bit, and, in my mind, thought to myself that if I ever got a chance to preach to a congregation, I would like to give a sermon combining common sense dog training ideas with a more philosophical view of the morality of men and dogs."

I gestured toward the door by which the associate producer had exited the room after giving us the news about the impending delay in our schedule, and said, "It looks like it's going to be a while before either of us gets called into the studio, so, if you're willing, I wouldn't mind hearing a version of what that sermon might sound like."

He laughed, replying with, "This is certainly unusual. In all of the time I was associated with the monastery, I don't think anybody ever asked one of us to spontaneously give a sermon. However, if you really want to hear it, the one I had been shaping in my mind was based on a parable that I heard someplace, or maybe it was a snippet of folklore, or maybe it was just some philosophical musings. Anyway, the sermon would go something like this . . .

"As human beings, we all like to feel we are good and moral, and certainly have a sense of morality which goes beyond that of animals. After all, it was humans who wrote the Bible, and the Bible is our source for determining what is right and what is wrong. And it is humans who write laws, codes of ethics, and rules determining what honourable and good behaviour is, and what it is not. Animals are beneath all this, and the idea of even attributing morality and a sense of righteousness to an animal probably does not occur to most of us. But are you sure that it is we humans who are moral, and it is our pet dog who is lacking in this virtue?

"I heard a story once which began when one day a man walked into his kitchen, and found

Gods, ghosts, and black dogs

that his dog had made a mess on the floor during the night. In great frustration he turned his head to the sky and shouted to God, 'Why is it the case that dogs have no respect for man? Where is the canine sense of morality? Why do dogs have no dignity or honour, the way that humans do?'

"As chance would have it, this was a slow day in heaven, and, since there were few crises to attend to at that moment, God decided he had time to answer this man. A flash of light and a divine musical chord sung by a choir of angels gave way to the voice of God, answering the man's question in his mind.

"So it was that the voice of the Lord said to the astonished man, 'You talk of the fact that dogs have no dignity, honour, respect, or morality, at least in comparison to human beings, or at least as seen from the pedestal that you have placed mankind upon. Why don't you talk to the buildings and the monuments that your species erected to honour the best of humanity to see what man is really like?

"'Talk to the Great Sphinx and talk to the pyramids, and they will tell you that they have seen many men pass by, including a lot of ignorant, besotted pharaohs, who cared more about their own comfort in the afterlife than they did for the welfare of any of the people they ruled in this life, or those forced to labour on their behalf.

"'Talk to the gold-covered pagodas, the marble elephants, the jade statues of gods in China, and ask them about the noble people they might have met, and they will tell you stories of suave, self-centred mandarins who used their citizens as if they were tools to be thrown away if they were broken, or if their hands weakened too much to be of any use. Or they may speak of the cruel warlords in bright, painted armour, who were preceded by flowing silk banners to announce their presence: the very same warlords who used people as weapons and resources with no care for their blood or suffering.

"'Talk to the temples and forums of Greece and Rome whose face and style you still use today as the model for the buildings that house the courtrooms and the government offices which maintain order and justice. Those buildings will tell you of the men they have seen who owned other men and, in their time, bought and sold humans as slaves in open auction. Those slaves it was who constructed the great temples that you so admire, and whose hands carved the Doric, Ionian, and Corinthian columns which adorn these edifices.

"'Talk to the mediaeval Gothic cathedrals, and the great churches edged in gold, supposedly erected in my honour, but filled with priests who asked the population to pray for corrupt kings, self-serving politicians, and all forms of stiff-necked, drunken, robber barons. It was out of the doors of these cathedrals that the crusading knights flowed, with crosses emblazoned on their tabards, to begin their journey east to kill all of those who did not believe in the same God they did — not knowing or caring that the hated 'other' God is really me, but by a different name.

"'Talk to these great buildings about man; listen to their answers, and consider what they tell you. Then ask yourself might it not really be the case that, in comparison to dogs, it is people who have no honour, dignity, or moral sense? Dogs do not lie. Dogs do not betray confidences. Dogs do not buy or use or abuse others of their species for their own selfish concerns. Yet, people do all of these things. So who is the more moral?

"'Oh, yes, and to answer your question why your own particular dog seems to have not shown you any respect because of the mess he made on the floor during the night: you should know that, had you let him out into the yard for a few minutes before you went to bed, neither his sense of morality nor his bladder would have been so challenged.'"

With that he laughed, made the sign of the cross, and nodded his head at me.

I smiled and nodded back at him "Amen."

Are there dogs in heaven?

I was giving a talk at a book conference in Toronto, and was sitting at a lunch table with several other people who were also speakers at the event. I have no idea how seats were assigned for this event, but found myself sitting between a Protestant priest and a true crime writer. As is often the case in such mixed company, the talk at the table was fairly casual, and did not deal with any deep, significant issues.

However, I am always interested in the perspectives and opinions that people have about dogs, especially those in relatively unique positions in life, so when there was a lull in the conversation, I turned to the priest and asked, "As a clergyman, I was wondering whether you could tell me if there are dogs in heaven?" The man laughed, and put down his coffee cup. He paused for a moment, letting his fingers absentmindedly caress the surface of the carved silver cross which hung on a chain around his neck, before he looked up at me and responded.

"Now, that's a question which clergymen hear much more often than you might think. I am a Lutheran priest, and the founder of our sect, Martin Luther, even had to deal with that question once

himself. Martin Luther had a daughter named Mary, and a dog named Tolpel. One day, Mary came into his study with Tolpel. Mary loved the dog very much, but Tolpel was growing old and frail. 'Father,' she asked, 'what happens when my dog dies? Does he go to heaven?'

"I am not Martin Luther, of course, and God has not whispered the answer to that question in my ear, but, whenever I hear it, I think back to when I was still a student at the theological seminary, and someone in the class asked virtually the same question about dogs in heaven. To answer the question, an old priest told us a story: a folk tale he claimed came from Virginia, and it goes something like this.

"There was an old man named Sam who lived near the foothills north of Roanoke, Virginia. One afternoon, Sam was really tired, and lay down for a nap, during which he had a dream, only this was way too vivid for a dream, actually, and felt more like a 'seeing' or 'vision,' such as the prophets in the biblical era used to have. It felt so real, Sam had no doubt that this was something special.

Gods, ghosts, and black dogs

"In that vision, Sam reached up to wipe his face, but the hand he found himself looking at was that of a younger man: his own hand from when he was young and strong, and the skin wasn't spotted with age, and the veins didn't show so clearly. He was no longer old, and he felt vibrant and healthy. He noticed that he was standing in the middle of a dirt road, and the countryside looked a lot like what he remembered from wandering around near the Jackson River in the late springtime, and standing next to him was his big Bluetick Hound, Freckles. Now, that didn't make any sense, as Freckles had been Sam's companion in his late teenage years, and that well-loved dog was long gone now.

"Sam bent down and held the dog's head in his hands. He felt so real, and he heard himself telling the dog 'I really missed you, boy. You were my best friend for so many years.' It was then that Sam came to the conclusion that, if this was really happening, he must have 'passed on' and 'crossed over,', so he announced to Freckles, 'It appears that I have died, boy, so let's make the best of it,' and the touch of that beloved dog was so comforting, it seemed to keep him from worrying about this new and unknown situation.

"It was as if the dog understood exactly what he was saying, since he flipped his head up, gave a playful little bark, and made a dash to the side of the road, a moment later returning with a stick which he dropped at Sam's feet. The man picked it up and threw it, and this began what turned into a lively game of 'fetch.' Sam tossed and Freckles bounded after the stick, accompanied by the sounds of canine barks and human laughter. After the process had been repeated many times, Sam sank down to knees next to the dog and announced, 'I haven't had so much fun in years.'

"Freckles panted happily beside him, and Sam said, ' think we both could use a cold drink of water about now.' Sam looked around and, not seeing a creek or any other place to drink, stood up, called Freckles to his side, and said 'Let's head down the road and see what we can find.'

"Well, they hadn't walked too far when they reached a place where the land was fenced in by a large, white, marble wall, elegantly built and edged in gold. A short way further along there was a gate, which looked like it was covered in mother of pearl, and next to it was a saintly-looking man with a long, white beard. He was wearing a long, white robe, and sitting at a tall desk with a number of leatherbound books in front of him.

"Sam stopped in front of the man and asked 'What is this place?' and the man in white replied 'These are the Gates of Heaven.'

"'Wow!' said Sam, 'This is wonderful. May I come in?'

"The saintly man flipped a few pages, then said, 'Certainly, your name is listed here.'

"'Wonderful! My dog and I are kind of thirsty, and really could use a drink of water.'

"The man in white replied, 'We can get you some cold, fresh water, and even some ice, if you like. However, we can't let your dog in: we don't allow dogs or other pets in heaven.'

"Sam looked down at Freckles, then at the shiny gates which had opened a crack to reveal the sight of a tall, golden fountain with water bubbling over its edge. He scratched the dog's ears, and then said, 'Well, if my dog isn't welcome, then I suppose I don't belong here either.'

"The man in white looked surprised, and stood up. 'Now, that's a drastic decision on your part. We only offer to open the Gates of Heaven once for each person, so if you don't enter at this time, you won't have a second chance.'

"Sam had a real twinge of doubt about then: after, all no one turns their back on heaven! But then he looked again at his dog, and knew he couldn't leave him now that they were together again. So he gave Freckles a pat, and the two of them turned their backs on the pearly gates and moved on down the road.

"The man and the dog walked on for a while. To tell the truth, it wasn't hard travelling, since the day was still fine and the scenery pleasant. As they crested the top of a small hill they saw a farm, with a simple, white-painted wood fence, and a gate that was propped open. The place looked neat and well kept, if not all that prosperous. There were a couple of wooden lawn chairs under an oak tree in front of the house, and on one of the chairs was an older-looking man in jeans and a denim shirt wearing a straw hat. He was reading a book.

"Sam paused at the open gate, and said, 'Hi there. Is there any chance we could come in and get some water? My dog and I are really thirsty.'

"The man looked up and smiled pleasantly. 'Sure. You're welcome here. There is no need to go all the way back to the house to get a drink.' He gestured toward a nearby shed, and continued, 'There's a pump over there and some cups. There should also be a bowl for the dog.'

"Sam went to the shed and found an old hand pump, which he used to fill a cup with water for himself and a bowl for his dog. He then returned to the man, who gestured with his hand toward the other chair. Sam sat down with the cup still in his hand. A moment later Freckles left his now-empty water bowl, and came over and laid his head on Sam's knee.

"'What do you call this place?' Sam asked.

"'Well, sir,' replied the old man, 'You've just entered through the Gates of Heaven.'

"'Heaven? This is very confusing. There was a man in white down the road, who told me that the Gates to Heaven were back there.'

"'You mean the place with the pearly gates and all the gold stuff inside? Well, that is actually hell, and you were talking to the devil himself.'

"This bothered Sam. 'Well, why don't you do something to make him stop lying in order to get folks to leave the path and go into hell?'

"'No need to. He serves a useful function – a sort of screening service. Do you think that God would want to admit anybody into heaven who was willing to leave a good friend behind while he satisfied his own wants? No, sir! You *and* your dog are welcome in heaven; not just you without your dog.'"

The priest smiled, and continued, "I have always liked that folk tale. It is not biblical text or a theological analysis, but makes sense to me in terms of the way that I picture the will of God, and the nature of heaven – at least when it comes to people and their dogs in the afterlife. I think that you might also be happy to know that this brings us back to Martin Luther and his daughter, Mary's, question about whether her old dog would go to heaven when he died. The record shows Luther looked at his daughter and smiled. He then rose from his desk, walked over to the dog, and bent down to pat it. As he did so, he said with great assurance, 'Be comforted, little dog, come the resurrection, even thee shall wear a golden tail.'"

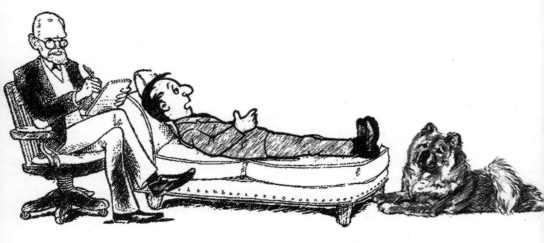

The dog who breached the gap

Animal Assisted Therapy is a technique used in clinical psychology, whereby companion animals — usually dogs — are used to help bridge emotional gaps in a person's personality, and thus help sooth individuals who are suffering from various psychological problems. It is a well respected and useful technique that might never have seen the light of day had it not been for an accidental encounter ... and a folk tale.

Before we get to that folk tale it's important to know that therapeutic use of animals has a long history. In ancient Egypt, the city of Hardai became known as Cynopolis (City of Dogs) because dogs were used as offerings in its many temples dedicated to the god Anubis (the dog-headed guide of the dead). However, dogs were also used in healing practices there: it was believed that being licked by a dog could help to heal injuries, or cure diseases, for example. This practice was picked up by the Greeks, and temples dedicated to Asclepius (the Greek god of medicine and healing), often contained dogs trained to approach suffering individuals, and lick their wounds.

Perhaps the most famous story of a dog healing a person is the tale of Saint Roche. He was born at Montpellier around 1295, and had a bright red mark across his chest in the shape of a cross, and many people believed this indicated he would be a holy man, destined to do great deeds. When he was about twenty years old, his parents died, and he wondered whether their early and tragic deaths may have been a judgement visited on him because he had failed to follow a life in the church, as ordained by his birthmark. Instead of joining the clergy, he had taken the easy path to a career in government, which was available to him because of his father's position as governor of the city. Eventually, however, Roche reconsidered his life choices, and decided to distribute his fortune among the poor, and hand over all of his government responsibilities to his uncle. The only thing that he kept as a reminder of his past life was the family dog. Then he dressed himself simply, and set out on a pilgrimage to Rome.

On the way he stopped at Aquapendente, which was suffering from the Plague of the Black Death. He tried to offer assistance to plague victims in the usual ways of that time, and noted that his dog had no hesitation about approaching the sick, and licked at the abscessed spots on their skin. The patients allowed the dog to do this since being licked by a dog was believed to have the power to cure. There is even a French saying, "Langue de chien, langue de médecin" which translates to "A dog's tongue is a doctor's tongue." To Roche, however, this ministration by his dog seemed to him a sign that what was needed was his touch, so he carefully traced the sign of the cross on the sick individual's body while praying for deliverance. The effect was miraculous: sores began to heal, and people began to recover from their illness.

He next visited Cesena and some of its neighbouring cities, finally making his way to Rome. Everywhere the story was the same. Roche and his dog visited the places where the sick had gathered, and the touch of the man and his dog, along with his prayers and sign of the cross, seemed to drive away the sickness. Roche now felt he knew what his calling was in life, and he and his dog continued to go from city to city on his healing mission.

Unfortunately, at Piacenza, Roche himself was stricken with the plague. He considered going into the city, but felt weak, and did not want to impose his own suffering on others, so, instead, he found a small hut: the kind of rude shelter used by foresters as a temporary shelter when the weather is very bad, or sometimes by woodcutters in which to store cut wood until it is dry and ready for sale. He crawled inside, covered himself, and went to sleep.

Some time later he awoke. There was a rain barrel nearby, so he had water, but he was now too weak to get up to forage for food. His dog licked at his open sores and seemed to want to comfort him.

As the sun dropped lower in the sky, Roche's dog got up and left his feverish master, wandering down the road, not more than a mile, to where a castle stood, owned by a minor aristocrat named Gothard. The dog entered the main gate and walked into the building. People were gathering in the dining hall for dinner, and, as they watched in amazement, the dog placed his paws on the edge of the table, and helped himself to a loaf of bread. Without stopping to eat it, he trotted back out of the open door.

Gothard was amused, but his amusement turned to astonishment when this theft was repeated several days in a row. The aristocrat went to the window to watch the dog leave, and was amazed to see that the animal took not a single bite out of the bread, but proceeded down the road and disappeared along a path into the woods. On the fourth or fifth night that this occurred, out of curiosity, the nobleman followed the dog. The faithful animal went directly back to the shelter where his master lay, and Gothard witnessed the dog drop the bread by Roche, and then proceed to tenderly lick his plague sores.

Gothard was so moved by the care shown by the dog, that he set about having Roche's needs met. To the amazement of everyone, Roche recovered, and did not even show any of the scars that the abscesses caused by the plague usually left. Gothard was so profoundly affected by this situation that he eventually entered the service of the church himself.

However, as I said when we began this discussion, animal assisted therapy as it is practiced today usually involves using pets to assist in the healing of human psychological and emotional rather than physical problems, and in this case there are also historical instances. In the late sixteen hundreds, John Locke (who introduced psychology to the concept of association in learning), suggested that small pet animals aided in the social development of children, including the development of empathy. In the nineteenth century, Florence Nightingale (the mother of nursing) suggested that pet dogs seemed to relieve depression in patients, especially for those with chronic conditions, such as those we associate with post traumatic stress disorders today.

Despite this, there was little data, and no widespread acceptance of the fact that the presence of animals could, and did, improve psychological functioning, although much anecdotal information suggested that this might be the case.

For example, during World War II, Corporal William Wynne was recovering from wounds in an army hospital in the Philippines, and, to cheer him up, members of his company brought his Yorkshire Terrier, Smoky, to the hospital. The effect was remarkable: not only did Corporal Wynne's mood improve, but there

Gods, ghosts, and black dogs

was a positive effect on the other injured soldiers in the ward. The degree of psychological improvement experienced impressed the Commanding Officer of the hospital unit, Dr Charles Mayo (who would later go on to head the now-famous Mayo Clinic in Rochester, Minnesota), and, as a result, he decided to regularly take Smoky on his rounds in the military hospital to act as a living antidepressant for his patients. Smoky became a therapy dog, in effect, and, as such, continued as part of a visitation programme for twelve years; well beyond the end of World War II.

This brings us to my initial contact with the idea of animal assisted therapy. It was quite early in my career – in the 1960s – and I was attending the American Psychological Association meetings in New York. Because of my interest in dogs, and their relationship to people, I was caught by the title of a talk to be given Boris Levinson, a child psychologist, who was at Yeshiva University.

Although I didn't know it at the time, this talk would turn out to be the first formal presentation of animal assisted therapy given before a national audience of psychologists. Levinson had observed that a very disturbed child was much more at ease and willing to communicate when the psychologist had his dog, Jingles, with him, and seemed to result in more productive therapy sessions. Levinson gathered data from several similar cases, and these formed the basis of the paper he presented at this APA meeting. His talk did not receive a positive response, however, and the tone in the room did not do credit to the psychological profession. Levinson was distressed to find that many of his colleagues treated his work as a laughing matter, with one even shouting from the audience, "What percentage of your therapy fee do you pay to the dog?" In my mind this did not bode well for the future of such research and therapy, and I thought it unlikely I would ever hear about such use of animals in therapeutic interactions again.

And I might have been correct in my assumption, except for the fact that a psychologist, whose voice could not be ignored by the therapeutic community, essentially spoke from beyond the grave in support of the concept of animal assisted therapy. Around 15 years after Sigmund Freud's death, by chance, several new biographies of Freud's life had been released, and translations of many of his letters and journals were just being published in English after being translated. There were also new insights into Freud's life in books published by people who knew him, and some even described his interactions with his own household full of dogs.

From these various sources, we learned that Freud often had his Chow Chow, Jofi, in his office with him during psychotherapy sessions. The dog was originally in the room as a comfort to the psychoanalyst, who claimed that he himself was more relaxed when the dog was nearby, but Freud soon began to notice that the dog's presence seemed to help patients during their therapy sessions as well. This difference was most marked when Freud was dealing with children or adolescents. It seemed to him that his patients were more willing to talk openly when Jofi was in the room, and also more willing to talk about painful issues if they could touch the dog while they were speaking. And the effect was not confined to children but also apparent in adult patients.

From this newly-available information it became clear that Freud had observed very much the same phenomena that Levinson described in his report. When Levinson and others learned about Freud's experiences with a dog during therapy sessions, it seemed like a form of divine confirmation that the presence of dogs *did* have a calming and therapeutic effect. Levinson's ground breaking book on what he called 'Pet-Oriented Child Psychotherapy' followed not long thereafter in 1969, and the climate now warmed noticeably to this issue. With evidence that Freud was willing to entertain the usefulness of animal helpers in psychotherapy, and Levinson's book collecting his case studies, the laughter ceased, and some serious work began.

By the year 2000, over one thousand animal assisted therapy programmes were in operation, and, today, such programmes are common, and not only include dogs who are brought into the psychotherapist's office as part of the treatment, but also visitation programmes where dogs are taken into hospitals and homes for children and the elderly.

The dog who breached the gap

There are also some rehabilitation programmes where the dogs are brought in as companions, to build morale and confidence for veterans returning from combat with stress-related psychological issues. More recently, dogs are even being used to reduce stress in educational settings.

By now you may well be thinking that, while this may be interesting historical information, it certainly has nothing to do with folklore, but here you would be wrong. At the time that Boris Levinson was writing his book, I was teaching at the Graduate Faculty of the New School for Social Research, located in a building at the corner of Fifth Avenue and 14th street in New York City. Yeshiva University was located only a few blocks south on Fifth Avenue. I had a colleague in the psychology department at that same university who was doing research very similar to my own, and we would meet occasionally for a cup of coffee, and, typically, spend an hour or so chatting about our research, and gossiping about what was going on in the psychological community. One afternoon, as we stood in line to pick up our coffee, we ran into Boris Levinson, and invited him to join us at our table.

Although Levinson was a specialist in child psychology, his physical appearance was far from the soft, welcoming visage that one might expect in a psychologist who would be accepted by children. His angular face, deep-set eyes, and severe goatee made him look more like the stereotype of an evil sorcerer. Nonetheless, quite incongruously, he had a merry note to his voice, and I later learned that most of his young patients referred to him as 'Uncle Boris.' As the three of us sat there talking about random topics, I congratulated him on his new book about animal assisted therapy, and took the opportunity to ask, "So, tell me, what made you think that the emotional bond between dogs and people would be strong enough to be of value in therapy in the first place?"

Levinson had obviously been asked that question before, and probably a number of times in a much more hostile manner. In the friendly context of sitting with colleagues, however, he smiled and replied, "I never really planned in advance to use a dog as a co-therapist. The patient was a nine-year-old boy who was extremely withdrawn. In the past, his therapeutic experiences had not been very successful, and a number of psychologists and psychiatrists had already given up on him. The child acted in the way that a lot of patients suffering from autism do: he simply would not communicate, and you can't do therapy unless there is communication. Anyway, the boy's mother was quite desperate, and asked me to at least look at the child and see if something could be done.

"Every now and then, when the opportunity arose, I would bring my Golden Retriever, Jingles, to work with me, and it just so happened that, on the day when that mother and son arrived at my office, I had Jingles with me. Jingles was a typical Golden Retriever, the sort of kissing-oriented dog who believes that 'You've got a face and I've got a tongue: I'm sure we can work something out.'

"When the boy walked into the room, Jingles jumped up and greeted him in the enthusiastic way that Golden Retrievers greet anything that might be alive. The results were remarkable, at least from a psychological point of view. The boy wrapped his arms around the dog's neck and actually spoke — not much, just two or three words — but it was a remarkable start, given the fact that previous therapists had found this child virtually impossible to communicate with.

"At the time I didn't know of any data or historical precedents where dogs had been used to establish an emotional link with people — or some kind of communication link that could be used therapeutically, at least. In fact, my first inclination was to think that the child was just having a particularly good day, or maybe even that the boy's mother had overstated the severity of his problem. The fact that my dog, Jingles, played such a significant role in the interaction really didn't occur to me until I thought about the situation later.

"It was when I was sitting down and organising my notes about that day's intervention with the boy that something popped into my head — a story, a folk tale I had heard, or maybe read, somewhere, sometime. From what I could remember, it belonged to the plains Indians, maybe the Sioux. Anyway, how I remembered the story was that, after

Gods, ghosts, and black dogs

the world had been created, after the mountains and lakes and rivers had been shaped, and the forests had been filled with trees and bushes, and the plains covered with grass, and all of the animals had been made, the Great Spirit, or whatever the creator was then called, felt that there was one more task he needed to complete. So he next sent out word that all of the different species of animals, and also the humans, should gather on one great plain on a particular day. On that day the Great Spirit placed the animals on one side of him, and mankind on the other, and then drew a large line in the earth. The line began to turn into a crevasse, which widened, and became deeper and wider by the moment, with man standing on one side of the fissure and the animals on the other. At the last moment, before the gap became unbreachable, dog leapt the chasm to stand alongside man.

"You know, this particular story, created by an unlettered and uneducated primitive group many years ago, seemed to me to epitomize our forced estrangement from nature in general, and from animals in particular. And this situation is worse now than it was back in the days when the story was created, since the difficulties and complexities of living in a highly technological environment have alienated us from our evolutionary origins, and broken those relationships with nature that are essential for our emotional, if not biological, survival.

"But according to that story, there is one major exception, and that is the bond which exists between humans and dogs. As the canyon between the rest of nature and mankind grows wider and wider, we can still look down and see dogs standing by our side. Our feeling for dogs is woven into the fabric of our souls, and, as I thought about this, I knew that this folk tale perfectly describes the emotional link that exists between man and dog: a connection that I could use as a psychologist. I felt that the presence of Jingles as my co-therapist would help to establish an atmosphere of trust that could serve as the basis of a solid relationship with the child.

"So, in the end I placed my trust, not only in my clinical observations, but in the truth that that little folk tale was wrapped around. That is what got me started, and it seems to be working."

It is interesting – and humbling – to think that a snippet of folklore might have helped create a therapeutic process that has helped hundreds of thousands of people through their psychological problems, and is still doing so today.

Index

Gods, ghosts, and black dogs

Visit Hubble and Hattie on the web: wwwhubbleandhattiecom
wwwhubbleandhattieblogspotcouk • Details of all books • Special oers • Newsletter • New book news

September 1943: German forces occupy Rome.

Gestapo boss Obersturmbannführer Paul Hauptmann rules with terror.

Hunger is widespread. Rumours fester. The war's outcome is far from certain.

Diplomats, refugees and escaped Allied prisoners risk their lives fleeing for protection into Vatican City, at one fifth of a square mile the world's smallest state, a neutral, independent country within Rome.

A small band of unlikely friends led by a courageous priest is drawn into deadly danger.

By Christmastime, it's too late to turn back.

Sunday 19th December 1943
10.49 p.m.
119 hours and 11 minutes before the mission

Grunting, sullen, in spumes of leaden smoke, the black Daimler with diplomatic number plate noses onto Via Diciannove, beads of sleet fizzling on its hood. A single opal streetlight glints at its own reflection in an ebbing, scummy puddle where a drain has overflowed. Pulsing in the irregular blink of a café's broken neon sign, the words '*MORTE AL FASCISMO*' daubed across a shutter.

Scarlet.

Emerald.

White.

Delia Kiernan is forty, a diplomat's wife. Doctors have ordered her not to smoke. She is smoking.

A week before Christmas, she's a thousand miles from home. Sweat sticks her skirt to the backs of her stockings as she pushes the stubborn gear stick into first.

The man on the rear seat groans in stifled pain, tearing at the swastikas on his epaulettes.

The heavy engine grumbles. Blood throbs in her temples. On the dashboard, a scribbled map of how to get to the hospital using only the quieter streets is ready to be screwed up and tossed if she encounters an SS patrol but the darkness is making the pencil marks difficult to read and whatever hand wrote them was unsteady. She flicks on her cigarette lighter; a whiff of fuel inflames his moans.

Swerving into Via Ventuno, the Daimler clips a dustbin, upending it. What spills out gives a scuttle and makes for the gutter but is ravaged by a tornado of cadaverous dogs bolting as one from gloomed doorways.

Squawking brakes, jouncing over ramps, undercarriage racketing into pot-holes, fishtailing, oversteering, boards thudding, jinking over machine-gunned cobbles, into a street where wet leaves have made a rink of the paving stones.

Whimpers from the man. Pleadings to hurry.

Down a side street. Alongside the university purged and burned by the invaders. Its soccer pitch netless, strangled with weeds, the pit meant for a swimming pool yawning up at the moon and five hundred shattered windows. She remembers the bonfire of blackboards, seeing its photograph in the news-paper the morning of her daughter's eighteenth birthday. Past the many-eyed, murderous hulk of the Colosseum like the skeleton of a washed-ashore kraken.

Across the piazza, gargoyles leer from a church's gloomy facade. She flashes her headlights twice.

The bell tolls eleven. She feels it in her teeth. Wind harangues the chained-up tables and chairs outside a café, wheezing through the arrow-tipped railings.

A black-clad man hurries across from the porch, damp raincoat clinging, abandoning his turned-inside-out umbrella to the gust as he scrambles into the passenger seat of the ponderous, boat-like car, trilby dripping.

As she pulls away, he takes out a notebook, commences scribbling with a pencil.

'What do you think you're doing?'

'Thinking,' he says.

Pulling a naggin of brandy from his pocket, he offers it to the groaning pas-senger who has tugged off one of his leather gloves and jammed it into his own mouth.

The man shakes his head, scared eyes rolling.

'For pity's sake, let him alone,' she says. 'Give it here.'

'You're driving.'

'Give it here this minute. Or you're walking.'

An eternity at the junction of Via Quattordici and Piazza Settanta as a battle-scarred Panzer rattles past, turret in slow-revolve as though bored.

'What does it mean for the mission?' she asks. 'If he's gravely ill?'

'We'd have to find someone else. Maybe Angelucci?'

'Enzo couldn't be trained up. Not in the time.'

Hail surges hard on the windscreen as they pass Regina Coeli prison. She lights another cigarette, veins of ash falling on the collar of her raincoat. He has his eyes closed but she's certain he's not praying.

'For the love of God, Delia, can't this rust-bucket go any faster?'

Steaming blue streetlights, alleyways snaking up hills, ranked silhouettes of martyrs on the rooftops of churches. It comes back to her, her second morning in Rome, when she climbed the staircase to the roof of St Peter's, every feature of every statue worn away by time and storm. Soot-stained, weather-beaten stalagmites.

Now, a farm gate blocking a driveway. He steps out into the furies of rain and tries to haul the gate open, trilby falling off with the fervour of his shakes. In the glim of the headlights, he wrenches at the bars.

'Tied closed,' he shouts. 'Would there be a toolbox in the boot?'

'Stand out of the road.'

'Delia—'

Revving, foot down hard, she *bolts* the massive car through the splintering, wheezing smash as the gate implodes and he clambers back in, shaking his heavy, wet head as a man wondering how his life can have come to this pass.

Through the long, flat grounds, where soaked sheep bawl, then the road climbs again and the hospital buildings loom, three blocks of brutal concrete bristling with empty flagpoles and monsters that must be water tanks.

A fluorescent yellow road sign commands in black:

'*Rallentare!*'

Up a short winding drive where the gravel is wearing thin, past a trio of diseased sycamores and the concrete hive of a machine-gun turret, to the floodlit portico by which a khaki-and-red-cross-painted ambulance is parked, engine on, three orderlies in the back playing cards. Inexplicably, on seeing the Daimler approach they pull the doors closed on themselves. A moment later, the floodlight is extinguished.

She exits the car but leaves the engine muttering.

The hospital doors are locked, the lobby beyond them in darkness. She tugs the bellpull three times, hears its distant, desolate jangle from somewhere in the heart of the darkened wards.

Stepping back, she looks up at the shuttered windows, as though looking could produce a watcher, the hope of all religious people, but no one is coming and as she approaches the shut ambulance for help a wolf-whistle sounds from behind her.

An orderly in his twenties has appeared from some door she hasn't noticed. Sulky, kiss-curled, cigarette in mouth, he looks as though he was asleep two minutes ago. The smell of a musty room has followed him out. The flashlight in his left hand gives a couple of meagre flickers, diminishing whatever light there is. In his right hand is an object it takes her a moment to recognise as a switchblade. He looks like he'd know what to do with it.

'I've a patient who needs urgent assistance,' she says. 'There. Back seat.'

'Your name?' he sighs, peering into the Daimler's chugging rear.

'I am not in a position to identify myself. I am attached to a neutral Legation in the city. This man is seriously ill, I had our official physician attend him not an hour ago. He says it's peritonitis or a burst appendix.'

'Why should I care? I am a Roman. What are *you*?'

'Matter a damn what I am, send in for a stretcher.'

'You come here with your orders expecting me to help a son-of-a-whore Nazi?'

'You've a duty to help anyone.'

He spits on the ground.

'There's my duty,' he says.

The man in black steps out of the car, heavy hand on the roof, gives a grim stare at the sky as though resenting the clouds, slowly rounds to where the youth is standing.

'You kiss your mother with that mouth?'

'Who's asking?'

'Name's O'Flaherty.' Opening his raincoat, revealing his soutane and collar.

'Father. Excuse me, Father.' He crosses himself. 'I did not know.'

'The German uniform that man in the car is wearing is a disguise. He was running a surveillance mission and became seriously ill.'

'Father—'

'Tough Guy, here's a question. Is there a dentist in that hospital behind you?'

'Why?'

'Because you'll need one in a minute when I punch your teeth through your skull. You ignorant lout, to comport yourself before any woman in that fashion. Go to confession tomorrow morning and *apologise this minute.*'

'I beg forgiveness, *Signora.*' Bowing his florid face. 'I haven't eaten or slept in three nights.'

'Granted,' she says. 'Can we move things along?'

'Our passenger is escaped British prisoner Major Sam Derry of the Royal Regiment of Artillery,' O'Flaherty says. 'The lives of many thousands depend on this man. If you love Italy get him into an operating theatre. This minute.'

The youth regards him.

O'Flaherty hurries to the ambulance, hauls open its doors.

'*Andiamo, ragazzi,*' he says, beckoning towards the Daimler. 'Off your backsides. Good men. We need muscle.'

Derry lurches from the car, blurting mouthfuls of blood, clutching at his abdomen and the night.

— 2 —

THE VOICE OF DELIA KIERNAN
7th January 1963
From transcript of BBC research interview, questions inaudible,
conducted White City, London

I probably drink too much. Which is the main thing to say. They'll have told you, no doubt. You needn't sham.

We were after setting up a mission – a 'Rendimento' was the code, the Italian word for 'a performance' – for that Christmas Eve, starting at eleven o'clock that night. But on the Sunday five evenings beforehand, Derry, our mission-runner, got sick while out on reconnaissance, and Angelucci was sent for, to stand in.

But you're wondering what led to it. As well you might.

Old age has made a bit of a hames of the memory, I'm afraid. Not that I forget things, but sometimes I remember them the wrong way around. So I'm not entirely certain when I first met the Monsignor. It was in Rome during the war. Don't ask me to work it out more than that or I'd need a long lie-down.

No, I didn't keep a diary, love. Never had the patience.

You wouldn't happen to have a cigarette? If we're going to get into it.

Thanks. No, I'm grand. I've matches.

As the wife of the senior Irish diplomat to the Vatican, you did a lot of standing about at official receptions being talked at by Archbishops and pretending to listen. But I suppose you felt it a sort of duty to do what little you could for the young Irish of the city, most of whom were in religious life.

Oh, I'd say a total of five hundred or so, priests and nuns. Many seminarians. What with rationing, you didn't have much of a good time in Rome during the war – you wouldn't see a head of cabbage or a bit of chicken in a month's travel. Scabby bits of turnip. Hard-tack biscuit tasting of sawdust and ashes. Sausages with that little meat in them, you could eat them on a Good Friday.

And so many of the youngsters I'm talking about were barely out of their teens. These days we'd call them teenagers. That word didn't exist back then. So they seemed – how to put it? – a bit lost. And exhausted. A religiously minded kid will often be good at lying awake all night because you need an imagination if you're going to believe.

One or two were scarcely into long trousers and they staring down the barrel of priesthood. Some of them, you wondered had it maybe been more Mammy's idea than their own. And, often enough, though some won't like me saying it, a nun was the youngest daughter of a poor family, with no other prospects. Or she's impressionable in adolescence, like most of us were. Some ould gull of a Mother Superior goes prowling for vocations into a little school in Hutchesontown, Glasgow. Annie raises her hand and she barely gone thirteen. Annie loves Our Lady and the flowers on the altar. And that's Annie despatched to the convent, for the rest of her life. Not in every case, obviously, but you wondered. You wondered.

Anyhow, there was all of that, just fellow feeling for these youngsters. You'd see an awful lot of fear and plain hunger in Rome at the time. It was also a hellishly hot summer, scalding, sapping heat. The gardens of our beautiful Legation villa had a swimming pool, and I let it be known at every function I attended that all Irish youngsters in the city could use it, and the numbers of the trams that would take them there from Piazza del Risorgimento, which is right next door to the Vatican. My poor Tom nearly lost his mind with me and insisted, at the very least, that the sexes must attend on different days. 'You're no fun,' I told him. 'But sure that's why I married you.'

To be serious, of course I was happy to agree to his compromise. Seeing their poor, scrawny bodies leapfrogging and splashing would have brought tears to a glass eye.

So, I started putting on a weekly evening for them, an Open House, if you like, at the Residence of a Thursday night.

I'd have tureens of delicious minestrone and that lovely long Italian bread, you know, a bit of fruit if I could get it on the black market – the Legation maids used to help me in that respect – a few bob will get you most things in Italy. Great cauldrons of pasta; a quid's worth of spaghetti will do you to feed a whole battalion. If you'd olives or a cheese or two, that was nice for them as well. A dirty big beast of a lasagne, piping hot. Also, sausages and rashers from Limerick the odd time, if I could get them brought in in the Diplomatic Bag. A table of ices or poached peaches with zabaglione, maybe a lemon tart. Yes, wine, too. Why not? I wanted them to feel welcome in my home. If they felt like *un bicchiere di vino rosso* or a bottle of stout, which most of them didn't, I wanted them to enjoy it, and to share anything we had ourselves. That's the way I was brought up.

I'm a Catholic, I love the faith as best I can, but I wouldn't be a great one for kissing the altar rails. Not at all. Wouldn't be a Holy Mary. There's good people of every persuasion, and there's 24-carat bastards. Life schools you the way no catechism will.

There was a modest enough budget provided for entertaining guests at the Legation. I drove my misfortunate liege demented by exceeding it every week. And then, Dublin could get a bit snippy, too, as I recall. There'd be these urgent cablegrams from the Department of Foreign Affairs demanding a receipt in triplicate for that bottle of Prosecco: viz, heretofore, moreover, block capitals. Oh, I didn't give a fig, dear. We'll be a long time dead. Here's a girl wouldn't be too renowned for doing what she's told. Some little jack-in-office of a penpusher thinks he'll lord it over yours truly? Take the back of my arse and boil it.

This particular evening, I'd plenty on my mind. I was after spending the morning in the recording studio at Radio Roma because I was making a record of two songs to be released back in Ireland. Yes. I was a professional singer before I was married. I didn't want to give it up fully.

That day? Oh, I can't remember now, love, I think 'Danny Boy' and 'Boola-vogue'. Maybe 'The Spinning Wheel'. I'd have to check.

I'd a grand little career going back at home and I got such fulfilment and excitement from that. To be honest, I missed it dreadfully, the concerts, the travelling around. But by '41 I'd had to take a break from it, between one thing and another, the war getting worse, Tom's posting to Rome. I was singing in Belfast the night the Luftwaffe firebombed the theatre. That's what you call a mixed review.

Wasn't a town I didn't perform in the breadth and length of Ireland. In the summers, the Isle of Man, Liverpool, Manchester, often Dundee or Ayrshire, maybe a couple of nights in Cricklewood at the dance halls. I've sung in Durham, Kilmarnock, Northampton, all over. A woman can lose her confidence in the house all day. And I always think, if singing's in you, you have to sing.

Anyhow, in comes this polite sort of fellow to my get-together that evening and introduces himself as Monsignor O'Flaherty of the Holy Office. Chilly words.

'Monsignor' is a title conferred by the Church on a diocesan priest who's been an administrator five years. So, it conveys a bit of importance. As for 'Holy Office', that's the department of the Vatican where they keep a weather eye on what's called 'adherence to doctrine' and ensure everyone's toeing the line. It's what used to be called 'the Inquisition'. So that carried a bit of weight, too. There's few of us want an Inquisitor at our party.

Normally at my evenings I didn't like too many high-and-mighty sorts, because the youngsters weren't able to relax and enjoy themselves if the quare ould hawks were along. Once, for example, a certain Cardinal who shall be nameless pitched up; a long drink of cross-eyed, buck-toothed misery if ever there was, he'd bore the snots off a wet horse, and the effect was like turning a fire hose on a kindergarten. He'd a way of smiling would freeze up the heart in your chest. As for smug? If he was a banana, he'd peel himself.

But this Monsignor fellow was different, down to earth. Affable. You get that with Kerry people, a sort of courtesy. Too many priests at the time saw themselves not as a sign of mercy but as grim little thin-lipped suburban magistrates. Hugh wasn't too mad on authority.

Another different thing, his means of transport over to us that night was his motorcycle. Here he's ambling up the steps to the residence and he grey with the dust from boots to helmet, huge leather gloves on him like a flying ace, and he blessing himself at the Lourdes water font on the hallstand. As though a priest dressed like that was the most everyday sight you ever saw. And the bang of motor oil off him. Unusual.

He spoke in beautiful Italian to my servants. I didn't know it yet, but I would never meet a brainier piece of work: Hugh had three doctorates and was fluent in seven languages, his mind was like a lawnmower blade; he'd shear through any knot and see a solution, if there was one.

Around the party he sallies, anyhow, tumbler of *limonata* in hand, a word of chat here, a joke or two there. Two Liverpool students were playing chess; he watched them for a while, and, when they finished, asked the winner to explain what the strategy had been. He didn't touch a drop but not a bother on him about anyone else having a glass of beer. Fire away. Whatever you're having yourself.

There was a young woman from Carrigafoyle, a Carmelite novice, they'd a great old natter; didn't it turn out he'd known a late uncle of hers through golf back at home. Hugh was brought up on a golf course as you probably know. His father, a one-time policeman, was the club professional in Killarney. Then Hugh and the young Carmelite – I can see them clear as you like, still, from that night in my living room – the pair of them demonstrating to the company how to putt with a walking stick. There was a bundle of talk about happy subjects and none of the war.

Oh, I forgot to say, when, later, we started having code names, his name was 'Golf'. He was obsessed with the notion the Germans were listening. Escaped prisoners were known as 'Books', their hiding places 'Shelves'. We never used the real names of the Roman streets but gave them names of our own, based on numbers, like the streets in Manhattan. Or we named them after the great Italian composers. And we had to keep mixing the codes to stay ahead of the Gestapo. But more of that, anon.

Tom was out that evening, visiting a trio of Dubliners who were after unwisely giving lip to the Fascisti and getting themselves chucked into Regina Coeli, the jail in Rome, after a hiding; and, anyway, he rarely attended my get-togethers. He enjoyed pretending to disapprove of them more than he actually did.

A point came in the evening when the youngsters started asking would I sing. Some of them had my 78s back at home in Ireland, or, likelier, their parents had. There was a recording of mine was after being played all that summer on Raidió Éireann, 'The Voice of Delia Kiernan', even on the Third Service and American Forces Network. The great Richard Tauber himself had said in an interview he liked it, so that was a feather in my cap. The Monsignor encouraged me to oblige them. 'Go on, Mrs Kiernan, before they start breaking up the furniture.' I answered that I had no accompanist and would feel nervous without that safety net. In truth, I'd a couple of whiskeys on me.

He answered that he was no Paderewski but would vamp along as best he could if I would tell him the key. What I had in mind was written in A-flat, which isn't easy for an improvisor, but I told him I could hack it in A. So, over with the pair of us to the piano, a lovely old Bösendorfer, and off we went. It was an old love song, an arietta by Bellini I've long had a place in my heart for – a lovely loose melody like a soft-rolling folk song. It always brings my father back to me, Lord have mercy on him, it was a great favourite of his. As a girl I learned it off a 78 he had in the house, John McCormack's version – and some of the younglings joined along.

Vaga luna, che inargenti
Queste rive e questi fiori
Ed inspiri agli elementi
Il linguaggio dell'amor

It wasn't false modesty from Hugh, I must say, about the level of his musicianship. Dear knows I've heard bad pianists in my time but he was cat altogether, God love him. He'd grand big hands on him like a pair of shovels but he was clumsy. All the same, it was a lovely experience. You'd remember it. In recollection, Rome comes to me always as everyday music: the clunk of a shutter on a sweltering afternoon, the gasps of wonder when you're inside the Pantheon and rain starts to fall. The hot pigeons warbling, the way the drinking fountains chuckle. But there was never music sweeter than hearing the room sing that night.

Something happens in a room when people are singing. It changes the air, like rainfall, or dusk. You've those say it's escapism but, to me, life seems realer, then.

Forgive me. Makes me emotional to think of.

Well, that's how we met, and we were soon good pals. He'd come along to my evenings the odd time, bring a chum or two with him. Priests, yes – a Japanese Franciscan came once – or pilgrims from the homeland or his beloved United States, and always a bottle of excellent Chianti, the dear knows how he laid hands on it, though he didn't drink himself, as I say. Often, he'd bring a naggin of brandy.

A well-placed Papal Count was after gifting the Irish Legation an expensive subscription to a box at the Opera House, to which we'd often invite other diplomats and their families. You've to remember that independent Ireland was still a very young country, having only won her freedom in 1921. The solidarity of others was needed and valued. Hosting was something a diplomat's wife was expected to do. Verdi sometimes proved an ally, you could say.

This one particular occasion the plan was for a party of seven, but the Portuguese Ambassador was under the weather with the awful heat, the filth of which brought headaches that would cripple you and made it hard to breathe, so I invited along the Monsignor to join the group, for I knew he loved Puccini, and *Tosca* is set in Rome as you know. We were the Swedish Ambassador and his wife, the Swiss Cultural Attaché – there's a part-time job if ever there was – and a lady friend, then the Monsignor and yours truly and my husband. 'A riot of neutrality,' Hugh joked, shaking hands. 'We lot couldn't shoot our way out of a mousetrap.'

Which the Swedish Ambassador laughed at. But not the Swiss Cultural Attaché, as I recall, who seemed understandably put off by the fact that Hugh had a little notebook in which he kept scribbling, all the way through the performance. It was an oddity of Hugh's: if a thing wasn't written down, it hadn't happened. Even his Bible, he'd be scrawling all over the margins. Anyhow. Another story. Where were we?

Yes.

Late in '42 it must have been, a kind of darkness I hadn't seen before came over him. For a while he'd been visiting the Axis prisoner-of-war camps in Italy as an official Vatican observer. But something happened to him that autumn. He wasn't the same. He stopped attending my evenings, went to ground a while. Someone told me he'd been sick, was after being in hospital with cancer or was considering going to Massachusetts to do parish work. My Tom heard on the Vatican grapevine he might be leaving the priesthood. But when at last he agreed to see me, he said that wasn't so; he'd been preoccupied with what he called a private matter.

It was after raining for days as we spoke, and the river was rising, one of those nights when the Tiber was tipping the tree-roots. Was he in trouble? I remember asking him. Was he in need of a friend?

Because, I'll be honest, sometimes you heard of a priest where a woman had come into the picture. Human nature is what it is. We won't change it this late in the day. There's many a good man discovered the celibate life wasn't for him, but they'd be shunned by the Church when they left. The routine was you'd be told to go to a particular room in some shabby back-street hotel, on the bed there'd be a suit from a pawnshop and three pound-notes. You took off your priestly clothes, folded them on the bed, got into the dead man's suit, left the hotel by the back door. It was understood no one from your old life would ever contact you again. They made it hard for you to leave. So, too many stayed.

I can say now, after all this time, I had a particular lady in mind, a young Contessa recently widowed who'd been seen in Hugh's company at art galleries and the like, around Rome, each of the pair for different reasons clad in black. A beauty she was, with something of what the French call 'gamine', slightly boyish film-star looks, like those of Leslie Caron. She and I became great friends; indeed, I was speaking with her on the telephone not two hours ago. The Vatican, like all kremlins, is a hive of whispers and envies. I know for a fact that her friendship with Hugh didn't merit the way it was sometimes talked about. 'No smoke without fire' is the way gossips put it. I always say, maybe it's not smoke, maybe your spectacles need a wiping.

Anyhow, he gave a laugh when I mentioned her name. The private matter he was after mentioning was nothing at all of that nature, he assured me. 'But thank you, Delia, for the compliment.'

When I persisted, he showed me a scrap of a letter that had been smuggled to him from a poor Scottish boy, a soldier in a prisoner-of-war camp, about to be executed. The lad wanted it sent to his mother. The words of it, the fact of it – forgive me a moment – had been coming between Hugh and his sleep.

I wept when I read it. Handed it back and wept. There's never a single day of my life I don't pray for that mother.

We'd go through American bombing attacks the following summer. Those I'll never forget. Because unless you've lived through an air raid, I don't think I can convey the terror. There's no film could capture it. The screaming. The smell. The nerves would be at you weeks afterward.

A B-25 Mitchell bomber is the size of a London bus. You look up and there's forty of them raining 500-pound bombs. So, a street isn't damaged, it's obliterated. Gone. A rubble of stinking smoke and pulverised bricks. The planes would come the night before, drop eighty thousand leaflets saying what would happen the next day. So you'd plenty of time for the dread to build up. One night an air raid came during one of my evenings. I'll never forget the young people's fear; they were weeping, terrified.

By now, Hugh had become aware that certain individuals in Rome – a person here, someone else over there – were helping escaped Allied prisoners and Jews get out of the country, into Switzerland, and he'd been giving them the odd bit of assistance on the QT. Things like buying train tickets in false names, getting clothes, nothing much more. It was ad hoc, you know, not organised. Hugh had a lot of friends in the city between one thing and another; he wasn't one of those priests that eat and sleep and die in the chapel. He was half-thinking of putting together a proper group that might raise a few bob for the escapees, the odd handout, at a distance, on the quiet.

Discreet. Nothing formal. All very hush-hush. Perhaps best not to mention it to Tom or anyone else at the embassy. There wouldn't be any danger, it would only be in the background, like a charity fund.

I didn't know what it would lead to or I'd have run for the hills.

He was after thinking of a cover for it.

The Choir.

— 3 —

Monday 20th December 1943
6.47 a.m.
112 hours and 13 minutes before the Rendimento

In the hours after the dash to the hospital, a head cold assails him. Racking sneezes, hacks, shivers, hot eyes. The fear looms that this is the onset of the dreaded Roman flu, which killed a dozen of his African First Years and nine of his Chicagoans last winter.

Minutes before dawn, exhausted, he forces himself to sleep. The Daimler roaring through his nightmares.

Somehow it becomes the Mercedes of Hauptmann, the Gestapo commander. They're driving long spirals of impossibly narrow streets in a city that is and is not Rome. Oak trees. Lightning. Bloodstains on sand. Rain patterning a window. Vast towers. A well as deep as the moon is high. Faces turning to stone as a Chopin nocturne plays, the settled, broken blankness of those without hope. Now Hauptmann is at his bedside, a presence, a virus. You'd be afraid to breathe in case you inhale him. *Tell me who you met. Tell me why you met them.* The Nazi's grey eyes. Grey infantry braid on his cuffs. Grey smoke of his grey cigarettes. The wolf feeding Romulus and Remus in a fresco comes to life and slobbers at her starving babies before devouring them.

At ten o'clock, he leaves his room, walks uneasily to the School of Divinity, starts into the three-hour lecture he must give on Aquinas, in Latin, to a class of ninety seminarians. Last night's sleet still beating in his head as he clutches the lectern for steadiness, the bleached-out yellow windows of the lecture hall throbbing. This term's Third Years are bright. Their questions swarm like wasps. The glass of hot water and lemon he has brought with him to the dais tastes of mud and pencil shavings.

Afterwards, wrapped in a blanket, he begins grading their end-of-term disquisitions but makes it through only thirty papers before retreating to his sickbed. The remaining sixty scripts he marks between bouts of flicker-lit half-sleep and fits of angry coughing. His wheezes cast a seething dog into the corners of the room. His ribcage is made of fire.

No word from Sam Derry.

Bombers overhead.

Perhaps news will come tomorrow.

Transcript of memorandum recording made on Allgemeine Elektricitäts-Gesellschaft AG Magnetophon

This is Obersturmbannführer Paul Hauptmann speaking. For the attention of Dollman, confidential. Twentieth of December, forty-three, Gestapo headquarters, Rome.

Himmler telephoned again. Ranting, threatening. Furious that enemy prisoners are escaping Italy-based camps in large numbers. Says most are heading towards Rome, seeking asylum in the Vatican. I appreciate you're busy but I have changed my mind and want you to look into a couple of suspects we discussed recently, including that nuisance of a priest I mentioned before. I know you think he's nothing. Let's find out.

Poke around. Bang heads. The usual informants. See if he's using a false name.

I'm sending you a dossier on him, into which I have written what I already know. Complete its currently empty sections and return it to me before Christmas.

Be discreet. Stay in backstage.

Let's get this weed uprooted.

We don't need trouble.

Heil Hitler.

Awakening in the early hours, he realises that today is the eighteenth anniversary of his ordination. Fevered, his thoughts skim oceans. He sees himself prostrated before the altar that morning in the cathedral, then walking back down the aisle, hands bound, the hawk-faced, candlelit Bishops.

Around sunrise he drifts into some zone of pulsing, crackled redness that is not sleep, some land where candlestands have voices. Surfacing, he stirs the tumbler of medicine someone has placed on his locker and manages two sips before dry-retching.

The lemon wedge in the copper spoon beside the alarm clock is the strangest object he has ever seen, so yellow it's green, so green it's blue, its aroma creeping up his sinuses like a midnight burglar until it sprouts a thousand insect legs and scuttles around the pillows, emitting a sordid, irksome buzz that becomes the reedy drone of an oboe.

A dream of words slithering out his ears like worms.

The air in the room is rank. He pushes open his window.

In the rainy street below, Hauptmann's black Mercedes.

As he watches, its headlamps are killed.

Transcript of memorandum recorded on Allgemeine Elektricitäts-Gesellschaft AG Magnetophon

Twenty-first of December, forty-three, Gestapo headquarters, Rome, Hauptmann speaking, for the attention of Dollman. Confidential.

Tonight, I was driving near the Vatican. On a hunch, decided to reconnoitre the College where HO'F lives. Forbidding-looking building. Own graveyard. Rather Gothic. Sort of place one imagines vampire priests. At midnight the porter came out but did not lock the door. Taking a chance, I entered. The hallway was dark. Religious pictures, a lurid crucifix, the usual tat. A pile of mail for residents; I looked through it but could find nothing intended for HO'F. I began to ascend the staircase, but the sounds of men talking (I assume the students) dissuaded me. See if someone working there can be compromised. A servant or skivvy. Maybe another priest. We'll pay.

Wednesday 22nd December
11.49 a.m.
59 hours and 11 minutes before the Rendimento

When he wakes, the fever has broken. His skin feels new. The air in the room smells of woodsmoke and beeswax.

The bells in St Peter's clang dolefully for noon. Women are singing the Angelus.

Pages from his jotter lie in flitters around the eiderdown. Horrified, he sees they are covered in his handwriting: names of the Choristers, locations of hiding places. He gathers and rips them, washes the ink from his fingers. The bedsheets and pillowcase are smudged with black, too. The tell-tale pen on his locker.

Some winter days in Rome have ice-blue eyes, a freezing stare.

From the bedside drawer he takes his darts, stands shakenly to the dartboard on the back of his door. The darts cold and weighted, *heavier* than they are, threading flight paths from his fingertips to the sockets of the board.

Fthunk.

Thrunk.

Double top.

One hundred.

Then the livid red iris of the bull.

Like writing something down. Nailing air into numbers. Little wonder it assuages his dreads. Pull the darts, they come out. Throw them sharp, they go in. A cork-and-wire battlefield where a squint is a rapier and the points stab nothing worth adding.

Long minutes, he plays. An hour disappears. Measuring, thinking, planning out the shots. Trying to think like Hauptmann, to reason like him, to *be* him. Trudges a thousand metres of linoleum between the mark and the board, the board and the mark, the oche and the door, feathered flights in his hands, hidden routes in his mind, and every time he throws one, a fugitive is rescued and the *fthunk* sends Hauptmann stone mad.

From his desk he takes the file of cuttings he assembled in the Germany section of the Vatican Library, clippings mentioning Hauptmann from the German newspapers: the regionals and locals, the Party publications, a one-line reference here, a brief paragraph there, even the entry from his School Yearbook back in Stuttgart. Know your enemy, they say. See through his eyes. A photograph of him leading a Hitler Youth hike. The announcement of his engagement to be married. Wife's name is Elise. Two children, one adopted. Joined the SS, '34. Graduated from the Führerschule der Sicherheitspolizei, '38. Former Kriminalkommissar. Boy Most Likely to Succeed.

From time to time, he dons a threadbare dressing gown and inches barefoot down to the hall, on the pretext of expecting a Christmastime letter from home, but no message about Sam Derry – about anything – has arrived.

He tries to place a call to the hospital, then to Delia Kiernan or the Contessa, but the Vatican's telephones are dead; no one knows when they'll be fixed. The editorial in this morning's *Messaggero* is hinting that the Nazis have cut the lines, that the invasion of Vatican City will happen within days.

Three weeks ago, at the start of December, he applied for a haircut pass, as all Vatican residents must, a complicated process involving a letter in triplicate to the Curia. Usually, he cuts his own hair in a shaving mirror, badly, but the students have begun to pass remarks. If granted, the permission to leave the Vatican and enter Rome will be for one hour and ten minutes. Armed guards will conduct him to the barber's and back.

At two, he goes out to the loggia to see if the pass has arrived and is surprised when the *portiere* finds it.

'You look poorly, *Monsignore*.'

'I'm improving, Giancarlo, *grazie*.'

'*Con rispetto*, I can cut your hair if you wish, *Monsignore*? To save you the trouble?'

'I could do with getting out.'

'Very good, I will send a message to say you're ready. Three o'clock?'

'Three o'clock it is. *Grazie*, Giancarlo.'

'*Prego*.'

The two troopers sent to convey him are clumsy and young. Helmets loose, grimy tunics ill-fitting. They stumble on Rome's cobbles, seem uncertain of the direction, their confusion occasioning halts and bleak, muttered squabbles over the blurrily printed military map they've been issued, itself twenty years out of date. He could indicate to them the right road, with gestures, a pointing finger, but he feels they'd resent it, as they about-turn and double-back, and he longs to happen into someone who might get a message to the hospital, but suddenly, as he and the soldiers pass through an arch into a high, cold piazza, they are moving through a party of black-clad SS officers taking photographs of the statuary on a church's facade, their death's-head cap badges shining. Now he sees that Hauptmann is among them, but alone, looking distracted, out of sorts, scrawling in a wire-bound notebook, conversing with no one.

The barber, Orlandi, wrestler fat, damply breathless, must be the only one of his profession in Rome with little to say. From the mirror a taped-up newspaper photograph of the Lazio soccer team stares down on his sink, beside an icon of the Black Madonna and a postcard of Betty Grable in a swimsuit.

'You're a Lazio man, Orlandi?'

'For my sins, Father.'

'I never saw a better striker than Piola.'

One of the troopers emits a hiss, puts a finger to his lips. No talking.

'These sausage-munchers think they can boss us,' the barber sings quietly, in Italian, as though half-remembering an aria he heard a long time ago. 'The kid's half my age, impudent prick, and he's telling me when I can talk? In my own place, too. You want me to shave you while you're here, Father?'

Mixing the soap in a pewter mug, he strops the razor seven times and croons onward. 'Turn your face for me, Father. That's it.' Shaving his nape hair. 'Be done soon. Kick this sausage-muncher's ass. Alleluia.'

Opening a package of Old Golds, Orlandi lights one, drags on it, places it in a scallop-shell ashtray – as an afterthought offers a smoke to the troopers.

'Go ahead, help yourselves,' he says amiably, in Italian. 'You ugly sons-of-bitches.'

'*Danke schön*,' they reply, understanding his gestures but not his words. Not that you can ever be sure of their ignorance. Some pretend not to understand; it's a part of their training, another way of listening to the conquered.

'And your mother,' mutters Orlandi. 'I hope you get shot.'

Through puffed smoke, they grin, nodding, coughing gratitude.

'*Allora*,' he says, 'Been to the movies lately, Father?'

'Not in a while.'

'Only, I wouldn't go tonight. If you know what I'm saying. Little birdie told me the picture house in Prati might be best avoided.'

'Why so?'

'Certain out-of-towners frequent the place. I hear there's a welcome planned. The kind of Christmas present where someone lights a fuse and starts running.'

On the way back to the Vatican he sees Hauptmann again, now seated outside a café with a man in plainclothes. The soldiers salute as they pass but Hauptmann and the other don't notice, Hauptmann taking minuscule sips from a tumbler of water, the subordinate drinking red wine and operating what appears to be an addition machine as he listens, nodding, unpicking a paperclip, pausing to smoke. A beggarwoman approaches. Hauptmann gives her a coin.

Half an hour after the priest and the soldiers have departed, the barber, whistling and cursing, goes to his till to fetch some change. On a banknote, six scrawled figures he didn't notice when the Monsignor handed it to him:

'Bach 21.'

In the code known to the Choristers' supporters, '21' means 'urgent'.

'Bach' means Enzo Angelucci is to make contact by any means available.

Orlandi shutters his shop and starts walking.

———

Thursday 23rd December
7.00 a.m.
Exactly 40 hours before the Rendimento

Fthunk.

Thrunk.

He pulls the darts from the board.

Throws again.

Still no message.

Last night's grenade attack on the cinema is not mentioned in the newspapers but he is certain it happened, one of the younger priests was called to the scene. Three German soldiers, a Roman woman and the projectionist were killed. He wonders why the news has been censored, what Hauptmann's reprisal will be.

Perhaps a deathbed summons will come today, a legal reason to leave the Vatican, the fifth of a square mile to which he has been confined for so long. It seems improper to pray that someone would be close to death, although many in Rome are closer than they know. Many more soon will be.

He lobs volleys of unseeable darts across the city to Angelucci. *Come to the Piazza. You are needed urgently. Derry is sick, for all I know may be dead. We need you to run the Christmas Eve mission. Come to the Piazza tomorrow at noon. Wait by the colonnade. Do not leave.*

Opening his Bible at random, he allows his fingertip to find a verse. Matthew 27:52. 'And the graves were opened; and many bodies of the saints which slept arose.'

He shaves in a bowl, dresses, hurries the rainswept hundred metres across the courtyard from the Collegio to the Holy Office, where he switches on the lights and climbs the marble stairwells and says Mass alone but for his lamplit shadow in the private chapel off the seventh landing.

His left hand is shaking. A flicker in his eyelids. A headache is creeping around his boundaries; he dreads its return.

The fox of his fears prowls a carpet of broken glass.

Some say the Renaissance crucifix on the altar has been seen to move. This morning, that could happen. Others claim the miraculous cross was swapped for a fake many years ago, that the real one is hidden so deeply that no one remembers where.

Glancing out the chapel window, he sees three German tanks nudge into place on Via Rusticucci. Troopers crowbarring up cobblestones, hefting sandbags into clusters around machine-gun posts. A *Panzerjäger* anti-aircraft cannon being aimed along the three hundred metres of space that ends at the doors of St Peter's. Last night Radio Algeria broadcasted 'on cast-iron authority' that an incursion into the Vatican is 'absolutely imminent'. The servants have stopped coming to work.

'*Look again,*' his shadow cackles. '*The crucifix does not move.*'

Mass said, he leaves the Collegio and crosses the passageway to the abandoned Annex, a quattrocento *casa del pellegrino* whose long-planned demolition was delayed by the coming of war. The Rector, a German, is given to joking that he wishes a bomb would be dropped on it. 'The expense saved would be considerable and welcome.'

Up the staircase, through a long corridor where dilapidated statues are stored, to the loft he has made his private nook. For months he has managed to put off the task, but several documents must be written now.

He will limit himself to what can be written in forty minutes, what might be read in thirty. If the invasion does come, he wants his family to know his mind at the last.

So as not to exceed the allotted time, he takes from his pocket and winds his alarm clock, its rusted ratchets rasping. The cockerel down in the yard gives a disconsolate squawk.

He writes hurriedly, in Latin, placing the papers one by one in a metal box, like a cashier's, which he locks with its fat, short key. In an hour, the key will be mailed to his sister in Ireland, with a coded message in mirror-Gaelic, the play language of their childhood, as to where the box is to be found.

He does not know that the key will be lost on its journey, that for decades the box will squat behind the loose wall-plank where in forty minutes he is about to place it, until many years later, when renovation work on the Annex will be halted by a pandemic, and a sinkhole will open, causing a buttressed section of the eastern gable to collapse, vomiting slates and ancient bricks and stained-glass window frames and ancient codices and Bibles and a crucifix said to be miraculous and a rust-blackened metal box and plaster haloes of statues into the mosaicked courtyard below.

MY LAST WILL AND TESTAMENT
23rd December 1943

Since I own almost nothing, I have little to bequeath. My books I ask be given to my sister, Bride, my brothers Jim and Neil, and my parents, James and Margaret, 11 Henn Street, Killarney, County Kerry, in Ireland. I request that, for three years, on the date of my ordination, a Mass for the forgiveness of my sins be offered in the church where I was baptised. The above is the entirety of my Will.

As to my Testament, I should like to tell of a man I never met, an orchestral conductor, a Roman by birth, whose presence in my life – whose absence from it, really – altered how I understood the world and how we are to act in it, if any single event other than the Resurrection may be said to have done that.

In my twenties, once a schoolteacher, now a student for the priesthood, I came to undertake doctoral study in Rome having never previously left my home place. With a cabbage for a brain and the stones of rural Kerry in my shoes, I gaped as the train pulled into Tiburtina.

The multitude of steeples, that pincushion skyline. I can never forget the exhilaration of those first weeks. That quartet of great and majestic basilicas in the gloaming, the hundreds of dark and beautiful churches, the food, the art, the zestful life, the many languages, the glories to be encountered in the Vatican Library: it was like awakening in a land of wonders.

Rome for me is a painter's palette, a chiaroscuro of burnished pinks, old copper, walnut, honey, ivory, mocha. It is also its own music, a piano sonata. I can never hear Clementi without the sight of my beloved adoptive home and the pierce of a spear of longing.

After periods of ministry in Palestine, New York, Haiti and other places, in my early thirties I was summoned to return here. On the evening when I arrived, it happened that a small electrical fire had broken out at the dormitory intended to house me, in a poorly modernised medieval friary, and so I and seven fellow priests were lodged in an old *pensione* on Via Pompeo Magno in Prati, not far from the Vatican. But far enough.

As is the case with all marriages, priesthood has its seasons and tides, the gravities no one warns you about. Yes, there are summer evenings when the stars in the sky may be stirred by the outstretch of a hand, but there are Februaries, too. You'd want to father yourself when those happen. The lonesomeness of priestly life can at times freeze the heart. My Rome thawed it out, helped me breathe again.

I lived in a boarding house for pilgrims, managed by Congolese nuns who had taken the holiest oath of all, an oath of silence. They would point you to the dining table or the sitting room in which we had a wireless, or with a pencil indicate on the map the ancient church you sought. Gentle, unsettling ladies, they ruled with their eyes. I pray God for their safety in the coming days.

Joy it was to live in that house with my good-humoured Mauritian and Romanian confreres and the travellers who came and went. As Chaucer knew, only rarely are pilgrims the drearily spotless saints we imagine; usually they are people who have lived with whole heart. I loved my lecturing work at the College for the Propagation of the Faith, the intelligence of my students, their courage and simple likeability, but, more than that, I loved the Rome I had been given, the bell-song for vespers, the faces of travellers from every land, their languages so strange to me that one wondered *were* they languages, how any two people ever born could have even begun to learn them, the theatre of going through the streets.

There was an ease to Roman life, a taking-in through the senses, the very name of the city a metaphor for patience. The place that wasn't built in a day.

My walk would take me by way of the Spanish Steps, where I would say a silent prayer for that haunted man, John Keats, who died in a house nearby. A sinner, as who is not, but a greater poet than Wordsworth, whom I was never able to forgive for the daffodils.

The place names and direction signs were as jewels set into a mosaic: the Quirinale, the Orti Farnesiani, the Fontana di Trevi, the Arco di Costantino, Santa Maria Maggiore. To say those words aloud was to fizz.

To walk the Via Cola di Rienzo or the aisles of the Mercato Rionale, the great beauty and profusion of the produce, the sweet *prosciutti* and bursting cheeses, the intense sensuousness of any place in Italy where food is bought or sold, to watch the handsome women going about, the mocking way they argued with the stallholders, hefting an avocado here, a stem of luscious tomatoes there, or to cool by the cascade in the Piazza Navona, to sit a while by the Tiber, not a half-hour's walk from my room. Ardent lovers, hand in hand, glitter-eyed and gesturing, alive in the radiance of their need for one another, or the youths full of peaceful silences, as Italians against expectation can be, staring contentedly into a fountain. Romans are like people stepped out of a Caravaggio, long-nosed, alluring, courtly. The street singers, the vagabonds, the bawling men arguing. A painful difficulty about happiness is that we so rarely notice its arrival. In Rome, we would soon know it was gone.

In those days, for a couple of coins, one could attend the Opera on weekday afternoons to watch rehearsal. It was something that gave me immense pleasure. I liked seeing the young music students, their attentiveness and seriousness – we are all drawn to those skills that we do not ourselves possess – and I found it fascinating to hear but also to *see* the orchestra. Once you did not interrupt or make your presence too intrusive, you were permitted to walk right up to the lip of the pit and watch. Their carefulness touched me, their meticulousness in small things. It interested me, for example, to see that the musicians had a particular way of turning the page of a score, double-tapping it with a finger or a violin bow, so that the breeze would not turn the page back.

Such occasions were often used by the company to try new, young conductors from the Conservatorio. Their role enthralled me in a particular way.

What is the conductor doing? I had little idea. Despite what we think, erroneously, when we are children, he is not providing the rhythm or beating out time, but is editing, italicising, adding emphasis, a style. His version of the piece will not be the same as anyone else's on this Earth, though both orchestras are playing from identical sheet music. For that reason, his knowledge of the score must be total, more even than the composer's. Is there any more difficult calling?

The chief tutor of these young conductors – all of whom, notwithstanding his strictness, adored him – was a professor named Vittorio Proietti.

Proietti, an imposing man in his early forties, was a figure one would notice in a room. He was what was termed in those days 'a confirmed bachelor' and had the sensitivity and great graciousness one often encounters in homosexual people. An artist of courtesy and distinguished, dignified fervency, he was the sort of person for whom the Latin noun *gravitas* was coined, a word that has entered many languages because we know it when we see it. Once, I was outside the Teatro, just passing the stage door, when I saw Maestro Proietti step out of his long black Maserati, in his long black cloak, long black cane in hand. It was a sight to make the waves dance.

That evening, I had gone for a simple meal at a trattoria near Piazza Mazzini with two companions, my visiting friend and fellow Kerryman, Dr Maurice 'Moss' Trant, with whom in happier days I studied as a seminarian, and another man whose name I cannot quite recall now, a Chicagoan, a Father Valentini, I think it was. Often when people came into my orbit who were new to Rome, I felt it a pleasant obligation to show them one or two of the little museums that are not in the guidebooks, the hidden chapels and galleries, to break bread with them in the wider city.

Not long before that night, the Fascist emblem had been nailed onto the crest in the Royal Box at the Opera House, a desecration that caused offence to many regular attenders, and gladness, I would hazard, to others. As for me, in those days, I saw all political systems as more or less the same, forms of foolishness, the prattling of apes, designed to keep the lesser chimps down. This was a shameful foolishness of my own. I have come to see that neutrality is the most extremist stance of all; without it, no tyranny can flourish.

When my two companions and I arrived at the Teatro that evening, many of the orchestra members were already in the pit and there arose that special sound that brings such joyous excitement, appealing as it does to the child in every heart, the noise of an orchestra tuning up. The sound that says Reason may be left at the door, Wonders are about to witnessed. A stately, bright trumpet. The seethe of impatient violins. A crescendo of harp arpeggios arising like wavelets and the answering foghorn of a bassoon. God, to be alive at such moments.

A coven of Fascist roughnecks now appeared in the Royal Box, ostentatiously smoking, opening a jeroboam of Prosecco, making self-important nuisances of themselves, but people pretended not to notice. The house lights were extinguished. Out strode Proietti. He stalked to the podium like an early Roman king, half-nodding to the audience with that curious mixture of acknowledgement and disdain that the greatest performers evince.

The overture began, then the first act of the piece, Bellini's *I Capuleti e i Montecchi*. All progressed sumptuously until fifteen minutes into the performance, when from the box came brays of loutishness; the Fascists were drunk. They had brought along as guests certain ladies of the pavement; the misfortunate women themselves were embarrassed by the Fascists' inebriated catcalling and entreated for it to stop, a plea that only seemed to stir the boors on.

At a certain point, one of the yobs called out '*Me ne frego*', a slogan of the Fascists, 'I don't care', and the imbeciles about him whinnied into coarse laughter and bleary cheers. The remark, hitting its target, was shouted a second time. Again, the explosions of glee. The fleeting appreciation of his fellow nonentities is always a powerful fuel to the bullyboy, living as he must with his greatest fear, the dread that even among nobodies he is nothing.

The third time the Fascist motto was howled, Proietti rapped his baton eight or a dozen times against the lectern. The orchestra stuttered to silence, the soprano stopped singing; Proietti folded his arms. He had the air of a person awaiting a tram but not in desperation, a nobleman not bothering to look at his watch. Some in the audience began to hiss, others murmured or shushed. Without turning to face the auditorium, he called out with brisk sternness, '*Signore e signori, silenzio! Abbiate rispetto per gli musicisti!*'

Applause and cheers arose. The orchestra resumed.

As he left the theatre that night, Vittorio Proietti was seen getting into a car at gunpoint.

His body has never been found.

───

In dreams, I'd often see Banna Strand or the rocks of coastal Kerry, the tiny islands like inkblots splashed by a careless cartographer. The corner of the world where I was reared is known for its stern, stark mountains and mirroring lakes, its raggedness on a map, the attack of its fiddle style, for an imperiousness of character that is sometimes mistaken for mere pride, though it is something far stronger, a pagan identification with place. There's a notion of land and person as expressions of one another, translations.

Kerry people are Kerry people first.

In my childhood the neighbouring counties were lampooned and done down, their indigenes, often our own relatives, the butt of only partly good-natured quips. Corkonians? Arrogant. Limerick people? Sanctimonious. As for derision of the capital city, that was part of the weather. Dublin was 'West Britain'. Her citizens had sold themselves. Prancing like show ponies for their overlords across the water, while the overlords snickered at the effort. My father used to joke that there was only one circumstance in which he could ever bring himself to cheer for England; that would be if an English team were somehow opposing Dublin in the All-Ireland Gaelic football final. 'I'd be draped in the Union Jack.'

Otherwise, England was despised, Perfidious Albion, a despotism. As my poor, ardent grandmother, God be good to her, used to vow into her teacup: 'I'll burn everything English but their coal.'

No matter that our uncles were digging the streets and drains of Coventry, our aunts nursing the sick in Poplar and Camden Town. Their youngsters, our cousins, had the accents and outlooks of England, as how would they not. Money sent home from the kingdom of the conqueror bought shoes for children that were otherwise patriotically barefoot, saved many a widow from famished destitution or the assiduously rationed mercy of the ratepayers. But we in my homeland have a limitless capacity for self-delusion, as all once-conquered peoples have.

England's junta was hated; being hated was its purpose. Hating it drew us together, gave us a banner under which to congregate, when we feared, indeed were coming to see what some had long known, that there was little but clichés and superficialities to bond us. Differing from your enemy is the illusion of a powerful unifier, the moonshine passed around the campfire as the cold dawn comes.

Tens of thousands in my townland had been permitted to starve, whole families my grandmother knew in her girlhood; a million starved throughout the island. They had been informed to their surprise that they were not Kerry folk at all but something called 'British', whatever that meant, subjects of a family living five hundred miles away in one of its many palaces, claiming your allegiance despite doing nothing to earn it. You had never seen any of them. They had never seen you.

But your contract with this London-based family of unemployables was binding. You would work every hour; they would do literally nothing. The fruits of your work would be sent to their acolytes in the form of rent so as not to inconvenience them too much. Had you land, it would be stolen and given to their henchmen. Your religion would be crushed, theirs raised; your language outlawed, theirs established; but when hunger arrived to destroy you the picture would become clearer, that you were not British in the same sense as were the good people of, say, Hampshire. You were a surplus, a sort of trash, the sooner exterminated the better. In every one of her dozens of colonies the whole world round, England and her owners toiled hard at being hated. In Ireland, they received their due.

For this hatred, as constant and intoxicating as the turf smoke in October, we may blame proximity or history or everyday human feeling; but that history sharpened malignly in the years of my youth, when a force of reprobate mongrels, the scum of England's jails, was sent to assist Ireland's constabulary in pacifying the colony, by the jackboot and the noose if needs be. Not for the first time in the star-crossed story of the archipelago, the bout did not come out as planned.

Their viciousness against the people of the countryside was infamous. If one Tan had a stone thrown at him, a village was burned. Prisoners were shot without trial, Catholics arrested without cause, women aggressed, men beaten. Once, in my twenties, a friend and I were walking back to the seminary having paid our respects at a funeral in Limerick city, when a Tan patrol happened along the street and dragged us away to a cell, getting in a good rake of rifle blows and cannonades of cockney spittle along the way. Next morning, an urgent telegram from the Abbot secured our release. It was not a night one would quickly forget.

Hatred of England was deep as the graves, hatred of her armies, deeper.

Thus, when two years ago I was ordered by the Papal Secretariat to serve as an official Vatican visitor to the Italian concentration camps for British prisoners of war, I found myself not wanting to comply. I was in favour of the Vatican's neutrality, and in favour of Ireland's, not that, in either case, anyone outside the rulership was asked. Spells of ministry in London and the New Forest had planted a fondness, indeed a love, of those places and their people in me. But it wrestled with inherited darknesses. And Vanity, the siren of ego, goaded me like a leashed dog: these Vatican appointments are rarely given to non-Italians. But how could I dishonour my home place? I was on the point of writing to His Holiness to ask that I be released from my obligation when the Rector of my college gave me stern, correct counsel. A priest takes a vow of obedience.

The appointed day came. I set out with the Vatican driver, an official photographer and another priest, a Milanese, to the Passo Corese camp some thirty kilometres from Rome, in the countryside. I will say that I had not slept well.

The lands immediately beyond my beloved city are some of the loveliest a weary pair of eyes will ever see: olive and lemon groves, fields of aubergines, vineyards, the ruins of aqueducts, scenery like the background of the *Mona Lisa*, roadside stalls piled high with artichokes and pumpkins. The hot musk of citrus and pine nectar as you open the car window on the winding, high-hedged lanes in summertime. You imagine that if you stuck an old man's walking stick in the earth it would sprout into a gorgeous willow.

I was raised among country people; to me, there is no glory like a farm. Those of the Roman hinterland are so beautiful and pleasing, with their red, loamy soil and well-kept fields, little barns painted ochre, and fat, peaceful cows, the countryfolk handsome and strong. On another day, one's spirit would have soared to the skies. But what was coming would be scorched into me like a branding.

I had ministered in jails before. Not like this. In Durham prison, I once sat a terrible night with a man who was to be hanged at dawn. In Haiti, I saw unspeakable things. But the afternoon that I spent at Passo Corese took five years from my life in as many hours.

Four thousand frightened prisoners crammed like abused beasts, half starved, into a couple of barbed-wired stony fields. One doctor, a drunken pervert. No letters. Two latrines. Compulsory hard labour. Frequent beatings.

Perhaps cruellest, nothing to do, as a matter of policy. No newspapers, no writing materials, not a playing card or a prayer book. Possession of a chessboard meant ten days of solitary confinement in a punishment cell scarcely larger than a coffin. No curtains on the shed windows, so that the wretched men could not even attempt to sleep away their boredom. Each inmate was given one litre of water daily, about two pints, and no more, so that he could not even clean himself, again a deliberate policy. The guards' leader was a vicious, dull-eyed brute, one Müller, later commander of the regional Gestapo before he was sent to the Russian front. One imagined him as a disturbed schoolboy hacksawing the legs off cats.

The photographer and I walked in silence as he made his pictures. I found I was incapable of speech.

What could one say to those emaciated, skeletal men, some of whom were in age no more than boys? I entered their sheds, the yards, saw their bunks, their gaunt bones, their good-fellowship to one another, their dread. The rule was that I was not to speak with them on any matter but might make notes if I wished to and could offer Holy Communion. My notes would be compiled into a report.

The priest who was with me, I do not judge. He had family in Milan and did not want Nazi trouble for them, so he looked away towards the olive groves and the ruins of the aqueducts, his spectacles misting with shame. I am no better than him, as God knows, and might well be worse. I burned to look away, too, but was unable to.

It would have been evident to a blind man that the prisoners had been threatened that they must lie to us. This all of them did, insisting they were in good spirits, well treated and adequately fed. I nodded and uttered my platitudes. There are times when we must permit one another to lie. I wanted none of them to suffer a beating for telling me what I already knew.

The stench in those sheds, I shall never forget, and the fear in the eyes of those prisoners. Their dignity had been systematically stripped from them; they were as whipped orphans. Even some of the guards had the decency to appear ashamed, refusing to meet my stare. Presently a seventeen-year-old boy from Liverpool came to me. About his throat was a medal of St Michael, patron of airborne warriors, and he requested me to bless it, which I did. As we conversed, it transpired that the boy had in fact the same name as my father. He asked to receive the Eucharist.

I knelt there in the filth, and we prayed, James O'Flaherty and me. The German guards did not like this, sent me angry glowers and coarse whispers. Some began barking at me like men trying to take bites out of the air. But the courage of the boy gave me strength, and I continued.

We offered a decade of the rosary together, him counting off the prayers to Our Lady on a length of knotted twine, then he began gently to sing the old hymn 'Abide With Me', and despite having the voice of a jackdaw, I joined him.

A moving custom of the crowd at the Cup Final in England is the communal singing of this hymn before the commencement of the game. Never has it been sung by anyone in Wembley Stadium as stirringly as by Private James O'Flaherty of Bridgewater Street, Liverpool, that day.

God bless that boy, wherever he is as I write. He showed more Christlike manliness in one moment than I have shown in all my life.

Soon, his bravery strengthened his fellows, too. Some limped from their sheds, in nervous twos and threes at first, blinking in the painful sunlight, helping one another along. One prisoner, a Dundonian who was unable to walk, was taken to me in a wheelbarrow. Before the war, he had been a schoolteacher. Others had improvised crutches from tree branches or broken planks. Their accents were of Birmingham, Manchester, Coventry, London, Tyneside, every corner of England, and among them the intonations of Scotland and Wales. They had been captured in North Africa, a good number at El Alamein or in the desert south of Tobruk. Many men, intending respect, addressed me as 'Padre', a term used in their own Church if not mine. Some spoke with hesitant affection of Ireland or of sporting contests between our two countries, in football, steeplechasing, rugby, boxing; others said nothing because they were dumbstruck with fear but looked at me with pleading glances.

I found myself telling them the war was going well, that the Allies would soon wrench Italy back from Fascism; that before long they would be home again with their families. In my pockets I had bars of chocolate and a couple of packs of American cigarettes – I do not myself smoke but they are a currency in Rome, as in all prisons, and I make it my business never to go out without them – and I distributed these among the men, who fell upon them. I had brought a bottle of Sulfaguanidine, diarrhoea medicine; this was received with pitiful gratitude. We spoke again of football and cricket. Some of the prisoners had boxed. A middle-aged man who had been blinded, his head wrapped in russet, bloodied bandages, held my hands as we spoke of Everton, Stoke and the Kop, the glory days of Freddie Steele and Tommy Lawton. A bantering argument began about the ill fortunes of Manchester United, and it was good to see the prisoners laugh and mock one another, pointing and mimicking, to the bemused chagrin of the guards.

Too soon, the appointed time came for us to conclude the visit, this fact being communicated to me by a Nazi sergeant who tapped on his wristwatch and briskly jerked his thumb toward the tall iron gates, which he stalked off to open. I said to the prisoners that we might gather in a circle and say the Lord's Prayer together, that everyone was welcome to stand with us, men of all creeds and none.

One prisoner, an East End Londoner, a fighter pilot downed in Tunisia, whispered to me that he was of the Jewish faith, was being protected by his comrades who told the guards he was a Methodist, but he wanted me to know the truth, he could not pray with us for he did not know the words. I said the greatest Being ever to set foot on the Earth was born a Jew, that it was not important to know the words, we would each of us pray in our own private manner or simply be silent together in examination of conscience and the will to do one another good when we were able.

Now one of the guards ordered me in angry, bitter German to cease what I was at, jolting forward and aiming his rifle at my face. I asked if he would like to join us in the prayer. For one moment, I thought he might.

'I offer you my hand,' I said. 'Take it. Let us pray.'

'I do not need your prayers.'

'Soon enough, you will.'

'What is that supposed to mean?'

'What it says, no more.'

'Are you threatening me?'

'With a prayer? You are easily threatened.'

By now, the camp's commander, Müller, had been summoned from his office, which, I recall, was in the foot of one of the watchtowers overlooking the main gate. He strode towards me with the false bonhomie that is always the mark of the secretly gutless, raising his right arm in the Nazi salute.

'*Heil Hitler*,' he uttered, attempting but not quite succeeding to click his heels.

I offered no reply.

'*Sie sind willkommen*,' he said.

I said nothing.

'Your papers, Father.'

'I presented them on arrival.'

'You will present them on departure, please. To me.'

'Why should I be asked to present my papers on departure?'

'To ensure that you have not given them to a prisoner.'

'You are accusing a representative of His Holiness of breaking the regulations?'

'I hope I never have to.'

'Your discourtesy to an emissary of His Holiness shall of course be noted in my report.'

'No discourtesy was intended. The Reverend Father will excuse me.'

From my briefcase, I produced my wallet of Vatican credentials, and I watched as he pretended to read them, now also pretending to make notes. I could see that he was worried. This pleased me.

'Reverend Father is an Irishman,' he said.

'My nationality is of no concern to you or anyone else. I am here as Envoy Representative of the Vatican City.'

'The Party and the Führer have many admirers in Ireland. Your people have of course fought the British dogs many centuries. Ireland's struggle is well known and admired among all right-thinking persons.'

I did not accept the invitation.

'The prisoners have made no complaints, I assume,' he now remarked, handing me back my documents, refusing to look me in the eye.

'No one has told me he is being ill-treated,' I said. Which was true.

'Good. Excellent. That is gratifying to know. We are not of course –' he gave an unctuous, buttery grin – 'a luxury hotel. That much will be obvious.'

'Yes,' I agreed. 'That much is obvious.'

'Nevertheless, we do our best. With straitened resources. My requests for food and medical assistance are often not listened to, by Berlin. And I have not enough men, as you will have seen for yourself. I send a telegram once a week. One may as well throw it in the river. Many in Berlin are of course careerists and bureaucrats, nothing more. They have no understanding of war. One may as well be dealing with women.'

'You dare to criticise the Reich,' I said. 'That fact, too, shall be entered in my report.'

One could almost hear the cogs squeal in the private hell of his mind. Crows on the barbed-wire fence squawked bleakly.

'Of course not,' he replied. 'I am a loyal servant of the Reich. It was merely that I wished the Reverend Father to know of the background to the work we are doing here. It is not easy, you know. Wartime, so on. Often our hands are tied.'

'I am to inform His Holiness the Pope that wartime means these men may not be given water?'

'There must be discipline,' he said.

'Must there?'

'Of course.'

'Where do you see the line between discipline and torture?'

'No man here has been tortured. To say so would be a slur.'

'Five minutes ago, I was ordered to leave. Stand out of my way.'

'But in honour of the Reverend Father's visit and as a mark of respect to the Vatican, I shall increase the water ration to two litres today. There is no need for undue harshness, after all.'

'You are a disgrace,' I said, then. 'You miserable, pitiable coward. You would be wise to un-holster your pistol and shoot me, this minute. Because, if it is the last thing I ever do, I will have you dismissed. I give you my solemn word. You vermin.'

'Reverend *Father*—'

'I shall return in one week. Have this abattoir in decent order. And make certain you're not here. *Auf Wiedersehen.*'

———

I visited many more of the prison camps, some eighty installations across Lazio and beyond. If there were occasions when I witnessed the prisoners treated properly in accordance with international law, I am sorry to say they were few. Fewer still were the times when I saw anything like the simple human decency that should not need legislating for, but usually does.

Mostly it was a matter of dismal, everyday belittlement, guards lording it over prisoners, standing in their way, making schoolyard remarks about their wives and mothers back home and so on, rather than outright physical violence. But there were times when one encountered a little Göring who needed putting in his place. At any rate, thus I saw things.

Meanwhile, things in the city were worsening.

It was my habit at that time, for the sake of my health, to walk briskly every day from the Collegio to the Victor Emmanuel monument ('the Altar of the Fatherland') and back, a trek of six kilometres or so. If it was hot, I broke the ordeal with an orange juice at a little bar on the Via del Portico d'Ottavia, in the quarter of the Jews, one of those places where you stand at the zinc and engage your neighbour in the talk of the day or are pleasingly left to mind your own business.

One noontime, I was at that counter, reading a copy of the *Chicago Tribune* someone had left behind, when a commotion out in the street took my attention. A group of the Fascist police had stopped and emptied a tram and were forcing a Jewish lady and her husband, a Rabbi, to their knees, mocking these elderly people and calling them vile names. One swine handed the old couple a toothbrush and instructed them to clean the pavement, his fellows having a mighty laugh at his brilliance. I went out and demanded the bullies' names and that of their superior officer – I had on priestly clothing, which fact I thought might soften their cough for them – and, during the noisome squabble that ensued, the old couple managed to make away into a side alley. But it was a sickening piece of casual cruelty. The fact that these innocent Romans had been abused in a busy street, at noon, as hundreds passed by, was itself a sort of poison.

One afternoon in late '42, just over a year ago, not long after I had returned to my quarters in the Vatican from a prison-camp visit, the Rector of the College, a good man now deceased (he died of influenza two months ago; Lord have mercy on his soul) sent a message requesting my presence. I was hungry, weary, dishevelled with dust, had been on the road nineteen days and was low in my spirits, wall-fallen a little, the camps having brought this about. The pleas made to me by the prisoners had kept me awake many nights. But I washed at the sink as best I could and put on the cleanest soutane I could find. Seeing the Rector, a learned theologian and exegetist if a somewhat humourless Berliner, was rarely an occasion of light chat.

As I entered his study, he appeared troubled, more anxious than I had seen him. It disturbed me a little that he was smoking. He beckoned me to his desk, gestured that I was to be seated. We had always got on civilly enough, the Rector and I, despite my lack of capacity in German, perhaps *because* of it, in an odd way. Sometimes, I have found, when people are not fluent in one another's languages, conversations become limited to bald pleasantry.

On his desk was an unruly stack of the reports I had compiled on conditions in the camps. It struck me as odd that the Rector had read my despatches, that someone must have had them translated, for I had written them in English. I had not sent them to him. I wondered who had.

Addressing me by my forename, he said he was *in Schwierigkeiten*. Which I knew meant 'in difficulties'.

I indicated as best I could that I saw distress in his face, that I was sorry to know he was burdened and would consider it a blessing to share the weight if he would permit me.

He began speaking to me in Latin, quietly.

Was it true that, some time ago, I had interfered with an attempted arrest of a couple in the Jewish quarter? An official complaint about me had been made by the authorities.

I answered that the elderly Rabbi and his wife were being victimised in the street, that I would interfere again if such an outrage required me to do so.

'You would?'

'Yes, Rector.'

'I see.'

He made a note.

'You surely know,' I said, in Latin, 'what is being planned and done to the Jews.'

Refusing to answer appeared to give him almost physical distress. Eyes shut, he rocked a moment, inhaling through his nose.

Was it also the case, as the official complaint asserted, that I had distributed books and food among the Allied prisoners of war in the camps on dozens of occasions, in defiance of the agreed regulations?

'I suppose so.'

A further note was made.

Then pausing, he tore out the page on which he had scribbled, carefully shredded it to pieces, and looked at me.

'These are not the correct answers, Hugh.'

'With respect, Rector, what are?'

At this point he picked up and rang a handbell that sat on his desk. A very young nun I had never seen before came into the office and stood by the window. She explained that she would be acting as interpreter for this meeting.

Adding to the surrealism of the moment was the terrible detail that the young Sister's right hand was missing.

The Rector touched his fingers together and told me he was not a Nazi.

I did not know how to reply.

He despised the National Socialists and all they were doing. 'To my Germany, to Europe, to the People of the Book.' Everything about them was *schrecklich*.

'Horror,' said the Sister.

'*Abscheulich, entsetzlich, fürchterlich,*' he continued. '*Grässlich. Schauderhaft. Widerwärtig.*'

As she translated these words, all variations of the same word, the Rector's whole face became slick with grief. He wept.

The Papacy was neutral, he continued. This must be respected. It was a matter of international treaty, was not open to debate. The Vatican ('our Mother') must be protected from Nazi invasion or bombing. Beyond the pastoral realm, visiting the sick and so on, what happened in wider Rome or Italy was none of our proper concern. In any event, there was nothing we could do about it.

But the Vatican, we must defend, as was her God-given right and our solemnest duty as Christ's ordained soldiery. Provocations of even the smallest kind were to be avoided. The Nazis were burning for a pretext, 'like a dragon lusting'. Imagine what would happen were *they* to disrespect the treaty, perhaps cross the boundary, roll their Panzers into the square. The Musei Vaticani might be burned to the ground. Or worse.

'Picture it, Hugh,' he said, 'the swastika flying from the dome of St Peter's.'

That would be a special obscenity, I agreed.

'So, you will give an assurance that you will desist from doing anything that could cause difficulty. Won't you, Hugh?'

'It has never been my intention to cause difficulty,' I said.

'Does that mean yes?'

'I would rather you did not ask.'

'Why so, Hugh?'

'Because I should prefer not to tell you anything that would bring you distress.'

He nodded.

'Stand up, please, Hugh,' he said, and he crossed to the door of the anteroom. Into the study strode the Holy Father.

The young nun genuflected. I was unable to move.

His face always has austerity when one observes it in photographs but is capable of tenderness, too, when one sees it in person, which I had only ever done once, from a fifty-metre distance, while assisting with a hundred other priests at High Mass for Easter. But there was nothing at all of kindliness that evening in the Rector's study. He looked as one carved of granite.

Like a slow-moving cold front he walked to the leaded window, now peering into St Peter's Square below.

I swallowed beady tears. Blood throbbed in my eardrums. A sudden and dreadful thirst possessed me, so that I would have drunk from the blackened ocean I found myself picturing.

He turned.

For what seemed a long time, the Holy Father looked at me without blinking, an expression of stony disapproval flinting his eyes, long arms by his side, like a soldier's in an honour guard. The gold crucifix about his neck caught the twilight. From far above us, I heard a bomber, then the dull wail of the air-raid siren from Parione. Even these did not cause him to flinch. The young Sister brought a chair. He nodded gratitude to her but ignored it. When, finally, he moved, it was to brush something invisible from the skirts of his impossibly white robe.

'The celebrated Monsignor O'Flaherty,' he said. 'We are honoured to make your acquaintance.'

I approached and kissed his hand but felt him draw away.

'Do you know Shakespeare, my son?' he asked, quietly, in Latin, and I said I knew a little, had read some of the plays as a young man training for school teaching.

'Which ones?'

'*Macbeth*, Holy Father. *The Merchant of Venice*.'

'You would appreciate that one,' he said. 'It being about a Jew.'

The air in the room seemed to be changing colour.

'We used to act,' he said now, with an icy smile that unnerved me. 'In High School. We were not very gifted.'

He paused as though providing a space he expected me to fill, but I felt that, if I did, he would interrupt immediately, which I had heard him do many times during the wireless broadcasts of his weekly audiences with the faithful. It is a thing done by men as a way of italicising their power.

'And then,' he continued, 'in the seminary a little. We were permitted a Drama Club. Supervised by the authorities, of course. The milder classical plays. Things like that.'

I was lost as to what response was required.

'Did you ever act, my son?'

'No, Holy Father.'

'Truly? Never? That seems odd.'

'In the Christmas play as a boy, nothing more than that.'

"'In the Christmas play as a boy, nothing more than that,'" he repeated, another tactic I have witnessed him deploy.

'Yes, Holy Father.'

'I have the feeling that you are acting now,' he said.

'Holy Father, forgive me, I do not follow.'

'*NO, YOU DON'T!*'

I had never heard him shout. Hearing it shocked me. It was not a raised voice but a furious bellow, almost a scream, that made something glass in the room vibrate. The Rector bowed his head, the young Sister appeared terrified. The Holy Father dried his mouth with a handkerchief.

'Do you wish to ruin everything?' he said. '*Answer when we address you.*'

'Holy Father—'

'You wish to see our Vatican, where repose the bones of our greatest pontiff, a saint who knew Jesus Christ *in person*, a man who witnessed the very trans-figuration itself, in smogs of flame and poison gas? The storm troopers' jackboots trampling the martyrs' graves. Two thousand years of Christ's dominion destroyed in a single night of firestorms.'

'No, Holy Father.'

'No, *Holy* Father. No, Holy *Father*. The sour, black irony of your pretended respect. But why do you address us thus, when you are evidently the only priest in the world never to have undertaken the vows of submission? When you have a special dispensation to formulate your own rules and procedures. To ignore decisions and orders deliberated by your betters. Surely it is we, the Bishop of Rome, who should genuflect before *you*. *È bene.*'

At this, he put his hand on the desk and made to kneel down, until the nun and then the Rector hurried over and pleaded with him not to do such an appalling thing. The young Sister's lips were trembling, her face contorted in shocked sorrow.

'Surely the Saviour Himself and all the saints should offer prayers to O'Flaherty,' he continued. 'We beg you, O'Flaherty. *Ora pro nobis*, O'Flaherty. Intercede for your inferiors from whatever pulpit of vainglory you preach from. *Have you an explanation you would like to offer for your filthy arrogance and insolence?*'

I began to speak. He interrupted me.

'We hereby strip you of your authority as a Vatican representative. Until further notice you will remain in this college or go one hundred metres to your work in the Holy Office every morning and home from it every evening, nowhere else, I say *nowhere*, without written permission in advance. You will not set foot outside the walls of Vatican City again until we permit it. You will reflect on the gravity of your errors and atone for them. *Do you hear me?*'

'Yes, Holy Father.'

'Because of *you*, those prisoners are to have no further visits.'

I felt that he was about to strike me across the face.

'How sharper than a serpent's tooth it is, to have a thankless child,' he said, bitterly. '*King Lear*. Act One. Scene four.'

With that, he swept from the office. The Rector said nothing. His silence, his very decency blazed me like a furnace, as he looked at his hands and the floor. He was merciful enough not to say that I had brought shame on the Collegio as he murmured that our meeting had concluded.

I went at once to my room and tried to sit with the shock of what had happened, as well as the grave sin of my disobedience. The Holy Father's words had scalded away my egotism, and I prayed that his indomitability would be rewarded. It came to me that what we find convenient to call charity is often vanity in camouflage, merely a way of floating up smoke signals of superiority about ourselves, or *to* ourselves, so that the smoke will conceal our ugliness.

Weeping, I pictured the men in the camps, their worn faces and wounded hands as they had reached to me in supplication or simple friendship. I prayed hard for all prisoners, as hard as I could, for the circumscribed of the world, this wretched sinner included.

———

For six months I remained in Vatican City. In time the Rector took pity and mitigated my sentence. Following the commencement of aerial bombing in July this year, I was permitted to attend the Irish Legation fortnightly, then weekly, there to offer pastoral support to the young Irish Religious and their hosts, if solemnly I undertook not to speak with anyone else and not to come to the attention of the authorities.

I can say with honesty that I gave the latter undertaking every effort I could. On the former point, I need now to confess that, while en route to or from the Legation, I would sometimes permit myself to converse with individuals whom I knew were in small ways aiding escaped prisoners and other fugitives to make their way to the coast. It was at that time a matter of a few lire here and there, sometimes a change of clothing. I knew I was in contravention and nevertheless continued. I ask prayers for the forgiveness of my disobedience.

On 13th September, a couple of days after the Nazi invasion of Rome, an urgent note came to this house that many of the Dominican friars at San Clemente had fallen gravely ill with the consumptive flu, which of late seems rampant around Italy. There being a contingent of pilgrims trapped in the city at that time, an English-speaking helper was needed to hear confessions. A pass to leave the Vatican and enter Rome for two hours would be arranged for the acceptor of the message.

That Monday was on the roster as a day of rest for me. I had intended to study and pray, for I was very afraid of what the German incursion might mean, but I decided that I would instead offer to volunteer at San Clemente. At the back of it, I think, was the hope of perhaps encountering someone from home. Perhaps, too, I wished to test if I had been forgiven by now, if the sentence of internal exile imposed by the Holy Father might receive official parole. I telephoned the Papal Curia and explained the pressing need of the Dominican Brothers. An hour passed before my call was returned. Permission was given for me to accept, but I was to speak with absolutely no one outside of San Clemente. Would I promise before God not to do so? I did.

Setting out on my motorcycle, I saw many German soldiers in the streets around the Vatican, dishevelled and unshaven, a rabble. Some were manhandling women or roaring for drink at the proprietors of cafés. Others were older than me, gaunt men in their fifties, or were boys in ill-fitting grey drabs. At one point I saw a man I know, John May, on the street, and our eyes met in greeting but neither of us made to stop and engage the other in talk. He looked fearful and exhausted, and this pained me to see, for usually he is a cheerful, bright Londoner.

Chillingly, as I passed one alleyway, I heard an abrupt burst of machine-gun fire.

Arriving at the church, I went directly into the sacristy. Often, I think of San Clemente as my most beloved Roman place of worship. It is far from the most beautiful, the largest, the most ornate, but always seems cooler and airier than it is, an atmosphere that raises the exhausted spirit, like a ladling of cold water after a banquet. There were indeed many people coming in and out, praying quietly, some admiring the frescoes or waiting in lines at the confessionals, but none of the monks was about, so I entered the first available confession box I saw and began to minister.

For an hour, all was normal enough. It felt a blessing to offer the mercy of the confessional. There arose the unearthly beauty of the choir and organist practising a piece I have loved since boyhood, Perosi's *Missa Eucharistica*, beautiful baritone timbres thickening the sound. And then, a thing occurred that was so frightening that I must commit report of it to paper. Should anything happen to me in the coming times, this event may explain it.

I opened the small, grilled hatch separating priest from penitent. As is the best custom, I did not look through, but continued facing ahead of myself, eyes closed. There was silence for some moments, an occurrence not all that unusual. People can be troubled before confession.

'Friend,' I said, at length. 'Leave anxieties beyond. Know you speak to the Unending Compassion, not to me.'

The voice, a man's, commenced reciting the introductory prayer monotonously, as though reading it out from a card.

In the usual way, I asked how long it had been since the person's last confession.

'I am not here to answer questions,' came the reply.

'My brother,' I responded. 'You are a long way from home.'

'So are you.'

'Come with openness. Our sins are a tomb. Roll back the stone.'

He said nothing.

It was so quiet that I could hear the ticking of his wristwatch from the other side of the hatch. To my astonishment, I now saw, when I glanced through the grille, the livery of a Gestapo commander.

'My name is Paul Hauptmann,' he said in English.

I made no response.

'We have not met,' he continued.

'This is a place of worship.'

'The door was open. I entered.'

'How dare you.'

I went to slam closed the grille, but his gloved hand stopped it.

'I have not finished speaking, Monsignor.'

'I want nothing to do with you.'

'I should like you to know something. A fact that is important. When two years ago you were selected as Vatican Envoy to our prisoner-of-war camps, it was I as Gestapo Officer overseeing Lazio who made the appointment, from a list of suggested persons.'

'You?'

'I wanted an Irishman leading the delegation. For reasons that are obvious.'

'Such as?'

'Unlikelihood of undue sympathy with the enemy.'

'Leave this holy place.'

'I misjudged you. You were weak. I had forgotten that an intelligent man can also be – in fact, usually is – naive.'

'I have nothing to discuss with you.'

'Nor I with you, Monsignor. But I will offer a piece of advice. *I* run this city now. You would be wise to remember it. In future do not go making trouble, for yourself and others.'

'Meaning?'

'Meaning we must have responsibility, cool heads. Respect for realities. Your addiction to belittling Wehrmacht commanders of the prison camps in front of their soldiers made you feel better, perhaps. I am aware that you did this often. Know, the commandant who succeeded Müller when your report recommended his dismissal is the most brutal thug ever to don a uniform. All your stunts ever accomplished was the worsening of conditions for those prisoners. The measurable worsening of thousands of lives. When there was no need for that. A pity.'

'Have you finished?'

'Ask yourself sometime, who brought about your removal from the delegation.'

'The Papacy brought it about.'

'You think so?'

His question, which was not a question, floated between us for a moment.

'I know there is an Escape Line,' he said. 'I will crack it. Believe me.'

I offered no reply. His voice became quieter.

'Berlin has ordered, no Escape Line. Or I shall suffer harsh consequences. Which means my family would suffer in turn, and I do not permit that to happen. I do not suffer consequences. I inflict them.'

'So I notice.'

'Order in Rome is my duty,' he continued. 'Do not make further difficulties, Monsignor. The slightest cooperation with an Escape Line would result in sentence of death. If you find that your friends are tempted – if you are tempted yourself – remember this conversation.'

'There are people awaiting confession. Again, I ask you to leave.'

'Your stubbornness, Monsignor, is standing in your way. Clouding your thinking. You are drunk on false virtue. Our movement will not be halted. Indeed, we have many priests, many Roman Catholics who support us. You would be amazed if I told you.'

'I would be disgusted and ashamed but not amazed.'

'My own wife is a Roman Catholic.'

'In that case she, too, should be ashamed.'

'Of her husband? Of her country?'

'And herself.'

'Rome fell, Monsignor. The British Empire will fall. So, too, the Soviet Union and the United States. All empires will fall. But one.'

'Yours will fall, too. Sooner than you think.'

'Not certain, are you, Monsignor? I hear the doubt in your voice. It is part of my training, to hear the doubt in the voice. But it is part of your own training, too, no? To listen to the poor captives? As they stutter their little failings in this box.'

'There is no captive here but yourself.'

'Be part of the march, Monsignor. Or don't stand in its way, I warn you.'

'You are part of nothing at all but your own self-hatred and irrelevance. Parades and processions and games of dressing up.'

A sob of grim laughter. 'Says a priest?'

'You are each of you alone in the pit of your inadequacies.'

'Rhetoric, Monsignor. Get down from your pulpit. I am not one of the sheep to be impressed by old women's prattle, and in truth you're not much of a sheepdog.'

'Get out,' I repeated. 'Before I kick you out.'

'You like hearing yourself say that, don't you, Monsignor? Not that you'd try it. All posturers are cowards. And all priests are afraid of life.'

'We'll see who the coward is when they're dragging you up a gallows.'

'Only know that you can be liquidated at any instant, Monsignor. It would be like snuffing out one of the candles those deluded outside pay a few lire to light, as they cower before gilt-stained idols set up by you and your ilk to frighten them into doing your will. You are alive because I tolerate it. You are the candle I burn. And I can choose my moment carefully for when your extinguishment is most useful. In the meantime, good day to you, Monsignor. Consider yourself advised.'

'I am not afraid of you,' I said.

'You will be,' he replied.

After he left, I stayed where I was for a couple of minutes, trying to calm myself. When I went outside, my motorcycle was in flames.

From the distance, the stutter of machine guns.

As he walks away from the burning motorcycle outside the church of San Cle-mente, Paul Hauptmann wipes his fingers on a scrap of paper he rips from a loose-flapping poster, 'DEATH TO THE FASCIST INVADERS'. Glad he didn't take the car. A good day to stroll a few kilometres.

The September sunshine is warm and golden, autumnally Roman; laurels sweeten the air as he crosses the little park near the marble staircase on which, people say, Christ once walked. Nonsense, of course, but let them have their stories. A line from Shakespeare arises at the thought. 'What fools these mor-tals be.'

From time to time, they stare at him, the conquered Romans and their chil-dren. Let them stare. They'll get used to him. No choice. He is new, unfamiliar, only a few days in command of their city; they can be forgiven a slight sullen-ness; their situation is not easy. He could go about with a bodyguard but that would be seen as weakness. The Luger on his hip is all the bodyguard he needs. That, and the reputation he's been careful to stoke through his leaks to the Fascist press. Should a Roman attack the Gestapo, the reprisal will be the dynamiting of seven city blocks and the hanging of the attacker's parents.

At the headquarters he's established at the German Cultural Institute on Via Tasso, he issues a directive to his men: no looting, Rome's businesses are not to be thieved from. Women are to be respected. Proven rape will be pun-ishable by death. The enemy shall be permitted to bury his battle-dead with dignity. Furlough will be allowed, but you will behave as a soldier of Germany. I am proud of you. Commander Paul Hauptmann.

It rankles, the priest's accusation about being alone. He shouldn't let it bother him but when one is tired and under strain, nonsenses can hit home harder.

Typists have arrived, radio engineers, Nazi clerks. Wehrmacht masons are mortaring bars into the windows of the smaller rooms on each floor, installing manacles and leg-irons, draping the walls with horse blankets for soundproofing.

A dentist's chair has been requisitioned and is being bolted to the floor of the cellar, restraint straps and a strangle-wire will be added soon. His second-in-command, Dollman, wants a gallows erected on the stage of what used to be the concert room, more for the dread its sight will induce in prisoners than for everyday usage, but that might be a bit much, the room adjoins the typists' office after all. The electrical supply to most of the building has failed; men are coming to get it reconnected. It pleases him to see the work being done, the set-up of governance. A lick of paint would be good; he records a memorandum on the subject. Perhaps a bit of new furniture. Those curtains are shabby. The sundial in the garden is broken.

As for those cheap, horrible reproductions adorning every wall, have them removed, he tells a secretary, we are in the city of Michelangelo. Fresh flowers and a borrowed Madonna in every public room of the headquarters. 'My wife says I'm inhuman,' he deadpans, 'before my coffee in the morning. Be sure I never need wait too long.'

At three o'clock, a captured deserter is brought before him, a young soldier from Bremen. He listens to the weeping boy's case, wishes there was an option for clemency. 'I will write to your parents to say you died in battle,' he says, 'so there will be no disgrace. It is sad we've come to this, be brave at the last,' shakes his hand before sending him downstairs to the yard to be shot. The sordidness of war. The wretched, filthy waste. When *all* of us have moments in which we would desert our lives if we could, if only it weren't too late. But it is. The crack of the pistol volley appears to upset one of the typists, but that can't be helped. Christ, the squalor things come to. War is war.

An idea has been nudging him, to bring the family to Rome. Is it feasible? Where would they live? Would the danger be immense? It's a balance, but isn't everything, now. The warmth, the sunlight, the statuary, ancient temples. Perhaps good for the children, to live a season or two abroad.

On the telephone from Berlin, his wife seems distracted. Their daughter has a cold, their son is in trouble again at school, very slow with his letters, disobedient, introspective. In her voice, he hears anxiety, a sort of false glee she attempts when he calls. He wonders if she's drinking again. She sounds tired.

'Are you eating properly, Paul?'

He tells her he is.

'Is your barrack all right?'

'It's good.'

'I miss you,' she says. 'I wish you were home.'

'*Wenn ich mir was wünschen dürfte,*' he whispers, the title of an old love song they associate with their courtship. 'If I could wish for something.' The phrase has become a sort of private tenderness between them.

'You're sweet,' she says.

'Because I love you.'

'Paul, did Himmler call again?'

'I can't say on the telephone.'

'Are we in trouble, Paul?'

'No.'

'Then, why does he keep calling you?'

'There's no need to worry. It's only a difficulty.'

'That's why they pay you the big money, my darling,' she jokes. 'To solve them.'

'That's why they pay me the big money, you're right.'

A line from an American gangster movie they saw while on honeymoon in Guernsey. Somehow it became part of their couple-talk.

'Have those prisoners stopped escaping?' she asks.

'Sweetness, I can't discuss it.'

'So unfair of them, rotten nuisances, causing problems for my Paul. You'd tell me the truth, wouldn't you? If we were in trouble with Himmler?'

'I'd tell you the truth. We're not.'

'If those prisoners keep escaping—'

'Elise, let's not speak of it.'

'Are the Roman women beautiful?'

'Not as beautiful as you.'

'Liar.' She laughs. 'I wish I could kiss you.'

'I wish that, too, darling. To cover your body with kisses.'

'Don't say such things, Paul, when I'm lonely without you.'

'Sweet girl, get some rest. I adore you.'

'I, you.'

'Goodnight then, little dove. Let's speak again tomorrow. I've an idea to put to you, might be a nice thing for the family.'

'One last time, can you tell me we're not in trouble with Himmler? Because

I'd worry myself sick, Paul. Those rotten, escaping troublemakers. Why can't they *stay* in their prison camps, must they always cause a problem? Don't they *want* their wives and girlfriends to know they're safe, away from war? If *you* were in a prisoner-of-war camp, I'd be glad you were safe.'

'Elise—'

The line goes dead.

On his desk, Himmler's telegram:

'Führer incensed by these recent escapes. STOP THIS EMBARRASS-MENT. I warn you.'

From a drawer he retrieves a file of photographs he's been collecting in recent months. People worth looking at again, possible collaborators, suspects. Placing them painstakingly into alphabetical order by surname, he pauses from time to time, to extract a photograph from the folder and pin it to the cork board above the desk. Persons of Particular Interest. His Portrait Gallery.

He pauses at 'O'.

Pins that photograph to the board.

'O'Flaherty, Hugh' is the name on the label. In pencil he adds the words: 'Troublemaker. Stubborn.'

He blows out the candle.

To bed.

But hard to sleep tonight. Difficult to say why.

It isn't quite anxiety. Not wakefulness alone. It isn't the solitary church bell that tolls the hour through the night, or the silence that follows it, the wait-ing. Some unease for which he has no name has entered him like a splinter.

Darkness.

Fox bark.

Three-in-the-morning Rome.

A man in a box, saying, 'I'm not afraid of you, Hauptmann.'

The silence that follows the bell.

6

THE VOICE OF ENZO ANGELUCCI
7th November 1962

From transcript of BBC research interview, tape 1,
conducted Bensonhurst, New York City

Speak in here? Like this? You hearing me okay?

So, my name is Enzo Gianluca Alessandro Angelucci. Age, fifty-four. That's right.

I'm living seventeen years in Brooklyn but I was born over there in Rome. People in the States call me Johnny.

Italian-American? Sure. Put the 'Italian' in bold.

When I first came I worked construction, a sheet-rocker, good money. My three brothers and me lived in one room over a deli on the corner of Mulberry and Broome, on boloney and cans of tuna.

Later, things came up. I done good. These days my wife and I got a used restaurant-equipment business on the Bowery and a hardware store on Mott Street. Angelucci Paint and Tile. We don't owe nobody nothing.

Before the war I had a newsstand on the corner of Largo del Colonnato and Via di Porta Angelica, right there on the edge of St Peter's Square, a good sit. You got a lot of passing trade with a sit like that. It was hard, honest work. I liked it. My parents established the business. Their names were Sandro and Antonella, *che Dio li benedica.*

And my mother was the toughest business person you ever met. Her thing was work hard, God gave you two ears so you'd listen twice as much as you talk. Get up early, love your family, don't bullshit.

My old man built the stand from old oak barrels that was rescued from a winery on the Principe Pallavicini estate out in the countryside, the Castelli Romani, so the walls was kind of curved, a nice talking point. The people liked that. It was good for trade, a conversation starter.

Me and my sisters and brothers worked there on weekends and in the summers or after school, and when my parents got too old, I took it over. I guess I was twenty at the time. Young punk. Full of piss and vinegar. I built it up over eight, nine, years, something. I was married on my twentieth birthday, my wife died in a bombing raid on Rome in March '44. We was only kids when we met. Yeah, I still think of her, sure.

Kind of stuff on the stand? Oh, everything, everything. All the newspapers we sold. Italians are crazy for newspapers. Even second-hand, I'd sell those if some guy was buying. Even a week or ten days old, you might get five lire for it. Sure.

Fashion magazines. Guidebooks. Crosswords. Dirty books for old men. Tickets to the Vatican. Biographies of the Caesars and saints. Holy pictures. Old maps. Everything.

Yeah, that was how I met the *Monsignore*.

He starts coming by my stand every other morning for the *Gazzetta dello Sport*. Tall fella, well built. Little red in the face. We true Romans are small-boned. But this guy's the size of a door. Stands out. This blue-and-white golf umbrella, huge thing, when it's raining.

'I got a spare ration card for today,' he tells me. 'You want it? Take it.'

I tell him I don't need nothing, I'm good.

'Take it for your children. Get a little extra milk. Or bread. It's going to waste right now.'

Hair's a little thin but it's black as the Sicily grapes, as we say. These old-fashioned, horn-rimmed glasses, bifocals. Sense of humour he got. Made you grin.

'Say, friend,' he goes. 'How much are your postcards?'

'Five lire for two.'

'How much for one?'

'Four.'

'I'll take the other.'

Sometimes he whistles as he looks over my stock. Or he sings to himself. I like a man who sings. I'm Italian.

Another thing I remember, he got this strong, distinctive walk, manly, you know, head up, swinging his arms. Confident. When we introduce ourselves, one day after he's been coming to my stall for I guess a week, his handshake is firm, like a farmer's selling you a cow. His eyes don't move while he's talking to you; the guy scarcely blinks through them glasses. There might be fifty, sixty thousand people in the Piazza; you're the only one there. You can tell he's taking you in, with the cash-register eyes. In Italian we got a word for it, *sprezzatura*, that's a word I like. Means knowing how to come across casual.

Stands to reason in St Peter's Square, you're seeing priests all day long, right? I was Communist at the time, but they didn't bother me none. You want to buy a newspaper, brother, I'll sell you a newspaper. I want confession? I'll let you know.

And this one, the *Monsignore*, he's hard to dislike. Such a big, laughing countryman, got no airs, he talks to you like an equal, in Italian. *Come sta, Signor Angelucci, amico mio? Come stanno sua moglie e i suoi figli?* Oh, swell. No, we didn't talk politics or religion, just the everyday shoot-the-shit.

Soon afterwards I found out, from the other guys in the square, he's giving away his ration card every other morning. What's happening – we figured it out – is the guy's only eating every second day. The other, he's hungry. Swear to God.

Another thing I liked, he was crazy for sports. Boxing was his thing. Regular encyclopaedia of fights. The Cuban fighters he loved. Also football as we call it in Italy, by which we mean soccer. Then tennis, cycling, the Tour, any contest. The ponies not so much. I don't know why. Because plenty of priests, let me tell you, they go nuts for the ponies. But the boxing, oh, baby. He adored it.

Talking your arm off about the great heavyweights. Joe Louis, guys like that. Loved the welterweights too, he seen Rocky Graziano fight amateur. Graziano was born right here in Brooklyn but as a kid moved to East 10th Street and First, over the bridge, a big Italian neighbourhood, where my own sister and her husband lived. She cleaned house for a family called Barbella, which was Graziano's born surname. The *Monsignore* loved hearing all that.

For a foreigner, he had an incredible, I mean incredible, knowledge of Rome. This street, that block, the little '*vicoli*' as we call them, *vicoli e incroci*, the passageways and criss-crossings between the old houses and around the backs of churches, some of them too narrow to ride a scooter through. Rome is like a cheese, you know, full of holes. You could live in Rome a thousand years and not know every alleyway. But this guy came close, let me tell you. His hobby was studying old maps of the city; if I came across one on the stall, I'd give it to him. Always he tried to pay me, but these was just pages cut out of books, not originals. You'd frame them and hock them to Americans. His big thing was breaking my balls that the guidebooks I was selling on the stand was garbage. He wanted to write a guidebook himself one day and maybe I'd sell a thousand copies at twenty lire a throw and we'd both get rich and have ringside seats at the fights. Type of guy he was. Down to earth.

We'd pass the time, have a conversation, compare the reports of the bouts in the different newspapers. If I was making coffee on a cold morning, he'd take a quick cup with me, sure. When war came, the coffee was horrible, you couldn't even call it that. Made of acorns. But we'd force it down, it was something, at least it was hot, right? We'd have a bet now and then. It was part of his playfulness. One morning he says to me, 'Angelucci, you're deluded, Armstrong won't last four rounds against Montañez, let's bet on it.' Now, I'm joking back to him, just bouncing the ball. 'Brother, you're a priest, ain't betting a sin?' He says, 'Not with invisible dollars.'

So, he bets me fifty invisible dollars, like a yank, and I give fourteen to one, like a bookie. Next day he says to me, 'Angelucci, you made me a Rockefeller, hand over my invisible winnings,' or 'Enzo, you broke my bank.' We actually kept account, in a notebook. He never went nowhere without his tiny notebook and a pencil stub behind his ear. And we'd bet, like two dukes. It was ridiculous, you know. Just a way of passing the time. I'd write him an IOU for a million dollars and change. He'd say, 'Give me a cup of your rotgut coffee, we're even.'

Well, the Fascisti kicked my stall down and burned what was left. Because I wouldn't quit selling foreign newspapers. But you don't tell no Angelucci what to do. Like we say, '*O mangi questa minestra o salti dalla finestra,*' kinda means you deal with the shit or you jump out the window. My wife had a cousin worked in a chandlery, an old factory in Trastevere where they made church candles, and he'd let me have a box or two, cost. I'd get them blessed and go around St Peter's Square like a pedlar selling them for a couple of lire to the pilgrims queuing in the line. Two babies at home and another on the way? You do what you do. Feed your family. I'd say, '*Buongiorno, Signora,* inside the Basilica these are ten lire each. How about I give you two for five. These were blessed by Cardinal Ventucci.'

Because people like a bargain. You learn that in business. Specially the old ladies, see, they don't have much dough, so you cut them a deal, we're all happy.

'*Nonna*, I give you four for eight, *che Dio protegga tutti*.'

I won't lie, sometimes them candles was blessed by Enzo Angelucci. But if I could find a priest to do it, I did. Strange to say, I don't remember never asking the *Monsignore*. Maybe I didn't want to, whatever, compromise him I guess. But I'm sure he would have done it if I asked.

Allora: here's one hot afternoon I'm down in the square and, hand to God, the sun's beating me like I owe it money. It's one of those Rome days when even your sweat burns. I'm working the line, when I seen, near the colonnade, trying to get some coolness in the shadow, here's this young guy alone, in shabby, dirty clothes, and he's looking so sick, face white as the moon, arm in a sling made of a potato sack. You get tramps in Rome, same as everyplace else. But something about him. His eyes.

Tell you the truth, I'm busy; the people are buying candles – beautiful – but something in his face is so sad, so broken. Only nineteen or twenty. Handsome kid. Floppy hair. Reminds me of my brother, Marco, always getting in trouble. So, what are you going to do?

I go over in his direction and he's backing away scared. Sweating like a waterfall. He's got fever.

'What's the matter, kid? You hungry?'

I offer him a pear.

Kid looks at me a long time before taking it, eats it down in five bites. Tattoo on the back of his wrist says '*Viva l'Italia*'. In my pocket I got a porchetta sandwich she made for my lunch and I give him that, too, and a flask of cold water, and my kerchief for his face and his neck.

'Sit down a minute, *Paesano*. Take it easy. Bathe your forehead. You got sunstroke? You want a cigarette maybe?'

It's like he don't hear me. Eyes rolling like a doll's. I'm thinking he's going to faint. Jesus Christ.

I mean, he's terrified. Shaking. And your heart is going to crack. If I live to be two hundred, I'll never forget what he's about to say.

Forgive me, it still . . . When I think of it.

[*Subject becomes emotional.*]

'For the love of God, brother, I beg you, don't betray me.'

Those were his words. Like flames.

He's an escaped prisoner of war, a Jew, half-Italian. They catch him, he's dead. We both know it. It's over.

I mean, what am I to do? I'm some guy who hawks candles. I don't got no powerful friends or money or connections. My place is five kilometres away near Termini and anyhow there's no room, and my wife is going to kill me if I bring this kid home. That's not going to be happening. Impossible.

I mean, I'm tempted to walk away. I got a family, a life. Italy, now, is a place where you're careful. Don't go looking for trouble, you won't find no trouble. All kinds of thoughts go tumbling in your mind. Suddenly you're in a sand-storm. Until you're a grain of sand yourself. Or you're staring at a moment. And you better believe there's consequences. These guys of Hauptmann put a bullet in your head before breakfast then sit down to eat. You're dirt on their floor. But I can't help it.

I'm looking across the square – I'm desperate, confused – and, right then, three hundred metres away, I seen the *Monsignore*, by the fountain, pacing and reading his holy book – the breviary they call it – the holy book a priest got to read from every day. I tell the kid come follow but not to say nothing, just pretend he don't know me, and we cross, in and out of the crowd, and it takes a while because he's limping so bad. Nazis every which way. Fascist police. The works.

The sun is blazing down on the granite like a bastard. The kind of heat you can feel through the soles of your shoes. You'd give a lot to be far away, in a cool room with the shutters closed, and your wife. When I'm maybe twenty paces from him, the *Monsignore* looks up from the book, like he's been expecting me all along.

'Say, Angelucci,' he goes, like good-humoured, poker-face. 'You're come here to rob me on the Sugar Ray fight, you bum. And you owe me four million already. You finagler.'

I go closer and explain what's going down over here.

He looks past me at the kid. Then he looks at me, angry. I ain't never seen this expression in him before.

'Are you out of your living mind?' he says. 'To bring this man to me?'

'They'll murder him,' I say. 'Let's not let that happen. Got to be something we can do. You're a priest.'

I swear to you, I can see the thunderstorms lighting up his eyes. I'm not sure if he's going to agree with me or punch me. We're there two, three minutes. A long time to stand in sunshine. Try it.

Then with his expression he beckons. The kid nods and follows. And off they make tracks, in the direction of the Basilica, this big, tall countryman the size of a door and this limping, broken kid beside him. There's a little bridge to the left of St Peter's, which leads into the Campo Santo. Little bridge I can't remember the name of. That's where they go.

I say to my wife what happened, she goes crazy that night. I'm this, I'm that. She could cuss, for a girl. Rile up an *Italiana*, you'll hear about it. But she'd have done the same thing, is the truth. I know it. She was a good person, full of kindness. She'd have done the same thing. Elisabetta Monti. *Possa riposare in pace.*

Next time I see the *Monsignore*, couple days later, he tells me, 'Angelucci, the kid is safe, in the Vatican infirmary, been given false papers. Only thing he needs to worry about now is some Carmelite falling in love with him. And I've decided to form a choir.'

'A choir?'

'You're one of the members.'

'But *Monsignore*, I can't sing.'

'I can't dance and I'm dancing. You're about to learn.'

'I'll think about it,' I tell him.

'Don't take long,' he says back. 'Storm's blowing out there. I need help.'

No wind where we're talking. Nice sunshine. Calm day. But yeah, course I know what he means.

Was I scared? Bet your ass. Who wouldn't be? Times was bad. Hauptmann finds out you're fooling, it's curtains, *ciao a tutti*. No trial, no sentence, you're dead. But then, that kid's eyes. So, what the hell was your life? Was there anything you ever believed in, any moment you stood up? Because, brother, the day will come when your children be asking, and you better believe you'll need an answer, so what's there to say? In my head I went back and forward, but in the end, I agreed. That was that; I joined the Choir. Once in, I was in. It's like taking a penalty in soccer: choose your spot and aim hard, let the goalie dance around if he wants to, that don't change your decision. So, yeah. I'm on board. *O la va o la spacca*. Better or worse. *Il Coro*.

Every day from then on, as the bells rang for noon, he'd come out from the Collegio and start pacing the Basilica steps. Or he'd stand there, big and tall, in the black cassock and red sash, so anyone coming into the square could see him, couldn't miss him if they tried. He hid in the open. Like a lighthouse.

If it was raining, he'd have that huge golf umbrella with him, like a giant blue-and-white toadstool. He might as well be standing in a spotlight on the Pope's balcony, he's so visible. Like some goddamn soprano up there.

So, in twos and threes they'd appear. Or, some by themselves. Guys escaped from the prisoner-of-war camps. Out the side streets, the laneways all around St Peter's. In disguise as Roman workmen, trashcan collectors, coal heavers, streetcar drivers, housepainters, *muratori* – our word for a stonemason, a wall-guy – farmers in town for market, hawkers, priests, I got no idea where they got the clothes. They'd make their way to the *Monsignore* and he'd lead them through, under the bridge.

Soon it got out among the escapees, don't know how, that I was one of his helpers, and they'd come up to me in the square, saying they wanted to buy my candles but needed 'to get them blessed'.

I thought, I'll bless you in a minute, with my boot up your ass. But then I'd point out the Boss.

That's how it got started. The Choir.

Every day they kept coming, one after the other. Before long, I couldn't keep count.

But that Christmas Eve Rendimento. Christmas Eve '43.

We planned it so careful. All the time, fate was laughing.

Cuts me to pieces to think of it. Still can't believe what happened.

And that was the *Monsignore*. Irishman. Crazy. Type of guy wouldn't listen to reason.

7

Christmas Eve 1943

9.11 a.m.

13 hours and 49 minutes before the Rendimento

The refectory is empty but for three Japanese priests conversing anxiously in their language over a newspaper. Avoiding them, he fetches an ersatz coffee from the bulbous copper urn on the counter, a steamy blast of chicory odour and potato peelings assailing him, now following him to one of the long tables down the end of the room, over which glowers a reproduction of van Craesbeeck's *Temptation of St Anthony*. A hang-around smell of old mops taints the air. Three fluorescent tubes emit a bile-green unpleasantness no one could define as light.

A Sister he's never seen before approaches and addresses him in German but in a moment apprehends that he doesn't understand and translates herself into Italian. Would he take a piece of biscuit?

'*No, grazie.*'

'We have no other food today, Father.'

'I'm fine. Would there be a sheet of notepaper?'

She brings it.

What he needs is to be alone at the long table with his thoughts, the space to spread out a contingency. Time to think.

At the top of the page, he writes one word:

'RENDIMENTO'

The Choristers' code for a mission.

With no news of Derry, the plan must be recalibrated, and, if Angelucci doesn't show, changed again. One by one, he considers the possibilities, his associates, the understudies. The Rendimento is too dangerous for any of the women to be asked but all of them are too brave to decline it, he knows. Perhaps Delia? The Contessa? What about Marianna? She's tougher than any man, a fast-thinker, clever. May couldn't do it, he doesn't yet know all the back streets. Asking Osborne is out of the question. Or is it?

Yes, it is, Marianna de Vries seems to say, pushing to the front of his mind. *He's too old and he talks too much.* Her Dutch briskness makes him laugh, though not today.

Scribbling, sketching, scoring, cross-hatching, blackening every millimetre with spirals, altered lists. The Rendimento *must* take place tonight, any later is too late. Hauptmann will never expect anything on Christmas Eve. No matter how the sum is done, there is only one answer.

It adds up to Enzo Angelucci.

He gets himself another coffee, thinks toughly about Angelucci. Loyal, courageous, brimming with righteous hatred – but he lacks Derry's cunning, the discipline-under-fire drummed into their officers by the British. Derry can climb facades, get through barbed wire fences, evade a pursuer, disappear into shadow, has seventeen Rendimenti under his belt already. Angelucci doesn't have combat training or counter-espionage expertise. Might he brag a bit in advance or let something slip later? Would his hot head be a vulnerability?

In the credit column, he's a Roman, knows every alley and nook. His impatience to run a mission should be used without further delay, months have passed since it started becoming dangerous. He's bored of being a watcher, a glorified tout, noting the movement of Nazi trucks, counting the numbers in a patrol, smashing streetlamps with a catapult so the police don't see who's entering an apartment building. All Italians talk in emphases but when Angelucci gets frustrated, hands windmilling at the air, his undulations overwhelm him. 'Like a *school*boy,' he often complains. 'I am treated as *a child* here. For *pity's* sake, *give* me a *Rendimento,* Father. A *solo.*'

Captured by Hauptmann, would he break?

Who wouldn't?

Even Derry might break. Always says it himself. *Don't tell me everything, Padre, because they'll start with the pliers and blowlamp. I'll hold out as long as I can but you know what Jerry's like. Once he gets you to Via Tasso, German efficiency's rather efficient.*

The former German Cultural Institute, Via Tasso. As a young seminarian awed by the city, he had often attended concerts there, Brahms, Schubert, the lattice-like fragility of the music. Now there will be no more concerts.

Barbed wire, hooded sentries, the windows bricked up. People living three blocks away awakened by the screams. A baker's truck materialises every dawn to collect the carcasses that were once the bodies of students, Partisans, resisters. The van is said to have been made leakproof by casing its interior in rubber, but even such orderliness doesn't always prevent the trail of scarlet splashes from Via Tasso to the squares and parks of the city, where Hauptmann has the disfigured bodies placed so they'll be widely seen.

On benches. In bus shelters. Hanging from lamp posts.

Would Enzo be one of them?

A married man, could he be asked?

What of his wife and children should the worst thing happen?

Derry knows precisely how many Books are in hiding, and where, has some memory system he learned during his training at Sandhurst, but whenever he tries explaining it, the other Choristers plead with him to stop. The speed of the number's growth is too frightening.

At the table up the hall, the Japanese priests are chuckling, pointing. It seems a mouse has been spotted in the corner nearest the lectern where the Rector, before the war, used to read aloud from the scriptures during supper. The unknown Sister hurries out from the kitchen and a pantomime of mouse-hunting commences, colander as snare, egg-whisks as cudgels, but the mouse, if it ever existed, proves unwilling to appear despite the shrieks and multilingual cajolings.

People would delight you if you let them. Their innocent foolishness. That, and his tiredness, threaten his eyes with tears, face turned to the frosted window.

Via Tasso feels close.

A baker's truck, revving.

He goes to the public telephone in the cubbyhole under the stairs, expecting that the line will be down, but no, it is working, a burr, like a dozing animal.

He wonders why the Nazis have switched it back on. Bait, he supposes. Hauptmann's fishing for something. At this stage, there is no choice but to bite.

Placing a code-call through to the Contessa's private number, he hears her pick up, so he knows she is at home, then he disconnects and dials again, letting the ring sound four times. This is the most urgent of the signals they share.

One ring. Two rings. Third ring. Four.

It's urgent. The usual place.

Receiver replaced, he stays where he is for a moment, in the telephone cubby under the stairs, among raincoats and yellowed directories. He prays for her, or tries to, as he does every day of his life, but the words turn to smoke as he thinks them. She feels oddly present, somehow; he can sense her reassurance, *I heard you, I'm on my way, don't worry.* Sees her putting on her gaberdine in the dark old house, running down the marble staircase that's too steep to run down, emerging into the street, the hurting brightness, the noise, and the old door slamming behind her. He's too shy to put a name on the fondness he feels for her and often wonders if it's true. There is an ache in many hearts where a daughter might have been. He never knew it before he met Giovanna Landini.

He returns to his room, collects his breviary and rosary beads, then back across the landing and down the squeaking stairs, through the chatty tempestuousness of the busying male house, students jostling and joking on the ashy cold corridors or hurrying out to the last of this term's lectures.

'*Guten Morgen, Monsignore. Guten Tag. Salve.*'

In the gardens behind St Peter's the stilled fountains have frozen so that the water is the same sooty grey as the marble containing it. Gravel scrunches as he walks, thoughts monkeying at him, mocking; the cold stone bench a taunt.

A dream he had of London looms up from old leaves: mist rolling across Hyde Park, cavalry horses exercising, a young, veiled woman seen as from a great distance across the lake. He wants her to unveil, but she won't.

Farm Street, Brompton Oratory. Old bookshops. Cricket scores. Charing Cross Road in the autumn, dusk bringing on lights in the theatre foyers. The consoling bleakness of slate-grey skies. A night on Leicester Square Tube Station when a woman fell ill, he knelt by her on the platform and waited for the ambulance men to come but she had said with immense gentleness, English politeness, that she would prefer him not to pray, just to converse with her or remain silent, that she was not a believer, and even if she were, 'God has better things to be doing.' They talked of Handel and wildflowers as she died.

From the pocket of his soutane he takes an unopened stack of blank postcards and the fountain pen his mother sent last Easter, bought on a trip to Dublin for surgery, and begins ticking through eventualities.

He checks from time to time that no one is coming. Birds wheel and shriek above cypresses.

Osborne and Giovanna have between them arranged the last of the money – he doesn't know how, doesn't want the burden of knowing – which will arrive in used notes via an unidentified city this morning. Delia Kiernan has a contact at the American Express office who has agreed to look the other way when a certain package comes in. John May will see it delivered to Operations HQ.

If they can find him, Angelucci will undertake the Rendimento. If not, they will gamble on a former soldier known to Marianna de Vries, a tough, committed sniper, knowledgeable of the streets, who's been pushing a long time to join the Choir. A baptism of fire might be the only option. Far better if it were Angelucci.

Three drops, one in Prati, the second in Parioli, then a 'refuelling stop' to take on more cash, then the largest drop in Campo Marzio but no one will know exactly where until the final moment. Then rendezvous with a getaway agent, 'the pilot', for the last kilometres home.

If everyone's still alive.

In the distance, the same distance as the veiled young woman in the dream, he sees the slim, deliberative, white-clad figure of the Pope, walking alone near bare olive trees, from time to time stopping, glancing up at the sky like a farmhand expecting it to tell him something about weather.

Normally there would be guards. Why are there no guards?

He moves painfully, stiffly, as though much older than he is, towards a bower of tied-up roses near which someone has left a barrow with a spade shoved into muck. He seats himself on the rim of a fountain, long arms by his side, before rising again and going to the barrow and shovelling out a hefty spadeful of manure. As he digs and thrusts, steam globing from his mouth, he turns his weary torso in a slow, steady circle.

Two Swiss Guards and a nun hurry out from the palace doorway with an overcoat. The old man ignores them, digging, digging, his skullcap the colour of dirty snow.

Bombers overhead, high above the range of the ack-acks. An old man hoeing at thorns.

THE CONTESSA GIOVANNA LANDINI

From an unpublished, undated memoir written after the war

We had been married less than a year when my husband died. The day after his funeral, I lost a longed-for pregnancy. I was thirty, in storms of grief.

I had servants, gowns by Chanel and Elsa Schiaparelli, jewels, a palace, a villa at San Casciano dei Bagni, a yacht moored at Ostia, a prosperous vineyard. Without Paolo, it counted for nothing.

When war came, I volunteered in the Ambulance Corps as a driver. Without that, I would have gone mad. The irregular hours were a cover for the fact that sleep had become a stranger to me. There was no fire towards which I wouldn't drive. In the end, they had to dismiss me.

For a time afterwards I assisted as a motorcycle despatch rider for the Red Cross, delivering medicines about the bombed parts of the city where a truck could not go. Paolo had taught me to ride the Triumph Tiger I had given him as a wedding gift, a small, fast, good-handling machine. But war made it impossible to find British spare parts, and, following a fuel line malfunction that burned out the engine, his steed had to be glumly stabled in the old coach house at the end of my garden, where the spiders found its wheel spokes the perfect lattice for their webs, and mice gnawed the saddle leather to black lace.

If you know Rome in high summertime, the weeks leading up to Ferragosto, I don't need to explain the vampiric, exhausting heat. My house on Via del Corso, built around a quattrocento courtyard, had a fountain and a colonnade in which bleary peacocks sulked, but I couldn't abide the courtyard, young and jealous as I was, for it had been remodelled by a former lover of Paolo's, a girl who had left him, rather too glamorously I felt, to become a nun and die in China, on the missions.

Instead, on those scourging afternoons of heat, when most of Rome retires to a café or to bed in a shuttered room, I would bicycle to the gardens of the Villa Umberto and lie in the grass between the lordly pines. The heat would coax loamy musk from the earth. I felt close to Paolo then. It was as though I could hear his whisper. The agony of life would abate.

Mostly, what I wanted was to follow him, wherever he was. The only thing I had not decided was the method of my self-destruction. I had a pistol he had given me, a small, jade-handled Beretta. Perhaps that would return me to his side. In the gardens, he would whisper that I was to remain; hope would come if permitted. The heat, the aromas, the earth beneath my body made it possible to believe in a ghost.

There was no need to bring a bundle of his love letters with me; in truth, I knew every one of them by heart. Blushed into my memory, as pomegranate juice tinctures Prosecco in the cocktail we shared on the Terrazza dell'Infinito at Ravello before retiring on our wedding night.

Those gardens were where Paolo and I had met, on an autumn day in 1936. I was walking with my sister when a blazingly handsome soldier approached, pushing a wheelchair in which was a blanketed old gentleman, his father. Elisabetta asked them for directions to the Casina delle Rose – a concert we wished to attend was to take place there – for we were lost and had been going in slightly argumentative circles, as sisters sometimes like to do. His eyes had a fierce gentleness, if such a contradiction is possible, and his manner such gallantry and what I can only call acumen – but enough of happier days.

On those afternoons of my raw widowhood, when I would go again to the Villa Umberto gardens to weep on a park bench with his absence and the sirocco, I would sometimes after an hour or two go into the Galleria to wash my face or to look at the beautiful things. On a hot afternoon, the great rooms were often empty, lending the statues a pleasing sadness in that particular redolence of old, heated dust that, for me, will always be Rome. Or, a couple of students might be sketching them, a tousled boy, a smoking girl; I found envying their youth a healing heartache.

One Thursday (I remember it well), as I entered the Sala Bernini, the only person there was a priest. A tall, high-coloured man, in wire-rimmed spectacles, he was clad in a black cassock that must have been making him broil; his face was red as the monsignorial sash he had on and his thick, black hair looked damp. He was standing before that disquieting masterpiece of statuary, *Apollo e Dafne*, which Paolo had always loved and often bribed the attendants to be allowed to photograph.

Obviously, one sees priests every day in Rome. But something about him took my attention. He was not a particularly striking person to look at. Perhaps it was simply that he appeared hot and uncomfortable or that seeing a priest in an art gallery is for some reason not all that common. Anyhow, he glanced towards me and smiled.

'Did you ever in your life see anything so beautiful,' he said, in good, very formal Italian that had been learned from a book, in that it lacked the jaunt with which we speak. 'If one lived a million years and had lessons from a master every day, one could never do a single square millimetre of that. Imagine, it was once a block of stone in a quarry.'

'*Vero*,' I agreed, '*è bellissima*.'

'*Meravigliosa*. The detail takes one's breath; one would swear they are alive.'

'I have sometimes seen them move and breathe,' I said. 'If you watch for an hour that happens. Or, when you enter the room very suddenly.'

With a look of joyous bafflement, he indicated the most miraculous detail of the piece, where the fingertips of the god's left hand touch Dafne's flesh.

'Miraculous,' he said. 'One doubts one's own eyes. Such softness could not be marble.'

Shaking his head as though in disbelief, he then turned to me again.

'Madame is French?' he asked amiably.

'*Sono italiana*,' I said.

'Forgive me, *Signora*, I misheard your accent.'

'My family are Parisian on my mother's side,' I told him. 'My sister and I attended school in Nantes.'

'The Oblate Franciscan Sisters, I am guessing? Excellent ladies. Not to be trifled with.'

'A little strict,' I agreed.

'Very good.'

By now, we seemed to have steered ourselves into the sort of conversational blind alley that often, among the newly met, preludes a departure. But, oddly, I did not want him to go. Equally oddly, I felt he knew that.

'Have you lived in Rome long?' I asked. 'Do you like it?'

'I studied here as a seminarian in the late Prehistoric era and returned a few years ago for post-doctoral work. I am attached to the German College, do you know it, in the shadow of St Peter's? I like Rome very much. But then, who wouldn't like it?'

'May I talk with you, Father?' I blurted.

Suddenly I was weeping. He did not look taken aback. What I can only describe as a sort of fit assailed me. I had a feeling that I was drowning, and it frightened me. I remember a woman attendant hurrying in but then leaving the room just as quickly, perhaps to seek help. The old, hot dust stung my eyes.

'*Signora*,' he said, gently, with intense respectfulness and grace. 'Of course. Shall we walk a while outside?'

In the garden, I was unable to speak for a time. He cooled a handkerchief in the fountain and gave it to me silently, then led me towards a granite bench under cherry laurels. A minute or two passed before my weeping subsided a little, a minute or two that must have had their difficulties for him, heaven knows; more than one passer-by glanced with what the English call dagger eyes in our direction, as though my tears had been caused by their consoler.

'You are young to be so troubled,' he said. 'I am sorry you are in pain. It walked into the room beside you. Like music.'

My voice would not come, only bitter, anguished sobs. I realised I was tearing his handkerchief.

'Try to believe me, *Signora*, that your burden will pass.'

'I fear it won't.'

'In time.'

'You don't even know what it is and you speak to me of time.'

'That is true. *È vero*. Forgive my presumption. It seems to me that there is only one thing that causes us such pain. To lose someone dear to us. Too soon.'

'*Why?*' I wept.

'I don't know,' he replied.

'Why don't you know?'

'I don't know that, either.'

There was a pause before he added, 'It is not given to us to know. There are those that would say, to share the crucifixion is a great blessing; it is also to share the resurrection.'

'Enough,' I retorted. '*Don't* tell me such lies.'

He nodded, gazed about. 'We need not talk at all if you wish; I can sit with you here and watch the trees.'

This we did for a time, during which we said nothing. I smoked. He did not. I wept. He bowed his head. Presently he went to the railings where a battered old First World War motorcycle was parked, held together with bits of coat hanger and Scotch tape, fuel tank badly dented, handlebars mismatched, puncture patches on both tyres; from its panier he took a pad of notepaper on a page of which he wrote the address and telephone number of his Collegio.

'May I ask that you accept these, *Signora*,' he said, resuming his seat beside me, 'in case I or a confrère can ever be of assistance. I apologise with all sincerity if I have been presumptuous or intrusive. Sometimes I jabber clumsily without thinking. You have heard of the Roman flu, of course?'

I nodded.

'The condition I have myself, you see, is the Irishman's flu.'

'What is that?'

'The brain takes itself on holiday while the mouth works overtime.'

The ridiculous image could not help but make me laugh. I told him my late husband had been a motorcyclist, that I was one of sorts myself. If I am honest, he seemed a little shocked that a woman could advance such a claim but he made a reasonable fist of disguising it.

'Need you go?' I asked.

'Soon enough,' he replied.

'Perhaps you would hear my confession,' I said.

At this request, he looked surprised but without delay he agreed, turning from me, closing his eyes and murmuring the prayer in Latin. I noticed that he had taken a set of wooden rosary beads from his pocket and was holding them as he listened to my words.

A priest may never reveal what is said in confession but of course a penitent may. I had never killed anyone, nor, I hope, had I ever sinned against the most important of all commandments — for me the only truly unbreakable commandment — *Thou shalt not bear false witness against thy neighbour.*

My transgressions against the other edicts, which seem to forbid everything from loneliness to human nature, I listed as thoroughly as I could. I conceive of these transgressions not as sins but as ghosts who draw us in to their orbit. And there was one great ghost that had me in its grip in those days. The high prince of ghosts. Despair.

Despair, in his diamonds of ice and grief, his robes of shimmering mist. In his eyes the strange light that draws ships to the rocks, in his mourning, ten thousand choirs. You may gamble a hand with him but the cards are all marked; he knows he will win at the close. What he's offering is opium, but many times stronger. There is no intoxicant quite as numbing as perfect despair.

You don't understand the fact that hope, if it is ever encountered, is in the small things of the everyday, not an announcement from on high. In the aroma of cooking, a phrase from Vivaldi. A handclasp. A conversation.

This is what happened in the gardens of the Villa Umberto that day. Hope was waiting in the Sala Bernini.

Entering the park, I didn't know him. Leaving it, I had shaken hands with the greatest friend of my life, who in those terrible months would give me purpose, a reason to go on living. We can never know the miracle that is hiding in the everyday. Sometimes, it is a matter of looking.

I handed Hugh the pistol that had been in my haversack, loaded with one bullet only, all I would have needed to put an end to myself. My plan had been to go to the pine groves, to wait until no one was about.

Unloading it, he threw the cartridge in the laurels.

I still think of it, rusting there, all these years later, through rainstorm and sun-blast and the nights of my Rome. Perhaps a scavenger will one day find it and wonder at its journey, the story that brought it to the place where it now lies.

No one will know.

But you, reader, know.

These words would never have been written without Hugh O'Flaherty. Their author would be dust in Rome's air.

9

Christmas Eve 1943
11 a.m.
Exactly 12 hours before the Rendimento

From far across St Peter's Square, he sees her at the café table. Dressed in black, she is reading a magazine, smoking. She pushes a strand of hair behind her ear. As though sensing his presence, she glances up but does not wave. He sets out hurriedly towards her through a cloud of uprising pigeons but, approaching the barriers at the edge of the Piazza, is halted by a German trooper who holds up a gloved hand.

'Remain inside the Vatican, *bitte*. You are not permitted to cross that line.'

'I am on a mission of the cloth.'

'With respect, direct orders from Obersturmbannführer Hauptmann are that no one is to come over the border today. There may be an opportunity tomorrow, or later in the week.'

'For God's sake, "border". It is a line on the ground.'

'I apologise, Father. Strictly no exceptions today. Come back tomorrow, around noon.'

'May I speak with your superior?'

'There would be no point, I assure you.'

Now he notices that she has called for her bill, is paying the waiter, who peers after her with a glower of mournful lustfulness as she tosses a banknote onto the saucer and heads away. A corner boy gives a wolf-whistle, she doesn't even glance. Black pillbox hat, black pearled mantilla around her face, grey overcoat open, stylish black oxfords negotiating the glassy cobbles, umbrella under her arm like a swagger stick.

Don't approach me, he thinks, they're watching.

She approaches.

To be still? Or back away? Pretend not to know her? Suddenly it is too late, she's only metres from him, nodding.

'*Signora*,' says the trooper, 'I warn you, remain in Rome. Do not cross the borderline into Vatican City. If you do, you will need a formal permit to return.'

'I am *Contessa*,' she says. 'Not *Signora*.'

'*Contessa*, then. Excuse me. The instruction still applies.'

Shaking her head without looking at the trooper, she lights a fresh cigarette, exhales a ring of smoke that wreaths itself around her, the same colour as her scarf and eyes. A breeze raises an ivy leaf against the collar of her polo coat.

'*Buongiorno, Monsignore*,' she says, in a formal tone, for the trooper's benefit. 'You won't remember me but we have met once, at a function with my late husband, the Count. It was some years ago, I think at the San Giovanni Hospital.'

'Good day, Contessa Landini.'

'What a pleasant surprise to run into you so unexpectedly. How have you been keeping of late?'

She stands on the Rome side; he stands in the Vatican, like people looking over a tennis net.

'Don't you have anything to do, yob?' she snaps at the trooper. 'If you don't, go and wash your filthy face.'

A century passes. The soldier nods, turns his back, trudges away.

'What is it?' she asks.

'Did you hear about Derry?'

'Perhaps he'll recover.'

'Is there a way of finding out?'

'I'll see what may be done. Leave it with me a day.'

'We need to find Enzo.'

'Didn't you receive my message?'

'No.'

'I telephoned the Collegio and left a message for you yesterday morning. I found him near his house. He agrees.'

'To what?'

'The Rendimento, of course.'

'But, what else did he say?'

'"Don't worry."'

'How in hell am I not to worry, I haven't heard a single word from him?'

'He'll be in touch today.'

'What time?'

'I don't know.'

'Do you know where the devil he is? He hasn't been around the square all week.'

'I'll go by his house again in an hour.'

'Careful not to get tailed. They're watching.'

'I won't get tailed.'

'How can you know?'

'I hid a change of clothing behind the cistern in the ladies' lavatory of an *osteria*. I'll slip in for a moment. You look ill.'

'I had fever.'

'Get better. I have a thousand dollars here in my handbag, is there a way you can take them?'

'That soldier's watching, I tell you. Better go.'

Lightning crackles over the Basilica, a bellowing groan of thunder. Waiters outside the cafés retreat beneath awnings. A mounted Fascist policeman emerges from the gloom of a side street, black horse steaming as it ponderously clops. Behind the centaur a ragged parade of barefooted children, high-stepping, cartwheeling, invisible rifles over shoulders. Handing him the umbrella for a moment, she pulls over her hat a capacious hood he didn't notice her raincoat having, and, without another word, she is walking away, past streetcars and dustcarts, through the parade of goose-stepping urchins, towards Via dei Penitenzieri.

Minutes later, returned to his room, he opens the umbrella. Inside is an envelope containing ten hundred-dollar bills, which he hides beneath the floorboards of his wardrobe.

Leaving the room, he hurries to the Vatican hostel where the British Ambassador and his servant are in refuge, but the Ambassador is not available, the servant, John May, insists. Sir D'Arcy is writing his December report, which is late. He is not to be interrupted.

From there, to the Lecture Hall, an hour on St Catherine of Siena with the Fourth Years but answering the seminarians' questions is like juggling with mud. His mind keeps ratcheting back to the square. Something not quite right; he's not sure what it was. Did the sentry notice anything? Was the waiter a tout? The Fascist on horseback, why was he there, and that object he pulled from his greatcoat pocket as the rain began to surge, was it a radio mouthpiece or a camera?

Ending the seminar, he wishes the students a peaceful Christmas and returns to the square.

Mirrors of grey rainfall.

The same trooper on duty.

Still no sign of Angelucci.

'You've returned,' says the trooper. 'I was hoping you would.'

'Why so?'

Reaching into a pocket, the trooper produces a fountain pen.

'You dropped this. Earlier. I called after you, but you'd gone.'

Gulls swoop.

'Mightier than the sword,' says the trooper, eyes cold. 'Don't let me see you here again.'

10

SIR D'ARCY OSBORNE
Christmas Eve 1943
12.32 p.m.
Coded communiqué sent by diplomatic courier

From: Sir Francis D'Arcy Godolphin Osborne, His Majesty's Ambassador to the Holy See, now in refuge in Vatican City.

To: The War Office, Italian Section, Whitehall, London

On: 24th December 1943, 10.32 hours, GMT; 32 minutes past noon, Rome time

I should like to commence by apologising for the delay with this report. Winter has been uncommonly harsh here in Rome this year, and I succumbed to a most debilitating dose of bronchitis. The lack of fresh or adequate food has made life difficult from time to time, as of course has the fact that, following the German invasion of the city on 10th September, I and my staff had no other recourse but to move into the Vatican, where we are now living at close quarters.

We share a four-floored former hospice (in the Roman sense a house for pilgrims), with multitudinous mice and flying fleas, also with the diplomats of Portugal, Bolivia, Uruguay and Cuba, and so, as will be imagined, we have a certain amount of noisiness to contend with.

There is something wrong with the water. We all have eczema.

Not to dwell on misfortune but it does need to be added that we possess no means of heating any part of this building or of heating the water. Nearby is a bakery where, daily at dawn, the dough for bread is steamed. Every morning a good Sister goes there to collect the hot water that is a by-product of the process. It is only by dint of this that we are able to wash or shave. A litre of this water costs about the same as a bottle of Veuve Clicquot 1929.

A fortnight ago, as I was watched from my window, I saw that the Nazis had ordered a work detail of prisoners to paint a two-foot-wide white line around the edge of St Peter's Square, indicating the borderline between Vatican City and Rome as established by the Patti Lateranensi or Lateran Treaty, 7th June 1929. Notices on wooden posts have since been erected, to the effect that the citizens of one city must not enter the other city without applying for a written permit, which must be triple stamped by the military authorities and accompanied by a hefty payment. The Swiss Ambassador went down with several witnesses and asked the SS Officer Commanding what was the meaning of this outrage, were we all to be kept in?

'*Nein*,' the Hauptsturmführer replied. 'Kept out.'

But what about pilgrims?

Arrangements would be made.

'Of what nature, these arrangements?'

'You will know when you know.'

'I am a credential-bearing diplomat of the Corpo Diplomatico.'

'I don't care if you are Jesus Christ Almighty. Cross that line and you're in a concentration camp.'

An Associated Press newsreel crew had assembled their camera not far from where this exchange was taking place. They were commanded in plain terms to be gone. When they offered resistance, the Hauptsturmführer smashed their lens with the butt of his pistol, his subordinates chuckling as they watched. 'You show *lies*,' he screamed. 'Back to Hollywood.'

Since then, German patrols have been guarding the line, standing along it making louts of themselves or having their photographs taken with, or by, priests and other passers-by. Many of the representatives of the Master Race that end up here in Rome are generally of the stupider, box-headed sort, a clottish assemblage of conscripts pining for lederhosen and lager. Alas, some are more than that.

One week ago today, at 15.00 hours, I and my factotum, John May, went to the obelisk in St Peter's Square to meet with Golf, as had been arranged by coded message that morning. Golf had expressed himself reluctant to meet at the two rooms doing duty as Legation and Official Residence, feeling certain

80

that they have been planted with transmitting microphones by undercover Gestapo. I am of the view that this is fanciful, that he attends the cinema too often. But after all, one can't be too careful.

Golf was late, as he too frequently is. As May and I conversed, we smoked several of the American PX cigarettes of which he seems to have a bottomless supply despite severe rationing. I did not like them but, as many of us will recall from when we schooled, it is good to smoke with another fellow, it fills in the time and gives him a reason to like you.

I should like to place on record that May, an inscrutable native of Whitechapel, has proven a veritable genius of on-the-quiet, resourceful scrounging, a filcher the like of whom has not been seen since the Artful Dodger. He is, after a fashion, quite the classicist, and is wont to quote or at least paraphrase the old saying one had caned into one at Haileybury College: *Dii facientes adiuvant.* The gods help those who help themselves.

Items procured by the great May to date include: drum of petrol, drum of grease, drills, metalworking tools, Benzedrine tablets, boots, shirts, magnetised razor blades capable of being used as compasses, underclothing, penicillin, ration books, running total of thirty-two thousand cigarettes, Andorran and Swiss identity cards, maps and ordnance charts printed on silk (of the type issued to Bomber Command to meet the eventuality of having to parachute over open water), lady's bicycle, Fascist police uniform (one), German uniforms (three), Swiss Guard uniform (one), Dominican friar's habit (one), box of N82 Gammon-bomb grenades. I will add that His Majesty's Legation on retreat in Vatican City has an uncommonly well-stocked drinks cabinet since May's arrival here, including a quite exceptionally fine Strathisla 1937 Scotch, aged in 34-year-old sherry casks, fifty guineas the bottle, not a libation encountered frequently these days outside the finest Whitehall clubs. One doesn't ask questions of a talented man.

What is more, May has the most likeable quality in a servant, in that he always goes one better. Lost in the jungles of Amazonia following an aeroplane crash, if you asked him to go away and come back with a guide, he would return with Rita Hayworth.

When at length Golf turned up, he was in a strange, quiet mood. I asked if he was well and what he had been doing. He looked exhausted, a little dishevelled and had in fact not shaved, the first time I ever saw such a slip in a man of the cloth. He fidgeted as we conversed, clearly is under strain. We went over the ground of a problem.

The number of Books in the Library was increasing by the day, he told me, and it appeared that we were approaching capacity. Two Books had arrived that very morning (both British), thus Golf's unpunctuality, and had asked to be shelved in the Vatican.

United States Books had been flooding in of late. The Library was running now to more than seventy, perhaps eighty. Even keeping an accurate tally was by no means without difficulty and would become impossible following the sharp and irreversible increase he predicted, which presently would see thousands of Books entering Rome. At that point we would be counting the loops in the Gordian Knot. No more could be accommodated within the Vatican itself, which, being neutral, is not supposed to harbour any Books at all. The solution was for all Books shelved currently throughout wider Rome to be moved out into the countryside in order to make space. This achieved, we would re-shelve those at present lodged in the Vatican in the vacated Roman billets.

A sum of money would be required to bring this about.

Ah, I quipped. The root of all evil.

Eighty thousand American dollars.

At this, I gave a chortle and asked if there was anything further Golf would like, perhaps a pixie or a couple of gryphons?

One's attempted witticism was met with a scowl.

I pointed out that such a sum was not to be encountered down the sofa cushions at the Legation and that the matter would have to be sent Upstairs.

There would need to be committees, I insisted, oversight, paperwork, carbon copies, a system, a way of doing things, or Whitehall would send for the smelling salts. These days one could not purchase a mousetrap without a receipt. I reminded him that I am a Civil Servant not some lonesome Man of Action in a Western. Nor was May my Tonto.

May now uttered a sort of barking, uneasy chuckle like a dog having a dream of cats.

At this, Golf became a bit schoolmasterly, which I did not like, now hectoring, now vengefully mimicking, now wagging his finger and scolding. There was a good deal of Might I Bring To Your Attention and I'll Have You Know, like a housewife returning something defective to a shop and wanting to be noticed by the queue. Golf is a reasoning and calm sort, usually, the finest company one could imagine for a round on the links (which is how I met him), but he does have this tendency, not unknown among one-time schoolteachers, who sometimes mistake uninterruptable blather for persuasiveness. He is one of those men possessed of the ability to deploy the word 'sir' as an insult, by a sort of wheedling, half-ironic inflection of voice accompanied by a low-lidded, unblinking, slightly deranged stare. One sees it in his countrymen frequently.

A volley of frightened shouts from just beyond the Piazza now drew my attention. Golf fell silent at the sight that had inflamed them.

Through the colonnade, on the corner of Largo del Colonnato and Via di Porta Angelica, I saw perhaps a dozen Hun motorcycles roar up, with two Sturmgeschütz armoured cannon, known as 'Stugs' by the Romans, and I should say thirty machine-gun-bearing, helmeted troops, some with Dobermann dogs (what a ghastly 'yike yike' bark those brutes have), and a large consignment of the Questura, the Fascist police. Also, several truckloads of the GNR, the National Guard, and a dozen shipped-in German Polizei. Out of his armour-plated black Mercedes stepped Hauptmann, the Gestapo chief of Rome, in mufti for some reason, and wearing dark spectacles. But I am certain that it was he.

Not a career police officer but a professional Nazi who joined the Party a little later than most Gestapo men, he evinces the zeal of the convert in intimate proportion to the arc of his personal advancement. Formerly a technical draughtsman with the Berlin electricity authority, he is of slim, athletic build, slightly shorter than he at first seems, high-cheek-boned, alert-looking, threw the javelin at school. Widely known in Rome to be a black-market king, he controls large warehouses of goods, foodstuffs, tobacco, spirits and medicines, and has access to considerable amounts in forged currencies, chiefly sterling. His speaking voice is quiet. His favoured interrogation tool is the blow-torch. He sends the occasional Renaissance altarpiece or Etruscan statuette to Hitler. One of Hauptmann's two children, an adopted daughter, on whom he is said to dote, is the product of the Lebensborn, the Nazi breeding programme. His wife, formerly a Berlin fashion model, is known to drink. (Despite the Reich's avowed disapproval of 'non-Aryan' modes, her cosmetician of choice is Elizabeth Arden and her favourite couturiers, Kuhnen, Goetz and Grünfeld, are Jewish.) On Hauptmann's left hand he wears a death's-head ring given to him in appreciation of his role in the release from captivity of the dictator Mussolini. It is said to bear the inscription, 'To Hauptmann, from Himmler' and an assortment of allegedly Viking runes.

Hauptmann is a regular visitor to Regina Coeli prison where one entire wing of the four has been commandeered by the SS. Here he takes time to peer through every individual spyhole systematically, one landing per night, making notes on the prisoners' appearances, in a shorthand of his own devising. He is said to have a photographic memory and is known to drive about Rome in the early hours by himself, observing curfew-breakers to see if they match the faces in his files. Petty criminals and the sexually compromised are lifted, beaten and brought by his henchmen out to the cave system close to the Domitilla catacombs, where they are offered the choice of being shot or becoming his tout, as a result of which he is reputed to have a tout on every block in Rome. Suspected Partisans and collaborators are interrogated at Gestapo Headquarters on Via Tasso, Hauptmann sometimes delegating the vilest tortures to a German-Italian, one Dollman, the obscenely depraved Chief of Police.

Both ends of Via di Porta Angelica were barricaded quickly, making access or egress impossible. Jerry riflemen appeared on balconies and rooftops. *'Alzate le mani'* rang out. It was clear that we were witnessing what the Italians call a *rastrellamento*, a dreaded blitz-raid or round-up. A systematic search began, conducted at gunpoint; men without identity cards were dragged away. A boy of perhaps fifteen years who was working on a miserably provisioned fruit stall cried out for his father not to be taken; he was pistol-whipped. A woman, protesting copiously, approached Hauptmann in remonstration. With his gloves, he slapped her face. At that thuggish affront, Golf bowed his head and cursed the Nazi.

I noticed that Hauptmann appeared to be looking at us, now. That is not an agreeable thing to notice.

'Steady, old man,' I whispered to Golf.

From the corner of my eye, I saw a trooper pass a pair of binoculars to Hauptmann, who raised them to his eyes, regarding us. I indicated to my two colleagues that we should turn our backs.

May began speaking as though in a light way, gesturing and laughing about his team, Tottenham Hotspur, the Spurs, and I joined in the effort, but it was hard. By these means and by his sparrow-like persistence, he persuaded Golf back down towards terra firma.

And I was glad of May's presence for a more personal reason; had I a revolver on my person I would have walked the fifty yards to the Vatican border and given Hauptmann a faceful of lead.

I asked Golf how many Books are shelved in our Library at the present time. He answered that he did not know for certain since some had been moved out and others were always coming in, but he would make enquiries. I suggested he do that expeditiously.

I feel something is up. It might be a most opportune moment to re-accommodate these Books, I added, for if the Gestapo were to discover their whereabouts, their fate would be sealed; so too would be that of many others.

Furthermore, the day was fast approaching when the Nazis might invade the Vatican itself. Anything we had by way of papers must be burned without delay. Here there is a difficulty, for in the Pilgrim House where we are living there is only one fireplace and the chimney is blocked. Golf said he would see what might be done about burying them in the Vatican gardens.

At that moment, a Sister in a navy-blue habit approached and asked with discreet decorum if I was I and if Golf was Golf. We said that we were. Indicating in unconventional language that she was glad to make our acquaintance, the holy lady proffered a hand. 'She' was in fact Joseph Thomas Coleman, a Shrewsbury-born Private of the Queen's First Infantry, captured at Tobruk, escaped from the prison camp at Bussolengo near Verona, now presenting for refuge in the Vatican.

The words uttered by Golf as he led our new friend away were unusual for a man of the cloth.

Life, May remarked, is getting odder.

Quod scripsi, scripsi, as Pontius Pilate is said to have remarked. What I have written, I have written.

11

Christmas Eve 1943
2.06 p.m.
8 hours and 54 minutes before the Rendimento

The needle is rusty and warped. His eyesight is poor. Difficult to find good spectacles since rationing worsened. As he bends to darn the frayed vest, he pierces a fingertip, utters a curse.

Blood beads. It won't stop.

Downstairs, there is no one in the refectory. Its fourteen tables have been reset after the lunch he now realises he forgot to come down for. Ghost-priests were seated in the room until the moment he switched on the light.

Hungry, holy ghosts. Meals don't take long anymore. Almost nothing to eat. Not for weeks.

He enters the cold-smelling kitchen, finds the First Aid box in its cupboard, unspools a sticking plaster, notices his face in the kettle's bloated reflection. Filling the kettle from the pump, he sets it on the burner; a sharp, yellow odour of gas moistens his eyes. From his pockets he takes the envelope of tea he's been saving for a month, a gift from his parents back in Ireland.

The odour, perhaps the blood, raises a realisation.

He goes to the swing door to check that no one is coming, returns to the greasy sink, the unruly cupboards, begins searching the drawers. Fingers clattering greasy cutlery.

A short, thick knife with a shellac handle and serrated edge.

Elena, a half-lame orphan, was kitchen maid here for a while. Three months since she stopped coming to work. He used to like watching her sharpen implements with that brick-shaped granite strop, her skill in the act, the nearly musical fluency; she could natter away to the other servants while sharpening, not even look at what she was doing. He goes to the brick-heavy strop, commences rasping the butcher's knife, sideways, but the knack of the motion eludes him and the act feels weirdly inhuman even though it must be old as the apes. The *rasp* draws the elderly cat, the College ratter, from the wine crate that serves as her basket, and she regards him with the green-gold-green assessing eyes that, years ago, made a young priest from Ruanda-Urundi give her a new name.

Cleopatra.

Approaching, she utters a purr, tendrilling her tail around his lowered hand before the shrilling of the kettle unsettles those eyes and she slinks for whatever Nile is contained in the pantry.

Slipping the knife into his breast pocket he goes to the bread press, finds a length of staling focaccia from two days ago.

Tea and bread. Could be worse. Probably will be.

Alone in the long, thin room, he eats, the heft of the butcher's knife close to his heart, the scald of tea dislodges an icefloe of childhood. That gypsy who'd return to the village every year in December, a black-haired, mauve-eyed, elderly man home from England, unable to read but gifted with the curing of horses, the ability by magic to help women in childbirth. He worked on the canal in Manchester. In Exeter, they jailed him. His hands had been blessed by the seventh son of a seventh son. He claimed to be able to make cider by looking at a barrel of apples, or the Cornish drink, perry, by looking at pears. For a shilling, if you gave him a knife, he would sleep with it beneath his pillow, and it would never again dull, the blade would slit diamonds. But greatest of his wonders was the tale he had in twelve parts, one for every night of the Christmas season: how the magi met a wren on their way through a forest and she led them to the clearing from where the Bethlehem star was sighted.

On the way, the Eastern Kings christened the nameless lesser stars and the wildflowers that sprouted in the forest track before them: calamint, celandine, aubrieta, bedstraw, the words perfumed as the flowers themselves. Their names in the gypsy's accent, tinctured by Manchester and Munster, made music. Juniper, arrowglass, purslane.

The people would crowd into the cottage where he stayed every homecoming, a bothy inherited by his widowed sister once married to a settled man, a miner from Cornwall. Others clustered to the lamplit windows like a murmuration of moths, no matter the weather or the lateness of the hour, many clutching bottles for him, or pipes of tobacco, or handfuls of ivy leaves, said to be lucky. He started when he started, he finished when he finished.

Some years, the whole townland arrived, there'd be throngs in the lanes, but if no one came it was the same to him, the story would be told anyway. 'I'd tell it to the hearth if I had to. Many's the time I did. I was in the Queen's navy one time, been up to the Arctic where it's blackdark half the year, Chicago, Guatemala, Australia, America. I been all over England and back ninety times, Coventry, Birmingham, Hull, pick your card, I seen things in Jakarta would grow a corpse's toenails, and there's no place like home, boy, I'd know for I was there and told my story in every kip and hive along the way.' It was always the same story. Everyone had heard it. But there was something in the telling made it sacred.

One year, a professor came all the way from Sweden to write the tale down, but the travelling man would have none of it, the scholar's pen must be broken and put in the fire, his notebook thrown in the river. The story of the stars and wildflowers must never be written. If it were, he'd forget how to say it.

Tea drunk, he rinses his cup, peers out the broken-shuttered window, through the hurtful winter daylight. In the distance, the grey expanse of the Vatican gardens, silver-blue lawns, gravelled pathways. Eleven escaped prisoners are hiding in those gardens, in outhouses, potters' sheds, the greenhouse, the empty icehouse. He wonders how long it can last.

A gruff purr from behind. He turns, to an offering.

Cleopatra, in her maw the veiny mangled mess that used to be a rat.

Making his way through the corridors, he hears laughter and coughing above him, the slam of a door. Not wishing to encounter anyone, he detours towards the back staircase, but the new Rector, an elderly, ostrich-eyed South German Jesuit, is descending in pyjamas and dressing gown.

'Ah, Hugh,' the Rector says. 'You have been busy in these past days.'

'Yes, Rector.'

'Very good. You are an example. What plans?'

'Catching up on the filing that needs attention before the Christmas recess. I have letters that must be in the post by this evening.'

'Again, very good. Was there something you wished to say?'

'Rector?'

'You appear, what is the word. Expectant?'

'No.'

'Did you sleep well last night? My own sleep is disturbed of late. Since the bombings commenced, I find that I have most vivid dreams.'

'I have heard that said by many.'

'Most vivid. Disturbing. But this is not your own experience?'

'No.'

'Very good. Go along.'

As he leaves, the Rector calls him back.

'Forgive me, Hugh. A possibility occurs. Might one ask?'

'Of course.'

'I am scheduled to celebrate a wedding this afternoon but a difficulty has arisen. I feel unwell, as no doubt you have inferred from my clothing. This sleeplessness, as I mentioned. And headaches. Also diarrhoea. Might you be able to stand in? Half-past three in the Chapel of the Relics. I am sorry it is such short notice. It is not too sudden?'

'No, Rector.'

'*Vielen Dank.*'

As the bells toll for three, he crosses the College cemetery, blessing himself hurriedly, then through the side gate that leads to the white expanse of the square, where pilgrims are already gathering at the vast doors of the Basilica. The queue spreading around the colonnade and beginning to double back on itself. Hawkers assailing them with medals and prayer books.

A hundred and fifty metres away, just over the boundary line, three open-backed trucks, spewing spectres of exhaust, flanks boasting the red-and-black swastika.

A trio of German soldiers with their backs to him, slouch-hipped, smoking, arms about each other, having their photograph taken by a fourth. St Peter's as backdrop to the comradely mirth. A tannoy in one of the trucks playing 'Lili Marlene'.

He circles the Piazza quickly, head up, breathing hard, is approached by a woman selling bottles of holy water shaped like the Virgin Mary.

'*Grazie, no.*'

'Do you wish me to give you holy water for nothing, Father?'

'I don't,' he replies. 'But I haven't any money.'

'Ten lire,' she says.

'Really. I have nothing.'

'Five.'

'I can't.'

'*Madonna mia.*'

With a roll of the eyes, she leaves, swishing at the non-existent flies, her sandalled feet dusty, tiny bells tinkling on her heavy velvet skirts, clutch-sack of plaster Colosseum paperweights banging her thigh. Pigeons rise around her as she goes.

At three-fifteen, the huge, heavy doors are pulled open. The maw of the Basilica yawns. He has his pass, but he waits in line with the pilgrims. There is solace in hearing the clamorous orchestra of languages, hopeful, excited, as people entering a theatre, or moved to silent tears by the immensity.

Women in front of him grasp hands, stifle sobs. An old man is murmuring the paternoster. Girl Guides praying in French, in every dialect of Italian, children dark-eyed with frightened awe, clutching their fathers' cuffs. A solemn priest in gemmed vestments stands sentry in the doorway, ensuring the rules concerning dress are observed with full propriety – no short sleeves for women, no men with hatted heads – and he nods like a metronome as they enter the cavernous space, its lungs breathing incense and age.

An unseen choir is singing plainchant and it echoes around the apse. Pilgrims gape up at the vaulted ceiling; the faraway frescoes shimmer, the air so very cold, so stern. In less than a minute, fifty candles are lighted, soon a hundred, then a thousand, a salt-shake of light in that lake of shadows and gilded murk. Weeping, a young woman kneels, kisses the feet of a statue. The susurration of seven thousand whispers.

He joins the line at a confession box near the *Pietà* side-chapel, for a priest about to celebrate a sacrament must always have confessed. His confessor listens in silence, gives five decades as penance – 'offer them for the conversion of Russia, my son' – and utters the final blessing and absolution hurriedly, as one trying to get through them before the shops close.

Leaving the confessional, he notices, in a pew near the candle table, the seated figure of D'Arcy Osborne, half-nodding, removing his spectacles. Taking a navy handkerchief from the breast pocket of his Savile Row suit, the Ambassador polishes the glasses lightly, holds them up to the stained glass.

The move is a signal. All is in place.

The Rendimento may proceed tonight.

Clusters of cooing pilgrims before the life-size manger, the chipped wise men, the camels. The young woman he saw kissing the statue – she looks like an art student – walks away from the railing, leaving a satchel by the marble steps. Crossing to the Madonna, she makes the sign of the cross.

The plainsong soars. He leans, picks up the satchel.

When he turns, the Ambassador has gone.

— 12 —

THE VOICE OF JOHN MAY
20th September 1963
From transcript of BBC research interview, Coldharbour, Poplar, East London

But people take a liberty. Making assumptions, all that. Down the years it's been presumed I only joined the Choir seeing I had to. Me working for Sir D'Arcy at the time.

Not so.

It don't go with no job that you do what you're told outside hours. What happened was, he's asked me. Sir D'Arcy, I mean. Tell a lie, that ain't fully true neither.

Before the war, I worked nightclubs in Soho, up west. I was trying to make it as a musician – saxophonist – but there wasn't no wedge in it. So I've done security to make ends meet. The Shim-Sham, the Windmill. Valentino's Nude Review. I was hospitality steward and doorman, which is a nice way of putting it. Chief knuckleduster more like.

One particular place, Billie's on Denmark Street, things could get a bit tasty. Particular sort of clientele if you know what I mean. Actors, jazzmen, queers, mad poets, villains, bent coppers, nervous wrecks. Nothing very wicked, the odd magic cigarette. You didn't shine your torch in the corners.

Mainly blokes, but you'd get the odd stripper or tart come in. Never met a nicer bunch, as it goes. But sometimes you'd have aggravation off drunks on the door. Some dummy has a skinful, wants to give you the great benefit of his views. Bam. Out of order. Couple of dry slaps. Sleep tight. Most punters are on the level but you'll always get one where it's lights, camera, arsehole. That's when you bang your clapperboard.

No queer's never done me no bother, I say live and let live. Leave them people alone, mind your business. Old music-hall song was popular here in the East End when I was a nipper. 'A Little of What You Fancy Does You Good.'

Sir D'Arcy Osborne's a regular. Big tipper. Nice man. Respectful, good-humoured. Very civil to the staff. Which I've noticed. If you're looking for a sign that a bloke is a chuntering tosspot, it's the way he treats the people who can't answer back, like waiters or cigarette girls. Sir D'Arcy treated them civil, always time for a smile or a kind word. Sort of thing gets appreciated. Manners don't cost. Some of the punters was married, others wasn't. Obviously. Sir D'Arcy used to say he never met the right girl. Or was 'married to his career'. You didn't push.

Blokes dancing with blokes in a nightclub don't bother me none. If you're bothered yourself, don't go, mate. Have a dance with your bloody wardrobe as far as I'm concerned, and take it to bed with you after, if it's willing to go. Best of luck to the pair of you. Free country.

So, Sir D'Arcy's in one midnight with a couple of his old school muckers and they're larking about with the drag boys. It's coming on a bit fairyland and hark-at-her, Gladys, and they're calling Sir D'Arcy 'Francesca', just good clean fun, but there's trouble outside as they're leaving. Gang of Blackshirts wants to give them a talking-to. With a brick. I've dealt with the difficulty efficaciously, as Sir D'Arcy puts it later. I wasn't what you'd call the most elegant pugilist, but let's just say they wouldn't have been doing the foxtrot for a while.

The surprise was Sir D'Arcy, he's gone off like a ten-bob rocket. During the ruckus, I've looked up, he's battered one of the tosspots half-stupid, stuffing his face through the hole in a letterbox. Roundhoused him. The other, he's give him an unmerciful bunch of fives up the bollocks. Queensbury rules? Not tonight. After they've scarpered, he's doing his cufflinks, straightening the dickey bow in a barber's shop window, cleaning blood and snot off his wingtips with his cravat. Tell you, I'm impressed. 'Boxed at school,' he's explained. 'Never cared for a bullyboy.'

Well, we've needed a couple of stitches, nothing major, just a graze, so it's cab down the hospital, long wait. Porter asks him, 'Is that your son, sir?' Sir D'Arcy goes, 'No, but I should be proud if he were. Might I introduce to you my associate, John May Esquire of Whitechapel, a goodly knight and true.' Sign on the wall says 'Silence', but Sir D'Arcy won't stop talking; he's either burbling away in Latin or he's making me laugh. 'Those ruffians, all they want's a good shagging. Why don't they just *ask*? One might *like* a bit of rough. Ah, nice to see you, Matron, good evening, *enchanté.*'

Couple of nights later, he's asked me to come and work for him, been posted to Italy, do I fancy it? As it happened, I'd a spot of bother going on over a matter of missing gelt from a certain enterprise, mate of mine's happened to accidentally wander into a spirits-and-fags warehouse down Deptford with a crowbar, wandered out with a truckload of Scotch. Fortnight later give us the loot to mind, Old Bill's sniffing around, then there's a concatenation of misunderstandings. Also, I'd be overdoing it a bit on the giggle-smoke of late. Also, a woman I was involved with told me she's stopped loving her husband. I stopped loving her, right then, if ever I had. Be handy to get out of Soho.

'Tiny matter – my handle's a bit of a mouthful, John. I am Sir Francis D'Arcy Godolphin Osborne. Ordinarily, as you know, I am addressed as "Sir D'Arcy", but I prefer to be called "Frank" by my friends.'

I said I shouldn't think it quite proper to address a Sir as a friend.

'I do wish you would, John.'

'Thank you, no, sir.'

'What about "Sir Frank", then? As a workable compromise?'

I've thought about that. Felt acceptable. Had a ring to it.

'Sound,' I've told him.

'Excellent.'

We shook hands on Sir Frank and a week later off to Italy. But things didn't turn out simple. Never do.

What's occurred, we was there in Rome when Fritz come rolling in and we've had to scarper into Vatican City a bit lively. Fairly cramped, I'll be honest. But needs must. That's that. I've kipped in worse places than the Vatican. I've even kipped in Chislehurst. Spent forty years there one evening. Long story.

You might think the Vatican would be boring. You'd be sodding well right. Bugger all to do at night if you ain't a bat or a bellringer. That's what got on my wick, the monotony. Do your head in something proper. Another thing, I'm Jewish, not that I'm religious, never was. So there wasn't even Catholicism to get the horn about.

Young gun at large in Rome, the evenings tend to be full, if you know what I'm getting at. Presentable-looking fella with a few pound in his pocket? You'll have a good time in Rome, never fear, and a story to tell after. Suddenly, all that's gone.

It's me and Sir Frank and his horrible little dog, Sirius, cross between a Jack Russell and a gnome. Most kickable living thing I ever had the misfortune to know. The sheer amount of shit come out of this dog? Had to be seen to be believed. Go out for a stroll, it's priests and nuns everywhere. Nothing against them, like I said, but we ain't having no bottle party. Knees-up with a nun? Ain't fun.

Sir Frank, see he's lucky, able to go into his own imagination. Talking to you about the Riviera, the nightlife in Cannes, skiing with the sodding Kaiser in Switzerland, all that. One morning I've come in and he says to me, 'John, I'm off to Locarno tonight for the spa and the baths, going to have a lovely time, come back slim, fit and handsome.' I've said, 'It's Locarno you're going to, not sodding Lourdes.'

At least I had the sax, so I'd practise, do my scales. Chromatic, octatonic, pentatonic, the lot. Two, three hours straight. I'd blow till my lips hurt. Flaming sax would be speaking. Or squeaking. But you can't practise all night on your tod like a pranny. You're missing the drummer, a pianist, the double bass. Belting out a blues in the Vatican felt dodge. Also, you've come over a bit sad. Blow an F-sharp, you're seeing Greek Street, punters in the clubs, some killer-diller brunette giving you a smile through a sandwich-bar window across Dean Street. A sax can get into you that way.

So it's me and Sir F, staring up at the walls. There's a gramophone record of some Scottish bird wailing about the glens, the way they do, but we ain't got no gramophone to play it on. Only one solitary book any normal person would read, history of the Vatican down the ages. Tell you what. Cassocks up. *Buongiorno*, darling, I'm a Cardinal. There was Popes got banged more times than an anvil. Well, it's power I suppose. And they're sharp dressers, Popes. A bloke in a frock can do well.

Apart from that, a load of books on theology and eschatology and epistemology and bollocksology, tripe no one would read except at gunpoint. Pneumatology, ecclesiology. Right page-turners. We've smuggled in a radio but the crystals ain't working. One night he's come in, all smiles, silly berk. 'You'll never guess what I've found at the back of the sideboard, John. A special treat once you've finished sweeping the chimneys.'

This was his little joke. We'd had a row about the way he was overworking me.

'Our entertainment difficulties are a thing of the past, John, dear boy.'

Five-thousand-piece jigsaw.

Of the Vatican.

Do what?

I've said thank you very much, leave it out.

Soon after, I've noticed this particular Padre's started hanging about like cheap aftershave. This big Paddy, dropping in now and again on Sir Frank for a cuppa. Bit funny, my pal. Bit odd.

Or Sir Frank's having a natter with him down in the courtyard late at night when no one's still up, just him and the Padre, rabbiting away in Latin, playing *darts*, and the cats in a circle staring up at them. Or Ancient Greek. Couple of nights, the same, then he don't come near or by. Then he's back. Now he's gone. Bit curious. I think they'd met before, on the golf course, it was. Seemed an all right sort of bloke. Fairly nondescript, I'll be honest. Bit serious for a Paddy. That worried me.

Paddy's all right when he's cracking jokes. When he's serious, it's a worry. When Paddy's quiet, watch out, he's doing one of two things. Resenting you, or scheming. Or priming his bomb. Not being funny. Watch your Paddy.

In the pictures, a Paddy priest, he'll be played by Bing Crosby. This one was more your George Raft. Tough. Quiet. Wouldn't want to mess him about. Touch of the Robert Mitchums. Not a talker.

Soon after, I've started noticing something odd in Sir Frank. His requests and that. Seem unusual. One morning he's asked me on a sudden if I can lay hands on a couple of shirts. Course I can, sir, how many would you like?

He's looked at me in a funny way and said, fifteen.

Five small, five large, five medium.

Kind of thing makes you think. You've time on your hands. Fifteen shirts, what's he at? Forming a rugby team?

But if the boss wants fifteen shirts, then fifteen shirts he gets. That's part of being a manservant. You don't ask no questions. I know this second-hand clothes geezer down the market, the Mercato Rionale, and he's fixed me up handy. Fifteen shirts. In a bag. *Grazie, Luigi.* Here's a tenner, have a good drink. There's always a Man to Know in Italy.

'For the poor of Rome,' Sir Frank's told me, later. 'Even in adversity, we must think of those less fortunate than ourselves, John.'

As a manservant, you come to expect things. It's part of the job. Discretion. You saw nothing. Keep shtum.

You'll find bosses might ask you to lay hands on a case of vodka. Packet of

French letters, a particular cigar. Stockings for his bit of frippet, sleeping tablets, a girlie film and projector. Or if he's the other way inclined, what used to be called a weightlifting magazine. It ain't Jeeves and Wooster no more, if ever it was.

Done a spell in the army as a batman for a titled gentleman, you'd have heard of him. One day he's sent me down to the chemist in the village.

For what, sir?

Nothing.

Beg pardon, sir?

Nothing. Simply ask for the chemist in person, explain you're from the Manor, you'd like the usual nothing, and wait for the package.

The package, sir?

Yes.

Of what, sir?

Nothing.

Nothing, sir?

Stop complicating matters, are you deaf?

But it's come to the point with Sir Frank where I can't go on remark-less. Thirty pairs of trousers. Forty sets of underwear. Train tickets to Zurich in the name of everyone on this list, memorise the list, then burn it. Forty overcoats, all different. Forty cardigans. Forty hats.

I'm to bag the stuff up and cart it over to the Padre's rooms in the Collegio. Leave it outside his door. Knock twice. Disappear. All a bit secretive and mysterious, that Paddy. I've give him the nickname 'Hughdini'.

Suits. Jackets. Train driver's overalls. It's coming obvious by now, they're running one of two things. An Amateur Dramatic Society or an Escape Line.

I've tried dropping the hint, I know what's going on, but Sir Frank won't give me no gen. I mean, nothing.

I ain't stupid. Course I knew. Impossible not to. So, one morning I've said to him, pouring the nettle tea for his breakfast, because you couldn't get coffee in Rome for love nor cash money, 'I've a surprise for you, sir. Here you go.'

What I've put on the table is a shopping bag from Barbiconi, a posh shop for priests near the Trevi Fountain. A priesty boutique, if you will. The clobber in Barbiconi, it's none of your muck. Silk soutanes. Hand-stitched shoes. Black cashmere gloves. Velvet slippers. The Pope gets his socks and drawers off Barbiconi, so they say. Upscale clerical schmatta, no fannying about. You want the

Mae West? Look no further. Only, it's come to my attention from Luigi down the market that stuff can be arranged to fall off a lorry now and again. What I've got in the bag is two dozen priesty shirts, nice texture, charcoal grey, assorted sizes.

I've said, 'I should like to assist more fully in the endeavours of your good self and the Padre, sir.'

That's how I've put it. Nice and discreet. You didn't want to startle him, dear me, no. Sir Frank wasn't a man for startling early in the morning. He felt things heavily then.

Well, his newspaper's twitched – a copy of last week's *Times* – and slowly he's lowered it, dramatic like, *tense*, and the eyes behind the specs are giving it large.

'To which endeavours in particular do you allude, John, may one enquire?'

Public school is marvellous, though, isn't it?

'The work you and the Padre are up to for the poor of Rome, sir. If you take my meaning.'

'Ah.'

'Yes, sir.'

'I had rather formed the impression that our work was a secret, John, old thing.'

'Any secret's quite safe with me, sir. As you know.'

'John, dearest, one's been waiting so long to hear those words from your lips. How deliciously you flirt.'

'I'm serious.'

Well, he's looked at me a while. I can hear his brain turning.

Because it's a crossroads, when you think. A moment like that. You'll remember it the rest of your life, depending on how you chose. There's a swamp between you and the right thing; how far out are you going to wade? It matters, what you did. Always will.

'Fetch another cup, would you, John?'

'We expecting a guest, sir?'

'I should like you to have a cup of this ghastly brew with me, John. Be seated.'

'What are we going to talk about?'

'Nothing.'

13

Christmas Eve 1943
3.29 p.m.
7 hours and 31 minutes before the Rendimento

In the sacristy, he dons the heavy vestments, begins preparation for the wedding. The ledger must be completed in Latin, and, since Fascism came, in Italian. As he turns through the ancient book, a scrap of hand-drawn manuscript that someone folded into the pages is revealed, a fake signature half-obscuring the watermark.

He recognises the script as John May's. A couple of minutes to decode the message.

Sam Derry is back but weak and in pain. These addresses are to be avoided. Angelucci's on his way.

Taking an empty shampoo bottle from his pocket, he quarter-fills it with altar wine, screws it tight, slides it into his soutane.

A knock, and the best man returns, now accompanied by the mother of the bride, expensive hat in hand, her hair a sprayed-on grey helmet.

'I understand we have a difficulty,' she says.

'Not a very important one. The position is as I explained to this man.'

'What did you mean, "ill", Father?'

'My title is Monsignor.'

'Monsignor, this is my daughter's nuptial Mass. His eminence, the Rector, was asked a month ago to perform the ceremony.'

'I understand, *Signora*, but illnesses do happen.'

'My guests have been informed that the priest will be a Rector.'

'That won't be the case, I'm afraid.'

'What am I to tell them?'

'Whatever you wish.'

'Fetch the Rector quickly, Monsignor, he won't be needed longer than one hour.'

'That is not possible.'

'My husband is high up in the Party, I warn you. We are friends of Obersturmbannführer Hauptmann.'

'The Party has no authority here.'

'I – beg your pardon?'

'You are in the house of the Almighty, *Signora*, not a Meeting Hall.'

'The Party has laboured endlessly for the betterment of Italy.'

'God has no country.'

Shock lights her.

'Where are the altar boys? I ordered six.'

'One does not "order" altar boys, *Signora*, they are not frittata sandwiches.'

'I shall have to cancel the ceremony. The Party shall hear of this affront.'

'As you wish.'

She turns to the best man. 'Guido, take that idiot's look off your face and wait outside for them as they arrive. Don't "but" me, do as I say. My good God, the shame. Get going, don't stand there like a lamp post.'

'Monsignor, what shall I do?'

'I warn you, son, *Tra moglie e marito non mettere il dito*. Woe to those coming between husband and wife. *Signora*, if you wish to cancel the ceremony, I insist that you discuss the matter with the couple. Stop wasting my time. Out you go.'

'You dare to speak to me like what, an old mongrel?'

'I will not permit you to send a proxy to do your bidding. If the bride or groom come to me in person with word that we are not to proceed, their request is granted and the subject is closed. But if they prayerfully aspire to be husband and wife, they are already married in the eyes of Almighty God and the Church. All the celebrant does is bear witness. Be he Curate, Rector, Cardinal or Pope.'

At the deployment of the final word, she gasps as though spat at.

'Perhaps,' the best man ventures, 'the *Signora* and I might step outside for a moment.'

'There's the door. Don't let me detain you.'

As they leave, he resumes work on the parchment, filling in the date, the place, the names of the couple, then his own. It is one of those moments when writing your name feels strange and you wonder how it belongs to you, if it does. John May's radiant frown seems to flicker at him from the flame of a candle. 'Chin up, Monsignor Mitchum. There's my boy.' His Londoner's courage. The music of his English. Even his way of lighting a cigarette has a sort of correctness and suavity, a physical grace, an ease. 'Monsignor Mitchum, you're a jazzman only you don't know it yet. We'll go down Soho when this is over. Never fear.'

Guido returns with a message. The wedding is to proceed.

An unsmiling, frock-coated Don who can only be the bride's father is ushering guests to seats in the side chapel, accepting their kisses to his hands. The Man Whose Daughter Was Married in St Peter's. Lengths of white ribbon have been draped through the ironwork of the gates. Almond sweets are being placed on dishes, for luck. The groom, a moustachioed Private, is missing a leg and is leaning on a crutch. A bridesmaid offers to fetch a chair but he insists on standing. Peaked cap beneath his elbow, hair black and lustrous as his epaulets. Dress sword glinting on his hip. Behind him, six comrades, polished as new plums, at red-faced, high-necked attention.

The bridesmaid and maids of honour in a line by the altar rail, rosary beads dangling from gloved, slender wrists. Old uncles suited like disappointed bank managers beside their disappointed wives, glaring sullenly from the benches or staring hard at their prayer books as though apparitions are happening in the margins. It is a way of not noticing the unannounced guest. Despite the best efforts of the couturier, it is evident that the bride is pregnant.

Shining with hurt handsomeness, the soldier's face is that of a Raphael archangel, but his accent is southern, *Siciliano*. His voice quivers with feeling as he utters the vows, and the bride clutches his hand in a lover's reassurance.

Drawn by the bride's beauty and the magnetism of weddings, pilgrims stop to watch, to the evident irritation of her parents. The first marital kiss raises cheers from the aisle. *Viva gli sposi!* Long live the newlyweds.

The couple sign the register and ask him to stand with them for a photograph. The soldier's arm about his shoulder, the warm, sweet strawberry scent of the bride's perfume.

As the show of politeness required in Italy, he at first declines the offering made by the bride's father, and the Don in turn insists, handing over the envelope.

'A discreet word, *Signore*? Step into the corner with me a moment?'

'*Monsignore?*'

'A minor difficulty.'

'How?'

'That amount is not sufficient.'

'*Mi scusi?*'

'The offering to a priest for a marriage carried out in St Peter's is customarily three times that sum. Naturally I do not wish to embarrass you in front of your guests.'

'That is all the money I have with me.'

'Then you shall have to ask your friends.'

'Can you be serious?'

'The labourer is worthy of his hire.'

'You think yourself clever to quote scripture? Even Jews can do that.'

'That is hardly surprising since they wrote a great deal of it.'

Muttering, the Don turns his back, rummages in his wallet, hands over a wad of bills the thickness of a roof slate.

Not the worst feeling to know that a Fascist's money will be given to a Jewish escapee.

Hollow victories are not quite defeats.

Changing out of the stiff vestments, he hangs them in the sacristy garderobe, locks it and leaves the room, re-entering the transept, satchel in hand.

The Basilica heaves, pilgrims crowding into every nook, surrounding the vastness of the altar to take photographs of the statues and monstrance. Swiss Guards hissing them to cease. A souk in Palestine comes to mind, where he once got lost. Far above, the bells toll four.

A German naval officer in black uniform leads a woman from chapel to chapel, gesturing up at foreshortened, hair-lined frescoes, the fine lace of an altar cloth, his black-gloved hands pointing out the numerous intricacies no guidebook is able to show. From time to time, she leans her head back in almost convincing imitation of hanging on his every word.

An African Sister in a white habit kneels alone on the stone of the aisle as the choirboys loft a harmony towards the dome. Old vowels lengthening, *In Excélsis Deo*, the 'o' echoing back like a recollection. A party of bored-looking schoolchildren tolerate the remonstrations of their teacher, who had to bribe someone to get to the top of the Christmas Eve queue but now feels her money was wasted.

> *Laudámus te,*
> *benedícimus te,*
> *adorámus te,*
> *glorificámus te,*
> *Dómine Deus, Rex caeléstis,*
> *Deus Pater omnípotens.*

Outside, he stands a moment on the steps, in the smoky minor chord of a Roman winter. Larks rise from the colonnade, circling the Piazza, or swooping over the gypsies selling chestnuts at braziers. A band of pilgrims brandishing a tricolour he doesn't recognise are trying to get a communal hymn going, howling it at the vast and roiling crowd, but not many are taking it up and after a minute, it dies, replaced by the mass murmur of prayer.

With a start he sees Angelucci, a hundred metres away.

Slouched against the rim of the fountain, hawking candles and Mass cards at the foldable card table he brings to the square. The red hunting cap means he's received the message, knows what to do. The pilgrims try again with the hymn.

Emerging, the German officer and his lady notice a Monsignor descending the steps hurriedly, now pushing through the people and the smoke of the chestnuts, towards the fountain, where he turns his back on a candle-seller and makes the sign of the cross towards the Basilica before heading on, in the direction of the Holy Office.

The huge, studded door of the sombre fortress is hard to push open, heavy as it groans closed behind him to sepulchral silence. The city vanishes. Like being inside a pyramid. After four on a Christmas Eve, no one will be here.

Caged light bulbs hum as he flicks the switch. An elephant's-foot umbrella stand containing a single umbrella and a cluster of canes. The concierge's desk is draped, the porter's counter untended. He enters the lodge, checks his pigeonhole.

A Christmas card from his Fourth Years, a Waugh novel from the Book Club, a circular from *Newsweek*, a late-delivered essay on St Theresa, a loaned-out volume of Housman's poetry that a seminarian is returning after almost a year. A scrawl in the Rector's handwriting, on the back of a reused envelope, 'Hugh, I have a favour to ask. Come and see me.'

Six months ago, a lift was installed in what some of the older priests don't like calling the foyer, but he distrusts it, finds the mercilessly efficient turn of its wheel and greased cables threatening, like a machine encountered in a Breughel purgatory. Anyhow, it often breaks down.

He climbs the steep, granite staircase through the many-roomed emptiness, the walls around him substantial, four hundred years of silence. Well-connected Cardinals used to live at the Holy Office. Since the invasion, they've all moved away.

On the fourth floor, breathless, he unlocks the scriptorium and enters. The vast shutters of his workplace half-closed.

Bowed bookshelves. Onyx inkwells. Stacks of mouldering files. Mouse-gnawed dissertations on Christology.

Quills and their sharpeners. Letter-openers. Ledgers. Spiderwebbed portraits of virginal martyrs. A knot of tangled scapulars dangling from a doorknob, near a trinity of rickety candlesticks. Relics and rat traps. A skull doing duty as *memento mori*. Tomes. Bones. Combed texts of encyclicals. Leaded windows left unwashed for as long as anyone can remember. Only the heavy shellac telephones and the red metal fire-bucket announce the twentieth century as fact.

A young priest from Melbourne used to refer to the room as 'The Old Girls' Dormitory'. He didn't last long in the Vatican.

An empty ashtray on a windowsill.

A copy of the Catechism.

A teacup with something growing in its depths.

The old painting of St Cecilia that always reminds him of Marianna de Vries, his Dutch comrade from the Choir. When he told her, she laughed, 'I am no saint, my dear friend.' And yet, the woman in the picture has the same stoicism and strength, the jaw of a survivor, someone not to be fooled. Not exactly matter-of-factness but a high cognisance of realities, an absence of hate, a sort of reasonableness in the place where prejudice should be. If the world were governed by women like Marianna, he often thinks, famine would long ago have vanished. 'That is nonsense,' she tells him. 'But you tell charming untruths. Since I irritate myself so much, I will try to believe.'

On his Dickensian accountant's desk, a head-high stack of parchments, petitions for the granting of annulment. His task and that of the twenty other functionaries who work in the scriptorium is to read and reflect, to evaluate and categorise, most petitions to be dismissed, others considered by canon law scholars, a small few to be adjudicated by the Papal advisors.

It is work he loathes, as anyone would. Doing it feels the burden it is.

A woman in Toulouse wants her marriage ended because her husband is a violent drunkard. A man in Guatemala 'has become separate' from his wife. Sexual relations have 'long ceased' between a couple in Ottawa, never took place between a couple in Chicago.

He checks his watch. Already four-forty. The telephone will ring at five. Important to fill the time, to settle.

He pictures Angelucci in the square. Hopes he's ready for the danger. That lofty-browed, umber-eyed, unimpressible Roman, face made to be stamped in profile on an imperial coin, his nosebone the length of Italy.

Give me a shot, Monsignore. I despise these bastards.

That's why you're a risk.

One chance.

There is a last task to be faced before the Rendimento is able to be launched, but he'll wait until after the telephone call before taking that on, so he faces into a clutch of subpoenas from a woman in Paterson, New Jersey, but can't settle or think, mind flitting like a wasp. The couple's children, a boy of seven and a nine-year-old girl, seem to knock on the windows of what their mother is saying, frightened, pleading, contriving bad bargains, not wanting the marriage that gave them life to be ended, no matter its imperfections. He considers the Bishop's letter carefully, weighing, sifting. There are no grounds; the application for annulment will be refused. But after a moment of nagging conscience, he changes his mind. For pity's sake, let the poor woman be free.

Five o'clock comes rowdily with the Basilica's bells. He crosses to the telephone, ready to snatch it and respond to the code word with his own.

A minute past.

Nothing.

Five past.

Silence.

Dread creams in his stomach. He swallows it down.

On seven minutes, he lifts the receiver, taps the cradle, hears the purr. Quickly he dials the exchange to confirm the line is working this evening. The operator assures him that it is.

Quarter past. Twenty past. Twenty minutes to six.

The task must be done now, while the building is empty.

Approaching the ancient bookshelves behind the oaken screen in the darkest corner of the scriptorium, he pulls over the sliding library ladder, climbs. A powdery reek of mildew cracks open his headache and he sneezes so hard that the ladder rocks and creaks and he grasps it like a mast in a storm. On the penultimate rung, he steadies, reaches for the hefty book shoved in hard at the back, a folio of a medieval codex.

The cover, faded calfskin, is shredded and mottled, the heavy, atlas-sized lectionary is hard to manoeuvre down the ladder.

Still no call.

Hefting the book onto a table, he opens the cover, turns carefully. Illuminated grinning evangelists, scarlet dragons, silver gryphons, the rook-black of the text, the black of burned coal. Then a carnival of ornamented capitals wound in eagles and serpents, the haloes of archangels forming ivory O's, to the hollow where the middle quires have been patiently razored out, in which eleven folded pieces of architectural paper are hidden.

Each piece, the size of a tablecloth, covered in his minuscule handwriting.

Names, contacts, hiding places, dates. Regiments, ranks, camps from where each man escaped. Amounts bunged as hush money, bribes, rents, payments for forgeries of passports. Monies In as donations, Monies Out and to whom. When, which currency, what for. The code he uses is complex, mirror-writing and musical notation, but Hauptmann at the Gestapo has opened a sub-office in Via Tasso dedicated to the breaking of codes. The papers must be destroyed before tonight's Rendimento. Too late to bury them in the Vatican gardens with the rest.

Each sheet is too large to be burned in one piece. From his pocket he takes the carving knife filched from the kitchen, begins hacking the papers into halves, quarters, then eighths and sixteenths, slow, tedious work but the fragments can be placed one at a time in a candle flame, then the ashes in the wastepaper basket, which he can empty every few minutes out the window.

The stench of ashen scorch in the room is heavy, more lingering than he expected, and he wishes there were something he could do to disguise it. But on Christmas Eve, no one will come, not the cleaning ladies, not the guards; anyway, he will leave the window open. He works his way through the first sheet's tatters in just under seven minutes, sweat stippling his brow, slickening his upper lip; finds a rhythm as he moves to the second. But the paper is now damp from his perspiration and won't light. Cursing his ungainly fingers, he tears it into the tiniest pieces he can contrive, a confetti he flings from the mullioned oriel window, now drying his hands on his soutane.

The telephone trills.

Crossing, he grasps the receiver.

'Good evening, Monsignor, just to confirm, the piece is in G-sharp,' the voice says.

Blon Kiernan, Delia's daughter.

'Understood,' he replies.

'Happy Christmas, Monsignor.'

The line goes dead.

Important to hurry on.

Slashing the remaining sheets into rough eighths, he balls them, scrunching tightly, forces them into the red metal fire-bucket. Unwise, he knows, but time is running down.

Angelucci is now in place. Derry is briefing him.

As his match yellows the paper, an unmistakable *clank* floats its way up from the lobby, magnified by the soundbox of the lift shaft.

He stalls.

A mishearing?

The cables grind and buzz.

Iron gears whingeing with exertion.

Rain pelting the windows.

He hurries to the scriptorium door and locks it.

The dull metallic *thunk* as the lift bumps to its stop at the end of the corridor. The clank of the caged door yanked open. Slammed shut.

Footsteps, then.

A middleweight.

Booted.

Slowly along the landing, as a jailer on his rounds. Opening and entering the rooms in turn as he goes, the clank and rattle of a great chain of keys. Now pausing outside the scriptorium door.

Nothing is said.

A cuckoo-clock chirps.

The pages in the fire-bucket smoulder but don't light.

Smoke whirls.

The handle turns.

Quickly sits to his desk, spreads a parchment before him, black words and accusations seeming to spin, a miasma of recriminations. Fingers trembling, he pares a quill, rearranges a jug, pours himself a tumbler but the water slops on his wrists and tastes old and rancid and glassy and greasy, and the children of the unhappy couple in New Jersey pulse with him, somehow, like the after-image of something dark seen in light.

. The handle is tried again.

Twice.

Three times.

A rattle in the lock. The door is pushed but doesn't budge.

The intruder utters a sigh, now clomps away down the corridor, slowly, with eerie stateliness, hobnails clicking on the mosaic.

The *huff* as breath is sucked in, the quickening, running boot-steps, and the pummel of the body charging the door like a stabbed ox and the metre-high plaster statue of St Anthony of Padua topples from an alcove overhead and smashes on the desk and again the body withdraws, again bull-slams the door, now grunting, moaning, seething, screaming, but the studded oak, the door of an imperial bastion, refuses to give, and the architrave is granite and the frame is heavy marble and the volley of hard, sharp kicks rattle the vehement lock in its cast-iron moorings but nothing more and the ox-man retreats.

The lift gate whangs open, and, after a moment, closes, and the cage whines its descent to the foyer.

He creeps out to the stairhead. Two cats in a doorway. He can hear the intruder downstairs, going about in the foyer, rummagings and burrowings, opening and slamming drawers in the concierge's desk, going in and out of the porter's lodge, wrenching open the filing cabinet, then the cannon-boom slam of the closing front door.

From the scriptorium window, he peers down but the rainfall is heavy and his spectacles fog. The figure, beneath the umbrella from the hallstand, is making its way across the Piazza, with odd daintiness, avoiding puddles and dogs, like a murderer pretending to be a lady, in the direction of Largo degli Alicorni.

Sleet hisses hard on the ivy-choked skylight.

He empties the fire-bucket of the smouldering, stinking pages, stamps them out on the floor, bundles them as best he can, places the mess under his arm as he leaves the scriptorium, now hastening, half-tripping down the staircase. Best to dispose of them later, get out of the Holy Office while he can. The intruder might return with a Luger or a crowbar. Any sort of incident must be avoided.

Several times tonight, he will wonder what force drew him back to the porter's lodge, to glance a last time into the pigeonhole he emptied only an hour beforehand.

In it now, a brown paper bag, plump as a pouch. The handwritten name and address are very slightly inaccurate.

Hugo Flaherty

Personal

The Holy College

Roma

Inside is a small envelope, which he doesn't open immediately, containing what he thinks, from the scrunch beneath his fingertips through the paper, must be rosary beads.

The sheet of white airmail flimsy is folded into careful quarters, feels delicate as a page torn from a Bible. Three words, in the same hand, underlined in red ink.

YOUR

LAST

CHRISTMAS

The smaller envelope contains thirty-two still-bloodied human teeth.

Hail beats the stained-glass windows.

ACT II

The Solo

14

MARIANNA DE VRIES
November 1962

Written statement in lieu of an interview

During the war I was a freelance journalist based in Rome. I was introduced to Hugh O'Flaherty at the opera. *Tosca* was the piece. I do not recall the singers' names.

I attended as the guest of a Swiss diplomat who had been invited by Mrs Delia Kiernan, wife of the Irish Diplomatic Consul. There were some other Ambassadors and Envoys there. I don't remember now.

Sometime afterwards, I was commissioned to write a series of articles for an American newsmagazine on the artistic treasures of the city's lesser-known churches. 'Hidden Rome' was to be the title. Monsignor O'Flaherty did not of course carry a business card but had obligingly, at my request, that evening scribbled instructions as to how to get to Ostia Antica, on a scrap of the Holy Office headed notepaper that had been doing duty as bookmark in the Louis MacNeice book he was reading, *Autumn Journal*. The telephone number was visible on the scrap, so I called.

That morning he was on the way to a doctoral student's viva voce at the Angelicum, therefore was too busy to converse, but in the coming days he dropped me a note, advising me to undertake the Walk of Seven Churches, a pilgrimage established in the sixteenth century by St Philip Neri, but even though the walk included such beauties as San Sebastiano Fuori le Mura and San Giovanni in Laterano, there was nothing I wanted to write about. There were too many visitors. Nothing here was 'Hidden Rome'. I telephoned the Monsignor again.

We met in a café near Piazza Venezia. When he regarded you through those horn-rimmed spectacles, the effect was a little forbidding, like a torch being shone on you at a midnight roadblock. We spoke of Auden and MacNeice. In the Monsignor's leisure hours, which I gathered were few, for interest he had been working on a translation, *Diario d'autunno*. He felt that 'we don't really know a language until we can translate a poem into it'. Like every priest I have met, he was not without oddities, but I found him warm, genial company, a thoughtful man in both senses of the word. He said that I should feel free to address him by his first name, 'if you are comfortable doing so'. I wasn't, fully. 'Ugo' was the compromise.

At the time I was having an unwise love affair with a married contact, in fact the diplomat with whom I had attended the opera on the night that Ugo and I met. The matter ended when the man was summoned back to the bureau in Zurich. I had suddenly more freedom and time.

I am myself Swiss by birth, which meant that my passport had to be respected by all sides in Rome; I could go about the city, not exactly as I pleased, but with a good deal more latitude than others. Over a couple of weeks and two or three meetings, Ugo assembled for me a list of what he thought the most interesting if less frequently visited churches – there might be a Caravaggio Virgin and Child, say a fresco by Raphael, or a neglected but imposing piece of pre-Renaissance statuary – and I commenced a rigorous process of visiting them. The English church on Via del Babuino was a great favourite of his, for example. I had never heard of it but found its simplicity beautiful. He knew every Abbot and Reverend Mother, wrote letters of introduction or placed somewhat furtive preludial telephone calls requesting that I be assisted.

'Ask for Brother Such-and-Such. Avoid Sister So-and-So.'

One felt he rather enjoyed the skulduggery.

I and the roster of commissioned photographers were shown turrets and secret chambers, hidden crypts, disguised vaults, cupolas where medieval lovers were whispered to have trysted, bookshelves that, when a concealed lever was pulled, creaked open into cobbled passageways that led to Rome's sewer system, from there to the banks of the Tiber. Some disclosures were made on condition that precise locations were not revealed; others, custodians insisted, were only for our eyes 'as friends of the Monsignor' and must never be published or hinted at. In one chapel we were permitted to see, set in a wall behind a candle table, a grating no larger than a woman's headscarf. The person squeezing through would find himself in a marble bedchamber which, delightfully, had a skylight and its own tiny fountain. In my mind, Rome turned itself inside out, if one can put it like that. Europe's most majestic city is wearing a face. Behind it, she has numerous secrets. One biblical text, John 14:2, came to have resonant meaning. 'In my Father's house are many rooms.'

Ignorant as to how remunerative matters should be raised with a priest, I suggested that I might pay him five per cent of my fee for the set of articles, a proposal he dismissed with a woof of shocked laughter before proposing that I would instead, if I wished, make a donation to charity.

'Which charity?' I asked.

'Buy yourself a hat. As my gift.'

I donated five per cent to the Blue Nuns for the hungry people of Rome but I did buy a hat, a fedora by Borsalino. As for Ugo, he continued to refuse any payment but once, perhaps twice, permitted me to buy him tickets for the Hospitals' Sweepstake, a sort of lottery involving horseracing. He never won, a fact he liked joking about. 'If I backed the tide, it wouldn't come in.'

My series on 'Hidden Rome' was well received by readers, therefore was popular with my editor. Quickly it threatened to become a book of the same name. The advance I accepted was generous, the work would be pleasant. Ignobly, I was pleased that my former lover, back in Switzerland with his wife, would hear of this success and have the smooth lawns of his life disturbed by it, since the more independent a woman is, the more a certain sort of man will resent her, and resentment, for such a man, is part of what sexually attracts him. But as every guilty-hearted author will know, there are afternoons when you are supposed to be writing when all you can face is a cup of tea and a walk. A book rather gets its hands around your throat and shakes you until your fillings fall out. Some writers are skilled with words, but all of us are skilled with procrastination. What I wanted was to postpone the inevitable.

I kept in touch with Ugo now and again, until we were lunching fortnightly at Rompoldi's bar in Piazza di Spagna or the Trattoria Il Fantino in the Jewish quarter, a down-to-earth place he liked. The quarrelsome waiters flicked beer-towels at the flies or sighed with magnificent and vengeful gloom into the nicotine-stained Coca-Cola mirror.

Having lived in a great many places, Ugo had what is sometimes called a well-stocked mind but his knowledge had not the prim tidiness the phrase connotes. I had never been west of Cape Finisterre but at school had been special friends with a girl raised in San Fernando in Trinidad, the daughter of diplomats, so I was fascinated by Ugo's recollections of the Caribbean. He spoke vividly of the purple-and-ochre sunsets of Port-au-Prince and sombrely of the Vodou priests. I was intrigued by his photographs, of which he had a great many, all monochromes. His was an old Brownie box camera he had picked up in a junk shop on London's Portobello Road. You held it at the waist and looked down into the lens. The click the shutter emitted when you pressed it would have wakened the dead. He was endearingly a little boastful of being rather a good amateur photographer.

Clearly the poor of Port-au-Prince had permitted him to go among them: there were studies of women carrying water jugs, boatmen on a rainy dockside, ragged fisherfolk hauling and mending nets. His photographs of Czechoslovakia riveted me with a different sort of force, the farmwomen stonily stoic, their pebble-eyed children mirthless. He had many pictures of New York, iron skeletons of yet unfinished skyscrapers groping at the air, tenement fire-escapes on the Lower East Side, a whole album he had taken during a World Series baseball game contested by the Brooklyn Dodgers. I had little idea what the World Series or even the Brooklyn Dodgers might be, and, like all males, dear Ugo rather overenjoyed filling you in, not realising that I didn't know because I couldn't be bothered knowing and I not realising at the time that he had little interest, either; it was more that he liked having something to talk about. Pretending to love the Dodgers gave him that.

Ugo did not like silences; they made him uncomfortable. Soon, in Rome, they would become essential.

My favourites of his photographs were those of London, a city I always feel is most glamorously conjured in black-and-white: Soho doorways. Tower Bridge. A cinema queue in Leicester Square. Actors in a coffee shop. Spivs at a boxing match in Limehouse. He was able to gift you Chelsea, Tottenham Court Road or Primrose Hill as you sweltered in that workmen's café in Rome and the Nazi advance on the city commenced.

Before long they were only two kilometres from the walls. Still Ugo and I continued to meet. He would bring along a wallet of his photographs and we looked at them over coffee, even as we pretended not to hear the artillery in the distance, the shriek and burst of shells.

Indeed, on the afternoon before the Germans overran Rome, I remember him disconcerting a barman. The fellow had joked with him in the manner of the typical Roman male who believes he has invented flirtation and for some reason would like you to think him oversexed: 'Is this beautiful lady your girl-friend, Monsignor?'

Ugo answered, 'Her twin sister.'

The friendship was comfortable but was not close if I can put it like that. One was always aware that Ugo was an ordained Roman Catholic cleric, with the outlooks and boundaries of his calling. These he did not push but, as with all unseen foundations, one assumed they were implacable, no matter the grace of the edifice they supported. He was in many ways a rather conservative person.

Another important element was that I had no religion myself, had been raised contentedly atheist. My view of the universe was, as it remains, that there is nothing to hope for and nothing to fear; to live just once is miracle enough. So, we came up to one another's walls but did not go through the gates. In some ways, it was what made our friendship a happy one.

My father, from Rotterdam, and my mother, born in Harlingen, in Fries-land, were research physicists at the university in Zurich. My parents were both born deaf, and so I knew sign language, a mode of communication that fascinated Ugo. He and I spent a number of enjoyable but profitless hours in Piazza Navona, me attempting to teach him the rudiments over cappuccino, to the waiters' bewilderment, but, like most languages, sign language takes from the start or not at all. After the Choir was formed, John May and Delia Kiernan proved good, sensitive learners. As May liked pointing out, the Italians have vivid hand signals of their own. 'You see them when you step in front of a car.'

Ugo's Italian was the most perfect I have heard spoken by a non-Italian, zestful, performative, alive to the juiciness of Roman common speech (although Roman friends we were to have in common would tease him for speaking the language dully). It gave me great pleasure to hear him speak in the clear, grace-ful English of rural Ireland, full of timbre, subtle expressiveness, friendly seriousness.

Part of the journalist's training is to notice what is unusual. Sometimes it occurred to me that Ugo, by his own account, had embarked on priestly for-mation at a relatively late age, in an era when most seminarians went immediately from school, a fact that explains much, but not all, about what is dismal in the Roman Catholic Church. One wondered about his early twenties, was tempted to think of them a bit melodramatically as the Missing Years. It was not that I was imagining a tour of duty with the French Foreign Legion, but his silence on the matter inflamed the nosiness it was presumably intended to dispel. I knew he had worked as a schoolteacher, but he volunteered little more. You wondered. That is all I can say.

It was understood between us, as perhaps between all friends, that there were questions not to be put until the time became right, which would either never happen or happen so far into the future that we would both be different people, so the questions would not matter anymore. On one of the only two occasions when I transgressed the unwritten law – a glass of wine with lunch was perhaps the instigator – I worked my impertinent schoolgirl curiosity up into a query of hideous clumsiness, on the matter of priestly celibacy. Had he known, as a young man, a physically intimate relationship?

He stared coolly in response. 'A policeman wouldn't ask me that.'

When Ugo changed the subject, it stayed changed.

I remember to this day the one moment on which his guard slipped, also how thrown I was by the remark in question because it was so unexpected, by him (I feel sure) as well as me. We were exiting St Peter's Square on a bright, cold afternoon, the time of early evening when schools have just finished. Ugo had been asked to give the sermon at a funeral Mass in St Monica's, had requested moral support from the Contessa Landini and me. His apprehensiveness was justified, the sermon had been poor. Not long after Mass concluded, the Contessa left for an appointment and Ugo set out to walk me to the tram. Many Roman mothers and one or two slightly embarrassed fathers were waiting at the gate of the schoolyard for the emergence of their little darlings, who were biting and fighting and insulting each other, as their misfortunate teachers scuttled about like shepherds attempting to corral them. Traffic lights stopped our path for a moment.

Noticing his priestly attire, some of the parents nodded in courteous respectfulness or blessed themselves at his presence, a well-meant Italian custom I think he always found a little discomfiting. A certain amount of anti-clericalism has long been known in Italy; as a result, its mirror has existed, too, an unhealthy over-reverencing of clergy. As we waited for a green light, we watched the bellicose goings-on in the playground, and he asked me if I wished to be a mother.

Rather, he assumed that I did, and enquired as to when I might marry. It was not wise to wait too long, he added, in a meaning way. I was then aged thirty-four, a fact that seemed to dangle in the air for him, somehow. I replied that I was not the marrying sort, was adequately content single and intended to remain so all my life.

'Then, you would not like to have a child?'

I did not tell him that, in fact, a year previously, I had had an abortion.

'No,' I said. 'I would not.'

He attempted what I suppose must have been a diversionary nod but clearly was unsettled by my words or my certitude. The unsettlement, I think, brought his next remark. 'I would have loved to be a husband and father.'

It took me aback. He rarely spoke about himself without veils, evasions, ironies, the easier modes of concealment. I would say that it changed how I saw him. Until that moment he had seemed to me maddeningly rocklike, bulletproof in his self-certainties, impregnable as to his choices, especially the main one of his life. If Ugo had a fault, and who does not, it was perhaps this slight air of the loftily seigneurial, the superiority of the hermit. We like haloes in old pictures, rarely in our friends.

But suddenly, that afternoon, he was a person without a family. What I had seen as solidity came from a depth where there was something bereft. In a way, he *had* married. It was the first time I saw it. With another, one might have taken him by the arm or spoken a gentle word. The fact that he was a priest would have made that feel improper, would have embarrassed him, I felt, or given him the script to rebuff consolation, which perhaps was what he wanted. But often I wish I had. I would, now.

We continued our walk. I was going to the tram. At my flat, I knew, was the draft of an article for which the deadline was pressing. Time seemed to scrunch into a ball. As ever he doffed his trilby as he bade me farewell and we made conversational nothings for a final minute or two, I think attempting to find a bridge back to what he had told me. But the bridge, once noticed, was burned by the noticing. I think we both knew we would never speak of the matter again.

On the tram, I thought of him walking back to his room, alone. He was going to listen to the radio. I pictured him doing so with the lights off.

My parents worked hard to become scientists. I do not believe in ghosts.

But at the end of my journey, I went into the church near my flat, where I lit a candle for Ugo, knelt, and said an unbeliever's prayer. My story was late. But another had revealed itself. In as much as it ever would.

That was in the autumn of 1943. Soon, the Nazis – he pronounced the word 'Nazee', without the 't' – swarmed in. I became aware that Ugo and a number of associates intended doing something small to stand against the plague, and I resolved that, whatever it was, I would help. In this, I was motivated by the thought of my parents, whom the Nazis would have thought nothing of murdering.

I was motivated, too, by a certain Rubicon I had crossed in relation to my private life, central to which was a reality I now found myself wanting to articulate. Certain friends knew of it; most of course did not. My mother I think had long known but persuaded herself otherwise. Perhaps the resolve had been in part sparked by Ugo's and my conversation about marriage, perhaps by the proximity to death that war brings about. In any case, I wished to be truthful. On the morning of the Nazi invasion, we met at my request. I told him I had something to say, to which I wanted him to listen; I had known and loved men and could see their special beauty but had long preferred the companionship of women.

Who in their right mind would not, he remarked.

It took a moment for what the English call the penny to drop. One almost heard the clunk.

'Oh,' Ugo said.

That monosyllable, in its glorious rotundity, was that. The matter, being raised, was not mentioned by him again.

Ugo lived at the time in the Collegio Teutonico, under the right arm of St Peter's Basilica. The Choir, soon established, would meet for 'rehearsal' in a tumbledown, long-abandoned annex of the College, not a wing but a separate building, a fortlike block that had at one time been a hospice for fever victims, in another era a lodging house for pilgrims. It was whispered by many in Rome, a city of ghost stories, that the stark Gothic edifice was haunted by a sixteen-year-old girl who had fallen pregnant by a Cardinal and been banished to the nunnery that once stood on the site. Poor Emerenzia, as she was known, had starved herself to death and been interred in a cobbled wall.

I used to imagine what she saw as we rehearsed.

Three flights of cracked marble steps like a dinosaur's spine climbed up through the torso of rotting landings. You ascended to a long, gloomy corridor, five metres wide, like a passageway in a gallery but with smashed or crumbling tilework and many of the oak floorboards missing. Vast tapestries of queer toadstools spread themselves along the wainscot. Glassed arrow-slits admitted something that had once been light but was now an oyster-coloured, smoky, oppressive miasma, by which one could see, through astonishingly thick drapes of spiderweb, that the passageway had long ago been pressed into service as a storehouse for unwanted church statues, too broken or ugly for anyone to want them. Yet no one could throw them away.

Decapitated Madonnas, Christs with one hand. Wingless, chipped angels. Toppled, lurching prophets. Disciples and evangelists with sockets for eyes, a Sacred Heart missing its halo. Crooked, plaster martyrs. St Sebastians with snapped arrows. A John the Baptist with the face of a lavatory attendant. St Peter writhingly raving in chains long rusted away. A rat-gnawed Mary Magdalene, nest of wasps in her bosom.

Lazarus stolen from Mexico, throttled by woodworm, in a shifting bib of paint flakes explored by seeping ants. A lacerated donkey from a mahogany crib. A Christ-child's murderous eyes.

At the end of the passageway, you encountered an oddly modern door, like the flimsy timber door of a 1930s Mussolini schoolhouse, but whitewashed, badly, and, like the wainscots, mushroomed. This opened to an old Symposium Room that contained a long wooden table and a wheezy harmonium carved with owls and angels.

If she watched us, Emerenzia saw an odd, lamplit coterie.

The Choir comprised eight including our *Kapellmeister*, Ugo, whose custom was to sit facing the doorway. Delia Kiernan, Enzo Angelucci and I tended to place ourselves on his right, D'Arcy Osborne and John May to his left. May, a gifted musician, sang in his cello-like bass voice or trilled and weaved on his saxophone. Sam Derry toiled at the harmonium, perhaps the only person in history to have done so with a stolen German army 7.63-millimetre Mauser semi-automatic pistol in his belt. The eighth person, her back to the door, was always my dear friend the Contessa Giovanna Landini ('Jo', she preferred, for Jo March in *Little Women*, one of the only titles ever improved upon by its Italian translation, the lovely *Piccole Donne*) whose bleak joke was that if she was going to be shot by the Gestapo, she would rather it came from the back so that she might have an open coffin at her funeral.

Strange, the family we made.

The long, oak tabletop had an archipelago of antique ink-stains and scratchings, some in what I supposed must be Ancient Greek. That broken-down, yellow-keyed harmonium gasped beneath a skylight which had not been cleaned since Garibaldi was a baby. When a strong wind rattled the attic, as happens in a Rome winter, the harmonium uttered a lugubrious groan of complaint like a walrus prodded with a stick. One October evening, into a corner Sam Derry lugged up a potbellied stove, where it pretended with great valour but little effectiveness to heat the room. If anything, whenever that grate was lit, our eyrie seemed colder. Mostly, you wore your overcoat.

It was understood between all eight Choristers that questions about matters other than the weather were forbidden. The Nazi occupation, the war itself, the atrocities of the Gestapo, the controlled starvation that was the food ration, must never be discussed at all. The atmosphere before the music commenced was one of restrained geniality, like a bridge party or a dinner engagement between people who do not know each other very well and are on that sort of questing start-of-the-evening best behaviour. If talk threatened to drift in a direction that Ugo thought unhelpful, he would shoot you a look or draw his fingers across his throat. J. S. Bach and the weather were the permitted topics. If you didn't know anything about them, you had better learn quickly. Few of us being musicologists, we became meteorologists. Anyone can be one of those.

At the time, coffee in Rome was as desert sand in Antarctica, a matter of agony to the Romans, a most caffeinated people, but now and again John May or Delia would have somehow managed to get their hands on some, and Jo Landini might bring a plate of cannoli she had made. Sir D'Arcy often brought wine, but I remember nobody drinking it. Ugo would stand at the head of the table, handing out sheet music, explaining the background to the pieces or giving potted biographies of the composer. As though it truly *was* a rehearsal. Which, in a way, it was.

What was being rehearsed would have got us tortured to death by Hauptmann.

Presently Ugo would call the group to order and play the keynote on a harmonica. As the singing began, which usually happened ten or fifteen minutes after the last of us had arrived, sometimes white-faced and breathless, up the haunted steps, his practice was to systematically make his way around the table, from one of us to another, talking in whispers or showing scribbled notes on lavatory paper, which he would tear up and burn in the stove when we had memorised them. Rome was of course a nest of spies in those months; Hauptmann's Gestapo had planted microphones widely. It was common knowledge that they had taken over the telephone exchange, that every operator was now an SS agent, every call monitored, every meeting of more than six people covertly photographed. A secured radio-transmitter at Nazi Headquarters in the fashionable hotel neighbourhood had a direct channel to Hitler's lair, the Berghof at Obersalzberg. In the streets and markets near the Vatican it was whispered that Himmler himself eavesdropped on Rome every night, moving around the dial at random. Here, in the forgotten loft, we could be reasonably certain that nobody but Emerenzia was listening. In case we were mistaken, we sang.

Allegri's *Miserere*, Dowland, bits of plainsong. Early Elizabethan madrigals and Alleluias. The usual repertoire of an amateur chamber choir or singing society such as you might find in a small town in England, but sometimes we stretched to an attempt at that glory of glories, Palestrina's *Stabat Mater*. The occasional *Tantum Ergo*. A motet of Josquin or a Gregorian chant, some weeks a medieval carol. The Cornish anthem 'Trelawny'. That enchanting Welsh song, '*Ar Hyd y Nos*'. 'The Braes of Balquhither', a beautiful love ballad of Scotland, though Ugo insisted it had Irish cousins. As a piece of insurance, if I can put it that way, we did a German song, '*Hupf, mein Mädel*', but then one evening on my way to rehearsal I heard a Nazi column sing it as they goosestepped down Via Flaminia. We didn't do that one again.

Not entirely jocularly, John May objected to Bach on the basis that he had been 'a Jerry'. Dear John. But when he heard '*Wenn ich einmal soll scheiden*' from the Matthäus-Passion, the most austerely magnificent two minutes of music ever created, he lowered his gaze in awed reverence and hummed solemnly along, as anyone who has ever heard it must. I do not believe in God. But when I hear that piece, I do.

We were no Coro della Sistina but we brought heart to the effort. Lotti's '*Crucifixus*', Byrd's '*Haec Dies*'. Ugo would conduct, lilting along, a competent tenor, but mostly his approach was stern. We took the music seriously, in our way. If the hymn included harmonies, we practised them assiduously at home. He made clear that our rehearsals were not occasions for learning or pleasure; our time together was precious; it must be used to form plans. So, you came to rehearsal 'on book', as professional singers put it, knowing your part so well that you could sing without thinking about it at all, could sing it while thinking about something else.

But, even if the singing was a camouflage and not at all the true purpose, I must say that I adored it, even came to depend on it. And I believe I was not alone. In those dark, violent times, I longed for our weekly rehearsal. I would burn for the night to come.

Some consolation of the spirit, some release happens when human beings sing in a group, wherever and however that occurs. In a place of worship, on the terraces of a football stadium, in a cramped and draughty attic, bombers droning overhead. Nearly all music has beauty, but when it includes the marriage of baritone and soprano, of bass and alto, chorus and soloist, it becomes something more than merely the upliftingly beautiful. Harmony is an everyday, achievable miracle. Imagine having been the first person to think of it, to attempt it with another. *I* shall sing this. *You* sing that. Something greater than I or you will result. And, as everyone who has ever heard singing in a classroom knows well, when we are not wonderful singers, are in fact not musically gifted, singing has a special sort of sacredness that is impossibly moving. When we sing, we cease to be scum.

We sang, Delia Kiernan leading, in her pure, strong, soprano. I loved watching at such moments, her eyes closed, hands clenching and unclenching, the light, coltish gentleness of how she swayed her shoulders. The serenity of her smile between lines. I swear that when she sang, any wrinkles left her face, she was twenty years younger, somehow became her own daughter (who herself sometimes attended our gatherings). Delia was no longer someone's wife, a troubled woman in wartime, but a person in the radiance she believed she had been given. Little wonder we refer to music as 'a gift'. My make-up was often ruined as I listened to my wonderful Delia. I don't know how I held back from applauding her.

One night, D'Arcy Osborne did so. Ugo shot him a terrible glower. 'Couldn't help myself, old man.' Dabbing his eyes with a handkerchief. 'Reminds one why one's alive.'

'*Bravissima*,' the Contessa whispered, also moved to tears. Angelucci and Johnny May stared hard at the floor. Derry shook his head in awed, stunned reverence. The harmonium wheezed its low-toned whistle.

Ugo would move between us under cover of the music, explaining plans, routes, false names, contacts, addresses we were to memorise but never to write down. This escaped Sergeant had emphysema and, by nightfall tomorrow, must be moved from the damp garage in which he was lodged; that American Corporal had gone 'doll dizzy', sexually obsessed, and must be warned to stay in the safehouse on Via di San Marcello and not venture out to visit either of the girlfriends he had mystifyingly acquired since going into hiding. A South African Private had a septic gum infection and needed a dentist. Another had syphilis and would die without penicillin. All of us knew *something*, one element of that week's plan. Ugo was the one who knew everything.

At the start, numbers varied, swelling occasionally to sixteen or seventeen, sometimes other priests but mostly everyday Romans. Then, things would get too hot for a particular Chorister; perhaps the Gestapo had been observed watching her apartment from the upper windows opposite or had been asking questions at her husband's workplace or child's school. In such cases, retirement came early, as Ugo put it. Sometimes he met objections, but the Choir was not a democracy. No matter the asset, he wouldn't take the risk. The core remained the same, the octet mentioned above.

It was Angelucci's task to scrutinise the newspaper classifieds that offered lodgings or to walk about Rome identifying flats that might be rented in a false name. Sir D'Arcy and Jo Landini were assigned the duty of fundraising among sympathetic donors; Sam Derry collected the money in secret, commonly going under disguise, and delivered it to the safehouse's owner or landlord, whom we called in code 'the Benoit', the name of the landlord in *La Bohème*. Whenever the Benoit was a woman, it seemed easier, for some reason. Not that it was ever easy. The penalty for 'false renting', as it was termed by the Nazis, was death. So, the rent money would need to be substantial.

Then – this was work I frequently did myself – a dossier of abandoned houses and other possible hiding places had to be compiled. I must have walked a thousand kilometres about Rome that autumn, protected by my Swiss passport and my international Press Card, noting bombsites, manholes, follies in public gardens, rusted cisterns, gullies, storm drains behind apartment blocks, stables, henhouses, viaducts, storerooms, disused barges on the Tiber, a crashed train carriage, derelict factories, the abandoned traffic-tunnel on Via del Traforo. The parks were a sorrowful sight: all the benches had been ransacked for firewood; there might be a potting shed or dilapidated conservatory where prisoners could hide. Rome is built on a warren of volcanic rock, in which are scores of age-old subterranean quarries; asking around, I learned of several ways in. Beneath the Basilica dei Santi Giovanni e Paolo is a network of preserved ancient Roman streets; these, too, went on my list. The hidden aqueduct behind the Spanish Steps. The marble sewer-tunnel that, long ago, served a bathhouse. I made it my business to befriend the Fascist structural engineer commissioned to blueprint Rome's metro system, and to – shall I say – borrow his drawings.

Forgery was another important element of the repertoire. Often, while the Lord was being glorified in plainchant, Ugo would quietly make his way around the table – you slightly dreaded his approach – and whisper that this week we needed a Vatican City Employee card, two Swiss passports in the name of Franz and Heinrich So-and-So, ten hundred-franc notes and a set of Fascist Party membership documents with an early serial number. Had you any ideas?

It was expected that you would have. He became surly if you hadn't.

John May knew a crooked printer in Trastevere who, as he put it, 'would knock you up a Gutenberg Bible for three quid'. May was a good-looking man but, oddly, that was not what made him attractive; rather, it was his gloomily humorous manner, the sort of confidence that, in men, masks itself as self-deprecation. Seldom short of female companionship, for a time he knocked about with a *signorina* who worked as a typist in the Mayor's office. The Mayor liked a good lunch and was one of those gentlemen who do not attend too closely to the paperwork placed before them for signature during the afternoon session, particularly when an embodiment of Roman pulchritude is doing the placing. A number of our passes were signed by that Mayor, I regret to say, without his knowledge.

There was the exhausting, unending demand for clothing, and for it to be distributed without anyone noticing. Ugo instituted the practice that every Chorister turned up for rehearsal bearing at least a man's shirt or jacket. You found them in the second-hand markets or wherever you pleased. The booty was conveyed by May to a laundry where dyers and seamstresses got to work.

Indeed, a seamstress would play a central role in the Christmas Eve Rendimento. But here I get ahead of myself.

Rome, for obvious reasons, has a good deal of male prostitution. Several of these men, at appalling risk, were helpful to the Escape Line, and some met terrible deaths as a result. As for the women of that profession, I think it no exaggeration to say that their courage and tenacity, and the invariable accuracy of their information, saved hundreds of lives.

During every rehearsal, Ugo and I would find a few moments to go through the latest scheme. Rome contains thousands of religious institutions – monasteries, convents, pilgrim houses, seminaries, generalates, colleges, abbeys, individual churches – some of which had made it known they would be willing to assist our endeavours but were anxious to limit the danger. Ugo, Derry and the Contessa contrived a sort of timetable, a traffic-light system, by which a premises would be brought into play.

First, we would anonymously report the convent or church to the Gestapo as a place where late-night arrivals had been noticed. The ensuing German raid found no fugitives. A week or ten days later, the denunciation was repeated more ardently: a poison-pen letter reporting the monks as harbourers and black marketeers, possessors of an illegal radio or a hand-operated printing press. A detailed map of the building's floorplan and hiding places was provided; the abbey's doors would be kicked in by Hauptmann's search squad. This time, in addition to there being no escapees, there would be found on the Abbot's desk a well-thumbed copy of *Mein Kampf*, with warm annotations in the Abbot's own hand. Our forger ran us up six dozen autographed photographs of the Führer; we ensured that these were displayed in many of the nunneries where prisoners were reported to be hiding. War brings strange sights, but one does not expect to encounter a framed portrait of Hitler outstaring you over Reverend Mother's bed. We arranged for that treat to befall quite a number of German soldiers.

The fake report might be repeated four times, until we felt certain that the Germans had lost interest. At that point, the monastery would be flooded with escapees from crypt to belfry, and the fictive denunciations continued elsewhere.

There was another silent legion of brave Romans, often the poor, those who lacked space at home to hide a fugitive, but who wished to assist us all the same. Derry and Ugo came up with a means by which anyone living in the city could help. If you were willing to endure the unpleasantness of a Gestapo raid on your apartment, we asked that you anonymously denounce yourself or get a family member or neighbour to do it. The raiding party would arrive, smash down the door, empty out the wardrobes, clamber into the building's loft or descend to its cellars, but it could take them half an hour to discover that you were hiding nobody, that the denouncement had been groundless. To waste the enemy's time was to deplete his resources. Into the night with the Germans, but Angelucci would by then have made certain every urchin in the neighbourhood had sprinkled the street with caltrops – cross-pronged nails and bent screws – so that the tyres of their jeeps and motorcycles would be punctured. The caltrops were an idea of Sir D'Arcy's, adaptation of an ancient Roman sabotage weapon he had first read about as a boy at his mortifyingly expensive school and then seen in the Musei Vaticani.

There were bad days, many of them, when plans went wrong. Mistranslations. Slips. A misremembered sequence. A terrified Book in hiding – we termed the escapees 'Books' – might lurch towards losing his mind and have to be moved at short notice, or spoken to harshly, even threatened with court martial and execution, but his fellows in the same attic must be protected. Books under lockdown bickered and often enough came to blows. No privacy, little space, stale air, perhaps nowhere to wash. The natural desires of young people, given no outlet. One's face heats a little as one recollects the moment when Derry brought us the grave complaint that an escapee had been seen by his cohabitors indulging in a not unknown practice, one Derry refused to name except to say the man had been 'doing as a schoolboy does'. It was Osborne who, without deciphering, at least broke the tension. 'Darling, if everyone guilty of *that* were to suffer eviction, every room in bloody Europe would be empty.'

No news; rotten food, weeks of silence, warring rumours. Ten or a dozen palliasses crammed into a room. These were not professional soldiers but enlistees or the drafted: tradesmen, schoolteachers, postmen, farmers' sons. Their training for an existence in hiding was scant; their eyes had seen the horrors of battle or the *Stalag*. In stories for little children who know nothing of the world, the suggestion is often made that adversity stirs the best in the human person, but in war this is not always so. Envy and resentment sprout when men are shut in together, bullying, boredom, anger, restless fear, the exhaustion of literally never sleeping a full night, the famishment of sharing rations among eight that were intended for one. There is unease about status; who is in charge? Rank is exposed as a fiction.

Men of numerous nations and colonies served in the Allied forces. If colour prejudice began its hideous writhing, we crushed it. Ugo was vehement on the point; no excuse was given ear. Any man voicing such bigotries would be evicted. An Alabaman once made the error of exculpating away a filthy remark he had uttered, on the basis that in Alabama it was 'how folks do'. Ugo told him in blunt terms understandable anywhere in the English-speaking world that he was not in Alabama now.

There were other forms of behaviour that drove Ugo and the rest of us to rage. Often, they were explained as playfulness. Escapees who were sworn to maintain the secrecy of their hideouts, tossing a baseball back and forth, across from balcony to balcony, or firing golf balls in catapults to crack the windows opposite. Donning the landlady's wig and underclothes to pirouette on a rooftop. Dancing galliards with one another. Kissing brooms. Emptying chamber pots or armfuls of homemade tickertape into the street. Did they *want* to be caught? Was the boredom that poisonous? In prison, might these men feel freer?

As for the Choir, we lived with the never-ending dread that an escapee might die, which, given that some were wounded, seemed grimly inevitable, and would need to be buried covertly in some equivalent of a potter's field. These possibilities loomed, always. My nightmares were terrifying. I grew addicted to the barbiturate methaqualone, which made them worse.

There was also, it must be admitted, the constant fear that we were compromised, that an apparent supporter, perhaps even one of us in the Choir, might be a Judas. Stranger things have happened and always will. Often, as we met, among the ghosts and dead statues, Mistrust sat down with us at that long oaken table. A hard guest to banish. He convinces you he's a friend.

A good day occurred when the Contessa received word from a hawk-eyed informant of a certain large apartment house near the casern in Prati, in which sixty German conscripts were billeted. It was their habit to shine their boots last thing at night with a polish that was quite wickedly malodorous – human urine was rumoured to be one of its ingredients. So vile was the stench that the men would leave the boots out in the rear courtyard until reveille at dawn. One morning, they and their *Oberstleutnant* received a surprise. A crack squad of layabouts had been paid by Angelucci to scale the moonlit wall, each mountaineer bearing a pillowcase that was empty when he commenced his climb but clumpy and full when he came back. 'Booty is truth,' Sir D'Arcy remarked. 'Truth, booty.' The ghost of John Keats gave a groan.

Some will aver that far worse should have been done to those German soldiers. If you have murdered a man in cold blood, I will listen. If not, I suggest you admire yourself in the mirror of your certainties – but know where the light is coming from.

We were not paramilitaries. Our purpose was to hide fugitives from the tyranny. Doubtless, we had members that were also supporters of the Roman Partigiani, the largely Communist armed resistance, a body from which the Choir turned its gaze. Rightly, wrongly, that was not our business, nor was the matter debated at rehearsal.

What I see is a group of slightly odd people singing in an attic, Ugo O'Flaherty circling the table, looking stern.

I can picture that room to the tiniest detail. Moonlight silvering the ancient, dented table. Stove-light yellowing the keys of the decrepit old harmonium and purpling Jo Landini's eyes. Sometimes, as we sang, I would reach out to clasp her hand, for I knew that her departed husband felt close to her then. Dead statues, broken crucifixes on the landing outside. A ring on Angelucci's finger. The glint of D'Arcy Osborne's spectacles. Some nights, the certainty that Emerenzia was watching.

For always I felt watched.

Recorded.

Observed.

Lamplight on seven faces.

The Choir.

Together, but, in the end, one was out on one's own.

Always there would need to be a solo.

15

Christmas Eve 1943
5.47 p.m.
5 hours and 13 minutes before the Rendimento

Dusk is descending as he takes a glass of hot water and cloves, alone at a rusting garden table in the refectory's allotment. Ravens strut and squawk. Smoke on cold air.

Seeing him through the windows, the other priests look away, sup a snout-and-lung stew in silence, play draughts. It is not unknown for those of their calling to turn introspective at Christmastime. When your only home is a linoleum-clad room up a landing, festivities can be trials of endurance.

At six o'clock he is seen walking in the Papal gardens. Soon afterwards he calls into the Montessori School for the children of Vatican employees, where the usual seasonal play is being subjected to production. He makes conversation about A.S. Roma with the father of St Joseph, a driver, blesses rosary beads for the shepherd's twin brothers, both sick from sweets, permits himself to be photographed with the innkeeper's aunt, a Sister home from Africa, a trainee radiographer in a Nairobi hospital, at whose mother's funeral Mass he assisted last April.

A cadaverous, broom-waving Befana, the bountiful witch of Christmastime, is borne in on an ecclesiastical sedan chair, brandishing the school's heavy handbell. Bambino Gesù is a little girl's doll and is missing a leg. As the nuns announce the *limonata*, they call for '*nostro amico, il Monsignore*' to say a few words, give a blessing. It takes a few moments for people to realise he has left.

At quarter to seven, he is covertly filmed crossing the gardens in the direction of the infirmary. Rain is falling but he is wearing no coat.

In the lobby, he is approached by a Polish Nursing Matron whom he's known a long time. She tells him he's looking terrible, insists he sit a moment, examines him. His blood pressure is 160 over 90, his heart is 'banging drums'. She advises him to return to his room, 'avoid all anxieties', otherwise a coronary might be his Christmas present.

In the ward, he prays the rosary by the deathbed of an elderly gardener, assuring him from time to time that there is no need to utter the responses: 'I can do it for both of us, Gino, rest your spirit.'

An applewood bowl of winter laurels on the bedside locker, beside a stone jug of water from the spring the man unearthed behind the Basilica with his sons some thirty years ago, on a morning when a sinkhole opened, the dawn after a thunderstorm, and they dug into the sandy, rasping schist, joyous as Texan oilmen.

Nurses come and go amid the reek of disinfectant. The gardener accepts the Communion host, strange roses in his eyes, touches a napkin dipped in the chalice to his parched, pale lips.

'*Grazie*,' he wheezes. 'Now my bag is packed.'

'The Lord doesn't want you yet, Gino. Bad manners to arrive early.'

'I'm on my way, anyhow.'

'We shall walk to your spring again, my friend.'

'Remember the newspaperman, *Monsignore?* Who sold papers in the square?'

'Angelucci?'

'Came to me in a dream last night. Guy liked boxing.'

'Still does.'

'Liked boxing. Can't remember his name. I never did, myself.'

'Why not?'

'*Bontà mia*, life is full of fights already. Why invent them?'

'For sport.'

'Liked boxing, that guy in the square. Newspaperman. Can't remember his name.'

'This beautiful nurse is telling me you must rest yourself, Gino. You don't want to disappoint her.'

'Think I'll have a little siesta.'

'Do, my friend. Rest.'

'Thanks for coming, *Monsignore. Buon Natale*. Goodbye.'

'I'll come again soon.'

'You won't,' mutters the gardener. '*Paisano*, you're betrayed.' As he slips into morphined sleep.

———————

At the College, the furnace has chugged on. Pipes crossing the ceiling of his room give their clicketting hum; the aroma of roasted dust arises. In the swelter, he strips to his underwear and socks, lies on the narrow bed.

Just ten minutes.
Rest his eyes.
Try to calm.
Long night coming.

A whirl of propellers
chop crisp London air
The engines cough
a scutter of smoke
and weep an oily tear.

Knowing he is dreaming, he turns, attempting to surface. The gardener is here, in groves of winter laurels. The children from the nativity play, toy Nazis in their hands.

Far below, the river
winding like a sentence
etched by the jeweller
in spirals of mind
a ribbon of silver
on a ballgown of rushes
laid on a springtime featherbed

Out, over townlands
football fields, estates
manses, cattle marts

brickfields, farmlands
the miracle irregular of new forest fields
grown glorious now in a lamb-bleat of March
as the farmer looks up,
scythe in hand, from his bees
at the fall and the all of the SCREEEEEEE—

Shuddering, wrists thrusting, handcuffs of damp sheets. The vast bells of the Basilica tolling for eight, answered by every other chime in the city.

A certainty, like the memory of a broken bone in midwinter, that he does not belong here, has never belonged.

B'long, say the bells. Rolling, tolling, with clappers the size of a battleship's anchor or the tinkling of a porcelain thimble. *B'lung. B'lang.* Orchestra of bell-song. Lambastes of blowsy gong-song, the jangle of Rome. Pealing. Clanging. Booming and bawling, spangling from steeples, dovecots, turrets, the billow of bell-song so you feel it in your coccyx, the shock, the mockery, in dour oratorios, knells, dirges, tolling, rolling, piping *soprani* or piccolo jingle, rolling the *doloroso* of orotund bass, over martyr's bones, immemorial stones, pulsing out spheres of iron unseen, Atlantics of sound every second.

The bells roar for eight.

The dream roils again.

In the clouds, a dead gardener, howling, *pointing.* But his words can't be heard for the bells.

———

Across the city, a man enters an improvised office that used to be the kitchenette of the German Cultural Centre. Removing his cap, he crosses to the sink.

Evocative, the bells.

He counts them down.

Eight.

Christmassy, of course, like cinnamon turned to sound. Berlin will be lovely tonight but cold, damp, foggy. Mother and Father having the neighbours in for a little glass of schnapps. Sad time for some, Christmas Eve.

The gramophone plays Grieg's A minor Piano Concerto, Op. 16, the

Schnabel recording, a little old-fashioned, but muscular and finessed. The blurt of water against metal is pleasing, a comfort to the senses, blanking, as it does, the screams from the cells downstairs. He washes the butcher's-shop smell from his hands. But now it occurs to him that he has forgotten to buy a Christmas present for Elise. He curses his stupidity and forgetfulness.

What would she like? Shoes? A piece of jewellery? A pet, perhaps? An antique? If he could summon from memory her dress size, perhaps a gown? Or stockings. It is only eight o'clock, some of the merchants will still be on their premises.

A fortnight ago, while leading a kidnap squad to Trastevere, he happened to notice, on a mannequin in a couturier's window, a tight-fitting, ruched ivory silk ballgown, slit to the thigh. A woman of Elise's figure would appear a goddess in such a garment. And it would be a way of asserting that he still found her physically attractive, which she sometimes says he doesn't, 'since pregnancy destroyed my body'. At such moments, he embraces her, covers her hands with kisses, thanks her for the strength and affection she shows their children, thanks her for coming to Rome to be with him at this trying time. The gown would be a sort of lovemaking.

But where would she wear it? It is not as though they go out. The opera is far too dangerous, too public, he has been advised. A Partisan sniper in the wings, a bomber in the box above. The Communists are getting reckless; they no longer fear reprisals.

Perhaps at a ball in the Villa Farnesina for the Führer's visit in the spring? Humming along with Grieg, he rinses the iron-smelling blood from his knuckles, bundles the reddened tissues, drops them out the window, before noticing, on the carving table now doing duty as what he calls 'the Urgent Desk', a document needing his attention, the now-completed dossier on the priest.

Damn that wretched typist, why couldn't she go home early for Christmas as ordered?

Now he will need to read it, Elise's gift will have to wait. An idea occurs to him. Is the typist still here? She is the same sort of height and build as his wife, perhaps she would accompany him to the couturier's, try on the gown for him? He sees her standing very straight, graceful hands on her hips, dark Italian smile in the long slim mirror.

For God's sake, man, that would be disrespectful. Improper to ask a woman to do any such thing. Get a grip on yourself and grow up, you are not sixteen.

Strange, the background thought that haunts his reading of the dossier. Bells and the blood taste the same.

INTELLIGENCE REPORT
CONFIDENTIAL ON PAIN OF DEATH

File commenced: P. Hauptmann, date redacted. Information added: E. Dollman, 24th December 1943.

Subject: Hugh O'Flaherty (surname on certificate of birth is 'Flaherty'; has been checked in person by agent of the Reich, Public Records Office, Dublin).

Date of birth: 28th February 1898; i.e. subject is aged forty-five.

Place of birth: Kishkeam, County of Cork, Ireland/Éire, but was raised in County of Kerry.

Address: Collegio Teutonico del Campo Santo, Via della Sacrestia, Rome. Informant confirms the subject's room is on third landing, eleven paces from stairhead, door numbered '15'; two small windows. Subject eats (often alone) in communal refectory, ground floor, five large windows. Often walks unaccompanied in cemetery garden. Wall is two metres in height; one gate leading to passageway. Gate often locked, soap copy of key to be investigated. See sketched map and floor plan supplied by informant. (Building is an extraterritorial property of Vatican City, i.e., not legally part of Rome or Italy.)

Subject's Occupation: Roman Catholic priest, ordained 1925, now '*Scrittore*', clerk / lecturer / diplomat of the Curia, rank of Monsignor. Has worked previously in Haiti, San Domingo, Palestine, Czechoslovakia, London. Summoned to Rome 1934.

Place of Work: Office of Marital Nullity, Supreme Sacred Congregation of the Holy Office and Propagation of the Faith, Piazza del Sant'Uffizio, Rome, known as 'The Propaganda'. Building is extraterritorial property of Vatican

City. Calls to and from telephone on subject's desk are monitored (commenced seven weeks ago), transcripts available within thirty-six hours.

Passport: Ireland /Éire. Is thought may possess counterfeit Swiss papers and Vatican Secretariat *carta di identità* in false name but with own photograph. (Subject speaks Italian, Spanish, French, Czech. No German. Is conversant in Latin and Ancient Greek.)

Height: 1.88 metres.

Weight: 90 Kilos approximately.

Eyes: Blue. (Subject is short-sighted, wears spectacles. Photograph of recent prescription attached.)

Complexion: Ruddy.

Medical Condition: Doctor's records (photographs attached) indicate tendency to high blood pressure, varicose vein in left thigh, bronchitis in wintertime, otherwise reasonable health. Capable of withstanding very severe interrogation.

Pursuits: Reads, goes to art galleries (holds three doctorates), conducts a choir. Rides a motorcycle in countryside around Rome. Known to attend boxing. Does not consume alcohol, does not smoke. Opera, bridge, golf, through which he has met and fraternised with Rome-based enemy sympathisers including Sir Francis D'Arcy Godolphin Osborne (British Envoy Extraordinary and Minister Plenipotentiary to the Holy See), Mrs Delia Kiernan, née Murphy (professional singer, wife of diplomatic 'Minister' of Ireland, formal term for de facto Ambassador), the Contessa Giovanna Landini and her circle (Communist apologists).

Political beliefs: Pro-American. Frequent attender at American motion pictures. Was official Vatican visitor to Allied prisoners of war in Stalag 369, Trieste, and many other concentration camps, but raised morale of prisoners, distributed books, cigarettes, sheet music of songs, accepted letters for posting, in disobedience of Papal policy of strict neutrality, attempted to demoralise guards. Was disciplined by Vatican late '42, removed from role as visitor and has been confined to Vatican City since but is rumoured to disobey under darkness. Informants have heard him deride Mussolini. Has been seen not to stand in the Cinema Clodio while Fascist anthem 'Giovinezza' is played. Claims to have visited British Navy submarine docked at Ostia in 1934. Has been observed in possession of *Avanti*, socialist degenerate newspaper. For some time has been suspected of being complicit in the hiding of escaped enemy prisoners and Jews, in disobedience to martial law decree section IV, paragraph X, punishable by death.

In recent months, complicity has intensified.

On foot of recent intelligence gathered by surveillance and other methods, subject now thought to be centrally involved with well-funded Escape Line, operational methods and precise source of monies as yet unknown. Co-conspirators refer to escapees collectively as 'The Library', to individual fugitives as 'Books', to hiding places as 'Shelves'. Chief mission-runner thought to be escaped British officer, surname possibly 'Kerry', 'Terry' or 'Bury' (as in the English place name). Several substitutes in training, all Italian.

Subject's Vulnerabilities: Yet to be uncovered. Investigations continuing. Is not thought to be homosexual, molester of children, or womaniser. Evinces no interest in money.

Suggested Action: Subject received shock-visit at his workplace this evening with purpose of inducing fear / disorientation. Advise close surveillance of subject, three weeks, commencing immediately on receipt of this now-completed dossier, followed by covert night arrest of subject and intensive Gestapo interrogation.

To be shot while trying to escape.

16

Christmas Eve 1943
8.31 p.m.
2 hours and 29 minutes before the Rendimento

On the roof of the hotel across Via di Porta Cavalleggeri the German sentries switch on the arc light.

Through the gaps in his shutters the beam comes glaring, grids of chemical whiteness along the marble floor and up the wainscots. Over the face of the Sacred Heart, the sad eyes of St Bernadette Soubirous. A tin-framed wedding photograph of his parents.

It started in mid-September. Every night since. That unblinking, unkillable stare. They stole the lamp when they ransacked the Cinecittà film studios, trucked it through the streets like a hostage, roped on the back of a flatbed, a deity of glass, the thousand-watt tungsten bulb of a lighthouse. The brightness confuses the birds, makes them croak and whistle all night, illuminates the facade of the Collegio, its entrance gate and garden, the graveyard.

At one time, until not long ago, the hotel was a *pensione* for pilgrims, now it is a brothel and drinking den. ('The wine list is said to have improved,' Jo Landini bleakly joked.) From his room, he sees the Fascist police arrive and depart, hears the maudlin, lurid singing about *Vaterland* and thunder, the drunken braying of folk songs.

The Steinway thieved from a Professor of Music, a Jew, was pulleyed in one midnight by prisoners at gunpoint, pawed at and mauled by some hammer-handed Klaus before being doused in gasoline and set on fire as a prank. Across the street, in his window, he watched the brave piano burn, smoke belching into the dawn amid the smash of shattering bottles. Every night since. The singing, the roaring. The Reich is cried up, the Communists cried down. Prostitutes are manhandled in.

On such nights, it brings ease to picture the five-hundred-year-old buildings around him. The empty churches and palazzos. The tens of thousands of empty rooms. He counts the cracks in the tin ceiling as he listens to Algiers Italian News or the BBC. Possession of a wireless has been made punishable by ten years in prison but the thought of life without it is unbearable. He pretends not to know that several of the younger seminarians have smuggled in their own radios or built them. Jazz is being quietly listened to in the darkened Collegio, sometimes with a cigarette or a shamefaced beer. It isn't his job to know.

Through the hissing weep of the airwaves, newsreaders talk of firepower and battleships. Pincer movements, fighter planes, pontoons. The crackle wefts and warps; strange interplanetary whoops. To hear the words 'London calling' consoles him, as a full moon at sea, or the boom of a friendly cannon. The wet streets of Piccadilly arise through the sibilance, in sepia, molasses-tinted, a watercolour of themselves, or Kerry sometimes comes to him, the coconut aroma of gorse on the bog road.

His father, putter in hand, on the fourteenth green at Killarney, dark glasses and spats, sunburned with August laughter.

A December evening when someone had been to Glasgow for a cousin's wedding and brought back a clockwork racing car that chuntered round the chair legs all St Stephen's Day, bumping into grown-ups' shoes. After the tea, a troop of mummers bumbled in, all straw masks and sackcloth tunics, to perform their charade of hunting the wren – as a boy, he had always found it more disturbing than it was meant to be – but they'd been stilled into marvel by the buzzing, insistent toy, as it nosed at the dozy cat and headbutted the fire irons. One by one they queued to take their own turn winding it, until a man named Mulvey whom people said was simple-minded had overwound the ratchet, wrenching the mechanism, and the car never raced again. He had wanted to strike Mulvey, to scream in his strange face. His mother warned him not to cry, it would make 'poor Michael' feel awful.

Across the street, the Nazis slobber, brangle, murder folk songs. Sometimes he hears them blamming their pistols and he wonders what they're shooting at – each other? the night? the paintings on the walls? – for the curfew has emptied the streets. Only the most desperate of the women appear beneath the lamp posts, skeletal, empty-eyed, offering themselves for a quarter loaf of bread, but they are beaten away by the Fascist Youth corner boys, the *squadre d'azione*, who burn to impress the Germans.

At nine o'clock, the Basilica bells roar like a vengeful immortal, raising jeers and choruses of mockery in the hotel. He finishes a letter to an old friend, Moss Trant, a man who left the priesthood to marry, became a dentist, is now living in Detroit. Then he reads over a single page of notes, commits to memory the three locations at which Angelucci must make drop-offs of money to buy safe passage for the escapees – a dustbin in Prati, a coalhole in Parioli, an address not yet known, over the river in Campo Marzio – tears the page to shreds, which he swallows. Along the way there'll be a stop to take on board more cash. Like the drop-offs, that will be a dangerous moment.

He looks at his watch, pictures Angelucci with Derry.

The Basilica is closing.

What will happen, will happen.

———

Remember me to your parents, Moss, when you are next in touch.
Sending you thoughts of happier days, and the blessings of the Prince
of Peace on Yvette and you and the children. I don't know when you'll
get this but may the new year of 1944 bring you and yours all you'd
wish. Pray for me, dear friend, and I'll pray for you.

Your old pal,
Hugh O'F

PS : I mean it about the request, Moss. Say a rosary for me one evening.
I feel certain I am in imminent trouble or danger this weather. If
anything does happen, I want you to know I'll be thinking of our
friendship at the end, and all the good times we shared, and that I loved
you dearly as my brother.

— 17 —

Christmas Eve 1943
9.17 p.m.
1 hour and 43 minutes before the Rendimento

He bolts closed the shutters, extinguishes the candle. In the slatted beam of the arc light, he disassembles his makeshift wireless, hides the coil in a bedspring, the valve behind a book, Dostoevsky's *Notes from the Underground*.

Forming a sphere of the knotted escape rope he keeps hidden beneath the wardrobe, he arranges it on the pillow and covers it with a sheet. The bolster forms a body; he drapes blankets, a bedcover. The result would not fool anyone coming into the room but a watcher glancing from the doorway might think the bed's occupant were asleep.

He unscrews the shampoo bottle, sprinkles altar wine about; a sudden silence and he hears the droplets splashing on the floor. This won't be the first room in a seminary to know that aroma. Good for any observer to think the sleeper is drunk. Raising the two floorboards, he retrieves the canvas knapsack.

Makes the sign of the cross.

Leaves the room.

At every point of what is coming, he will need luck to go undetected. Just walking down the stairs, he'll need luck. Long practised, he is careful to avoid the floorboards that groan or chirr, to zigzag where he needs to, not to cough.

In the hall, he slides the letter to Trant into the residents' post box, which is stuffed with Christmas cards and slim parcels. The casement clock bongs soberly for half past nine. Everyone in the house will be at evening private prayer.

Entering the cubbyhole beneath the old staircase, where the telephone for the use of residents is mounted to the wall, he pulls closed the flimsy curtain behind him. If the telephone should ring now, all is lost. Somehow, on these nights, it never has, but luck can be ridden too long. Sweating, he takes the penknife from his pocket. Three raincoats are hanging on the wall behind the seat. He parts them. It will take two and a half minutes to remove the eight screws in the panel.

He starts working.

Pipes clank in the wall. Somewhere above him in the house, a man is laughing. He fumbles, drops the third screw, bends to feel for it beneath the bench, and as he does, is ripped into by stomach cramp.

The telephone shrills.

Like a glass bowl smashing in the stilled, dark hall.

He lifts the receiver.

'*Pronto?*' he murmurs.

'*Mi chiamo Silvia,*' the young woman says. '*Posso parlare con Maria Elena?*'

'*Non è qui.*'

'*Ma . . .*'

'*Mi dispiace, Lei ha sbagliato numero.*'

Her voice takes on a tearful urgency, she must speak with Maria Elena. Through a chink in the curtain, he watches as the cat pads haughtily along the corridor, yellow-eyed, imperious, reigning. The caller disconnects. Wind buffets the house. He replaces the receiver but slightly off its cradle, so the telephone cannot sound again.

Removing the last of the screws, he lifts out the panel, climbs into the crawlspace behind it, to the odour of old plaster and damp. So quiet, he can hear the tippet of fleeing squirrels. Raising the panel behind him, he pulls it back into place, and, with a match, lights the stub of candle from his pocket.

Four metres take him to a junction where the crawlspace enters a down-sloping cobbled passageway echoing of dripping water. In a cleft in the brickwork, his electric torch. He switches it on – the battery is weakening – and continues into the murk.

Descending into the shaft by the iron ladder on its wall, he enters a cellar system that has not seen light in seven hundred years. Long ago, Vatican servants lived here among the pantries and wine vaults, the ice rooms, vats and ship-sized casks; there is no plan of this warren, at least none he has ever seen. Not even the fleets of Roman workmen who came in to shore it up following a collapse thirty years ago were able to count these passageways.

Passing a grotto, he glances in. Three men in ragged RAF uniforms are playing cards by candlelight. The Sergeant salutes him wordlessly; he motions back for the man to keep silent, and the Sergeant nods gravely, returning to the game as though the intruder was only a shadow.

Eyes behind gratings.

Thumbs-ups from alcoves.

Hammocks and blanket-rolls.

A chalked Stars and Stripes on a cavern wall.

Nooks where a whisper is heard.

Soon he is under the cobbled yard separating the College from the Basilica. Above him, the Swiss Guardsmen will be on duty, he knows, the arc light on the roof of the conquered hotel picking out the blue, red and orange of their uniforms. Tiredness washes over him, and again the pulse of stomach cramp through the sharply sluicing fear; it is still not too late to turn back. A moment. He goes on.

Lichen on wet slabs. Rugs of hairy white weeds. There must be rats here, but in all these months he hasn't seen one; perhaps never having known light they are afraid of his torch. The beam yellows plasterwork, ancient crests, skulls-and-crossbones, a carving of Romulus and Remus on an ancient man-hole cover. He approaches the oaken door into which someone centuries ago carved an obscene cartoon: Gluttony Forced by the Devil to Drink. The hinges are rusted to powder; he wrangles the door ajar. Behind it, as in a mine, a vented crawl-way extends into the stark, cold crypt of unremembered Popes, their strange names graven into the marble coffins.

Through the sepulchre, torch struggling, his gasps are orbs of steam, and he slides behind the sarcophagus of Pius II, a tight, painful fit that can only be accomplished by inhaling as hard as he can. Through the squeeze, into an opening like the burial chamber of a passage grave, from there through the culvert and into a smaller, lower crypt where a pirate crew of disgraced Cardinals sleep their last. The fourth marble casket has a fake lid of painted plywood; he removes it, climbs inside, drops down slowly on the knotted rope through the false floor and into a bat-flickering passageway beneath.

Thirty-two metres brings him to an X-junction. Then eleven metres west.

He knocks four times on a length of broken pipe.

Three knocks come back.

He knocks again, once.

'Beethoven,' he says.

'Evening, Padre,' comes the echo.

Behind him, the black curtain is parted.

The ancient Romans believed ghosts looked like living people, only wearier. The figure parting the curtain has that hauntedness. In the candlelight, Sam Derry is old-porcelain grey, looks exhausted and breakable, like the flawed hero in the final scene of a tragedy done in military dress. Shirtless but wearing his officer's khaki jacket, bandages around his abdomen, long-john underpants, stolen Wehrmacht boots.

Five months ago, he jumped from the moving prisoner-train into a ravine; his limp has never healed. He gives a shuddering wince, like a man nodding away a mosquito. His Shelley-like hair in wet straggles, spectacles repaired with wire. He is not religious ('part-time Church of England') but is wearing a St Christopher medal about his muscle-roped throat, gift of the Genovese medical student who four nights ago performed his appendectomy herself, no surgeon being obtainable, and who, early this morning, helped smuggle him into the hidden floor of the laundry truck that returned him over the Vatican line.

'Major Derry. How are you keeping?'

'Mustn't grumble, Padre. Yourself?'

'Right as the mail.'

'You don't look it.'

'Never did.'

They shake hands, then embrace. 'You had us up the walls with worry, Sam, I thought you were a goner.'

'The things I have to do to get noticed around here.'

He is fond of Derry's turn of phrase and glum humour, his seriousness. Easy to see why he was appointed OC by the men in the prison camp. The guards would have found his solidity unnerving.

'How's the pain, Sam?'

'Worse at bloody night for some reason, so sleeping is hard. But they gave me a bucketload of sedatives to bring home. There's also gin. So, I'm keeping sedate. Speaking of which, could you or the excellent May lay your hands on a bottle of disinfectant, even a floor cleaner, and bit of gauze and a needle? Need to keep the wound clean. For when I take out the stitches.'

'Of course.'

'Soon as you can, Padre, bout of sepsis could complicate matters.'

'Sorry I'm late, by the way.'

'Oh, my social diary isn't too busy these evenings, Padre, don't worry.'

'I wasn't.'

'*Molto bene.* Stands the Eternal City as it stood?'

'Bread and oil are gone invisible. We heard there might be rice. A bold butcher in the Mercato Rionale fairly got himself lynched for admitting he'd a kilo of guanciale hidden behind the counter. Oh, I forgot. A Christmas banquet.'

From his pockets, he takes a bread roll, a hunk of cheese wrapped in a page of yesterday's *Corriere della Sera*, a pack of Woodbines and a pint of Scotch.

'Riches,' says the Englishman. '*Grazie mille*, Padre. You won't object if I don't stand on ceremony?'

'Tuck in.'

'Onward, Christian Soldiers.' Uncorking the Scotch, downing a glug.

'Get a bit of air yet, Sam?'

The Englishman shakes his head. 'Tried this morning around eleven but the gardeners were about. Saw them through the grille, didn't like the look of their slash hooks. Thought it might be best to spend a few hours with the thoughts and my Eye-tie grammar.'

'How did that go?'

'Entertainingly enough.'

'Introduce yourself to me, so. If you dare.'

'*Mi chiamo Samuele Derry e sono inglese. Buona sera.*'

'You have to put a bit of bodily *feeling* into it, Sam. It's why Italians talk with their hands, they're conducting themselves.'

Derry gives a gruff chuckle, gnawing on the bread. 'Afraid I shall never conduct. Well, perhaps on a bus. Oh, this afternoon I finished the Marcus Aurelius you brought the other week, rum stuff, a lot of it. But food for thought, too.'

'I'm fond of old Marcus.'

'You would be.'

'Why's that?'

'One assumes he was a Mick. With a name like O'Relius.'

'After the war, don't attempt a career as a comedian, Sam, will you?'

'One of his sayings rather struck me as worth putting on a poster in the Underground or somewhere. "Think of yourself as dead. Now, return and live your life."'

'We'll natter about that again. There isn't much time. How's your student getting along?'

'Come and see.'

Derry leads him into the rock-lined passageway, now through a high-roofed, flooded, taper-lit cavern over which a bridge of roped-together pallets has been slung. Up a shingled, slippy embankment, into the cell-sized alcove.

Angelucci is seated on the narrow outcropping ledge, chain-smoking. The glow of the cigarette reddens his glittering eyes as he mutters at his shadow, an actor learning lines.

Behind him, on the wall of the cave, a tin Peroni sign and a pin-up of a tight-sweatered Jane Russell. Somehow an electric bulb has been wired from a length of flex. The battered ice-bucket pressganged as ashtray is overflowing. Damp items of malodorous clothing have been draped on the rocks to dry by a nest of whitened, sighing coals. A kettle gives an incongruous hoot.

'Enzo.'

'*Monsignore.*'

'Ready?'

'Sure thing.'

'Know your stuff?'

'Back to front.'

'You look anxious.'

He drags on a cigarette, eyes widening. 'I'm not.'

'You should be.'

He shrugs. 'Then I am.'

'Did you tell anyone?'

'No.'

'Your wife?'

'Are you nuts?

'So where does she think you are?'

'Drinking with the boys, playing cards.'

'She doesn't mind?'

'I didn't ask her.'

'Enzo—'

'When I need advice on the Immaculate Conception, I'll ring your doorbell, *Monsignore*. On my girl, you leave it to me, good idea?'

Derry utters a chuckle, cups his hands, lights a Woodbine, with a click of his chin expels smoke rings. Some trick of the breeze brings the gurgle of running water into the cavern and the candle flames gutter, casting lambent purple light over the crevices. Angelucci's wearing a look that even his friends don't like to see, a sharply defiant smile that could change at any moment.

'You look worried, *Monsignore*. For a guy with God on his side. What's rattling your cage over there? You having doubts?'

'Tell the itinerary, Enzo. Don't pause.'

With heavy, pantomimed patience, Angelucci shuts his eyes, raises his face to the dripping roof, begins intoning the route as though a litany, his drawl studiously colourless, rote-learned, unexcited. Counting off the street names and back alleys on his fingers, as though if he ran out of fingers he'd run out of alleyways, now staring at the icon of half-reclined Jane Russell as though the list is being addressed to her as a homage. The circuit is so detailed, it takes four minutes to recite. He never falters or stammers. It's perfect.

'Then home.' He grins defiantly. 'To the wife.'

'Via Orsini is blocked,' Derry counters. 'What's your alternative? Quick.'

'So I take Farnese, then left. Nothing simpler.'

'The Jerries have barricaded the Ponte Cavour.'

'They'd never do that.'

'Say they do.'

'I take the quay. Figure it out. What's this, a competition?'

'That won't work.'

'Madonna mia, *I'm a Roman*, I know *my own city*. Give me a chance to damn well *breathe* here, why can't you? Hand to Jesus Christ Almighty, you two are worse than the Gestapo. The way you *look* at me, *Monsignore*. Calm down.'

'Three hours from now, I'm Hauptmann walking into you on Lungotevere Michelangelo. Show me your card. State your name.'

'We've been over this a hundred *times*, Derry, what's the matter, you deaf?'

'State your name this minute, Enzo. Or the Rendimento is off.'

'Francesco Lynch.'

'That's it?'

'That's what?'

'I'm Paul Hauptmann, you ignorant bastard, your life and the lives of your comrades are in my hands. You address me as sir or I'll take three days to bleed you to death.'

'Lynch, *sir*. Francesco.'

'Occupation?'

'Technical Operative, sir, Vatican Radio, sir.'

'The man on this identity card is older than you.'

'*Con rispetto*, that is me, sir.'

'I don't think so.'

'Yes, it is.'

'What keeps you looking so young?'

'Your wife riding my face.'

'Enzo—'

'I've grown out my beard, sir, since that photograph was taken. People say it makes me look younger.'

'That seems strange.'

'Strange that I look younger, sir? Or that I grew out my beard, sir?'

'Both.'

'Razor blades are hard to come by since rationing, as sir knows.'

'Date of birth?'

'Seventh December '22.'

'Where?'

'Bologna, sir.'

'I know Bologna well, I was stationed there for a time. What street?'

'Milazzo.'

'There is no Via Milazzo in Bologna,' the Monsignor says. 'You are lying to us. Why?'

'With respect, sir, there is, it's off Via dei Mille.'

'Current address?'

'My apartment block was destroyed in an air raid, so I'm living in a storage room at the radio station, until I get back on my feet. Sir will see a telephone number there for my manager, Father Rainaldi. He's well connected in the Party.'

'Married?'

'Sir, yes.'

'Your wife also lives in this storage room, as you call it?'

'Sir, she went back to her parents.'

'I have heard your wife is a whore,' Derry says. 'How much does she charge for an hour?'

'Sir's joke is amusing, sir. Thank you.'

'I daresay she'd like a proper German who could satisfy her, not a puffed-up Italian queer.'

'I daresay you're right, sir. Who wouldn't?'

'Where is Vatican Radio located in relation to St Peter's Cathedral?'

'St Peter's is not a cathedral, but a basilica, sir. The radio station is a five-minute walk from there. In the Vatican gardens.'

'Your citizenship?'

'Vatican City passport, sir. I am legally a neutral.'

'Why are you breaking curfew? You are unaware of the rules? *Stand up straight when you are addressed by an officer of the Reich, you Italian son-of-a-bitch.*'

'With respect, sir, there is an exemption under article nine, "technological necessity". We have an equipment failure at the station and it is my responsibility to get it fixed.'

'At two in the morning? Do you think me a fool?'

'All I need is a metre of electrical cable, sir, and a length of copper wiring. I can find them on any construction site or in a builders' yard, sir. The matter is urgent.'

'Surely the construction sites and builders' yards are locked up for Christmas.'

'Perhaps not all, sir, it is my duty to look.'

'How is it so urgent that you presume to ignore the curfew?'

'We at the radio station will broadcast the Christmas message of the Holy Father at noon tomorrow, as I'm sure sir is aware. The Duce mentioned the fact in his article in Wednesday morning's *Regime Fascista*, as sir will have seen. There will be a worldwide audience of forty million listeners. It would be a mortifying embarrassment to Italy and the Duce were the broadcast to be cancelled.'

'I glanced through the *Regime Fascista* on Wednesday and there was no such article.'

'Sir, a copy of it is here in my pocket. Should sir wish to see it?'

From his jacket Angelucci produces the scissored-out sheet of newsprint, handing it across with the inscrutability of the poker player presenting a royal flush.

'Think that's clever, Enzo?'

'Who are you now, sir? Hauptmann or yourself?'

'Hauptmann would have put a bullet in your guts the moment you reached for your jacket, Thickhead. Stick to the script. *Don't improvise.*'

'I knew you'd say that. Turn over the paper.'

Scrawled on the back, in Angelucci's handwriting: 'GIVE ME MY CHANCE.'

'It's the smart lads get people killed, Enzo. I told you that before.'

'Then you don't need to worry, *Monsignore.*'

'Sam, what do you reckon?'

'Above my paygrade, Padre. Your decision.'

'What's your instinct as lead mission-runner? Is he ready?'

'We've gone through it two dozen times. I say put him in.'

'Cargo here, is it?'

'Last consignment arrived this afternoon. I sent it up top as agreed. Francesco, tell the holy gentleman where you'll find it.'

'In the fourteenth nook along, in the cloakroom near the exit door of the Musei, a postman's sack, canvas, the notes are wrapped in stacks of five thousand each, I could recite this whole thing *in my sleep.*'

'Thirty thousand American dollars,' Derry says. 'Believe me, Padre, I had time to count them. He collects the remaining fifty along the way.'

'My feeling is to postpone, Sam. It feels ludicrously risky.'

'It's not ideal,' Derry concedes. 'But Jerry might storm the Vatican any day, any hour. Then it's curtains to our little Glee Club and we're probably dead. With every escaped prisoner in Rome.'

'We *can't* postpone,' Angelucci says. 'Let's stick to the plan.'

'A plan should never be stuck to just because it's a plan,' Derry says. 'That's the Catholic in you talking.'

'Go to hell.'

Something stirs in the shadows. The three men snap silent, Derry's hand goes to his inside holster, pulls out his Webley.

A starling, lost, butts its way through the crypt, trilling in panic, and enters a grating.

Derry lights a Woodbine on the one he's already smoking, the glow illuminating the isobars of his face, the scars and broken teeth he received from his captors in Camp 21. On the train, they threatened to give him a death that would turn his children's hair white when they heard of it. Not that anyone would hear of it, the chief torturer assured him. 'What's left of you will be poured down a sink.'

Angelucci regards him. Water gurgles on rock.

'I'll go with him,' Derry says. 'Down a couple of painkillers.'

'Sam, you can barely walk. That's the worst idea of all.'

'Why?'

'If one of you got lifted by the Gestapo, he might just about stand a chance of not breaking. Not two.'

'We'd be halving their chances.'

'We'd be doubling them.'

'I'm granite,' says Angelucci quietly. 'I despise these whores' bastards. The chisel to crack me has never been made. If you think I'll let these nobodies catch me, in my own city, you know nothing. They're scum. They're zero. I'll go through their locks. Like smoke.'

'Take this,' says Derry, offering his pistol.

'I won't need that peashooter.'

'You might.'

Angelucci shakes his head.

'*Buona fortuna*, Enzo,' says the Englishman. 'Whatever else happens.'

'My name isn't Enzo. I'm Francesco Lynch.' He stares. 'Thought you'd catch me out, *inglese*? Try harder.'

'Good luck, Francesco Lynch. Hope to see you tomorrow.'

'Not if I see you first. *Andiamo*.'

18

THE VOICE OF ENZO ANGELUCCI
8th November 1962
From transcript of BBC research interview, tape 3,
conducted Bensonhurst, New York City

That night, I'm in condition.

Best shape of my life.

I been training two months, flat out.

In the apartment block, we got a stairwell right outside our front door, I hung a twenty-metre knotted rope from the eighth storey, down into the lobby. Seventeen seconds, whole climb. My neighbour Mike Festa used to time me, friend of my old man. By Christmas week, I could do it in eleven.

Squats. Sit-ups. Lost four kilos. Got strong. If my time slipped? I wouldn't be intimate with my wife for three nights. We were young. That time ain't slipping.

Ran barefoot up the staircase without waking a soul. I could run up them steps like a *bat* wouldn't hear. Guy name Crivella lived on the block, good long jumper, this guy. Starts giving me lessons, chalking out lengths right there on the street. He don't know it's the distance between two rooftops.

Fast? I could catch a fly between my fingertips, not kill it.

This means everything to me, the chance I might get my shot.

I can stand forty minutes holding two saucepans of water parallel to the floor. Think that's easy? Go ahead. Try five.

We say *arrivederci* to Derry. It's quarter to eleven, something. I can see he don't got full confidence, wishes he's running the Rendimento himself. But what's he going to do? No choice. Got a hole in his belly the size of a sundial, and a head full of black-market morphine.

Heart whomping against my ribcage as the Monsignor and me climbs into the tunnel. He's going like a train, you want to see this guy move, in front, and he's urging me all the time, hissing over his shoulder, 'faster, Enzo, faster, *Più veloce, andiamo'* and we come to this stretch where we got to crawl along through a grid of old sewer pipes, like snakes. I'm thinking of my wife, picturing her at home with the baby. The Gestapo don't kill me? She will.

Here and there, they got them guide-ropes, like below deck on a ship. But other places, nothing. Just the darkness. How in hell he knows where he's heading, I got no faintest idea. Like a mole, this guy. Like a sandhog. Guess he'd studied it all out, saw the map in his mind. Him and Derry knew the necropolis every which way and then backwards. Like you'd know your own reflection. Like they *created* that damn warren.

Before long I see an elevator shaft, old-fashioned cagework, black. We go in and climb up the bars one storey. Now we're in some type of basement, wooden boxes and crates. Electric light bulbs in muzzles. Is that the right word?

Fire Exit signs on the walls, dust-buckets, janitors' carts. Like an industrial type of feeling in the way it's been painted, this green-blue porridge-gloss everywhere, and fire extinguishers and fire buckets. The place smells of cats' piss and lonely old men. An axe in a glass case on the pillar.

I always thought it would be like I'm Sugar Ray walking into Madison Square Garden. Name in silver on my back, tricolour on my gloves, double-shuffling down the tunnel, punching air. The crowds, the flashbulbs, the cheers, the applause, here comes the hero. Stupid fool. There wasn't no flash-bulbs, there wasn't no ring girls. No one's clapping my shoulders, massaging me with towels. Only second I got in my corner is the *Monsignore*. I'm scared. It ain't no night at the Garden.

He hands me an envelope and I ask him to bless me. Communist as I was. Who cares? There's free insurance going? Brother, I'll take it.

I thought it would make him feel better, if you want to know the truth. So he says the stuff in Latin and does whatever he does. I don't feel no different. But that ain't the point. Someone wants to give you something, accept it, let them give. Sometimes that's all they got.

What he's giving, it's his conscience, he wants to feel he done his best. That's the difference between us and the animals, you want to do more than the least you can get away with.

Says, 'Enzo, stay where you are for *exactly* twenty minutes. Then, open that envelope. Couple of last-minute instructions. And be brave.'

He gives me this big bear hug. And I hug him back. Sure.

Because I loved the guy to pieces. Though he'd drive you batshit nuts.

In a Dick Powell movie I seen one time, this cop says about the gangster's wife, 'She'd make a Bishop kick a hole through a stained-glass window.' Guy wrote that must have met the *Monsignore*.

After he's gone, I stay where I am for ten minutes, fifteen, like he told me. You never saw time go so slow. There's this clock on the basement wall – I can still see it, clear as day. Man, the second hand on that clock is moving like it's glued.

I slide over to look at the fire-axe in the glass case on the wall. Thinking, maybe I'll take it, break the glass, could be useful. They got words stamped on the shaft, so now at least I know where I am. 'Property of the Musei Vaticani'. So I'm under the Museum, right next door to the Basilica. All kinds of crazy things, I'm thinking about, in a tumble, up and down. My parents, my babies. Of course my wife. *Her* parents. They ain't never liked me none. Feeling's mutual.

And I'm thinking, could you take that axe and smash a human being in the face? Angelucci, or Francesco, whatever in hell you're called, could you murder a fellow creature, even a Nazi, with a hatchet? Tough guy, you could? Who you kidding? One time your grandmother told you, wring the neck of that chicken. Remember the shake in your fingers? What in hell do you think you're doing, about to run a Rendimento like this? You couldn't run water. You're weak. This Hauptmann, he catches you? He got ways of making you die take a long, slow time. You'll beg to be dead. He won't let you till he's done. Empty you out like a suitcase.

What I do, I'm scared, so I picture the whole world. It's a thing my old man used to do when he had worries. Starting out right here in Rome, then up to the north, then all around Europe, Norway, England, then up to the Arctic, then over to Canada. Through the States, Chicago, the Great Lakes you seen on the globe in school, across the oceans, then Australia, China, Burma, huge seas full of islands, all these other places I'll never see and the people there won't see me neither. And, who cares? You got people live in igloos, tepees, caves, mansions in Los Angeles, mud huts on islands. They ain't thinking about you, *stronzo*, you ain't thinking about them. They all got their problems, you got yours. They fight, they fool around, they figure it out. I'm saying, Angelucci, you ain't nothing, you're a speck on the ass of the world, you're zilch. And in some ways, you know? That's fine. The world been here a long time, got no plan to go nowhere, *vaffanculo* to the Nazis, so they catch you and kill you. At least you died fighting. Let's go.

Ring the bell. Round One, come out swinging, drop your jaw.

See, I'm young and dumb, too. Wanted in. Be the tough guy. Made it to nineteen and a half minutes before I opened that envelope. There it was, in his writing. Man, I'll never forget it.

I cried. Like a baby. Guy broke my heart in ten pieces.

'Enzo, you're a hero. But you're not ready. Another time.

Go home a different way.

Respects,

GOLF'

19

Christmas Eve 1943
11 p.m.
The Rendimento

In monk's cowl, he opens the air hatch, admits himself to the vast, cold, resonant silence, screws closed the grille behind him.

Ninety metres away, on a pillar near the steps to the altar, the scarlet lamp glows in its high, silver bowl.

His torch beam illuminates smoke-grey marble sconces as he crosses the Basilica, hurries along the nave. Past the rosewood murk of side chapels, the confession boxes and stacked collection plates, the squat, iron tables of extinguished candles.

Past the wild eyes of martyrs, the crossed hands of virgins. Raised swords, crushed snakes, burning pyres. A hundred graves are stared down on by the ceiling-high organ, its flues whisperingly hissing at his trespass. Candle stands and candle racks throw shadow as he goes. The marble-stern Madonna cradling her broken son.

Over flagstones worn smooth by pilgrims' sandals. Tombstones whose names have long been ground away. Moonlight glows the indigoes and ochres of stained glass, the purples, the fiery gold of the pulpit. So quiet that he can hear the swish of the cowl. Ghosts look down on the beforelife.

An affront to some immensity to be the only creature drawing breath in a fortress the size of a stadium. Long benches have been placed for High Mass tomorrow; the tall, black cross, the long, empty benches, the glaring, pointing Pharisees, the nailed-through hands. Something about the candlesticks and the frescoed Roman spears gives the aura of an execution chamber.

Wind squalls outside. Mammoth organ pipes groan. Pages of ten thousand prayer books riffle on their pews. He sees himself as from above, a grain of sand in a Colosseum, Angelucci's insulted rage, Derry pacing and smoking in the depths, the Contessa at silent prayer. Delia Kiernan drinking. Marianna typing words. D'Arcy Osborne and May saying nothing.

Through the linger of incense and candlewax, the colder smell of rain, like a secret refusing avoidance. He genuflects before the red lamp, hurriedly, shivering, now making a way up the steps and into the shadows of the sacristy, where heavy silken vestments draped from railings dangle in a draught and the sherryish odour of altar wine thickens the air. Dark sideboards return the moonlight. An alarm clock ticks.

The tabernacle's studded doors. A medieval hassock. Two wardrobes like upended coffins.

Opening the first, he finds nothing but an accusation of chattering clothes-hangers, in the second the working man's grey suit, homburg and overcoat. Quickly he changes garb. In the fourth Bible down, on the eleventh shelf, near the monstrance, a key is hidden, which he retrieves and uses, opening the door to the stairwell.

At the top of the stairwell, the gate to the Sistine Chapel is bolted; from the breast pocket of the jacket he takes a copied wooden key for the padlock. The key is long and gaunt and must be turned with great care or it will snap. 'Imagine it is made of water,' the lockpick told May.

He prays as the key turns, feels the action's heavy click; hurries into the vestry of the chapel. Above him in the darkness, the Creation of Man, the fingertip of God outstretched to awakening Adam. Hell behind the altar, reddened tridents, flayed pelts, the torture house shadowed by age and night.

Two kilometres above that ceiling, the heavy bombers droning. He pauses, uncertain, listening.

Luftwaffe returning to base? RAF? The Americans?

The drone brings his room to mind, the coil of rope on the pillow, the arc lamp gridding the shutters. But vital to hurry, the plan must be followed. The security guards' round will bring them through the Basilica in seven minutes. Then will come the octet of silent, elderly monks whose duty is to prepare the altar for Christmas Mass.

He takes the staircase that leads into the Musei Vaticani, the long, narrow corridors, through the Sala di Mappa, charts of all the oceans and known lands of the world, cartouches, sea monsters, legends, mottoes, then he's moving through the dust of the Sala Rotonda, by manuscripts in glass cases, rubied reliquaries, chalices.

Roped-off masterpieces, 'FORBIDDEN TO TOUCH' signs. A tapestry in which Christ's eyes follow him along the passageway. Alcoves of crewel and lace.

Past the nook where it is said Michelangelo lived seven years, past twisting marble torsos, castrated Grecian huntsmen, armless naked goddesses, lapis lazuli urns the size of tramcars, a swan raping the Spartan queen.

His meek torch flickers, threatening to die. Switching off, he goes by the moonlight that pearls the long windows from the fairyland of the Vatican gardens.

Men speaking.

The murmur and low laughter of the security guards on their rounds, and he slides behind an alabaster pillar as they pass. Two minutes have been wasted. He opts for a shortcut.

Through the side door, into the boudoir of the old Papal apartments and out into the ceremonial corridor. Approaching slowly, heads down, hands in their cowl sleeves, the octet of blindfolded, barefoot monks, before them, three candlelit nuns, chanting an Ave Maria, and an Abbess carrying a plaster Christ-child half her own height.

Stepping backwards into the darkness, he waits.

Et benedictus fructus ventris
Ventris tuae, Jesus . . .
Ora pro nobis
Ora pro nobis . . .

Hurrying through the Museo Gregoriano Egizio. Past mummies and death masks of dog-headed pharaohs. Nobodaddies, ibises, a leering, bald sphinx, jagged panels of cracked hieroglyphics. Into the marble entrance hall, past the ticket booths and coat shelves. Entering the women's public lavatories, he checks each stall before opening the mop room at the back.

Brooms in metal buckets.

Overalls hung on hooks.

The words '*Uscita di Emergenza*' in fluorescent green on a door.

Which he pushes.

The door clicks open.

Night tries to come in, cold and foreign.

Taking a matchstick from the box in his pocket he places it in such a way that the dead-weighted door will remain infinitesimally ajar. Steps out into the street.

But the money!

Hastens back through the lavatories, gapes for the alcove Derry mentioned. Again, he hears the security guards talking, again he retreats, into a long, narrow anteroom that has no windows.

Through the darkness come strange sounds – gasping, a moaning. A young woman, dress opened, leaning back against a sarcophagus, a security guard kneeling before her, their urgings and whisperings, her fingers in his hair as she shakes.

What shocks him is not the sight alone, but the word they are passing to one another.

Sì.

Sì

Dio.

Sì.

Hurrying from the anteroom to the lobby.

Dazed, among the shelves where pilgrims stow jackets and hats, he sees the folded canvas sack.

Minutes later, the moment of maximum danger returns, for there is no way of seeing outside to the street, no means of knowing what awaits.

A patrolman. A Nazi. A rainstorm of bullets.

He steps through the door.

The night smells bitter.

A tram's bell clangs.

Sparrows mimic a machine.

From somewhere in the middle distance, the bawling of youths.

A rat scuttles out from the foot of a municipal tree trunk and into a broken manhole beneath a house-sized mural of the Duce.

The street falls silent, as though obeying a command.

Weak legs carry him across the Via dei Bastioni di Michelangelo. He enters a butcher's doorway, tries to calm. Counting backwards lowers the heart rate, Derry once told him.

Backwards from a hundred, blinking hard, he counts. Through the windows, he sees the aprons, the hooks and glinting cleavers, the massy bronze hulk of the till. On a blackboard at the back of the shop, on which the butcher chalks his prices, someone has scrawled a lewd cartoon.

The couple in the Museo shimmer and writhe, their trembling, the fire of that *sì*.

A street-cleaning truck trundles past, spraying hoses over the kerb, the stink of disinfectant assaulting his eyes and throat, raising his gorge, and he swallows, retches, coughs into his gloves, hoping the men in the truck haven't heard him above the cacophonous engine.

It slows to a shaking stop, black windows rolling open, and it shudders as though digesting the rubbish in the back, crimson winkers in the mirrors behind the butcher's counter. The daubed names of meats, a statue of the Infant Jesus of Prague.

The black-masked driver climbs down from the cab, his apprentice, in balaclava, from the footplate at the rear. They swish at the pavestones with long, filthy brooms, the older man whistling a folk song, the other muttering blasphemies. Dabbing at the telegraph poles with a rag on a stick, kneeling to scrape gum from a grating. The truck's engine grumbles. Scarlet lamps click. An old garbageman sings of the sea:

> *Andiamo a vedere la spiaggia*
> *mentre splende la luna piena*

He watches as the dustmen edge nearer to his doorway. Now so close he can hear their banter.

People are animals. Look at this filth. Mother of Christ, the stench off this trashcan is worse than your breath. Shut your beak and get mopping, you donkey.

Above the butcher's, on the third floor of the apartment block, a window is tugged open and a woman caterwauls down at the disruptors.

'*Deficienti*, it's Christmas Eve, must you make so much racket, go home to your slum and leave good people in peace.'

The older dustman, disguising his hurt as amusement, shouts back.

'Why don't you have a husband? Oh, I think I got the answer. I'm doing you a service, lady. Shut your mouth.'

Soon his decrial becomes a performance intended for the entertainment of his trainee. *Get your backside to Mass tomorrow, missus, and pray for a new face. The one you got there would crack a bell.* He enjoys this self-awarded role, the Man Who Speaks his Mind. But after a burble of dutiful laughter, the lad isn't interested. On the pavement, he's found a broken cigarette, pulls askew his balaclava, lights up with a Zippo, smokes hard, deep and long, stares up at the moon, crushes out the butt, back to work.

Sweeping lazily, steadily, outside the trattoria, the grocer's, the tobacconist's that had its windows smashed because the proprietor was a Jew, outside the hardware store where sweepstake tickets are sold beneath the counter, then the bar, the boarded-up travel agency, the office of American Express. Steadily, lazily, lazily, steadily, the steadiness feeding the laziness. He pauses with the broom, as a crooner into his microphone, whispers a phrase from a Hollywood love song, clawing at the air.

Sinatra of the sidewalk, star of a mind's-eye Manhattan. Lazily towards the butcher's doorway, lazily, steadily, a drummer using brushes, doobie-dooing, la-la-la-ing, now spitting on the pavement he's just pretended to sweep. Closer every second, until he has entered the doorway.

Cold, curious eyes through the holes in the mask.

Unblinking.

Expressionless.

Two search-lamps.

A century passes.

'Antonello,' yells the youth.

'What's happening?' the old garbageman calls.

'Nothing,' shouts the younger, gaze not leaving the man in the doorway. 'For God's sake, let's get on. We've wasted enough time here already.'

'Lazy bastards, you kids. If there was work in the bed, you'd sleep on the floor.'

'We need to get back to the depot.'

He turns, leaves the doorway, cricket-bats a pebble across the street with his broom, climbs up into the cab and waits for his galumphing captain to join him, which he does in a fanfare of valedictory denunciations of the woman in the apartment above.

'*Puttana*,' he yells.

'*Cornuto*,' she shouts down.

'Get yourself a husband. *Shut your mouth.*'

The truck judders awake with a storm of racking coughs. For badness the driver tugs hard on the claxon as they inch away. He doesn't know there's a third rider on board, a man on the rear footplate, holding fast to the handgrips, vibration through his torso, face a concealment of dirt.

The reek of fetid rubbish Sometimes the rider half-turns, gulps the night. Past churches and empty piazzas, by Swastika banners and machine-gun posts.

At the roadblock, the truck is waved through, the German sentries chuckling at the stink. Pinching their noses, miming vomiting. Middle-aged men, the weird excitability in their eyes. Six of the seven will die in March, blown to pieces by a Partisan bomb in the Via Rasella. The seventh will lose his hearing and sight.

Past palaces, monasteries, a closed-down nightclub. Fountains that have sparkled for three thousand years. Past a nunnery from which four hundred eyes are watching. Down a laneway off Via Segundo.

A left turn into a barbed-wired, filthy, gull-assailed yard where a dozen similar trucks are parked in an unruly line, the green-blue stench almost visible. The two dustmen alight, pull their sodden mops and buckets from the cab, trudge towards the corrugated-iron hut near the crooked back gates.

The yard falls silent.

Pulling up his coat collar, he goes.

Through the reeking fetor, the zizz of a million flies, along a passageway to Via Agazzari.

Again, the moan of bombers, heading out or returning.

He crosses the street, turns onto a tiny laneway behind Via Alessandri, through the bullet-strewn yard of a derelict hotel. Up the crumbling wooden steps, through the devastated kitchens, their sinks, taps and refrigerators crowbarred out by looters, the pantry used as a latrine by people of the street, past weird, scarlet lichens sprouting on scorched tiles, through the vandalised circular lobby and the shattered, reeking ballroom, a burned-out double bass and smashed chandeliers, glass tables upended, stacks of rotting velvet chairs, past a line of bedroom doorways, paint shorn by the fire, doors with withered spats and melted stilettoes still outside for the bootblack, along a corridor where larks have nested and some predator has clawed tatters of mouldering silk off the wainscots, emerges down the shuddering fire-escape onto Via Vittoria Aleotti.

A black Mercedes passes.

Then an empty tram.

Fifty metres south before squeezing through the gap between two tenements, then across the Z-shaped patch of filthy wasteland behind them, where old bicycles and lengths of chain and beer kegs and pram wheels are strewn. Spools of rancid wiring, sheaves of radiator pipe, the skeleton of a Fiat cannibalised for parts. A tramp asleep in a hammock between cadaverous trees.

Back lanes and alleyways, across a vacant lot.

Wind gusts up as he makes for the passageway called Vicolo Cozzolani, so narrow that it appears on no maps. Crossing now by the entrance to the Cavalry Academy, slowing his pace as he approaches every streetlamp, quickening as he passes, recollecting Derry's words after a Rendimento that had to be aborted. *Light is the enemy, it must always be avoided. Every time you see your shadow, you're in trouble.*

Now, as he hurries, the shadow starts whispering.

You're condemned by your own vanity. What did you think you were at, playing God? Derry's a hero; you're a pretender, a clown. When they catch you, as they will, that stupid collar won't save you. Every one of those prisoners will be tortured to death. So will you. As an offering to your pride.

Via Stolto. Via Tonto. Via Balordo. Via Morte.

You're stumbling down Death Street. You blindman.

The Contessa had an idea but you shot it from the skies. Didn't like someone bringing something useful to the table? Beggars to be paid ten lire for every street bulb smashed, that way a completely dark route across the city could be cut. But Monsignor didn't listen. Monsignor knows best. Monsignor's the conductor. Bow your heads.

The shadow-voice flames, refusing to let him alone. He turns towards the gust from the river.

A deadly stretch now, the long, broad thoroughfare. Elegant couturiers, jewellers, shirtmakers, fine hotels. A German machine-gun turret on high black stilts at the northerly junction sixty metres away. He can see the three soldiers in the watchtower.

Silhouettes against the moon.

Night-binoculars glinting.

Around the corner, onto a side street of high-bourgeois apartment blocks. Gleaming motorcars beneath elms. Rampant stone lions above mullions.

Brass panels of doorbells shining. On a manhole cover, the letters 'SPQR'.

A baby is yawling but quietens as he passes.

The mewl of cold cats, the swishing of restless leaves. Something boils in his stomach. He looks at his watch. One-seventeen. Hurry on.

In Kerry, they've the three miles from the chapel walked by now, will be coming in from Midnight Mass. Frost on sacks of caustic by the half-door to the stable. Your mother making tea in the aluminium pot got from Limerick. The maple smell of the lake by the water fields in wintertime. A glaze of frost on the yew berries but your father's warning that they're poisonous.

See the pictures? Stop walking. Give in.

You remember it, don't you, that night you couldn't sleep and you stole down for the sup of milk.

Heads bowed, murmured words, Daddy and Mam praying. The votive lamp before the picture of the Sacred Heart making the wireless dials glow red. Bread had been baked; the air over the kneading-board was like gauze. The kitchen smelt floury like a cakeshop.

The sweetness of that milk, your father's mild admonishment, the low of the calves made nervous by starlight. Your mother fetching milk to the pair of you.

You and Daddy out the back yard, him smoking a Players, Mammy accepting the odd puff like a girl outside a dance hall. He was tracing you the stories of the stars, the Hunter, the Plough. Beards of cloud and they rolling past the gleaming coin of the moon. Birdsong and horses nickering. The three of you there a good hour, so you thought, but Mam's watch said only ten minutes. In the India-blue darkness, the silky-blue blackness, and you marvelling at the whistle of a pair of stubborn blackbirds that refused to return to the nest.

The Christmas you turned fourteen.

'You'll have lovely nights like this with your own children, please God,' Daddy said. You didn't want to tell him, but already you felt you'd be a priest. There wouldn't be children or wife or home. It frightened you, didn't it? You couldn't tell anyone.

In the same kitchen now. Two old people praying.

Our son, a priest in the Vatican.
Stop this madness.
Turn around.
Go home.
Grow up.
It can yet be yours again, that night of the milk.
I'm your shadow.
You'll never lose me.
Stop walking.

20

THE VOICE OF JOHN MAY
20th September 1963
From transcript of BBC research interview, conducted Coldharbour,
Poplar, East London

There's an exam you need to pass if you want to be a London cabbie. Sorts the sheep from the goats. Called 'The Knowledge'.

Takes three years of graft and practice. Moves in like a lodger. You're *dreaming* the streets, the railway stations, the terraces. Five hundred hotels in London, you've got to know the address of every one of them. Cinemas, football grounds, theatres. Whole lot. Twenty thousand streets in London. Ain't easy.

Your missus is demented because you've roped her in and all. You've told her, ask me surprise questions. Catch me out.

Then the morning comes around when you show what you're made of. You're washed, scrubbed, combed, polished, best bib and tucker. Game on.

You're sitting there in front of the examiner and he's got a map of London the size of a tabletop. Every laneway, back street, alley, crescent, streets you ain't never seen, where no one's ever going. Streets that don't bleeding *exist*. It's formal, no chit-chat, he's an experienced, senior cabbie, a professional. He's asked you what's the route from Piccadilly Circus to Brickfields Terrace in Maida Vale. Nice, simple start. Draws you in.

You tell him left, then right, then round by the park, then right, then left, then north, then west, then straight along Whatever You're Having Yourself — only you can't go by Queensway being it's one-way at the moment — so you turn down Westbourne Gardens and you're there.

You ain't got no map yourself but the one in your head. You do it from memory or you're stuffed. Fastest way from Rupert Street to Craven Hill Mews. Simple? Only, now he's throwing googlies. Watch out.

I'm at Royal Oak station, need to get to the tailor's in Duke Street, St James, then Caulfield Gardens, Earls Court, look lively, I'm picking up the wife, then Cropley Street, Shoreditch. In rush hour.

'The Knowledge', like I said. Sorts out your contenders.

That's the way the Padre knew Rome.

Avenues, alleyways, parks, tram routes. Near on a thousand churches. I swear he knew all of them. In Dublin – anywhere in Ireland – they give you directions by the pubs. 'Turn left at John Grogan's, take a right by the Palace.' The Padre was like that with the churches in Rome. 'Go straight at Santa Maria, cross the lane behind Sant'Ivo alla Sapienza.'

Don't ask me how he learned it. But he did. Had the nous. You didn't fanny about with Hughdini.

Also, a walker. Shanks's Pony, all that. Wasn't a cobblestone in Rome he didn't know. People *born* there would be stopping him in the Piazza to ask the best way from Trastevere to Prati. I used to tell him, 'If you wasn't a man of the cloth, you'd have made a pukka cabbie.' He'd be tickled. 'Maybe it ain't too late, John.'

When he was bored or couldn't sleep – this is what he told me -- he'd lie awake driving his taxi from Buckingham Palace down to Deptford and back. 'That usually does the trick.' We was fishing when he told me that, it was one day in the country, Sir Frank, the Contessa, the Padre and me. Miss de Vries and Delia come later. At Ostia, near the seaside. String quintet on the bandstand. Wurlitzer horses, a roundabout. Kiddies running around. Almost normal. Delia sang 'Danny Boy' and the girls all cried. The Monsignor sang 'Take Me Back to Blighty' in a terrible cockney accent. *Take me over there, Drop me anywhere, Put me on the train for London town.* I'm giving him stick. Calling him 'Aitch' for a laugh. He's calling me 'Johnjoe' like they do in Ireland. Happy day.

Funny, it was always London, not Rome, when he couldn't sleep. I think he found London a comfort, a mother. You'll get that with the Irish. They're free here.

Another thing, he was on the level. Down-to-earth bloke. And it don't show in photos but the Padre was tough. Like they say where I'm from, he had bottle. I was thinking before about Shackleton, the poor sods in the Antarctic, their whaleship was hulled with this Guyanese wood, greenheart, so hard you can't hammer a nail in it. That was the Padre. Proper greenheart. An old-fashioned, stand-up, don't-take-liberties sort. Dressed like it, too. Yes, he did. All the photos, he's in priest's clobber naturally enough, but a different story when he was off duty, in mufti. Camelhair coat and black trilby. All that. Shoes you could shave in. Sharp dresser. The moxie.

Short-back-and-sides once a fortnight, hot comb, touch of Brylcreem. Maltese I knew as a nipper done a seven-stretch in Pentonville for a bank job in Mayfair, when he's come out, he's like royalty, cock of the walk. The Padre had shades of same. A good front.

Seen him down Whitechapel, you'd say, that's a Face. And you wouldn't want to cross him, he'd have a razor up his cuff. Funny thing to say about a man of his profession but he walked like what the Italians call *il capo dei capi*, the godfather.

That's the way he'd come over, 'I ain't scared of bugger all.'

But that night, I'm telling you, he must have been scared. I don't like to think of it.

Can we stop?

———

Let the bridge be open, let the bridge be open, let the bridge be open, he prays.

The identity card was forged with skill and its photograph is real but that won't be enough. If he's stopped, there'll be questions.

Who is your father? In what city was he born? What is your brother's birthdate? Are you married? To whom? How is that spelled? What age is your mother? Which soccer team do you support? Who's their captain?

Every non-Italian in the Choir has been given an alias in case it's ever needed. Delia Kiernan's is Mary Lavelle, Sir D'Arcy's is Robert Melmoth. May becomes Kenneth Oliver, valet to a difficult Cardinal. ('It ain't far enough off the truth,' he says.) Marianna is Ann Brunner, an actress and dramatist, whom she says she prefers to herself.

In the mornings he and Derry ('John Atkinson', Vatican librarian) work an hour on the aliases alone. Fine-sanding their stories to smoothness takes detail. The date of the first Fascist rally I attended, the city, the friend I went with, the length of the Duce's speech. The number of bodyguards, the reasons why I joined the Party, the names of the businesses I've burned, their addresses.

169

One night at rehearsal, he made the Choristers imagine their aliases meeting in a room, told them to sing as their Others, in character. Each alias was then subjected to a public questioning from Derry in the meticulous briskness of his own. The Contessa left the rehearsal. There was a bitter, loud argument, 'We are not staging *an operetta*, Hugh, what time-wasting idiocy is this?'

'For God's sake, Jo, would you calm yourself, we've *work*.'

'Stop "Godding" me! You talk as though you *invented* God.'

Out spilled their exhaustion, the terror they carried, a closeness turned inside out.

'Must you always be the diva?'

'You know *nothing* about me, Hugh, you never have.'

'How can you speak in this manner to someone who cares for you?'

'Cares? How, *cares*? I am to be a puppet in your drama, robbed of even my name, my meaning, because you deem it better?'

'It's your name could get you *killed*. Don't you *see*?'

'Then *let it*.'

'What?'

'I am Giovanna Landini and I bear my husband's name.' Her quiet, cold words seemed to cut the dusty air. 'I will bear it until I die, come Nazi, thug or priest. The name I freely took, that is mine. *Do you hear me*?'

'There's someone ninety miles away can't hear you, woman, why don't you *shout a bit louder*.'

'People call you "Father", Hugh. You are *not* my father.'

'Thank God.'

'You will not dare to baptise me. Get it into your brain.'

'*At least I've a brain to get it into.*'

'Would you like the last word? You can have it, *Monsignor*. Do not tell me what I am, or who I am, ever again. *I* shall decide who I am.'

'I can see who you are, never fear.'

'Hugh.' This was Delia, gently. 'Let's ease down the gears. We're tired. There's no harm meant. Come on. Back to work. Jo, love, I've water in a flask out beyond. Dry your eyes, there's my girl. *Andiamo*.'

For an hour after the mutual apology and the continuing of rehearsal, the quarrel had remained between them, a stranger in the room. At midnight, they shook hands, then embraced, swallowing tears.

Let the bridge be open, let the bridge be open.

Turning right onto Piazza Corelli, he puts on his Other and feels it envelop him like a cloak.

Marco Mancuso, translator, Vatican secretariat, born Glasgow, Scotland, of Italian immigrant family, came to Milano '33, parents Gianluca (meaning 'gift of God') and Elisabetta. One brother, Giancarlo, deceased, two sisters, Catalina and Elena. No registered political affiliation but strong admirer of Fascism. Unmarried, former seminarian, left a month before ordination, brother-in-law a minor Party official in Brindisi. Manager of the Italy team in the 1934 World Cup was Pozzo; midfielder was Bertolini.

Illegally open, the last cafés are closing. From an upper room comes the blared bay of a mediocre tenor mangling '*E lucevan le stelle*', counterpointing the bayed blare of groaners asking him to stop. Two drunkards plod the footpath like men treading water. No licensed premises anywhere in Rome may be open after the curfew, but in Italy, as in most places, there are always exceptions. The manager is connected. The magnate brings his mistress. The bribe has been generous. We'll dynamite you if you refuse.

Crossing the tramlines, he falters, happens to raise his glance.

A woman in a window is watching.

The glow of her cigarette, reddening, fading.

She bites her thumb, a gesture of contempt, at someone in the *strada* behind him.

The unease is so sharp, it's like encountering a stench. When he glances over his shoulder, no one's there.

Wind billows, blowing folds of old newspaper across the Piazza like weird birds.

In the distance the Musei, the scowling dome of St Peter's.

A Stug truckles past, leaking oil.

Marco Mancuso walks on.

On the quay, facing into the slab of a growing storm, he tosses a Lucky Strike packet stuffed with hundred-dollar bills into a dustbin daubed with a treble clef – first drop-off accomplished, almost on time – as he passes the padlocked gates of an Augustinian chapterhouse where seven escaped paratroopers have been hiding out for a month.

Across the street, over the bakery, two Iowan rear-gunners and a B-26

Marauder pilot from New Orleans whose ulcerated wisdom tooth is giving him agony. Something will need to be done for him. Not tonight.

In the wine cellar beneath a trattoria on Via Geminiani, three; in the stock-loft above a shop selling priestly vestments and fine chalices, nine; behind a false partition in an art gallery on Via Bellini, one, in the coal bunker of a tobacconist's, two.

Seventeen in the pilgrims' dormitory of the Capuchin Monastery on Borgo Scarlatti; nine in the monks' quarters, four beneath the kitchens. Two in a tailor's back room amid the mannequins and spools, seven in a fruiterer's warehouse. Nine in the grounds of the Palazzo Leoncavallo, two in a mechanic's workshop behind Via Palestrina, three on a half-sunken old sightseeing boat moored on the Tiber. Fifteen in the three-bedroom apartment of a Maltese widow and her children, who every day go without food so to feed them.

Men disguised as friars, sleeping on granite shelves in belltowers. In bivouacs on rooftops, among the chimney stacks and pigeon lofts. Bayonet blades in their cassocks, or billhooks beneath pillows. Men with hidden pistols and one remaining bullet. Making garrottes from piano wire, shanks from chisels. Men dossing under bridges, on park benches, in sewer-shafts, on rusted trams, in burned-out ticket offices and ivy-swathed graveyards, on crashed buses in side streets. The army of the attics.

It feels to him as though every last one of them is parading behind him now, down Corso Paganini, roaring to be noticed.

A torch-flash in the highest window of an apartment block on the corner is answered from a rooftop several houses down the street. Three glints, four. Four glints, three.

Derry has sent urgent messages warning them to stop; this behaviour is endangering every escapee in Rome. But the men it's endangering never stop for long.

High windows flicking Morse messages over a deserted piazza, across the wide banks of the river, all night. If one Nazi clocks your whereabouts, a hundred of your comrades will die. A thousand could die. So could you.

A couple of nights, then, when the signalling fades. But soon it returns like the tide.

Injunctions to keep up the spirits. Obscene jokes. Requests for news. Sports results. Ribaldries. Mock insults.

How do they find each other? He hasn't an inkling. Some nights it's worse – 'Christ's sake,' John May sighs, 'it's like Times Square on New Year's Eve' – but every night you'll notice it if your eyes are halfway open, the shooting stars sent by the frightened.

It's the only thing he has ever seen to make Derry lose his temper. How strange to hear the Englishman curse. 'Don't the bastards realise what they're *doing*? Don't they *know*? Fucking *idiots*. They want shooting, the selfish pricks. Why bother?'

What he knows is that if you confiscated their flashlights, they would signal with matches. They'd set bonfires on the rooftops that protect them. He has come to accept it, wishes Derry would, too; opposing it is like countermanding gravity. A vow of silence, like most vows, is not workable all the time. He hurries on beneath the bantering beams.

A streetwalker is watching as he passes on Via Boito, through the shadow of broken bottle-ends on walls. Moving quickly, head down, as though that posture will take up less space, he looks, she will say later, 'like a man with a target on his back'.

Where are the Allies?

When will they come?

They're not coming, says his shadow. *You know it.*

Who do you think you're fooling? Your feeble, murdered God? Derry is at least a man, you're not even a footnote. Afraid to live life. Snivelling behind vows. Your fool's errand means nothing. Too late.

He reaches into an Ave Maria, blindly, afraid.

A foxhole *prayer, my favourite, go ahead, deluded fool. I'll say the words* with *you, they're mimicry, an idiot's cackle. Your gruntings mean nothing, they're* noise, they're bad music. *A chimp hurling shit at the bars of its cage.*

I was here long before you. I'll be here when you're gone.

Shapeshifter, they call me.

Changeling.

Turncoat.

I am not your shadow. You are mine.

His reflection passing the windows of a knife-grinder's premises. Spits of rain on the dust-smeared glass.

Left onto Via Martucci.

Blood in his stomach congeals.

The roadblock has been set up from pavement to pavement. The belch of a brazier spluttering into ashen, wintry gloom. A golden-sepia flicker across the sky-high brickwork and the flanks of an open-backed truck.

Smoke pulses from the exhaust. A Stug's engine grovelling.

He can see, in the lorry, a dozen cowed prisoners, cuffed wrists, hands up, lowered heads. A gnarled, chained Rottweiler snarling before its handler as the man lights a cigarette at the brazier. An order is screamed for the captives to kneel – *knien!* – but some don't understand or are too petrified to move, so the handler and his comrades truncheon them down and the dog lifts its leg to a tyre.

Too late to step into a doorway. If he fled?

No time.

A dark-featured welterweight with the blunt head of a bull shark sees him first and beckons coolly, in no hurry.

The dog tugs on its restraint, now turns its dripping maw, trying to gnaw through the rope-thick chain.

The trooper's breath reeks of rancid cheese, of old, stale coffee.

'Name?'

'Mancuso.'

'First name.'

'Marco.'

'Identity card?'

He presents it.

The trooper glances down through the fiery shadows at the photograph, muttering to himself in what must be some obscure dialect of German, now regarding the nightwalker assessingly and repeating the name 'Mancuso' as though doing so might weigh it on a scale. With a yelp he summons over a younger comrade, who examines the document. A long look is shared between them. They hold the card up to moonlight.

'You are aware there is a curfew,' the welterweight says.

'I have an exemption. As you see.'

'Where are you going?'

'To collect an item of medicine.'

'Excuse me?'

'Sir will have seen that Cardinal Hinsley of Westminster is on a private courtesy visit to the Vatican with the Papal Envoy to Nairobi and his sister and father. The Cardinal became ill this evening with suspected malaria. No physician was available but a well-wisher in the city has quinine. His Eminence's valet requested me to collect it.'

When lying, as Derry says, you have two options that might work. Keep it simple or make it complicated. Then stick to it.

'How long will you be out, Mancuso?'

'Two hours at most.'

'Make sure it's no more. Move along.'

'Who are those prisoners?'

'Curfew-breakers. Undesirables.'

'What will happen to them now?'

'A little sightseeing trip.'

'Where?'

'Somewhere that doesn't concern you. Get going.'

As he passes the rear of the truck, he hears the whispered word in Italian.

'*Salvami.*'

Nothing he can do.

If he pauses, all is lost.

'Save me.'

Stars glint.

He keeps walking.

Let the bridge be open, let the bridge be open, let the bridge be open, he prays.

21

THE VOICE OF SAM DERRY
27th September 1963
From transcript of BBC research interview,
conducted Newark-on-Trent, Nottinghamshire

Seven weeks beforehand, an informant had passed us the word, through Miss de Vries I think it was, that on the night of Christmas Eve, between midnight and two in the morning, certain strategic points around Rome would remain unguarded by Jerry or be only sporadically patrolled.

She was a typist at Nazi headquarters, the young woman I'm speaking of. She couldn't be certain fully, didn't overhear every word of the order Hauptmann gave, but over cigarettes in the courtyard one of the junior Gestapo officers seemed to confirm it. The important bridges would be roadblocked but not the Ponte Sant'Angelo.

This had formed part of our thinking.

An unbarricaded bridge can of course be a significant opportunity. It is also, in classical warfare, a trap.

Previous information from this young woman had sometimes proven unreliable. Sir D'Arcy had in fact wondered if she was a double dealer, a Fascist. I never liked trusting an informer I hadn't personally met but obviously it wasn't possible to waltz her into the Vatican for a chinwag over tea and it could have fatally imperilled her to meet anywhere else. All you had in the end was your instincts, I suppose.

I do remember the Padre insisting, 'She's a risk, Sam. A very real risk.'

I said, 'Who bloody isn't, when you think?'

'We can't trust her,' he repeated. Back and forth it went, like a slugfest. The disagreement in fact threatened to become quarrelsome, accusatory. In the end, time pressed, we agreed to the pull of a playing card. The Monsignor drew a three, I drew the Queen of Spades. The plan would be retooled in line with the young woman's information.

'And if the Tiber can't be crossed, Sam?'

'We abort.'

'That's that?'

'A gamble, I admit.'

'Much more than a gamble.'

'My lookout, I suppose. Since, my life on the line.'

'It isn't only yours.'

'No, I don't suppose it is.'

'She's not to be trusted.'

'We'll see.'

In the end, all you know for certain about an informer is one thing: they're an informer. It's like falling for a proven liar, don't be surprised that they lie. It's something they do well, they've had practice. And it's easier the next time to break what's left of their word. They know what it feels like and it isn't that bad. Leopard and spots. Old story.

So, there you have a bridge. And here, you have a story.

———

Quietly along Vicolo Sgambati.

Let the bridge be open.

Adrenaline boiling in his stomach as he steadies himself in the bus shelter, gathers, counts to five, turns the corner.

Ahead of him, the searchlights, the trio of armoured cars with their red-and-black swastikas. Magnified silhouettes of police horses on the far riverbank's wall.

The informer got it wrong. Or was lying.

Away to his right, the course of the Tiber takes a sudden, wrenching turn, and he can see that the Ponte Vittorio Emanuele II, too, is barricaded, by a Panzer, as is the Ponte Umberto a few hundred metres to his left.

Down the slick, crooked steps to the riverside path, the rank stench of damp and wet rotting moss. A line of bollards in the gurgling darkness, the stilted croak of ducks.

Could you swim it? A hundred metres? Two hundred? More?

Try, the shadow snickers. *I'd like to see you drown.*

In the seethe of black water before him, a nest of punts and chained rafts, bow-seats improvised from lengths of plank and sawn-apart fish crates. A trio of low-floored dinghies, clumping together in the wavelets.

The ropes, thick and wet, in his cold, ignorant fingers. The harder he twists, the harder they entangle. The old boats rock with mockery.

Now he sees, far to his right, two soldiers descend the staircase beneath the bridge, rifles shouldered, black helmet rims low. Behind him, between slabs of ancient embankment wall, a crevice the height and width of a man; he backs into it, waits.

The murmur of conversation as they approach.

He tries not to breathe.

They can't be more than twenty paces from him; he hears the word '*Huren-haus*', answered by a bark of spluttered, coughing laughter. A cigarette is lit; he can smell the match's sulphur. They come to a pause with their backs to him.

Begin to kiss.

Moving against each other, groping, pretending to moan, and they resume their patrol and an empty bus passes, above on the windswept quay.

Thirty metres away from him now, receding into darkness. He steps into a filthy dinghy, the nearest one, black, 'Santa Maria' painted on its prow by an amateur. It bobs in a sickening sway that makes him throw out his arms and flail.

Kneeling, he goes at the rope again; it refuses to loosen. From his pocket he pulls his torch, smashes the glass, starts sawing at the knot, but it's the thickness of an oak root, refuses to fray.

Down the path, the soldiers reappear, rifles shouldered, walking slowly. He lurches, sags forward, arms by his side, face an inch from the briny slops. A long two minutes later, the thunk of boots as they pass, and the clank of a buckle, and the scraping of a rifle as it grazes the riverside wall.

Peering, he sees them ascend the crooked, stone stairs to the bridge. How long before the next patrol?

A plash. Hard and cold. As though someone has flung a stone into the Tiber.

Again, comes a splush, then a volley of spatters. A pebble strikes the boat. Another lands behind him. The moon sails from behind a cupola.

Looking out through a knothole in the side of the smack, he sees a steady rain of pebbles being thrown from the bank.

Now, a battery-torch signal. Three dots and a dash. The opening notes of Beethoven's Fifth.

The password employed by members of the Choir at the door of the rehearsal room. Derry chose it because everyone knew it, the signal was unforgettable.

Again come the glimmers. Three shorts and a long. The sharp, yellow pin-prick through the murk across the bank, where a row of shacks or crumbling warehouses is too vague to be made out.

Kneeling up, he sees now, emerging from the shadow, the black prow of a skiff being rowed with firm, strong steadiness in his direction, the rower bent low, straining, back to him. An eerie skreeking grind as the rowlocks give and swivel. The skiff enters an eddy, turns in a sudden, wild circle. The rower pulls down a balaclava before continuing, oaring hard, coughing breathy grunts at the Tiber as it is fought and overcome.

A trick? A trap?

The shadow gives a chuckle.

Who put that three of diamonds in your hand? I hold all the cards.

He glances towards the bridge, where a *Panzerkampfwagen* is nuzzling into position.

'Padre,' hisses the voice from the boat. 'Look lively. Step aboard.'

A volley of mumbles as the figure rows closer.

'Top o' the morning, Aitch,' he whispers.

22

THE VOICE OF JOHN MAY
20th September 1963
From transcript of BBC research interview, conducted Coldharbour,
Poplar, East London

See, the Tiber ain't no river you want to go swimming in. You could develop film in the Tiber. But not swim in it.

I don't want to dwell on this particular episode. Had my sources, that's all. Move along.

Well, it ain't nothing mysterious, just a personal matter. Let's just say there was a certain young lady in Rome and we'll leave it at that.

She was a cashier in the bank where the Embassy had our accounts. They had to be in fake names, which she must have known well – the Escape Line account was Vincento Bianchi and Company – but she never asked no questions, just a firework display of a smile. That's how we met. No, I won't give her name. Rather not. I believe she's still alive.

Burn you down to the floor, that smile.

I'd say she was maybe thirty. Not that I've asked. Her husband was indisposed, being as he happened to be in a prison camp at the time. Needs must, as they say. War is war.

I wasn't no matinee idol to look at. Whereas she was a proper dinger. Like the actress Laura Nucci, with the brown eyes you could drown in. Lovely lady, she was. I like the Italian people. You know where you stand with them. Got a natural love of life. They don't mess about. They're exuberant.

So the afternoon of Christmas Eve, I've arranged to make my way over to see her, quiet like, and we'll have a discreet little celebration, is the plan. I've ways of getting about the city in the daytime. False card. Fake name. Don't matter. I've a bottle of bubbles, a nice box of chocs and the natural instincts of the season. Well, we've had a little dance, and we've had a little drink, and one thing's led to The Other. As it does.

Only afterwards, we're laying in bed and we're listening to a record, and she mentions she's heard the Teds are closing the bridge tonight.

'Teds' was what the Romans called the Jerries.

Chiedo scusa? Do what, love?

Barricading the bridge. She's had it off her mate, bird works down the hairdresser's dyeing wigs. Apparently, it's all over the quarter. So, I'm welcome to kip over with her, and we'll have a bowl of grub and play an Ella side she likes, once I've scarpered before the sister and the nasty brother-in-law and the army of nasty kids trundles over in the morning to fetch her off to church, then the mother's.

I've gone, are you certain?

About kipping over?

No, about the effing bridge.

Sì, sì, this bird down the hairdresser's heard it off her brother and her brother's heard it off Pierluigi and Pierluigi off Massimo. Ted is barricading that bridge tonight, sure as eggs.

Well, now it's on my mind, see. I've a fair inkling of the plan. After Derry got sick, it was obvious the runner would have to be Angelucci, who I liked. You didn't need to be no supernatural medium or nothing; it's plain as your face he's going to need to cross the river at some point and it's plain he ain't sprouted wings.

So what I done, I went down there, and waited, that's all. Wasn't expecting trouble. Just go down for a butcher's.

That quiet, you'd hear a mouse piss on cotton.

It's got darker and darker. Sky black as your boot. Ticker's doing the tun and I'm frozen to buggery. It's that cold, I can't even feel my fingers no more. I'm thinking of my hero Shackleton and the poor sods in the Antarctic. I've seen a snap of their ship, in a book Sir Frank was reading. Their ship in the ice. Stuck there. Break your heart. 'Beset', the chapter was called.

And I'm thinking of *la mia lei* a few streets away in the flat, in a nice big feather bed with more pillows than you ever seen. In the green silk pyjamas I've give her. Dear me. *Madonna mia.* Wouldn't mind getting beset over there.

We've had plans for the evening. Ain't going to be happening. I'm starving, too, nothing to eat since a bit of heated-up bucatini and spam at lunchtime, which I've had to pretend to like if I know what's good for me. So, the picture ain't good. Not at all.

I'm waiting and waiting.

Suddenly, what's this?

I've recognised the gait. Think I'm losing my reason. Christ on a bike. It's the Padre.

There he is, across the Tiber, prancing up and down on the walkway like a tit. And the Teds not a spit away on the bridge.

What's happened to Angelucci? Where we going now?

I fling over a few stones but he don't see me, the blind sod. Now what do I do? I can't shout. Giving it large with the torch but he ain't seen that either. Waving my arms. Leaping about. *Willing* him to clock me. I'm dancing the bleeding fandango the other side of the Tiber but he won't look my direction. Blind sod.

Now there's action up on the bridge, I've seen the lights moving. I've scarpered up the embankment behind me.

What do I see then? Pair of Jerries coming down the steps, that's all. His goose is bleeding cooked, it's curtains, *arrivederci*, but they've passed him and headed away, and he gets in a boat.

Don't be a tit, Aitch. The current's too strong.

Big bloke, the Padre, but he ain't got the strength for rowing. Where I'm from, you build your arms as a kid coming up. You don't win no fights with weak hands.

I've seen this little skiff there, ten yards down from me, and managed to get open the ropes. But now, there's no sodding oars.

So, what does Muggins do? I've rowed across the bleeding Tiber using the bench of the boat. True as you're sat there. What happened.

They was having problems with their tank, the turret wouldn't stop revolving. Snag with the gears. You get that with the Panzer, a lot of them had been in the desert, gummed up with sand. So, all eyes was on that, Jerries coming and going. And I've weaselled across the Tiber. Loaded up the Padre. Crossed him over.

He was shook something awful. But he insisted on going on. I asked him where he's headed but he won't give us no gen, 'need-to-know only', all that. He'd cut his hand on broken glass, I asked him if it was okay, he said he'd get a bandage later on the night 'from Lonnie' if he needed one. I didn't have a monkey's who that was, and in the Choir you didn't ask. He shouldn't have mentioned no name, it was a slip.

No, I didn't offer to go with him, I won't lie. I didn't. And he wouldn't have let me if I had. He must have thanked me a dozen times, then off he heads on his tod. He's insisted. I've begged him not to go, but he wasn't a bloke for persuading. And I've took myself back to the flat.

No, I didn't see it as no heroism. Nothing like that. Mate of yours is in trouble, you front up.

See, people had their different reasons for being in the Choir. Some reasons was religious – not being funny but you're going to get that in Rome – and some was whatever they was. Political. Patriotic. Bleeding-heart do-gooders. Me, I was none of the above.

I daresay some was Communist, others was Labour, some Tory. Sir Francis D'Arcy Godolphin Osborne? Ain't from the Old Kent Road. But I never ask your politics, they're all the bloody same in the close. To me, there ain't no reason people has to like each other's countries. Look at the Welsh. Don't even like their own. What's the first thing they done when they got to Australia? Call part of it 'New *South* Wales'.

Don't give a monkey's what church you go to, or don't go at all. Synagogue, Chapel, Methodist, what you fancy. As for me, I was in the Choir for one reason and one reason only.

Won't lie to you, darling. Fritz ain't my cup of tea.

We ain't supposed to say it but at my age you do.

Funny thing, I felt different way back as a youngster. After I got the jazz trio going, we'd get the odd gig in Germany, string a night or two together, make a tour. The money was fair, they paid you same night, they listened, applauded, all handsome. Very polite people, never no bother. The other lads would scarper home just as soon as they could, I was footloose, no ties, hang about a day or two, go mooching. One day – we'd been supporting Nat Gonella and the Georgians – I'm in Düsseldorf, lovely old part of town, wander into a fish restaurant on my tod. Lovely piece of *Seezunge mit Mandeln*, sauerkraut, pickles, bit of slaw, nice capers, black rye. Done with a bit of care. You respect it.

Half-bottle of Weissburgunder, pack of smokes, article on Coleman Hawkins I've been saving. Wintry day outside, plan is to settle in until the train. But then there's this noise, out the window.

Gang of numpties in lederhosen, shouting at everyone. Singing '*Die Fahne hoch*', big Swastika flag. I thought they was funny, like Morris dancers back home. Blockheads. Bit pathetic. Half-extinct. But soon it gets angrier. Spitting on old men passing by. I didn't know German. But I know what '*Juden*' means.

I turn to the waiter, ancient geezer in a suit, and ask what's occurring, is this some kind of sodding joke? He says, 'That's the future, *mein Herr*.'

I'm an East End Londoner. Tell me Hermann's on the level? I got two words in reply. With three effs.

It wasn't the Quakers firebombed Whitechapel. We all know who it was.

Oh, I'm sure there must be good ones. Well, there was. Before they murdered them all.

That's Jerry; only following orders.

Forgive the enemy, turn the other cheek? Off you pop, love. Not John. Once bitten, twice bite, that's my motto.

I ain't British, not first. Ain't English. I'm London. Come at me and mine and I'll forgive you with a machine gun. Take a knife to my mother's throat? You'd better hope you're struck by lightning. Bet the rent I'll catch up on you one night.

Jerry's good with the smile these days. Giving it all that about peace and starting again. Flannel. Stroll along. Not buying.

My grandkids sometimes ask me what I done in the war. I tell them, every single day I could balls up a German, I did.

And I tell them, so should they.

That's my politics.

Wouldn't give you half an inch of Whitechapel for the whole of sodding Germany. Welcome to it, Ted. Get fucked.

So, that's the way it was. I'm back at the flat with *mia bella amore*. Only, soon it starts nagging me, he's out there on his own with the Teds, the Fascisti, God knows who else. Nagging like a bastard. He's alone. And, who's this 'Lonnie' he was on about?

When you think, might be the last time I'm ever going to see him. Should have gone with him, or stopped him. And I didn't.

It was all so quick. I wasn't thinking rational. Now it's nagging me something awful. A torment.

I've no way to contact Derry. And Angelucci don't have no telephone. I could go after the Padre but I ain't got the foggiest where he's gone, who's his marks. I kick myself for not going. But I know he wouldn't let me. And I kick myself for not making him call the whole Rendimento off, come back to the flat, lie low.

But that's cobblers, too. He's stubborn, the Padre. Wouldn't never see reason, drove us all flaming scats. Typical bloody Paddy. World of his own. Ask Pat to do the sensible, obvious thing? May as well dig a hole in the sea.

Now it comes to me, on a sudden, the neighbourhood he's heading for. It ain't 'Lonnie' he's mentioned earlier, it's 'Blonnie'. 'I'll get a bandage from Blonnie.' Tell you plain, I've sat up in that bed like a vampire on Methedrine. 'Blonnie' is Delia's daughter.

I've asked *carissima* for a map of Rome but she ain't got one in the flat so we've found a fountain pen and notepaper in a drawer. Funny thing to remember, she can't find no ink, so she gives me an eyebrow pencil, all she's got. I can still see the two of us, sat there, stark bloody naked, sketching out the districts, and she's telling me the names of the streets.

Now I'm certain I know where he's headed.

What I've done, I've asked her to place a call. If it's a woman's voice, an Italian, Jerry won't be so suspicious. I've told her speak quick as you can, love, Italian's hard to follow when it's quick. Which was lunacy, an impulse. The whole idea was lunacy from start to finish, as it goes. But there wasn't no choice. Needs must.

I tell her the code words. She puts through the call. And I'm watching her fingers as she turns that dial, it's like seeing in slow motion, and waiting for the answer, and thinking this could be the biggest mistake of my life.

Place that call and two hundred prisoners might be dead by tomorrow.

Half of me was hoping there wouldn't be no answer.

But there was.

And I swear I didn't sleep one second the rest of that night.

The not knowing was the torment.

Always is.

Clambering from the rowboat, he gestures wordless thanks to May and mimes for him to get going, which after a moment or two of remonstration May does, sidling away from him, hands in pockets, down the path, into the smuts of cold, as the Panzer on the bridge judders a metre forward, gears clanking.

Sleeves soaked, he ascends the steps, crosses the quayside, takes the laneway beside the fishmonger's a winding, narrow *passaggio* lined with warehouse doors.

Nineteen minutes behind schedule.

He breaks into a run.

A person running at night is always suspect, Derry says. No Chorister on a Rendimento is ever to run unless under fire.

Twenty minutes behind schedule is fire.

His feet sound to him like whip-cracks as he trots across the Piazza, head low. Past the hulks of shuttered souvenir stalls and tarp-wrapped news-stands, the statue of a forgotten General, plinth bespattered with hammer-and-sickles, the fountain giggling at the swear word daubed across its cherub's abdomen.

Skidding, he steadies.

Ghiaccio.

Ice.

Gashing into his cheekbone.

Head fills with asterisks.

A moment, and the pain comes. Shocking, dredger-like thirst, and the bounced-around echo of his howl.

The rim of the fountain smashed him in the chin as he fell. Pain again, blazing, like a truncheon to the spine. Pain roaring through his jawbone, through the bones of his cranium. Tiny, incendiary lights, the audible *slosh* of his eyeballs, the fading, blackening Piazza, the *cut* of that swear word. The shimmer of the General on his shimmering horse.

Don't let me pass out.

You're passing out, goads the shadow.

Thirst battling nausea. Blood in his throat.

Elbowing up, he vomits, right trouser leg ripped from ankle to knee, livid handprint-sized graze down his calf. Manages to stand. Rinses his mouth in the bitter water of the fountain that floored him. Pain grasps him by the ribcage, monkey-wrenching his spine, but he's able to limp onward through the sleet-slick Piazza, past a church whose name he knows but the fall has banged it out of his head, into the dark, narrow mouth that is the rendezvous street, high dwelling-houses on both sides, crossed clotheslines.

Three seconds, four.

He knows he's been clocked.

A boy on the fire-escape whistles, chucks a pebble across the blackness and it lands with a clatter by the finial on the opposite rooftop.

There, a girl peers over the edge, now whistling back.

The shadow gives a scoff.

Night swims. The smell of coal.

23

MARIANNA DE VRIES
November 1962
Statement in lieu of an interview

The first drop was in Prati. I lived on the edge of Parioli and had volunteered to receive the second. Added to the danger and anxiety was the fact that the Choir never met for a week before a Rendimento. So, you were going on trust and whatever instincts you had. And the plan you'd dinned into yourself.

At the appointed time I went from my apartment, leaving the front door slightly ajar, as agreed, and made my way down the maid's back stairs to the communal coal cellar next to the boiler room.

To pass the hours beforehand, I had been reading *Romeo and Juliet*. 'Afore me,' says Lord Capulet. 'It is so very, very late that we may call it early by and by.' That line was lodged in my head.

It was by now a quarter to one on Christmas morning, but some of my neighbours were playing radios, others quarrelling. My plan, if I was discovered, which I thought unlikely, was to say that my room had become unbearably cold, that I thought the house's furnace must have gone out. For that reason, I had left the radiator off all that day and night, in fact broken its valves with a screwdriver. The apartment was indeed so cold that ice was forming on the insides of the windows, something I had never seen in five Roman winters.

Down I stole, teeth knocking, blanketed, to the darkness. I found the key to the coal cellar, on the frame over the door, where I knew the janitor kept it – he did not live in the building. I unlocked the cellar, entered and waited.

It was dusty, hard to breathe, appallingly cold. On the street, a few curfew-breakers passed but no sign or sound of Angelucci. I could tell from their footsteps that all the passers-by were women or slighter men than Enzo. A Stug trundled by, slowing as it passed our building. Its terrible gurgling whine and the crew shouting in German made me sick with fear. Where was Enzo?

The plan had been worked out to the tiniest detail, and yet Angelucci, after Derry the most dependable man in the Choir, was not here. A sometime hothead, yes, but that was a mask. If Angelucci told you he would do something, it was done, no question. What had gone wrong? I began to dread the worst. Despite being in a coal cellar, I had to smoke a couple of cigarettes, but I was careful as to where I extinguished them.

At length, some thirty minutes late, I heard the pipe in the ceiling give a rattle. This meant the girl watching from the rooftop had seen Angelucci turn our corner. With some difficulty I crawled across the crunching mound of anthracite, to the coalman's hatch in the wall, and pushed it a couple of centimetres open.

I heard a man draw closer. It was unmistakably not Enzo. Foreboding seized me like a monster, should I follow the plan or not? Were we betrayed, was this limper a Nazi, a tout? On the point of fleeing the cellar, I heard one short, barked word.

'Sol.'

My Chorister's code name.

I could not make out who the barker was, I knew only that it was not Angelucci. The queerest feeling possessed me, that it was, of all people, Ugo, but my assaulted rationality told me this could not be the case, he was in the Vatican, no doubt pacing his room. All of this happened in seconds. I must make the most dangerous decision of my life.

When I guessed that the man was two metres away, I took the chance and pushed the hatch open further, as far as it would go. Without a word, he dropped the satchel through, and I bundled it into a pillowcase I had brought in the pocket of my dressing robe. I left the cellar, locked the door, restored the key to its dwelling place over the frame, and crept back up through the night-sounds of the house, to my apartment.

Luigina, the girl from the roof, was now in my bedroom, with a good-looking boy I had seen in our neighbourhood but did not know by name. They waited while I quickly showered (in cold water) and put on clean clothes, then, at my signal, followed me into the bathroom.

The boy, whom I should say was seventeen, was dressed in a workman's blue overalls. The girl addressed him as 'Eugenio' but another time as 'Beppe', so at least one of these must have been a *nom de guerre*. Without speaking, we put the grimy satchel in the empty bathtub and spilled out its contents, bundling the dollars into careful stacks, which we sealed with rubber bands. I helped the girl conceal three of the stacks in her underclothes; the boy took four, placing them in the large, loose pockets sewn into the thighs and calves of his trousers. Producing a switchblade, he deftly hacked the satchel to shreds, some of which he flung in twos and threes out the window, handing a bundle of others to the girl, then off they went via the roof they had come from. I hid the remaining stacks in the lavatory cistern and dumped my coal-dirtied clothes.

In the coming days, I distributed the dollars, one or two hundred at a time, in small bills, around the contacts I had learned by heart over many a night from Derry and Ugo's list. It was a matter of leaving an envelope addressed to a false name with the barman at such-and-such a café near the Fontana di Trevi, of folding a couple of fifties into a copy of Dante's *Inferno* and replacing it on the shelf in the back of an antiquarian bookshop in a side street by the Scala Santa. An elderly Carmelite Sister visiting the Colosseum stood close to me as our impromptu group listened to the guide conjure the well-worn marvels: eighty thousand hooting Romans, brandishing fists, eating still-warm entrails, the flooding of the arena for naval spectaculars. The Sister returned to the convent with three hundred dollars she hadn't had when she arrived and an escaped Canadian tail-gunner disguised as a monk.

On the Sunday I went to Mass six times, five in the morning, once that evening, an unusual practice for an atheist. As had been arranged, I gave plump envelopes when the collection plates were passed around, the sacristans in each case being friends of the Choir who had instructions on where to further dispense the money: ultimately almost all of it would be used for bribes and forged papers, to get the escapees out of Rome and hidden in the countryside.

It was an interesting Sunday. Well, that is not quite true. The shattering level of its boredom was interesting. It put me off plainchant for life. Also, each of the six priests preached a sermon on that day's appointed reading from the Gospel and all differed in their elucidations, in some cases markedly, as in the various lengths it took to loft them, one good man needing five minutes, another, half an hour. It made me wonder what would happen if a sinner attended confession ten different times to as many different confessors, uttering the same set of sins each time. Would the penance be different depending on the listener, on his mood, his age, the quality of his breakfast? But I believe we know the answer. Wittgenstein (I think it was) once put it rather tartly: on subjects about which there is nothing to say, it is wisest to say that.

One morning as I went to meet a source for an article I was preparing, I noticed the boy from the roof, now outside a bar in my neighbourhood, but he looked through me, as though I were weather. What was odd was that he was in the company of a group of youths singing the Fascist anthem while banging down dominoes in a desultory fashion. I was alarmed and for a day or two wondered whether we had been compromised.

Every footstep on the stairs of my apartment house had me swim-headed with fear. If a woman glanced at me in the Piazza, I was seized by the impulse to run. A counter assistant at the American Express office asked me, somewhat briskly, to repeat the spelling of my surname and then appeared to check it against some list she had in a file; I broke into a heavy, headachy sweat that came and went all day. Panic blooms during wartime, particularly, some would say, when one lives alone. But perhaps it is worse for the married.

I came in from a walk one night and convinced myself that the typewriter had been moved during my absence, that the sheets of carbon paper on my desk had been shifted and examined, that a cupboard containing medicines and personal items in the bathroom had been opened and interfered with. It seemed to me that there were fingerprints all over its mirrored door, that the whole apartment stank of stale sweat and cigar smoke. The pillow beneath which I kept my nightdress had been moved, I was certain. Maybe I was watched even now.

Was there a hidden camera, a microphone? A minuscule spyhole drilled through the wall? There is no paranoia like the one that festers when we fear that our privacy is stolen. The Gestapo were well capable of that, as Ugo had long warned. 'Walls Have Ears' was his watchword.

When I tried to sleep, the intelligence photographs I feared had been made flashed at me, wrenched me awake. Strange whispers, mocking leers haunted my insomnia. Soon I had in mind to go *myself* into hiding, or get out of Rome altogether, so chilly my certainty that we were duped and betrayed. Indeed, I would have done so were it not for the fact that we in the Choir were sworn not to contact each other for a full fortnight after that night, and I did not want to imperil my friends or disappear without them knowing, for that would inflame suspicion.

All that unending week, the boy stalked my nightmares. I even went looking for him about the neighbourhood, intent on some sort of insane confrontation. A grown woman drifting the streets, peering in through slatted windows like some lunatic in a Gothic novel, or a peeping nuisance. I don't know what I should have said to him, perhaps did not know even then. In any case, my walks did not find him.

On New Year's Eve, it was made known to me – I do not wish to say how – that the boy was secretly a Communist, a plant in the Fascist ranks. We had given him eight thousand dollars. I hoped my informant was correct.

The coalhole was the second of the three drop-offs poor Ugo would attempt that night, a night when I feared the dawn would never come. When I think of it, I remember the girl, who would one day become a renowned actress, and the boy, who would be tortured and murdered by the Gestapo in the first month of the new year, his body dumped near the back of the Stadio dei Cipressi, which was later named the Stadio Olimpico. So long as there is air in the sky, the five rings of the Olympic symbol will for me always have private meaning: that boy, his defiance, his calm, his courage, his love for his magnificent country.

I do not think I shall ever forget the cold of my flat that late December. And the dread of not knowing what would happen.

It was a few days that changed my life. I did a great deal of thinking.

If I survived the war, I resolved, new roads would be taken. I would return to the university, complete the studies I had abandoned in my early twenties. I would end what I privately knew to be my dependence on barbiturates. I would write in a different way. I would live as myself.

Dawns could be imagined, but it was still the night.

I heard nothing from any member of the Choir.

The fear came, then, that all my friends were dead.

Was Ugo alive?

Was anyone?

———

He crouches behind a line of dustbins as a quintet of armoured Nazi bulldozers roars past, along the quayside.

Up ahead, like a battlement, a cluster of darkened lockups. Behind him, the stinking breeze off the Tiber.

He enters the Campo di Giuliani, uncertain, eyes pounding.

High on a stone loggia off a long, ivied rooftop, a flautist, an elderly, white-bearded Moses from a Raphael, in moth-eaten dinner jacket and cloak. Beside him a lop-shouldered tenor singing '*Una furtiva lagrima*', outstretched hands squeezing teardrops from the air. Far across the Piazza, in a candlelit upper window, a young woman in harlequin mask is accompanying them on piano. The spangling, clear chords and dulcet arpeggios echo on old, cold stone.

Every other window in the Piazza is shuttered. The residents must be able to hear, yet no one is listening, unless listening beneath blankets, in the land of counterpane. Perhaps they don't mind being kept awake.

> *Un solo istante i palpiti*
> *Del suo bel cor sentir.*
> *I miei sospir, confondere*
> *Per poco a' suoi sospir!*

Stilled by the fragility, he looks up from beneath an awning as the aria starts to soar, every vowel blade-clear, the coo of the flute like a dove's call at dawn through the dewfall of the tenor's *esses*. It shimmers, unwinds towards the sob of its climax, and the pianist and the flautist and the tenor bow stiffly, first to one another, then to the empty Piazza, before withdrawing to the darkness they came from.

The clack of shutters closing. Then birdsong. Then silence.

Did it happen?

It must have.

The windows are empty.

The music has opened something he wants closed, postponed.

Slithering on greasy cobbles, stumbling, he steadies.

A boy shinning across a washing line five storeys up in an alley.

Two brothers in a courtyard, cutting each other's hair by candlelight.

A rat staring up at a steeple from inside a gnawed melon.

Moonlight on tombstones.

Stone wolves over a doorway.

A woman on a balcony, being murmured to by her lover, an eternal eight feet away, in the opposite window.

24

THE VOICE OF SIR D'ARCY OSBORNE
14th December 1962
Interview with BBC researcher, recorded 66 Via Giulia, Rome

It is not, with respect, a matter of my being evasive. When one signs the Official Secrets Act, one signs it for life. You will appreciate, therefore, that there is a limit to what one wishes to say – or would be permitted to say, even now, after a not inconsiderable time has passed – on the question of how monies were put in place for the mission undertaken by the Monsignor on the night of Christmas Eve, 1943. Secrecy exists between countries for good reasons.

I daresay people will come to their own conclusions on the matter. Some realities will be so obvious as to hardly be worth denying. For example, it would not be ten million miles wide of the mark to assert that most of the monies were shall we say brought into Italy through the offices of various neutral or friendly Ambassadors, in small enough amounts at first.

It will be evident, too, that individuals were involved. That part of the thing was coordinated by me. As an Englishman, I am free to speak with whomsoever I wish once no law of my kingdom is broken.

Owing to currency fluctuations and what shall we call it, the lightfingeredness one can encounter in my beloved Italy, there proved to be a shortfall, which arose at the last minute. The Contessa will not mind me placing on the formal record that it was she who, as it were, rode to the rescue. I believe the selling of jewellery given that good lady by the late Count was part of it, but one was never quite told, for good reason. I should like to add that this was an exceedingly dangerous thing for my friend the Contessa to have done. The SS watched the bank accounts of all non-Fascists assiduously. The consequence for Allied collaboration was death.

Around that time, I became aware, I do not wish to say precisely how – and again, I will ask you to forgive my tergiversation – it will be obvious that the intelligence services and counter-espionage were involved – that Hauptmann, the SS commandant in Rome, was being telephoned with notable regularity by Himmler himself. This fact disconcerted me considerably.

On a nightly basis, sometimes twice nightly, the Reichsführer – after all the second-most powerful man in the Nazi empire – was raging at Hauptmann and his odious deputy, Dollman, about the Führer's perception that Allied escapees were waltzing about Rome at will – 'like whores in a *Bierkeller*' I seem to recollect was one haunting phrase. He threatened Hauptmann that, were the situation not resolved expeditiously, the Führer's displeasure might narrow down to a rather tight focus, in effect, that Hitler had Hauptmann in his crosshairs.

One had known for some time that Hauptmann was developing what the renowned Professor Freud might have termed 'a complex' about the Monsignor. We had a plant in Gestapo headquarters, a courageous young woman, indeed a heroine, whom I do not wish to name or otherwise identify. I neither confirm nor deny that she was herself German. I will say nothing whatsoever of her, except that she had informed us that, among other things, the Nazi would stride about the office ranting about 'that bastard priest' and glaring at surveillance photographs of him like a druid trying to set them on fire. I apprised the Monsignor of the facts, but, perhaps like others of his countrymen, if I may say so, he was not always the sort to take facts in.

There it is.

The Celtic peoples – and one admires them – excel as exponents of bard craft. But as rationalists? *Satis dictum.*

I wish to state for the record that the Monsignor had an eminently clear picture of the peril he was facing on Christmas Eve 1943. Any suggestion that he did not is, frankly, horse-feathers. What I mean is that such an insinuation would be totally unfounded. I warned him, and he knew the danger.

That is my solemn word. After that, cleverer people than I must believe what they wish. As Mr Orwell is supposed to have said (though I have never found the reference), 'There are some ideas so stupid that only an intellectual could believe them'. Mr Orwell attended Eton, thus must always be trusted.

Not long after the series of angry telephone calls from Himmler commenced, the unfortunate Jews of the ghetto, most of whom were very poor, hard-working Romans, were ordered by Hauptmann to collect up a preposterous amount of gold so as to avoid deportation to the camps. With a great deal of trouble, this total was raised. Again, the Contessa was involved, at least peripherally, or so I have reason to believe. It was obvious that matters were now spinning very fast.

I have never stated previously – none but the Monsignor and Derry knew at the time –that an approach had been made by the Nazis to compromise me. This took place one afternoon some months before that Christmas, I should say in mid-October, perhaps later. I was noodling through *The Times* over a gin and French in a little café I liked under the colonnade of St Peter's Square, a fortnight-old copy my man May had somehow got his hands on, but one had to make do. A crossword need not be up to date.

It was one's custom, at the café, to spend a little time simply looking about and doing one's best to enjoy the fact that one was there. The Italians are an eminently social, embracing, demonstrative people. Part of their culture, their identity, is to be communal. Eating together is important to them. They kiss, they embrace. Men, women, the young and the elderly. They display their feelings, their emotions, in a way we in England generally do not. For me it makes Italian life most attractive and uplifting. So, that is what I was doing. Taking in the scene. Suddenly, an interruption arrived.

This louche-looking Johnny with something of the pimp about him strolled up and asked if *mein Herr* would mind him sharing the table. Since he was already doing so, indeed had his elbows on the place mat, there wasn't all that much one could say. He did not introduce himself but I was aware of who he was. Dollman, Hauptmann's deputy.

The cigarette was slim and black with a gold-coloured tip. The cufflinks were miniature theatrical masks, a downcast Tragedy and its smirking cousin. Presently he ordered a cappuccino, a further lapse of taste. Italians, correctly, regard that beverage as suitable with breakfast only. No cultured Roman would order it after eleven o'clock. In any event, as the waiter told him, coffee was not to be had anywhere in the city, owing to rationing. Dollman took from his pocket a pill bottle and handed it to the man.

'Inside you will find three teaspoons of hundred-per-cent Costa Rican Arabica. Make me a cappuccino. Do it quickly.'

Pretending that a thought had just this moment occurred to him, he turned his sluggish eyes in my direction. Might he have the honour of buying me a cup of coffee as his neighbour?

'*Nein danke*,' I replied.

'Later, then,' he said, placing a second pill bottle by my saucer. 'That is a little gift for *mein Herr*.'

He spoke with a cultivated Kraut accent that was at odds with his spiv appearance and deportment. The nails of his many-ringed fingers were untended, I noticed, and his expensive-looking spats had not been polished since the fall of the Weimar Republic. Aptly named, he had curiously puppet-like movements, frequently nodding his head, as though his strings were being jerked. A sulphurous reek of what I suppose must have been cologne or after-shave wafted across, battling with another, less mentionable odour. He was at least wearing a tie, if overly vivid, like a shred torn from an artiste's bodice during a striptease. Apart from the sad, tawny eyes, somewhat syphilitic but thoughtful, he was as one of those types hanging about the back door of a nightclub in Berlin being buzzed at by gnats and jazz.

Would I care for a cigarette? Was *The Times* of London interesting today?

At this point I beckoned for my bill.

'You find your new life in the Vatican amenable, *mein Herr*?'

A revealing question. He knew precisely who I was.

I said that living in the Vatican suited me adequately for the moment.

'Yes, you Englishmen like a monarchy,' he replied.

'Sir, you are inside the boundaries of an independent, neutral state,' I reminded him. 'If you are a combatant in the present hostilities or any sort of Axis operative, your presence here without advance written permission from the Vatican authorities is forbidden under international law. I must bid you return to Rome. Over there. Good day. If you don't, I shall have you arrested.'

'An understanding between men of the world, Sir D'Arcy,' he replied. 'That is all I seek. Perhaps you will indulge me one moment.'

A fat, weary bluebottle happened to be inching across the red-checked tablecloth, and as my intruder waited for my reply, he pointed to it, now hold-ing up his nicotine-stained fingertip and grinning at me with disturbingly porcelain-like teeth.

'"Mark but this flea and mark in this, how little that which thou deniest me is." That is a couplet of your English clergyman and poet, Donne, I believe. From a poem of seduction. Is it so?'

I told him I was not in the habit of indulging in literary disquisition with strangers (although, in fact, I am, when the opportunity arises), he must say what he wished, then cut along. A diplomat must sometimes tolerate persons one would rather slap across the face. That is why we have diplomacy, after all. One felt a certain degree of apprehensiveness, naturally enough, but would not give him the satisfaction of showing it. Most probably he had a Luger in his armpit; all Gestapo men had. But even a Hun would be on balance unlikely to shoot me in St Peter's Square. Not during daylight, at any rate.

'I would like to speak with you concerning the matter of another clergyman,' he said.

'There are many of those in Rome,' I replied, kicking for touch like a springbok, if I say so myself.

'Not all of them so troublesome, *mein Herr*.'

I said I hadn't the foggiest inkling as to the advertence of my unwanted visitor. He nodded in an overly mild manner, like a bad actor nodding mildly, and muttered, 'Of course.' Then he took from his inside pocket what I thought was a piece of card, which he pushed across the table, now fingering the tips of the toothpicks in a sherry glass and squinting hard at the menu a waiter was attempting to give him, as though being offered a menu in a café was an event of inexplicable strangeness.

The piece of card turned out to be a reasonably well-defined photograph of the Monsignor, the Contessa Landini and me, on the putting green of the eighteenth hole at Viterbo. It had been taken from a distance through a window of what I knew must be the clubhouse. The Monsignor had a putter over his shoulder, rifle-style; he'd been heavier at that time. Rationing thinned him considerably. The Contessa's head was leaning back and she was laughing with abandon, a sight I couldn't remember having seen. Odd, the things that strike one under stress.

'We are in what I believe is termed a "pretty pickle",' the Kraut said, pleased with himself for knowing the expression. 'A spot of bother, don't you know, old sport.'

'How so?'

'There are laws, after all. International conventions. Germany does not assist German prisoners of war in your country to escape.'

'I shouldn't think they'd want to.'

'It is a question of mathematics. Also of perceptions. One man's happy situation is another's little difficulty. Much depends on the vantage point from where one is observing. Thus the common ground must be sought in all things, must it not.'

'Go on.'

'It is quite evident that an Escape Line is being operated, illegally, from within Vatican City. Do you agree?'

'Do I agree that that is evident?'

'Do you agree that it is being operated?'

'I have never heard of a body called anything as vulgar as an Escape Line being operated in the Vatican. Elucidate a little if you wish?'

'We believe that this is a photograph of three of its leaders. The Holy Trinity, one might call it.'

'I would call it a trio of casual acquaintances playing golf.'

'Dear sir, I do not think so.'

'I don't give a fish's tit what you think.'

'Admirable,' he said with a facial movement that I think was intended to be a smile. 'The British independence of mind, what? The refusal of convention. This extends to other areas, other *aspects* of your life, I think, *mein Herr*. Your nightlife in particular. Does it not?'

'You're the expert.'

'No crime to like the gentlemen, *mein Herr*. Well, strictly speaking, yes. To be "cut from the different cloth", as the Englishman says. You have homosexual friends and associates, who does not, after all?' He chuckled. 'Here we are in the Vatican, are we not? Boys' Town.'

'You can tell all that from a photograph of three people playing golf, can you? Wondrous. Ever think of taking up clairvoyance in a bunko booth?'

'Yes, the evidence is circumstantial. But more shall be found. The proposition I now put to you, and, if you wish, to your comrades, is that a certain number of Allied escapees shall be permitted by us to go their way. "Nod as good as a wink", as it were. On the strict proviso that fifty or sixty a week will be handed back to us for immediate return to the camps. In this manner, honour is satisfied.'

'What would happen to those returned?'

'Exegution.'

'Your pronunciation is lamentable,' I said. 'Do you mean "execution"?'

'I mean being shot. Or hanged.'

'You would term such a bargain honourable?'

'War is war, *mein Herr*.'

'Is it?'

'We must all swim in the same sea. Come, let us take a coffee and discuss.'

I picked up and unscrewed the pill bottle, poured the ground Arabica into my cupped palm, inhaled. It was rich, cherry-ish, sumptuous, finely roasted, with notes of chocolatey sandalwood, a truly exquisite blend. *Puff* – I blew it in his face.

'Run along, darling,' I said. 'You're smudging your lipstick.'

He responded with a volley of filth I shan't repeat.

At that, I stood up and called out affectionately to a duo of the Swiss Guard who happened to be patrolling nearby, picturesque gentlemen in their quaint medieval livery but well known in Rome for carrying Thompson sub-machine guns sequestered in their cloaks and not being afraid to use them if told the Pope or his State is being assailed. As they approached, giving me a cautious version of their fist-to-forehead salute, the Kraut slipped from the table and hurried across the boundary line, where he stood for a moment, grinning his puppety grin in my direction, before slouching away through the construction site of the Via della Conciliazione.

The guardsmen asked if I wished to report him but I told them not to bother with his ilk. One day a slighted Roman would deal with him face to face, I felt. Not the most diplomatic of thoughts. There we are.

Returning to my quarters in the Vatican, for a time I paced and smoked, in a condition of some anger and vengefulness. Again, these are not good traits to be allowed to seed themselves in an Envoy of His Majesty. But they sank in deep that day.

Nonetheless, in one respect, the vile upstart had done me a favour. I would go so far as to say that, without his attempt to corrupt me, I am not sure that I would have permitted myself to become too involved in the Escape Line. But then I thought: ruddy nerve. Ruddy *nerve* of the bastard. It ate at me all afternoon. It enraged me.

They would murder every Jew, every gypsy, every artist. If ever they got to London, they would go directly to Soho and murder a number of my closest friends. And then, they would murder me.

I think you know what I am referring to.

I seemed to see them, one by one, old classmates, colleagues, companions. Decent, good men, witty, loyal, brave. Some had fought for their country, for the decency of many of her values, our system of parliamentary government, our non-hatred of our opponents. Our very-far-from-perfection but our wish to do much better.

The laughter and late nights we had shared in better times.

I said 'no'. You fucking thug.

Not without a fight.

So I went to the Monsignor and told him to count me in, as it were. I had of course known of the Escape Line, had, I dare say, assisted it in small matters, but had officially looked the other way so as to preserve a certain, shall we say, deniability. But no more. He was praying in the garden of the Collegio, at least I assumed it was prayer. Seated on a bench with a Bible on his knees.

We talked for a while about missions that had already been run, the hiding of prisoners in such and such a convent, the moving of escapees or medical supplies at night. Then we spoke of a mission that was coming. A Rendimento.

After an hour or so, a man in gardener's overalls happened along the path and was introduced to me as Major Sam Derry of the Royal Artillery, 'the Gunners', my own former regiment, an escapee hiding in the Vatican *scavi*, the excavations.

What took me aback was how quickly he and the Monsignor told me everything. They and a helpmate in the city had been putting together monies for some time. There were too many prisoners in hiding, they would need to be moved out of Rome into the countryside, before an expected large influx of Nazi reinforcements early in the New Year. The cash facilitating this would be dropped on Christmas Eve night.

There would be three drops, the smallest in Prati, the medium in Parioli, the largest in a location as yet undecided. The round trip would be a walk of fourteen and a half miles. Arrest would result in prolonged torture and death. Derry had volunteered for the mission.

A grisly part of the business was what we did next. It turned out that, in the Bible on the Monsignor's knees, he had underlined many names in red ink, which Derry was committing to memory, in their Italian versions. Luca. Paolo. Marco. Matteo. Giuseppe, Elisabetta. Pietro, Stefano.

Why was he doing this? I asked.

'In case I find myself in Club Hauptmann, sir.'

'Beg pardon?'

'Slang some of the boys use for Gestapo headquarters, sir,' Derry said, in a matter-of-fact manner that floored me. 'Club Hauptmann, they call it, or Doll-man's Basement. If I get tortured, I want to have actual names to give up. So that I don't betray my friends. I meet the Monsignor here every day for my homework. Bloody tough taskmaster, too.'

We sat beneath the cypresses, the Monsignor, Sam Derry and I, as the nightingales came and went, and the Roman sun gleamed, Derry reciting the names, I testing him on their fictional addresses. At one point, I was unmanned, gave in to my emotions. With gentleness the Monsignor took my hand and murmured, 'Courage, old man.' Derry said, 'Chin up, sir. We're Gunners.'

And I told them something which was true, that I missed my brother back in England. But that I loved them as my brothers and always would. To the end of my days. Beyond, if possible.

They indicated to me that that was a comfort, and on we went. Speaking names and addresses, by birdsong.

25

A left off Via Boccherini, through a gap in the barbed wire, now picking his way across the bombsite. Notices say the ruined schoolhouse could collapse at any moment; loitering and 'immoral behaviour' are punishable by death.

The rocket crater overflowing with oily, littered water, islands of mould-covered plasterboard, broken boxes. The bomb shattered the building into diagonal halves, the corkscrewed central staircase now exposed, half-collapsed, the shattered sinks and exploded lavatory cisterns blackening with rust. Obscenely, a child's tennis racket dangles from a window sash.

Graffiti splatters every millimetre of the shrapnel-scarred walls – *'Viva l'Italia!' 'Morte al fascismo' 'Roma '27' 'Libertà, sempre!'* – Six of the seven oaken buttresses brought in to shore up the gable have had their cast-iron brackets stolen by looters; the seventh has been attacked with a chainsaw. Discarded French letters lie in profusions of broken glass like jellyfish torpedoed ashore.

A spectral nun intoning the alphabet arises from the rubble but he blinks away the memory, if that's what it is.

'*Hände hoch!*' snaps the voice behind him. 'Hands high. Do not turn.'

His arms anvil-heavy as he raises them. Mind ticking. Stomach boiling. In the ruins, a starling chirrups and a mongrel gives a scuttle. Boot-steps crunch through the rubble.

'Keep your back to me,' now in Italian. 'Spread your feet.'

The voice is brisk, local, sickening in its confidence. A careful, probing hand pats the rear pockets of his trousers. A pistol presses his back. Fingers grope his jacket.

'Take three steps forward and kneel.'

Prickles tingle his jaw. Bracing for the bullet, he speaks.

'I am content to step forward, not to kneel.'

'You'll do as commanded.'

'In that respect, no.'

'*Mi scusi?*'

'Have respect for a man twice your age, you ignorant lout. Or I'll do what your father should have done.'

A mangy, three-legged vixen trots out from the rubble, whining with hunger or pain.

With a roar, she explodes, blood slops across brickwork. The pistol shot echoes. The voice gives a sigh.

'*Allora*. Remain standing. Now, turn to me, *slowly*. Try to run and you'll get the same treatment.'

What he sees when he turns is a moustachioed, pig-eyed, twenty-year-old bruiser, in the drabs of the Fascist police. Stocky, long-reached, adept in a brawl, a human hammer in search of a nail. Some emptiness of the eyes is like the bombsite's broken windows.

'Grandad,' the youth sneers, 'why are you not wearing the Party insignia?'

'I dressed hurriedly. If it's any of your business.'

'How is your trouser leg torn?'

'I slipped on the ice.'

'You slipped?'

'That's right.'

'You are aware of the penalty for disobeying the curfew.'

'My profession is such that I am exempt.'

'You speak stiltedly. You are not an Italian. Where are you from?'

'That information is on my identity card, which you will find on a string around my neck, inside my shirt.'

The Fascist reaches and finds it, reads the lying words by torchlight.

'Mancuso,' he says. 'Kind of name is that?'

'You tell me.'

'We have reports of Communist activity in the city tonight. Partisans, terrorists, they attack us like cowards from the darkness. Know anything about it? Signor so-called Mancuso?'

'Forgive me, what does a Communist look like?'

'Got a mirror? You'll see.'

'I pay no attention to such matters. I only do my work.'

'It says here you grew up in Milano. Is that right?'

'That's what it says.'

'Which is your football team?'

'Inter.'

'What's the name of the church in Milano where *The Last Supper* is?'

'Santa Maria delle Grazie.'

'Bullshit. This card is a forgery.'

'Why would you say such a thing?'

'You are not an Italian. I can tell by your accent.'

'I didn't say I'm Italian. Can't you read?'

'You shall come with me to the police headquarters. *Andiamo.*'

'Mother of God, degenerate criminals are walking the street. Not ten minutes ago, on Via Peri, I passed a prostitute openly revealing her body. Half-naked in a doorway. On Christmas Eve. You tell me there are Communist insurrectionists and murderers at large. And you wish to arrest an innocent man at his work? *È bene,* I have tolerated enough, let us go to the station. We shall see what your superiors say to this time-wasting.'

'Think you're cleverer than me?'

'I think a sack of stones would be that.'

'Quite the stuck-up, aren't you. *Professore Partigiano.*'

'Let me tell you something, son, before you embarrass yourself further. Today I was one of a small group invited to a wedding in Saint Peter's—'

'Big deal.'

'The bride was the daughter of Traetta, yes, the Fascist official. A close, personal friend of mine, since before you were born. Take me to the police station, I will telephone him from there.'

'I don't believe you. What's she called?'

'My goddaughter's name is Alicia.'

'You're Traetta's girl's godfather?'

'Her husband is Luca.'

'Anyone could know that. You're trying to trick me. Stay *back.*'

'In my breast pocket, you will find a copy of the Order of Service. Signed and dated by the happy couple. And Traetta.'

'Take it out. *Slowly.*'

He does. Hands it across.

'There. You see the words. You have made a mistake. Tomorrow I shall telephone Traetta to commend your dedication and hard work.'

'Say "Damn the Jews".'

'Why would I say that?'

'Because I told you to.'

'That is no reason to say anything. Another man might tell me to say "Damn the Duce".'

'What?'

'You heard me.'

'Withdraw that remark.'

'What remark?'

'"Damn the Duce".'

'Now you've said it yourself. Do you think that is wise? Someone could be eavesdropping and denounce you.'

The Fascist reaches out a fingertip, touches the top button of his prisoner's jacket.

'Big-Brains Mancuso. Big men fall hard.'

'Touch me again, son, you'll know all about it.'

'You're threatening me, Professor?'

'Not threatening. Warning.'

He touches him again.

Mancuso lunges.

Grabs the index finger, bends it, *hard* back against the wrist, and the youth utters a scream of shocked, gulping pain, falls sideways, arms flailing, somehow regains his balance, manages to haul out his pistol from its underarm holster but he can't get the safety catch off. Eyes rolling, he totters, spews blasphemies and avowals, Mancuso hits him again, a battering parry at the temples, but the Fascist ducks, swinging, they're into a bad wrestlers' clinch amid the stench of unlaundered linen and dirty pomaded hair, as he gropes at the pistol butt, bites at Mancuso's ear, fingertips clawing towards eyes.

A masked figure looms from the schoolhouse, length of scaffolding in gloved hands. As the Fascist turns toward the footsteps, he's struck hard across the chest, staggering backwards into a pile of toppled bricks and slates and the assailant seizes him by the windpipe, kneeing him hard between the legs, and the Fascist sinks, retching, in agonised gasps as the figure unleashes a kick at his head.

A roar in German from the laneway, *Hands up or we shoot!* and the figure hurtles into a run, clambering over the broken wall.

From the street, three German soldiers, a storm-lantern, rifles jutting.

'What is going on here? Do not move. Raise your hands.'

'My name is Mancuso, this officer was being beaten as I passed and I came to his aid. He needs an ambulance, he's concussed, have you a radio-set at hand? His attacker fled away in that direction.'

Two soldiers hurry towards the wall. The third utters a long sigh.

'Your identity card, *bitte*?' he says.

26

THE VOICE OF DELIA KIERNAN
7th January 1963
BBC research interview, recorded White City, London

A Roman winter, you see, throws a lot at a building. The Embassy, an old villa with no heating system and clanky piping the age of your granny, was receiving a sorely needed renovation at the time. Buckets up and down the corridors, we'd that many leaks in the roof. A burst water-main in the cellar. Rats you could saddle. The swimming pool froze solid and became a right, effing nuisance, pardon my French, because the mosaic in the floor cracked and the *caementicium* was destroyed.

My husband felt he should remain onsite, in the servants' flat, which in truth was little more than a boxroom; you'd fit a camp bed, nothing more. Our daughter Blon and I had taken an apartment in the city for the ten weeks. That's where I was on Christmas Eve.

It was a night you wouldn't put a milk bottle out. Sleet. Bitter cold. Pulverising furies of wind. My father used to joke that the rain is liquid sunshine. That Christmas Eve it was liquid depression.

Half past two in the morning comes a battering on the front door like an army of angry devils. When I open it, there stands Hugh, by his lonesome own, and he blinking at me like a lighthouse, eight to the bar, as though trying to signal me something urgent.

'Good evening, Signor Mancuso,' says I, with any calm I can muster, though the fear is making me unsteady. 'I assume you are here for the bottle of quinine, as arranged?'

The look on his puss.

'Thanks indeed, Mrs Kiernan,' says he.

'Won't you mosey in for a moment?' says I. 'It's a chilly night, so it is. You'd take a little nightcap for the road?'

That's when the three Nazis step into the porch. Well, maybe not Nazis, three German soldiers, conscripts, I'd say.

One from the right, the other pair from the left. They were after waiting, hidden, the way I wouldn't be able to see them but they could hear anything I was saying to Hugh, or he to me.

Pistols in hand.

Not saying a word.

Two of them were unattractive lads, may God and Mary love them, but the third, their superior, was an absolute fright. A haddock-faced, lumpen-shouldered, *Wurst*-fingered corner boy, that ugly the tide wouldn't take him out. He'd a face like a Lurgan shovel.

'Good evening, gentlemen,' says I. 'Or an early *Guten Morgen*, I suppose. And how may I assist your excellencies?'

They said nothing.

'You are associates of my husband's friend, Signor Mancuso, I assume?' says I. 'Well, thank you for escorting him to my door, very considerate of you altogether. There's a horrid lot of thievery and crime these nights in Rome, so there is. A body would be afraid to go out.'

They're gawping at yours truly, then at Hugh, then at each other. Fine examples of the super-race. Three wise men. But you want to be good and careful when you're dealing with the stupid. Stupidity has cunning, otherwise it would have disappeared a long time ago. Stupidity is a shark. It outlasts.

The problem was to get Hugh into the house without making them more suspicious, which wouldn't be easy, for by now he was beside himself with anxiety. Also, I was needing to think on my feet. Christmas isn't an easy time for me, I was after having a few brandies to try and help me get to sleep. I wished I hadn't, for now my thoughts were all in a hames. At that moment, it started to snow.

It was a dirty, bitter night, the snow was the wet sort that soaks through your clothes, and the soldiers were white with the misery. There was that awful smell you get off filthy socks once the wetness gets through boots. One of them now asked me in very broken and embarrassed English if he might step in for a moment and avail himself of the lavatory. That was when the solution occurred to me.

'Sure wouldn't you *all* come in?' says I, and I sobering fast as a cat. 'I've coffee got for Christmas, you'll take a cup just in your hand.'

'I don't think that would be proper, Delia.' This was Hugh talking now. 'These men are on patrol. They've their duty to attend to.'

'Arra, Marco, don't be so dry, sure it's Christmas Eve night,' says I. 'Let them come in and stand by the fire ten minutes itself and get a thaw in their bones, the poor dotes.'

Well, the murderous look he gave me. But I knew what I was at. Or I thought I did, anyhow. Either way, the bolt was shot.

The three start colloguing together in German a minute, then in with all four to the hall. The fellow in need takes himself off to the closet below the landing. Blon, who that moment came down the stairs, helped me take the soaked overcoats of the other pair and put them below in the cloakroom. I winked her to be calm.

'There's a German gentleman in the lav, dear,' I said, for we hadn't a lock on it. 'And may I introduce you to Mr Mancuso,' meaning Hugh, whom she knew well enough to regard as an uncle. She nodded as she shook his hand.

Blonnie had turned nineteen that October and was what used to be known as a knockout. The Italians have a phrase, *fare bella figura*, which means looking your absolute utmost all the time. That's how she was: confident, in control. She'd sell a double bed to a Reverend Mother. Blon had every bit of her father's handsomeness, and something of the defiant spirit of the women in my family but was lovelier than anyone I had ever seen. Her father used to say she had the sort of beauty that machine-guns a room, a quip that always drove her batty, but you knew what he meant, for you'd seen it. Hearts had been broken from Bundoran to Bologna. Brown eyes you'd drown in and a heads-up-straight walk and a figure like Veronica Lake's. Fluent in three languages, halfway through her science degree. As for charm? She'd talk rain out of wetting her.

Introductions were made and the visitors bowed and clicked their heels. You could tell the poor looders were machine-gunned. Trotting after her, the creatures, bumping into each other, into the living room, where the hearth was angel-bright and the Christmas tree lit and the Waterford crystal plates of candies and apples, and Blon's harp under its cover by the window. I did up a plate of proper sandwiches you'd need a weightlifter's fist to hold, and put a mutton soup on the boil, and got the trifle out of the refrigerator.

'*Freunde*,' says I. 'Fill your boots.'

Appetite?

Man dear, you'd want to have seen them. They'd ate the leg off the lamb of God.

Like most in Rome that time, they were half-starved alive. Hunger was rampant, you'd see people faint in the street, even die. Worse was coming, too, it would be a famine by March, and, like many a famine before and since, the people did the starving were the poor. It was well known the Nazi officers stole any decent food for themselves and their families, the conscripts in the lower ranks could hang, they lived on the dregs. These three, shall we say, were not officer class.

By the time I got the gramophone going, there was scarcely a crumb on a plate. I thought they'd eat the cushions. It was pitiful. I saw hungry people when I was a girl, they eat calmly and quickly, not stopping to talk, not wanting to waste. As though someone will take it away from them. Like automatons.

Blon, wonderful Blon now pushed in the drinks trolley, which I may add was plentifully supplied. Scotch, vodka, schnapps, grappa, whatever you fancied and more besides, port, chartreuse, Bourbon, Dutch gin, and the pride of the bundling, three naggins of Powers White Whiskey, the most exquisite occasion of sin you ever savoured. It was Johnny May got them for me, on the Roman black market, where they cost a sultan's ransom, ninety-five dollars the bottle. But they earned their keep that night.

'You'll take a drop of this, boys. It's very rare,' says I. 'Indeed and you will. Don't be girls. *Prost!* The traditional way is down in one. Do it fast.'

A grand hole was soon made in the first naggin, the lads nearly lowing in pleasure. Before long we were punishing the second. The daggers Hugh was shooting me would have cut through a safe. Blon brought more scoff, dishes of tiramisu and panna cotta, and had by now been prevailed upon with beckons and leery smiles to give us a tune on the harp.

Blon is classically trained and had played in the university orchestra; her end of the forest being that dreadful modern stuff, what do you call it, atonal, like a bag of blind cats mating, but she obliged with a few gobbets of misty-eyed Celtic bilge, which foreigners, especially Germans, seem to like. And when you've never seen a harp played, it's really and truly remarkable, especially if you're a bit scundered at the time. You sort of think, that's impossible.

It's like watching a unicycling juggler. I didn't sing myself that night – I'd a touch of laryngitis – but Blon rose to the occasion, lots of *mavourneen acushla*, and her voice was light and lovely. Soon the lads were humming along, pearly tears in the peepers, as though the gentle grey-haired mammy in the songs Blon was singing was their own little *Mutter* back in Nuremberg.

Second bottle down, we uncapped the third. They started appearing a little, shall we say, woozy. Powers White Whiskey is not for the faintheart. It's what they use to eke the rust off old coins.

An aunt of mine used to say so-and-so was 'drunk as a boiled owl'. I never knew what it meant before that night. I was able to take Hugh aside and put him in the picture. Ten minutes before himself and the Teds appeared at the door, Jo Landini knocked on my bedroom windows, which were at the back of the house, having come in through the garden and crossed the courtyard. Johnny May was after telephoning her, she'd slipped straight out to Angelucci's apartment, then the pair of them went searching my neighbourhood with the hope of finding Hugh, when the sound of a pistol-shot a few streets away drew them to the ruined school.

Angelucci was at a safehouse, was after escaping the pursuers, was delighted to have cold-cocked a Fascist policeman before taking flight. As a travelling man that used to camp on my daddy's land used to put it, 'he left him for priest and doctor'. It would be a consolation for not being permitted to run the mission. He intended to lie low for a fortnight, get out of the city, would be in touch when the coast was clear.

I gave Jo a hug, the dear mite; she was cold and gone quiet. She said, 'Delia, your arms are springtime,' and we laughed a little moment. 'When all of this is over, invite me to Ireland?' she said, and I promised I would, never doubt it.

'What shall we see there, Delia?'

'Muddy lakes. Scrawny cows.'

'Will you find me an Irishman to marry?'

'I'd never inflict that on you.'

'Have you a cigarette, *carissima*? I'm gasping for a smoke.'

It was an Irishism I'd taught her, well, hadn't *meant* to teach her, but I suppose she picked it up, she was always listening out. I gave her a Woodbine, and she coughed as she lit it. It was a moment I saw the girl in her, and also – this was strange – the old lady. I was so fond of her, somewhere along the way we were after becoming great pals. Tough, she was. Witty. Never back down. It's hard when you're beautiful, I saw that with my own daughter, because a beautiful-looking person will always attract trouble. But Jo had more sense in one fingernail than anyone I ever met. I loved the bones of that woman. Never more than that night.

She was now upstairs, I told Hugh, hiding in a crawlspace behind the ceilings and attic. I said I'd send Blon up to tell her to either stay hidden or make her getaway, for there was by now no way that our visitors would be able to see a staircase, never mind climb one, let alone conduct a proper search when they got there. They had been with us less than an hour but were scuttered.

But when Blonnie went up, she was gone.

Hugh said he was leaving, too. Blon brought in an old overcoat of her father's, a heavy frieze ulster patched up here and here.

'This is for yourself, Uncle.'

'I'm grand,' he told her.

'I'm not asking. I'm telling, put it on.'

I nodded for him to do as commanded.

Too large, it wasn't a great fit, but it was adequate for purpose, if I can put it like that. I could see him start to twig what was happening.

'Is it altered?' he asked us.

I told him it was.

'Nice bit of tailoring,' he said.

'We work cheap.'

Presently, he slipped away, through the pantry at the back and into the laneway at the rear of the house. By now it was gone three in the morning. Soon our other visitors departed, too, by the more orthodox exit. Off into the night, with a fanfare of confused and confusing salutes and rebuffed attempts at embraces. I regret to say that they would receive an unpleasant little surprise when they got back to barracks, for their ration books, German currency and military identity cards would somehow be missing from the greatcoats Blon and I had put in the downstairs cloakroom to dry.

Opportunity must be availed of, especially in wartime. The Powers had been expensive, after all.

Which would have been fine, in its way. But you know what happened next.

213

It turned out that one of the boyos had not been quite as drunk as I thought, or the cold night sobered him fast.

At the Carabinieri headquarters on Via Busoni, he radioed the Gestapo.

It was Christmas, so most of the regular goons were off. The message went direct to the SS commandant at his villa.

The most dreaded man in Rome.

Paul Hauptmann.

ACT III

The Huntsman

27

On Saturday 6th March 1475, two peasant boys were swimming in a lake seven leagues south of Rome when they observed what they described as 'a scarlet light' in the depths and tried to swim downwards to investigate.

The distance was too far.

They were idiots, their parents said.

In the coming spring and summer, the boys trained themselves to dive a little further each day, to fill their lungs like swollen wineskins and keep open their stinging eyes in the murk, until the afternoon arrived, near the start of that autumn, when the younger made it down to the sandy, silty bed, and, gasping, trembling, slick with weird weeds, brought back a ruby the size of a grapefruit.

Even the wisest of the village could not explain the find.

Rubies in a lake?

Impossible.

No ruby mine existed in all the lands of Lazio. Some Caesar long gone to dust must have dropped it while charioting or hunting, or flung it away, a sacrifice, perhaps, to Diana, goddess of love, who lowered the moon into the water on the nights of her unhappiness. As with all inexplicable finds and all facts resisting reason, the ruby of the lake inflamed stories. Children of that lakefront were lulled to wondrous dreams by legends of the red dragon's eyeball.

Ninety years later, on the morning after a bad storm, the net of a weary fisherman pulled out no fish but an object that turned out to be, when he wiped off the mud, an opal-encrusted, golden goblet. Rowing out to the middle of the lake, he looked down into the depths, and saw, far below him, a presence that had not been visible before, 'the dragon's long black shadow'.

Terrified, he fled, through the splashes of his oars. 'I heard it roar behind me,' he testified. 'I was too frightened to turn and look.' Breathless, he hurried to the elders. Warriors were given harpoons, ordered to dive down to the dragon, measure and observe it, come back with sketchable details. A scribe would be sent to consult the bestiaries at the ancient library in the Vatican to see if the lake's beast had precedent or name. But the divers, when they surfaced, nets heavy with gemstones, said the dragon was not a dragon but a ship.

For days afterward, the townspeople crowded into the lake, returning with crystals, jade goblets, terracotta tiles, plump diamonds and opals, silver statuettes of leering pagan deities, jewelled daggers, golden platters depicting copulations. One morning, a thirteen-year-old farmgirl, the deepest diver yet, reported seeing the vast hulk tilt. It turned appallingly onto its starboard side and broke into three, an immense billowing cloud of black, rotting splinters, half-sunken into the muck it must have come from. A hunk of iron that had belonged to the anchor was dragged to the shallows by the girl and her father. The oxen that pulled it from the mud all died within a week. On its length was stamped the name 'Caligula'.

In 1927, the Duce, avid for the past, commanded his archaeologists to drain the dragon's lake. Through a radius of ten kilometres, the fields were dammed or flooded. Two pleasure-ships were found, the larger the size of an Olympic soccer pitch, the smaller not much smaller, a barge. There was also an ancient rowboat filled to her oarlocks with stones. A museum was built on the lakeshore; the three vessels pulleyed out of their long, dignified slumber, the restful sleep of antediluvian secrets, and placed on display like captured princesses, in the bleak, cold stare of touristry.

It was at Nemi that Obergruppenführer Hauptmann established his weekend home, in the pleasantly appointed cut-stone villa constructed in 1929 for the Museo's Chief Curator and his family. The master bedroom and reception rooms overlooked the lake; the little kitchen faced south and was sunny and dappled, perfumed by a herb garden and lemon groves. The house was cool and shaded, had an electricity generator, efficient plumbing, its own well. Importantly, it was three kilometres from its nearest neighbour. Hauptmann did not like to be observed.

Here he could be himself, could loll about in a dressing gown, playing his beloved gramophone records as loudly as he pleased. From hidden loudspeakers, Mozart and Beethoven boomed through the forest, frightening the nightingales and water rats. It was not done in Party circles to admit anything non-Aryan as having merit, but here, by the lake, his guilty secret, Verdi, could be indulged in private, a peccadillo no one would uncover. A great pity that Verdi had been Italian, member of an inferior race. But no one is perfect, Hauptmann told his children.

Only one person in the history of this world has ever been perfect. That person suffered unimaginably but has risen again, and we must follow him without the slightest question for he is leading his people into the future-

'Daddy means Jesus,' his wife interrupted. 'Don't you, dear?'

'What? Oh, yes. Our Lord.'

He loved his retreat, half an hour's drive from hot, filthy Rome with its battalions of tireless beggars, the reek of shit and olive oil. The crumbling, dusty piles of mediocre, popish rubble. Machicolations and murder holes, the never-ending bells and processions. An apparition here. Some saint's liver there. Touch that statue with your forehead, you'll suffer a thousand years fewer in purgatory. Talking crucifixes, bleeding friezes, barred windows, mouthy gargoyles. And always, *give us money*, at every turn, money. The incessant, donkeyish bray and hand-waving inanity that passed for talk. The only city on Earth founded on superstition and fleecing credulous old women. Rome was a capital of stupidity and childishness. Nemi was a world made for men.

Swimming naked in the lake, the whiff of blood would clear, the tang of the cell and the torture room. The gape of a prisoner as you attached electrodes to him would be rinsed away. The rasp of the file as you worked his teeth to pulp. Cold water was so replenishing that your whole head felt new.

He began to spend more time at Nemi, reduced the size of his establishment in the city to a single, small room on the top floor of Gestapo headquarters to be used in case of absolute necessity, if an interrogation, say, were running on late, or a captive was close to breaking. It was understood among his men that he was living at his retreat. Summoning his wife and children from Berlin, he installed them at the villa. They arrived on the morning that the telephone was installed, a symmetry he often quipped about, for it pleased him.

'Now, I have everything I need.'

'Thank you, Daddy.'

Often as he strolled in the cypress woods with his wife, one of those odd tricks of water would bring them the children's echo-splashed laughter as they played tennis or dress-up or tag with their governess, a local girl, and the world seemed sanctified, restored. At great cost, his official Mercedes was armour-plated, fitted with bullet-resistant windows, a lead floor, bolt-on cage

work tyre-protectors of his own design; the mouth of the fuel tank was moved to the dashboard so no one could push a burning rag down it. Now the car was too heavy to manage the pine-needled country tracks or the fragile wooden bridge leading over the streamlet, so it had to be garaged in the city. But, as Elise pointed out, this meant a healthier, more wholesome life. At the weekends and in the evenings, he walked.

Since boyhood he had loved a book by an American author, Strauss, entitled *The Huntsman and the Lake*. A presentation copy had been sent to him by an aunt in Plainfield, New Jersey, for his fourteenth birthday; perhaps one day he would come for a visit, she wrote. She directed the *Turn- und Gesangverein*, the gymnastics and singing club, in Plainfield; her young people would love to meet him, New Jersey was a welcoming place for the Germans. The excitement of seeing the American postage stamps, the franked words 'Liberty and Prosperity', the blue scrawlings of the customs official across the packet. Often, he thought the book's title the loveliest in all of literature. Simple and clean like its subject.

The huntsman as an orphan had been adopted by the Iroquois but now lived in the Great North Woods on his own. His longing was to return to the Southwest Miramichi River, where his parents had lived on a houseboat near Push and Be Damned Rapids, but the thaw required for the trek never came. You wanted it never to come because then the book would end. It was possible for you and the hero to want different things even though the side you were on was the same. By day he fought bears and rattlesnakes, by night, mountain lions and coyotes. His truer enemy was 'the do-gooder', a schoolteacher from the town twenty miles away who was always trying to tempt the huntsman back to the falsehood called civilisation. The lie of bank managers, conformity, medicines you didn't need, cages called houses, opium dens called saloons. It was a novel of fishing and trapping, of landscape and water, but could be read in another way, too. Indeed, that was part of its magnetism to the lonely, fatherless, privately troubled, teenaged boy. This was the first time he realised that a book *can* be read in more than one way, is often about a secret at which the title does not even hint. A story was a bottle, a way of storing something valuable; what was printed on the label was only part of the preciousness, if that. The discovery was so thrilling as to feel almost sexual, like coming to understand the new things your body was doing. It was not a book about a lake but about how to be a man. Life was an accommodation with vast, roiling systems, most of which wanted you dead. Now he had his own lake, and the lake had its stories. It was not unlike owning a world.

Prisoners were brought from the camps to construct a sauna cabin of pine logs, and an elaborate treehouse he designed for his son and daughter, with staircase, heart-shaped portholes, battlements, retractable ladders. In the garden, he lifted barbells, bammed at a punchbag. He picnicked on the shore with his wife, their children and the nanny, beneath wild-grown figs and olives. Salami, fine cheeses, succulent San Marzano tomatoes, glinting aubergines, grapes, *pepperoncino*, *arrosticini*. The cook made a *sgroppino* that would coax sighs of bliss from a rock. Truffles from Piedmont. Basil pesto from Liguria. The glory of a hunk of ciabatta dipped in olive oil and salt, eaten in ecstatic sunshine, with a glass of something crisp. A corrupt race, the Italians, but by God they knew how to live.

After lunch, he and the children would kayak in the cool shallows beneath the willows or swim near the lemon-wood dock. Elise smoked, or wrote letters home, and read on the shore, sometimes played cards or talked clothes with the nanny, gave the girl fashion magazines. On warm autumn afternoons Hauptmann taught the children to fish. His daughter was better than his son, who lost patience, grew petulant. She was clear-eyed, persistent, watched the surface like a gull. He saw a great future in the Party for his daughter.

Perch, roach, bream, squalius. He loved saying the Italian names of the lake fish to his children, how his son and daughter ran to their mother with a wriggling bream in their hands, calling, '*Mutti, Mutti, wir haben einen Fisch gefangen!*' Since coming to Rome, she had been drinking too much; sometimes he noticed her stumble, slur her words. One night, they'd had a disagreement, he had asked her to stop reading the Grimm brothers' stories to the children: 'They need something more modern, Elise, something of the *now*.' He gave her a young people's book he had sent to Berlin for, Hiemer's *Der Giftpilz*, *The Poisonous Toadstool*. 'As it is difficult to distinguish the deadly mushroom from the good one,' he read aloud, at random, 'it can at first be difficult to tell the murderous outsider from the friend.' She had countered that the Grimms' stories taught the most important lesson any child, especially any girl, would ever need.

'What is that, Elise?'

'Men are beasts.'

She had the cook gut the catch, the children would roast it on a campfire. A motorcycle outrider would be sent into the city for *cioccolato* ice cream and cannoli, to the Piazza Navona, where the children's favourite gelateria was, across from the Fontana del Nettuno. Often the rider made a stop at Gestapo headquarters in Via Tasso on the way back, where he collected that day's file of intelligence reports and bloodstained confessions, fetching them out to Nemi by nightfall.

Night fishing was a particular pleasure, the velvet of the forest in darkness, water moving the rushes; the fireflies. You didn't have the assistance of a cloud of bubbles on the surface. If a breeze came, you couldn't see the lapping wavelets because you couldn't use a torch; the fish would be watching through the water. Light made them scatter. You needed to learn how to listen.

He had a feel for it. *Einen Instinkt.* His son would never have it, Hauptmann knew, but he hoped that his daughter would. Often, he sensed he could angle without bait, a true master. He *knew* where the fish were, how they moved, at what times, which pools they liked, which currents, what sort of moonlight. It was simply a matter of waiting.

He could sense in his daughter the same knowledge.

She was thirteen now, and, as Elise phrased it to him one morning, had recently 'become a woman'. Her bedroom door was to be knocked upon before entering; she must have a small allowance of her own. Important to afford a little independence, a space into which she could grow. There were times when she mentioned that she would like to be either a structural engineer or a Luftwaffe pilot. It unsettled her mother. The latter was no job for a girl, Elise would say. Hauptmann disagreed, why not?

At night he walked the museum with her, explaining the glass cases of swords and cracked oars, the helmets, the battered platters, the ancient ships themselves, their black, broad beams and long hulls. Nineteen hundred years beneath the water, but they had held out, not disappeared. He would smoke and talk, she would listen and nod. The future would knock on the windows. Many visits concluded with him showing her the exhibit he valued most. A cracked terracotta tile the size of her lovely face, but graven with a line from the Roman poet, Accius.

Oderint dum metuant.

Let them hate once they fear.

'Say it for Daddy.'

She did.

A dozen of his most trusted plainclothesmen patrolled the barbed-wire perimeter, with Rottweilers kept perpetually half-starved. In concentric circles reaching outwards, a squadron of elite Panzergrenadiers guarded lanes and old roads, approaches through the forest, the warren of cart-tracks. The instruction was 'shoot to kill, presume guilt'. Pictogram signs of the death's head were nailed to the larches. Poachers in the woods were horsewhipped.

Trenches were dug, the surrounding meadowlands mined. *Chevaux de frise* barricaded the laneways where the vines sprouted so uncontrollably that they wound themselves about the spikes like garlands. Prisoners from Regina Coeli were trucked in and forced to build a breastworks and moat.

The Museo, of course, he closed to the public. You didn't want the conquered getting ideas. Sometimes, late at night, he walked its moonlit aisles, alone, enjoying a last cigarette before bedtime or a glass of fine Amaretto with the ghosts of Caligula's ships.

The artefacts thrilled him: broken daggers, little axes made for use by children. A parallelogram of jagged terracotta, somehow still intact after its centuries sunk in sediment, depicting the sloe-black 'O' of a goddess's eye or part of a peacock's wing. Elise found the Museo intolerably eerie at night, the writhe of looming shadows in its windows made strange by some effect of lake water, the faint but unkillable odour of rot, the lecherous grins of the figure-heads. Hauptmann found the place arousing to the imagination, the faculty his wife called the soul.

In some night-lake of his mind, the ships still plunged, vast, Herculean, unearthly in their awe, powered by the oars of a thousand snorting slaves, manacles carved from queens' bones. Little wonder the peasants had glimpsed a dragon. Sometimes even Italians were right.

One day soon, the Führer would return to Rome. Hauptmann would give him a conqueror's welcome. Here at Nemi a grandstand would be constructed, there would be fireworks, a procession, a naval rally filmed by that Riefenstahl woman. *Why not?* 'Elise, that is my motto, why not?'

The ships would be re-floated. The impossible would be done. It must happen at night. The drama.

Piped march tunes and Bach. Handel's 'Zadok the Priest'. The Führer will glimpse what could be forged for the Reich here in Italy. Arc-lit on the stage he will scream paternal thankfulness to *our greatest of Germany's sons, Paul*

Hauptmann. Elise by Hitler's side, with her husband and the children, all standing to attention, saluting the Führer. An example to the whole Fatherland. The Hauptmanns.

His career will be strengthened; the family will prosper; the only roadblock is the matter of those accursed escapees. After Christmas, he will refocus, bear down harder on the problem. What he's planning is a January that Rome will never forget: hourly raids, a thousand interrogations, total war on the Escape Line's leaders. Kill the snake by cutting off its head.

Soon will come the turn of that interfering Irish priest. Like all troublemakers, a self-important little gnat. There is enough in the dossier alone to have him in front of a firing squad; that's before an interrogation extracts the full story of his involvement. Which it will. One of these nights, he'll flit out of the Vatican; the vain are unable to stay long in a room. He'll never see daylight again.

Perhaps, after the war, a Ministry in the government – he had discreetly let it be known in the sections of the Party that mattered that he was interested in the Education portfolio, had been reading up on pedagogy – or an Ambassadorship somewhere. *Why not?* Elise had often told him he was a man of charm and force, attractive to women, envied by men, no mere soldier to do the dirty work required of the present but a superior who should be raising his eyes to the future, when this terrible war would end, and there would be no one left to butcher, and strong, clever leaders would be needed by Germany. Times would be happier. No more awful duties. Their children would fondle the Führer's dogs.

In the early hours of Christmas morning, he is working at the drawing board in his study, small glass of whisky at hand. His pencils moving carefully, cross-hatching, filling in. A slide-rule measuring out the distances and scales, a compass tracing circles that will be artificial islands for the cameramen. The larger of the ships will be launched down a gangway, the smaller, the more fragile, lowered into place by three vast cranes, the whole spectacle enthrallingly torchlit from a diagonal line of pontoons moored across the surface of the lake.

Lately he has been suffering a recurring irrational dread, that an air raid is unleashed as the Führer takes his seat in the grandstand. Those prows and poop-decks and figureheads burning. Turrets of sparks gushing into the sky over Nemi. Yellow-black flames, Elise's silhouette weeping. The stench of ancient pitch. It is hard to sleep. So he draws, pyjama sleeves up, measures the angles, sips whisky. It helps to kill the time.

At noon yesterday, the scheduled telephone call came from the Duty Officer in Rome. The city was unusually quiet. No burglaries for two nights, little of the usual seasonal drunkenness or curfew-breaking, no women reporting molestation, no petty thefts or public disorders.

'It would almost make one wonder, sir.'

'I know what you mean.'

'I feel something might be afoot, sir. We have a prisoner here, a Communist, he might be close to talking. What are your orders?'

'Cancel all leave, will you, and shut the main highway. And close all the bridges. I'll be with you in half an hour.'

He had led the interrogation personally, but the student did not break. The body was taken away in a mailbag, so the neighbours wouldn't notice. One doesn't want to discomfit people at Christmastime.

It is to the Nemi house that the second telephone call comes from the Gestapo sergeant-on-duty through the cold, sleety hours after midnight on Christmas Eve. A patrol trooper has reported an unusual nightwalker, a man bearing a false identity card. Through a misunderstanding he has not been arrested, is at large in the city. At present thought to be heading for Trastevere.

Hauptmann doodles on the drawing board, scrawls a triple spiral while he listens. Call completed, he enters the living room. Three-thirty in the morning – far too late for the children to be awake – but they've been unable to sleep, Christmas has taken hold. He blames himself for overexciting them earlier by his talk of the astonishing gifts they'd be receiving: chocolate money, clockwork soldiers, a doll with real hair, a fort, a toy aeroplane that flies. By firelight, Elise is reading them a story, 'Hansel and Gretel', and sharing their daughter's mug of hot chocolate. He does a thing that always makes them laugh – *Oh, Daddy's making a moustache of the whipped cream!* Part of being a father is to clown for them, don't pitch yourself too high above the weak. Children must never fear Daddy.

The aromas of cinnamon and cloves, an incense of burned brown sugar. Foil stars and scarlet candles have been placed in the living room windows, a line of lemonade bottles on the sill. He hears the telephone buzz briskly again, down the corridor, in his study. Elise stumbles away to answer it.

'Are you and Mummy friends again?' his daughter asks.

'We are always friends.'

'Are you going to fight again?'

'No, we're not.'

'I hate it when you fight.'

'Even friends have fights sometimes.'

'Are you getting a divorce?'

'Don't be silly.'

As he ruffles his daughter's yellow hair, she yawns and curls up. Her brother gives a chuckle, bulge-eyed with tiredness, and squeezes his father's hand. Their hair smells of the carbolic shampoo Elise makes them use. How miraculous, these children, with their mother's charm and witty serenity. If only she would not drink so much. He wonders what the matter is.

To hear their breathing lengthen as they approach sleep is one of the great and healing pleasures, often raises tears of raw protectiveness. Elise enters the living room, haughtily beautiful, in a powder-blue dressing robe and pyjamas and a mismatched pair of slippers. 'Paul,' she murmurs. 'They say it's an emergency.'

'Damn them,' he replies, unpeeling himself from the sofa.

'I'll make coffee,' she says. 'In case you need to go in.'

'I shan't be going anywhere.'

The Duty Officer apologises. A further report has arrived. The curfew-breaker observed earlier would seem to match the appearance of the priest whose photograph is on the office noticeboard.

'The priest? You're certain?'

'Reasonably certain, sir.'

'Where is he now?'

'Not quite sure, sir. We're looking.'

'I'll be there in thirty minutes.'

He hurries up the stairs to his bedroom, takes off his pyjamas, hands shaking. From the clothes-rail near the window he pulls his pressed uniform, dons it quickly. Wind rattles the windowpane. Mice tippet in the walls. In the pier glass, he adjusts the death's-head epaulettes, shines the peak of the black cap with a spat-on handkerchief.

'What has happened, Paul,' she says, slurring. 'To make you smile so?'

'It seems Christmas has come. Kiss the children goodnight.'

28

The moon creeps behind a drumlin of smoky cloud.

Blon Kiernan leads him by flashlight through the darkness of the rear garden, the munch and champ of icy gravel underfoot, marram grass through stones, the croaks of woken birds, to the rusted old gate that opens onto the coach alley.

As the gate clunks behind him, he hears the heavy working of the lock, the thunk of old bolts being pulled, her receding footsteps.

Solitude clutches like a jailer.

The alley is narrow and furrowed. Ruts filled with filthy ice. He makes his way past the stable doors and along to the street, which he reckons must be Via Cimarosa, and edges around the corner, heading north.

Stops.

That sound?

Over there, from the doorway.

The click of a pistol's safety catch.

Or the whirr of an insect?

The broad street is empty, traffic lights clacking from green to orange.

He waits thirty seconds.

No one there.

Mind playing tricks. He hastens onward, coughing. The fabric of the unfamiliar coat smells of pipe smoke and sweat, of hedgerows and mothballs and mildew. Tired, you sense the fairies, an old saying of his grandparents. He gulped a bowl of rigatoni before leaving the Kiernans, now regrets the onsetting heaviness, the longing for sleep.

Again comes the *snick*. He turns.

The heat of his breath mists his spectacles to fog. Cleaning them on his handkerchief, he hears a *cha* that might be a suppressed sneeze. Fifty metres behind him, near that news-stand outside the side entrance to the chapel.

Should he run? Stay silent? Could he make it back to the Kiernans if he bolted?

A skeletal fox hobbles out from behind the news-stand, gull in maw, urinates on a fire hydrant, gives a dull, rasping bark.

Now, the moan of the bombers, high above Rome. Goggled, starey men in their cramped glass cockpits, ten miles up, beyond the range of the ack-acks, fingertips poised on release buttons. In the bowels of every death machine, sixteen tonnes of dynamite. Enough to obliterate half a town.

Seventeen years ago, that night flight from Orly. Not long ordained, he spent a winter ministering at St Gabriel's in Archway, standing in for a curate who was ill. He and two confrères, a Glaswegian and a South African, had gone to Paris for a rugby international, had stayed at the Collège des Irlandais. En route back to Beaconsfield, a storm raged up out of the Channel without warning; the little Airco 16 had been battered. The dizziness, the nausea. The wrench of timber splintering, the screams of the passengers. He had prayed, had pleaded. Felt certain he would die. Somehow, inside the terror was a bead of certainty that he was redeemed, the afterlife was real as that storm. But the other priests had not felt that; the Glaswegian left the ministry a year later and married. The South African had taken to drinking.

Turning, he faces into the blackness of the side street, crossing quickly to the shadows by the chapel's high wall, past the railings of the Franciscan cemetery. Bleak statues of the martyrs adorning the mausoleums. Broken, marble fingers groping at the boughs.

So cold now, and silent, as the moon reappears. Its shadowed, unblinking eye.

Across a piazza where every shutter is dark.

A strange fluttering above him.

At first, he thinks they're moths.

In spiralling, dreamlike, downward glide, white swallows in a murmuration, or a flock of youngling doves, silver in creaming moonlight.

Dozens become scores, hundreds, thousands, swooping, coasting, dipping, rustling. As the first of them float within reach of his grasp, he sees they are pieces of paper.

Falling, they flutter around him, drifting, dancing, a snowfall of black-smudged white.

Flapping against the windows of apartment blocks and cars, into dustbins and prattling fountains, over park benches, steeples, the domes of old Rome, the ghetto, the empty tables, the parks and palazzi, the slopping, gurgling Tiber, the barracks and pillars, the highway towards Nemi, to the cobblestones in waterlogged silence.

A moth dances before his eyes, floating on the breeze, backing and forthing, upping and downing, as though animated by his desire to clutch it. When, finally, he grasps it, the paper is damp; ink blackens his fingers as he reads.

PROUD ROMANS!
TAKE COURAGE
THIS IS YOUR FINAL CHRISTMAS UNDER TRYANNY
LIBERATION IS COMING
SABOTAGE THE ENEMY IN EVERY WAY YOU CAN
THE DAYS OF THE NAZIFASCIST OCCUPATION ARE DYING
HAPPY CHRISTMAS TO YOU AND YOUR FAMILY
DESTROY THE INVADER
LONG LIVE ITALY
LONG LIVE THE ROMANS
GENERAL CLARK
UNITED STATES ARMY

The memory comes back to him through the sleet and the fall of wet leaflets. That dark October afternoon, two months ago, the week the Jews were deported. The young Ethiopian seminarian had found him in the Library to say there was a visitor in the Reception Room, a lady that appeared distressed. The rain was atrocious, had emptied the streets. Choir rehearsal had been postponed. Danger felt close. By now, the patrols were passing the gates of the Collegio three times hourly. Fascist police had been seen photographing the building.

In the large room downstairs, she was seated by the window, which someone had forgotten to close. The rain brought in the aromas of earth and the garden. Her hair was wet, in string-like straggles, and the shoulders of her raincoat, which was too large for her, were dark. He asked if she wanted a towel.

'*Bitte*,' she replied quietly. He rang for the servant.

Nothing was said while they waited. He knew who she was. She smoked, stared into the ashtray. He wondered what she would say. The servant came in, listened, hurried from the room, came back a minute later with the towel, went again.

He turned toward the empty fireplace while the visitor dried her hair. The act seemed too intimate to be watched.

When she had finished, she asked with her eyes if she might light another cigarette. He nodded, pushing the onyx ashtray across the table towards her.

'Thank you,' she said, 'for agreeing to see me at such short notice.'

He offered no reply. It was probably a trap.

'You are wondering, I think, why I am here,' she continued, her clipped, formal English plain and elegant.

'I have not had the time to wonder that.'

'I am most anxious. Forgive me.'

'Frau Hauptmann—'

'Might I ask a glass of water?'

He filled a tumbler from the stone jug on the table and she drank it in three swallows. It occurred to him that he should have requested the servant to remain, or that he should send for the Rector; that this conversation should be witnessed. Her wedding ring was unusually slender, like a piece of bronze twine. It brought the presence of who had placed it there into the room.

'There is a matter I would like to discuss with you,' she said. 'A private, family matter. If I might ask your assistance.'

'Are you a Catholic?'

'A bad one.'

'Is it a spiritual question?'

'In its way.'

'Does he know you are here, Frau Hauptmann?'

'No, he doesn't. Not yet.'

'There is nothing that I wish to say to you, Frau Hauptmann, but I am willing to listen. For ten minutes, no more. By that clock on the mantelpiece. After that, if you wish I will send for another priest, a confrère. You may speak with him in full confidence, of course.'

'It is you and only you that I wish to speak with, Monsignor.'

'Why is that?'

'Because I am lost and do not happen to know another priest in Rome.'

'You don't know me either.'

'I have heard my husband mention you.'

'Charmingly, I'm sure.'

'Violently. Angrily. But not always. There are moments.'

'Are there indeed.'

'He sometimes says that in different circumstances you and he might have been friends.'

'Rubbish.'

'In another life.'

'This is this life.'

'Unfortunately.'

'Frau Hauptmann—'

'I have come to ask your protection.'

'In what sense?'

'I wish to enter the Vatican City as a political refugee from Germany. To repudiate National Socialism. With my family.'

A door slammed in the room above. The heavy clock placked.

'I have considered the matter thoroughly,' she said, 'and am ready.'

'You expect me to believe this?'

'It is true.'

'With your family, including your husband? The commander of Rome's Gestapo?'

'I believe his wish is the same as mine but that he is afraid to face it.'

'What is the basis of this belief?'

'A wife's instincts.'

'Have you discussed this matter with your husband or not?'

'The fact that you have never been married is clear. If one may say so with respect.'

'What does that mean?'

'Merely that sometimes in a marriage there are understandings. Silences. The couple are moving towards a moment that has not been articulated in words. But they know it, all the same. What was once believed is over. Sometimes not discussing a subject is a way of discussing it.'

'I ask you a last time. Have you discussed it with your husband or not?'

'I intend to do so this afternoon.'

'Frau Hauptmann, you'll forgive me for not seeing you out. I have pressing matters to attend to. Good evening.'

'He is a caring, considerate husband. A most utterly devoted father. That is his essence, his true nature. He supports his parents financially, also mine, from a salary that is not large.'

'Don't talk rot, would you, Frau Hauptmann. Now I insist that you leave. Take your farrago of untruths and self-deceptions with you.'

'I did not marry a Nazi.'

'This conversation is over.'

'We shall be in St Peter's Square at five to midnight tonight. All I ask is a chance. Do not close the door on us. I beg you. Mercy for my children, if not me.'

'Go now, Frau Hauptmann. Never come here again.'

Angry, he left the room and returned to his work but at quarter to midnight had entered the square, pretending to take photographs of the full moon.

He drifted between the hissing fountains, the obelisk and the steps, aiming his camera at the ocean of the sky. Rain and the curfew meant nobody was in the vast space but for a trio of street sweepers who worked a slow way around the colonnade, occasionally calling out instructions to one another or crossing to their arch-backed truck to empty out a bag of rubbish. By midnight, they too were gone.

The October moon in his lens was a yellow-tinged coin. The great bells tolled. No one came.

The fountains slowed to a dribble. Then, silence.

Had she been fishing for intelligence? He tried to remember what he had said to her in the Reception Room. He wouldn't put it past Hauptmann to use his own wife as a tout. Perhaps he should go to the Rector this minute.

Ten past. Quarter past. A lone cormorant squawked.

A vision assailed him of the obelisk toppling into the square, bombs exploding around it, hails of shrapnel. Augustus's armies had brought it from Egypt on a vast silver barge, the largest vessel the world had ever seen. For twenty centuries the pillar had been tortured by the weather of Rome. Any night, it might fall. Would he see it?

Twenty past.

Half past.

Photographs of the moon.

At quarter to one a gust blew around the square, raising cold and grit. As he pocketed his camera to leave, and lifted his collar to the night, the black, bulletproof Mercedes purred into view, halting at the Vatican line.

Steam rose from its hood. Headlamps darkened.

The two children emerged abruptly, as though someone had pushed them, each bearing a cardboard suitcase. The girl had with her a doll, the boy a teddy bear. Then came their mother, then Hauptmann in civilian clothing.

All four walked to the perimeter, Elise Hauptmann fighting tears, the children bumping their cases along the cobbles. On her back was a hiker's rucksack, under her arm an umbrella. Hauptmann did not wave as they walked away. Tugging a bottle from his pocket, he took a long, spilling swig, hurled it through the air in the direction of the obelisk but it smashed on the wall of the fountain.

'*Are you happy, Priest?*' he roared. 'To have stolen my family? Planting stupidities in my wife's head in order to trap me? I see you there in the darkness, you skulking, sly bastard. Come out, you filthy thief. Here's your loot.'

Elise Hauptmann bowed her head, sobbing hard, as she kept walking, children beside her.

'I told her, *go if you wish,*' her husband howled, 'only *never come back*. Never contact me again. Desert me and you're dead. *You think you can bait me, O'Flaherty?* Take them. Do your worst. *I'm still here.* You have murdered me, Priest. But look hard, *I'm still here*. Be afraid, there is nothing else you can do to me now. *You have shot your last arrow.* You cur.'

Returning to the Mercedes, Hauptmann entered. The engine chugged on. The headlamps glowed large as he began the very slow three-point turn, their yellow beams sweeping the square.

Imploding into tears, the little boy turned and ran for the car, hurtling, spilling his suitcase, crying out '*Vati, bitte geh' nicht,*' followed by his weeping sister, and now, by their mother, whose left shoe came off as she ran through the billow of her children's spilled clothes.

The boy pounded on the back window as the Mercedes continued inching away. He followed, begging his father to let him in, not to go, and his sister wailed, too, in a terrible rending scream, '*Verlasse uns nicht, Vati. Es tut uns leid!*'

Daddy, don't leave us, we're sorry.

The Mercedes paused for a moment before permitting them to enter.

Then heavily, slowly drove away.

October. Two months ago. Taillights in the mist.

The crossroads, rejected.

The last chance, declined.

Now, in the small hours of Christmas morning, he seems to remember a sight he never saw, Hauptmann at that wheel. Driving in silence.

Cigarette smoke. Gear-grind. His children's sobs.

Why didn't you stop him? mocks the shadow.

There was more you could have done.

He walks on, towards the backstreet, feeling followed.

———

The sidecar in which Hauptmann is being carried feels frail as an egg. On the ride down from Nemi, through the dark, wet meadows, away from the lake and the cinnamon-scented children, he loads his Luger with seven high-pressure cartridges, checks there are more in his tunic pocket, calculates the hour to come.

He has given his orders. No arrest, nothing hasty.

The priest is to be tracked; a list of his movements compiled. The message is going out over the radio now. Commander Hauptmann will take charge of the surveillance when he arrives in the city in twenty-seven minutes. Wake his driver. Prepare the Mercedes for collection at Gestapo headquarters. Be sure Interrogation Cell Zero is free.

The forest track wends down towards the highway for Rome and the pillion car bounces with every jounce and sharp swerve, bolts and rockers creaking, engine razzing like a hornet, but the rider, a heavy man, stands hard on the accelerator and soon they are gunning towards the amber glint of the *autostrada* lights, up ahead, through the winter-thinned trees.

'Faster,' calls Hauptmann. 'Get your foot off the brake.'

The box of ammunition in his pocket gives a glum little rattle as though wanting to assent to the urging.

Over the speed-mounds leading to the barricade at the edge of the clearing, the troopers Hitler-saluting as the red rail is lifted, the orange-purple glow of a brazier on their helmets. He greets their raised arms with a wave. Brave lads, so far from their parents at Christmastime. Tomorrow he will get the cook to bring them a turkey, plum cake, a bottle of schnapps. But better — *why not?* — to serve them himself. He and Elise will visit the barrack-house, perhaps bring the children. An old military nobleness, to swap roles on Christmas Day. All officers should remember they were once common soldiers. They'll sing '*Stille Nacht*' together. He hopes Elise won't slur.

As the compound's exit gates are approached, the dirt track becomes gravelled, and the floodlight blazes on a young woman pinned to a pine trunk by two troopers. She fights back with such vigour, landing punches and head-butts, that a third trooper, a veteran old enough to be her grandfather, approaches with a truncheon, smashing her into a hedge.

Hauptmann barks for his rider to stop, steps out of the pillion car. The air smells of cold and petrol.

'What is going on here?'

'Sir, we came upon this trespasser twenty minutes ago, in the woods. This man was with her.' He nods towards a handcuffed, face-beaten youth. 'Courting couple, they said. He was armed with a shotgun. And making his way towards your house.'

'That's a lie,' the youth insists.

'Shut your mouth.'

As Hauptmann approaches the young woman, she goes to speak but lowers her head. The children are so fond of her, it will be hard to administer punishment. But perhaps there is an innocent explanation.

'Maria?' he asks the nanny. 'What were you doing in the forbidden zone? And who is this man?'

She says nothing.

'Shall I ask him?' Hauptmann says. 'Is that what you suggest?'

The youth displays no fear but stands straighter, taller, his lean torso visible through the ripped shreds of shirt. It is hard to dislike him. Something admirable about a streetfighter.

'Explain yourself,' Hauptmann says quietly. 'And tell me the truth.'

'I was out setting traps. I am a hunter. As I told them.'

'A poacher?'

'I strayed into these woods by accident. My torch stopped working and anyway, there is no fence.'

'Sir, there is,' a trooper snaps.

'It was cut.'

'Because *you* cut it.'

'Every farmer for ten kilometres around knows the extent of this property,' Hauptmann says. 'It is clear you have been lying to my men.'

'I am not a farmer. Until recently I worked at the cement factory in Velletri. Before it was bombed. My livelihood is gone. And this has nothing to do with Maria, she's just a girl I know from the village.'

'What was she doing here with you?'

'Walking.'

'You are aware of course that poaching is a capital offence.'

'What is a man to do when his children are hungry?'

'Hold out your hands.'

The youth does as commanded.

'I do not think you work in a cement factory. You look soft. Like a city girl.' Hauptmann's men laugh, a sound he enjoys hearing. A good officer should always be admired by his soldiers. 'You are a Partisan. A Communist. You know the fate that awaits you.'

'I am no Partisan, no Communist, I cannot afford politics. I am nothing but a father desperate to feed his children on Christmas Day. You have children yourself. For pity's sake, let me go.'

'How do you know I have children?'

'Someone told me.'

'Who?'

'Sir, I – can't remember, it's well known, people talk.'

'Try a little harder. *What concern of yours are my children?*'

'I was speaking in a general way; they are none of my concern.'

'What is your name?'

'Luca Ricci.'

'You swear to me on your eternal soul that you are not a Partisan, Luca Ricci?'

'I swear it.'

'On your children's souls, too?'

'Of course.'

'Very good. You may leave. Just this once. Happy Christmas. Never again make the mistake of trespassing onto this compound. Understand me?'

As Luca Ricca turns to go, Hauptmann steps forward and fires through the back of the neck. Crossing to Maria Esposito, he shoots her in the forehead.

'They tried to escape,' he orders the sentries. 'Now, quickly. To the city.'

29

Crossing the tram tracks, breathless, he hastens through the passageway and into the Via Ventinovesimo.

Two figures are huddled near the advertising sign for the *Corriere della Sera*. Seeing him, one drops a lighted cigarette to the pavement; the other picks it up, tosses it into a stone trough by the garage.

The signal.

A heron gives a shriek. Wind blusters up. Approaching, he now sees that the figures are both in priestly clothing.

Without acknowledging him, they start northward, quickly, almost lurching, in the direction of the widening, statue-adorned end of the piazza. A dozen paces behind, he follows.

Ahead of him, they bolt into an unseen laneway. When he catches up, rounding the corner, one figure has vanished. The other is revealed to be a young woman.

'*Andiamo*,' she says, nodding briskly towards the half-opened shutters of the abandoned theatre.

Through the glass-strewn foyer surveyed by a vast, shattered mirror, the moon in a hundred shards on the floor. Down the aisle through the burst-apart, burned velvet seats, scorched putti capering on opera boxes. Up the carpeted steps to the stage, the slink of a dozen meagre cats around a papier-mâché shipwreck. Pools of fallen plush.

Now into the wings, her torch-beam on bare, knotted boards. A stench of mould, of blue-rotting oranges. Past hulking, draped shapes, plaster heads still bewigged, the haggish ghoul of an upturned mop in a bucket. Down a flight of trembling wooden stairs, through the fire-escape doors, into a yard giving out on an alley.

Turning, she asks, 'Are you ready? It will be difficult.'

'I understand.'

Nodding, she pulls a hessian hood from inside her jacket, places it over his head, tightens the fasten-cord.

'Take my arm,' she whispers. 'Two steps down. Then left.'

In blackness, he feels himself led, but he falters, stumbles, hot mist in his eyes, the tutting impatience of the young woman. Then someone else has joined, is clutching him by the left elbow, and they're flurrying him through what feels like a garden or a terrace, through a smell of wet vegetation and oversweet winter lilac. He asks them to slow, but the woman says they can't. Time has run on, they are late.

Ropes of pain in his thighs. A firestorm in his lungs.

He's aware of being helped across streets, the change from tarmacadam to cobbles. For a minute, the river feels close.

Not water, but sopping sedge and the tinkle of halyards. The thought looms that Mark Antony knew the stench of that sedge, that it pinkened the night-mares of Nero.

He does not want to get into the motorcar, feels a hand pressing down on his head. *We're lying you on the back seat, be quiet.* As he obeys, a heavy blanket stinking of wet dog is flung over him. The car jolts away; a bad driver, young? The woman whispers in staccato; the driver hisses back, coughing. After ten or a dozen minutes, the rear door is opened. He's hauled out, legs unsteady. She checks the hood is still tight.

'Careful,' she murmurs, 'do not be afraid,' as he's led into a building he can tell by the reek of smoke is a bombsite, and now up spiralling stone stairs as in a medieval castle's turret. He feels his spectacles slip loose, gropes through the hood of sacking to get them back on, begs the duo leading him to pause even a moment but they don't. The smell of their perspiration, the aroma of washed hair. Wooden doors roll open. A chain is clanked free.

Down what might be a concrete ramp, the stench of gasoline and auto grease; bolts being unshot, the heavy *skreek* of metal gates. A blinding wash of thirst. Cold air. He's outside.

'All right,' says a man's voice. 'You're here. Count to twenty. Then take off the hood, not before.'

'Where do I go, then?'

'Count to twenty. *Buona fortuna.*'

By the time he has unhooded, there is no one on the long street of apart-ment blocks. Its thousand shuttered windows are dark.

From somewhere in the middle distance, the bleat of a police siren. He blinks, after-images of hydrants and doorways on his retinae. Behind him, the locked gates of a mechanic's workshop, the '*O*' in the '*AUTO*' sign a cartoon archery target.

Wiping runnels of sweat from his forehead and arms with the hood, he pushes it into a dustbin.

On the corner, a scallop-shelled fountain in a little archway set into a cobbled wall. The coldness of the water. He bathes his wrists and throbbing face. Wheezing, sneezing, he looks at his watch. Twenty minutes to five. The stillness of Rome before dawn.

Across a wall, a stencilled notice in German exclaims:

'*Strassen gesperrt. Bandengebiet.*'

Streets closed. Gang Area.

Their code for the Partisans.

The thrown pebble turns him.

Fifty metres away, between the tramlines, a bin lid is rolling.

Slow as a rowboat, he approaches.

He halts at a gateway, through which he can see a Fiat up on bricks, a relic from the twenties, cracked windscreen, gull-ripped soft-top.

After a moment, the signal.

So quiet; hardly audible.

A scratchy gramophone record playing the *Moonlight Sonata*.

He enters the arched portico, past the mailboxes and dustbins, crosses a tidy, pave-slabbed courtyard, the glazed pots shining.

Behind him, he hears the heavy gate being shut but he doesn't turn. Ahead, the door opens, a bulb blinks on in the narrow hallway. He enters, walks through the corridor, out the back door, across a laneway, into the courtyard of a much older house.

In a window, a middle-aged woman in an indigo dressing gown and hairnet is smoking, avoiding his glance, looking up at the dawn. They don't know each other's names, never will.

Pushing open the door, she crushes the cigarette out beneath her slipper, steps backwards.

Entering the living room, he crosses to the fireplace.

The curtain to the courtyard has been pulled closed by a barefoot teenaged girl in boy's trousers and work shirt. It is clear she and the middle-aged woman are mother and daughter.

The gramophone plays. Framed tintypes on the walls. Old men in military uniform, children in First Communion clothes by a lake. A poster for a performance of *Tosca*, 'Beniamino Gigli' in bold red. A dog-basket under a rococo mahogany table. A twelve-armed candelabrum.

A lidless, pewter teapot bristling with pencils and pens. In the corner, an eerie, firelit, cast-iron-wheeled apparatus that it takes him a moment to recognise as a sewing machine.

She asks with her eyes if he is ready. He nods that he is.

Pulling a scissors from her pocket, the seamstress approaches. He takes off the old overcoat, hands it to her, she lays it on the workbench, parts its pleats, begins cutting, from its depths. She retrieves the taped packets of banknotes, working carefully, methodically, in wordless concentration, now circling steadily around the laid-out coat. The deft, slick snip of the scissor-blades. Frayed lengths of fabric fall to the rug. The girl kneels, brushes them into a large metal dustpan, empties it into the seething hearth.

Through a door towards a candlelit pantry, he sees that a third woman, far older, in housecoat and pince-nez spectacles, is standing over a table, slicing open the stacks of banknotes with a steak knife. Distributing them between envelopes, which she places in a shoebox. Glancing up, she wordlessly offers a glass from the bottle of wine at her side and seems unsurprised when he shakes his head.

Nearby, on marble platters, three fruitcakes cut into hollowed-out halves. She wraps bundles in foil, wedging them into the cakes, pushing the halves back together, now sheeting them with wraps of yellow marzipan. The girl enters the pantry, fetches a bowl of unset icing from a cupboard; starts into icing the cakes as the old woman nods approbation, sometimes guiding her, now taking her wrist, showing her to move the spatula smoothly, deftly.

The Beethoven skips, returns to its beginning.

A new old coat is brought for him, and he dons it.

Not one word is uttered during the drop, which takes less than a hundred seconds. As he goes, the seamstress dips her fingertips into a Holy Water font by the door and touches them briskly to his forehead.

Two masked youths are waiting in the street, he permits them to blindfold him; he is walked for a time, then driven in a car, then walked again until he hears the river. 'Count to ten,' they whisper, 'good luck,' as they go, and he waits for the receding footsteps to be no longer audible before he uncovers his pulsing eyes.

Ahead of him, the Tiber. Over rooftops, the dome of St Peter's.

Quickly along the quay, into strong slabs of wind, past the high, rusted gates of the prison. Up the steep steps of the passageway, through a sloping street so narrow that the front rooms of the apartments look into one another, and the washing lines strung between them are hard to tell apart with their buntings of grey chemises and socks.

Some brave Roman has draped a tattered tricolour over a half-collapsed balcony, the red, white and green faded by laundering and quarterlight. Across the flag, the patchwork words *'Viva l'Italia!'*

The clank of a shutter. He stops.

Birds churring faintly.

So quiet.

He can hear the river moving, the shush-and-lapping on old, cold stone, the swaying of sedge in the shallows near the banks, water rats nuzzling beneath the bridges.

Twenty past five. Vital to make haste.

He turns. Via Segundo. Rain starts to fall.

The back streets that lead to the Basilica.

Ambling towards him out of the shadows, at an easy, measured pace, two men in grey raincoats, homburgs low. He knows they have seen him; too late to turn back. They pause beneath the only lamp left unbroken on the street, light cigarettes, begin to talk, gesturing, nodding, as though explaining something contended, but their voices are so low that he can make nothing out.

They're standing sidelong, half-facing away from him, but he knows that doesn't matter. Gestapo men can see out of the backs of their skulls. Don't pause, walk steadily. If you bolt, they will catch you. They're armed and half your age. You are Marco Mancuso.

'Buongiorno,' one of them murmurs.

'Buon Natale,' he replies.

They're not SS, he sees now. Too relaxed, conversational. An older woman with a suitcase approaches from the end of the street, they greet her with filial embraces and stroll away together in the direction of town.

He hastens around the corner.

Into Hauptmann's jutting Luger.

Everything is quiet. The Nazi's eyes shining.

The shock is like a punch. A pummel to the stomach. A thousand times, a million, he has anticipated this moment, but the scald of it shocks him, the physical closeness of the other, the veins in his eyelids, the pallor of his lips, the throbbing worm in his temple, the whiff of his steadying breath.

Far above, the drone of bombers, grey light in the sky.

From the gun battery dug into the peak of the Palatine Hill, the searchlights spring on, white beams criss-crossing the clouds, and the ack-acks begin to rattle. Hauptmann half-turns, oddly childlike, as though magnetised by the music.

'Walk,' he says. 'Ahead of me. Hands high.'

Down an alleyway reeking of bins. The Mercedes waiting at the end.

Hauptmann opens the rear door, kicks him into the seat, climbs quickly in beside him.

'Proceed,' Hauptmann commands the driver. 'Gestapo Headquarters.'

The car moves off, at first slowly, then climbing sighingly through the gears, Hauptmann lighting a cigarette, now seeming to frown at the match before blowing it out. For a time, he says nothing, as though comforted by the soothe of the engine. The car stops at amber lights, allowing an early tram to truckle past.

'I can answer the question that is upmost in your mind,' Hauptmann says. 'Your friends are as good as dead. By tonight or tomorrow morning I shall have extracted from you their names and whereabouts. Their final knowledge will be that you betrayed them.'

The walkie-talkie receiver crackles on the Nazi's left lapel, then a softer sound, murmurous, like a waterfall heard from a distance.

'Perhaps it is even yet not too late, Monsignor. Are you prepared to be reasonable? I am a believer in mercy.'

'Go to hell.'

'Ah, here is Via Tasso, Monsignor. Your final address on this Earth.'

The driver gets out, ascends the three steps into the building. Lamps go on in windows. Now Hauptmann steps out, yawning, walks around the back of the Mercedes.

'Exit slowly, Monsignor. With your hands on your head.'

He does as commanded, Hauptmann regarding him.

'The high-and-mighty Monsignor. Where is your Choir now?'

'You poor man,' O'Flaherty says.

'Why so?'

'Have you truly not realised what this entire charade was about?'

'Enlighten me.'

'What time is it, Hauptmann?'

'Thirteen minutes past six.'

'Just so.'

'Meaning?'

'Thirteen minutes ago, your wife entered Vatican City with your children and sought asylum. All we needed was a decoy you'd bite at, to get you out of the way. Elise swore you'd fall for it. I didn't believe you'd be so gullible.'

Hauptmann smiles bleakly. 'This is the best you can do?'

'News of their defection will be announced on the BBC World Service in seventeen minutes. The Vatican photographer is with your wife and children now at the British Ambassador's apartment. A sea plane is waiting at Ostia to take them to Dover. Your wife intends to seek British citizenship.'

'Monsignor, don't you know that it is a sin to lie?'

'Telephone your villa. No one will answer.'

'You think me so weak-minded that I would actually test this nonsense?'

'A photograph of your family with the British Ambassador has just now been cabled to Berlin. To every newspaper in Europe and to the Führer's personal office. Your wife's statement condemns National Socialism and predicts its imminent defeat by the Allies, a defeat she now pledges to do all in her power to support. She adds that you yourself know the war to be lost by Germany. That you plan the assassination of Hitler.'

'Rubbish.'

'I have a signed copy of her statement, here in my breast pocket. Would you like to see it?

'DON'T MOVE.'

'Calm down.'

'Do not tell me what to do.'

'Step closer, take it out of my pocket. Or I'll do it? As you wish.'

'Be silent, I warn you. *No more of your lies.*'

'I realise this is a dreadful blow to you. The loss of your family. Never to see them again is a terrible fate, I know. She asked me to say that she left a goodbye letter for you. On her dressing table at your villa. With her wedding ring.'

Hauptmann makes for his radio mouthpiece, O'Flaherty uppercuts the

Luger from the Nazi's right fist, not a heavy punch, but fast and accurate, an ice-hard, driven drub, the gunmetal slicing open his own knuckles so he cries out in pain, the pistol somersaults into a wall before clattering to the gutter, and he dummies, as though making a snatch for it, as Hauptmann dips, grasping, but the slimy handle is slippery and the pistol spins in gutter water and the priest is *in the car, at the steering wheel*, revving, spots of blood on the bullet-proof windscreen and now the Mercedes is moving.

Hauptmann grabs at the door handle. The jolt rips his left shoulder from its socket.

Is the screech out of his own mouth? Is it tyre-rubber shrieking? The choke of black smoke as the car jounces away from him, sheering like a colt unleashed. That stench of burned Firestones. The bawl of the engine. Smoke spewing from the wheel-wells. Vomit of exhaust in his face. The *blam* of his Luger, stink of cordite, wet lead.

Now he's running after the Mercedes, swim-headed with pain, but running, *running*, shooting into the blackness, the car strikes a news-stand, graunches, reverses, he kneels, like a marksman, one accurate shot is all he needs, bullets crunching off its armour, sparking away in silver flakes, and the Mercedes squeals and rasps around the corner whose name he doesn't know and his Luger screams its fury but the Mercedes is gone, roaring down the blitzkrieg where his shoulder socket should be, in the direction of the rain-boosted Tiber.

He bellows for help, the SS driver runs from the building, stupefied, cursing, the priest has escaped, Hauptmann staggers from door to door along Via Tasso, but nobody answers.

Pounding, threatening.

'*I need help.*'

Somehow, in the agony, he sees the Mercedes speeding through Rome, saluted by sentries, barricades lifting. Tottering after it, he's lost on a filthy back street, a hail of bricks and chimneypots raining on him from the rooftops. Minutes later, delirious with pain, he is encountered by German patrolmen to whom he manages to stammer what has happened, but when the Sergeant radios for the Mercedes to be stopped at any cost, the troopers guarding the bridge are discomfited, sensing trickery.

Fire on Hauptmann's car? The Gestapo commander? Sign your own death warrant first.

Now the Mercedes has crossed the Ponte Cavour, has been logged approaching the Interior Ministry at speed. A sentry in a third-floor window radios an emergency. 'Hauptmann is running amok.'

Over the bridge, the Contessa is waiting in the rendezvous place, the porch of an abandoned bakery. Right hand bleeding, he jumps from the Mercedes. Reaching into it, she plunges her lighted cigarette down the maw of the fuel tank, leads him through the maze of passageways and cloistered footpaths where the stolen motorcycle is waiting, climbs onto the bike, he behind her; she kicks the starter, swerves, curses over her shoulder, 'Head down, Hugh, head down,' gunning along the passageways, the labyrinth of dark lanes, as behind them the explosion roars, smoke roiling and dense, blown down through the narrow back streets into the Piazza del Risorgimento, where it stains the awnings black.

In the shadowed doorway of the Musei Vaticani, Derry and Osborne are waiting, beckoning, waving, faces etched with anxious joy, summoning their friends in from out of the rain that is pouring its coldness on Rome. He staggers, slammed by breathlessness, the Contessa's shoulder supporting him. 'Gentlemen,' she says, 'may I present the doer of the impossible.' Embraces and back-slaps, towels, flasks of tea – well, not exactly tea, as Sam Derry puts it, not the tea they deserve, but cloves in hot milk – well, not exactly milk, as Osborne remarks, but sock-flavoured toothpaste, dissolved. Through the corridors of the museums, keeping quiet, moving quickly, stumbling, gasping, a deep diver surfacing, half-carried by his companions, in serious, efficient silence, for the security guards are on duty and not all to be trusted, down the landings, up the staircase, through the Cappella Sistina, where he pauses a moment in the numb, white blaze that is the prayerfulness of a survivor, a joy that includes grief and loss. For his parents on Chrismas morning, for every friendship not made, for the escapees who will now live and the thousands who need them, for the numberless, nameless, suffering fallen for whom no one but their comrades ever fought. For Derry, Angelucci, Delia and May, for Osborne, Marianna and Giovanna Landini, praying beside him now, hand in his hand, who, often, when she recollects their dash to the Vatican that dawn, the Roman sky purpling the silhouetted statues, hears him singing a Puccini aria behind her, though she knows that can't have happened. For his sister and brothers, for everyone a prisoner, for all starved of mercy or force-fed on lies. But it's time to hurry along now, Derry says, quietly, arm around his shoulders, 'Lean here, Padre.'

'I do think you might address him as "Hugh" at this stage,' Osborne chuckles.

'I've a better idea,' says Derry. 'Been practising my Italian. Give me your arm, *mio fratello*.'

At Lake Nemi, Frau Hauptmann and her children sleep late on Christmas morning. Daddy won't be home for a while.

Near five o'clock that evening, Hugh O'Flaherty climbs to the roof of St Peter's, alone.

Domes and high dovecots. Campaniles. Seven hills. Stately, grey seabirds whirling in the mist. Chimneypots and steeples. The glister of early stars. Dusk is coaxing lamps on, all over the city. Torches glint from attic windows, carving lines through the smokefall. From Flaminio to Ponte, from Prati to Campo Marzio. Bridges. Palaces. Tenements. Fallen temples. He waits for the great bells to salute the close of day.

Afterwards, such silence.

Almost music.

———

Dear Mam and Dad,

Just a note from snowbound Rome.

I said Mass for you this morning, the feast of St Stephen.

In case I never told you: No one ever had more loving parents.

Thank you for my life.

Happy 1944.

Your Hugh

30

MARIANNA DE VRIES
November 1962
Statement in lieu of an interview

More die coming down Everest than perish on the way up. A fact known by soldiers and bank robbers everywhere. Every raid needs its getaway driver.

From the outset it had been agreed that Jo Landini would rendezvous with the mission-runner two kilometres from home and that a motorcycle was the best option, or at any rate the least-bad. One would never plan a Rendimento without plotting with fanatical assiduousness the safest way back to base. That was at Derry's insistence, fruit of his Sandhurst training. A mission-runner can get sloppy at the very end of the run; he's exhausted, falsely elated; it's the most dangerous few minutes. He needs help getting over the line.

Jo, as I have said, was a woman of immense personal courage. She insisted that she would be what we termed 'the guidelight' for the Christmas Eve Rendimento, a role she had fulfilled on seven previous missions and would reprise on a further five in early '44. Usually, we stole the motorcycle from the German army. A certain Londoner whom I need not name assisted in that respect. 'All's fair in love and war,' was his watchword.

I lay low for ten days, then fled into the Vatican. Delia Kiernan and her daughter had done the same. Apart from the further Rendimenti with which she was centrally involved, Jo did not leave Vatican City for the remainder of the German occupation. She and I lodged in May and Sir D'Arcy's quarters, to the amusement (perhaps the envy, she used to say) of certain ordained observers. An eminent Cardinal was once seen not quite kneeling to the keyhole but hanging about in the corridor as though awaiting an invitation to join the non-existent orgy. 'Perhaps we'll make it existent one evening when we're bored,' Sir D'Arcy said.

'One would need to be *quite* bored,' Jo rejoindered.

The flat, which had three rooms, was cramped enough but comfortable. Its little circular windows gave out on a garden. We played backgammon and parlour games. There were books. Sometimes we gazed in companionable silence at the mint-and-cherry Roman sunset, an event for which Sir D'Arcy always donned his Black Watch tartan smoking jacket. The peak of nightly excitement was choosing which pair of his carpet slippers to borrow and enduring his eye-watering tales of the corns that made his frequent recourse to such footwear inevitable. ('Good ladies, I have had bunions one could place a hat on and put up for election.') Food was in short supply and what passed for coffee tasted like sludge. But we had plenty of Piper-Heidsieck '33, thanks to May. The King was toasted respectfully by our British hosts at six every evening. People had worse early 1944s.

We became a quintet when Angelucci, too, took refuge with us, having got his wife and their children out to the relative safety of the countryside beyond Viterbo. She would die in a bombing raid in March, having briefly returned to Rome to visit a family member who was ill – this tragedy was some months ahead of us, as were many more.

For now, Angelucci proved an excellent cook – the art of eating well is to the Italians one of the highest arts. He was able to do a lot with very little ('like all Marxists,' Sir D'Arcy used to quip). Enzo could make a pasta of wheat and water, without eggs, a luxury we didn't possess, that, with a little pepper and Parmigiano, if we had it, would make one sing. Sir D'Arcy would wickedly tease him by saying, 'Dear boy, *all* the finest people in England are Communist these days, why, one can't throw a stick in the Magdalen dining hall without hitting a comrade or whatever they are. Pass the Nero d'Avola, there's a love.'

Angelucci was a magnificent person whose contribution was beyond measure. Even his habit of going about shirtless was forgivable. There are unfortunate people one meets who see food as merely bodily fuel. The Italians know that it is a very great deal more than that. When asked if he believed in God, Enzo used to answer that he believed in *risotto al radicchio e Gorgonzola* with a glass of something fragrant and one's friends. For him, there was no holier word in any language than '*mangiamo*'.

'Best answered with a silent Amen,' Jo Landini answered once, serving out the food.

'Contessa, we'll make a Communist of you yet,' Enzo responded.

'My dearest chef, you wouldn't have terribly far to go. Now for pity's sake, put on a shirt, we're eating.'

'Come the revolution,' remarked Sir D'Arcy, 'everyone shall travel First Class.'

'Count me out,' said Johnny May. 'I ain't toiling for the masses.'

'*Toiling,*' mocked Sir D'Arcy. 'You think being handsome is work.'

'If it is,' said Jo, 'he works hard.'

'Don't be talking of Communism in front of my daughter,' Delia said, both Kiernan ladies being our guests that night. 'She'll assassinate me in my sleep.'

'Mother, for God's sake.'

'Is there e'er a drop of wine? I've a thirst would sink ships.'

'Mother, you've had *enough.*'

'If I'm not given a drink this minute, it's my *own* shirt I'll take off.'

'Jesus Christ Almighty.'

'More pasta?'

There was not much room. People could become irritable. But if some of us jumped our trolleys, the others were forgiving.

In truth I remember it as a not unhappy time. Major Derry would often surface from his lair in the excavations, Ugo might pay us a visit for a hand or two of poker or lansquenet, games he played with unpriestly vehemence. In the end, at our insistence, he joined our household at the lodgings, a place to which he referred as 'the digs'. It was evident from intelligence reports that he was in very grave danger anywhere else. Indeed, it had been brought home to us rather sharply.

One February afternoon in St Peter's, two Nazi operatives in plainclothes arrived, with the intention of hustling him out of the Basilica and over the boundary. Thankfully, Enzo had by then assumed responsibility for Ugo's protection. A squad of fourteen escapees dressed as cowled monks – Enzo favoured Glaswegian dockworkers and Yugoslav miners – formed a covert diamond-pattern around the Monsignor whenever he entered a public area. The two plainclothesmen were shall we say assisted out of St Peter's that afternoon, unfortunately tripping on the steps. Several times. Nasty men, in a most unsporting manner they kept attacking Enzo's fist with their faces. I would imagine they recall the occasion now and again, even yet, for example whenever they need to move their jaws.

The bunks and hammocks in the flat – indeed, the little round windows, too – gave the place something pleasing, the feeling of a ship. In the evenings, to sustain the spirits or to tire ourselves towards sleep, we often sang an old Scottish song from those nights of rehearsal, gentlemen taking the verses, ladies the chorus.

Let us go, lassie, go
To the braes of Balquhither,
Where the blueberries grow
'Mong the bonnie Highland heather;
Where flie the deer and rae
Lightly bounding altogether,
Sport the lovelorn summer day
On the braes of Balquhither.
Let us go, lassie, go.
Lassie, go.

Funny thing, none of us had ever been to the Scottish Highlands, a place I never think about without hearing that song, near the end of the war in Italy, among backgammon pieces and glasses of Chianti, in our little *ménage à huit*.

The Christmas Eve mission succeeded. Hundreds of Books were safely moved from Rome into the countryside. We ran many further Rendimenti, perhaps fifteen or two dozen, between that Christmastime and late spring, 1944 – including one mission to steal or destroy Hauptmann's hoard of forged currency, another to smuggle a surgeon into a safehouse not two minutes from Gestapo headquarters, to attempt a lifesaving procedure on an escapee. But this is not the time to speak of those terrifying nights. Doubtless there will be other occasions. It became an era of great personal pain.

I suppose that what must be called tensions came to exist in the Choir, as the Allied advance on the city progressed. Ugo wished to aid deserting German conscripts, every one of whom was in peril of being beaten to death. Sir D'Arcy saw matters differently. The Monsignor and he quarrelled.

Cracks worsened. Foundations shifted. Harsh words buckled pillars. Things were said in the heat of argument that would have been better left unspoken.

Over the subsequent months, the Choir fell apart, as all good things will. Ugo and Sir D'Arcy stopped speaking. Ugo departed the flat.

There was innocence on both sides rather than guilt on either. Poor Sir D'Arcy, I believe, had misunderstood, had all along not quite seen the point. One can persuade oneself for a moment that the same song is being sung. But that is rarely the case, alas. What is happening is little more than the concretisation of a Venn diagram. Which isn't nothing, by the way. But there is more to life than geometry. My enemy need not of necessity be the enemy of my friend. But it helps, I suppose. There it is.

Attempts were made by the redoubtable Delia to mend burning bridges – I seem to remember a luncheon or something of that nature being mooted – but for some reason it never happened. I became so distressed by the implosion that, in the end, on an early June morning, I left, returning to my old apartment through the cold, scarlet dawn. On the way, I saw the spectral and astonishing sight of a lone American Army jeep heading towards St Peter's Square. Liberation had come to Rome.

Enzo and Jo would be awarded high honours by the Italian government, as was Ugo.

Dollman was lynched while trying to get out of the country. It was widely felt in Rome that he was in as much danger from Hauptmann as he was from the Romans, the two having fallen out badly when Hauptmann began suspecting his second-in-command of touting on him to Himmler. Sometimes I have seen it written that the National Socialist movement was a brotherhood. In fact, it was a hate-gang, led by inadequates and psychopaths, loyal as that species of poisonous frog that eats its own siblings after it has devoured everything else it can find. What is chilling is how many people permitted themselves to be led. 'Permitted', in fact, is not quite an active enough verb. Agreed in warm enthusiasm to be led.

Hauptmann was tried in 1948 for the murder of three hundred and thirty-five Romans in one night, retaliation for a Partisan bombing that killed thirty-three German soldiers. In the court it was detailed how he spent hours in his office that day, among his beloved files, compiling the death list, including Jews, old men, children, prisoners from Regina Coeli, several helpers of the Escape Line. Ten for every German. Plus five, to make certain. Taken to the Ardeatine Caves and gunned down.

He was tie-less in the dock, spoke quietly, often blinking hard or glancing about the courtroom in an odd, intense manner as though startled by something nobody else could see.

During the lunch break in the proceedings, I filed my report. The act of writing out what had happened made me vomit.

When the hearing resumed, it returned quickly to events at the caves. Photographs were displayed but it was difficult to look at them. A Nazi officer had waited at the entrance, Hauptmann's list in hand, on a clipboard. Most methodical. The prisoners were beaten from trucks, roped together in groups of five, led into the darkness, shot, bodies dumped where they fell. Hauptmann led the shootings in person, to give an example of leadership to his men.

Even working with such efficiency, the killings took all night – sometimes a prisoner did not die immediately and had to be finished off – but yes, Hauptmann said, probably some were buried still alive. The task was so arduous that, in order to complete it, he and his gunmen had to get out of their minds on brandy. At dawn, the mouth of the caves was dynamited and blocked with cement, and the Germans drove back to the city. Thousands of copies of a poster were already being plastered on the walls of Rome, warning that further reprisals would follow any Partisan attack.

There was an intense silence in the courtroom as sentence was handed down, apart from the faint sound of a stenographer trying not to weep. Hauptmann in the dock displayed no emotion whatever but turned the winder on his wristwatch as though correcting the time.

Life imprisonment without parole, to be served in Modena prison. Other Nazis involved in that night's horror escaped to Argentina.

Following painstaking work at the Ardeatine Caves, many belongings of those murdered there were recovered and identified. Pocket books, crucifixes, combs, gloves, love letters, paperbacks, pens. Some were placed in the Museum of the Occupation, the former Gestapo headquarters on Via Tasso, a place I have never been able to visit.

During the nine-month occupation of Rome, eighteen hundred Roman Jews were deported to the death camps. Fewer than twenty returned.

CODA

This is Your Life

31

THE CONTESSA GIOVANNA LANDINI

From an unpublished, undated memoir written after the war

There are cities where we feel part of the streetscape, not visitors but returned exiles. We are at home so completely yet inexplicably that fond thoughts are permitted: we must have lived here in a previous life or were conjured into being by one of the metropolis's pantheon of artists or poets, sculpted from its ancient stone.

When I was younger, London was that, for me.

In my twenties, newly a wife, I went four times with Paolo. We had visited during our courtship, too. The grey of the stately terraces was restful after Rome. The hymn of London rainfall on a gallery roof stirs recognitions, is somehow the music of the sublime. If there is a peace that passes all understanding, it is to awaken from lovers' bliss in London during murmurous rain, to stir in bed and hear it.

We spoke often of purchasing a town house, perhaps in Chelsea or South Kensington, but our marriage was to prove so brief that we never began the quest, and, for a time after he died, I was too broken to go there anymore, for always I felt he would come walking around the corner of Sloane Square, or wave to me from Claridge's window. Or step down into fog from one of those wonderful buses whose reds are always redder in memory.

But in the years after the war, I Londoned again. I felt I was returning to faith.

Old friends were looked up, concerts attended. Two brief love affairs (the phrase is not quite correct but things have to be called something) were had and were gently unregretted when they came to a courteous close. I was not free to fall in love. I never would be again. London gifted me that realisation, among others.

The last time I went there was early in 1963. The circumstances were unusual and memorable. I had by then taken a permanent apartment in the penthouse at the Savoy, with views over the Strand and the Thames. On the day I wish to tell about, a wintry Thursday in late February, my London chauffeur's wife had recently given birth and I did not want to bother with arranging a replacement so I rose early and started out for London airport on the Underground.

On that morning, the beeches and elms were just commencing to put on their spring finery: yellow chiffons, white buds that would be blossoms. But I was anxious. There was a question I needed to ask Hugh, a question I suspected he would not welcome. But I had made up my mind: it would be asked.

As I waited with my magazines and newspaper in a corner of the arrivals hall, my heart bumped like an ingenue's in a novel. I had not seen my friend in two years. Ill-health had assailed him, as I knew from his increasingly rare but increasingly amusing letters. His handwriting had deteriorated badly but he was still able to type.

Retirement, back in Ireland, was not suiting him well. He was living over a hardware store with his widowed sister, of whom he wrote in affectionate, slightly tolerant tones, as though she were a creature from a distant galaxy. (As no doubt she would have written of him!) But he missed his Roman life.

When he came through the gates, he looked irritable and alert, ruddy of face as ever, but was of course in the wheelchair to which his most recent stroke had consigned him, a vehicle he insisted on referring to as *la biga Romana*, the Italian word for a chariot. He had lost a little weight. In all my life I have never seen whiteness akin to the merino-wool-white his thick hair had turned to. The airport had provided a porter to push the chair, but Hugh would not hear of the possibility and kept flapping him away, insisting on 'going by my own steam'. As we embraced, tears overcame me. He gave the exasperated sigh I had long adored.

'Sweet Mother of James's Street, is this the way it's going to be?'

As we made our way through arrivals, the porter and Hugh conversed of something that I realised after a while must be the West Indies cricket team. I tried not to reveal that even the most rudimentary rules of cricket were as a long-dead language to me, a tongue I had no interest in acquiring.

Outside, the man fetched us one of those magnificent London taxis. My old friend and I climbed aboard into that ecstasy of blackness and leather-polish. The wheelchair was placed in the boot.

It was obvious that his speech had been affected quite severely by aphasia. He had told me of this in letters, but hearing it was another matter. I would not say that he was slurring; that would be inaccurate. It was more that he seemed uncommonly reluctant to speak, spoke with slowness, over-enunciation, not-quite-necessary deliberation, like a man who has taken too much wine but must converse with his wife's awful family. He permitted me to hold his hand as we rode into London.

He had not seen the city in a good many years. I was touched to hear him greet it again. 'Ah, there you are, Hammersmith. Ahoy, Shepherd's Bush.' The poet best-loved by Hugh was always Louis MacNeice, whom he more-than-slightly misquoted as we approached Hyde Park, 'her eyes saw all my waterfalls'. It enthralled him to notice, near Paddington, an Indian restaurant; such wonders were not to be encountered back at home in Cahersiveen, County Kerry, where a bottle of tomato ketchup would be considered exotic and possession of a clove of garlic would have you burned as a witch. This led him into a reverie on the food of beloved Italy: fat figs and *baccalà mantecato*, the fish in lamplit markets.

How was such and such a street in Prati? Were there fireworks in Piazza Navona for a festival these nights? He had been told by a Kerry neighbour recently returned from pilgrimage that the Trevi Fountain was fenced off for renovations; when would it reopen? He spoke of the city with such affection and everyday knowledge, as though he had departed it only yesterday and would be returning tonight, although in truth he would never again see Rome, except in dreams, a fact I felt he was coming to final terms with.

But Ireland was beautiful, too. He had been thinking of his childhood, the people in the town, the February light on the lakes. To awaken on a summer morning to the chaffinches in his sister's garden, her roses.

'At the back of it, the old motto is true, there's no place like home,' he said.

I asked if there was a particular part of Kerry for which he felt this home-comer's affection.

'Oh, I didn't mean Kerry. I meant Rome.'

As he said this, our taxi was passing St Francis House, a hostel for men on hard times. He mentioned that, as a young Deacon, he had once spent a winter in ministry there, living alongside the guests in a bleak plywood-partitioned cell off their dormitory, which rang nightly with threats and uncorkings.

'What was that like?' I asked.

'Bloody awful.'

One November evening, a stern Redemptorist Abbot from Belfast had loomed in from the bleak and angry rain, to inflict upon the residents a soul-improving tirade of the blood-and-thunder variety then popular. My friend was a good storyteller, the scene soon swam into being. I saw the cadaverous, thin-lipped ogre as he ascended the rickety steps to the pulpit, his mirthless, glinting eyes on the upturned unshaven; his ghastly little knuckles clutching the lectern.

'Look at yourselves,' he commenced. 'A nice pack of Fancy Dans.'

Alcohol was evil. The pub was 'Satan's waiting room'. Whiskey was 'the sweat of the devil'. There were more Fancy Dans in hell because of drunkenness than there were stars in the sky. It led to fornication, disobedience of the authorities, marital disharmony, impurities of thought, unhealthful association between the races and creeds, hair-raising sicknesses, early death. The ruination of women, the degradation of men, the starvation and orphaning of the infant. On the Final Day of Judgement, the drunken would be punished. Scripture had assured it. No escape would be possible. 'Lo, there shall be a weeping,' threatened the Redemptorist, 'and a gnashing of teeth.'

One of the older inmates, emboldened or bored, had the temerity to raise his hand. 'Saving your presence, Father,' he said, 'but I don't *have* any teeth.'

Hugh was poker-faced but corpsing a little as he delivered the sermoniser's punchline. 'Teeth shall be provided.'

At the apartment, he was tired and, after a sandwich lunch with me on the balcony, went in to take a siesta. His overnight bag containing clothes and shaving things had been mislaid by BOAC, a matter about which he was fretting, for his medicines were also lost, but while he rested I saw to matters. The Savoy had its own pharmacy and a collection of upscale shops, including a tailor's. Hugh's measurements were duly taken, and he was kitted out by Anderson & Sheppard of Savile Row, in a charcoal lounge suit and slightly racy polo neck, like a raffish uncle home from the theatrical tour of the provinces that ended in gossip. Dignified ties and fine-cut shirts were also provided. He delighted in the louche cravat.

Thus attired, he asked in a throwaway manner if I wished to say a rosary with him. I have always loved the rosary, finding its incantatory aspect transporting to the spirit, sometimes soothing, sometimes sad, always bringing the strange consolation of repetition but in truth I had never prayed it with Hugh, a fact he appeared to have forgotten. From his notebook he took a postcard depicting a Russian icon of Our Lady, which he placed against the carriage clock on the mantelpiece. Then he asked if I would help him to kneel down.

I ventured the view that Our Lady and Her Blessèd Son would find Hugh's prayer as acceptable if offered from the wheelchair but, in his quietly obstinate way, he insisted. It may have been the only time the holy rosary was prayed by two people in a bedroom at the Savoy, one in a fine lounge suit, the other in a dressing gown, hair still wet from her bath, while the traffic noises and police sirens arose from the Strand below, through the shining opened windows.

Years later, I saw that this was the moment I should have asked my difficult question of Hugh. Perhaps I knew this even then but was afraid. In any case, I did not ask it and on went the day. On go all the days. Alas.

At that era, there was on the English television a programme entitled *This is Your Life*, the premise of which involved a surprise being unleashed on some misfortunate personality of note, who would be whisked from the fake appointment at which he had innocently presented himself and conveyed to a studio where he would be confronted by the friends of his youth, as the Christians were confronted by the lions.

If anyone needed proof that no good deed ever goes unpunished, a conspiracy had been concocted to anoint Hugh the latest victim, in recognition of his leadership of the Escape Line. The researchers had done extensive preparatory work, tape-recorded the recollections of several of the Choir, sent us transcripts for correction, unearthed writings one or other of us had published (or not published) down the years. An assistant producer travelled to New York for a lengthy interview with Enzo Angelucci, and to what was by now West Berlin to meet Marianna de Vries, who, under a name changed by deed poll, had become a university lecturer, then a distinguished novelist and member of Parliament.

But, trove of research assembled, wiser counsel had prevailed. Vascular neurologists were consulted. Hugh was in no condition to endure the planned shock and the subsequent sixty minutes in the footlights. It was decided, instead, that Major Derry, our indomitable Choir colleague, would receive the BBC's laurels, if laurels they were, and that Hugh would be the surprise guest who always appeared through the curtains at the denouement, reducing everyone to lachrymose ecstasies as the credits began to roll. It really was a most vulgar programme. People adored it.

Hugh managed the experience admirably, as I knew he would, shyly passing around signed copies of *O Roma Felix*, a little guidebook he had written some years previously, and refusing to accept the compliments of his friends. (Its blunt subtitle, *'Practical Guide for Walks in Rome'*, was amusingly typical of him and, to we veterans of the Escape Line, not without ironies.) In addition to Sam Derry, who had grown ever more spectacularly handsome as he aged, a good number of our old Choir-mates were along. Delia Kiernan, her daughter Blon, Enzo Angelucci now of Brooklyn, John May of Whitechapel, dapper as a film star, and the inimitable but frequently imitated Sir Francis ('call me Frank') D'Arcy Godolphin Osborne, KCMG, soon to be named 12th Duke of Leeds. His Grace amused everyone, especially his most treasured audience, himself, by pretending never to have heard of the programme and insisting on addressing the presenter by surname. 'I say, Andrews. You're Irish? Ain't we all, what! Libations!'

Johnny May, in houndstooth mohair, was suntanned and splendid, although the years had not always been kind to my diamond. 'Evening, Treacle,' he twinkled, introducing me to his wife, Janine, whom he had met when she auditioned to sing with his bop quartet. Oesophageal cancer meant that he was no longer playing in public, had become a London cabbie, 'But I blow a bit at home.' Janine's parents had a sweetshop-and-tobacconist's in Loughton, a town in Essex, and Johnny did the weekly run to the wholesale. He and Enzo greeted each other with kisses and back-slaps, Enzo doing a lot of 'Willya take a look at this wiseguy,' Johnny affectionally telling him, 'Sod off.'

'Big occasion, Angelucci,' Delia said. 'You're wearing a shirt.'

'Don't look at me with those beautiful eyes or I'll drown,' Enzo countered. 'You remind me of a beauty I used to know but you're too young to be her.'

She pucked him, before they embraced, and afterwards too. And he lifted her, laughing, in his tender Roman arms, calling her *'bellissima* Delia'.

'God almighty,' she said, 'I'm glad my husband's not here to see this. Come over here, Jo, till we get a photo of the old gang. Stand in the middle, that's right.'

Delia, me, Enzo; behind us Johnny May and Frank Osborne, Johnny making the V-for-Victory sign, Frank raising a wine glass. In front of us, in his

262

wheelchair, a blanketed, stone-faced Hugh, mug of tea in one hand, Lazio soccer pennant sent to him by dear, brave Marianna de Vries, who could not be with us, in the other. Hunkered beside him, Sam Derry, stern, mild and knightly, arm about Hugh's left shoulder.

Apart from a picture of Paolo and me, taken on the morning of our wedding, it is the only photograph I have ever had framed.

One of Johnny's subsequent remarks was excised from the programme as broadcasted but I have checked with my darling Delia, with whom I am still in monthly contact, and she is quite certain that my memory of it being made is accurate. He was recalling to the genial presenter a spirited quarrel he had had with Hugh on one occasion, because a promised couple of hundred dollars for the Choir had not been delivered on time.

'So, the Padre, he says to me, Johnny, we ain't got no money. Ain't you listening, Dobbin? It's a serious situation. And he spells it out for me, lively, in case I don't get the point. No M. O. N. E. F. Y.

' "Padre," I tell him, "there ain't no eff in money."

' "Exactly," he says. "Go and *get* some!" '

'I'm sure it didn't happen quite like that,' the presenter laughed, a little anxiously.

'It did,' Hugh replied. 'And worse.'

A little party had been arranged in a room above a local pub after the recording, the George in Portland Place, a premises haunted by BBC types and their forlorn-looking girls and radio scriptwriters in Aran sweaters wanting their multisyllabic bawlings to be commissioned. For some reason, it was almost empty that night. I seem to remember a severe rainstorm, or perhaps the forecast of one. It was thoughtful of whoever had organised things but Hugh was tired, a bit distracted, disconcerted I should imagine, by such a sudden re-exposure to the past and the gale of raw goodwill to which he had been subjected.

The room was up a flight of stairs once fallen down by Dylan Thomas, and they were difficult for Hugh to manage, even with the help of Blon Kiernan and Frank Osborne. A reporter from the *Standard* materialised, wanting to interview him, and had to be shown the door. Sandwiches failed to arrive.

After a time, Johnny May and the inexhaustible Delia got a sort of singsong going. Things cheered up a little, or pretended to. Somehow, perhaps through some influence or intervention of the programme's host, a relative back in Ireland was spoken to on the pub telephone. Enzo sang something from Verdi down the line. Later, I seem to remember dear Frank making a speech peppered with quotations from Demosthenes and the like. Usually he did. Easier to stop the sunrise. Unlike most men, Frank became more attractive as he drank, his auburn eyes glistening like demerara sugar, and his gestures more Italian, vowels voluptuous and rich, like a man doing an impersonation of himself, as he almost certainly was, almost all the time. After a distinguished Foreign Office career, he retired to Rome. Sam Derry's children thought him a sort of astonishment. The boy, a long-haired bohemian, the girl, a short-haired bohemian, appeared not to understand at all.

Towards the end of the night, Frank proposed that the Choir all stand together and sing one last hymn for the old days, 'Abide With Me'. ('You too, Andrews!') With mild firmness Hugh let it be known that he didn't want that, and Frank, a skilled backtracker like all his profession, with silken elegance retreated.

'Friends, Romans, countrymen,' he said. 'Memory Lane is a thoroughfare best visited fleetingly. But permit me, gentles all, one valediction of the heart. When I have been requested down the years to define the Rome Escape Line, I have always said the same thing. And I always shall. It was my dear friend Hugh O'Flaherty and a number of us who loved him.'

Hugh's head was bowed. When he raised it again, his whole face was wet with tears.

A taxi drive through the West End in the rain is not the worst way for a night out to conclude. I recall a forest of umbrellas, as in an impressionist painting, the silver and amber shadows of Oxford Street, young people going into nightclubs in Soho. The London of my salad days was changing.

I asked if he had enjoyed the evening and he conceded that it had been a pleasure, if a painful one, to see old friends again, but felt that too much limelight had been shone on him, not on the wider doings of the Choir. Quoting his favourite Shakespeare play, *Coriolanus*, he said he did not like to see his nothings monstered.

'Don't you think you did a lot?' I asked.

'Not enough,' he replied.

Again, my unasked question loomed. But by the time I had framed its words, he was pointing with delight. 'Oh, look, Berwick Street, will we get a fish supper, do you think the driver would mind? Lots of vinegar on mine, no salt.'

The following morning, I let him rest; in fact he slept until noon, emerging then from my bedroom with mole-like blinks, like one uncertain as to how he had arrived here. The fantastically expensive silk pyjamas he was wearing had been ordered but never paid for by a Socialist cabinet minister, now disgraced, a matter the tailor had slyly let slip to us. My own bed had been the couch in the sitting room, a fact that appeared to appal Hugh, but in truth I am rather fond of dozing off on a well-upholstered old couch in firelight, a ghost story or a book of poems I don't understand by my side and a small whisky and water on the ottoman. A certain amount of sleeplessness seems to suit me.

We breakfasted simply – one can breakfast at any time from sunrise to midnight at the Savoy – on the terrace overlooking the Thames. He told me he still suffered nightmares, dreams of Hauptmann and his thugs, the caves, the deportations, 'the more we should have done'.

Eichmann had been executed the previous summer, in Israel. Hugh followed the trial in the newspapers. One of the Israeli soldiers given the task of committing the Nazi's cremated remains to the sea, six miles beyond Jaffa and therefore outside the national waters, remarked in an interview that he had been struck by how minuscule is the handful of ashes left by a human being. Hugh had seen a news-magazine photograph of the vast mountain of ash at Auschwitz. 'Everyone should look at that picture,' he said. 'Is there someplace we could go and say a prayer?'

'We can pray here,' I said.

'I'd like to be in a congregation.'

At that time in St Paul's, Bedford Street, known affectionately among London's night-people as 'the actors' church', a service was held in the afternoons. Actors being actors, as the vicar once told me, there would be little point in holding it in the mornings. 'St P's', the place was termed by those in the know. The atmosphere was bohemian-thespian-diva-fallen-on-bad-times. Monogamy, one felt, was not the universal practice, nor perhaps was heterosexuality, though nobody called it that in those days.

It bothered Hugh that he had missed Mass and so we went together to St P's, I having warned that this would not be vespers in a nunnery.

The meagre congregation of shatter-eyed nightclub performers and jaded dancers delighted him, the bleary jazzmen and five-o'clock-shadowed blues shouters. In the porch arose a distinct aroma of something that may not have been frankincense. Hugh was the only gentleman in the church wearing a collar and tie, indeed one of the relatively few not wearing rouge.

Afterwards he got into a conversation with a sort of bedraggled busker, a former mathematics professor, or so the man said, about the accursed heavyweight boxing they both liked. During this ordeal, I looked at the stained-glass windows and the tombstones. Protestant tombstones are so touching, full of tenderness and anecdote, their euphemisms for death so hopeful. *My son who fell asleep. Returned to the Light. His beloved wife departed to that further shore. Gone away to glory. Called home.* It is one of my lasting postcards of Hugh. Chuckling about boxing, in stained-glass dapple, with a person many would have termed a tramp.

That evening I achieved a long-held ambition to take Hugh to Covent Garden. It was a magnificent production of *Tosca*, featuring Tito Gobbi and Callas, and he would have been enthralled by Act Two, his favourite forty minutes in the history of music, had he only not fallen asleep shortly before *'Vissi d'arte'*. I hadn't the heart to wake him.

After the performance, I recall a strange moment that I still think about from time to time. We were making our way along Wellington Street, Hugh blanketed in his wheelchair, I pushing, when, through a cracked dirty window on the ground floor of the old Lyceum, he thought he saw a white-faced adolescent girl staring out at us. That theatre had been derelict for many years by then. But he was convinced. She seemed to have shaken him.

I had asked the concierge to book Montinari's for supper, for Hugh, like all admirable and trustworthy people, liked his food – he once signed an antiquarian book of Artusi's recipes, a birthday gift to me, with a beloved quotation he translated from Wilde, *'Dopo una buona cena si può perdonare chiunque, persino i propri parenti'* – 'after a good dinner, one can forgive anybody, even one's own relations' – and I wanted him to see that great ocean liner of a restaurant that sailed so many years on the Strand. Signed photographs of unremembered actors bedecked every wall, often a troubling signal in a restaurant, like having photographs of the food, but Monty's whilst past its best was still by some distance the finest Italian in London in those days, meaning that it was almost as good as the worst railway station café in Italy. Their famous *Penne all'arrabbiata* had been retired from the menu by the night of what would be our only visit, but the maître d, whom I knew of old, arranged its fleeting resurrection.

Hugh and he conversed in Italian, a delightful exchange to hear, Hugh telling him of the filming of *Quo Vadis* in Rome back in '50, the Metro-Goldwyn-Mayerification of the city, the suave limousines and swarms of helmeted extras, the ranked paparazzi, the stupefying sets, the terrifying detail that went into the gladiatorial fight scenes. 'The lions were brought from Germany, the bulls from Portugal, and the four white horses from Ireland.' Robert Taylor and Deborah Kerr had stayed not far from the Collegio; he had seen them walking with Nero, the actor Peter Ustinov, in the gardens of the Villa Pamphili. When the penne arrived at our table, he dutifully pronounced it unsurpassable, though in truth it was mediocre at best. As always, he refused even a half-glass of wine, and as always, insisted I have one. I had two while he sipped at rather dusty-looking orangeade, containing, marvel of marvels – again, unknown to the indigenes of rural Kerry, who seemed to be managing without it – crushed ice.

I recall his suspicious glower in the light of the crêpes Suzette that Luigi Montinari himself would do at your table. Monty's was the only 'Italian' restaurant I have known where the menu featured 'jelly', and even, if one asked carefully, that culinary abomination which young people were learning to call 'fries'. One was oneself learning, of course, to call these people 'teenagers', and to call their music 'music' through a tight smile of unfelt empathy. Born after the war, they knew literally nothing. There were times when one was glad to be childless.

Coffee was called for. The floor show began. A handsome big-eared lunkhead in a once-black dinner jacket sang Gershwin, in the finger-clicking, low-lidded, crooning style of his grandparents' remote youth, often smirking at his pianist, a cadaverous ghoul in a cummerbund, who *hulked* over the keys as though resenting them for some crime, or shooting what I suppose he must have thought were enticingly boyish winks at the vodka-soaked dowagers and one-time flappers and chain-smoking Henrys and hooting Wilfs who were among the last remaining denizens of Monty's in those days, exotics possessed of the strange, poignant beauty of creatures becoming extinct.

From time to time the singer attempted a Charleston or did that hands-criss-crossing-on-your-knees trick so beloved by very little children, and the old people chuckled dutifully, Hugh and I among them. The satirist David Frost came in, with his mother, as I recall. I had seen a photograph of him in the newspaper with several Beatles.

I do not know how it got about the restaurant that Hugh was who he was – some years previously he had written a regular column for the *Sunday Express*, 'Our Correspondent in Rome', his by-line including a rather flattering photograph he never liked – but drinks with fruit segments and tiny Japanese umbrellas and miniature plastic swords in them started to be conveyed to our table. There were collegial waves across the hors d'oeuvres and the odd cry of 'Well done, that man.' Thankfully, no one went so far as actually to approach; Hugh seemed to be emitting a force field. But it was wonderful to see him contend with his suddenly arrived celebrity by appearing to turn quite luminous with embarrassment, like an angry squid. The coffee bean in the Sambuca someone sent over burned less hotly than my friend.

'You should hold my hand,' I teased. 'We'd be in the *News of the World* on Sunday.'

'I don't want to hold your hand, thanks,' he confirmed.

With a final murdering of Cole Porter, the singer departed the dais, tripping on his shoelaces as he went. The conversations over which he had been performing intensified quickly. Candles glowed in Chianti bottles.

A young woman came through the kitchen's swing doors, wiping her wet hands on a cloth, crossing quickly to our table in a way that made clear she had been watching us for some time, and enquired in a reticent, apologetic way if she might speak a moment with Hugh.

She was already battling tears.

He asked if she wished to be seated.

Shaking her head, she indicated she didn't.

She wished to thank him, she said, for having saved the life of a nineteen-year-old Glaswegian, Private Michael Robert Connolly, First Battalion, King's Fusiliers, on 20th September 1943. Did Hugh by any chance remember him?

Hugh said that in plain honesty he did not – there had been so many prisoners – and she nodded as though having expected this answer.

He had escaped from Modena prison camp while on a forced labour detail, made his way towards Rome, barefoot, by night, exhausted and starving, snatching whatever rest he could in haggards and hedgerows, found the strength to stagger across the Vatican boundary and into St Peter's Square, from where the Monsignor had smuggled him into hiding at a convent near the Holy Office, St Monica's. He slept in the ruined dovecot that had once been a Roman *columbarium* and recovered from the scores of gangrenous wounds that his scramble through the barbed wire had wreaked on him. In a military hospital near Croydon aerodrome, en route home after the war, Michael Robert Connolly met a nurse a year older than him, a girl from the New Forest. They married after a month; their first child, a daughter, was standing before us now.

'I wouldn't be here,' the young woman said, through rivulets of tears, 'if you hadn't done what you did. Neither would my children. So, thank you.'

She was named Monica, after the convent. Her sixteen-year-old brother was Hugh, after Hugh.

Every year on 20th September, they prayed thanks for their father's deliverance, and for the man who saved his life.

'Dear child,' Hugh said.

'God bless you,' she whispered.

'Is your father in good health?'

'Yes, he is. He's very well.'

'Will you give him my best. And your mother. And your children.'

'Of course.'

A lovely thing happened, then. Hugh began to speak to her of his own time in the New Forest, the six months he had spent as a young priest in Brockenhurst. I had not known of this before, did not even know where it was.

He spoke of wild ponies, I remember, and the seasons of forest life, the customs of that part of England. Clearly it gave him pleasure to say the names of the local towns, as it always gives us pleasure to say the names of places where we encountered the fleeting ghost that is happiness. Lymington. Beaulieu. Lyndhurst. Hythe. Keyhaven. Barton on Sea.

I am bitterly sorry to say that, later that night, back at the penthouse, Hugh and I had a very serious quarrel. There was a question I had long wanted to ask him, I said; he raised his voice when I did. Nevertheless, I persisted.

I had heard certain whisperings, which I detailed; would he confirm they were false? He would not speak of the matter at all, he replied. 'It's nobody's damned business what I do.' The moon, if there was one, went down on our anger. Doors were slammed in the penthouse that night.

Next morning at London airport, I bade him farewell. A bundle of opera records, a gift for a neighbour back in Kerry, was wrapped in brown paper, there was also a present for his sister, a fine linen tablecloth we had bought in the hotel lobby. It was Hugh's manner, following a disagreement, to pretend it hadn't happened. So that's what we did. I was glad.

We spoke of the weather, as often we had done in the Rome days at rehearsal. Did I listen to Bach anymore? No, I didn't.

A fine, soft day. Yes, it was, I agreed.

But in England you'd never know, he said, it could be thundering by noon.

He was trembling when I embraced him. So was I. He kissed my hand.

I murmured, '*Grazie mille.*' So did he.

As he trundled down the departures corridor, and away from me, he raised a clenched fist in salute. The last time I would ever see him, we both knew.

In my head was an old ballad we used to sing at rehearsal.

It seemed a long time before his flight went, but I waited, every minute.

Now the summertime is come
With the laurels richly blooming,
And the wild mountain thyme
All the moorlands all perfuming;
To our own beloved bower, let us journey altogether,
Where the wild lilies bloom
'Mong the braes of Balquhither.
Let us go, lassie, go.
Lassie, go.

———

Cathair Saidhbhín
County Kerry
October, 1963

Cara Giovanna, my Jo,
My dearest old friend,
I don't think there have been such lilacs since the year I met you.

By the time you receive these words, I shall have departed this weary body and gone wherever we go when evicted from it. I have left instructions that this letter be sent to you three days after my funeral. Forgive my sloppy typing. It is late.

Always, as you know, I have been a neurotic writer-down. Things didn't seem quite real unless written.

It has lately been at me a bit that those lovely few days in London may have been spoiled for you by our quarrel, by my adamant silence on the question you asked. For my stubbornness, I apologise, you know how pig-headed I always was. But there were other reasons why I was reluctant to speak.

The truth is that, yes, I did attend Hauptmann in Modena prison. Nine times in all – there was to be a tenth but I cancelled the arrangement. The visits were made at his request.

During the first, we scarcely spoke. In the second, he was self-piteous and vengeful, pacing the cage, smoking, ranting that he had done no more than obey orders, spewing obscenities I felt had been meticulously contrived to shock and hurt a celibate person in a particular way (but they didn't). Some men adjust to being in a cell. He hated it.

Did I understand that he was married, had responsibilities, onuses? He could no longer see his wife and children! How was this justice? My daughter who has done nothing is denied her own *father*? My parents are elderly! I am to excrete in a bucket, like an animal. For doing as legally ordered! There were many worse than I. Do you know what it is like, to exist in a cage?

I did not go again for two years.

He wrote asking for a third meeting, I discussed this with my Rector. It was decided that I would go, and I went. At that time, the burial places of many disappeared Romans were still unknown; there was talk that Hauptmann might supply details so the proper rites could be done. I knew he wouldn't, but hope is hard to kill.

Hauptmann greeted me as a beloved cousin returned from long abroad – an act, of course – 'Sit down, let's play chess.' Somehow, he had organised a cake, I seem to remember, and 'a pot of your English tea'. What he wanted, of course, was for me to tell him I wasn't English. I told him I wasn't thirsty. This defeated him. He claimed to know nothing of the disappeared. He knew nothing of anything. He asked would I shake hands. I would not.

At our fourth encounter the chessboard and pieces were again produced – he had fashioned them himself, during woodworking class – which gave him the opportunity to deploy the Italian proverb any psychopath would find meaning in: '*Alla fine della partita il re e il pedone vanno nella stessa scatola*' He then said it in English, as though I did not know Italian anymore. 'After the game, the king and pawn end up in the same sack.'

I told him his accent needed work.

He was able to pretend to be mentally troubled if he thought that might be useful, but was in many ways a rather humdrum, sane, mediocre individual, a manipulative narcissist with, like many such people, a remarkable capacity to attract. The guards would sometimes confide that there were moments when they found him hard to dislike; 'irresistible', I remember one warder saying. He had a way of exuding vulnerability, a babes-in-the-wood incognisance, and a particular mode of not-quite-apologising in which 'all of us' had been victims and of generalising outwards with deft, disingenuous cunning. 'Of course, always where there is violence everyone seeing it is maimed. This has been observed by psychiatry.' His magnetism made him a very frightening person to be near. You felt your edges blurring.

I suppose it should never begin to surprise us that the murderer wears a mask. Yet it does. We all of us wear so many, of course. Perhaps that is the definition of the human being, a mammal able to alter its face. Only one person in all of history went entirely without mask, was always His very self, come betrayer or killer. He was murdered by power, on a tree.

Soon afterwards, I noticed the décor of Hauptmann's cell had begun to change, gradually at first, but noticeably, calculatedly, postcards of the saints and martyrs had been taped to the walls. One sees this often enough in a prison. One morning I arrived, reluctant as always, to find a photograph of myself in their midst.

'You are where you belong, Monsignor. I pray to you, daily.' Here he paused. 'Forgive my English, I meant *for* you.'

It will be obvious to you, perceptive Jo, where matters were heading. Soon, I was proven correct. Hauptmann asked if he could be received into the Catholic faith, as I had known from the very outset he would. No doubt it is cynical to notice that the discovery of the Lord by murderers and liars happens with predictable regularity once the judge passes sentence, rarely beforehand. With an eye on the Parole Board, the killer arrives at realisations the Sermon on the Mount did not provoke. Hauptmann insisted he was sincere, wrote long letters to Rome, saying he wished me – and me only – to be the priest who would prepare him.

The decision brought me agonies. In the end, I agreed.

We went through the required formalities, I gave him a Catechism, which he studied most assiduously, often asking deep, knowledgeable questions, as the sly faker and the truly earnest both must.

The morning came for his baptism, which took place in his cell, the prison chapel having suffered a collapsed ceiling. Hauptmann and I were alone. He had not shaved or washed. His lank hair was greasy. He had a bad cold and felt unable to face the shower block, he said, but his lack of proper deportment seemed to me a way of transmitting his contempt. Perhaps it was not.

He snuffled and mock-solemnly stared, misremembering the vows. The moment arrived at which the priest must summon two witnesses to the sincerity of the person entering the Church. He had hoped I would find a couple of guards to fulfil the role, but, without telling him, I had made a different arrangement.

'*Bitte*,' I called.

Two young people entered the cell. His daughter, now aged twenty, and her brother, seventeen. Both attempting not to weep. Neither able to look at him.

'Your children will witness your solemn oath,' I told him.

He was taken aback and did not address them, which I thought was strange, and he waited a fair while before nodding his head. As they watched, I concluded his baptism.

Perhaps he was not duping me. Perhaps he was. So be it. I do not understand or even like several of my Redeemer's teachings. Think yourself not much better, offer good to those that hate you. Like many of my sex, I have often felt profoundly that God made a terrible mistake in not making me God, that the world would be without darkness or difficulty if only I ruled it. Had I been the Almighty, I would have put several matters rather differently. But I wasn't.

God was.

And is.

The moment the baptism rite was complete, his children departed the cell, his son having shaken hands, the girl still refusing to touch him. He asked if I would hear his first confession. This I would not do, but I summoned a confrère, the prison chaplain, as I left. In the end, the priest later told me, Hauptmann declined to confess.

The day of his baptism was the last time I saw him, I am happy to say. Some years ago I heard that his wife had applied to dissolve their marriage. She may since have remarried, but I don't know.

These are the painful events I should have told you about in London. I am not certain as to what prevented me from doing so. Perhaps I thought you might be angry that I had given him any attention at all. Often, I was angry with myself for that reason. More recently I have found that I do not wish to think of him, and there are many days when I do not, for which mercy I thank the God of Silences. As I come closer to the Light, I have grown uninterested in the Dark. Always I used to fear it, and fear is a connectedness.

I am sorry that I hurt you. When in this world I ever doubted the existence of anything good, I thought of you, your kindness, compassion and grace, the love you showed a friend who was prideful and mean, your forgiveness, ardent bravery and guts. Many people never meet a hero. I met heroes. I loved them.

Arrivederci, my friend and comrade. I did many things wrong in my life. But my Father's house has many rooms.

Be kind to yourself, bellissima. You're not kind enough to yourself.

Sing your song, taste the wine.

With all love and respect.

Che Dio ti benedica sempre,

Your H

Caveat, Bibliography, Acknowledgements

While real people and real events inspired the work of fiction that is *My Father's House*, it is first and last a novel. Liberties have been taken with facts, characterisations and chronologies. Incidents have been concentrated, characters amalgamated, renamed, adapted or invented. The Hugh O'Flaherty, Sam Derry, John May, Delia Kiernan and D'Arcy Osborne in these pages are my versions and are not to be relied upon by biographers or researchers. This novel is not intended to be a source for students of wartime Rome or the Nazi occupation of Italy. The letter reproduced as epigraph is quoted on page 197 of Sam Derry's memoir *The Rome Escape Line* (1960). The writer's surname is not listed. He was 'a Glasgow boy'. All other sequences of *My Father's House* presenting themselves as authentic documents are works of fiction. Readers in search of nonfiction on Hugh O'Flaherty and the Rome Escape Line, or reportage on life in wartime Rome, are directed to the following works, which of course do not agree on every aspect, and to the references, notes and bibliographies they contain:

Fergus Butler-Gallie, *Priests de la Resistance!* (2019), Victor Failmezger, *Rome, City in Terror, the Nazi Occupation 1943-44* (2020). JP Gallagher, *Scarlet Pimpernel of the Vatican* (1967), republished as *The Scarlet and the Black* (2009), Stefan Heid, Johann Ickx: *Der Campo Santo Teutonico, das deutsche Priesterkolleg und die Erzbruderschaft zur Schmerzhaften Mutter Gottes während des Zweiten Weltkriegs* (2015), Robert Katz, *The Pope, the Resistance and the German Occupation of Rome* (2003), Borden W. Painter, *Mussolini's Rome* (2005), William Simpson, *A Vatican Lifeline* (1995), Stephen Walker, *Hide and Seek: the Irish Priest in the Vatican Who Defied the Nazi Command* (2012), M. de Wyss, *Rome Under the Terror* (1945). This list is far from exhaustive.

I express heartfelt gratitude to the Monsignor's nephew and namesake, retired Judge of the Irish Supreme Court, Hugh O'Flaherty, and grand-niece Catherine, a filmmaker, for granting me an interview and making available to me their collection of Monsignor Hugh's unpublished papers, including his letters, diaries, notes, telegrams and other writings and his published journalism (for some years he wrote a newspaper column) as well as audio and other recordings that Catherine O'Flaherty found while researching her documentary about the Monsignor (*Pimpernel sa Vatican*, 2008), including a full audiotape recording of the 1963 *This is Your Life* programme for Sam Derry, a fictitious version of which concludes this novel. I thank archivist Mark Ward for the skill and professionalism with which he facilitated the family's sharing of this material with me. I thank Flor MacCarthy for alerting me to a letter to the Monsignor that I had not seen before, from Irish president Sean T O'Kelly, and for sharing an inherited collection of remarkable unpublished 1930s and '40s Rome photographs. All the book's errors are my own.

I thank Liz Foley and Mikaela Pedlow at Harvill, and Isobel Dixon and Conrad Williams and their colleagues at the Blake Friedmann Literary Agency. The closing chapter's threat that false teeth will be provided on the Day of Judgement is borrowed from the work of that virtuoso of storytelling, the late Dave Allen. I have altered it a bit for my purposes. A special pleasure of writing this book was the warm helpfulness of Ireland's former ambassador to the Holy See, Emma Madigan, and her husband Laurence Simms. I thank them and their son Cormac, whom I first met when he was a tiny Roman, for their friendship. The arrangement on page 101 is by maestro Brian Byrne, to whom I offer heartfelt gratitude. I thank John Bowman, Bert Wright, Prof Diarmaid Ferriter, Monsignor Stefan Heid (see list of reference works, above) and the librarians at the Collegium Germanicum in Rome, Monsignor John Kennedy in Rome, Kathy Rose O'Brien, Mariachiara Rusca, Anna Loi, and my sister, Dr Éimear O'Connor. As ever, I thank my sons James and Marcus, and my wife, Anne-Marie Casey. *Vi amo, dal profondo del mio cuore.*

Joseph O'Connor was born in Dublin. His books include *Cowboys and Indians, Inishowen, Star of the Sea* (American Library Association Award, Irish Post Award for Fiction, France's Prix Millepages, Italy's Premio Acerbi, Prix Madeleine Zepter for European Novel of the Year), *Redemption Falls, Ghost Light* (Dublin One City One Book Novel 2011) and *Shadowplay* (Irish Book Awards Novel of the Year, Costa Novel of the Year shortlist). His fiction has been translated into forty languages. He received the 2012 Irish PEN Award for Outstanding Contribution to Literature and in 2014 he was appointed Frank McCourt Professor of Creative Writing at the University of Limerick.

www.josephoconnorauthor.com